The State and Legal Traditions of Mongolia

The State and Legal Traditions of Mongolia

An Historical Overview

Jigjid Boldbaatar and Danzan Lündeejantsan

With an Introductory Essay by Rüdiger Wolfrum and Naiade el-Khoury

MELROSE
LEGAL PUBLISHERS
THE HAGUE

ISBN 978-90-834075-2-4 (hardback)
ISBN 978-90-834075-3-1 (e-book)
DOI 10.63006/ALTU7609

Contents

Preface

This volume, *The State and Legal Traditions of Mongolia: An Historical Overview,* appears in English for the first time. It was released originally in Mongolia and in the Mongolian language in 1997. This publication was recognised in 1998 as the Top Book by Mongolia's Science and Technology Foundation. A second Mongolian edition was published in 2011 in response to the increasing demand among scholars and students, post-graduate and doctoral degree students.

In the period since then, much new research on the history of the State and the law came into circulation and many laws and much legislation in the sphere of the State system were revised and changed. Changes and amendments were also made to the Constitution of Mongolia. At the same time, international interest in these topics and demand for information about them has been growing steadily.

We are therefore very glad to present this new, revised and updated, English-language version of our book to our esteemed readers. It brings a wealth of otherwise inaccessible sources (ancient and modern), research, ideas, facts and information to an international scholarly audience. We thank Chanravyn Bürenbayar, who supplied the initial translation from Mongolian; and the editors at Melrose Legal Publishers who further improved the text for publication. We welcome any feedback at info@shihihutug.edu.man.

Preface to the Mongolian Editions

(translation)

This humble servant, having read through and analysed this book, created through the hard work and diligence of my spiritual guru, Member of the State Great *Khural*, Doctor of Legal Science, Professor Danzangiin Lündeejantsan and my spiritual comrade, Doctor of Legal Science, Professor Jigjidiin Boldbaatar, feels honoured and proud to pen this Preface.

It gives me utmost pleasure to note my feeling of deep appreciation for this book, written by the two scholars, as a work that takes its source from invaluable ancient materials, rich collections of works by learned men of the Occident and the Orient, the extremely rich treasure trove of national Mongolian laws and legislation, and which is based on contemporary research methods and methodologies. The work looks into the evolution and growth of the national Statehood, its legal foundations and the last 20 years of the modern history of Mongolia.

The work is invaluable because it considers the development of the State and legal traditions of Mongolia from the entire gamut of such sciences as philosophy, history and the science of law. It is a priceless work because it analyses a rich collection of historical documents and draws important conclusions based on facts and evidence.

The book looks into each and every stage and period in the development of Mongolia's Statehood from the perspective of historical processes, and its legal traditions in close connection with the culture and civilization of the Mongolian people. It contains weighty, evidence-based conclusions and the book has been penned in a style that meets the standard of a textbook on "The History of Mongolia's State and Law," especially for students of higher law schools, which is evidenced by the fact that it has been a part of the curriculum now for more than a decade. The newly edited Second Edition of the book contains thoughts on the latest accomplishments in the science of State and legal history and has been further enriched with new documents.

This book has been and continues to be the only work that covers all the stages and periods in the State and legal history of the country.

I am positive that the work *An Historical Overview of Mongolia's State and Legal Traditions* will bring enlightenment and blessing to the people of Mongolia, its scholars, intellectuals, students and law experts who wish to and are studying the history of the national State and law.

Professor Ishiin Dashnyam
Merited Lawyer of Mongolia, Doctor of Legal Science

List of Diagrams

About the Authors

Jigjid Boldbaatar is a member of the Mongolian Academy of Sciences and holds a Doctor of Historical Science (Sc.D.) degree. With over five decades of teaching experience in universities and colleges, he is a prominent expert in Mongolian and political history. Professor Boldbaatar has authored some 170 monographs and brochures, and over 200 research articles in English, German, Russian, Japanese, Chinese, Korean and Hungarian.

Danzan Lündeejantsan holds a Doctor of Legal Science (Sc.D.) degree. He is a distinguished scholar renowned for his expertise in Mongolian State history, constitutionalism and constitutional law. Moreover, Professor Lündeejantsan is a seasoned parliamentarian, having been elected to the Mongolian State Great Khural (Parliament) eight times. He has authored over 80 monographs, textbooks, brochures and research articles on the above subjects.

Naiade el-Khoury holds a Master 2 in Law from Paris X Nanterre, an LL.M. from Potsdam University, and a Ph.D. in International Law from the University of Tübingen (Germany). She is currently a Senior Research Fellow at the Max Planck Foundation for Intrernational Peace and the Rule of Law, specializing in comparative constitutional law and public international law.

Rüdiger Wolfrum Professor (Em.) Dr. Dres. h.c., is Professor of Comparative National Public Law and International Public Law at the University of Heidelberg, Faculty of Law; Director (Em.) of the Max-Planck Institute of Comparative Public and International Law; former President of the International Tribunal for the Law of the Sea and Judge at this Tribunal for 21 years; Judge ad hoc at the International Court of Justice; arbitrator and conciliator in several cases; and Honorary Director of the Max Planck Foundation for International Peace and the Rule of Law in Heidelberg.

Introductory Essay

Professor (Em.) Dr. Rüdiger Wolfrum and Dr. Naiade el-Khoury

*A tentative analysis of how the Mongolian Khans legitimized their exercise of public authority (nationally as well as internationally) from 1206 until the end of the IL Khans, and how they and their counterparts saw the status of the Mongolian Empire in international relations.**

1 Introduction

The following contribution will attempt to put the governmental activities of the Great Khans from Chinggis Khan to Kubelai Khan into perspective. This is, admittedly, only a brief period in the history of the Mongolian Empire. However, it is a formative period since Chinggis Khan was successful, as we will demonstrate, in transforming an unorganized system of nomadic tribes into a State. To do so successfully he had to establish his legitimacy as the superior ruler *vis-à-vis* other tribal leaders, and – which is often not honored sufficiently – to consolidate his government so that he could hand over his governmental power to his successor. As already indicated, from the point of view of general political theory, he transformed an area in which loosely coordinated or competing tribal groups had existed into a State with a governmental structure, even with a dispute settlement system, a legal system and a standing army. Under his successors the Mongolian Empire was acknowledged as a participant in the international relations as they existed in the 13th century.

We shall come back to this process and analyze it from the perspective of legitimacy to govern a State as well as from the point of view of the standing of Mongolia in international relations.

2 Symbolic Elements for Establishing and Upholding Legitimacy

All governmental regimes, including those in Antiquity,[1] expressed by symbolic acts or by proclamation or the combination of those that the leaders of these entities had the legitimacy to exercise public authority. The Mongols relied on symbols – such as the reference to turtles as the

---

* This Introductory Essay relies as far as historic facts, translations of diplomatic correspondence and specific Mongolian literature are concerned on a summary produced by Professor Dr. Dazan Lundeejantsan.

1 See on that in general, Roman Herzog, *Staaten der Frühzeit: Ursprünge und Herrschaftsformen*, 1988, on the establishment of Chinggis Khan as superior ruler, see p. 136.

foundation of the Earth. The capital which was established (Karakorum) in the Ochon valley was in sight of the 400 years older capital of the Uighurs, which the Mongols considered predecessors. We shall not elaborate on this point. However, it is worth mentioning that some of the symbols of the 13th century are still of relevance as the basis of the Mongolian identity today.

3 Establishing and Upholding Legitimacy

3.1 *Some General Considerations*

What do we understand under the term legitimacy? Legitimacy of the exercise of public authority means that those who are the addressees of the act in question accept that the institution or person having promulgated the act in question as a matter of principle has the right to execute public authority. This does not mean that the addressees have to accept each individual act of public authority. The notion of legitimacy can also be used in respect of actions of States in international relations.[2]

It is necessary to distinguish between various levels of legitimacy namely the legitimacy of the superior ruler in a State (internal legitimacy) and the legitimacy of the established entity (State) *vis-à-vis* co-existing organized entities (external legitimacy). It should be noted that originally no distinction was made between the legitimacy of the leader and of the entity he was leading. To be more precise – the legitimacy of the superior leader also covered the legitimacy of the entity (State) the leader in question governed.

The following considerations concentrate on the mechanisms or claims the Mongolian Khans used as a basis of their external legitimization, that is their legitimacy *vis-à-vis* the European States of this period, including the Vatican, as well as Japan and Korea, and States from the (today's) Middle East.[3] The understanding of the mechanisms and claims used to establish and to maintain their legitimacy will be deduced from the diplomatic interactions of the Mongolian Khans as expressed in their letters to foreign States. As will be shown the claim of Mongolia concerning its status in the international community was not static but developed from a

2 The notion of "legitimacy" has been introduced into the discourse of international law in particular by TM Franck, *The Power of Legitimacy among Nations,* OUP, New York, 1990; see also Rüdiger Wolfrum, "Legitimacy of International Law from a Legal Perspective: Some Introductory Considerations", in Rüdiger Wolfrum/ Volker Röben (eds.), *Legitimacy in International Law,* 2008, pp. 1–24.

3 See under 7.

system of co-ordination into one of co-operation.[4] To put it more precisely, the Mongolian Empire developed into a regime where the mechanisms of cooperation became more relevant. However, before we deal with the external legitimacy of the Mongolian Empire we have to establish whether there is a relationship between internal legitimacy and the external one.

Judging from today's international practice it can be observed that after a coup in a State (mostly a military one) other governments refrain from recognizing the new government as the legitimate government. This, however, does not mean that they deny the qualification of that State as being a subject of international law. This issue is being dealt with controversially in literature and in State practice.[5] However, in the end, considerations of Realpolitik prevail in practice. Considering that in reality there are many governments of States which cannot be qualified as being democratic and thus legitimized. It is necessary also to include all States into international deliberations. Otherwise dialogue oriented international relations as a mechanism to preserve peace would not be able to function.

States exist on the basis of established facts, a population, a territory and a government.[6] The people is an "aggregate of individuals who live together as a community".[7] In his famous statement *Ubi societas ibi jus* Marcus Tullius Cicero established an interrelatedness between the "existence of a society and the existence of a legal system".[8]

Seen from a today's perspective the meaning of this statement is not fully evident. What did Cicero mean with "*societas*"? Did the term "*societas*" for him include what today qualifies as community?[9] As far as the reference of Cicero to law is concerned, he meant that societies develop through law a minimum degree of cohesion necessary for their future ex-

---

4 It should be noted that the "law of co-ordination" and the "law of co-operation" do not identify different epochs in the development of international law but different mechanisms. For further details see Georges Abi-Saab, Cour Général de Droit International Public, *RdC* vol. 207 (1987).

5 For details see Dahm/ Delbrück/ Wolfrum, *Völkerrecht*, vol. I/1, 2nd ed.

6 See *Oppenheim's International Law*, 9th edition, edited by Sir Robert Jennings and Sir Arthur Watts, 1992, at p. 120 *et seq.*

7 Oppenheim (note 6) at p. 121.

8 (1988), pp. 196–7. Andreas Paulus, "International Community" in Rüdiger Wolfrum (ed.), *Max Planck Encyclopedia of Public International Law* (online edition edn, Oxford University Press 2011), para. 6.

9 Max Weber, *Wirtschaftliche Beziehungen in der Gemeinschaft*, Wirtschaft und Gesellschaft, Teilband, Gemeinschaft, p. 77 (78 ff).

istence. [10] The issues touched by Cicero are still valid perhaps even more so than at his time.

In today's understanding, the normative order of a community serves several interrelated purposes, which will serve as the basis of the research objective of this study. A normative order, which constitutes a value oriented organizational structure, is one of the preconditions of a community.[11] Such a value oriented normative order also establishes and reflects the identity of the community concerned. Such normative orders require legitimacy and at the same time, provide the legitimacy for acts on behalf of the community concerned. It should already be mentioned here that the legitimization of State power covers two aspects. It explains why State powers exist and also establishes the entitlement of the State power to act authoritatively *vis-à-vis* those under its territorial or personal jurisdiction. The decisive aspect is whether the State can be shown to be necessary and its government as well as the exercise of public authority at least legitimate.[12] In respect of Mongolia this means has the establishment of the Mongolian Empire by Temuddin (later named Chinggis Khan) been necessary for the peace and security of the area and its population in question? The answer is definitely affirmative. The fact is being highlighted in the letters (decrees) of the Khans still to be discussed.

There are different approaches concerning the elements, which may induce legitimacy of a particular authority. Theoretically they may be procedure or result oriented or a combination thereof.

Authority can be legitimized by its source of origin. As far as public international law is concerned legitimacy rests, at least according to the traditional view, in the consent of the States concerned. Concerning the national level legitimacy may depend on the procedure through which the act in question has been developed.

Authority can also be legitimized if its decisions are taken in a procedure which is considered to be adequate or fair. Finally, it has been argued that authority can be legitimized by the outcome it produces. This is a crucial issue and one which deserves further consideration.[13] An aspect frequently underestimated is that the legitimacy to exercise public authority has not only to be established but also sustained over time.

---

10 *Ibid.*

11 Jean Jacques Rousseau, *The Political Writings of Jean Jacques Rousseau, Contrat Social,* C.E, in: Kanghan, vol. II, p. 1 (7) ; see also *Rousseau's Social Contract, An Interpretative Essay,* Lester G. Stockes, 1968, p. 3.

12 Reinhold Zippelius, *Allgemeine Staatslehre in Juristische Kurz-Lehrbücher,* Beck, 1991, § 16.

13 Fritz Scharpf, *Governing in Europe: Effective and Democratic?,* OUP, 1999.

Legitimacy has both a normative and a sociological meaning. To say that an institution is legitimate in the normative sense asserts that it has the right to rule. To characterize an institution being legitimate in the sociological sense means that it is widely believed to have the right to rule. Such a belief may be based on the input legitimacy as well as output legitimacy, the latter may prevail. [14]

4 Mechanisms to Establish Legitimacy in the Period of the Establishment of States

4.1 *In Particular in Respect of Mongolia in the 13th Century*

It is evident that today's mechanisms for establishing legitimacy were developed only in the 20th and the 21st century.

There was a multiplicity of mechanisms employed in the period when States developed out of more loosely organized congregations as was the case with Mongolia. The most common mechanism to establish legitimacy was then the reference to God or to another spiritual identity. This was also true for the Mongols referring to the Sky as the source of legitimacy.[15]

Although it was generally common to legitimize the authority of the ruler of the given State (or an equivalent entity having for objective to unite a multiplicity of persons to serve a particular purpose) by reference to God or another spiritual authority there also existed in several States some form of an electoral process. An example for a formalized electoral process is the one for electing the King of the Holy Roman Empire. It existed for over 400 years. This process was codified in the Golden Bull of 1356. According to the written text of the Golden Bull:

> We have promulgated, decreed and recommended for ratification the subjoined laws for the purpose of cherishing unity among the Electors, and of bringing about a unanimous election, and of closing all approach to the aforesaid detestable discord and to the various dangers which arise from it.

---

14 Allen Buchanan/Robert O. Keohane, "The Legitimacy of Global Governance Institutions", in Rüdiger Wolfrum and VolkerRöben, (note 3), p. 25 at 29 *et seq.*

15 *Secret History of the Mongols,* translated by Francis Woodman Cleaves, Harvard University Press, 1982, p. 1: "There was a bluish wolf which was borne having [his] destiny from Heaven above." This is the beginning of the ancestral line of Chinggis Khan.

Although the election of the King of the Holy Roman Empire by the chief ecclesiastical and secular Princes was already established before, it was found necessary to codify the process. Today we would say the reason for codification rested in the need for clarity and transparency, elements derived from the principle of the rule of law, which was clearly in the 13th century not formalized on this abstract level. Although in the Mongolian Empire elements of today's rule of law thinking were omnipresent as we will demonstrate.

The Golden Bull identified the seven electors and decided that a positive vote needed the affirmative vote of four of them. At the time of the establishment of the Mongolian Empire the system of selecting the ruler in Islamic States had developed into a hereditary process. However, in the period after the death of the prophet Muhammed in 632 C.E. there existed a process of selection or election. Considering the number of persons participating in this process, one cannot put this process on an equal footing with election processes practiced in Rome in the Republican period. The limitations of the electors as provided for in some instances was based on the following considerations. The electors belonged to the wider family of the future ruler. Which means that this family as a whole had a spiritual blessing. An alternative was that the electors belong to the leading families (elite) of the population concerned. This reflected Realpolitik.

We will demonstrate in the following that Temudschin (as he was named originally) was elected as the superior ruler in a procedure involving other Khans. Part of Temudschin' s election was his change of name and from that point he adopted the name Chinggis Khan. However, on the basis of the *Secret History of Mongols*[16] and of the documents we are going to analyze, he upheld that he had a spiritual legitimacy. This system was maintained by his successors with one variation.

The normative understanding of the concept of legitimacy covers an aspect that refers to the particularly important purposes that can only be achieved through the existence of a State. The legitimacy of a State is justified by the purposes that outweigh the restrictions, which the existence of a State brings with it for the individual. This normative concept is based on the regulatory and ultimately peacemaking function of the State

16 *History of the Mongols*, note 15 above, reports two "coronations", namely at paras. 123; 202. At the second opportunity (in the year of the tiger (1206) he appointed the captains of the "thousands". At this occasion Chinggis Khan has been reported to say: For those who are gone with me, together "setting up a nation". The translation of *Die Geheime Geschichte der Mongolen, herausgegeben von Walther Heissig*, 1st ed., 1981, p. 112 speaks instead of "nation" Reich (empire).

community and the provision of a just community order in which the individual can achieve personal development. This understanding covers the actual functioning of social processes. Thus, legitimation answers to whether and for what motives a State order is acually accepted and approved by the legal community.[17] This reference to the results achieved so far as an element establishing legitimacy will turn out to be particularly relevant in respect of the Mongolian Khans' legitimacy.[18]

5 The Question of Legitimization of the Rulers of the Mongolian Empire and of the Mongolian Empire as Such

5.1 *Basis of the Legal Analysis Concerning the Legitimacy of the Relevant Khans of the Mongolian Empire and of the Mongolian Empire Itself*

We shall base our analysis on the letters (notes) sent by the Khans of the Great Mongol Empire (Chinggis Khan, Ögödei Khan, Güyüg Khan and Mönkh Khan); Letters of the Great Mongol Yuan Empire Khan (Khubilai Khan); Letters of the Khans of the Golden Horde (Bat Khan); Letters of the Il Khanate Khans (Il-Khan Khülegü, Il-Khan Abaga, Il- Khan Ahmad Tegüder, Il-Khan Argun, Il-Khan Gazan and Il-Khan Ölziit).

We have to point out that the foundation of our research is limited and therefore the results reached are preliminary and may require further research. The number of letters or notes by the Mongolian Khans is limited; there may have been more such letters and in particular there have been numerous treaties concluded between Mongolia and other States. However, since all the letters analyzed by us display a remarkably similar pattern it is to be assumed that other such letters, if they existed will have had the same or at least a similar format. Apart from that there are divergent views concerning the wording of these letters and their translation as well as their interpretation.

The analysis of the letters – some are construed as decrees – requires taking into account the development of the governmental system since Chinggis Khan took power. However, it cannot be the task of this contribution to reiterate the historical development of the governmental system of Mongolia.[19] We will only identify elements relevant for the legitimization of the ruling powers of Chinggis Khan and his successors and in

---

17 Max Weber, *Wirtschaft und Gesellschaft*, 16ff, 122ff; Johannes Winckelmann, *Legitimität und Legalität in M. Webers Herrschaftssoziologie*, 1952.

18 See below.

19 See on that Bawden, *The Modern History of Mongolia*, 1989.

particular those elements, which are reflected in the letters under consideration.

As already indicated, all these letters follow a similar pattern. They refer to the divine or rather spiritual legitimization of the Mongolian rulers concerned ("By the power of the Eternal Sky (Tenggeri)…") as well as to the successful exercise of public authority ("We the Oceanic Khan of the Whole People…") so far by the senders of the letter and by his predecessors. The letters following the ones of Chinggis Khan sometimes also refer to him as an additional means of legitimization.

The coming to power of Chinggis Khan is of some relevance in respect of his legitimacy although this is reflected in the letters only – if at all – indirectly ("We the… Khan of the Whole People"). After having established a military power base by alliances and by defeating competing tribes he called for an assembly of the tribal leaders associated with him. They offered him the position of the leading Khan, He first refused and offered such a position to each of the participants who declined. Only then he accepted the position. At this moment he assumed the name Chinggis Khan.[20]

Finally, it has to be noted that the Mongolian Khans succeeding Chinggis Khan were selected and acclaimed in a procedure specified in the *Secret History of Mongolia*. As far as the succession of Chinggis Khan is concerned he had decreed who would follow him, namely Ögödei and not his oldest or his youngest son. The youngest son would have been the appropriate choice according to Mongolian tradition. However, it was well understood that the succession would switch to the line of his youngest son eventually. The successor so identified required the acclamation of an assembly of the Empire. However, it would be unsustainable if one would equalize this process with a democratic election process. Eligible for the succession were only the sons and their descendants of Chinggis Khan and his wife Börte.

The selection process of the Mongolian Khans and the mechanisms for establishing their legitimacy were not unique. This combination of a spiritual legitimacy, an electoral process and the successful government were used and came to a test already in the 8th century for the Frank Empire. Pepin (le Bref) the Short, the son of the Frankish prince Charles Martel, was King of the Franks from 751 until his death in 768. He was the first Carolingian to become king. This position rested in the hands of the members of this family for several generations. Before that the kings

20 See on that fn. 16 above, as well as the *Geheime Geschichte der Mongolen*, edited by Walther Heissig, at p. 47.

of the Franks had belonged to the Merovingian family and had spiritual standing whereas the actual State power was exercised by members of the Carolingian family. Pepin the Short addressed Pope Zacharias with the question whether a leader having merely spiritual legitimacy should be regarded as King or the one who yielded the actual governmental power. The Pope ruled in favor of Pepin thus – at least indirectly – negating the relevance of a spiritual legitimacy. On that basis Pepin was crowned as King of the Franks.

In respect of the Mongolian Khans the spiritual legitimization and the success in government were both kept. Actually at the coronation of Pipin the spiritual legitimization was reintroduced by the ceremony of anointing.[21] Therefore one can conclude that the spiritual legitimization concerning monarchs remained dominant and still exists – now rather as a pure ceremony.

5.2 *Divine Legitimization Concerning the Exercise of Public Authority and Reference to the Power Already Exercised as Expressed by Individual Letters of Mongolian Khans*

The letters sent by Chinggis Khan and Ögödei Khan were directed to neighboring States covering particular situations. The letter sent by Chinggis Khan to the Shah of Khwarezm was about the killing of Mongolian merchants, who happened to be Muslims, too. The letter announced sanctions to be taken. The letters by Chinggis Khan and Ögödei Khan to the Goreo Dynasty (Korea) were addressed to a State having accepted the superiority of the Mongol Empire.

The first letter so far known from Mongolian Khans to rulers of States outside Asia is the one of Güyüg Khan to Pope Innocent IV via an ambassador from the Pope. It is to be taken from this letter that there must have been an exchange of views before. From the wording it is also clear that this is not merely a diplomatic letter but a decree. Güyüg Khan felt and addressed the Pope from a position of superiority.

Güyüg Khan's letter:

> By the power of the Eternal Sky (*Tenggeri*), [We] the Oceanic Khan of the whole great people. Our command. This is an order sent to

21 There is a rich literature on this issue. However, it is not so much concerned with the question of legitimacy. Worth reading are: *Pippins Königserhebung von 751 und der Papst. Die Narrative der Reichsanalen und der Friedegar-Fortsetzung*, Körntgen, Ludger, S. 39–68; *Das Konzildekret von Ver (755) – Ausdruck eines neunen Regierungsstils*, Glatthaar, Michael, S. 69–90; Semmler, Josef, *Der Dynastiewechsel und die Fränkische Königssalbung*, Droste Verlag 2003.

> the great Pope that he may know and understand it. You have said: 'Become Christian, it will be good.' This petition of thine we have not understood. Again. You have sent words [saying]: "Thou hast taken all the innocent lands of the Majar and the Christians by force and we are astonished at such an act. Tell – What was their crime?" These words of thine we have not understood either. They do not trust the command of Chinggis Khan, Ögödei Khan and the *Tenggeri*. The words in thy letters reckless; you have acted with arrogance. Haven't you all acted unfriendly towards us by killing our ambassadors? This is why, under the patronage of Eternal *Tenggeri* we invaded those countries. Who dare can disobey the command of the Eternal *Tenggeri*. By the power of the Eternal *Tenggeri* we were conferred the right to rule and administer all these lands from the sun rises to the lands where the sun sets. How can we dare fail to remember the command of the Eternal *Tenggeri*. We show mercy on those who submit with true intentions and without resistance. But, we deal severely with those who resist. I am not a Christian. I am someone who tries and judges others. If you have committed a sin, you have to pay for it. Thus We pronounce. The Eternal *Tenggeri* above knows what awaits your fate should [you] not follow my order.[22]

This letter is indicative of how Güyüg Khan saw his position in relation to the Pope and in respect of the rest of the world.

The paragraph in the letter "By the power of the *Eternal Tenggeri* we were conferred the right to rule and administer all these lands from where the sun rises to the lands where the sun sets" refers to a heaven-given mandate to the Mongols to conquer the world. The impression of the seal (the letter has been stamped twice with the Khan's seal) of the Great Mongol Khan is in the Mongolian language and reads "By the power of the *Eternal Tenggeri*, this is the Order of the Oceanic Khan of the Great Mongol Empire. All peoples, small and big, respect and fear the command."[23] There are further elements worth mentioning. The attacks on Hungary are justified by the claim that Mongolian ambassadors have been killed. It is interesting to note that belligerent attacks are considered to need a justification. Apart from that it transpires from this part of the latter that, according to the Mongolian tradition, ambassadors are considered as per-

---

22 Batsüren, B., Delgerjargal, D., Erdenebat, U. *History of the Mongol Empire. The Great Mongol State. Volume One*. Ulaanbaatar. 2006. p. 245.

23 Batsüren, B., Delgerjargal, D., Erdenebat, U. *History of the Mongol Empire. The Great Mongol State. Volume One.* Ulaanbaatar. 2006. pp. 478–479.

sons who ought to be protected. This was in fact a principle of the Mongolian tradition. Further, the letter refers to Chinggis Khan and Ögödei Khan as additional references. This has to be seen as an element confirming the legitimacy of Güyüg Khan. Finally, the last lines of the letter express a warning due to the seemingly traditional Mongolian principle that before sanctions may be taken a warning has to be expressed about what would be the consequence of any lack of obedience.

Mönkh Khan continued the policy of his predecessors: expanding the lands under the Mongol rule. He dispatched a letter to King Louis IX of France who equally was interested in establishing contact with the Mongols in order to use the Mongol troops in his crusades. First attempts at contacts failed. Louis IX, finally, appointed Guillaume de Rubrouck as secret envoy to Mönkh Khan. After having received the ambassador he sent a letter to Louis IX via this ambassador.

This letter followed the same lines as the letter we have already discussed namely in that it repeats the mandate of the Mongols to conquer the whole world. However, the letter (again a decree) is remarkable for two points. It is part of a diplomatic exchange of messages, in this case initiated by the King of France and it refers to Chinggis Khan as one of the sources of legitimacy.

Khubilai Khan communicated and engaged with the major European monarchs and religious figures through Nestorian Christians who served as envoys. From among them perhaps the most important one was Rabban bar Sauma, Nestorian Christian ecclesiastic.[24]

At that time, the Pope, the King of France and the monarchs of the Byzantine Empire sought contact with Khubilai Khan in order to engage in the Great Mongol Yuan Empire. Mikhail Pravdin had written, *"In the first half of the fourteenth century envoys were sent from Europe on nine occasions and the Mongol khans had reciprocated by sending envoys on 15 occasions, who had travelled to Rome, Barcelona, Valencia, Paris and London."*[25] In his desire to enter into contact with the Pope Khubilai Khan made use of the assistance of the Venetian merchants Niccolò Polo and Maffeo Polo.[26] The letters exchanged have not yet been recovered but it seems clear that Khubilai Khan asked for cooperation. In particular, Khubilai Khan had asked

24 Ider, D., Chinzorig, B., Sodbileg, Ch. *The Great Mongol State Called the Yuan Empire*. Volume Two. Chief Editor Delgerjargal, P. Volume Editor Bazarsren, J. Ulaanbaatar. 2019. p. 71.

25 *Ibid.* p. 71.

26 *Ibid.* p. 70.

the Pope to dispatch missionaries, and to send some sacred oil from a particular lamp of Jerusalem.[27]

This letter constituted a revolutionary change of attitude compared to that of his predecessors. Khubilai Khan considered himself as a member of the then existing system of State governments and the aggressive attitude – including the emphasis on the mandate to govern the world – was not upheld. This may have been a reflex of the territorial dominance of the Yuan Empire.

Khubilai Khan also tried to establish contacts with the Emperor of Japan. Although Khubilai Khan emphasized his superiority, he first and foremost sought cooperation, albeit not on equal terms. As far as legitimacy is concerned, he referred to his predecessors, the fact that he is governing a vast empire and that today's Korea (Goreyo) was already under his dominance. The following excerpt of the letter is of interest in this respect:

> ... Let us pay mutual visits and let us greet each other. We think all countries belong to one family. How are we in the right, unless we comprehend this? I call upon thee the King to carefully think which would you choose – make friendship or take up arms?[28]

The reply of the Emperor of Japan was unfriendly while pointing out the Emperor of Japan also claimed a spiritual legitimacy "Great Divinity Illuminating Heaven", the celestial sun goddess from whom the Japanese imperial family claims descent).[29] Even after his failed invasion of Japan, Khubilai Khan unsuccessfully continued to establish contact with the Emperor of Japan.

A decisive turn of attitude is to be witnessed in the initiatives the IL-Khans took.[30] The letters of IL-Khans indicate that the IL-Khans were well

27 *History of the Mongolian People's Republic. Volume One. One. From Early Times to the XVII Century.* Editor Sh. Natsagdorj. Ulaanbaatar. 1966. p. 298.

28 Pagma, N. "Extremely Interesting Documents Have been Sent". An article published in the daily newspaper Ödriin Sonin. Issue No. 274/91776 of 6 November 2004.

29 Ider, D., Chinzorig, B., Sodbileg, Ch. *The Great Mongol State Called the Yuan Empire.*Volume Two. Chief Editor Delgerjargal, P. Volume Editor Bazarüsren, J. Ulaanbaatar. 2019. p. 87.

30 The IL-Khanat was established at the south-west of the Mongol Empire in 1295. The core of the IL-Khanat was what is today known as Iran, Azerbaijan and Turkey, later it also included today's Irak and Syria. The last ruler converted to Islam. The IL-Khanat fell apart in 1335. Despite its short period of existence it had a comparatively long list of rulers.

integrated in the political affairs of what is now referred to as the Middle East. There have also been contacts between the Khans of the Golden Horde and European countries but documentary evidence in this respect is scarce.[31]

We shall concentrate on the letters of the IL- Khans offering an alliance to the Kings of France. A relevant letter in this respect is a letter of Il-Khan Argun. [32]

Il-Khan Argun's letters were written in a similar pattern to the other ones of Mongol Khans reflecting the custom and tradition of referring to the Heaven Tenggeri.

As regards his foreign policy, Il-Khan Argun actively pursued the traditional policy of establishing ties with the Crusaders against the Mamluks of Egypt. He dispatched ambassadors to the West several times and one such mission to Europe was led by a prominent Nestorian Rabban Bar Sauma who called on the Byzantine Emperor Andronikos II, Roman Pope Nicolas IV and King Philip the Fair of France in 1287 proclaiming "Be known, there are many Christians Mongols and among them are quite numerous khans, queens and their children who were baptised and converted to Christianity. In every camp they have their own churches and places of worship. The Khan seeks help from you all in conquering Egypt and delivering Jerusalem to the Europeans." In 1289, Argun Khan sent a letter to King Philip the Fair from France through Buscarel of Gisolfe, who was a European and who had settled in Persia in the thirteenth century while it was part of the Mongol Il-Khanate. He was a Mongol ambassador to Europe from 1289 to 1305, serving the Mongol rulers Argun, Ghazan and then Ölziit.

Il-Khan Argun reminded King Philip the Fair about his promise and called for the formation of an alliance.

> Under the power of the Eternal *Tenggeri*, the message of the great king, Argun: ... We welcome your commitment to join forces if the warriors of the Great King move towards Misri (Holy Land) and *Tenggeri* willing, we shall go there in the first month of the Tiger year's winter, and settle in Damascus on the fifth of the first spring month.

---

31 The Il-Khanate and the Golden Horde were the European dependencies of the Mongol Empire; they maintained intensive relationships with other countries of the Middle East and Europe. Both were the result of the division of the Mongolian Empire after the death of Chinggis Khan.

32 IL-Khan Argun was enthroned on 11 August 1284.

Although contacts were established with King Edward I of England, the latter having expressed its the readiness to combine forces with the Mongols the plans of a military cooperation were never implemented. The Pope had issued an ultimatum that Argun convert to Christianity, in response to which Il-Khan Argun argued that he would "not obstruct his own Mongols from being converted to Christianity, but I will not become a Christian" and continued that"We, Chinggis Khan's descendants, will not let anyone preach us which religion to follow, as it is not important what your belief is, but what is important is to remain true to your beliefs and achieve noble deeds."[33]

From a letter sent by Il-Khan Argun to French King Philip the Fair in 1281 (First version of the translation):

> Under the power of the Eternal *Tenggeri*, the message of the Great Khan Argun, to the King of France…, said: I have accepted the word that you forwarded by the messengers under Saymer Sagura (Bar Sauma), saying that if the warriors of Il Khan invade Egypt, you would support them. We would also lend our support by going there in the first month of Tiger year's winter [1290], *Tenggeri* willing, and settle in Damascus on the fifteenth of the first month of spring [1291]. If you send your warriors as promised and conquer Egypt, *Tenggeri* willing, then I shall give you Jerusalem. If any of our warriors arrive later than arranged, all will be futile and no one will benefit. If you care to please give me your impressions, and I would also be very willing to accept any samples of French opulence that you care to burden your messengers with. I send this to you by Myckeril and say: All will be known by the power of the *Tenggeri* and the greatness of kings. This letter was scribed on the sixth of the first summer month of the Year of the Ox at Khöndlön.[34]

A second translation of this letter exists, which is not fully identical. However the discrepancies are without relevance for the subject matter dealt with here.

Il-Khan Gazan being the fifth generation continued the policy pursued by his predecessors. He exchanged letters with and campaigned against the Mamluk Sultan al-Nasir Qalawu.

---

33 Ankhbayar, D. *History of the Mongol Empire*. The Il-Khanate Dynasty. Ulaanbaatar, 2019, p. 53.

34 Bayarsaikhan, D. *From Khülegü Khan to Abu Sa'id:Articles on Il Khans*. 2016. p. 103.

In 1299, Gazan Khan sent emissaries to Roman Pope Boniface VIII (1294–1303), Henry II of Cyprus, (he died in 1324) who was also the crowned King of Jerusalem seeking alliance against his enemy Mamluk Sultan al-Nasir Qalawun.

From among the Il-Khanate rulers, Ölziit Khan changed his religion to Shi'ism in 1310 with the objective of preventing conflict and maintaining a balance among different religions and religious sects. He sent emissaries and maintained links with King Philip the Fair of France and King Edward I of England in 1305 in order to form an anti-Mamluk alliance. This letter contained a new element. Ölziit Khan had been the first Mongolian ruler ever to promote the idea of peace. It is worth noting that although the Khan had changed his religion and referred to himself as a sultan in his letter, he still referred to the "Eternal Tenggeri" thus still relying on the chain of legitimacy already established by Chinggis Khan.

The letter of Ölziit Khan sent to the rulers of European countries soon after his enthronement is "specially interesting"[35] since it refers to previous contacts thus establishing a network of contacts.

> Hearken, Ölziit Sultan, our word to the Frank sultan.
>
> How could it be forgotten that from ancient times you Sultans of the Frank citizens have dealt peacefully with our good great grandfather, good grandfather, good father and good brother, and although we have been far away, we have always been close to each other and exchanging various words, envoys and gifts of well wishes. Today, with the power of the Tenggeri we have ascended the throne and without disregarding the orders and instructions of (our) previous khans – (our) noble ancestors, (our) good fathers and when I have become their khan, we have followed the well-established rules (and) and without neglecting the agreement of allegiance (with your consent) that we had reached with the kings that ruled in the past, we are planning to exchange ambassadors so that we could be friends. We, brothers and sisters, because of (owing to) the souring of relations and exchange of fallacious (toxic) words (in the past)we began to detest each other. Now all of us, Tömör Khan,Tsapar (also written as Chapar), Togtoga (also written as Tokhtogha, Toqta) and Togba and ourselves, main descendants of Chinggis Khan, all of us, descendants and brothers, are reconciled through the inspiration and the help of Tenggeri after past forty years and five of odd with each

35 *History of the Mongolian People's Republic. Volume One. From Early Times to the XVII Century*. Ulaanbaatar, 1966. p. 379.

> other until nowand we have built highways (relay stations and have revived communication) from the land of the Nankhiad (China) in the east from where the sun rises upto Talu (Red) Sea and our nations have been now connected. We have agreed that whoever interferes (with ill intentions) in our affairs we shall come together (to withstand against them). Today, with a strong feeling why we should not remember that (our) good ancestors, (our) good fathers and (our) good brothers have been in friendly relations (with you all), I am hereby sending my two ambassador Mamal and Toman to you all. You have said (to us) that the many kings of the many Franks are in friendship and agreement with each other. In truth, can there anything be better than concord? If anybody was not in concord with either you or ourselves, then we would defend ourselves together. Let the *Tenggeri* decide! This letter has been written on the old eight day of the first summer month of the Year of the Snake (1305) in 704 while I am in Alivan.[36]

In their book *Letters sent to French Philip the Fair by Il Khan Argun and Ölziit Khan in 1289 and 130,* Mongolists A. Mostaert and F.W. Cleaves had written: "The common initial formula "With the power of the Eternal Tenggeri", The destiny of the Master Khan are to be found in the letters of Gazan Khan and Ölziit Khan, and also the words "Eternal Tenggeri" in the seal of Ölziit Khan and his son Abu Sa'id, but the word "Tenggeri" that is to be found in the letters and other documents of the khans and princes, who had converted into Islam, could be interpreted as the Allah."[37]

These letters to the West-European States were supplemented by letters to the Sultans of the Mameluk.[38] As indicated, all the attempts made by the IL-Khans and their diplomats to convince the West-European powers to join the Mongols in an alliance failed. One can only speculate about the reason. Perhaps the ultimate reason was that the Mongolian leaders would not convert to Christianity although they were religiously tolerant in respect of the population they governed.[39]

---

36 Mostaert, A., Cleaves, F.W. *Letters sent to French Philip the Fair by Il Khan Argun and Ölziit Khan in 1289 and 1305*. Translated by Tömörkhüleg, T. 1998. pp. 86–87.

37 *Ibid*. pp. 86–87.

38 Edited by Ai-Preiss, R.A & Morgan, D.O. (1999). *The Mongol Empire and Its Legacy* (*Islamic History and Civilization*. Vol. 24). Brill, Leiden, Boston, Koln.

39 Denise Aigle. "The Letters of Eljigidei, Hülegü and Abaqa: Mongol Overtures or Christian Ventriloquism?" *Inner Asia*. 2005. 7 (2). pp. 143–162.

6 Standing of the Mongolian Empire in International Relations

It would not be adequate as regards the standing of the Mongolian Empire in international relations to rely on the letters between the Mongolian Khans and the leaders of other States alone. Equally important in this context would be an evaluation of the treaties between the Mongolian Empire and other States.

According to historical evidence there must have existed many treaties or treaty-like arrangements between the Mongolian Empire and other States. They vary in substance and they have changed in this respect over time. The treaties already concluded between the Mongolian Empire under Chinggis Khan as well as Ögödei Khan with today's Korea regulated the relationship between these two States. It is evident that the relationship was not one of equality. Other treaties of later periods dealt with economic matters, specific fields of cooperation and – as was demonstrated by activities of the IL-Khans – cooperation in respect of a perceived common enemy. However, such type of treaties even existed earlier. For instance, Mönkh Khan and Hethum II of Armenia concluded a treaty in Kharakhorum in1253, according to which the Armenian King took commitment to convert Mönkh Khan into Christianity, establish eternal friendship and comradeship between Christians and the Mongols, relieve Christian churches and priests in the land occupied by the Mongols and those lands the Mongols plan to occupy from all kinds of taxes, liberate Jerusalem and return it to the Christians, wage a war against the Caliphate of Baghdad, render, when necessary, military assistance to Armenia.

7 Some Tentative Conclusions

As indicated at the beginning the conclusions, which may be drawn from the exchange of letters/decrees started by Chinggis Khan can only be tentative ones. They should be supplemented by an evaluation of the treaties concluded by the Mongolian Khans. However, the material before us allows us to answer the questions raised at the beginning.

Chinggis Khan established its legitimacy to rule by reference to a spiritual entity – the Eternal Sky (Tenggeri). In that respect his legitimization did not differ from the approach followed by the European Rulers referring to the Grace of God. It is telling that even when the IL-Khan became a Muslim and referred to himself as a Sultan he still used the traditional reference to Eternal Sky as an element legitimizing his governance. However, the Mongolian Khans also used other mechanisms of legitimization, namely a form of an electoral process and an acclamation at the assembly. In one respect their legitimization was different. They referred to the pacification of the areas und their governance. This element had its starting point in a declaration by Chinggis Khan himself:

> When I was 13, I waged wars against some seventy revolting countries in all the four directions and against the twelfth king, and after 32 years of effort, made the northern territory into a peaceful realm. All the people of the tümen (ten thousand) state giving credit to me, an uneducated being, for suppressing the enemies once and for all, thus making the tümen land peaceful and tranquil, for which they elevated me as the Khan and out of great respect named the country Khökh (Blue)Mongol and named me Chinggis Khan. Thus, this humble self with utter disregard for my own sufferings and toil, for the good of hundred tümen people, following the command of the Tenggeri, became the Khan, which was proclaimed to lands near and far. To be brief, this humble servant will rise and destroy all those who go against the Tenggeri.
>
> Humble servants shall respect and carry high those who follow the Tenggeri. For this, our Great Mongol State has sent messages to the Song Dynasty, the Jing Dynasty of China, Koryo, Tibet, Nepal and Kashgar.[40]

The standing of the Mongolian Empire developed in connection with its expansion and some time even before. The Mongolian Empire became a partner of its direct neighbors already in the period under Chinggis Khan and reached a peak under Khubilai Khan.

As referred to in the letters of the Mongolian Khans they saw it as their mandate to conquer the whole world. However, it would not be adequate to reduce Mongolian foreign policy to expansion. It transpires from some of the letters that Mongolian Khans felt that expansion would lead to an establishment and preservation of peace (as it had been a fact with respect to the Mongolian homeland) and to an increase of the freedom of trade. In this context it should be mentioned that under the Mongolian Khans a legal system had been established. The applicable laws had been codified (the *Great Yassa*);[41] that Chinggis Khan and Khubilai Khan were interested in fostering international trade relations is well established.

40 Jügder, Ch. *The evolution of the socio-political and philosophical thoughts of the Mongols*. Ulaanbaatar. 2006. p. 151.

41 As to the interest in a legal system see Rüdiger Wolfrum, *Das Recht der Mongolei unter Dschingis Khan und sseinen Nachfolgern: Die Bedeutung des Rechts in nicht-staatlich verfassten Gesellschaften, Verfassung und Recht in Übersee,* Vol. 39/40 (2006/07), pp. 5- 17, where I referred to the integrating force of law.

On the whole, the Mongolian Khans were – in respect of their international relations actions – guided by several principles.

They were committed to the sending and receiving of envoys (ambassadors). A whole regime had been established including details concerning a diplomatic passport, credentials etc. They protected these envoys and expected their protection. Such envoys enjoyed certain privileges as far as travelling was concerned. It should be mentioned in this context too that the Mongolian Khans concluded agreements of various kinds and expected them to be observed.

Another feature, particularly relevant in respect of their expansion policy was their tolerance concerning religious freedoms with respect to exercising religious services as well as adhering to particular religions. In this respect the Mongolian Khans did not receive a reciprocal answer. As a matter of fact, it seems that the insistence of the various Popes that the Mongolian Khans were to become Christians constituted a major hindrance for a closer cooperation.

As far as military warfare is concerned, practice shows that for the Mongolian Khans it was necessary that a military attack had to be justified. Mostly the violation of Mongolian ambassadors and the interruption of international trade was considered sufficient to justify an attack. Today's invocation of proportionality clearly played no role. Issuing a warning before an attack was launched was considered necessary.

Considering the development of Mongolia under Chinggis Khan I would argue today that Mongolia had achieved statehood at the end of the reign of Chinggis Khan.

Introduction

1 Why This Research?

The prism of history does not look at the present from the past. Rather, it looks to the future from today's perspective. When a person wakes up, he/she thinks of the things done the day before and contemplates the actions for today. This is where the thought process about history and historical lessons begins. The deep internal link between history and the contemporary gives the possibility to discover the past. Remember what the great writer William Shakespeare wrote in his play *The Tempest*: "What's past is prologue." The present becomes a direct continuation of the past; it includes in itself many aspects of past society and inherits them, which is proven by the science of history. Hence it follows that the science of history is a science that studies the historical processes of various developmental aspects of humankind, nations and social relations, and the lessons learned from them.

To be more precise, history is a science that considers the organic links between the past, the present and the future of humankind; in short, the history of science can very well be defined as a science of human life. The fundamental science about Mongolia is its history. Its scientific disciplines include the archaeology of Mongolia, the ethnography of Mongolia, the political history of Mongolia, the State and legal history of Mongolia, the history of the economy of Mongolia, the cultural history of Mongolia, the history of the art of Mongolia and so on and so forth. There is also the applied science of the history of Mongolia, including the chronology of Mongolia, historical anthropometry, sigillography, numismatics, and paleography of Mongolia etc. The applied science of history is the key to unlocking the mysteries of history. In this respect, the State and legal history of Mongolia is a branch of the science of the history of Mongolia.

The subject of study, the State and legal history of Mongolia, the sources and the methods of research are, first and foremost, invariably connected with the theory of Statehood, the theory of law, and their traditions and customs. They are the prologue to studying the course of the development of statehood and law.

The juncture when Statehood and law appeared from phenomena, which had occurred before the evolution of law, is today studied through such applied sciences as legal archaeology and historical legal research. Such research can yield tangible results only when a comparative research method is applied in studying the history of the Statehood and law of Mongolia, and other nations and countries. It must also be noted here that the outcome would have a far-flung impact if the study were based on a broad background of Mongolia's history.

The historical comparative research method makes it possible to identify the unique features of the general rules of the Statehood and legal development of the different States that existed on the territory of Mongolia during different historical periods, and how they differ from that of other nations and peoples.

Historical continuity forms the key pre-condition for the methodology of the history of the State and law. All State and legal phenomena are born from the past and they determine their future shapes and forms. The "connection between times and periods" makes it possible to consider all social phenomena in a single historical perspective. Different times are the telescopes of history.

A legal environment develops as a result of differing customs, actions, rules and institutions, which act as a means of carrying out legal activities. A person's actions are based on the notion of honesty and dishonesty, on what is legal or illegal. The legal environment, at various levels of development, has been non-identical, and was either conventional or compound. Its central component is a precedent, which is one of its key legal sources.

Another important source are customs and traditions. These notions are non-legal phenomena in a given society. But whenever the State takes them under its patronage, they become the legal source for and the legal standards of customs and traditions.

The "law," broadly speaking, becomes a legal source when the legal environment reaches a higher level of technological development.

In brief, in the history of the State and the law, the theory of the State and the theory of the law serve as prelude to a comprehensive study of the branch sciences of law and tune the strings of the State and legal thinking of a given jurist. A jurist ignorant about the history of the State and the law of the country is like a parrot that mindlessly and mechanically repeats what others have said.

2 The Chronology of the State and Legal History of Mongolia

Putting the state and legal history of Mongolia into chronological order is helpful in specifying the general and separating the inevitable from the accidental, which is dependent on multiple factors. The most important and decisive factors among them are socio-economic and political development factors, including the level of economic, technical and technological development, and the forms of ownership. In this respect, researchers of the history of the State and the law focus their attention on the different forms of the State and the laws, facts and phenomena.

The State and legal history of Mongolia, with due consideration for the general principles of the history of humankind and Mongolia, as well as the special features of history, can be put in the following chronological order.

1 *The Ancient Period of the State and legal history of Mongolia (3rd century BCE to 13th century CE).* This period starts with the formation of the first Empire in the history of Inner Asia, the Hunnu Empire (209 BCE-9 CE), and covers the period up to the establishment of the Great Mongol Empire in the 13th century. During this period, ancient societies made up of people of Mongol and non-Mongol origin existed on the territory of Mongolia, during which Statehood took shape, and a transition was made from customary law to written law.

2 *The Medieval Period of the State and legal history of Mongolia (13th to early 20th centuries).* This covers a period roughly extending for more than 700 years. This was a complicated period marked by ups and downs in the Mongol Statehood. The Great Mongol Empire was established in the 13th–16th centuries, which formed a large State that ruled almost one half of the world, and where people of different races and ethnic groups lived under the might and grandeur of a fundamental law called the *Ikh Zasag* (*The Great Yassa: A code of honour, dignity and excellence passed by Chinggis Khan. Tr.*). But the principles of Mongolia's Statehood began to weaken, starting in the 15th century when Mongolia came under the domination of the Qing Dynasty of the Manchus, from the 18th to the early 20th centuries. In such a complicated twist of destiny in their history, the Mongols aspired to preserve and continue the traditions of Mongolia's Statehood and enforced a whole set of codes of laws tinged with nationalistic feelings and colours, which played an extremely important social and legal role in the history of Mongolia.

3 *The Near Period of the State and legal history of Mongolia (covering the period from the 1920s of the 20th century to the early 1990s).* A new period in the State and legal history of Mongolia began on March 1921 with the establishment of the People's Provisional Government in Mongolia. This period covers the years up to 1990 when the country made some fundamentally important changes and amendments to its Constitution. Mongolia, at this juncture, opted for a constitutional State system, which was unquestionably an important historical and progressive move. However, the social structure of the country gradually started to follow the polarised line of Communism (orthodox Communism), which led to a serious distortion of the natural course of development of Mongolia's Statehood and had a very se-

rious negative impact on the country's progress and development. This historical period witnessed the evolution and growth of a modern legal system based on the Romano-Germanic legal system and the theory of Socialism. In the course of the development of the new State and legal system in the country, laws and legislation became distinguished for their class and party differentiation, and the trend towards imitation and formalism took the upper hand, as a consequence of which the legal system of the country became totally alien, non-Mongolian. However, we cannot overlook the many important and progressive changes that also took place in the evolution of our Statehood and legal system, which in many ways were unprecedented in nature.

4 *The Present Stage of the State and legal history of Mongolia (covering the period from the 1990s to the present time).* The Constitution of 1990 did away with the system of one-party rule and later in 1992 the country's Parliament adopted a new Constitution that holistically reflected the universally acknowledged and accepted norms and standards of human rights. According to this Constitution, Mongolia, as a Parliamentary State, is a Parliamentary Republic and is a unitary State in terms of its State structure.

The highest State legislature, the State Great *Khural,* is formed through free and democratic elections. The Head of State, the President, is elected through universal suffrage. Legal reforms have been carried out in all the domains and branches of our social life, and this process of reform is taking deeper and stronger root in the country.

1 The State and Legal Systems of the Early Mongol Empires and Dynasties (4th Century BCE–12th Century CE)

1 Historical Summary

The first ancient social structure of Mongolia emerged on the basis of blood relationships. This was a system of clans where people came together to engage in joint production. Those clans that became stronger and more powerful brought other weaker clans under their rule. This led to the disintegration of the system based on blood relationships, resulting in the formation of a distinctive unity of people, which was at a much higher level that the ancient tribal and clan systems. The disintegration of the clan system appertains to almost one thousand years BCE, which coincides with the historical period of transition from the Bronze to the Iron Age. The union of tribes and military democracy became the pre-requisite for the evolution and growth of Statehood, especially in the final stages of the collapse of the clan system.

The alliance of the Hunnu, which originated and was established in the 4th century BCE, created the first major State composition in Central and East Asia. Starting from the period of the Hunnu, clans and tribes adapted the decimal system of ten thousands, which was an administrative and military division. Kinship among the clans and tribes could very well be defined as the State administrative unit of the Hunnu people. This is why Hunnu researchers and scholars, such as L. N. Gumilyev, having studied the Hunnu State structure, have concluded that the social structure of the Hunnu was not based on classes, but on the union of tribes or the so-called "military democracy."[1]

However, the Mongol tribes in the 6th to 12th centuries were patrilineal, predominantly made up of members of one family, descendants of high nobles, in which men held primary power and predominated in roles of political leadership, moral authority, social privilege and control of property, by bringing under their control other people, households, clans and tribes.[2]

---

1 L. N. Gumilyev, *Hunnu in China*, St. Petersburg, 1994, pp. 71, 83.

2 Ts. Gombosüren, "Was the Traditional Mongolian Society Feudalism?" Ulaanbaatar, 1995, p. 27.

This period witnessed the appearance of ever new tribes. This did not mark the formation of the tribal system, but rather the formation, in the real meaning of the word, of the lineage of the nobility in the ancient nomadic society. Some of them had features and qualities of Statehood. In this sense, we can assume that with these features and qualities, the relatively unitary nature of the tribes was the defining (social) organisational set-up.

The Mongol tribes of this period, although quite homogeneous, had a much simpler structure than the tribes in terms of their social organisational set-up, and some of them, with their military prowess, outstripped some larger tribes and even advanced far beyond them. Doctor (D.Sc.), Professor Ts. Gombosüren drew the following interesting conclusion: "The life of the tribes and their economic activities passed and organized through relatively independent aristocrats and powerful people, who collectively (by the entire tribe) took care of and tended their livestock on the land that belonged to them."[3]

Apart from the Hunnu, a number of Mongol and non-Mongol States existed on the territory of Mongolia during the period under consideration and the Mongol khanates and tribes somehow maintained their Statehood during the period from the 6th to the 12th century. Let us now summarise in chronological order the history of the Statehood and legal traditions of the ancient societies of the Mongol nomads.

2 The Hunnu (Xiongnu) Empire (4th century BCE–2nd century BCE)

2.1 *Historical Sources*

The Hunnu (Xiongnu) are one of the oldest tribes that lived on the territory of Mongolia from the 4th century BCE. For the first time in the history of Central Asian nomads, the Hunnu established the first State in 209 BCE and established codes of laws, leaving behind an indelible footprint on the culture and civilization of not only Mongolia but also of the whole of Central Asia, thus playing a historically important role. The history of the establishment of the State by the Hunnu is believed to be the very beginning of the development of Statehood and the rule of law in Mongolia, which became a fertile soil for their further growth. Research conducted in recent years reveals that the State of the Hunnu was a mixture of different peoples and races, predominantly the Mongols, who held the reins of power. Scholars are also attempting to prove that Mongolia's Statehood began much earlier than that established by the Hunnu.

3 *Ibid.*, p. 29.

Modun, who acceded to the throne as the Khan of the Hunnu in the year 209 BCE, was a historical figure who established the first nation State. The State of the Hunnu, under the power and might of their Khan, the Modun, united different clans and tribes, introduced the hierarchy of nobility and the principle of military and administrative divisions. It formed an army designed to use force, replaced the common gathering of the people with the assembly of the princes and nobles, the so-called *Ei,* and introduced a rule of law on the foundations of the norms and standards of tribal customs. Worldwide, there is a growing interest in the study of the Hunnu.[4]

2.2 *State Formation*

In terms of State system, the Hunnu were a monarchy. The ruler or the Khan of the Hunnu was called the *Shanyu*. The Shanyu conducted internal State matters through the Council of Ministers by appointing, dismissing, punishing and even executing major government officials, such as the leader of the *tümet* (10,000), replenishing the State (Khan's) coffers, and pacifying the subordinate subjects. The Shanyu exchanged letters and notes with the Chinese emperors, established treaties and agreements, played host to and saw off visiting foreign envoys, and declared war and peace with other States. In other words, the Shanyu exercised a supreme right in handling matters related the State's foreign policy.

The Hunnu believed in the Eternal Blue Sky and revered their Shanyu as a celestial Emperor with exceptional power. This is why the Shanyu was even called *Chenli Gutu* (meaning "Son of Heaven"). This was a method by which the exclusive authority of the Khan was justified from the premises of shamanism. The so-called concept of the "Son of Heaven" was embedded in the consciousness of the Mongols over many generations. This later led to the appearance and the establishment of the fundamental idea of eternal rule, and respect and reverence for the State.

In terms of origin, Modun Shanyu belonged to the so-called Xyuilianti tribe. And so men from this tribe alone, and primarily the prince, were nominated and elected as the Shanyu. In other words, the Shanyu's son mostly inherited the throne. Disregard for this tradition, in some way or other, became frequent in the last years of the existence of the Hunnu. Up until the rule of Huhanye Shanyu (58–31 BCE), 8 of the 14 Shanyus were direct sons who inherited the throne, while 3 of the Shanyus succeeded their elder brothers, and the remaining 3 Shanyus acceded to the throne in different ways.

---

4 *The History and Culture of the Hunnu,* Collective Work, Ulaanbaatar, 2011, p. 9.

The Shanyus, who succeeded Modun Shanyu, began to use additional titles. For instance, Modun's son Qiyui Shanyu had the title of *Taoshang*.[5]

The State symbol of the Hunnu Shanyu was a jade seal and the nine symbols of an Emperor included among others a banner, stool, and sunshade. We know from historical sources that Zhizhi Shanyu had a banner of five colours.

The main (palace) residence of the Shanyus was in a place close to present-day Khöshöö Tsaidam in Arkhangai *aimag* (Central Mongolia). Modun was the first among the Shanyus to establish a State, for which he is not only distinguished as having a lot of merit, but also as being the most pragmatic and prudent among all the Shanyus. In order to maintain good relations with the neighbouring Donghu people, he offered them his best horses and married off his beloved wife, but when the Donghu people contemptuously asked for a slice of land, Modun Shanyu said that "Land is the bedrock of a nation" and mobilised his army to crush the Donghu people. Since then, the conventional phrase "Land is the bedrock of a nation" has remained the spirit and soul of the concept of Mongolia's Statehood. It must be noted here that the Treaty signed by the Hunnu with the Chinese Han Dynasty in 198 BCE established the "Great Wall" as the border between the two nations.

2.3 *Administrative Division and Officialdom*

The Hunnu Empire, from the very beginning, had an organised administrative system, with relevant procedures and principles. Once established as the Shanyu, Modun immediately carried out his reforms by dividing the country into three parts, Central, Eastern and Western territories on a regional basis, taking the Central area under his own rule. The Empire was made up of 24 *tümen*[6] (a unit of ten thousand troops each). The unit system of tens, hundreds, thousands and ten-thousands was a unique military and administrative set-up, which was best suited to the nomadic mode of life.

A system of ranked officialdom was established under the State apparatus of the Hunnu Empire. This meant that officials with special skills and knowledge, expertise and experience were assigned to carry out administrative managerial functions; in other words, this was a set-up to exercise special executive powers on behalf of the State and the legal

5 *The History and Culture of the Hunnu*, Collective Work, Ulaanbaatar, 2011, p. 103.

6 G. Sükhbaatar, *Anthology of the History of Mongolia, Book One*, Ulaanbaatar, 1992, p. 84.

system. Under the Shanyu, big and small government officials, according to their ranks and titles, served in the Empire. The government officials were even divided on a regional basis as leaders of the Eastern and Western territories, which included the so-called Eastern and Western Setsen Wang, Guli Wang, the Great Commanders, the Great Duwei, the Great Danghu and the Guduhou.

The four Wangs – Tutsi (Setsen) Wang of the East and the West, and the Eastern and Western Guli Wang – had the largest pieces of land under their control and had the most lavish (*ger* or *yurt*) palaces and they were appointed by the Shanyu himself. The Wangs also commanded more than ten thousand cavalry and they were of noble origin and so had a better chance of acceding to the throne as a khan. From among these Wangs, the most powerful was Setsen Wang with extensive authority, who was appointed by the eldest son of the Shanyu. These Wangs were also called the "Wangs with Four Horns," and after them came the Great Commanders, the Great Duwei and the Great Danghu. These officials holding the title of "Great", who commanded ten thousand warriors, were called the "Wangs with Six Horns." The use of horns was in fact related to totemism, which was a legacy of the clan system.

Leaders with "Ten Horns" commanded the *tümen* (ten thousand) followed by the commander of the 140 thousand. The commanders of the *tümen* were small Wangs who commanded several thousand soldiers; however, the Wangs with the highest ranks were the Guduhou of the Eastern and Western territories. The Guduhou policed the alien tribes and were responsible for administrative matters as well as for the judiciary. Under each commander of the *tümen* were the commanders of the units of thousands, hundreds and tens, and smaller ranking Wangs, key assistants, Duwei, Danghu and Tsetsui. There are indications that an envoy with the title of Tsetsui visited the Han Dynasty in 62 BCE. Although the commanders of the 24 *tümen* were from the noble tribes of the key tribe of Xanyui, they had different ranks, titles and categories according to their authority and office, the number and kinds of soldiers they commanded, and the land under their ownership.

The Hunnu Empire, after overrunning a foreign land, appointed the so-called *Jizhu Wang*. From historical sources, we know that they also had officials, the so-called *Dinlin Wang, Dunhu Wang* and *Hutse Wang* who directly governed the occupied lands. The current level of research does not make it possible to determine precisely and accurately for what kind of matters all these numerous ranking officials were responsible.

DIAGRAM 1 State structure of the Hunnu Empire

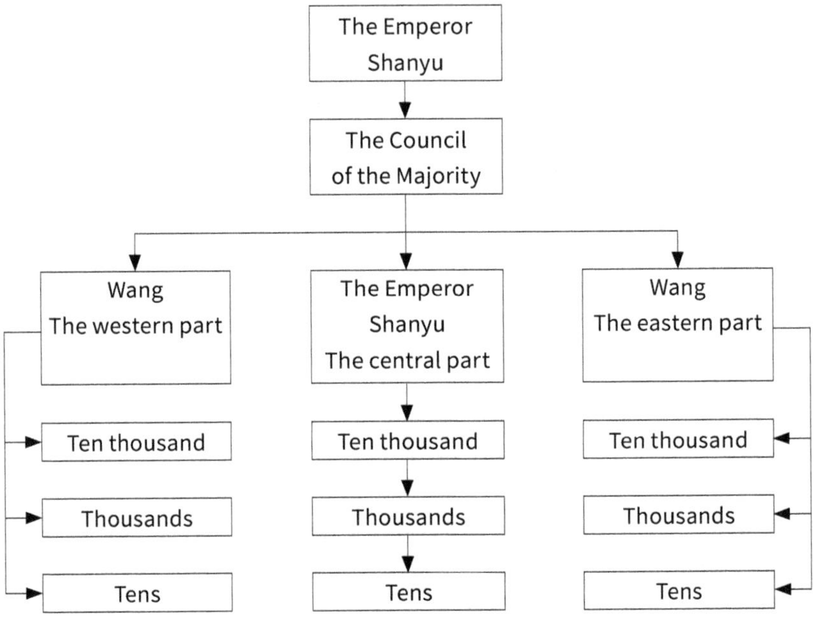

2.4 *The* Khurildai

One form in which the Hunnu conducted their State affairs was through the *Khurildai* (meaning assembly). A book called "Historical Notes" *(Xizhi)* writes that "All the leaders and commanders gathered in the *ger* of the Shanyu during the White Lunar month to make offerings. They meet for a great assembly in Lu in the month of May to make offerings and sacrifice to the elders, the Heaven, the universe and the mountain spirits. In fall, when the steeds have put on weight, they gather for a great assembly at Dailing to carry out a census of population and livestock animals."[7] Judging by this documentary evidence we know that the Hunnu had two gatherings, the great and the small *Khurildai* (assembly). Commanders of the *Tümen* – ten thousands – apparently gathered in the *ger* of the Shanyu for the small *Khurildai* to greet each other on the occasion of the New Year and to discuss important issues of State. This could have been the maiden form of the switch-over from the assembly of the people during the period of the clan system to a restricted form of assembly or gathering of the ruling nobles. O. Pritsak, who carried out research into the official bodies of the Hunnu, has noted that the Hunnu had a council of 24 mem-

7 G. Sükhbaatar, *Ancestors of the Mongols,* Ulaanbaatar, 1980, pp. 73–74.

bers (commanders of the detachments of a *tümen* or the ten thousand), which met in the town of Lunchen on the banks of Onon River three times every year in the first, fifth and ninth months of the year to consider important State matters.[8] Judging by this, one gets the impression that the small *Khurildai* and the State council were one and the same thing. The fact that the assemblies held at Lunchen and Dailing have been qualified as the great *Khurildai* supports the assumption that they were not only major large-scale events for making offerings attended by the entire population of the Hunnu, but a continuation, even in a formal manner, of the assembly of the people that was held during the clan system.

However, neither the great nor the small *Khurildai* passed the final judgment on the issues discussed, as they were institutions that only had the role of advising the Shanyu. With the deepening of the process of Statehood, the role of the small *Khuraldaa* or the State council increased, thus laying the foundations for the future Great or *Ikh* (Supreme) *Khurildai*.

2.5 *The Army*

The formation of the army, an institution of force, was an inseparable component of the State structure of the Hunnu Empire. A key duty of the Hunnu army was to safeguard and protect the country from foreign aggression, and to expand the Empire by invading other nations and peoples.

The army was organised in the unit of tens, which made it more versatile and effective as compared to the combatants of the older systems of the clans and tribes. In other words, the administrative unit of the Hunnu during this period was gradually being turned into a military set-up. It appears that at one time the Hunnu had as many as 400,000 soldiers. Modun Shanyu with his 400 thousand cavalry laid siege to the town of Pincheng (the present-day town of Datong) of Gaodi (Gaozu) Emperor of the Han Dynasty, locating cavalrymen with white horses on the Northern part of the two, horses with a white patch on the forehead in the Eastern part, black horses on the Northern and grey horses on the Southern part.[9] This was a proof of the highly organised nature of the Hunnu army. A soldier who failed to report at the designated time and place was put to the sword. The Hunnu soldiers, when they were on the move for a battle, brought along their wives and children to take care of the carts. Such combatants were called the *ger* (yurt) soldiers. From the "Historical Notes" we

8 G. Sükhbaatar, *Anthology of the History of Mongolia, Book One,* Ulaanbaatar, 1992, p. 73. (Indirect quote).

9 G. Sükhbaatar, *Ancestors of the Mongols,* Ulaanbaatar, 1980, p. 69.

find that the cavalry of the Hunnu were armour-plated; they used long-range bows and arrows, and for close-range combat, they used swords and armoured shields with wooden handles, but their horses were not armoured. The Hunnu were expert horse riders and could shoot arrows from their bows from the back of a running steed. They used whistling arrows to intimidate their enemies. The cavalry, if required, could cover from 200 to 250 kilometers in one day on horseback.

2.6 *Basic Legal Features*

The first State founded by the Hunnu was a legalised expression of the social system of the given period and so they left behind some concrete sources of legal history. The "Historical Notes" (*Xizhi*) writing about the legal sources of the Hunnu mentions that "according to their law, a person who dared to use a sharp-edged tool was executed, and a person who has committed robbery, depending on the severity of the crime, the property of the convict's family members was confiscated and those thieves whose crimes was severely grave, was sentenced to death."[10] Also the convicted were made to toil in the handicraft and house industry.[11] From this, it follows that the Hunnu had four kinds of punishment, which included flogging, confiscation of property, forced hard labour and capital punishment. Also, an analysis of the statement that "a criminal would not be detained for more than ten days, or the number of prisoners in the entire empire would not exceed certain number" we can assume that incarceration had not quite become an independent form of punishment given the unique nature of the mode of life of the nomads, and so detention was a kind of preventative measure executed for a certain period to determine the seriousness of the offence. On the other hand, the law of the Hunnu was very strict and so there were very few who dared to violate it.

Traditional and customary rules and principles lay in the origin of the legal norms and standards of the Hunnu. In this regard, it can be assumed that their legal sources were not literal, which had elements and features of customary legal norms based on the tradition of taboo that had been inherited from the tribal system. Hence, the legal norms of the Hunnu can be included in the category of special law.

The Shanyu served as the supreme judge of the Hunnu Empire. This is identical to traditions in ancient Oriental countries, where the head of the State served as the supreme judge. The "History of the Former Han Dynasty" (Qian Han shu) notes that "The Huyan' tribes of Eastern Han,

10 *Ibid.*, p. 71.
11 Ts. Dorjsüren, *Northern Hunnu*, Ulaanbaatar, 1961, p. 80.

the Lan' and Xiubei tribes of Western Han were executors of court of law, who passed sentences, which was orally reported to the Shanyu, but was neither written nor any book used."[12] This means that the Shanyu listened to the special cases in the kingdom that were handled by the court, monitored the court proceedings and appointed the judicial authorities. This also reveals that the judicial power was concentrated in the hands of the ruling Huyan tribes in the empire. The Shanyu also passed sentences, overturned or mitigated sentences passed by other judicial officials, and anyone who had committed a serious crime detrimental to the vital interests of the empire, or who contemplated such a crime was sent to the gallows. For example, some important officials who had suggested that a piece of land be given to the Donghu people were given capital punishment by Modun Shanyu. However, in the initial period of the growth and development of the Hunnu Empire, the suspects were judged by the elders. The responsibility of these elders was somewhat similar to the judges who determined if a suspect was guilty of a crime or not.

We have to admit that the severity of punishment in the Hunnu Empire depended on the origin and social status of the convicted, which was one way of protecting and giving priority to the interests of the nobility.

The law of the Hunnu society was not only related to the traditions of the tribal system, but also, to a certain degree, to religious beliefs similar to that of the law of slave societies, such as Greece. For example, in the year 47 BCE, Hulugu Shanyu of the Hunnu entered into a treaty with the Han Court pledging allegiance by slaughtering a white horse and licking a knife.

2.7 *Duties and Taxes*

One of the principal State functions of the Hunnu was to replenish the State coffers by levying duties and taxes, which is pursuing an economic policy. Under the Hunnu Empire, the land belonged to the State, in other words, the Shanyu. As important government officials, such as the commanders of the *Tümen* (unit of ten thousand) owned pasturelands, they were obliged also to pay both rent and tax. Internally, the Hunnu Empire levied duties, the size of which was determined by the size of human and livestock population, and that is why a human and animal census was carried out in the fall. Apparently, the size of the "privately owned land" was not taken into consideration.

The Hunnu Empire also accepted tribute from the nations they had occupied. For instance, in the year 198 BCE, the Han Dynasty, according to

12 G. Sükhbaatar, *Ancestors of the Mongols*, Ulaanbaatar, 1980, p. 72.

the bilateral treaty, paid tributes in measures of silk and silken goods, which can be classified as an "invisible duty." The Hunnu Empire had conquered a number of countries of Central Asia, where they installed the Jizhu Wang and accepted rice and grain, and handicraft works in tribute.

2.8 *Religious Beliefs*

The State humanitarian function of the Hunnu was related to religion and religious beliefs. The Hunnu primarily believed in shamanism. They made offerings to their elders, the heavens, the universe and the mountains during the Lunar New Year, and in the fifth and ninth months of the year, and the Shanyu would pay obeisance to the Sun in the morning and the Moon in the evening. When the Shanyu fell ill, the Hunnu shamans would make the captured Chinese commanders the death-escorts. The headgear and boots of a shaman were recovered from grave number 6 in the Noyon Uul Mountain.

In the early period of the Hunnu Empire, shamanism was the State ideology. This is confirmed by numerous facts, including the fact that Shanyu was regarded as the "Son of Heaven," that shamanistic rituals were used in diplomacy, Modun Shanyu in his letter to the Han Emperor signed it off as "The Great Shanyu under the Power of the Heavens," and shamanistic rituals were performed when bilateral agreements were concluded. However, in the later period of development of the Hunnu Empire, Buddhism came through Central Asia and China. The upper echelons of the Hunnu nobility considered Buddhism as important for the consolidation of the State structure and unification of the society, and therefore made efforts to turn Buddhism into the Empire's fundamental ideology. Syuchuge Wang of the Hunnu, who then lived in the neighbourhood of Hoh Nuur Lake and Gansu, had a deity, a 3 meters high painting of a god, which was the painting of the Lord Buddha,[13] according to Chinese scholars in the 3rd to 5th centuries CE. The Hunnu Empire disintegrated in the year 93 CE and was succeeded by the Sumbe (Xianbe) State.

13 *The development of state structure and political thinking in Mongolia (3rd century BCE–20th century)*, Volume One, Ulaanbaatar, 1995, p. 13.

3 The Sumbe State (2nd century–4th century CE)

3.1 *The State System, The Khan*

The State of Sumbe (Xianbe)[14] was an ancient State of Mongol origin that succeeded by adapting the Statehood and code of law norms and standards of the Hunnu Empire on the present territory of Mongolia. This State existed from the second to the fifth centuries CE and as the people of Sumbe lived in the neighbourhood of the Sumbe Mountain, they acquired this name. The Sumbe people have one and the same origin as the Hunnu and their customs and traditions were also identical, meaning they were adapted from the Hunnu people. Tanshihuai (136–181 CE) founded the State of Sumbe.

The State of Sumbe, in terms of its political governance, was quite similar to that of the Hunnu; that is, it was a monarchy. The Sumbe people called their leader the *Tolgoilogch (in Mongolian this means the Chieftain. Tr.)*. But after the death of Tanshihuai, the khanship became hereditary; however, the accession process passed through an assembly of the nobles. According to historical sources, the Tabgach clan, the aristocratic Sumbe people, elected their leader by making seven descendants of the Khan sit on a black felt carpet looking towards the West, and after they paid obeisance to the Heaven, they would be declared their Khan.

There was a common belief among the Sumbe people that their leader Khan was the Son of the Heaven, who was blessed by the Heaven. For example, when Tanshihuai's father Toluhou returned home after serving for three years in the army of the Hunnu, he was enraged to find his wife had borne him a son, whom he attempted to kill. His wife said to him: "In the afternoon, when I was walking, suddenly there was a thunderburst and when I looked up a hailstone fell in my mouth and I gulped it and then I became pregnant, and I gave birth to this boy after ten months. He might be an exceptional prodigal boy, let us wait for him to grow up." Toluhou did not heed his wife and abandoned his son in the wild. His wife sent her maid to find her abandoned son and took care of him secretively. This boy was Tanshihuai. People were amazed at the wit and valour of the boy when he reached the age of 14–15. A legend goes that one day when a stranger from an adversary tribe robbed his mother of her cow and sheep, Tanshihuai hunted down the stranger on horseback and brought back the animals, after which the people of Sumbe made him their Khan.[15] This is one different version of the legend of Alun Goo (*Alan Qo'a or Alun Goo is a*

---

14 The name Sumbe for the State of Xianbe was used as chosen by Professor G. Sükhbaatar.

15 P. Delgerjargal, *The Early History of Xianbi, Book Two,* Ulaanbaatar, 2017.

mythical figure from The Secret History of the Mongols, eleven generations after the grey wolf and the white doe, and ten generations before Genghis Khan. Tr.).

The title *Tolgoilogch* or Chieftain, as the Sumbe people named their leader, must be distinguished from the simple term chieftain that was used under the tribal system. This is because the leader of the Sumbe people had enormous wealth and power, and actually carried out the functions of a Head of State.

3.2 *The Khurildai*

The *Khurildai* (Assembly) in the Sumbe State had totally lost its tribal democratic features to become, to all appearances, a gathering of the ruling nobility. At times, the *Khurildai* proceeded amid severe struggle and antagonism. Kebinen (?-235 CE) at one such *Khurildai* killed the tribal chief Fulokhan and took his subjects under his control.[16]

3.3 *The Land and Administrative Division*

Tanshihuai organised his State in a military-administrative system and similarly to the Hunnu, divided his land into Western, Eastern and Central parts, installing in each centre the great leaders and the great commanders.[17] The great leaders were apparently the commanders of the unit of ten thousand. There were more than 20 tribes in both the Western and Eastern wings, and 10 thousand or so tribes in the Central part. The Central part of the nucleus of the State was under the direct rule of the leader (the Khan), but all the three parts were managed through 12 chieftains. A Russian scholar, N. Ya. Bichurin, basing himself on Chinese sources, wrote that the organisational set-up of tens, hundreds and thousands was predominant in the Togon tribe of the Sumbe State in the initial stage.[18] Therefore, it can be assumed that such an organisational division existed in the early period of the establishment of the Sumbe State. The Muyon tribe, who were a part of the Sumbe State, had a title called the Eastern Setsen Wang; it is possible that this title was used for the Sumbe people.

The Sumbe people and their Tabgach clan had their own writing, and there existed a Mongolian word *bicheechiin* (meaning a scribe), which meant that they had a copyist who maintained records. This word has been transliterated in Chinese as *bidezhen* and so it can be said that the Mongolian word for "scribe" was first being used by the Sumbe people

16 P. Delgerjargal, *The Early History of Xianbi*, Book Two, Ulaanbaatar, 2017.
17 *Ibid.*
18 N. Ya. Bichurin, *История Тебета и Хухунора, (History of Tibet and Huhnor)*, I, St. Petersburg, 1833.

and they also used such words as *uizen* (name of a title conferred on members of the nobility. Tr.), *yamutan* (staff of a ministry), *khorchin* (name of a tribe, basically quiver-bearers), *buurchin* (an owner of an inn), *zamchin* (a guide), which were later used by the Mongols. Judging by all this, an organised social community – the State – was established in Sumbe, which laid the foundation for the formation of officials who would work permanently in the State.

3.4 *The Military*

The Sumbe State expanded its territory by invading and occupying other nations, and it had its own military in order to protect itself from the encroachments by its southern neighbour. In 178 CE, Qan Yui, a Minister of the Han Dynasty, wrote in his submission that "With the downfall of the Hunnu, the Sumbe State gained strength, occupied the land previously under the Hunnu and had set up an army of ten thousand men... Their weapons are lethal, the steeds fleet footed, far stronger than the Hunnu Empire."[19] Judging by this, the Sumbe State had a strong and organised military. The book *The Annals of Three Kingdoms* states that Kebinen had a hundred thousand cavalry armed with bow and arrow, which in all likelihood were a kind of comrade soldiers (*нөхөр цэрэг in Mongolian: warriors of other tribes who had voluntarily offered allegiance to Kebinen. Tr.*).[20]

3.5 *Basic Legal Features*

The Sumbe people, based on the code of law and traditional law, made treaties and agreements, rules and regulations, and finally, codes of law. Scholar Ch. Jügder believes that the Sumbe, in the beginning, had a customary law, and later wrote codes of law.[21] According to historical sources, Tanshihuai "had passed codes of law to judge the right from the wrong, and there was no one who dare infringe them."[22]

After the death of Tanshihuai, his successor Kebinen in 228 CE passed a law banning the sale of horses to the Wei people, which later founded a dynasty in Northern China. This law was in the form of an oath treaty and Kebinen urged strict enforcement of the law by all to ensure the security of the State of Sumbe. In other words, this was a preventative measure

---

19 *History of the MPR (Mongolian People's Republic)*, Volume One, Ulaanbaatar, 1966, p. 100.

20 歷代各族傳記會編，編者霧伯贊、陳述孫鐵，楚明善、汪公量、吴恆。第一編、上海 1958, p. 753.

21 Ch. Jügder, *Social, political and philosophical mentality during the feudalism in Mongolia*. Ulaanbaatar, 1987, p. 83.

22 G. Sükhbaatar, *Xianbe*, 1971, p. 155.

against cavalry aggression from the neighbouring East. However, Sulin, one of the leaders of the Eastern tribes of the Sumbe State, violated the treaty and sold 1,000 horses to the Wei Dynasty, and Kebinen mounted his army to suppress Sulin. All this goes to show that the Sumbe State had quite a strict legal standard, which was enforced without hesitation.

3.6 *Religious Belief*

The Sumbe people, like other nomadic people of Central Asia, believed in shamanism. During the reign of Tanshihuai, the Sumbe people visited the Jaole River, where they made their major offering, a proof that they believed in shamanism. The ruling elite of the Sumbe State used shamanism in favour of their own interests and even used it as a State ideology. The gold portrait of Lord Buddha with the Hunnu people belonged to the Tuguhan' tribe of the Sumbe State. It therefore follows that the ruling elite of the Sumbe State not only had knowledge of Buddhism, but also believed in Buddhism to a certain extent.

The State of Sumbe disintegrated at the end of the 4th century CE as a result of its internal crisis as well as the splinter policy conducted from the south in China.

4 The Great Nirun State (4th century–6th century CE)

4.1 *The State Structure, the Khan*

The Great Nirun State (also *Rouran Khaganate*) occupied the central regions of the Hunnu and Xianbe Empires, which we have discussed above, in the 4th to 6th centuries CE, and played an important role in the history of Statehood of Central Asia. The Niruns are the ancestors of the core Mongols. Their first leader is Mongol *(Mugului)* during the period of Ilug (304–316 CE) Khan of the Tabgach clan. The word *Mugului*, as transliterated in Chinese characters more than 1,600 years ago, stands for the word "Mongol". In the beginning, this was a general nomenclature for the clan; it later became the name of the entire race,[23] according to Doctor G. Sükhbaatar.

The Nirun Khaganate was established by Mugului's son Charagui around 330 CE. The Great Nirun State had an administrative-military setup based on the units of tens similarly to the Hunnu and the Sumbe people.

The Nirun had a monarchical form of government. There were 23 Khans during the entire period of existence of the Nirun State (from ap-

23 G. Sükhbaatar, *The Mongol Nirun (330–556)*, Ulaanbaatar, 1992, p. 24.

proximately 330 to 550 CE). The Niruns were the first among the nomadic tribes to use the title of *Khagan* to showcase superiority. The Khagan or Khan was the highest supreme leader of the State, which according to Buddhism, descended from the Heavens and so the supreme leaders were revered as *Khutaktai:* "blessed", "honourable," and "heavenly." If the Khan deemed it vitally important, he would submit issues of important domestic and foreign State policy for consideration to the gathering of ministers and listen to their opinion. The Khan, however, made the final judgment.

Although there was an established system of succession to the throne, there were times when this rule was abused. For instance, the first five Khans acceded to the throne as per the established rules and procedures, but after them, power struggles led to the violation of the rules. Take, for example, Tatar, who became the Khan in 414 CE and violated the rule and came to power with the use of arms.[24]

The Nirun Khans, according to Buddhist practice, used such titles as *Ashid Amgalan* [meaning eternally serene] (464–485 CE), *Mashid Tüvshin* [eternally tranquil] (485–491 CE), *Mashid Taivan* [eternally peaceful] (492–506 CE), *Enkh Tüvshin* [peaceful] (506–508 CE), *Mandan Badrakh* [flourishing] (508–520 CE) etc., which was a novel phenomenon in the history of Statehood of the nomads of Central Asia. The Nirun also considered the supreme ruler of their State – the Khan – as a symbol, and even named the *ger* (yurt) of the Khan as *khatan* (*khagtagun*).

4.2 *Officialdom and Officials*

Officialdom developed in the Great Nirun State, and there were both lay and religious officials working for the State. The State Minister was the highest ranking official after the Khan. During the period of the Liu Song dynasty (420–479 CE), Silin', the State Minister of the Nirun Khaganate, was a pre-eminent scholar, who was well versed in astrology and mathematics, and who had mastered several foreign languages. There were high-ranking officials such as Mohe and Xyzhin among the envoys who were dispatched to the Wei Empire. However, it is not clear what their responsibility and functions were.

We have discovered evidence that in the year 534–537, Amgai Khan had appointed court officials, gate-keepers and scribes, which goes to show that by the middle of the 6th century CE the system of officialdom had become much more refined. Since the Great Nirun State had an administra-

24 *Ibid.*, p. 101.

tive and military system based on the unit of tens, it is quite obvious they also had the unit divisions of ten thousands, thousands, and hundreds.

4.3 *The Khurildai*

The Great Nirun State had a supreme *Khurildai* (Assembly) of the nobles that oversaw such important State matters as ordaining the Khan, and declaring war and peace with other nations and peoples. Chounu Khan (508–520 CE) called the supreme *Khurildai* of the nobles for celebration when he found his son, and honoured shamaness Divan as a blessed lady and gave her the title of Khatan (queen) and her husband was appointed as a high-ranking State official.

Besides the supreme *Khurildai*, the Niruns also had a smaller assembly of the nobles to consider matters within a restricted framework. For example, in early 540 CE when Amgai Khan wanted to enter into a relationship with Zha-Huizuan, the envoy of Eastern Wei, the smaller assembly of the nobles was called to discuss the matter. However, researchers have not been able to discover definite evidence on how the supreme *Khurildai* and the smaller assembly of the nobles of the Nirun were conducted and how participation in them was ensured.

4.4 *The Military*

The Great Nirun State had a permanent army organised on the principle of the unit of tens. The military consisted of light and heavy cavalry. The light cavalry did not have their horses in armour, while the warriors were in armour and wore helmets, armed with bow and arrows. The heavy cavalry had armoured horses and the warriors were also fully armoured. In 402 CE Jarun Khan (Shelun) lost more than 2,000 armoured cavalry to the Wei dynasty, which proves that the Nirun State then had a large army of armoured cavalry. The history of the Southern Qi dynasty notes that the Niruns "had exceptionally excellent war horses."

The Great Nirun State had a common border to the south with the Wei dynasty, and with the Central Asian nations to the West and in order to protect their borders, they had sentries who were responsible for their safety and the security of the State borders. We can state that the military of the Great Nirun State, in terms of their organisational set-up and weapons, were far superior to the Hunnu and the Sumbe Empires.

DIAGRAM 2 State structure of the Great Nirun State

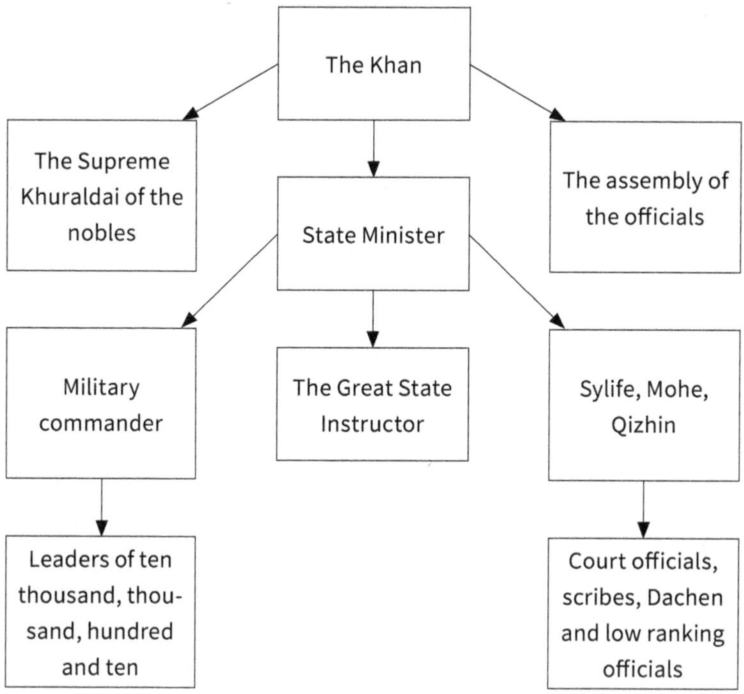

4.5 *Religion*

Buddhism made up the ideological foundation of the state policy of the Nirun Khaganate. Fertile social grounds had already been created for the inception of Buddhism in the Nirun Khaganate. This was possible primarily because of the Buddhist traditions among the Hunnu and the Sumbe people, the spread of Buddhism in the neighbouring countries, as well as because of the realistic social development needs.

The Khan of the Nirun Empire in approximately 438–489 CE, appointed a learned monk Dharmapiya (?–489 CE) as the State Tutor, who was well-versed in the religious sutras, Abidharma and the philosophy of Samkhya, gracing him with 3,000 households. In this manner, important state religious figures were installed, who had enormous influence on the State and ideology of the Khan and government officials, as well as the masses. In other words, the Khans and nobles of the Nirun Khaganate, through these religious figures, were exposed to a certain extent to Buddha's teachings, Indian philosophy and culture.

Doctor G. Sükhbaatar, who studied the spread of Buddhism in the State of Nirun, came up with the following conclusions:

a) Buddhism became a state religion and the ideological foundation of the Nirun State;
b) Nirun became the centre of Buddhism in Mongolia;
c) The people of Nirun had already been exposed, to a certain extent, to ancient Indian philosophy and thinking;
d) Buddhism had had an impact on shamanism in the Nirun Khaganate;
e) Buddhism started evolving as a constituent of the culture of the Mongols.[25]

With Buddhism becoming the State ideology of the Khaganate, shamanism, in general, continued to remain a predominant belief in the daily life of the Nirun people; however, shamanism under the influence of Buddhism had undergone some drastic changes. For instance, shamaness Divan of the Nirun Khaganate carried out her shamanistic ritual during the one-week fasting observed by the Buddhists and shamans as well as some common Nirun people who had visited the city of Loyan were appreciated as well-versed in Buddhism by an Indian monk Ratnamanithi, which proves that that were was a merging of Buddhism and shamanism among the Nirun people.

4.6 *Legal Foundations*

There are almost no or extremely few historical and legal sources about the legal system of the Niruns. Jarun or Shelun Khan, who ruled the Nirun State from the year 402–410 CE, had introduced a military-administrative type of code of law. According to the military code of law, one thousand men came under one regiment, which had a leader, and a hundred men formed a banner, also with one leader.

This was one form of the traditional nomadic division of the units of tens. According to the aforementioned code of law, warriors on the frontline were entitled to take possession of the spoils of war, while deserters were killed by throwing stones on their heads or were put to the sword. Judging by the above, based on some rare documentary evidence, execution by stone throwing and flogging of especially military deserters was one of the many forms of capital punishment in the Nirun Khaganate, where wrongdoers among the nobility were condemned to suffocation. Chinese sources have made specific notes about the military code of law of the Nirun, which means that the Nirun Khaganate had a special military law. Already in the early 5th century, the Nirun Khaganate had ministers well-versed in astrology, mathematics and foreign tongues, and so it cannot be denied that they had written law as well.

25 G. Sükhbaatar, *The Mongol Nirun State (330–556)*, Ulaanbaatar, 1992, p. 36.

5 Other States of Non-Mongol Origin (4th century–9th century CE)

The Great Nirun State collapsed to the Turkic Khanate in the year 555 CE. The Turkic Khanate existed on the present territory of Mongolia from the year 552–745 CE and after its decline, it was succeeded by the Uighur (Uyghur) Empire (745–840 CE).

The Turkic people and the Uighurs in terms of their language and origin were people of foreign race, but they were included as parts of the States founded by the Mongol people, and they made history after destroying the people of Mongol origin. They also brought under their rule some of the tribes of Mongol origin. In this sense, it can be believed that they preserved and further refined and developed, to a certain extent, the traditions of statehood and laws of the previous periods. It is therefore important to study, even superficially, the status of the statehood and codes of laws of these people.

5.1 *Basic Features of the State and Legal Foundations of the Turkic People*

The first Empire built by the tribes of Turkic origin on the territory of Mongolia was the First Turkic Khaganate. Buman, the chief of the Dulag clan, which was under the Nirun Khaganate, revolted against the rulers and captured the Telee tribes, whereby the first foundations were laid for the establishment of an independent State. In 555 CE, they led the Great Nirun State to its downfall, settled down in the Basin of the Orkhon River and established their empire after conquering some Central and Middle Asian countries. However, in 630 CE the Turkic Khaganate were occupied as a result of the policy and trickery of the Tang Empire in China.

In the early 80's of the 7th century, the Turkic Empire's independence was revived as a result of a powerful revolt spearheaded by King Kutuluk (Qutlugh) and his adviser Tonyukuk. In around the year 690, the *Khurildai* (assembly) of many different Turkic clans and tribes was held where Kutuluk was proclaimed the King, who was given the title of *Ilterish* (meaning "Collector of Nations"). This new Empire has gone down in history as the Second Turkic Khaganate.

In the Second Turkic Khaganate, the tribal nobles in the beginning used the name "*Il*" but later on this name was used only by the people who were from the lineage of the Khagan, and only those who carried this title in their names would choose their Khagan from amongst themselves. The Khagan had a council, which also included people of his lineage, leaders of the clans and tribes, craftsmen and the *Beg (roughly meaning "governorate" in the Turkish language. Tr)*. In the beginning the Khagan would heed the words and suggestions of the council members. With the development of the State, the Khagan's political and economic might, power and authority grew to deciding matters on his own. Gradually, the procedure of appointing the Khagan changed and it became hereditary. Those from the Khagan lineage started using such titles as *Tegin*, *Yabgu*, or *Shad* who ruled over the occupied lands. At a later period, the *Beg* switched to the practice of succession through inheritance.[26]

The State structure of the Turkic Khaganate was multi-tiered and the government officials had many different classes and grades, which is evidence of the deepening of its statehood. In general, a central State apparatus had been put in place with the Khagan as the supreme leader of the State, followed by the Khagan's advisers or vice ministers, high-ranking officials such as the Yagbu and Shad, who commanded the occupied lands, the *Tudug* who were the chiefs of the tribes that had submitted to the Turkic Khaganate, *Darkhan* or the tax collectors, and judges called the *Buyuruk*.

DIAGRAM 3 State structure of the Turkic Khaganate

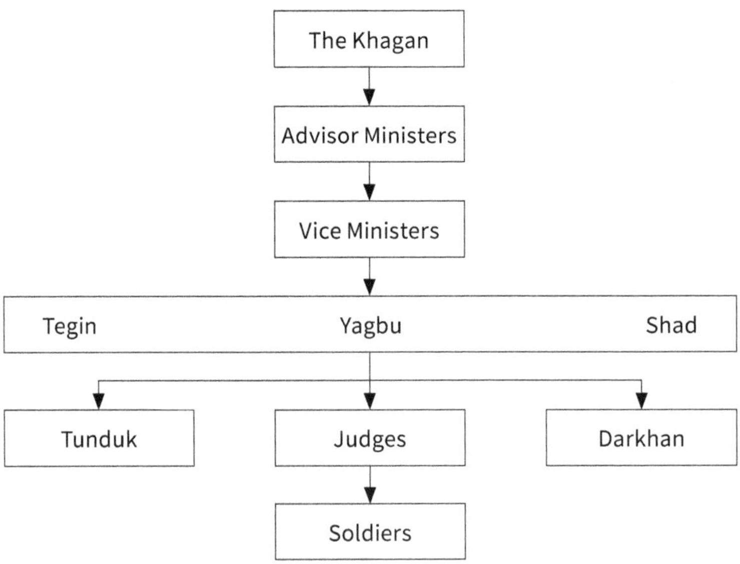

The Khan was the supreme leader in the Uighur Khaganate. Peylo was proclaimed the Khan of the Uighur Khaganate in the year 744 and assumed the title of *Khul Bilge*. Following him, his son, also known as *Bayan*

26 *History of the MPR*, Volume One, Ulaanbaatar, 1966, p. 129.

Chor, took over the reins of the Khaganate (747–759) and he became a popular Khan vested with powers to manage a heavenly kingdom.

Under the Khan there were many ministers and officials with the titles of *Tuntuk, Elteber,* and *Darkhan.* Judging by a so-called *Suuj* inscription from the northern banks of the Selenge River, which reads "I served as the higher commissioner,"[27] the Uighur Khaganate had a supreme judge or a high commissioner. Furthermore, the inscription has the words that "Kutuluk was the small *Darkhan* official of Öge-Buirug,"[28] which is another proof that tax was levied on the people and the subjects of the Uighur Khaganate.

The Uighur Khaganate had a powerful army. According to a Tang Dynasty manuscript "The Uighurs were courageous... they were good at robbery and banditry, they had a total population of one hundred thousand and half of the population served in the army."[29] The Uighur tribes initially elected their own leaders and heads, who were given authority to supervise military and administrative matters. But when it became united and grew into a Khaganate, the army came under one command and management.

Historians and researchers maintain that the Uighurs did not have a single legal system and did not have any written law that they followed. However, we consider it highly unlikely that the Uighurs did not have a written code of law, as they had their own script, they maintained official records, wrote books and even translated books from foreign languages. Most importantly, there is a lack of substantial research. However, it can be assumed that various cases were predominantly considered and resolved through the application of traditional legal norms and standards. Although this traditional legal norm among the Uighurs had many elements pertaining to the primitive community society, it also contained many elements of the newly forming relations based on serfdom.

---

27 Malov, S. A. *Monuments of Ancient Turkic Writings of Mongolia and Kyrgyz.* M. L. 1959, p. 77.

28 *Ibid.*, p. 77.

29 *History of the Mongolian People's Republic*, Vol. 1, Ulaanbaatar, 1966, p. 136.

DIAGRAM 4 State structure of the Uighurs

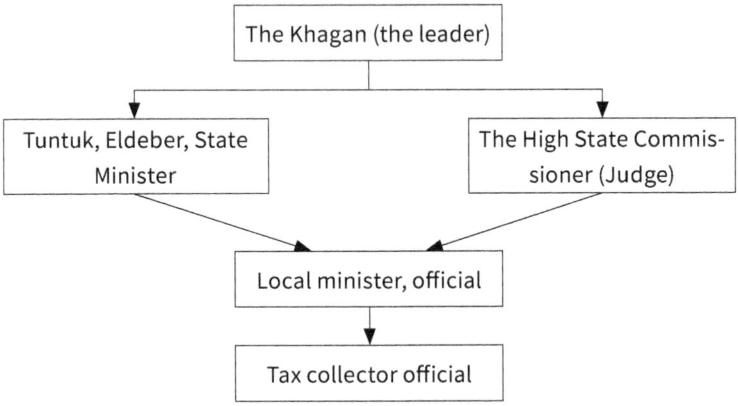

5.2 *Basic Features of the State and Legal Foundations of the Kidan (also Khitan)*

The Kidan Empire (907–1125 CE) existed on the territory of South East Mongolia and North China for more than 200 years, and made an important contribution to the culture and civilisation, development of the statehood and legal foundations of the Central and East Asian countries. Scientists have established that the predominating Eastern Hu tribe of the Kidans originated from either the Sumbe or the Huns. But the Kidans had broken away from the Mongol race quite early on to live as neighbours with alien races and peoples, like the Chinese, and through such intermingling the Kidans had developed into a unique race of people, different from the Mongols.

The aristocrats of the Kidans took the different Kidan tribes under their control in the seventh to ninth centuries to become the ruling elite. Starting from the year 80 to 718 of the 6th century the Da-He tribe became the ruling tribe, who were then replaced by the Yaoniang tribe, and then by the Elui tribe in the 10th century. The Kidans were composed of eight tribes and the head of the predominating tribe became the Khan who ruled the rest of the seven tribes. A banner and a drum were placed in front of the *ger*, which symbolised that the *ger* belonged to the ruler, the Khan of the Kidans, and this period pertains to the 7th–8th centuries.

In the year 750, major social and political changes occurred in the Kidan Empire. According to the writings in Gang-Mu, 1. The *Ilijin* (El Ezen), the next in authority after the Kidan Khan was re-appointed; 2. A clan of the *Ioni* was created from among the *Dela* tribe, who were hereditarily appointed into the office of the *Ilijin*; 3. The so-called *Khem Khemjee* or "standard" was introduced; 4. The Kidans for the first time used pictographs even for recording purposes; and 5. Prisons were built and criminals were incarcerated."[30] All the above was evidence of the deepening of the statehood and the legal system of the Kidan Empire.

The growth and strengthening of the Statehood and law of the Kidans are directly connected with the period when Ambagian (Abaoji) of the ruling Yelü tribe was made the Khan of the Kidans in the year 901 CE. Neglecting the established tradition of electing the leader of the Kidans once every three years, Ambagian became the Khan of the Kidans in 917 CE by force, and starting from this period onwards, the rule of the Khan became hereditary.

Ambagian renamed his Empire as Tayan Kidan and divided the Empire administratively into two parts, the Northern and the Southern States. These were ruled by an official called the *Zaisan* – the Northern and the Southern *Zaisans* – which laid the foundation for the administration overseeing the nomadic and settled Kidan people.

Ambagian, with the objective of further strengthening the statehood, passed a code of law in the year 921 CE and accordingly introduced the ranks and titles of the state administrators and officials. In 936 CE, the Kidan Empire mounted attacks against the Kyrgyz, Bohai, Zürchid tribes and finally China occupying the 16 northern prefectures to assume the resemblance of an empire. Since then, the Kidans began calling their Empire the Great Liao Dynasty.

Judging by historical sources, the Kidan Empire included 55 tribes and States, which were divided into 16 tribes of the South, 28 tribes of the North and 8 foreign tribes. The Great Liao Dynasty was divided into three parts, the Great Tribe or the main tribes of the Kidans, the Small Tribe and the dependent alien tribes, who were conquered by the Kidans, and each one of them had their own State administrations. Each Great Tribe was led by an *Iljin* or El Ezen, who had under him the Eastern *Zaisan,* the Western *Zaisan* and such officials as the *Tai-shi, Situ* etc. The administration of the alien tribes did not differ much from that of the Great Tribe. The administrations of the smaller tribes were simple, and were managed by such officials called the *Situ,* the *Sykun*. Normally, a person of Kidan origin would be re-appointed in a high State office.

The Kidan Empire had a well-organised permanent army. The army of the Kidan Empire was called upon to perform three kinds of duties, which were 1) provide well-equipped soldiers who guarded the Khan's residence;

30 Kh. Perlee, *The Kidans and their relationship with the Mongols*, Ulaanbaatar, 1960, p. 32.

2) ensure the Empire's soldiers would rise to the occasion of defending the country; and 3) provide soldiers who served as personal guards and soldiers of ministers and high-ranking officials. The male folk of Kidan would all take up weapons should a threat be posed to the country. A golden tablet with an engraved image of fish was given to the men who were mobilised into the army, while silver tablets were used for buying horses for the cavalry. A Kidan soldier would have 3 horses, metal armour, 4 bows, 400 arrows, one long and one short wooden pole, an awl, a small banner and a set of metal with flint. The Kidans are believed to have had almost ten thousand armoured horses. The cavalry was divided into four units, each unit consisted of 500–700 warriors and 10 units were united to make up a *zam*.

In the year 922 CE, the Kidan Empire set up an army of 50 thousand men and a general commander was appointed to manage the army. The troops of the Kidan army had gunpowder weapons and the Kidans are believed to be the first people to use firearms.

The Kidan Empire, as compared to the previous dynasties and empires on the territory of Mongolia, apparently had a much more sophisticated legal system and structure. Plots of farmlands were given by a special decree of the Khan. According to a code of law on tax, the State of Bohai had to give to the Kidan Empire 150 rolls of fabric and one thousand horses every year in the form of a tribute.

According to a rule introduced in the year 1070, livestock breeding tribes were made to pay in tax as many as 300 to twenty thousand heads of animals every year, and in the year 1041 a decree was passed by the Khan according to which an official responsible for hunting was appointed and people were punished who hunted in protected areas. Those who tried to avoid service in the hunting department were severely punished. Salt use was widespread in the Kidan Empire during the tenth to eleventh centuries, and the Khan had the sole responsibility on how salt was traded and a relevant decree was also passed in this respect that meted out severe punishment to the violators. The Kidans also banned the use of tobacco and alcohol as hazardous to health, and there are historical sources that prove that in the tenth century, heads of households who moonshined were punished by decapitation.[31]

The laws of the Kidan on tax, farming, hunting, salt, liquor and tobacco played an important role in the life of the Empire and left behind a rich

31 Kh. Perlee, *The Kidans and their relationship with the Mongols*, Ulaanbaatar, 1960, pp. 47, 52.

legacy that had an important impact on the legal growth and development of the Central and Inner Asian countries, including Mongolia.

6 Basic Features of Statehood and Law of the Mongol Khanates and Tribes in the 6th to 12th Centuries

6.1 *The Mongols in the 6th to 11th Centuries*

The Turkic, Uighur and Kidan Empires were established on the territory of Mongolia and held sway during this period, the Mongols, in one way or the other, inherited the cause of the powerful State of Nirun and continued to exist in the form of a small Khanate, according to a Mongolian historian G. Sükhbaatar.

In the 5th century, the Mongol tribes included the Nirun and the Tatars, and the word Tatar originates from the name of the Tatar Khan of the Great Nirun Empire (414–428 CE). Mongol tribal confederations and tribes in the sixth to eleventh centuries have been recorded in historical sources as Tatars, and much interesting documentary evidence is being found evidencing how the Tatars had continued to maintain and promote the statehood of the Mongols over the centuries. For instance, the Tatars had attended the funerals of the Buman (Tümen) and Istemi Khans of the Turkic Empires and around the year 715 CE came into armed rivalry against Bilge Khan of the Turks, and during the rule of the Uighur Empire (745–840) the Tatars fought with the Uighurs and once they even joined hands with the Tan Dynasty of China (618–907) against the Uighurs, and they dealt with the Song Dynasty in China (960–1279) by sending envoys on numerous occasions, which all bear witness to the fact that the Tatars existed in the form of Khanates and had maintained their independence in one way or the other.

Beginning from the late 11th century, people of Mongol origin were recorded in Chinese historical sources as Mongols, they maintained equitable relations and traded with the Great Liao Dynasty (Kidan) and the Song Dynasty in China. After analysing such historical documents and evidence, historian G. Sükhbaatar drew the following conclusion: "after the Great Nirun state of the Mongol origin-people was destroyed by the Turkic people in the year 555, the Mongol tribes continued to maintain their state structure, the traditions and ideology of the state."[32] However, some researchers have maintained that the "... Mongol tribes lived in a state of fragmentation and disintegration in remote areas without a single khan and a single state after they were finally driven out of their heredi-

32 G. Sükhbaatar, *The Mongol Nirun State (330–556)*, Ulaanbaatar, 1992, p. 35.

tary territory by the Turkic people following prolonged struggle against the alien forces, and after more than 400 years of despair, they returned to their ancient land, established themselves in the basin of Gurvan Gol River and revived their identity."[33]

Statehood features of the Mongol tribal confederations and tribes that lived on the territory of Mongolia became increasingly prominent in the 11th to 12th centuries, and relatively independent and large tribal confederations of the Khamag Mongol tribes, Khereid (Keraites), Naiman, Ongud and Khonkhereid began to gain in strength and influence.

6.2 *Khamag Mongol*

Khamag Mongol, a major Mongolic tribal confederation in the basin of the Kherlen, Onon and Tuul Rivers, was established in the twelfth century. This is evident from a historical note which says that "Khabul Khan (Qabul Khan) has taken over the rule over Khamag Mongol." In the beginning, the core of this tribal confederation were the Darligin and Nirun clans, and perhaps followed by the Borjigin sub-clan. Over time, the Borjigin, Jadran and Taichuud sub-clans took on leading roles among the 19 Nirun clans and sub-clans. The Taichuud were the most powerful with more population than the other two sub-clans. The other sub-clans either submitted to or tagged along with the other sub-clans and tribes, and when the Great *KhurIldaI* (Assembly) was held to select the Khamag Mongol Khan, only the top and influential nobility of the three sub-clans attended the assembly. With the accession of Khabul Khan, the son of Tumbinai Setsen, as the Khan of the Khamag Mongol confederation, the foundation was laid for the rule by the Khans of the so-called Golden Horde or *Altan Orda,* who were believed to have been born with the destiny of the *Tengri* or the Sky (Heaven). The Khan of the Khamag Mongol, compared to the previous tribal confederation and tribal leaders or "Khans" had become much more capable and divine. The princes and nobles were given lofty titles and privileges by the Khans starting from the rule of the Khamag Mongol. The second Khamag Mongol Khan Ambagai carried out reforms in the military structure and instituted the rank of a military commander called the *Taishi,* who was second to the Khan in the hierarchy of the supremacy in the confederation. The *Taishi* was also responsible for determining the opening and closing dates for the *Khurildai,* he also had the power and the authority to declare war etc., according to the Persian historian Rashid al-Din. The princes and nobles were also

33 Ch. Dalai, *History of Mongolia, The Khamag Mongol Tribal Confederation (1101–1206)*, Book One, Ulaanbaatar, 1966, p. 37.

given the ranks and titles of *baatar* (hero), *mergen* (wise), *khölög* (steed), *setsen* (skilled), *Begi* (olden ranks of nobility).

The Khamag Mongol confederation, following the ancient traditions divided their State into Western, Eastern and Central wings, maintaining the military-administrative division and structure intact. According to historical sources, Hotula Gurgutas, the commander of the Western wing, oversaw matters related to land, while Argichiney, the commander of the Eastern wing, ruled over a territory called Adar Jubur, and the Central wing was under the jurisdiction of Khadaan Taishi, the son of Ambagai Khan.

The *Khurildai* of the nobles of Khamag Mongol began to assume the characteristics of the Great *Khurildai* of the future united Mongolian Empire. Judging by the manner in which the *Khurildai* was held where Khotula Khan was proclaimed the Khan, it was quite similar to the ceremony during which Temüjin was made the Khan and proclaimed Chinggis Khan of the Mongol Empire. However, as far as the right of the *Khurildai* was concerned, it followed the orders and the will of the Khan, and discussed and adopted them in a very formal manner.

Khamag Mongol had a well-organised and a powerful army, which is evident from the fact that military support was given to the Great Liao Dynasty (Kidan Empire) and by the repulsion of aggressions by the Jin Dynasty on three occasions. The concept of *comrade soldiers*, which was fundamental to the military structure of the Khamag Mongol confederation, arose from the groups or circles set up by a handful of warriors who trusted each other. Scholar Ch. Dalai has written that "Historical sources have defined the military units of the Khamag Mongol confederation as *Turkhag*, who were in the beginning primarily personal bodyguards of the leader of the ruling Mongol tribe, who were special-tasks forces with a small contingent intended especially for warfare and pillaging. Later when the Khamag Mongol confederation was founded, and when the statehood became more refined and organised, the *Turkhag* assumed the form of a permanent military. In this sense, the *Turkhag* were the personal bodyguard soldiers of the khan, who during peace times served as the bodyguards and during a war, they would follow the khan and lead the onslaught."[34]

The male folk of the Khamag Mongol confederation, during times of war, were mobilised into the army; during times of peace they would be engaged in their personal livelihood. In other words, the army carried

34 *Ibid.*, p. 80.

out its duty of protecting the confederation when the need arose while the soldiers of the *Turkhag* served on a permanent basis.

6.3 *Temüjin Proclaimed the Khan of the Khamag Mongol Confederation*

In 1189, when Temüjin was proclaimed the Khan of the Khamag Mongol confederation, the statehood of the Mongols was elevated to a qualitatively new higher level of its development. During this period, the might and the power and authority of the Khan also grew substantially. This accomplishment of Temüjin was possible thanks to proper identification of reliable comrades from amongst the nobility and the common folk, directing their courage and wisdom in the right direction, and ensuring they surrounded him in an unwavering manner. Soon after Temüjin became the Khan, he created the title of a Commander at-large and nominated his most reliable and trustworthy comrades, irrespective of their origin and background, as the overall Commander; that is, he delegated authority based on merit and loyalty, rather than family ties. This led to the creation of organised and disciplined military units, a necessity that arose from the imperative need of uniting the Mongol tribal confederations and tribes. In 1204, Temüjin created his own guard consisting of eighty *khevtuul* or night guards and seventy *turkhag*, streamlining their duties and responsibilities.

The Khan appointed six princes in his "Orda," who were individually responsible for the administrative affairs of the Khan, the Khan's kitchen, the herd of sheep, the herd of camels, and herd of horses belonging to the Khan, and a superintendent overseeing the production of arms and armaments, who were put under the command of Bo'orchi and Zelme (Jelme), which proves that the system of running State affairs was becoming much more refined. It would, therefore, be appropriate to review the history of the statehood of Mongolia in a sequential manner starting from this period onward.

The Khamag Mongol confederation did not have any written Code of Law, where traditional law was predominant. *The Secret History of the Mongols*, for example, cites how Targudai Khiriltug (Tarqutai-kiriltuq) captured Temüjin and made him spend one night in each *ayil* (household) in rotation, and how Khaatai Darmaala was seized and made to wear a cangue and banished to Khaldun Mountain. These depictions show the unique law practiced then and how the guilty were punished. Also, soon after Temüjin was declared the Khan of all the Mongols, a "herd of sheep was given in offering" according to a manuscript pertaining to the Yuan Dynasty, which was obviously one form of tribute. The introduction of the system of paying tribute is an economic expression of the establishment of a serfdom system. In this manner, the Khamag Mongol confederation became stronger as a State and progressed along the irreversible path of leading the tribal confederation and tribes of Mongol origin.

6.4 *Other Tribal Confederations and Tribes*

In the 12th to 13th centuries, besides the Khamag Mongol, there also existed other Mongol tribal confederations and tribes, such as the Khereid (Kerait), Naiman, Onguud and the Tatars.

The Khereids were neighbours to the Khamag Mongol and were therefore, compared to other confederations and tribes, more powerful. The Khereids lived on the territory in between the Khangai and Khentii mountain ranges, concentrated primarily in the forests of the Tuul River north of the Bogd Mountains, which is what the present-day Ulaanbaatar is. The Khereids were led by Toghril, better known as the Wang (Khan), who lived in the late 11th and early 12th centuries.

The confederacy of the Khereids existed between the Khangai and Altai mountain ranges and consisted of eight Mongolic tribes, but it was divided into two in the second half of the 12th century because of internal strife and disunity. Following this, the confederacy of Naiman to the east of the Altai Mountains was ruled by Tayang Khan and the part lying west of the Altai Mountains was ruled by Buyruk Khan of the Khereids. Historical sources mention that the rulers and Khans of the Naiman Confederacy were "respected and powerful, and they had a very good army." Tayang Khan's *orda* or palace, at one time, was in all likelihood located in Karakorum, but later it was moved deep into the Khangai mountain ranges.

The confederacy of the Ongud was located close to the town of Datong in an area lining the Great Wall of China. Rashid al-Din Hamadani in his *Jāmiʿ al-Tawārīkh* ("Compendium of Chronicles") mentions that the confederacy of the Ongud had a large population. In the second half of the 12th century, the chief of the Ongud confederacy was Alakushtigimkhuri (Ala Kush Tegin) and the confederacy was a vassal of the Jin Dynasty, but nonetheless the Onguds had close ties and relations with predominantly Mongol tribes.

The confederacy of the Tatars was mainly located in the valleys of Khölön Buir and Khalkha Gol lakes towards the east of Mongolia. At the crossroads of the 11th and 12th centuries, the Tatar confederacy was disunited and the different tribes under the confederacy broke away to form their own associations and unions. The Tatar confederacy was not a confederation of tribes based on military unity but was a union of individual confederations. In terms of their origin, the Tatars were related by blood to the Mongols living in the three-river basin, and owing to historical circumstances, they had become adversaries. There also existed the alliances of the Jalair, the tribes of the Merged (Merkit), the Oirads, Khori Tümed and the Khongirad (Qongirat).

Historical studies carried out in recent times have come up with different ideas on the formation, the disintegration and also the very existence of the States created by different confederations and tribes of the Mongols, who lived in the 10th to 12th centuries. Take, for instance, the following assumptions:

- Such tribes and confederations as the Khamag Mongol, Khereid and Naiman set up viable institutes of Statehood (Ch. Dalai, N. Ishjamts and others).
- These confederated tribes did not yet have institutes of Statehood (Scholars from Cambridge[35], Sh. Bira[36], and M. Sanjdorj[37]).
- In 1189, Temüjin did away with the concept of "chiefdom" of the Khamag Mongol and set up a strong system of statehood, thanks to which he was able to unite and bring under his fold the other Mongol tribal confederations and tribes (J. Boldbaatar and his associates)[38]. Dr. D. Gongor, after studying the nature of the statehood of these confederations and tribes, offered a new interpretation in his book entitled *The Khalkha Tovchoon or The Khalkha Summary* as follows:
- Each confederation was made up of a combination of tribes and clans, and so the different confederations could be considered as an alliance or union of the tribes of which they consisted. Alongside this, new groups branched off from such an alliance or union, which again called themselves a nation. The Jalair confederation, for example, had ten tribes, such as the Jat, Tukaraun, Kunksaut, Kumsaut, Uyat, Nilkan, Kurkin, Turi, and the Shankut. Each of these tribes had large populations.
- The confederations were non-identical in terms of the size of their territories and populations. The Tatars, for example, had many family lineages from early known times and had some 70 thousand households, while the Ongud confederacy had some 4000 households and had only border sentries.

35 *The Cambridge History of China – Alien Regimes and Border States*, pp. 907–1368

36 Sh. Bira, *Study into the History, Culture and Historiography of Mongolia*, Vol. 3, Ulaanbaatar, 2001, p. 245.

37 M. Sanjdorj, *From the History of the Statehood of Mongolia (13th-19th centuries)*, p. 30.

38 J. Boldbaatar, *Historiography of Mongolia, its Reform and Trends (from the 1990s to the present time)*, Ulaanbaatar, 2008, p. 10.

- The confederations were in the main and predominantly ruled by a noble elected from among the core tribe that had founded the confederation. The Khans had exclusive authority over the warriors, matters related to the courts and the person in charge of sacrificial offerings, and their duties and prerogative rights were dependent on many domestic and external factors, but nonetheless, the territory, the population and the economic might of the given confederation were instrumental factors.
- Each confederation had a generic name particular to the tribes united under that union, which unlike that of the tribes of a similar clan was not the name of an ancestor that had united that clan, but consisted of two combined names, one of which was the name of the predominating tribe in the confederation. For example, the core of the Khamag Mongol confederation were the Taichuud tribes, and the ruling clan were called the Mongol and therefore they were also called the Mongol Taichuud and when other many separate Mongol tribes and clans were united, their confederation was called the Khamag Mongol (*Khamag in Mongolian means "All". Tr.*). On the other hand, the Tatar confederation consisted of nine tribes, such as the Barkhui, Kamashi, Neuchi, Teritg, Tutukulti, Hoyin, Alchi, Airug, Buirug and Tatar and so it was called the confederacy of Nine Tatars, while the Merged (Merkit) confederation included three tribes of Uduid, Khaad and Uvas Merged, and so they were called the Three Mergeds. Some of the common features of the confederation and tribes included the following:
    - The different confederations maintained political and economic ties and these relations were expressed through promoting camaraderie among their Khans and chiefs, seeking blood revenge, becoming related by marriage, exchanging envoys etc.
    - A type of civil service originated under the confederation chiefs. For instance, although rural in nature, this system became slightly more refined starting in the middle of the twelfth century and such officials as the *cherby, korchi, zasuulch, tamgach,* scribe, *buurchi* (cook) *agtach,* and *tergech* were employed, and they were managed by a general commander of the Khan's bodyguard, called a *Cherby.*
    - A confederation, based on the unit system of tens, was divided into three wings, which were overseen by the close attendants of the Khans. The residences of the khans of the confederations were erected in the central part of the settlement, which were called the *Aurug Orda.*

- Confederations were based on unions or alliances, the alliance members were involved in the running of the affairs of the confederation, where they could table motions, and important public matters were considered and decisions taken collectively. The assemblies of the people eventually became the "*Khurildai*" of a restricted circle of the chiefs, nobles and princes, the chief shamans of the confederation. The *Khurildai* would meet from time to time to consider 'pressing" issues confronting the confederation, as well as for appointing a new chief or khan, declaring war or peace, and also deciding on hunting etc.
- Each confederation had a regiment of soldiers to protect their land and livestock animals from alien aggression. Such warriors were initially called the *Turkhag* and later they were called the *Nökhör* or "comrades". Each confederation had autonomous right over their political and military affairs.
- The tribal confederations apparently did not have written codes of law. According to *Jāmiʿ al-Tawārīkh* ("*Compendium of Chronicles*"), the Tatars did not have a written law, while the chronicle "Notes of the Khar Tatar" mentions that before the thirteenth century, the Tatars did not have their own written language. However, other historical sources mentioned that a criminal case, for example, was considered in keeping with the existing procedures, and the above is evidence that there was law and order in the Mongol tribal confederations.[39]

When Temüjin reinstated the unity of Khamag Mongol, he succeeded in establishing a strong State system on a territory, which was, however, small; but this became the precondition for the establishment of a united Empire of the Mongols after the other Mongol tribes and confederations, such as the Tatars, Khereids, Naimans and the Onguds, were united and brought under his control.

7 Historical Continuation, Common and Specific Features of Statehood and Laws of the Ancient Mongol States

Researchers and scholars, after studying the social and State systems of the ancient nomadic States on the territory of Mongolia from a Marxist theoretical and practical point of view, had come to a common conclusion that these societies, given the basic social production tools, forms of ownership, the difference in the classes and social segments, the nature of the

39 D. Gongor, *The Khalkha Tovchoo,* Vol. 2, Ulaanbaatar, 1976, pp. 32–38.

State and law, the class nature of the material and oral culture, were in a pre-feudal stage, and in terms of the pattern in which their States were formed, their forms, nature, the nature of oppressive tools, legal capacity and the manner in which their statehood had been formed, these ancient nomadic States had the elements of an early-feudal State system.

In recent years, efforts have been made to consider these issues from a totally new practical and theoretical approach. There are some scholars who maintain that feudalism did not exist in medieval Mongolia as there were no feudal lords then[40]. Basing ourselves on the viewpoints of these scholars, and on a cultural and civilisation attitude towards history, we have defined the social status of the States and Empires during this period in history as ancient nomadic societies.

The social and State systems of the ancient States with their internal, mutually inter-related and live connections were an inseparable component of the global historical processes of those times.

The development of the social and State systems of the ancient Empires that existed on the territory of Mongolia can be divided into the following general categories:

1. The first State-like structure of the Mongol tribes during the initial period of the ancient society (Hunnu, Sumbe, Nirun);
2. Alien Empires that existed at a time when the relations of the ancient societies were becoming increasingly refined (Turkic, Uighur, and some parts of Kidan);
3. The reinstituted Khamag Mongol and other tribal confederations (Khamag Mongol, Khereid, Naiman, Ongud, Tatar etc.).

The following common features are evident in the social and State systems of the ancient nomadic States:

1. In the ancient societies, the classical form of animal husbandry had turned into economic expressions that led to the division of the societies into major groupings. In other words, the gap in the level of ownership deepened, movable property and livestock came under private ownership to become a powerful material basis for the growth of certain groupings in the society;
2. The Shanyu or the Khan, elected hereditarily, assumed the nature of Head of State and monarchy, in its classical form, took shape. This led to the shaping of State consciousness in the ancient society and to the formation of a State ideology of single rule by a monarch or a Khan.

---

40 Ts. Gombosüren, *Is the Traditional Society of Mongolia Feudalism?*, Ulaanbaatar, 1995, pp. 7–11.

3 All the ancient States, in terms of their State systems, were united and centralised, and starting with the Hunnu Empire, the State was divided into three administrative and territorial units of Western, Eastern and Central wings. In order to prevent the turning of such a division into a fertile soil for secession, at the country's level the military was divided into the decimal system of tens, hundreds, thousands and ten thousands, designed primarily to promote and safeguard the independence and security of the State. This ancient system of decimal units contributed to the creation of an integrated military, administrative and economic complex, which made it possible for the nomadic State to be flexible, responsive and united in the face of danger, which prolonged the viability of the nomadic State.

4 During the period of tribal confederations, the previous form of people's assemblies changed into assemblies of restricted groups of the ruling nobility to become one of the most unique forms of conducting the affairs of the monarchy. Such assemblies held the supreme power during coronations, while during ordinary times these assemblies performed the role of providing advice to the Khans.

5 The States that were established, besides applying the ancient traditional legal norms and standards, also introduced new rules and procedures, which were strictly abided by and which performed the role of a high court of the Empire.

6 Sometimes, a census of livestock was carried out and the common folk had to occasionally pay tributes and taxes, which was a sign that the State was already carrying out its economic duties and functions.

7 Slaves failed to become the key productive forces; they were, however, being put to work. Slaves were basically confined to households.

Traditions of the tribal system continued for very long in all the ancient States and Empires, and accordingly, it can be said that the features of public statehood, their impact and power did not express themselves in an even manner in each of the ancient nomadic States that existed on the territory of Mongolia. This was evidence of the fact that the development levels of the ancient States were not the same because of their own unique features and characteristics. From the viewpoint of general classification, the Hunnu Empire, for example, was only at the initial stage of transition from a tribal system to an ancient nomadic societal system, while in the Sumbe Empire and in particular in the Great Nirun State, ancient social relations had deepened, and statehood was becoming relatively well-formed and organised.

The Khanates that were established on the territory by alien (non-Mongol) tribes and clans, such as the Turkic and Uighur Empires, appeared one after the other to play a very important role, in their own fashion, on the historical and political arenas. They not only inherited the traditions of the past but also came up with their own unique and new ideas and practices for promoting the Statehood and the legal systems. In particular, in terms of the system of monarchy, Statehood and legal status, these States and Khanates made considerably more progress than their predecessor Empires and States, and they were on an equal standing with the rival Tan Dynasty and co-existed with their powerful Empire as super-powers themselves. During the period of the alien Empires and Khanates, the former Mongol-origin tribes, such as the Hunnu, Sumbe, and Great Nirun, continued to exist in different parts of the territory, but they were outweighed by the Turkic and Uighurs, who were prominent politically and militarily, and who held the overall power and authority.

Although the Turkic and Uighur dynasties were of alien origin, they could be considered indigenous inhabitants of the territory of Mongolia, similarly to the Hunnu, Sumbe and Great Nirun people, and one cannot simply overlook the tangible contribution they made to the development of social and political systems. In this sense, these so-called alien non-Mongol tribes handed over to the future generations of Mongol people the traditions of ancient statehood, and so the history of their statehood and legal system can very well be considered a constituent component of the history of the statehood and legal system of Mongolia as a whole.

The Kidans, who ruled South Mongolia and North China from the 10th to the early 12th centuries, made a very important contribution to the development of the statehood and legal system of the Mongols. The system of officials with different titles and ranks, and code of laws on tax, farming, hunting, salt, alcoholic drinks, and tobacco were introduced, and the traditional legal norms and standards were mostly being transferred into written form, proving that the Kidans, in terms of statehood and legal practices, had advanced far as compared to the previous tribal empires.

The establishment of States and Empires of alien (non-Mongol) tribes in the central part of Mongolia in the 15th-16th centuries stagnated and disrupted the social and historical development of the Mongol-origin tribes, yet there is no reason to believe that there were regressions and disruptions to the traditional customs of the State system. During some 400 years in this period, some sections of the Mongol-origin tribes had been a part of the Empires created by non-Mongol alien tribes, and compared to other tribes and clans were better developed. The other section of the Mongol-origin tribes, for instance, the Tatars existed in the form of small monarchies and tribal confederations, and entered the 16th century having maintained their Statehood, in one way or the other.

In the 11th to 12th centuries, Mongol tribes and confederations began to revive, and the nomadic society, in terms of substance and set-up, increasingly became organized and structured. The issue of uniting the different Mongol tribes and clans, the internal unity of the nomadic society, the establishment of peace had then become the pressing social and political issue of this period.

Temüjin, a descendant of a major Mongolia noble family, (1162–1227), played a significant role in addressing this pressing matter of the time. After Temüjin became the Khan of the Khamag Mongol tribal confederation (1189), all the Mongol tribes and clans, after a long process, were united into one large Empire, which could very well be classified as a period of transition to the formation of the Great Mongol Empire.

Finally, it can be concluded that the States and Empires that existed in the period under review had, on the whole, an ancient nomadic social relationship. Why this kind of social relationship continued for more than one thousand years can be explained as follows:

- Most of the Mongol-origin tribes, after they were occupied by the alien tribes, lost their leadership status; some of them migrated to other areas, while some of them were either assimilated by the Turkic and Uighur peoples or became mixed up with them, as a consequence of which the social progress stagnated and was disrupted.
- Different forms of economic relations existed for a relatively long period of time in the nomadic societies.
- The nomadic tribes were constantly at war and in a state of rivalry with each other, which only contributed to their decline and weakening.
- The development of the socio-state structures of the nomadic tribes existed at various levels.
- The nomads, as compared to the sedentary societies, maintained tribal structures and systems for a longer period of time.

Proceeding from the above special features, it can be concluded that the Statehood and legal structures of the ancient Mongol States and Empires, on the whole, were quite unique.

2 The State and Laws of the Great Mongol Empire (13th Century)

1 Historical Summary

Soon after Temüjin was proclaimed the Khan of the Khamag Mongol confederation, the struggle for the unification of the "felt tent dwellers" charted an irreversible course. The social demands then as well as the vital interests of the Mongols demanded such a turn of events. Two poles of power led by Temüjin and Jamukha appeared in Khamag Mongol, and both men strove to buttress their power. But the tide of time favoured Temüjin and Jamukha's subjects began to follow Temüjin.

Cracks appeared in the unity of the Khereid tribal confederation and when Tooril Khan (Toghrul) became weak, Temüjin took him under his patronage and made him stronger again. And together with Tooril Khan he rendered assistance to the Northern Jin Dynasty in 1198 and routed the Tatars. In 1199, they together encountered and fought against the Naiman confederation, and also seized control over many other Mongol-origin tribes. However, the princes of the Taichuud, Khonkhirad, Ikaris, Gorlos, Tatar, Oirad and Naiman tribes formed an alliance against Chinggis Khan. In 1201, they assembled on the banks of the Ergune River and proclaimed Jamukha Setsen as the Gur Khan.

This alliance was defeated by Temüjin, who joined forces with Tooril Khan. After Jamukha's alliance was squashed, Temüjin took full control over the Tatars in 1202.

Jamukha once again forged an anti-Temüjin alliance in 1203 by winning over to his side Altan and Huchir, influential nobles of the Khamag Mongol confederation, and managed to win over Tooril Khan to his side by manipulating his son Sengun. In the fall of 1203, Temüjin, who learned about the plot, defeated Tooril Khan in a surprise attack along the banks of the Tuul River. In this way, having defeated the most powerful Khereid confederation, the strength, power and prestige of Temüjin rose among the Mongol tribes.

Finally in 1204, after routing separate forces of the various tribal confederations and tribes associated with the Tayan Khan of the Naimans, Temüjin was able to unite under his command the core sections of the Mongol tribes and clans.

Temüjin conducted thirty-two large and small-scale battles between 1185 and 1206, in the course of which he was able to bring under his control all the 81 Mongol tribes, and thus "accomplished the great cause of bringing together and uniting the scattered tribes and clans under one state." This period in history can be defined as a kind of period of transition in the process of the establishment of the Great Mongol Empire.

In the fall of 1206 or the Year of the Red Tiger, the upper echelons of the Mongol nobles gathered in Temüjin's *Great Ger Palace* for their *Ikh Khurildai* – the Great Assembly. An eminent scholar Saishaal portrayed the grandeur of the *Great Ger Palace* in the following manner: "It was a large palace in the shape of a *ger*, with a snow-white cover and the hems in gold, and the four pillars that supported the *toono* (*wooden roof ring of a ger. Tr.*) were decorated in pure gold. On the one side of the entrance to the *Great Ger Palace* the state banner of the Mongols – the "Nine White Standards" as hoisted majestically, and on the other side of the entrance, stood the "Four Black Banners" – the war standards of Temüjin. The large square in front of the *Great Ger Palace* was a site where the military held their parade and where the *Naadam* games were played."[1] The key objective placed before this historically important *Khurildai* or Assembly was to proclaim the establishment of the Great Mongol Empire, and to enthrone the Great Khan, who would reliably lead the nomadic Mongols.

Temüjin, who from a youthful age had led the great cause of unifying the core Mongol tribes for more than 20 years, made this endeavour a reality at the manly age of 45 and was unanimously elevated as the Khan of the Great Mongol Empire by the *Ikh Khurildai*. About this, *The Secret History of the Mongols* writes as follows: "And so, when the people of the felt-walled tents had been brought to allegiance, in the Year of the Tiger (1206) they all gathered at the source of the Onon River. They hoisted the nine white standards made of horse tails and there they gave Chinggis the title of Khan."[2] In this way, a new Empire of the Mongols, which had united and brought together under one control the many small and big Mongol tribal confederations, was established in Central Asia.

Chinggis Khan and his successors, waged wars towards the West and the East, and established one of the largest empires that ruled almost one half of the world. Their wars and onslaughts were in fact one of the basic means of pacifying the external situation of the Empire at the given time.

Broadly speaking, the establishment of the new Mongol State was the legitimate outcome of the more than one thousand and four hundred years of tireless effort and struggle of the core Mongol tribes, starting from the third century BCE. It was a qualitatively evolutionary change in the socio-political growth of the nomadic people and was undisputedly a

---

1 Saishaal, *Chinggis Khan's History,* Books One and Two, Huhhot, 1967, pp. 382–385.

2 *The Secret History of the Mongols,* Clause 202.

historically remarkable, landmark event celebrating the traditions and renewal of the Statehood of the Mongols.

Today, scholars have characterised the key qualities of the State system of the Mongols in the 13th century as follows:

1 The society during the period of the Mongol Empire can be considered a society prior to the formation of a State or Statehood. At that time, there was no State structure as such, but rather a general unity based solely on the charisma of Chinggis Khan.[3] There are even doubts whether the so-called *Ikh Zasag* or *The Great Yassa* (The Code of Laws) ever existed.
2 The Empire built by Chinggis Khan was a kind of an early State. Some scholars have used such a formulation ("Early State") and have divided it into three categories, a) In terms of origin, b) type, and c) transitional. The book, *The Empire of Chinggis Khan,* co-authored by N. N. Kradin and T. D. Skrynnikova (Moscow, 2006), notes that "… The Empire during the period of Chinggis Khan was, in the most common sense, not a state," and continues that "qualities of Early State were predominantly evident in the Mongol Empire during the rule of Chinggis Khan."[4]
3 The Great Mongol Empire fully meets the criteria of the modern concept of a State, which is composed of a population, territory, State and its legal status.[5]

The establishment of a united Mongol State was a natural phenomenon, born due to a multitude of socio-historical reasons, including the following:

- It respected the origin and background, language, and national interests.
- Realisation of the Mongol self-identity or the basis of the mentality of the Mongol race.
- Psychologically the Mongols became hardened to carry out any and all activities designed to safeguard that immunity.

3 T. D. Skrynnikova, *Харизма и власть в эпоху Чингис Хана, (Charisma and Power during the Epoch of Chinggis Khan),* Moscow, 1977.
4 N. N. Kradin and T. D. Skrynnikova, *The Empire of Chinggis Khan,* Moscow, 2006, pp. 502–504.
5 Sh. Bira, *The Establishment of the First New United Mongol State,* (From the Report presented at a Grand Assembly of the Members of the Mongolian Academy of Sciences commemorating the 790th anniversary of the United Mongol State and the 75th anniversary of the People's Revolution), Ulaanbaatar, 1996.

- Proceeding from the interests of the nation and the race, the entire people anticipated and supported the idea of establishing a united State system.

The entire people of Mongol origin were equally geared to and supportive of seeing a State system that united the society and the entire territory of the State.

Until recently, from the standpoint of historical materialism, it was believed that the process of the formation of the Mongol race and people had been completed with the establishment of the new Mongol State. In recent years, some scholars maintain that not only were the Mongol race and people formed, but a united State of the Mongols was created as well.

2 State Structure

It must be noted here that the newly established State, which was founded on the traditions of Statehood in the previous period, was a monarchy in form but a State in substance, encompassing in itself extremely unique qualities of various elements of democracy.

2.1 *The Great Khans*

The highest authorities of the new national State of the Mongols were Lord Chinggis Khan, his immediate successors Ögödei, Güyüg and Mönkh Khans. They were believed to have been born with destiny from the Heavens: Tengri. They were the supreme masters of the Mongol Empire, the Head of the State. The highest State powers were concentrated in the hands of the Great Khans and they were the supreme masters of the lands of the Mongols.

The Mongols, from ancient times, respected and worshipped the Heavens, considered their Khans as sons of the Heavens, and on this basis, an entire political doctrine, which scholars and researchers have dubbed as "Tengrism," formed the bedrock foundation of the State ideology of the Great Mongol Empire. Shamanism, which respected and worshipped the Heavens, was the predominating religion during the reigns of Chinggis, Ögödei, and Güyüg Khans. But from the time of the rule of Mönkh Khan this ideology evolved into a well-formed doctrine of Tengrism, which believed that the Tengri – the Heavens – were the eternal masters of all.

The highest State powers were concentrated in the hands of the Great Khans, who were the supreme masters of the lands of the Mongols.

The Khan, while he was still alive, would name his successor, which was a smart policy to prevent all kinds of rivalry and conflicts that would undermine the existence of the State before the Khan breathed his last.

However, as was customary in Mongol military tradition, all princes of Chinggis' line, better known as the Golden Lineage of Chinggis Khan, had to attend the *Ikh Khurildai* to elect a successor. The enthronement ceremony was regulated and managed by the chief of the *Khurildai*. The closest relative from among the family of the Golden Lineage, who was to be enthroned, would be supported from the left, right and the back of the to-be-Khan by his brother, elder or younger, and his paternal uncle. For instance, when Ögödei was crowned, he was supported to the throne by his elder brother Tsagaadai (Chagatai), younger brother Tolui, and uncle Otchigin. As soon as the Great Khan sat on the throne, all the princes and nobles present at the *Khurildai* would remove their belts and put them on their shoulders, kneel down and utter the words "Oh the Great Khan" three times in reverence. Such a custom, on the one hand, meant the recognition of the new Khan and on the other hand, meant that his subjects would spare no effort to serve the Great Khan in a most reliable manner, that is, expressing their invariable allegiance to their new monarch. Soon after this the Great Khan would 1) hold a feast and the *naadam* games to display the grandeur and might of the State; 2) officially announce his commitment to invariably abide by the traditional Statehood and legal practices, and would pass the first edit designed at further streamlining them; 3) hand out food and provisions to the poor and the needy; 4) review the cases of those previously convicted on false charges, and show them mercy and pardon them; and 5) strengthen the State apparatus with new officials and functionaries. These practices were strictly followed.

In particular, the Great Chinggis Khan was a prominent statesman, an outstanding military commander, a hero of the Mongol tribes, the founder of the modern world, a personality that brought together, united, created and reformed the world.

2.2 *The* Ikh Khurildai

This was a political and military council that advised and guided the Great Khan on pressing issues confronting the Empire by analysing and seeking new solutions to problems, and it was a forum that enthroned the new Khan of the Mongols. The *Ikh Khurildai* of this period, as opposed to the previous Mongol Empires and States, had become much more refined, organised, and had increasingly taken the form and features of the highest State body. This is precisely why some scholars even argue that the *Ikh Khurildai* was the ancient predecessor of parliamentarianism. Whatever the case, the *Ikh Khurildai,* at the given period of time, was a proof that democracy, in one way or the other, was developing in the Mongol Empire.

The *Ikh Khurildai's* members included the most important queens of the Khan, the crown princes, his siblings, uncles and other close relatives from among the Golden Lineage of Chinggis Khan. Its members also included the Khan's favourite nobles and aristocrats, important military commanders and the *Khurildai* participants could freely express their opinion, advice and guide the Khan. It can be said that the *Ikh Khurildai* played a very important part in preventing and averting any attempt to seize the highest State power by foul means, and laying the firm foundations for the continued rule by the Khan. Most importantly, no-one in the Mongol nobility had the moral and legal right to declare himself the Khan by by-passing the *Ikh Khurildai*. It is believed that the *Ikh Khurildai* convened, at least, seven times even since Temüjin was proclaimed the Khan of the Khamag Mongol in 1189, the Year of the Female Yellow Pig (in 1189, 1202, 1204, twice in 1206, 1216 and 1219).

The date and the agenda for the *Ikh Khurildai* would be announced in advance to give its participants enough time to prepare themselves mentally, psychologically and also physically.

Ögödei further refined the rules and procedures of the *Ikh Khurildai*, and had even drawn up a special list of the nobles who would participate in it. It is believed that it was a taboo to come to the *Khurildai* smelling of liquor, or to come late or create unnecessary or unfounded disorder. What is more, a rule had been introduced according to which anyone who intentionally failed to attend the *Khurildai* was even subject to capital punishment. After the death of Chinggis Khan, *Ikh Khurildais* were held several times in 1220, 1235, 1246 and 1251, which were extensive in scale and scope, during which Ögödei, Güyüg and Mönkh were crowned as the Mongol Khans and alongside this, the *Khurildais* considered many issues such as declaring war, introducing duties and taxes. The decisions of the *Khurildais* were immediately brought to the notice of the masses, while matters that related to State secrets were kept confidential. It appears that huge amounts of funds were spent when the *Khurildais* were convened. For instance, when Mönkh was made the Khan, daily 200 horses, 200 cows, 5,000 sheep, 2,000 cart loads of *airag* or fermented mare's milk, and traditionally distilled alcohol were served for the guests, according to historical sources.

2.3 *Council of Commissioners*

Although the Khan had enormous power and authority, the Khan would pay attention to and act on the advice and guidelines of the learned and the intellectuals. Chinggis Khan had in his court a similar Council of Commissioners, which included as its members important policy-makers, learned people and scholars. According to some sources, the Council included most of the four military leaders, the four heroes, the two top ministers, the nine paladins, and the eighty-eight persons of outstanding merit in the Empire. The Council was set up to advise the Khan on the gaps in his policies, and take rectifying actions related to them. During the reign of Ögödei Khan, the duties and responsibilities of the Council of Commissioners became much more precise and thorough. The Council became an important forum to consider vital issues of the Empire during the interim period between the breaks of the *Ikh Khurildai*. In particular, during the eastern and western military campaigns carried out by Chinggis Khan and his successors, the Council met quite frequently to consider critical issues and pass relevant decisions. In this manner, the Mongol Khans not only received "fresh intellectual charges" but were also compelled to improve their education and knowledge so they could have a meaningful exchange of ideas with the Council members. Proceeding from this premise, it became a tradition among the Mongol Khans to educate their successor sons in a manner so that they would be well-educated from an early age to continue the State traditions and practices. For example, Mönkh and Khubilai Khans had mastered three to four foreign languages, they were well versed in history, language, mathematics, astronomy, geography etc., and in the science of state management. It can therefore be concluded that the Council of Commissioners that was set up in the courts of the Great Mongol Khans played an important role in sustaining a Mongol Empire that covered almost one half of the world over many generations, and in ensuring that the Empire grew and became stronger.

2.4 *State Ministers of the Empire*

As a Khan with extensive powers Chinggis Khan was both the executive and judicial authority of his Empire. However, in order to exercise his executive authority, Chinggis Khan appointed a State Minister whose responsibilities lay in managing the multi-faceted practical issues of the Empire. In this respect, Mukhulai (Muqali) was given the title of Go Wang, a position that was second next to the Khan in terms of authority. There are some researchers who maintain that Mukhulai was the first Prime Minister[6] of the Great Mongol Empire. However, if we were to approach this matter from the standpoint of the modern separation of powers theory, the Great Khan had overall executive authority and thus also discharged

6 D. Gongor, *The Khalkha Tovchoon or The Khalkha Summary*, Vol. 2, Ulaanbaatar, p. 57.

the duties akin to Prime Minister. Therefore, we can say that Mukhulai was not a Prime Minister but the leading minister of the Mongol Empire, who directly managed the central organ and was key scribe, responsible for the paperwork of the Empire. A little later, a certain Chingai, who was the leading minister under Chinggis, Ögödei and Güyüg Khans, served the Mongol State for more than half a century. In this connection, it must be noted that the term key scribe did not necessarily mean that the person was responsible for only the paperwork of the Empire, but was rather the chief minister managing the State affairs of the Empire as a whole.

Shikhikhutug (Shigi Qutuqu), the stepbrother of Chinggis Khan, was appointed as a high-ranking judge: the Chief Justice. Some scholars maintain that this rank of judge was akin to that of a Prime Minister. However, it is quite clear this position cannot be identified with the post of a Prime Minister, but was equivalent to the post of a leading deputy minister. The above conclusion is connected with the translation of the term *chung shu ling* or judge as a Prime Minister as found in ancient Chinese manuscripts. A closer look at this term means deputy premier, the core minister, an administrative minister responsible for all matters under his/her jurisdiction.

Chinggis Khan appointed, one by one, other State ministers of his Empire. For example, Bo'orchi, Zelme (Jelme) and Naya were appointed as military generals under his command. A similar high-ranking minister was a man called Üsün Övgön, who was the State expert, who would make a calendar after studying the heavens and the stars, and even identified the days when there would be solar and lunar eclipses. Basing himself on all this, he would advise the Khan when to call the *Ikh Khuraldai*, when to go on a military campaign etc. It was a tradition for the State expert to wear a white gown and ride a white horse. An individual who was of equal power and authority was the shaman Khökhchü. A Mongolian historian, N. Ishjamts, wrote the following about this shaman: "A popular shaman Khökhchü by name held much more important positions than the other shamans in the Empire. This shaman, as was the belief then, communicated directly with the *Tengri* – the Heavens, and would pass on to the Khan the words and guidelines of the *Tengri*."[7] But shaman Khökhchü did not live long as he was executed for betraying the Great Khan and the Empire.

Chinggis Khan conferred on his childhood comrades Zelme (Jelme), Bo'orchi, Sorkhon-Shira, Badai and Khishleg special titles, which not only

7 N. Ishjamts, *The Establishment of a United Mongol State and the Formation of Feudalism*, Ulaanbaatar, 1976, pp. 57–58.

showed grace, but was a move to strengthen the State structure of the new Empire.

These people would call on the Khan whenever they wanted and enjoyed special rights as they did not pay any taxes or duties, and would take possession of the entire spoils of the games or the wars. What is more, they were not even subject to any kind of punishment. However, there is no written or other evidence that they actually exercised the special rights given them, which is perhaps an indication that they were only doing their best to live up to the expectations of their Khan. In this sense, it can be said that Chinggis Khan smartly used the ancient practice of "comradeship" and was able to win greater trust among his generals and ministers.

Such important sources as the *Erdeniin Tovch* (The *Erdeniin Tovch* or *Tobchi* is a national chronicle and set of Mongolian judicial laws over historical content in the 17th century. It was written by Saghang Sechen in 1662.) and *Lu Altan Tovch* (The *Altan Tobchi* or Golden Summary, is a 17th century Mongolian chronicle written by Güüsh Luvsandanzan) briefly mention the appointment of the nine generals by Chinggis Khan called the *Yüsön Örlög* or the "Nine Paladins." A lyrical poem entitled "A treatise on how an orphan boy had a debate with the Nine Paladins of Chinggis" gives the names of all the nine Paladins as Mukhulai, Bo'orchi, Zelme, Shikhihutug, Sorkhon-Shira, Sübeedei, Zev, Borokhul (died soon after), Khara Khirüge and a later edition Tsuu Mergen or Yelü Chuchai. Scholars N. Ishjamts and Ch. Dalai have apparently compared these nine Paladins to modern day military generals.[8]

The Great Khan regarded Bo'orchi, Mukhulai, Borokhul and Chuluun as his four trustworthy knights. They were always at the side of the Khan and especially during military campaigns or other emergencies, they would protect their Khan with their own lives.

Khubilai Khan even compared Khudus, Zelme, Borokhul and Chuluun to outstanding hounds. During a war, the Khan would send them to the most difficult and decisive part of the battle to tame the enemies. In brief, these outstanding military generals carried the onus of the burden of a military campaign, and displayed their unwavering loyalty to the Khan as comrades.

Chinggis Khan, besides military and administrative actions designed to buttress his Empire, also gave priority to economic, cultural and education matters, and even appointed the relevant ministers. For instance, according to scholar Ch. Dalai "Todoi Cherby had been appointed the live-

8 *Ibid.*, p. 48.

stock minister, while Tatatunga served as the head of the Khan's secretariat and also as a minister overseeing education matters."[9]

2.5 *Military, Administrative and Territorial Units and their Management*

In the beginning, when Chinggis Khan administered the vast territory stretching from Lake Baikal to the Great Wall of China in the south, and from the Greater Khingan Ranges in the east up to the River Öröngö and Ulinger Lake in the Altai Mountain ranges, he divided his territory, following the ancient traditions, into Central, Eastern and Western *Tümen* with ten thousand households each. The Central *Tümen* was the core of the Empire situated along the basin of the Gurvan River, while the Western *Tümen* occupied the lands in the region of the Altai Mountains and the Eastern *Tümen* were in a land along the Khingan Ranges called Kharaon Jidun. The Central *Tümen* were primarily ruled by the Great Khan while minister Naya would attend to all the State and official matters. The Eastern *Tümen* was under the rule of Mukhulai and the Western *Tümen* of Bo'orchi. These *Tümens* were the largest units of military, administrative and territorial divisions, which gradually became the ownership of the nobles. The Great *Tümen* was divided into a number of small *Tümens*, which were a special kind of military and administrative units that had possession over large tracts of land and that were able to mobilise ten thousand warriors when the need arose. However, within the military division, the small *Tümens* were the larger joint unit.

Chinggis Khan divided his subjects into units of ten thousand, thousands into hundreds, and hundreds into tens. Having further refined the traditional system of thousands, Chinggis Khan divided the "Felt Dwellers" into 95 thousands. Judging by such historical sources as *The Secret History of the Mongols*, we can assume that there were three kinds of units of thousands, a. the old unit of thousands that existed prior to 1200; b. the 95 thousands in the year 1206; and, c. the thousands composed of subjects who were "taken captive." In this manner, later on, the number of thousands reached almost 130. The introduction of this system of unit of thousands by Chinggis Khan became the foundation for the long-term existence of the Great Mongol Empire. The system of thousands was a practical means of mobilising, within a short spell of time, warriors during a campaign and in the cause of protecting the Empire, it was a system that

9 Ch. Dalai, *History of Mongolia. The Great Mongol Empire: 1206–1260*, Book Two, Ulaanbaatar, 1994, p. 57.

was conducive to levying duties and taxes from the subjects based on a refined military and administrative set-up.

The thousands were divided into domestic and external thousands, and the latter, in terms of their ranking, were one stage lower than the domestic thousands. Chinggis Khan's mother, sons and siblings and his uncle Otchigin had their own thousands. Soon after becoming the Great Khan, Chinggis gave his mother Öelün and his uncle Otchigin 10,000 households; he gave 8,000 households to his second son Chagaadai, 5,000 households each to his third son Ögödei and youngest son Tului, 4,000 households to his younger brother Khasar, 2,000 to his younger brother Alchidai and 1,500 households to his younger brother Bilgüdei as their "shares."[10]

Chinggis Khan made his close comrades Menlig, Zörchidei, Zev, Sübedei and Bala commander of a thousand households each. A Japanese scholar Ikeuchi Isao, referring to the "-dium of Chronicles" has added that Chinggis had divided his Empire into 95 thousands and has clarified who were appointed the leaders of the units of thousands, and went further to reveal that 65 per cent of all leaders of the Western thousands and 76 per cent of the leaders of the Eastern thousands were all "comrades" of Chinggis Khan[11]. The size of the land and the population of the thousands were not identical. Some of the thousand households had two leaders, while there were some nobles who singly oversaw 4 to 5 thousand warriors as one thousand. Proceeding from this premise, the status of the nobles in the society who led the households of thousands was not the same. And those nobles who did not have the right to govern their own thousand households were called the leaders of the external thousands by Chinggis Khan.

The units of thousands were divided into units of hundreds and tens. The leader of the unit of thousands would appoint the leader of the hundreds, who in turn would appoint the leaders of the units of tens. The leaders of the units of hundreds and that of the tens, who were appointed by the former, were simple military officers. Traditionally, units of tens were the smallest military and administrative units and these consisted of a group of households that would be in a position to mobilise at least ten warriors when the need arose. The leaders of these units, besides han-

10 *The Secret History of the Mongols*, Section 242.

11 Ikeuchi Isao, "Chinggis Khan" , Serial 25 of the series on historical personalities, Book One, Gakushyu Kenkyusha, 1991, p. 102 (Based on the translation into Mongolian by Ts. Munkhtsetseg).

dling military affairs, were also responsible for managing administrative and civilian matters.

The key three central *Tümens* were not only given lands of their own, but some of the nobles of the *Tümens* were favoured as compared to some others, such as Khorch, Sorkhon Shira and Iljigdei, who were allotted specially protected lands for their use. Given the fact that new *Tümens* were set up, Chinggis Khan made sure that they were allotted the relevant population and lands. While Ögödei Khan appointed a special local leader from each of the *Tümens* and further streamlined the process of distributing lands and territories to these units. Soon after he became the Khan, Ögödei passed a decision strictly prohibiting members of the ten thousand, thousand, hundred and ten units to change their division and join another unit. In this respect, in May 1234, Ögödei Khan once again passed a law at the *Khurildai* of the nobles and princes, held at a place called Dalan Dawa, reiterating strict punishment for switching from one unit to another. This was an action that deepened the process of owner relationship of the leader and the subject.

Professor I. Dashnyam has written the following: "The rapid institution of the system of thousands was an act that became the guarantee for the survival of the Great Mongol Empire. Chinggis Khan implemented the system of tens, which was the most viable organisational system capable of managing the scattered population of Mongol tribes, who practiced pastoral livestock breeding economy across the vast tracts of pasture lands. Such an organisational and management division of the land and population contributed to the revival and progress of the economy of the nomadic Mongol tribes, the formation of socialisation of the society, and organising the army in such a way that it could manoeuvre easily in times of crisis, which helped him win victories in his military campaigns."[12]

One of the ancient, but unique forms of the nomadic socio-political structure of the Mongols was the system of *Khishigten*. A precise definition of its origin and development would have both practical and methodological significance in revealing the distinctive features of the State structure of the Great Mongol Empire and also understanding how it functioned. Initially, the *Khishigten* was created by the chiefs of tribes and clans for protecting themselves and their property from their potential enemies. Even Temüjin, after he was proclaimed the Khan of the Mongols, created elite special forces called the *Khishigten*, which included 70 *torguud*, who were the day guards of the Khan, and 80 *khevtuul*, who guarded the

12 I. Dashnyam, *State and Law of Chinggis Khan's Empire*, Ulaanbaatar, 1997, p. 3.

Khan's headquarters at night, but not limited to other responsibilities and besides them, the Khan had about a 1,000 heroes who would spearhead and lead the military campaigns.

Soon after the establishment of the first Mongol Empire, the role of the *Khishigten* increased and their organisational set-up and rules also became much more refined. *The Secret History of the Mongols* notes: "Then Chinggis Khan issued a [further] decree: 'Formerly, I had eighty night-guards and seventy sentries [serving] in shifts. Now, by virtue of the strength of Eternal Heaven, my might and power have been increased by Heaven and Earth, and the whole nation is unified under my sole rule. Now choose sentries from the [units] of one thousand and enrol them in my service. Enrol night-guards, quiver bearers, and sentries to serve me, in units of a full ten thousand.'" "Then Chinggis Khan issued a decree to the [units] of one thousand [regarding] the choice of guards and their enrolment: 'Enrol guards to serve us. Enrol the sons of the commanders of the ten thousands, the thousands, and the hundreds and the sons of the junior free people. Let those who are skilful, strong, handsome, and fit to serve at our side enrol to serve [us]. Enrol the sons of the commanders of the thousands. Let [each] bring ten companions [and let each companion] bring one younger brother. Enrol the sons of the commanders of the hundreds. Let [each] bring five companions [and let each companion] bring one younger brother. Enrol the sons of the commanders of the tens and the sons of the common people. Let [each] bring three companions [and let each companion] bring one younger brother. Let each come from [his] original [unit] with a mount made ready, to reinforce [those] serving at our side."[13] One of the reasons the sons of the commanders of the ten thousand, thousands and hundreds were selected and inducted in the ranks of the *Khishigten* was, on the one hand, to keep strict control over the nobles and princes under the Khan's rule, and on the other hand, it was a psychological tool to prevent the nobles and princes from betrayal, and moreover, it was a far-sighted policy of training and educating the boys of nobility from an early age in the art of warfare and education, so that they would be well-prepared for all contingencies.

After the formation of the first Mongol Empire, the *Khishigten,* besides providing security for the Khan and his residence headquarters, were also responsible for ensuring internal law and order, and preventing all kinds of disturbances and rebellions. Until recently, this is how the duties and responsibilities of the *Khishigten* were defined by scholars and researchers. However, a thorough study reveals that not very long after

13 *The Secret History of the Mongols,* Section 224.

the foundation of the first Mongol Empire, the structure, duties and responsibilities of the *Khishigten* became much more extensive to become the central military and administrative institute of the Empire. Scholar Sh. Bira has noted that "... As regards Chinggis Khan, the *Khishigten* not only increased to one hundred thousand, in terms of its number, but its operational activities also became broader and it was transformed into a military and administrative organisation directly under the Great Khan. The *Khishigten* apart from performing the duty of royal bodyguard of the Khan and his headquarters, they also managed the administrative matters of the Empire, so they were a kind of "government" of the new Mongol Empire."[14] This definition is justifiable as the *Khishigten* included not only the State ministers, but also all other officials, such as the scribe, the announcers, the judges, *torguud, khevtüül* (night sentries), *khorchin* (quiver bearers), hunters, guides, shepherds etc. who served the Empire and the Khan. If necessary, they had the right to command any unit of the army. Higher ranking officials were appointed from among the members of the *Khishigten,* who were always alongside the Khan and served him and secured his safety throughout his life. In this sense, the *Khishigten* were the key support of the Great Mongol Empire.

Ögödei Khan further strengthened the *Tümen Khishigten* (ten thousand *Khishigten)* during his reign, both in terms of discipline and organisational set-up. He also passed a decree saying: "I pass this decree to the public about the *khevtüül, khorchin, torguud* who guarded and provided safety to my father Chinggis Khan. May you all follow and abide by the decree of the Khan father as you had done before! The quiver-bearers and the sentries shall join [their] shift and perform the day's duties in each direction, each [following] his own path. At the sun's setting, they shall yield to the night-guards and go outside to spend the night. At night, the night-guards shall stay with us. The quiver-bearers shall leave [their] quivers and the cooks shall leave [their] bowls and vessels with the night-guards before they go. Those who have spent the night outside—the quiver-bearers, the sentries and the cooks shall sit at the horse-tethering place until we have consumed our [morning] broth. As soon as [we] have consumed [our] broth, they shall report to the night-guard. [The night-guard] shall return the quivers to the quiver bearers, their places to the sentries, and their bowls and vessels to the cooks. Each shift shall follow this same rule as it goes on duty.' '[During] the night, the night-guards shall lie down around the palace, close by the door. Those night guards who remain standing

14 Sh. Bira, *The Establishment of the First United Mongol State,* Ulaanbaatar, 1996, p. 12.

shall smash the heads of any people entering in the night and slash at their shoulders until they fall, [before] casting them away. If [people] arrive in the night with urgent messages, let them tell the night-guards. Let them stand together with the night-guards at the rear of the yurt and report [to us].' [Then] he said: No one shall sit on a seat on the upper side of the night-guards; without leave of the night-guards, no one shall enter; no one shall walk on the upper side of the night-guards; may the night guards collect and take care of the banner, drums, stirrup, spear, cups and utensils! May the night-guards be responsible for the drinks, alcohol, *airag* (fermented mare's milk) and meat."[15]

The *Khishigten* were given high responsibility and had strict discipline, but at the same time they also enjoyed special rights and privileges. For example, Chinggis Khan passed a decree expressing his will by noting that "the *tümen Khishigten,* who were sent to me to be my close possession by the 95 thousands, should be regarded, after my passing, by my successor sons and by the generations to come, as my bequeathed memorial and they should be taken good care of without letting them to any misery." Chinggis Khan's successors strictly followed his will and over generations safeguarded and augmented the rights and privileges of the *Khishigten.* Ögödei Khan decreed "If you beat them with a rod, you yourself shall [be beaten with] a rod. If you [beat them with your fists], you yourself shall [be beaten with] fists... My guards are senior [in rank] to the leaders of thousands [of households serving] outside [the palace] and my guards' attendants are senior [in rank] to the outside leaders of hundreds and of tens. If an outside member of a thousand quarrel with my guards and [try] to equal and match them, [he]—the leader of a thousand—shall be punished."[16] Therefore, it can be inferred that the *Khishigten's* contribution to bolstering the Mongol State was substantial and was instrumental in ensuring palace security, carrying out official State duties at the royal palace, and training State officials.

As the Great Mongol Empire grew and expanded, its State structure also became extremely complicated and refined. For instance, after Ögödei Khan defeated the Jin State of Northern China in 1234, based on the State system of the Jin Dynasty, he set up a general administrative ministry called *Zhunshushen* and Yelü Chuchai was appointed its Prime Minister, according to Yuan Shih or the History of Yuan. This was in consideration of the suggestion by Yelü Chuchai that Ögödei Khan should manage his

15 *The Secret History of the Mongols,* Section 228.
16 *The Secret History of the Mongols,* Sections 227, 228.

kingdom using Chinese methods, Chinese laws, and adapting the traditional Chinese State structure and system.

Mönkh Khan (1208–1259), realising the significant importance of the capital Kharkhorum (*Karakorum in Western sources. Tr.*) in improving the State and administrative affairs of the Great Mongol Empire, appointed the general governor of the city, which was yet another proof the State system was becoming more refined.

2.6 *The Military*

The *Khishigten* formed the core of the army of the Mongol Empire, but the military affairs of the Empire, in their scale and significance, were much broader and more extensive. Earlier it was mentioned that the Mongol Empire was united and better organised both militarily and in civilian matters. It must once again be stressed here that the military set-up in the unit of tens, formed by soldiers mobilised from ten households, the unit of hundreds consisting of ten tens, the unit of a thousand composed of one hundred tens and the unit of ten thousand, consisting of ten thousand ten units had laid the foundation that ensured that the Mongol Empire would have a powerful army at all times. This system was designed to augment the defence capabilities of the Empire, ensuring that both soldiers and civilians alike came under one single command and rule, and making the military law much more severe than the civilian codes of law.

With the consolidation of the *Khishigten* and followed by the appointment of the officials called *Cherby*, the Mongolian army assumed the shape of a permanent army and was re-organised in a new fashion. First of all, a military policy department called the *Ildech* was set up which was composed of 12 high-ranking advisors. This organisation, similar to a defence ministry, was primarily responsible for improving the warfare skills of the soldiers, ensuring that the warriors were constantly on the alert for action, constantly upgrading the managerial and command skills of the military officers, streamlining the organisational set-up of the army, and maintaining an army that was highly resilient and combat-ready.

Chinggis Khan and his successors promoted the development of the war industry and re-organised the military units and formations. Some scholars have noted that Chinggis Khan's army counted as many as 129,000 men.

The creation and maintenance of a powerful army by the Great Mongol Empire was connected with the formation of an integrated military training system. This system basically consisted of the following two components: 1. It became the duty and responsibility of every individual citizen to ensure that boys, from an early age, were taught how to ride a horse, handle bows and arrows, and learn the art of hunting and combat warfare; in other words, every subject in the Empire had to master these military-related arts; and 2. There also existed a kind of official training, where boys were taught to become professional riders, perfect in the art of using a sword, and to master the art of puzzle games. Different contests and competitions were regularly organised not only for entertainment purposes, but also as events to review and assess the quality of military training.

The military tactics of Chinggis Khan included gaining a strategic location before the enemy did and mounting a lightning attack on the enemy to take the initiative into his own hands, taking smart decisions with due consideration of the geographical location and the current situation, utilising to the full the mobility of the cavalry, integrating political and military policy in a manner that would display the valour, courage, psychological fortitude, and the wit and intelligence of the soldiers. Professor Kh. Shagdar, who has carried out extensive research into the military tactics of Chinggis Khan, thoroughly analysed eight of the 19 military campaigns, and drew the following conclusion: "The Mongols used individually or in combination a dozen or more military tactics, such as launching a surprise attack on the enemy at night from the direction the enemy would least expect the onslaught would come; luring the enemy into ambush and attacking; lighting up many fires to give the impression that the army is numerous; sending false information to or misleading the enemy via psychological operations, information warfare, visual deception and other methods; relocating the warriors, and intentionally making the enemy capture cavalry horses etc."[17]

The army of the Great Mongol Empire consisted of both light and heavy cavalry. The light cavalry was extremely mobile and the tactics used were crafty, while the heavy cavalry consisted of heavily armed, special purpose soldiers. The core weapons of the warriors included bows and arrows, sabre, spear, axe, metal cudgel, truncheon, and helmets and armour. The Mongol cavalry had a special engineering unit to deal with fortresses and barriers, and in this sense, the army of the Mongol Empire created an unprecedented military and warfare culture.

2.7 *The Judiciary*

The Khan passed the final judgment and he also appointed the highest judge of the Empire. For example, Chinggis Khan said to his stepbrother Shikhikhutug (Shigi Qutuqu) "Punish the thieves and put right the lies of

17 Kh. Shagdar, *The Military Principles of Chinggis, (1179–1206)*, pp. 248–249.

the entire nation. Kill those who deserve to be killed and punish those who deserve to be punished" and he appointed Shikhikhutug to hold judgment over all.

The Great Khan said to Shikhikhutug: "'Are you not the sixth younger brother? On you, my last-born younger brother, I bestow the same shares as on [all my other] younger brothers. Furthermore, in recognition of your services, you will not be punished for [up to] nine crimes." He also said: "While I am setting in order the entire nation under the protection of Eternal Heaven, you have become [my] seeing eyes, [my] listening ears. Share out the entire nation among [our] mother, us, [my] younger brothers, and [my] sons. Divide up the [people] of the felt-walled *gers*, according to the names of their tribes. Separate the [inhabitants] of the board-doored [dwellings] and let none countermand your word." Then he said to him: "Write down in a blue book a list of the shares into which [you] divide the nation and of the judgments [you] deliver. Unto the seed of [my] seed, let no one alter the blue writing of Shikhikhutug, ordained in consultation with me, [written] on white paper in a blue book and made into a register. Anyone who alters it shall be [found] guilty."[18]

The Chief Justice, according to the edicts as spelled out in *The Secret History of the Mongols*, had the following duties and responsibilities:

- Advise the Khan and conduct court proceedings on behalf of the Khan;
- Protect the legally-approved interests of the State institutions and subjects from criminal attacks, and restore rights that have been breached;
- Become the "eyes" and "listening ears" of the Khan and safeguard the security of the Empire;
- Develop written codes of laws, get them approved by the Khan and enforce them.

Based on the knowledge that we have today, we know that although the *Ikh Zasag* or the "Great Yassa" of Chinggis Khan does not have clauses referring to the judiciary system of the given period and its organisational structure, the leaders of the units of tens, hundreds, thousands and ten thousands, according to existing practices, were responsible for managing court proceedings at their own levels, while serious offender cases were referred to the Chief Justice and the Khan. It also appears that the Khan appointed, when required, special-purpose judges with special duties and responsibilities. For example, when the first Mongol Empire was being set up Chinggis Khan appointed Chingai (approximately 1169–1252)

18 *The Secret History of the Mongols*, Section 203.

as a judge under Shikhikhutug to primarily oversee matters related to the *Khishigten.*

Shikhikhutug devoted many years of his life to the cause of strengthening the State and legal systems of the Mongol Empire, thus winning respect through the Empire. The famous Persian historian Rashid al-Din wrote: "At the age of 82, he (Shikhikhutug) he decided cases fairly, helping and showing compassion to the convicts. He used to say 'Do not admit guilt out of fear' and used to tell the convicted to 'Speak out the truth without fear'. It is quite clear from the arguments furnished by judges that the methods and principles applied by Shikhikhutug continue to remain the basis of the court rulings."[19]

Shikhikhutug upheld the law, was fair and compassionate, and developed his own school of court proceedings. Mongol judges and those of subject foreign nations followed this principle of judiciary matters.

DIAGRAM 5 State structure of the Great Mongol Empire (first half of the 13th century)

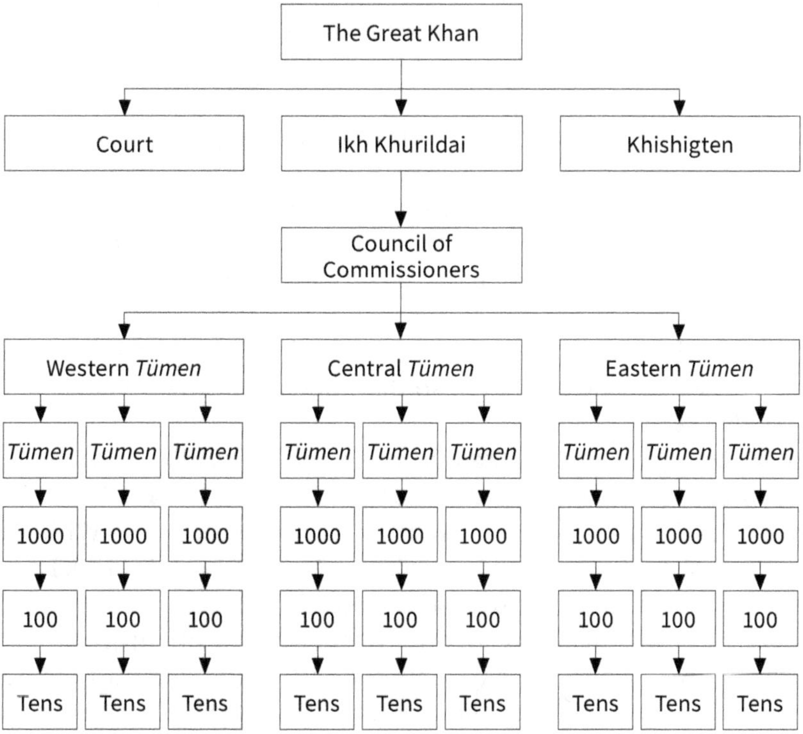

19 Rashi al-Din, *Compendium of Chronicles,* Vol. 1, Book One, (Translation in Mongolian by Ts. Sürenkhorloo), Ulaanbaatar, 1994, p. 61.

2.8 *The State Symbols*

The Great Mongol Empire used a state symbol that incorporated ithe lofty ideas and the grandeur of the monarchy. One of the symbols included the seal of Güyük Khan in the classical Mongolian script, as found in a letter sent to the Roman Pope Innocent IV in 1246, which was made of white jade and the inscription on the seal read: "Under the Power of the Eternal Heaven, if the Decree of the Oceanic Khan of the Great Mongol Nation reaches people both subject or belligerent, let them revere, let them fear." The seal was used in all state official documents together with the *Gerege (or a paiza was a tablet carried by Mongol officials and envoys to signify certain privileges and authority. They enabled Mongol nobles and officials to demand goods and services from civilian populations. Tr.)*

The **Nine White Banners** were used and revered by the Mongols since ancient times as a token symbolising the purity and eternity of the Mongol Statehood. This was composed of nine flag poles decorated with white horse tail hairs hanging from a round surface with a flame or trident-like shape on the top. White symbolised peace and the trident symbolised eternity. The banner was used with reverence in front of the *ger* of the Great Khan, during the *Khurildai* and during the great State *Naadam* festivities. The Nine White Banners were protected by a special team of warriors.

The grandeur and valour of the army of the Great Mongol Empire was displayed through the so-called **Four Black Banners**, which were used during times of war. This was made up of four flag poles decorated with black horsetail hairs hanging from a round surface with a flame or trident-like shape on the top. The two edges of the trident were sharp and in the centre it had a spear with symbolical flame tongues, which symbolised invincibility. The banners were placed on stone turtles and were always hoisted outside of the *ger*, so that they were always visible to the Eternal Blue Sky.

The Mongols, besides the State banners and the symbol, revered nine other symbols with deep respect. An important State, law and legal thinking source of the 13th century called the *Tsagaan Tüükh* or The White History, defines these nine symbols as follows: "1. The majestic black banner – the symbol of instilling fear; 2. The majestic red bugle – symbol of respect; 3. The powerful golden arrow – symbol of protection; 4. The splendid yellow cow – symbol of being *Exalted by All*; 5. The spanning diamond sword – symbol of conducting the government; 6. A reliable golden saddle – the symbol of events and happenings; 7. The majestic sash – the symbol of the sustainability of the state; 8. A tall and broad throne – the symbol of bureaucracy; and, 9. Reliable ministers – they are the ying and yang."[20]

The "palaces" of the Mongol emperors in those early days, were initially *gers* on wheels, a palace on wheels, and later, when the capital of Kharkhorum was built, a beautiful palace with 64 columns was built.

2.9 *State and Religion*

Shamanism was the central ideology of the Great Mongol Empire. The Great Khan believed in and offered prayers to the supernatural powers of the Heavens. Patronage and instructions from the Heavens were primarily transmitted through a shaman, and sometimes, it was also believed, that the Khans and nobles received guidance and instructions from the Heavens directly. The Mongols revered the Tengri – the Heavens – as their Father, and the Earth as their Mother, and were firmly convinced that their very existence and survival depended on the might of the Heavens. Chinggis Khan said "The Heavens bestowed on me the right to rule all the nations," which was an expression of his world outlook. Scholar Ch. Dalai attempted to justify the reason why shamanism had become the central ideology of the great Mongol Empire in the following manner: "The Khans of the great Mongol Empire primarily worshipped and revered shamanism, which although originated from their political policies, but at the given time, there were reasons why shamanism could not be abandoned altogether as well. For instance, only shamans and shameness' could be called up to raise the prestige of the emperor Khan, retaining the sacredness of the family hearth, worshipping and venerating the empire's banner and symbols, rousing and invoking spirits of good fortune, making offerings and sacrifices on the cairns, and to do divination. Other religions could not perform these rites as per the established Mongol traditions. What's more, the Mongol Khans were deeply convinced that the influence of all other religions may not be conducive to the unity of the Mongols and so they were strongly guarded against increasing their influence."[21]

Objects of shamanistic veneration were placed respectfully in the most important part of the dwellings of the Khan and common people in the early 13th century. Worshipping places were even created close to the dwelling *ger* of the Khans. William of Rubruck, a Flemish Franciscan missionary and explorer, noted that many shamans and shamaness would gather around the central dwelling of the Khan and one of them would

20 Kh. Nyambuu, *The Most Revered System of State of Blue Mongolia*, 1992, p. 74.

21 Ch. Dalai, *History of Mongolia. The Great Mongol Empire (1206–1260)*, Book Two, Ulaanbaatar, 1994, p. 219.

be the chief shaman who would be responsible for all matters related to offering prayers and sacrifices on behalf of the Khan and that shaman had become a leader similar to the Roman Pope. In the early period of the Great Mongol Empire, the Teb Tengri or Khukhuchu Shaman, under the patronage of Chinggis Khan, enjoyed greater privileges and authority, he had more influence in the Empire, and with his slyness he was able to bring many on his side. However, carried away by his power and authority, he was executed for his treachery and duplicity, as mentioned earlier.

As the Empire grew and became stronger, shamanism gradually was unable to meet the political and ideological requirements of the Empire and it was unable to bear the burden of the times. Peoples of different religions and faiths came under the domain of the Empire. Under such circumstances, Chinggis Khan did not restrict the practice of different faiths, which was appreciated throughout the Empire, and consequently, this opened up avenues for the coming of many other religions and faiths. The capital city of Kharkhorum, for example, besides Buddhist temples and monasteries, had two mosques and one Christian church, according to Marco Polo in his travel notes. Güyük Khan, in his letter to the Roman Pope Innocent IV in 1246, evidences the fact that shamanism then still remained the core ideology, as follows: "How dare you overlook the Decree of the Heavens? We both show mercy to those who are honest and follow the decree without any opposition. But we mete out severe punishment on the violators. I am a Christian by faith. I am a judge who supervises other's sentences … If someone has committed a sin, then that person should admit guilty of committing a sin. If you don't know your own abilities, if you do not follow my words and if you speak out against me then may the Heavens alone know what finally awaits your fate."

Chinggis Khan and his successors later on, when they realised that shamanism could not become the single State ideology of the Mongol Empire, gradually pursued the policy of making Buddhism the main religion of the Empire.

3 The Law

3.1 *The Legal Sources*

One of the main results of the Mongol Empire's growing strength was the establishment of legal norms that regulated social relations in detail.

These norms and standards were made up of codes of laws passed by the Empire as well as traditional norms and standards, which served the Mongol society then and thereafter for many centuries. As the great Mongol Empire became stronger and bigger, legal and traditional norms and standards became more distinct for their specific nature and features, they became mutually interdependent and played an important role in regulating the complicated relationships of Mongol society. In view of this, an analysis of the laws and their sources from a historical perspective has become one of the new objectives of the sciences of history and law. We would succeed in obtaining tangle results in this respect should we, first and foremost, apply historical and logical methods in analysing the factors that created the primary basis of the laws of Mongolia in the 13th-14th centuries.

Regarding legal sources related to the Great Mongol Empire, the following must be borne in mind:

1. The social life and the natural development trends of the Mongols and their empires in the 13th century must be studied from the intellectual level of the given period and the relevant conclusions can be drawn accordingly, which would become the legal material source.
2 The primary legal sources of this period are extremely rare and so study and research can only be done on the basis of third-party sources.
3 Concerning historical and cognitive sources, only a handful of documents, such as laws and customs, edicts, statements and letters of Chinggis Khan and his successors have come down to our times. Whatever the case, *The Secret History of the Mongols* remains the main monumental documentary source for studying the legal traditions of the Mongols in the 13th-14th centuries. Mongolian scholars Kh. Perlee and D. Dashtseden were the first to study quite extensively and exhaustively the legal traditions that are included in the above monument.

There are a number of important documents that shed light on the legal development of the Great Mongol Empire in *The Secret History of the Mongols.* Take, for example, the first edict passed by Chinggis Khan, other documents that set the legal norms, the notes on how the first chief judge of the Empire was appointed and specifying court proceedings, about procedures on convicting someone guilty of murder, mention about how Ögödei Khan established a fund for donations and grants, and about the law on horse-relay service, how some family-related relations were regulated and the adoption of relevant laws, decrees and edicts on granting pensions and benefits etc.

The *Compendium of Chronicles* by the Persian historian Rashid al-Din is the most important fundamental source material for studying the evolution and development of laws during this period. This monumental source document includes in detail norms and standards that outlined the rules and regulations of commanding the army, selecting and appointing the leaders of the units of tens, hundreds and thousands, the manner in which these leaders should manage civilian affairs and manage military and warfare affairs.

Scholars and researchers have also indicated that they have discovered some important documents related to the evolution of law in the great Mongol Empire from the book *The History of the World Conqueror* by Alauddin Ata Malik al-Juvaini as well as from Korean sources. In the late 14th century Al-Maqrīzī or Makrīzī, a prominent medieval Egyptian Arab historian of the Mamluk-era found fragments of the *Great Yassa* by Chinggis Khan, which was a significant discovery.

Therefore, the sources of legal norms and standards of the period under review are encapsulated in the integrated code of law, better known as the *Ikh Zasag* or the *Great Yassa.*

3.2 *What is in* The Great Yassa?

This code of law did not come down to us in its entirety. Judging by research carried out by different scholars, we learn that *The Great Yassa* was an integrated code of law, which regulated many different relations and not just social relations. *The Great Yassa* has always been a subject of keen research interest for international scholars and academics. We have found that scholars and researchers of more than 100 countries around the world, such as Russia, China, United States, Great Britain, Japan, Germany, Italy, Turkey, Egypt, Iran and others have either specifically studied these codes of law or have included them as references in their works and books.

The study of *The Great Yassa* can be divided into two elements. 1. as a source document; and, 2. as a research document. *The History of the World Conqueror* by Alauddin Ata Malik al-Juvaini, which was written almost at the same time as *The Great Yassa* was enforced, Rashid al-Din's *Compendium of Chronicles, History of the Mongols* by Magaki, *The Syria Notes* by Ab ul-Faraj and the *Yuan Shi* or *The History of Yuan* all contain direct quotes from *The Great Yassa* and so these works can very well be called source documents. There are very many studies on and a great deal of research into *The Great Yassa,* including books, articles, monographs etc. and we can name some of the following scholars for their enormous contribution to the study of *The Great Yassa,* such as Russian scholars V.V. Bartold, V. A. Ryazanksii, S. D. Dylykov, V. G. Vladimirtsov, Inner Mongolian scholar Saishaal, Taiwanese scholar Li-Qifin, Japanese scholars Sh. Ozawa and Murakami, American scholar J. Vernadskii, Mongolian scholars L. Dendev, Kh. Perlee. Sh. Natsagdorj, N. Ishjamts, D. Gongor, S. Jalan-Aajav, E.

Avirmed, G. Sovd, B. Chimid, I. Dashnyam, B. Sumiyabazar, N. Nyam-Osor, Ts. Minjin etc.

The Great Yassa was the result of the great historical process, that is, the establishment of the Great Mongol Empire. The term *Great Yassa* means the most important rules or principles. The word *Yassa* or *Zasag* in Mongolian has many different meanings, such as law, rules, procedures, and customs. A prominent American historian George Vernadsky, who specialised in the study of *The Great Yassa,* defined it as follows: "In my opinion, the *Yassa* as a whole can by no means be characterised as customary law. It was an integrated code of laws, based on customary law that covered the state administration, military and civilian affairs, criminal punishment, commerce, and customs." Professor I. Dashnyam defined *The Great Yassa* "As a law that defined the form of state of the Mongol, its structures, their duties and responsibilities, their *modus operandi,* ranks and titles of officials, their privileges, the prerogative rights and authority of the Khan, the principles of statehood, the empire domestic and foreign policies, the principle of rule and be ruled, land and ownership, customs and traditions, inheritance and succession, the rules and procedures of safeguarding and protecting the natural environment, rules and customs of social relationships, criminal policy, punishment, court proceedings etc."[22]

Professors of the School of Law at the Mongolian National University have researched source documents and books related to *The Great Yassa* and have classified the code of laws into 12 chapters and 216 provisions.[23] This does not in the least meant that *The Great Yassa,* after it was enforced in 1206, had a similar structure, that is, a similar number of chapters and provisions. Such a classification was created to better facilitate scientific understanding and conceptualisation of this monumental document by the general public.

Judging by the work undertaken by researchers and scholars, we can presume that *The Great Yassa,* in terms of its content, focused on the code of laws related to State affairs, civilian matters and the judiciary.

1. The code of laws related to State affairs could include such matters as the rights and authority of the Khans, the administration, military, foreign relations, judiciary and religion of the Great Mongol Empire.

---

22 I. Dashnyam *et al., The "Great Zasag" of Lord Chinggis Khan,* Ulaanbaatar, 1995, p. 7.

23 *Ibid.,* p. 15.

The process of proclaiming and enthroning the Khan, ordinances and decrees by the Khan, the effectiveness of the code of laws, decisions on appointment and demotion of high-ranking officials, the special rights of the direct members of the Golden Lineage of Chinggis Khan, and norms and standards of relations between the high nobles, the protection of State secrets etc., were included as the priorities in the *Yassa.* Provisions underlining the grandeur of the laws and ordinances passed by the Great Khan, their strict compliance can be found in the seals and *paiza* or *Gerege.* Legal provisions also note that the immediate successor of the Khan should be elected through the Great *Khurildai,* and the violator of this provision is fated with the strictest of punishment "without an iota of mercy." There are also provisions spelling out the requirements for State officials. For example, it was believed that a person who could manage his family well would be able to manage State affairs too, and so the belief existed that a leader who managed the unit of tens well could be promoted to be the leader of the unit of thousands, but if a noble is unable to manage his unit of ten, that person should be punished together with his child. Also an official would be severely punished if he/she transfers his/her duty and responsibility to another voluntarily.

The Great Yassa has special clauses concerning the misdoings of the immediate members of the Golden Lineage, and the punishment for the misdoing would be meted out within the Golden Lineage. "Should there be amongst our lineage who breach the *Yassa* or decree, first time violators shall be reprimanded by words, who commit the error the second time, shall be punished according to the gender, and the third-time repeater shall be exiled to the far-away Baljun Kholshar. Should they return from the exile, they shall be sent back. And if the violator still fails to understand his/her crime, shall be incarcerated handcuffed. It would be good if the convicted has developed some sense after he/she is released from imprisonment. If not, then let the entire member of the Golden Lineage decide on the action to be taken."

State secrets were heavily protected in the Great Mongol Empire, a person who disclosed such a secret was clubbed 100 time, and if a highly classified State secret was disclosed, the punishment was death by execution.

One of the central parts of the law on building the State and government included the code on administrative matters. For example, it was mandatory for "every single common person to be subordinated to the decimal system of the thousands, hundreds and tens." "No one, without the ordinance by the Khan, could change his/her geographical domicile, the chief of the thousands must guide and advise the chiefs of the hundreds, and the chiefs of the hundreds shall command the chiefs of the tens," and anyone who dared to violate this rule would be put to the sword. All individuals were assigned to the jurisdiction of administrations throughout the territory of the Mongol Empire, which is a sign that stage-by-stage administrative rule was strictly followed.

The code of laws related to military affairs has the most number of clauses and provisions in the part in *The Great Yassa* dealing with State affairs. This part of the *Yassa* includes the system of structure of the *Khishigten*, their duties and responsibilities, the rules to be abided by during the peaceful time when hunting, and during the time of war, as a matter of fact, this part of the code of laws includes provisions that primarily resemble strict military rules. The section on "State Structure" includes exhaustive provisions related to the *Khishigten*. Without going into their details, we would like to take up some aspects and matters related to the rules and regulations of the military during a war campaign. Hunting was regarded as a training for war and it was a litmus test to display the skills of a soldier, but "If an animal is intentionally let to escape while hunting, then the reason for this lapse would be carefully investigated, and the related chiefs of the thousands, the hundreds and the tens would be either reprimanded or even put to death," according to the *Yassa*. It also outlined the duties of a soldier, the rules to be followed during a war, and even the punishment that could be meted out should anyone violate rules, such as the following:

- The fighting men are to be conscripted from men who are twenty years old and upwards;
- During times of peace, when there is no war, all military personnel, starting from rank and file soldiers to commanders shall continue their military training;
- Warriors, who have been wounded in a battle, should not be left in the battlefield;
- If one retreats because of the enemy onslaught, the warriors must return to the place from where the offensive was launched, or else the violators shall be executed;
- Individuals or groups, who have defected during a battle, shall be put to death;
- No warrior shall abandon his post in search of booty while the battle is still on and such conduct shall be severely punished.

Judging by historical sources from Goryeo, a Korean dynastic kingdom, we find that the protection of people in occupied territories was regulated where training of warriors was given priority alongside the relationship between the commanders and the rank-and-file soldiers in the following manner: "...the warriors should be properly trained in the art of warfare, and they must be hardened to become outstanding soldiers… If a conscript is not mobilized owing to poor health, he cannot be substituted by someone else… when the warriors have already moved on and if a warrior finds a person, livestock animal or other bounty, they shall become the property of the warrior and his commander is prohibited to confiscate that property from his subordinate … the commander cannot take by force the horse belonging to his warrior, and exchange and use his horse for some other purpose, and the horse cannot be pushed to exhaustion … If anyone dare to take by force even a small portion of the property of the common people shall be put to death," as translated into Mongolian by B. Sumiyabaatar.

We assume that there was a military law, according to which "… it was prohibited to mobilise the warriors to physical labour, carry heavy loads," that is, making them perform non-duty work and exploit them for other purposes.

The Great Yassa contains provisions that focus on protecting the health of the warriors, and even providing incentives to medicine men depending on their merit. Take, for example, the following: "… should there be a sick warrior among the soldiers, he should be immediately referred to a good medicine man, and should be treated without delay. The award and the punishment for a medicine man shall depend on the number of warriors who have been treated or who have died from the time the patient was referred to the medicine man."

The Great Yassa specifically outlined the law on foreign relations. The *Yassa* covered issues related to the exchange of envoys and emissaries, rules and procedures of showing them respect as well as many issues concerning trade between peoples and States.

- Envoys and emissaries cannot be insulted and offended;
- Imposter envoys and emissaries shall be put to death;
- Officials and envoys, irrespective of their origin, shall be provided with transport means and food;
- The safety of trade among peoples shall be provided and guaranteed.

According to *The Great Yassa* all religions are to be respected and no preference was to be shown to any one religion, which bore evidence to the Empire's policy with regard to religion, where all religions and faiths were treated on an equal footing. The *Yassa* likewise stipulated that no taxes or duties should be imposed upon holy men, religious devotees, lawyers, physicians, scholars, people who devote themselves to prayer and points out that every individual person, as determined by the relevant unit of tens or hundreds, shall be liable to pay taxes and contributions, which is a sign that the inhabitants of the Empire were taxed and a proof of how taxes were regulated then.

2. The civilian statute as regulated in *The Great Yassa* included norms and standards related to customs, relations among the people, teachings and words of wisdom, pensions and benefits, property, property inheritance, marriage, family life, trade and commerce.

Norms and standards related to the livelihood, customs and traditions, beliefs and totems of the Mongols were duly reflected in *The Great Yassa.* "Whoever urinates into water or ashes shall be put to death," "When an animal is to be eaten, its feet must be tied, its belly ripped open and its heart squeezed until the animal dies; then its meat may be eaten; but if anyone slaughter an animal after the Mohammedan fashion, he is to be himself slaughtered," and the *Yassa* forbids the poking of fire with a knife or taking out meat from a cauldron with a knife – that is, practices and customs that related to shamanism are plentiful, which also goes to show the kind of respect and love the Mongols had for nature, the environment, fire and water. The victories and successes of the Mongols had always relied on their horses and so there were special codes of law that protected the horses. Take, for example, the following: "Take care of your horses before they tire when stating on a long-distance campaign," "As soon as the battle ends, the warriors must give their good steeds water and grass to drink and feed, and during this period, it is forbidden to ride the horses, and anyone who dares violate this rule shall be put to death," "Those who dare to beat their horses on their heads and eyes shall be put to the sword." Also there are strong warnings against those who cause damage to the environment, take for example, "A household that has dug holes after the grasses have turned green and who have put pasture fields on fire, shall be executed."

The ancient customs of comradeship and bonding, which were also practiced during the period of the united Mongol Empire, can also be included as a customary legal norm of relations among people. Also the *Yassa* apparently contained clauses and provisions of an everyday customary nature; for example, it says: "When a wayfarer passes by people eating, he must alight and eat with them without asking for permission, and they must not forbid him this," "It is forbidden to eat food offered by another until the one offering the food has tasted of it himself, even though one be a prince and the other a captive," "It is forbidden to step over a plate of food, those who do, shall be put to death."

The Great Yassa also contained words of wisdom and warnings, such as: "It is prohibited to take liquor. If unable to abstain from drinking, a man may get drunk three times a month, if he does it more than three times, he is culpable," "Love one another, don't lie, don't steal, do not betray one another, support and care for the elderly. Those who dare to disobey shall be put to death." It is clear from the following that there were statutes that allowed for benefits and compensations. "Sons, grandchildren and orphans of the warriors who have accomplished heroic feats in battles shall be supported."

The *Yassa* also has clauses and provisions that regulated ownership relations, in particular, inheritance of property, special privileges granted to those who have excelled in their fields. For example, "Give a restricted piece of land to Sorkhon-Shira for ownership for generations to come," and there were regulations of inheritance of property within a household, "A man who has many wives, the first wife shall be the most senior in charge". The *Yassa* prescribes that "Children born of a concubine are to be considered as legitimate," "The father shall decide and share the family property among his sons as he determines, the eldest son shall get more than his younger siblings, and the youngest son shall inherit the household of their father." What is extremely interesting is the clause, which is a kind of child-protection clause, that children born of a concubine are to be considered as legitimate.

Statutes related to families and households established norms and standards regarding polygamy, the superiority of the first wife over others, the taboo on committing adultery etc.

- A man, if he wishes, can have several wives. The first wife shall be the most respected among others with special rights, which is appropriate, and this special right shall be enjoyed by children born of her.
- After the death of his father, a son may dispose of the father's wives, all except his mother; he may marry them or give them in marriage to others. Two sisters can be married to make as one's wives.
- Anyone who, even if married, commits adultery shall be put to death.

The Great Yassa had clauses and provisions protecting the rights of women across the territory of the Great Mongol Empire. A historical document found by a Mongolian expert on Korea, Professor B. Sumiyabaatar, reveals that "... commanders and warriors, taking advantage of their authority, cannot marry by force women and girls of new towns and countries that have been seiged."

There are also provisions related to trade and commerce. "Whoever takes goods (on credit) and becomes bankrupt, then again for the third time takes goods and again becomes bankrupt is to be put to death after the third time." This shows that the first foundations of market, tax and monetary relations were already being established in the Great Mongol Empire, and consequently, there arose the need to regulate these relations through laws and legislation.

The question of protecting historical and cultural monuments was also taken up in *The Great Yassa*. For example, "it was prohibited to destroy and plunder graves and tombs." This is an illustration that the Mongols, since early times, had had a high level of culture when it came to protecting and taking care of historical and cultural values and monuments.

3. The criminal law of *The Great Yassa* had as its main objective keeping peace and order in the State and society. Chinggis Khan and his successors, while introducing provisions related to criminal law, were in all likelihood guided by the principle of safeguarding the first State of the Mongols and its independence, ensuring that it had a single leadership, reinforcing the customs, traditions and religious convictions and belief, and revering and upholding law and order. Dr. Kh. Selenge, having studied the legal norms in the *Yassa*, has defined the following special features of the Mongol society then:

1 Military-related crimes predominate in the criminal law of *The Great Yassa*. 14 of the 51, or 27.4 % of clauses related to criminal law deal with military crime.
2 Violation of customs and traditions, and established customs of shamanism were considered criminal offences.
3 *The Great Yassa* used capital punishment widely. 41 or 80.3% of the 51 provisions of the *Yassa* relating to criminal offences are subject to capital punishment. Perhaps this is quite a serious conclusion.
4 One of the special features of assigning punishment included the conviction of the entire family together with the person convicted of a crime.

The criminal cases, as listed in *The Great Yassa*, have been classified by researchers and scholars into the following six categories: 1. Crimes against the State and the administration; 2. Military crimes; 3. Property-related crimes; 4. Crimes against the life or health of a person; 5. Crimes against customs and traditions, and the practice of shamanism; and 6. Commerce and business-related crimes.

The *Yassa* also has provisions condemning violators who "go against the Khan and the State." If a *Khishigten* failed to appear for his shift, he would be thrashed three times by a stave. If he skips his shift once again, the *Khishigten* would be whipped by 7 staves, and if the *Khishigten*, although he is healthy and strong, skips his shift without the knowledge or the permission of his elder, he shall be hit by 37 staves, and exiled on the grounds that he is not to be relied upon anymore.

In *The Great Yassa*, abandoning one's position on the battlefield, retreating without the commander's orders, stealing war booty, exposing military secrets, absconding from military service, deserting, and searching for booty before victory in a battle were all considered military crimes, and the guilty were cudgeled, the booty they had captured would be confiscated and exiled, but in most cases, those found guilty of these military crimes were, as a rule, put to the sword.

Stealing the property of others was loathed during the period of the Great Mongol Empire and those guilty of stealing awaited harsh punishment. Punishment by death was prescribed for "third bankruptcy after safekeeping other's property, or concealing them...," "thieves were executed and his wife and his property shall be given to whose property had been stolen," "slaves who have escaped and their accomplices would be put to death," and so on and so forth. However, depending on the scale of the damage, the guilty were also whipped or fined.

The Great Yassa gave much attention to the life and health of man, and the maximum penalty was given to those who violated the related commands. "A murderer shall be killed," "A person who is guilty of taking other's life by foul means shall be executed," "A person guilty of extramarital and/or same-sex will be put to death," "A person guilty of bestiality shall be executed," "Persons giving false evidence shall be handed capital punishment." Furthermore, people who violated customs and traditions, and shamanistic practices were also considered as having committed grave crimes and so such crimes were considered under a special category. There are also numerous clauses and provisions in the *Yassa* that relate to business crimes.

Punishments outlined in *The Great Yassa* can be classified as disruption of comradely ties, offering as a sacrifice, condemning to wear a cangue, imposing a fine, whipping or clubbing, incarcerating, exiling and putting to death. Some scholars have further classified capital punishment as massacre, execution by not dripping any blood, breaking the spinal cord, chopping off one's head etc.

Nobles and princes, who had devoted their selfless services to the cause of building the first united Mongol State, were "not convicted for their first nine crimes," which is a proof of the existence of the principle of leniency and clemency by the Great Khan.

The Great Yassa is a significantly important document; in significance it is identical to the ancient Babylonian Code of Hammurabi and the ancient Indian Laws of Manu, which played a significant role in the evolution and development of integrated social and political structures in the history of global humanity. This is because the principles and concepts outlined in *The Great Yassa* left behind an indelible impression on the history of law and legislation of the world, given the impact the Mongol Empire had across the world.

3 The State and Laws of the Mongol Yuan Empire (13th Century–14th Century)

1 Historical Summary

The struggle for the throne began between Tului's two sons, Khubilai and Arigbökh (Ariq Bökh), immediate members of the Golden Lineage, after the death of Mönkh Khan.

When Arigbökh learned about the death of Mönkh Khan, he took advantage of the fact that he had stayed behind to take care of the main territory and the capital city as was decreed by his brother Khan and called the *Ikh Khurildai* in May-June 1260 and declared himself the Khan of the Empire. But when Khubilai learnt that Arigbökh wanted to become the Khan of the Mongol Empire, he immediately arrived at Kaipin from South China and on 6 May 1260 he also called the *Ikh Khurildai,* where he also managed to declare himself as the Great Khan of the Mongol Empire. In this manner, in 1260, there were two Great Khans in the Mongol Empire, which led to rivalry between the two Khans. This later became a bloody conflict that continued for almost four years and which ended with the victory of Khubilai Khan. He then moved the Empire's capital to China and as of January 1271 renamed the Great Mongol Empire as the Great Yuan Dynasty. The establishment of the Yuan Empire, centred in China, met with severe resistance from the native Mongol tribes.

There is a group of scholars who criticise Khubilai Khan for illegally using the title of the Khan, moving the capital city of the Mongol Empire to China and for leaving his native country to its own fate, while there is another group of scholars who give the title of *Setsen* or *Wise Khan* to Khubilai Khan, an educated person, who was able to manage State affairs in a proper manner and who reformed the laws and rules of the given times. It is high time that we scholars and researchers refrain from the old practice of either painting in great glory or downplaying historical events. Let us rather pose the question, what would have been the outcome had Khubilai Khan not moved the capital of the Mongol Empire from Kharkhorum and ruled the East?

As the rule is in a powerful monarchy, where centripetal force dominates, at least 2 to 3 million people from the almost 100 million population of China then would have moved and settled in Kharkhorum, as a matter of fact, in Mongolia. According to researchers, Mongolia's population then was in the region of about one million. Perhaps Khubilai Khan took into consideration the threat of assimilation of the Mongol tribes.

The Great Khan, when he moved the capital to China, may not have considered making China the centre of politics, but rather pursued a long-term vision of developing further the great Empire by occupying the Orient from the threshold of the ancient border of Mongolia and China. Subsequent historical developments have proved the correctness of such a policy pursued by Khubilai Khan. A Mongolian historian, Sh. Natsagdorj, who conducted a thorough study into the historical role of Khubilai Khan, has written that "There never was and never had been in the global history of any Empire, the like to Khubilai Khan with the size of lands that had been seized, and the role and impact on the occupied peoples and the world of the given times," and "Khubilai Khan was instrumental in regulating nomadic and sedentary cultures, finding a balance between the two and did everything possible to retain Mongolia in its unique form and saved the Mongol culture and civilisation from being assimilated into alien cultures and civilisations."[1] In the meantime, a prominent American scholar, Morris Rossabi, wrote that Khubilai Khan's successes and accomplishments cannot be denied, and that those successes and accomplishments, despite his short life, brought him eternal fame and that Khubilai Khan remained a Mongol, who never changed his inherent nature.[2]

Scholar Sh. Bira wrote that "Khubilai Khan, from among the other great Khans of the Mongol Empire, ruled the longest, during which he accomplished a lot in making the Mongol Empire into a global empire. Ten of his direct descendants became great Khans to continue the cause of the great Mongol empire for more than 78 founded by their great grandfather. Add to this the 35 years of rule by Khubilai Khan, we find that Chinggis Khan's direct descendants had, one way or the other, ruled the Mongol Empire for altogether more than 108 years. Apart from this, 20 years after the downfall of the Mongol Empire, as many as two direct descendants of Khubilai Khan were ruling the country. There were as many as 13 great and small khans, direct descendants of Khubilai Khan, who ruled Mongolia for Mongolia more than 128 years up until 1388 when the crisis of the small Mongol Khan began, which clearly illustrates the role of Khubilai Khan in the history of the state of Mongolia. There are at least 35 khans from the Golden Lineage of the Mongol tribes, starting with Chinggis Khan and almost 20 of these khans were the direct descendants of his grandson Khubilai Khan, while the others were the descendants of Chinggis Khan himself. Finally, it must be noted that Khubilai Khan, to-

1 Sh. Natsagdorj, *Khubilai The Wise*, Ulaanbaatar, 1998, p. 96.

2 Morris Rassabi, *Khubilai Khan: His Life and Times,* University of California Press, Berkeley, Los Angeles, London.

gether with his grandfather Chinggis Khan, were respected personalities not only in the history of Mongolia, but that of the world as well."[3]

And so, Khubilai Khan was:

- A wise statesman, who came to the helm of a great Empire through natural law and the law of competition of the given times;
- An outstanding thinker, who introduced the "dual principle", that is, the parity of power and dignity of religion and State in political affairs of the State;
- Spearheaded the spread of Buddhism in Mongolia for a second time;
- An enlightened and educated Khan, who strictly pursued the policy that a refined system of education can produce an educated nation, established the largest Oriental schools, initiated the introduction of a national alphabet, set up astronomy and history research centres;
- An outstanding personality, who spread the intellectual and physical might of the Mongols to the ends of the world and he was the second Khan after Chinggis Khan to elevate the name Mongol to the highest in the world. Some of our scholars have a misunderstanding of Khubilai Khan as a common traitor, which is unfortunate.

During the rule of the Yuan Dynasty, besides the consolidation of the Statehood, irrigated land farming and exploitation of natural resources were developed. Khubilai Khan was the first to establish country-wide use of paper currency; a horse-relay postal service was introduced and foreign trade was promoted; and all this helped cement the firm economic foundations of the great Mongol Empire. Mongol Khans, such as Khubilai and Togoontömör and other outstanding Mongol statesmen, set up astronomy centres in Kharkhorum, Shangdu, Beijing and other major towns, brought together scholars of different tribes and nations in prototypes of modern-day research centres and academies to bring out important works of science, which made substantial contributions to the growth of the Mongol Empire. However, during the rule of Khubilai Khan, the Golden Horde and the *Khülegü' Uls* or *Ilkhanate* gradually broke away from the Great Mongol Empire to become independent empires. During the last years of the rule by Togoontömör, from 1331 to 1368, the Yuan Empire became quite weak and it collapsed after the so-called "Red Turban Rebellion." Although the Mongol Empire disintegrated in 1368, there existed a State called the *Ar* or the North Yuan with Kharkhorum as its centre until 1387, which had under its control quite a substantial chunk of Chinese territory.

---

3 Sh. Bira, *Some Special Issues of History and Ideology of the Great Mongol State*, Ulaanbaatar, 2006, pp. 38–39.

In addition to the Great Yuan Dyansty, the State and legal system of the states established by Genghis Khan's sons and grandsons Zuchi State (Golden Horde established by Bat Khan), Tsagaadain State, and *Ile* Kingdom (established by Khulegu) are an integral part of the State and legal history of Mongolia. It should be noted that the ideals and principles of Ikh Zasag law have been used to some extent for many years in these countries.

Regarding the State structure of some of these countries, when the *Ile* emperors were finally installed on the throne (the second ceremony), the envoy of the Great Yuan king came to read the confirmation of the Great King[4], which shows that it had the characteristics of a confederation.

2 State Structure

2.1 *The Great Khan*

In terms of State system, the Yuan Empire was an absolute monarchy. The Great Khan had the ultimate power and authority of the Empire. After defeating his own brother Arigbökh in 1265, Khubilai proclaimed himself the rightful heir not only as the Khan of the Mongols but also of China. Khubilai Khan ruled the Empire for 34 years during which period, as evidenced by historical documents, he accomplished a great deal with regard to streamlining the State systems as a whole. The Venetian merchant and explorer Marco Polo gave a detailed picture of the grandeur and greatness of the Yuan Empire in his book *The Wonders of the East*. Regarding Khubilai Khan he wrote: "He was neither tall nor short, but of medium height. He was physically healthy and strong. His face was bright and shiny like a rose, the eyes were wise-looking and dark black, his nose was straight but high,"[5] and went on to describe the Khan's palace, the State principles and the titles and honours of the Empire. "The Chinese Emperor, who had ascended to the throne to rule the people 'waiting for orders from the Tengri' believed that he must tame not only humans, but also the nature. Time must also come under the jurisdiction of a Khan, who believed he had the right to rule nature as well. Immediately after becoming the Khan, Khubilai introduced a new calendar system called *Zhongtong (Chung-t'ung)*, which evidences that Khubilai Khan tried to use this unique Chinese idea that the emperor khan had immeasurable power. The new calendar system of Jong-Tong was used for five years, after

4 Rashid al-Din, *Compendium of Chronicles A History of Mongols,* (Translation into Mongolian by G. Akim), Ulaanbaatar, 2021, p.776.

5 *Yuán Shǐ* (*History of Yuan*), Beijing, 1987, p. 9.

which it was replaced by another system called Ji-Yuan. This signified the introduction of a new calendar system in the country after crushing the rebellion by Arigbökh,"[6] wrote a prominent Japanese scholar Otakhi Matsuvo, linking the power and authority of the great Khan with nature and time. This meant, that the Great Khan directly managed the domestic and external affairs of his Yuan Empire.

The State ideology of Khubilai Khan has been specifically and in detail explained in a book called *"Арван Буянт Номын Цагаан Түүх"* (literally meaning, *The White History or the Book on Ten Noble Deeds or Virtues,* Tr.), this was because *"The White History"* was a collection of laws and decrees adopted during the reign of Khubilai Khan on a dual principle; that is, it promoted the parity of power and dignity of religion and State in political affairs of the State. Khubilai Khan, as in ancient India and China, pursued, in all likelihood, a dual principle and made Buddhism the main religion of the Mongol Empire. Khubilai Khan defined the policy with regard to religion, which is spelled out in a book called *"Сувдан Зарлиг"* or *"The Decree of Pearls,"* which notes that equitable conduct of religious and State affairs signifies the establishment of an amicable parity between the religion and State, and pursuing them on an equal footing. "In the absence of religious affairs in the state, the living beings will be submerged in hell, in the absence of a monarchy, the country and nation shall break apart,"[7] wrote *The White History,* where religious affairs in the State mean the tantras and mantras of the God. The worldly State means a monarchy where happiness and progress prevail. In other words, it was believed that an individual can be happy and overcome pain and sorrow if the person follows the words of the God and the rule of the Khan. In order to pursue the dual principle, Khubilai Khan, first of all, placed State and religion on a par in his Empire. These two institutions played a principally very important role in further streamlining and strengthening the State. The basic principles of managing the worldly State, the concept of four great States, were developed by the ancient Indian King Mahasamadhi, which was revised by Shakyamuni and the foundations of which were laid in the land of the Mongols by Chinggis Khan. Khubilai Khan, during his reign, propagated that if these four great States were developed equally, then only the States created by Shakyamuni and Chinggis Khan would yield tangible results. In this manner, religious propaganda was promoted extensively so as to impact the spirit and mind of the common people,

6 Otakhi Matsuvo, *Khubilai Khan,* Ulaanbaatar, 1991, p. 98.

7 *Арван буянт номын цагаан түүх, (The White History of the Book on Ten Noble Deeds or Virtues),* Huhhot, 1981, p. 76.

which was a state policy of Khubilai Khan as a result of which religion and religious ideology were organised on a similar pattern as the State organisation, and religion became stronger and accordingly, it began to play a powerful role in the society. An imperial religious mentor and State tutor was appointed, who held a position as high as the Emperor himself. And so this kind of new organisational set-up of Buddhism grew to become an inseparable component of the social and State structure of the Yuan Empire of Khubilai Khan.

A key duty of religion in the Yuan Empire was to propagate among the people to follow Buddhist ethics. They preached that a human being can rid himself/herself of worldly pain if he/she can overcome the three evils or poisons – anger, delusion and desire. A person must refrain from ten black sins and accomplish ten good deeds by way of meditating and separating oneself from this world. The pains and happiness of this life are the result of the karma in the previous life, and as the next life depends on the karma in this life, it is important to accomplish good deeds and only through religion can one rid himself/herself of worldly pains and sufferings. For Khubilai Khan, who ruled over people of different origins and nationalities, such a single teaching was essential for his Empire.

According to Khubilai Khan, the core meaning of the worldly Statehood lay in peace and happiness. It was believed that the Mongol Khan incorporated in himself, physically and spiritually, all the "four basic qualities of a Khan", in other words, the Mongol Khan was likened to Mahasamadhi, the first king of ancient India, King Chakravarty, a heavenly king whose mission was to bring order to the world according to the words of the God, a noble king of noble origin like Siddhartha Buddha, who would bring peace and happiness to the world, an accomplished Khan who would tame and subjugate his enemies without much ado. In brief, the Mongol Khan was a Khan from the upper heavens, well versed in both literature and the art of warfare, and so invincible and with exceptional rights.

These are central ideas that are expressed in the book *The White History*. In order to ensure that this ideology would be pursued forever, Khubilai Khan decreed that "The true governance by the highest spiritual leader and the king of the world holding the state powers are as strong as the amulets of true faith, and the rule of the khan is unbreakable like a golden yoke."[8] Scholar Ch. Jügder, who specialised in researching the State ideology of Khubilai Khan, has noted that "Khubilai Khan, during his reign, introduced rules and regulations related to the actions, discipline and protocol that the khan must follow, and the state had defined

8 *Ibid.*, p. 76.

the three great deeds of the Khan, the Four Noble Polities, the Six Exemplary Actions, the Seven Great Mental Beings and the Nine Great Symbols."[9] These core principles and ideas can be explained in a much more comprehensive manner as follows:

I **The Three Great Deeds:** i. Ensure peace and tranquility according to the precepts of the State; ii. Rule according to the principles of Statehood to make the people happy; and, iii. Promote military policy and defend the country.[10]

Ensure peace and tranquility according to the precepts of the State: This meant that the State offices should be made to be managed by people who are knowledgeable and educated in the principles and ideas of Statehood, who must be rational and prudent in developing State policy, make the people appreciate the policy, implement it in practice and create peace and tranquility in the State.

Rule according to the principles of Statehood to make the people happy: This meant that the State offices should be managed by people who have both life and work experience, who would provide and extend services to the people without any hindrance or red tape and in a fair manner, but in keeping with the rules and regulations, and ensure that the opinions and suggestions of the people are put into practice.

Promote military policy and defend the country: This implied that every citizen should raise and educate their children to be healthy and strong, teach them the art of warfare, and educate them in the spirit of patriotism so that they would, without hesitation, come to the defence and protection of their homeland.

II **The Four Noble Polities:** The first two of the Four Noble Polities are being compassionate for the benefit of all the sentient beings, acting as a medical doctor when the need arises, showing the right road to someone who is lost in his/her life and acting as a lamp during the dark of the night, giving alms to the poor and the needy, and helping all beings equally like a Bodhisattva; 3. This implies that the Khan, when ruling the Empire, should strive for peace and tranquility; and

---

9 Ch. Jügder, *Social, Political and Philosophical Mentality during the Period of Feudalism in Mongolia*, Ulaanbaatar, 1985, pp. 122–125.

10 *State and Law History of Mongolia (Selected Works)*, Book One, Ulaanbaatar, 2006, p. 7.

4. One of the core duties of a Minister is to ensure that his officers work diligently for the benefit of the State.[11]

The first of the Four Noble Polities reflects the true nature of the State's social policy; however, according to the third polity, the Khan, while conducting State affairs, must be honourable, take wise decisions preventing issues from exacerbating and going out of control, and according to the fourth polity, make Buddhism the State ideology and ensure that both State and religions are given equal priority.

III **The Six Exemplary Actions:** 1. The historical examples of State management by the Mongol Khans; 2. The example of Buddha's teachings and ordinance on managing the State; 3. The example of the protocol and rules of managing the State and its affairs; 4. The example of preventing arbitrary actions; 5. The example of founding an army to protect the State; and, 6. The example of thriftiness to ensure growth.[12]

In particular, emphasis is given to ensure the continuity of the customs and traditions of Statehood, as well as the policy conducted by the former Khans, starting with Chinggis Khan, and alongside this, *The White History* notes the importance of studying and applying Buddha's teachings on managing the State and its affairs, and finally points out the importance of being exemplary in terms of the State demonstrating itself to be "honourable."

The next three exemplary actions include the importance of abiding by the law equally by the Khan and the common folk, walking the talk, preserving the heroic and combat traditions of protecting the State and the country with one's own blood and life, and ensuring the progress of the country by being economically thrifty.

IV **The Seven Great Mental Beings:** 1. The philosophy of researching into the past; 2. The science of understanding the future; 3. The art of unravelling secret mysteries; 4. The science of thoroughly understanding the present; 5. The capacity to guess beforehand other's thoughts; 6. The art of managing game hunting; and 7. The wisdom of mastering the five sciences.[13]

11 *Ibid.*, p. 10.
12 *Ibid.*, p. 10.
13 *Ibid.*, p. 10.

The first four mental beings outline the core principles of selecting and appointing State officials who are capable of learning from past history, appreciating the present, and appropriately planning for the future by acquiring knowledge on history and social science, have good management skills and proficiency, be gallant and valiant in a war and conflict, and have profound knowledge of language, philosophy, Buddhism, medicine and the science of art.

V **The Nine Great Symbols:** 1. The great black banner or standard to add spirit to the warriors; 2. The great red bugle that can put to motion everyone and everything; 3. The powerful golden fiddle that protects the body; 4. The giver of sun, the Exalted by All; 5. A sharp sword to run the State; 6. A strong and reliable golden saddle; 7. A heavy belt to sustain the State; 8. A tent with a raised platform of honour; and, 9. A trustworthy and a true friend. These are the nine great symbols that set aside a Khan from a common person.[14]

The great nine traditional state symbols of ancient Mongolia were changed with the seven Indian and Tibetan-origin symbols, such as the Dharma wheel, *Chintamani* – the wishing jewel, queen, noble prince, elephant, horse, a military hero during the period of the Exalted by All in Mongolia (1911–1919).

The three actions were the responsibility of a master of ceremonies, the four polities were overseen by the four *Taiji*, and the six exemplary actions were the responsibility of six *cherby* (*the supreme commander of the imperial guard called the khishigten. Tr.*), and the nine symbols were overseen by nine military commanders. These official positions, under the Yuan Dynasty, were given to the courtiers of the Khan.

Vice ministers of the Yuan Empire were *Taiji* princes, which included the following:

1 A supreme religious mentor *Taiji* whose responsibility was to propagate religion and ensure that life is managed according to religious tenets;
2 A supreme state *Taiji* who would protect religion and the great central State as the apple of his eye, appreciate the Khan's decree at the core of the heart, take care of the great Empire as if it were his own son, conduct the Khan's State affairs according to the established rules;

14 *Ibid.*, p. 10.

3 A supreme chief *Taiji* whose duty is to ensure the compliance of the laws and rules, settle cases honestly, and save the common people;
4 A supreme attendant *Taiji* who would suppress alien enemies during disturbances, who during times of peace would act as a warrior and keep the arms ready for action, and ensure there is vigilance and alertness.

Khubilai Khan deemed it important and essential for the local leaders and nobles to adhere to the dual principle while conducting State and religious matters, and passed a decree, wherein he proclaims "May the chiefs in the foreign (occupied) lands, leaders of the tens, hundreds, thousands and ten thousands, and those in their own tribes be aware of this (principle). If the principle of duality is not pursued then the people would not distinguish between good deeds and sin, between black and white. Between good and bad, and between happiness and suffering, but the state and religious affairs must be carried out on parity without interference between each other or else the state would not continue to progress in the manner it should, and the rule of the khan may not be invincible. So try and make effort all thee,"[15] ordained Khubilai Khan.

In order to ensure strict compliance and strengthening of the ideas of the dual policy and to put them into invariable practice, Khubilai Khan even set aside a day to remember and appreciate the propagated principles. For instance, the four most auspicious days (in the four seasons of spring, summer, fall and winter) for performing virtuous acts were devoted to Shakyamuni, and the four auspicious days for feasting (days connected with the most important landmarks in the history of Chinggis Khan) were devoted to the memory of Chinggis Khan, the founder of the great Mongol Empire, and strict rules were introduced for the commemoration of these red-letter days across the Empire.

Khubilai Khan had defined, in the book *The White History or the Book on Ten Noble Deeds or Virtues,* the rules and principles as well as the ethical norms to be followed by both State and religious figures in the Empire. He also introduced incentive and disincentive systems applicable to both a religious person and a layperson that encouraged promotion of the dual principle. "Identify upright lay person and a philosopher from across the entire empire. If an honest learned person is identified and encouraged, the khan's feelings would be promoted, which will make the nation lively. The Khan himself would become a gem for the masses. If an immoral person is made to serve the state, the state will suffer and so would the actions of the Khan. And the people become wretched and lawless. Ele-

15 *Ibid.,* p. 10.

vate a person to the rank of a lama if the person without fail propagates virtue. If a person has unblemished knowledge, promote him to the rank of a wise man. If not a single warrior is lost, promote the warrior chief as a hero. A person who passes judgment without bias should be promoted as the judge. If a person does not make errors in actions, promote him to the post a minister official."[16]

The significance of the dual policy of the Yuan Empire developed by Khubilai Khan is outlined below:

1. The policy was being applied in occupied lands with due consideration of the specific features of each individual occupied country and land;
2. Any official who dared to oppose the dual policy was castigated and punished, while those who strictly abided by it were promoted and rewarded;
3. It was believed that the real meaning of life of a State official was to sacrifice oneself to the cause of the Empire;
4. At the given time, although State policy aligned with religious ideology and teachings, the Empire gave priority to secular education, educated people were promoted to work as State officials and functionaries, and it was believed that the State should be strengthened with "education and knowledge" as in this way an honorary existence of the State be guaranteed.
5. In the course of the growth and development of the Mongol State, in the early 20th century the dual principle was revived with the establishment of an absolute theocratic monarchy when Mongolia gained its independence.

A special feature of the Khans of the Yuan Empire was that the Khans were all highly educated and erudite people who, relying on their education background, devoted themselves to the cause of the Empire State. (For instance, besides Khubilai Khan, the third Khan of the Yuan Empire Khaisan Khüleg (1308–1311) passed a decree according to which Buddhist scriptures as well as Chinese books and works were translated into Mongolian; the fourth Yuan Emperor Buyant Khan (1311–1320) personally oversaw the writing of the history of the Mongols; and Shadbal Khan (1303–1324) from early childhood had carefully studied Confucianism and he promoted educated people to manage important State affairs). The tradition of crowning the Khan at the *Ikh Khurildai* was practiced in the earlier years of the Yuan Empire. Earlier, we mentioned how Khubilai

16 *State and Law History of Mongolia* (Selected Works), Book One, Ulaanbaatar, 2006, p. 13.

Khan was proclaimed the Khan of the Mongol Empire at an *Ikh Khurildai* held at Kaiping (Xanadu/Shangdu) in 1260. There is some documentary evidence that the *Ikh Khurildai*, during the first years of Khubilai Khan's rule, continued to play an important role in addressing critical domestic and foreign policy issues of the Empire. For instance, Khubilai Khan submitted for consideration to the *Ikh Khurildai* issues related to declaring war against Japan, sending an envoy to the Java Islands, invading Annam (*Vietnam. Tr.*), as a matter of fact, matters related to promoting friendship or declaring war by the Empire. However, after Khubilai Khan, the significance of the role of the *Ikh Khurildai* diminished noticeably and was gradually pushed into oblivion.

2.2 *Officialdom and Central State Organs of the Mongol Empire, and the Sons, Queens and Hereditary Wangs (Princes)*

According to Marco Polo, Khubilai Khan had four wives, from whom he had fathered 22 sons. Seven of the 22 sons were wise, educated and honest, and had been given major provinces and countries to rule and justified their father's expectations. The eldest son of the great Khan was the legitimate successor to the throne. Khubilai's Khan's eldest son Dorj died prematurely and so his second son Crown Prince Chingim (Zhenjin) was groomed to become the next Khan. However, his inclination and favouritism towards China and Chinese officials caused the wrath of Khubilai Khan. As an atmosphere of mistrust and misunderstanding between the father and the son grew, Crown Prince Chingim also died prematurely and his younger brother Tömör obtained the right to ascend to the throne.

Khubilai Khan's four official wives were addressed as empresses. They had their own quarters and each of them had three hundred extremely beautiful dowry daughters. The empresses had more than ten thousand servants, eunuchs, maidservants, handmaids, and brothel women. The Khan himself also had concubines and from them he had 25 sons. However, according to some scholars, Khubilai Khan had eight official wives, two unofficial wives and scores of concubines. From among the official wives, the well-known and prominent empresses were Chabi and Nambui. Empress Chabi was the daughter of Alchi Noyan (Anchen) from Khongirad. She was wise, smart, and compassionate and acted as an assistant to the Khan Emperor. When Khubilai lost his beloved wife Chabi, he made Nambui, also from Khongirad, his wife. At that time, Khubilai had already reached the age of seventy and so he carried out his rule with the help of Empress Nambui.

Among the hereditary *wangs* (princes) were included the royal sons-in-law of the Khan. There were many *wangs* and they were collectively called the *"Numerous Wangs."* Civil administration was conducted, second next to the Khan, by three general ministers, who are mentioned as the "Three Princes" in Chinese sources. This official rank was introduced during the reign of Ögödei Khan. Eljigidei Noyan, a Mongol commander in Persia, Chingai, the commander of the Right Wing, and Shikhikhutug, the Chief Judge of the first Mongol Empire, served in this position. However, during the reign of Khubilai Khan, there was only one prince in this position, but during the reign of Tömör Khan, there were three princes serving in this position. Judging by the above, the Mongol tradition of State and civil administration was being continued to a certain extent in the Yuan Empire as well.

A Chinese official Hao Ching's document entitled *"Li Zhen-I" (Suggestion on building the State)* was primarily used for carrying out administrative restructuring within the Yuan Empire. The draft of the document was considered at a meeting of the council of Mongol noble officials during which a group of Mongol nobles, led by a military commander Bayan, had strongly opposed it.[17] Nevertheless, Khubilai Khan remained firm in his idea that China could only be ruled through Chinese methods and based on Hao Qing's document, and ordered Liu Bingzhong and Sui Heng, Chinese officials, to carry out administrative structural reform of China under the Yuan Empire. They spent almost one year from 1269 to 1270 developing the draft of the administrative restructuring reform and presented the draft to Khubilai Khan. The Great Khan and other Mongol nobles did not agree to implement the project in their forefather's land, but supported the administrative system reform in China under the Mongol Yuan Empire.

The central administrative office, Zhongshu Sheng or the Central Secretariat, was responsible for all civil administration of the Yuan Empire. We had mentioned earlier that this Ministry was set up by Yelü Chuchai during the reign of Ögödei Khan. The post of Director was held by an imperial prince (the Khan's son) or left vacant; however, the real work went to the right and left Grand Chancellors. Under the Grand Chancellors were five managers of governmental affairs, who were collectively known as State Counsellors. The Central Secretariat controlled the *Six Ministries* and was thus functionally the heart of the government. The Six Ministries included the Ministries of Personnel, Rites, War, Justice, Works and Revenue. *The History of Yuan (Yuán Shǐ)* outlines the duty of the Minister as "having an overall authority over the internal matters of the internal provinces, supporting the son of the *Tengri* (the Khan), and

17 D. Gongor, *The Khalkha Summary*, Vol. 1, Ulaanbaatar, 1970, p. 43.

handling tens of thousands of other matters."[18] The Central Secretariat had 22 Mongol scribes, 60 Chinese officials and 14 officials of Hoton origin from West Mongolia. The composition also included judges and medicine men. There were two other ministries with similar status as the Central Secretariat. They were the Ministries of Confidential Affairs and the Ministry of Officer's Affairs. The Ministry of Confidential Affairs *(Shu Mi-Yuan)* oversaw military and foreign relations issues, and *The History of Yuan* defines the Ministry as "responsible for specifically particular matters,"[19] apparently referring to the very important special responsibilities of the Ministry, such as overseeing the personal bodyguards of the Khan, the Khan's palace bodyguards, deciding on whether to station soldiers in occupied lands and provinces, whether to declare war or make friendship with other countries, and establishment of economic and trade relations. The Ministry of Officers' Affairs was responsible for monitoring the functions of the noble princes and officers, the question of their promotion and demotion.

The six ministries under the Central Secretariat, although they had their own specific duties and responsibilities, were ultimately accountable to the Khan. The Ministry of Finance, for example, was responsible for managing the Empire's treasury, carrying out census of households and population, while the Ministry of Works was responsible for "cottage" industry and handiworks industry, making irrigation systems, taking measures against water-related risks, building dams etc.; in other words, it was responsible for overseeing major public works. Organisationally all the six ministries were set up according to the ancient Chinese administrative traditions and practices.

2.3 *Organisational Set-up of Local Administrations*

Historical sources and research papers have quoted different figures as to the number of local administrative units and provinces, the number of officials working there, which perhaps is related to the fact that these data appertain to different periods in almost a hundred years of existence of the Yuan Empire. A Japanese scholar Otahi Mitsuo, for example, had written that Khubilai Khan, soon after he was proclaimed the great Khan, passed a decision instituting an official overseeing the administration and management of ten provinces, which included Yanjing, Idui Jinang, Henan, Beijing, Pinyan, Jendin, Dupnin, Damin Jande, Shichin and Jin-

18 *The History of Yuan*, Book 210, Section of Manuscripts of the National Library of Mongolia, Book 85.

19 *Ibid.*, Book 85.

zhou. The general administrator later on had a different responsibility and meaning, who in the very beginning was responsible for administration and management. Otahi Mitsuo noted that "the ten provinces with Yanjing at the lead, also included the whole of China with the inclusion of the Sun Dynasty."[20] However, Marco Polo had written that the Great Khan had "selected twelve well-known princes, who were given the overall responsibility of administering and managing the affairs of the thirty four provinces... Each province had one judge and a number of scribes, who managed all the matters of the appointed province... and strictly followed the wishes, desires and instructions of the twelve ministers. The rights and authority of these twelve administrators lay in electing the governor of the province, who were first nominated and their candidature proposed to the great Khan, who upon endorsement were each given a golden *paiza*."[21] However *The History of Yuan* notes that the local administrations were divided into twelve provinces, while other historical sources give a different figure altogether. Nevertheless, it is quite evident that a province was the biggest local administrative unit in the Yuan Empire. The central province was directly accountable to the great Khan, in other words, the Central Secretariat was responsible for the province. This is why it was termed as "Inner Province". There were 11 provinces other than the central one and they were called the "Outer Provinces". Besides these inner and outer provinces, there were a number of foreign countries that were under the administration of the Empire.

The central province included the Shandong, Shanxi and Hebei provinces of China with Hanbaliq as the seat of its government.

The second most important province was the *Dawaani Ar* (Beyond the Pass) province, or the proper Mongolia, with Kharkhorum as the seat of its government.

And the third province was that of Liao, which is Manchuria of today.

The fourth province existed in the land in between the two major rivers – the Yellow and Blue rivers – the so-called provinces south of the river. Besides the above, there were also the provinces of Shaanxi, Sichuan, Gansu, Yunnan, Jiangzhe, Jianxi, Huguang and Zhendong. The province of Zhendog, which also meant "Conquer East Province," was set up by Khubilai Khan in 1283 in the then kingdom of Goryeo when he was making plans to invade Japan, and Mukden was set up as the centre of its government. Goryeo did not become an ordinary province of the Yuan Empire, but it was a kind of a vassal State paying tribute to the dynasty. The

20 Ch. Dalai, *History of Mongolia*. (1260–1388), Ulaanbaatar, 1992, p. 100.

21 Marco Polo, *The Wonders of the East*, Ulaanbaatar, 1987, p. 115.

basic territory of Tibet, Vietnam, Burma, India, China and islands in the ocean were not the primary provinces, but were vassal States, who also paid tribute to the Yuan Empire. Marco Polo noted that the Yuan Empire had 34 provinces, which included both the principal and the appendage provinces, the so-called provinces of the occupied territories.

During the rule of the Yuan Empire, the provinces were administratively divided into the circuit, followed by *lù*, *fŭ* and *zhōu*, which are three kinds of prefecture-like divisions and the lowest political division was the *xiàn* or counties. The *xiàn* was divided into rural villages and these were administrative units that were better suited to the sedentary mode of life. Major administrative and political units as the province and circuit were administered by men aged 25 and above, primarily of Mongol origin. The creation of the post of administrator cum manager of the province laid the foundation for the introduction of the twelve general administrators of the provinces soon after the foundation of the Yuan Empire. The circuits, *lù*, *fŭ*, *zhōu* and *xiàn* were administered primarily by men of Mongol, Uighur and Turkic origin, while the official rank held by people of Han or Chinese origin was low. The rural villages and settlements with 50 and 100 households were managed by people of Han Chinese origin. In this manner, the Mongols applied Chinese methods to administer and rule the densely populated land of China; they took direct control of administrative and state matters, with people of Uighur and Turkic-origin serving under them as their assistants, while people of Han Chinese origin were primarily given executive responsibilities. The Khans of the Yuan Empire, in their administrative matters, had a different policy and attitude towards their native land and were inclined to maintain the Mongol traditions as much as much as possible.

2.4 *The State of Mongol Governance in the Yuan Empire*

In the first few years of the powerful Yuan Empire, which was built by the nomadic Mongols, present-day Mongolia was called *Yuan Chang Lu*, which was later changed to *Holin* (*Kharkhorum*) province. But in 1312 it was again renamed *Lingbei* or the "Province beyond the Pass". The territory of present-day Inner Mongolia was under the Chinese provinces and administratively, it was divided into several parts.

In the beginning of his reign, Khubilai Khan did not drastically change the original Mongol administrative divisions for the indigenous lands that were being ruled by his sons and princes, who were called the *Jing Wang* or the "Wang of the Roots" as *Jing* meant the "origin", the "roots", the "ancestors" and this Chinese word gradually became distorted to be pronounced as "Jonon" Wang.

The *Jing Wang*, permanently based in Kharkhorum, was the son of the Khan who was appointed to directly administer and manage the affairs of the province, and in this sense, this administrator could very well be regarded as the master and the holder of the golden seal of the Mongols.

The ancestral land of the Mongols was first ruled by Nomgan (Nomukhan), the fourth son of Khubilai Khan. But Nomgan did not live long and after his death, the great Khan's third son Chinghem (Crown Prince Zhenjin) was sent to Khakhorum to take over the leadership of the core land of the Mongols. But Chinghem also did not live long as he died after traveling to Tibet for Buddhist studies, and Khubilai Khan's grandson Tömör (Ölziit Tömör) was proclaimed the Crown Prince in 1295 and was dispatched to Khakhorum. Alongside this, Chinghem's eldest son Gamal was made the *Jing Wang* in 1292 to rule over the indigenous Mongols in Kharkhorum. He had spent his childhood growing up under Khubilai Khan and his mother was a noble lady of Khongirad (Qongirad), one of the major divisions of the Mongol tribes. Gamal ruled over Khakhorum, Gurvan Gol (Three Rivers), the Burkhan Khaldun Mountain, Kim-Hims, Selenge, Bayalik near the border of Kyrgyz, the Ikh Khorig of Chinggis Khan (*the site where Chinggis Khan and other great Mongol Khans are buried. Tr.*) and the Great Wall. Tömör Khan spent only one year administering over Kharkhorum after which he succeeded Khubilai Khan in 1295 as the Great Khan of the Yuan Dynasty.

In 1297, when Gamal passed away, his son Esöntömör succeeded as the *Jing Wang* to become the general administrator of the land of the Mongols. At that time, Khaisan was made the Crown Prince and accordingly, he spent more than a decade in the ancient land of his ancestors during the rule of Tömör Khan. During his rule, there were no major changes in the governance of the Mongols, but *The History of Yuan* writes that "In the 11th year of Da-De (1307) a province of the middle council was set up in Kharkhorum. Darkhan was appointed the leader or chéng xiàng of the Left Wing and the department of works and the circuit of general administration at Kharkhorum were dismantled, and instead a circuit of public authority of Kharkhorum was instituted."[22] From the present level of research, it is not possible to clearly determine the administrative divisions under the Yuan Empire. However, according to Volume One of *The History of the Mongolian People's Republic*:

22 *The History of Yuan*, Book 210, Section of Manuscripts of the National Library of Mongolia, Book 58.

> Outer Mongolia was ruled by the Great Khan, and the general government affairs ministry called Jung shu-sheng and the private affairs ministry called Sho mi-Yuan. From among these two ministries, the Sho Mi-Yuan was formed during the times of wars and dismantled during peace times.
>
> The Mongol branch of the Jung shu-sheng had two *chéng xiàngs* of the Eastern and Western wings, but later on only the *chéng xiàng* of the Eastern wing was left, and the post of the *chéng xiàng* of the Western wing was dismantled. Well before the institution of Jung sh-sheng, Khubilai Khan had established the Departments of Works and the Ministry of the Military at Kharkhorum, and they were responsible for the military and civilian affairs in the region. The Ministry of the Military came under the jurisdiction of the Works Department during times of peace, while during times of war, its duties and responsibilities became bigger, to individually handle all military and civilian matters.[23]

According to the *Yuán Shǐ* or *The History of Yuan*, the land inhabited by the Mongol nomadic herders was divided, like the branches of the central government, into *Lu* (Highway), *Fu* (District), *Zhou* (Banner) and *Xian* (Village). However, there are almost no evidence-based documentary sources as to how this kind of administrative division evolved further. A Mongolian scholar Ch. Dalai, having analysed this issue, has proposed the assumption that this maiden attempt to disseminate the Chinese practice of Statehood in Mongolia did not materialise[24] as was initially planned.

From research it has been found that there were roughly a little more than 60 Mongol tribes during the Yuan Empire. The names of these have almost not been written in their original form, they were named after the princes and the nobles to whose jurisdiction they belonged, such as the tribe under Qing Wang Esön Tömör or the *Aimag* under Olon Wang Tsagaan etc. It must be noted here that the ancient traditional practice of administrative divisions into the units of tens gradually took the form of military divisions. From among the numerous Wangs who administered Kharkhorum, only Esön Tömör Wang administered his subjects under several Mongol Khans in his native land. After serving as the Khan for four years, Esön Tömör (1324–1328) made his son Badamregzibuu the Qing Wang. He was dispatched to Mongolia and was responsible for reor-

23 *History of the MPR*, Book One of Three, Ulaanbaatar, 1966, p. 23.
24 Ch. Dalai, *History of Mongolia*. (1206–1388), Ulaanbaatar, 1994, p. 64.

ganising the Kharkhorum development department into a "Ministry of the Wang."

The second highest-ranking authority in Mongolia of this period after Qing Wang was called the *Chinsang,* who was responsible for the day-to-day administrative matters. In other words, the *Chinsang* was the key representative of the Ministry Jung shu-sheng in Mongolia and the key aide to the Qing Wang. It was not without reason that one of the ministers under the Khan was appointed to this post, which goes to prove that the affairs related to Mongolia were given top priority during the Yuan Empire. Khar Khason, from among the *Chinsangs* who were appointed by the Khaisan Khüleg Khan in 1308, played an instrumental role in matters related to administering the land of the Mongols. Khar Khason was the grandson of a horse-herder Khishleg, who was conferred with an honorary title during the reign of Chinggis Khan. Khar Khason was a smart and a clever state official, who is also mentioned in the *Yuán Shǐ* (*The History of Yuan*) as "somebody as tall as a noble mountain but with few words, who did not smile and he was a man who held in high esteem the culture of writing." Judging by the above, it can be presumed that the traditions of statehood were maintained in the indigenous lands of the Mongols during the Yuan Empire.

2.5 *The Military*

The military of the Yuan Empire was an indispensable instrument in carrying out the foreign and domestic policies of the Empire, and the "Ministry of Secret Papers" managed the military. The Empire too had a permanent and an interim organisation within the local administration that oversaw matters related to the military and war. "... in the remote outlying lands there were appointed officials responsible for conscripting, pacifying and administering purposes. The number of related officials was not the same,"[25] writes the *Yuán Shǐ.* During the period of the Yuan Empire, the traditional Mongol unit of ten formed the basis of the military organizational set up. But the unit of ten thousand, thousand and hundred had three distinct classifications, such as high, medium and low, and the unit of tens was called the *Pai* (platoon). According to the *Yuán Shǐ,* "ten men were made into one *Pai* which had a commander."[26] The commander of the unit of ten thousand had a general chief, and under the commander of the unit of thousand, there was a chief called the *bogtsot* and that of a unit

25 *The History of Yuan*, Book 210, Manuscripts department of the State Library, Book 91.

26 *Ibid.*, Book 98.

of hundred, the leader was called a *daranguilagch* (meaning a dictator), which was instituted anew and each of the officials, according to their ranks, wore hanging pendants to distinguish them from each other. For example, the pendant of the leader of the unit of ten thousand had the figure of a stylised golden tiger, the pendant of the leader of the unit of thousand was golden in colour and that of the leader of the unit of hundred was silver in colour. Different shades of the pendants signified separate duties, responsibilities and authority.[27]

The military of the Yuan Empire was, by and large, divided into two categories – Mongol and *Tammaći* soldiers – according to *The History of Mongol Soldiers*.[28] The Mongol soldiers included the *khishigten* (the imperial guard) and those soldiers who were serving in the indigenous original land of the Mongols. In other words, the Mongol soldiers were made up entirely of soldiers of Mongol origin.

There were 12 thousand *khishigten* soldiers during the reign of Khubilai Khan, and 3,000 *khishigten* soldiers guarded the "Great Ger" of the Khan three days and three nights in a shift. However, in later years, their number was reduced to almost 800 soldiers, especially during the reigns of Khaisan Khüleg (1308–1312), Ayürbaldbag the Buyant (1312–1321) and to almost 700 soldiers during the rule of Rinchinbal Khan (1321–1324). The Law of Yuan Empire points out that "many princes and nobles, who would bring along their sons and siblings to pay courtesy to the Khan, would make them the royal body guards,"[29] which goes to show that as in the previous times, the *khishigten* soldiers were basically made up of close relatives of nobles, princes, that is the aristocratic segment of the Mongol society then.

Mongol soldiers who were deployed to alien captured lands were called the *Tammaći* soldiers. They were primarily made up of security troops who were deployed in the neighbourhood of major towns of occupied lands; the so-called "tyrannical soldiers", whose primary responsibility was to bolster the rule of the Mongols in the occupied territories and also to suppress any or all protest movements. The *Tammaći* soldiers also included the border guards with the responsibility of protecting the borders of the occupied territories and also they were engaged in crop farming; the police force with the duty of preventing thievery and banditry; the

27 *The History of Mongol Soldiers*, Book One, Ulaanbaatar, p. 288.
28 *Ibid.*, p. 289.
29 *The History of Yuan*, Book 210, Manuscripts Department of the State Library, Book 210.

so-called gunners who possessed new, heavy artillery pieces, and finally there was the naval force, who served in the navy.

Young men aged 15 to 17 served in the Yuan Empire army. The Empire had its own conscription law as well, according to which "a household that had 2–3 sons, one of the sons had to serve in the army, 2 from a family with 4–5 boys and 3 from a family with 6–7 boys." The Mongol households that had moved to and settled in China as well as the families of soldiers who had surrendered their weapons and who formerly belonged to the Jin and the Song dynasties were called the "*Tseregchin* households" (*Tseregchin* or "*цэрэгчин*" in Mongolian means belonging to a family of military people. Tr.) The military commanders were all Mongols and although there were Chinese and Korean soldiers, they were under strict supervision, and were given weapons only when they went to war, which they had to surrender during times of peace when they were primarily made to work the crop fields.

The weapons, warfare methods, tactics and strategy leaning on the traditions had become increasingly refined and sophisticated during the time of the Yuan Empire. The key armaments of the soldiers remained bows and arrows, which alongside the shields and armour had improved significantly in terms of their quality. The Mongols started making metal radical cannons, which were used in their battles, which marked a turning point in the development of military hardware in the thirteenth century. The Mongols also started making warships. These developments helped bolster the army of the Yuan Empire with artillery, navy and foot soldiers, and with such a military might, the Mongols under the Yuan Empire worked to expand their Empire further.

2.6 *The Courts and Legal Proceedings*

The Khan held supreme power over legal matters, and he was responsible for appointing the judges. The supreme judge of the Empire ranked among the three key State ministers, who, on behalf of the Khan, managed the courts and legal proceedings of the Empire. In the early period of the foundation of the Yuan Empire, although of high age, Shikhikhutug remained popular and continued with his legal duties. Shikhikhutug was directly responsible for training Mönkhsar Noyon, an eminent lawyer under Mönkh Khan, lawyer Baiju during the reign of Khubilai Khan, including a number of Chinese legal officials who served in the court of the Yuan Empire.

The Ministry of Justice was under the jurisdiction of the Interior Ministry, and it had the overall responsibility of managing the judiciary and court matters. It appears that the Khan also appointed special judges. For example, Baiju, (1298–1323) the fifth generation official of the military commander Mukhulai of the Jalair tribe was responsible for overseeing the compliance and implementation of the *Ikh Zasag (The Great Yassa).* During one court session Baiju had asked "Why are we not following the old code of law in political affairs?" In this connection, it can be concluded that *The Great Yassa* was being enforced in the political policies and legal proceedings during the Yuan Empire.

In the local areas, the court had not become independent of the administrative affairs. However, there was one progressive element, and according to Marco Polo, each province and county had a judge. It appears that the leaders of the *zam,* province, banner, and village were also responsible for the courts and legal proceedings, alongside their administrative duties. Draconian measures, involving physical torture, were applied in the Yuan Empire during a legal investigation, which were unprecedented in the history of the Statehood and judiciary of the Mongol Empire before. This was because extreme Chinese torture and punishment methods were applied during legal investigations and this had, perhaps, become a necessity as an instrument for tyrannising different nations and tribes that were forcefully invaded and made subjects of the vast Mongol empire.

2.7 *State and Religion*

The Khans of the Yuan Empire continued the policy of the Chinggis Khan with respect to religion and belief, and they acknowledged the right to belief especially by the peoples of the occupied territories. What is more, Khubilai Khan sent letters to the Roman Pope asking the latter to dispatch Catholic priests in large numbers to his Empire. The Roman Pope responded likewise and many Catholic priests, side-by-side with the Mongol and Chinese astrologers, set up astrological centres and together developed calendars.

The Mongol Yuan Empire, besides respecting different faiths and religions, conducted a policy of making Buddhism the State religion. Soon after Khubilai ascended to the throne in 1260, he invited Phags-pa of Tibet and appointed him the supreme teacher of the Empire. From then, Mongol Khans, queens, princes and close aides and officials became students of the Phags-pa lama. Judging by the ordinances issued by Khubilai Khan in 1264 such as the "Pearl Order" and others, we can see that Buddhism had spread fast and began to play an important role in the Yuan Empire. Phags-pa lama's role was instrumental when Khubilai Khan launched the so-called "dual state and religion policy". Since the dual policy has been discussed in the previous chapters, we will here refer to some evidence of how the Mongol Khans were protecting religion. For example, in one of his decrees, Khubilai Khan announced draconian measures, including dismembering the hands of a person who dared to lay hands on Tibetan lamas and young monks, and cutting off the tongues of a person guilty of insulting them, thereby backing the inviolability and immunity of Buddhist monks.[30]

The policy of Khubilai Khan with regard to religion was continued by the Mongol Khans who succeeded him. The Mongol Khans maintained very close religious and political ties with important Tibetan Buddhist monasteries and made much effort to propagate Buddhism.

However, in the indigenous land of the Mongols, although Buddhism had become the predominating faith among the elite section, shamanism continued to be the main belief of the majority of the nomadic Mongols.

Although Khubilai Khan was an ardent Buddhist, he is believed to have continued to practice shamanistic rites, which is evidenced by the fact that the Mongol Khans of the Yuan Empire were active participants in rites and rituals performed by the shamans. They would also visit the burial site of a deceased on the 49th day after the demise of the person to offer prayers and sacrifice, where, as per the traditions, both male and female shamans would be present.

3 The Law

3.1 *The Evolution of Law*

With the deepening and strengthening of the principles of Statehood in the Yuan Empire, the law also reached a relatively high level of development. This is evidenced by the fact that the laws and legislation became much more polished and refined, and many written codes of laws were adopted. However, until very recently, scholars and researchers were of the opinion that the source legal documents of the Yuan Empire were mere "duplicates" or "carbon copies" of Chinese laws. Take, for example, Russian professor V.A. Ryazanovskii and other scholars, who maintain that the laws of the Yuan Empire had many similarities with the laws passed by the Ming and Qin dynasties, and some have even attempted to prove that the laws passed in the Yuan Empire were actually purely Chinese laws.[31] This was perhaps because many of these scholars and

30 Ch. Dalai, *History of Mongolia*, (126–1388), Ulaanbaatar, 1992, p. 164.

31 Обзор литературы по китаевадению, Харбине, 1932, Рязановский В.А проф-Библиография источников монгольского права, с. 286

researchers failed to carry out in-depth research into the laws of these periods, and had not done adequate comparative study in this respect.

Without question the laws passed, starting with Khubilai Khan and by other Khans of the Yuan Empire, were all based on the principles outlined in *The Great Yassa*. This is evidenced by the future trend of legal development of the Yuan Empire.

Khubilai Khan, from an early age, was familiar with and had studied at length ancient Chinese laws, was obviously aware that *The Great Yassa*, which was developed and adopted to suit the unique Mongol conditions and environment, could not be copied and applied without any changes or reforms in the then sedentary society of the Orient. This is why, even before becoming the Khan, he had instructed the Chinese official Yo-Shu and others to draft and develop legal instruments that would be applied when ruling the lands of the Chinese.

In 1262 a "Code of Compiled Law" developed by Yo-Shu, became the first ever law approved by Khubilai Khan, according to which social relations in northern China were regulated. After this, a number of other laws, such as the "Code of Newly Compiled Laws," (1264), "Code of Law Submitted by the Erken Council Province," (1271) and the "New Law of Zhi Yuan" (1291), were adopted, from among which the "New Law of Zhi Yuan" was an extended compilation of laws, which included provisions and elements from the earlier adopted smaller laws. Unfortunately, this law has not come down to us in its full original; however, about one hundred clauses and provisions of the law were included in the later laws that are available. Also during the reign of Tömör Khan, the so-called "Laws of Edicts of De-De" were adopted. In this manner, as new laws were adopted, they improved in terms of quality and substance, and became major codes of laws regulating multiple social relations in a refined manner. From among them, some of the largest laws, which have been inherited in full, include "The Veritable Records of the Great Yuan", "The History of the Great Yuan", "The Genuine Records to Restore the World".

3.2 *The Veritable Records of the Great Yuan*

This is a compilation of the laws and decrees approved by the Great Khan that were adopted prior to 1322. *The Veritable Records of the Great Yuan* towers on the same level with *The Great Yassa*, and is an important source of laws of Mongolia, which was enforced in the Eastern parts of the Yuan Empire, because these laws were developed and endorsed by the Mongol Khans of the Yuan Empire. This compilation of laws has 10 major units, with 60 chapters and 2,391 clauses, which cover the entire gamut of social life during the Yuan Empire of the Mongols.

Its Preamble notes that "From the ancient times, although the Khan has been extolled as the Sacred Master, his code of laws will not reach all the corners of the world and therefore, he should give priority to ruling the world through his intelligence and knowledge."[32] This means that a nation can be managed and ruled in a proper manner only when the law and knowledge are coupled. "If a subject does not follow the laws, then the subject would not doubt be castrated by law, and if the law is violated, then the guilty can be judged and put to death. Therefore, the Khans had introduced capital punishment not just to show that he is the supreme power but it is designed also at supporting and facilitating the state,"[33] thus outlining the inter-dependence and the significance of the relationship between the State, the law and the subjects.

The Veritable Records of the Great Yuan, first and foremost, legalised the rights and obligations of the State structure, and the central State establishments of the Yuan Empire.

Capital legal norms and standards related to the population, thievery, banditry, fraudulent activities, and deceit were established in Part Five of the Law.

The Law also divides the population of the Yuan Empire into four categories depending on their origin and tribal affiliation, and outlined their rights accordingly in a differentiated manner. For instance, the Mongols are listed in *the first class of people, the second-class citizens* included the Tanguts, the Turks, the Uighurs, Khotons and the Arabs, who were called people with "yellow teeth," and *the third class of people* included primarily the northern Chinese, who were under the rule of the Jin Dynasty, the Kidans and the Zurchid people, while *the lowest class of people* included the ethnic Hans from southern China. Such a classification of the population under the Yuan Empire according to different ethnic and tribal origin was done primarily to display the grandeur and might of the conquerors and is basically connected with the difference in classes and social segments that existed then. These differences as classified were clearly included in the clauses and provisions of the above law. For instance, "Curfew shall be imposed for the Chinese during dusk and night," "A tattoo shall be made on the left shoulder if a Chinese commits an offence for the first time, another tattoo shall be put on the right should for repeating crime the second time, and if the offence has been committed the third time

32 *The History of Yuan,* Book 210, Manuscripts Department of the State Library, Book 102.

33 N. Ishjamts, *The Establishment of a United Mongol State and the Formation of Feudalism,* Ulaanbaatar, 1976, p. 102.

by a Chinese, then a tattoo shall be imposed on the neck," if a Chinese person is incarcerated, then the punished shall be responsible for his/her food," "A Chinese person is forbidden to carry any kind of weapon, even a slingshot," "If a Mongol hits a Chinese, the Chinese cannot hit back,"[34] and in this manner, the law includes many clauses and provisions that openly discriminate against the Chinese.

According to *The Veritable Records of the Great Yuan*, a Mongol who had committed an offence would be given a lighter punishment. Take for example, the following provisions, "It is forbidden for an Uighur and a Chinese person to buy an offspring of a Mongol to use him/her as a servant," "Anyone who has betrayed a Mongol in an alien (occupied) land shall be deemed a serious infringer of law," "If a Mongol is incarcerated, then that person shall be provided with food and drink by the state," "If a household serving in the horse-relay service shall try to shun service, then that household shall be dealt with severe punishment, however, if that household is expelled, then the punishment shall be lighter."[35] This was nothing but the legalisation of the advantages of the conqueror.

3.3 *The Laws of the Great Yuan Empire*

These laws were drafted and had been adopted, in all likelihood, somewhere around 1271. The collection had 88 chapters and 2,539 provisions, but these laws never came down to our generation in their full original, and from sources, we believe that they were first published in 1323. Many of its clauses and provisions were identical and repetitions of the *Yuan Encyclopaedia*, and both of them were in force almost simultaneously as well. *The Laws of the Great Yuan Empire* also have quite a few clauses and provisions that safeguard and protect the rights of the conquerors. For example, if a Mongol had committed a grave crime that was punishable by death, the local official could not execute the death sentence, and if the face of a Mongol, guilty of an offence, had been tattooed according to Chinese law and customs, then the official in question would be clubbed 77 times, fired from office and would be made to remove the tattoo from the face of the Mongol himself. The part of the law dealing with criminal cases, also notes about the immunity and advantages of the Mongols, such as "If an indigenous Mongol, who has been incarcerated from crimes other than criminal offence, the Mongol must be securely protected. The incarcerated Mongol will not be subject to torture. Provide them with food

34 Ch. Dalai, *History of Mongolia*, (1260–1388), Ulaanbaatar, 1992, pp. 73–74.
35 *Ibid.*, p. 74.

and drinks and all that they require."[36] Furthermore, there were provisions that banned gathering and congregation of groups of people, which were apparently safeguards against any kind of revolt, uprising or mutiny, such as "Any person who dares to call the assembly of the state in one place shall be executed," "It is prohibited to gather in groups and hold assembly," and "Shops and market places where many people gather at one time, shall be closed down."[37] The Laws of the Great Yuan Empire likewise contained a provision that was designed to ensure the safety and security of the great Empire, such as "It is prohibited to practice using spears and clubs."

3.4 *The Genuine Records to Restore the World*

The original name of this law is *The Law on Transforming the Realm of the Monarchy*. The Khan had instructed Ayürbalba (1312–1321) to take the lead in compiling and printing this major law, which has 10 major units, and 800 chapters. This Law is also a continuation of the previous laws and incorporates many of the clauses and provisions of the laws that had been passed in the earlier period of the Yuan Empire. However, the Law has not come down us in its entirety.

All the aforementioned legal instruments also contain clauses and provisions outlining the kinds of punishment for all those who were found guilty of one or another kind of felony. *The Laws of the Great Yuan Empire*, for example, classified criminal offences and their punishments into five categories, such as hitting a criminal with a truncheon, clubbing the offender, making a criminal do heavy menial labour, exiling and execution, including 1. Hitting with a truncheon – hitting the criminal with a short truncheon up to 57 times by swinging the truncheon high; 2. Clubbing – Hitting the criminal 67–107 times by a club as if chopping something with a knife; 3. Heavy manual labour – making a criminal do heavy manual labour; 4. Exiling or banishing– Sending away a criminal to a land far away from his native place, with extreme climatic conditions and kept under strict supervision. *The History of Yuan* mentions the following about banishment: "Banish to the northern lands in the neighbourhood of Liaonin a person from the south who has been convicted. Banish a criminal from the north to the south in the village of Hugoang;"[38] and 5. Execution –

---

36 Documents related to the Laws of the Yuan Empire. Stock of manuscripts of the Institute of History and Archaeology.

37 *History of the MPR*, Three Volume, Book One, Ulaanbaatar, 1966, p. 307.

38 *The History of Yuan*, Book 210, Manuscripts Department of the State Library, Book 102.

there were two types of this kind of capital punishment, one of them was chopping off a person's head and the second type was cutting the criminal into pieces. However, *The Laws of the Great Yuan Empire* did not include ancient Chinese punishments, such as putting tattoos on the nose using old ink, chopping off the feet, and execution through suffocation or by hanging. In this sense, this law had progressed from the previous laws.

The Veritable Records of the Great Yuan had added a punishment, that is, canguing a criminal's hands and legs. A system of paying ransom was also introduced, under which a criminal could pay ransom and be freed. According to Dr. G. Sovd, "this was a much more humane and a flexible method of punishing a criminal without resorting to the use of any of the severe punishments meted out to convicts."[39] The method of paying ransom was in most cases included imposing penalty or cutting down on salary. For instance, "An official's punishment can be paid through ransom. People who are older than 70 and younger than 15 may not tolerate clubbing, so their punishment must be replaced with payment of a ransom. A person who is chronically ill, may not withstand punishment, so that person can pay a ransom instead."[40] According to the laws of the Yuan Empire, people convicted of serious crimes, such as thievery, had tattoos imposed on their face and neck, but this kind of punishment was not meted out to the Mongols and women folk. Furthermore, it was strictly forbidden to pass on the sentence of the father to his son, the sentence of the elder brother to his younger sibling, subjecting a convict to severe punishment, including torture other than in the law and to interrogate a suspect during the dark hours of the night.[41]

Based on the research and studies conducted by scholars, it can be surmised that the legal sources of the Yuan Empire were not developed on the principles and methods of ancient Chinese laws and traditions, but they were legal documents that were significantly influenced by the legal traditions of the Mongols and in particular, *The Great Yassa*.

This kind of conclusion can be backed by the following arguments:

1 It is quite clear that some of the ethnic groups and tribes, who had a lifestyle similar to or identical with that of the indigenous Mongols, were ruled by applying *The Great Yassa*. A Japanese scholar Tayama Sigeru had noted that "Chinggis Khan's *Great Yassa* was very much influential even during the period of the Yuan Empire, and this law

39 E. Avirmed, D. Dashtseden, G. Sovd, *Mongol Law*, Ulaanbaatar, 1997, p. 33.
40 *The History of Yuan*, 210, Manuscripts Department of the State Library, Book 102.
41 E. Avirmed, D. Dashtseden, G. Sovd, *Mongol Law*, Ulaanbaatar, 1997, p. 34.

was enforced among the Mongols by disseminating the substance of the *Great Yassa* through the traditional method."

2 Many laws that were adopted during the period of the Yuan Empire were influenced by the methods applied in the development of *The Great Yassa.* Take, for example, *The Laws of the Great Yuan Empire,* which contained identical copies of some of the clauses and provisions of *The Great Yassa.* We can see that the decrees and utterings of the great Khans had been sourced from *The Great Yassa.* Some of the provisions of the laws passed during the reign of Khubilai Khan, such as, the sentence passed to a person guilty of stealing livestock animals, the method by which to slaughter an animal for food and the prohibition of taking a bath in a running stream etc., have all been included from *The Great Yassa.*

3 Mongol officials, who were trained according to the school of drafting laws, such as *The Great Yassa,* were directly involved in the drafting of laws during the Yuan Empire, and some of the important laws and decrees were discussed at the assembly of the Mongol aristocrats and princes. As mentioned earlier, a Mongol official Baiju played a significant part in the development and compilation of *The Veritable Records of the Great Yuan, The Laws of the Great Yuan Empire.* What is more, there is plentiful historical evidence that a Mongol prince Shadbal Gegeen (1303–1323), who had great respect for *The Great Yassa,* brought together Mongol princes and nobles with a sound knowledge of *The Great Yassa,* for a discussion of major laws and decrees.

4 The laws of the Yuan Empire included Mongol terms and terminology in their original without their translation, and also words and expressions that had been obviously translated from the Mongolian. This is explained by the fact that a sizable portion of the laws of the Yuan Empire begin with orations, sermons, decrees and official documents in the Mongolian language. Scholar Ch. Dalai has noted that *The Genuine Records to Restore the World* in the beginning has numerous writings which were either initially written in Mongolian or could have been later translated from Mongolian."[42] In this manner, the evolution and growth of the laws of the Yuan Empire were important inseparable constituents of the history of the statehood and law of the Mongols.

42 Ch. Dalai, *Mongolia During the Period of the Yuan Empire,* Ulaanbaatar, 1973, p. 72.

4 The State and Laws of the Mongol during the Period of Political Fragmentation (14th Century–17th Century)

1 Historical Summary

In 1368, Togoontömör, the last Khan of the Yuan Empire, lost ground to the forces of the rebellion and left Beijing, which marked the beginning of the decline of the once glorious, united Mongol Empire. Until 1388, when the Mongols were confronting the forces of the Ming Dynasty, numerous court coups occurred in the Mongol Empire and within a mere decade there were five Mongol Khans. The key reason for the political cleavage in the Mongol Empire was the fact that influential Mongol nobles had basically taken control of the territory of the once units of ten thousand and thousands, and made the once soldiers and common subjects of the Empire their serfs, which led to the establishment of individual serfdoms where they fortified their economic and other bases.

During the political break-up, Mongol society was riddled with internal contradictions and struggles, and in particular, in the years from 1394 to 1399, beginning from the reign of Elbeg Khan, the monarchy became weaker and the Mongol nobles and princes almost did not follow his administration. The Oirads were the first to become fully self-independent. If we were to look into historical documents, we would find that the Empire was first divided into East and West Mongol, then the East and West *Tümens* (ten thousands) or the Oirads and finally, Inner, Outer and Western Mongols, and they were constantly at loggerheads with each other, at times merging and then separating from each other. In a word, as regards the monarchy, the centripetal force weakened while the centrifugal force predominated. This has been chatacterised in Mongolian history as the period of the "disintegration of feudalism." We would like to define this period as a period of "political fragmentation."

Yet D.Enkhtsetseg's research reveals that ancient Chinese historians referred to it as Mongolia during the Ming dynasty, but in more recent times, Chinese and Inner Mongolian historians have begun identifying it as the Northern Yuan.[1]

---

1 D.Enkhtsetseg, *History of the Mongols* (second half of the 14th century to the 17th century), Ulaanbaatar, 2022, p. 67–68.

2 State Structure

2.1 *Territorial and Administrative Organisational Set-up*

In the 16th to 17th centuries, the Mongols were scattered across a vast territory stretching from southern Siberia up to the Great Wall of China, and from the west from the Tian Shan (*Tengri Uul* in Mongolian) up to the Great Khingan Mountains in northeast China. The present-day territory of Mongolia and the Inner Mongolia Autonomous Region of China were inhabited by the so-called Outer and Inner Mongolians, and the lands west of the Altai Mountain ranges were inhabited by the Oirads. Although the Mongols were scattered, anyone who held the seal of the Great Khan always strove to maintain the country as a single administrative and territorial unit with due respect for the ancient traditions of Statehood, as well as the specific features of the environment, climate, population and the way of life of the people.

Scholars and researchers have been intrigued with the size of the Mongol population during this period, as well as the importance of the so-called unit of ten thousand. During the early 13th to 14 th centuries, when the Mongols conquered the world, it is assumed that there were forty ten thousand people living in the East of the country, and the Western Mongols numbered four ten thousand. This expression of the population in the units of ten thousand was also termed as "Two Forty Thousand." However, after the Yuan Empire, according to historical documents, there were six ten thousand Mongols in the east of the Empire and four ten thousand Oirads, as was documented earlier. For instance, there is mention in historical sources of the fact that when Togoontömör Khan fled, thirty ten thousand Mongols were left behind in the lands of Chinese, while he had fled together with him ten thousand Mongol subjects. Zhū Yuánzhāng (or Hongwu), the Emperor of the Ming Dynasty who had sent a letter to Togoontömör Khan in April 1370, had mentioned that the Mongol Khan had one hundred thousand subjects. In fact, the population of the Mongols had shrunk significantly, owing to a number of reasons, and primarily because many Mongols had stayed behind in the new lands occupied by them, and on the other hand, the ten thousand unit, which originally was responsible for mobilizing ten thousand soldiers, no longer remained a military organizational set-up, and also because the unit of ten thousand had been transformed into a generally larger administrative division. Since the administrative units increasingly became civilian in nature, it can be presumed that in the beginning of such a transformation, the number of people under the unit of ten thousand could have been either more or less. But in the 14th century, the term *Tümen* or ten thousand in Mongolian, was almost synonymous with the term State/country, as the territory of one *Tümen* was very large under one noble or prince, and the population exceeded a couple of ten thousands. For example, Altan Khan of the Tümed had more than 10 ten thousand households as his subjects, while Tümen Zasagt Khan had more than 13 ten thousand households. Also the Khalkha *Tümen,* after the Yuan Empire, had their own lands and subjects, military and administration, and with their own law, meaning they were relatively autonomous serfdoms.

The six ten thousands of Eastern Mongolia were divided into two, the so-called threes of the East and the West wings. The Tsakhar *tümen* of the East wing inhabited the lands of the present-day Shilin Gol province of the Inner Mongolia Autonomous Region of China, the Uriankhai *tümen* were in the Zuu-Ud province of Inner Mongolia, and the Ordos *tümen* of the West wing inhabited the land of Ikh Zuu province in Inner Mongolia, the Tümed *tümen* were in Ulaantsav province and the Yünsheebüü ten thousand inhabited the north of Kalgan or Zhangjiakou. The elder sons of Batmönkh Dayan Khan administered the southern or Inner Mongolia, while his youngest son Gersenz (1513–1549) ruled the Khalkha *tümen.* However, these *tümens* were at times merged and separated owing to various internal factors. For instance, when the Urainkhai tribes tried to revolt, Batmönkh Dayan Khan struck back and did away with the structural unit of ten thousand, which were merged with other *tümens.* And his successor Bogd-Alag Khan attempted to divide the three *tümens* of the West wing and merge it with the *tümens* of the East wing.

The *tümens* were divided into so-called *otogs,* meaning camps and the term "Otog" that became popular after the Yuan Empire was the continuation of the unit of thousands. Scholar Sh. Natsagdorj believes that the word *otog* means "fire," "hearth," "household," "a *ger*" in Mongolian, which in the beginning implied a group of households, which later became larger[2] as an administrative unit. But from the 16th century onwards, according to some historical sources, the term *otog* basically was understood as an administrative unit, while the term *khoshuu* or banner, was used as a military division. An *otog* did not consist of different tribes and clans, but like the unit of ten thousand in the past was made up of basically one and the same tribes and clans. Each *otog* had its own territory and all the people in that *otog* were direct subjects of the given lord of the banner. In the 17th century, the Tsakhar *tümen* of the three *tümens* of the East had 8 *otogs,* while the Khalkha *tümen* was divided into two, into inner and outer *tümens,* and the outer *tümen* had 7 *otogs,* whereas the

2 Sh. Natsagdorj, *The primary course of evolution of feudalism in Mongolia,* Ulaanbaatar, 1978, p. 147.

inner *tümen* had 5 *otogs,* and the *Tümed* had 12 *otogs.*[3] Yünsheebüü of the right wing had 5 *otogs* while the *Tümed* had 12 *otogs.* However, the set-up with the Oirads was quite different because up until the second half of the 17th century the *banner* was the key administrative unit among the Oirads. To be precise, from the 16th to the 30s of the 17th centuries, the *Choros, Khoshuud, Torguud* and *Dörvöd* were the four key aimags that made up the Oirads. At that time, the Oirads were also divided into two wings, each with 40 *banners,* including the 5 *banners* of the *Khoshuud, the 5 banners* of the *Torguud,* 5 *banners* of the Khoid and the 5 *banners* of the Jirem in the right wing, and the left wing or *Züün Gar* (Dzungar) included the 10 *banners* of the Choros (which later became *Dörvöd),* the 5 each *banners* of the Shiras and the Makhas.[4]

Galdan Boshogt (1644–1697) established the Züün Gar Khanate and made some changes to the original administrative divisions. He pulled down the structure of the *banner* and replaced them with the *otog,* which was directly under the rule of the Khan, and into *jis (Jas)* that belonged to important *Taiji* nobles. Professor A. Ochir, who is an expert in Oirad research, has noted that "In the beginning, there were 24 *otog* belonging to the Züün Gar Khanate and 5 *jas* of the monasteries and important lamas, but by the middle of the 18th century, their number grew and there were 24 *otog,* 21 units and 9 *jas.*"[5] There were on an average 9000 to 10,000 households in the *otogs* belonging to the Züün Gar Khanate, and the *otog* was further divided into the units of ten, twenty and forty.

But when Batmönkh ascended to the throne in 1479, he was given a reigning title of *Dayan* (meaning The Great Yuan) to symbolise that "he would become the universal ruler who would live a long life, whose state would be immortal, and the deeds good" and with the help of his wife Queen Mandukhai, he succeeded in stopping the fragmentation of the Mongol Empire. He ruled the Mongols for more than 40 years.

After the death of Batmönkh Dayan Khan, the land of the Mongols was once again divided into smaller khanates amongst his sons and the Oirads, which once again became autonomous, and was faced with the tragedy of further fragmentation. Tümen Khan (1558–1593), from among the successors of Batmönkh Dayan Khan, ruled the khanate for more than 30 years and during his reign he was able to shrink the size of the lands and subjects under the noble princes, and also kept strict control

3 *History of the MPR,* in Three Volumes, Volume One, Ulaanbaatar, 1966, p. 445.

4 A. Ochir, *Brief History of the Mongols and Oirads,* Ulaanbaatar, 1993, p. 6.

5 *Ibid.,* p. 7.

over the West and the East wings. Altan Khan (1507–1582), the leader of the Western *Tümen*, who had become extremely powerful like the Great Khan, to a certain extent acknowledged the rule of Tümen Khan, and consequently, became famous in history as the *Tümen Zasagt Khan*. It can be assumed that the Mongol State continued to retain signs of an absolute monarchy although it briefly ruled all the Mongols during the reign of the aforementioned Khans. However, during the reign of other Khans, they were only able to either partially or incompletely rule their subjects, as their reigns were riddled with internal disorders and conflicts. After the Tümen Zasagt Khan the power of the centralised government became significantly enfeebled and the political centre of the East Mongols switched into the hands of the *Tsakhar Tümed*, and the power and authority of the Great Khan did not reach beyond the bounds of this *Tümed*. Ligden, who ruled the country from 1604–1634, revived the unity of all the Mongol tribes and waged an unforgiving struggle against the aggressions of the Manchus to protect the Mongol homeland. But he eventually lost this battle as he failed to garner the support of other Mongol nobles and princes. In this manner, the once glorious Mongol Empire came under the yoke of the Manchus and the Great Empire, which was established in 1206, met its end. In the following chapter, we shall deal with the crisis and conflicts of the Mongols that ensued.

2.2 *The Assembly of the Mongol Princes*

The Assembly of the Mongol Princes replaced the earlier *Ikh* or *Great Khurildai* of the Mongol Khans. These assemblies were held in the eight snow-white *gers* built in memory of Chinggis Khan, which were also called the "Ezen Khoroo" (*meaning Committee of Masters. Tr.*), where the Khans were "crowned." The scale and scope of the Assembly of the Mongol Princes depended on the power, authority and grandeur of the Khan of the given times and was either held involving all the Mongols or just one *Tümed*. Compared to the *Ikh Khurildai*, which were held during the period of the Great Mongol Khans, the Assembly of the Mongol Princes had fewer participants, and the Assembly was not held at regular intervals. However, when a matter needed to be resolved and a decision taken, the opinions of the princes and nobles were given preference. In other words, apparently during the course of the Assembly, the Great Khans and the important princes made concessions to each other, which either led to consensus, or even to break-ups.

After the clout and authority of the Great Khans became weaker, the *aimags* and *banners* would individually hold their own assemblies among their nobles and princes. For instance, we can refer to a few documents related to the assemblies of the nobles and princes of the seven Khalkha *banners*. A member of the horse relay station would be sent as a messenger who would announce the date, time and venue of the local assembly, which were, as a rule attended by the Khans, the princes, *taijis*, sons-in-law of a noble. If a man with a black head (a person of lower social class) returned home without the consent of the nobles, the fine was an armour, four horses and one camel.[6] From this it is clear that the commoners also had an important part to play in the assembly of the nobles and princes. It appears that the assembly was divided into two, the great session and the common session. Anyone who was late without any reason or did not attend the session was dealt with severely. For example, according to a document called "A newly found Khalkha legal document"[7] if a noble prince did not attend the session, the noble should be punished by giving one hundred camels and one thousand horses, and if a noble did not come to a small session in the Year of the Pig (1611) within the first three days, the noble would be penalized with one hundred horses and ten camels. And if a prince did not attend the great session held in the Year of the Monkey (1620), he was penalized with one hundred horses and ten camels, and if a son-in-law of a noble missed the session, he would be penalized by submitting 50 horses and five camels.

According to a prominent Mongolian historian, Kh. Perlee, "In those days apart from the sessions, there were also held meetings. The meetings were normally held where an urgent message from outside would be delivered. The meetings, depending on the issue, would be held among three major *otog*, where representatives of outlying *banners* would gather, and if the meeting was planned to be held under the *black banner* then it would be held in the temple where sacrifices and prayers were offered to the *black banner*. According to the existing rule, a common noble could attend the meeting without any accompaniment, while a senior noble would come with four attendants, and a junior noble would be accompanied by two other people. And if the meeting was skipped of the noble did not come to the meeting on time, they were given sentences identical to the punishment meted out for those who violated the attendance rules related to the great session."[8]

---

6 *Ibid.*, p. 109.

7 Kh. Perlee, Sh. Bira, *Two rare documentary sources related to the history of culture of the Mongols and Cenrtal Asian nations*, Ulaanbaatar, 1974, p. 109–110.

8 Kh. Perlee, Sh. Bira, *Two rare documentary sources related to the history of culture of the Mongols and Central Asian nations*, Ulaanbaatar, 1974, p. 110.

A number of important sessions were held in the 17th century that had a direct impact on the future course of the Mongol nation. In this respect, we can name the session of the Mongols and Oirads held in 1640 at a place called *Tarvagtain Ulaan Buraa* and the session of the Khalkha nobles and princes held in 1688 at a place called *Zag-Baidragiin Khüren Belchir.* Originally, the session of the nobles and princes had the right to advise the Khan, but when the Khan had lost all his power and authority, the nobles and princes had the last say and passed the relevant decision.

DIAGRAM 6 State structure of the Mongols in the 14th–16th centuries

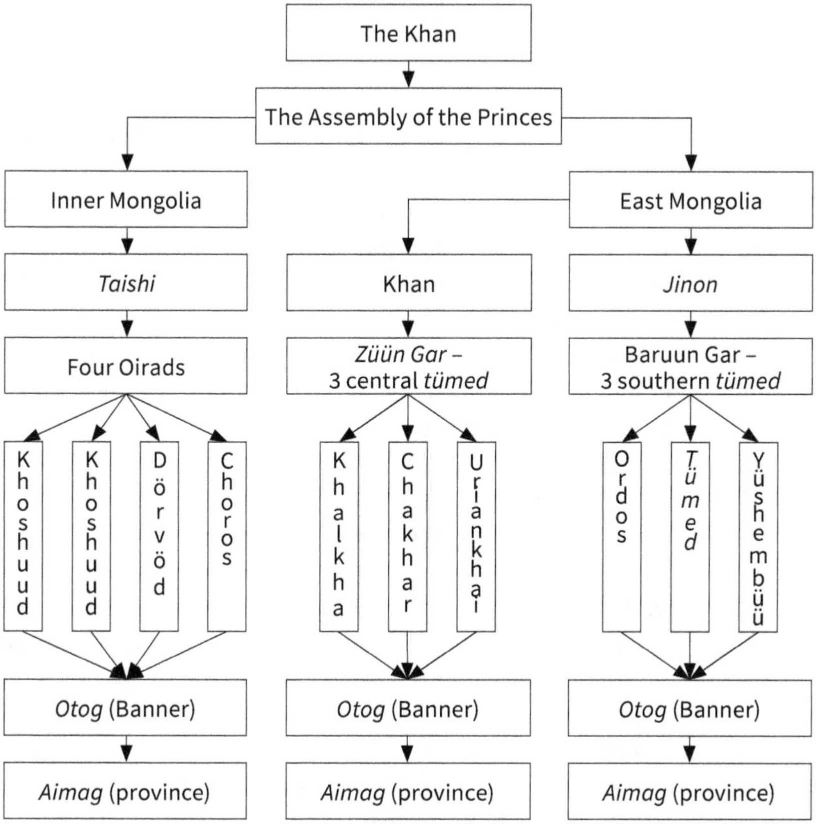

2.3 *Decorum Related to State Officials*

There are very few historical and documentary sources related to the rules and regulations, and the ranks and grades of the Mongol State officials in the period under review. If we summarise based on the documents available, we find that the *Züün Gar (Dzungar) tümen* were led by the Khan himself, while the *tümen* of the right wing were led either by the Khan's younger brother or his son, and accordingly a phrase was coined "In the heavens above there is the sun and the moon, and down below is the khan and the prince". In this manner, as per seniority in rank, the administrator of the right wing was second to the Khan in terms of seniority; in the Mongolian language he was called the *Jinon* (prince), and the four Oirads were ruled by a high-ranking noble called the *Taishi,* who was appointed by the Khan and this administrator was appointed for life.

The Khan had a close associate called *Chinsan* who was his immediate deputy, a chief minister, and was responsible for overseeing the administrative and military affairs of the State. A central government, composed of representatives from both the *Züün Gar (Dzungar) tümen* and the right wing *tümen,* was instituted, and this government was, in all likelihood, administered directly by the *Chinsan.* The Oirdas were also divided into two wings, right and left, and each of them was also administered by a *Chinsan.*

In those days, ranks and titles were conferred on the nobles and princes, other than the Khan himself. On the one hand, this was a sign of appreciation expressed by the Khan (March 26) for the services rendered to the State, and on the other hand, it could have been a last ditch effort to at least keep under control the nobles and the aristocrats who had amassed greater power and authority. What is more, Altan Khan of the *Tümed* (1548–1557) had also demanded that Daraison Khan confer on him the title of *Shidü.* According to Sh. Natsagdorj, the title of *Shidü* was the same title as the *Shad,* that was conferred during the reign of the Turkic Mongols. Judging by the fact that the Turkic title *Yavabgo* was used during the reign of Altan Khan, there is every reason to believe that the title of *Shidü* could have been adapted from the Turkic honorific title of *Shad.*[9] There is also a reference in a historical source that Bodi-Alag Khan (1506–1547) had conferred on Altan Khan the title of *Tüshee Setsen*[10]. Also, the Great Khan, starting from the 16th century, had been conferring on some noble princes the title of "Khan" in recognition of their exceptional services to the State. Besides the traditional honorific titles, such as *setsen, mergen, darkhan,* the Mongols were also using such other honorific titles as *khuntaiji, khoshuuch, erdene khöndlön, tsöökhör, ölziit, daichin tsogt, ilden* etc. Also, after Batmönkh Khan united the six *tümen,* he conferred on

9 S. Natsagdorj, *The Primary Course of Evolution of Feudalism in Mongolia,* Ulaanbaatar, 1978, p. 143.

10 *Epic of the Altan Khan Chakravardi.* Mongolian Historical Sources Series IV. Ulaanbaatar, 2006, p. 23–24.

some princes such titles as *dai darkh* and *al juukh,* and these titles were accompanied by golden seals; however, it is not clear what rank or grade these titles entailed.

The key administrative unit of *otog* was administered by a person called the *zaisan.* One *otog,* depending on the number of population and the kind of administrative services that were managed, had as many as three *zaisans.* In the *Züün Gar* khanate, the Khan even appointed the *zaisan* official of an *otog,* under whom there was the *demch,* who was the administrator of the next lower level or the unit of the forties, followed by an administrator called the *shüüleng* of the unit of twenties, and the leaders of the unit of tens. According to a Mongolian historian Kh. Perlee, such high-ranking officials as the *yambatan, güüsh, khonjin, shireet örlög, khötöltön* and the *khia,* as well as the father or brother of a prince, the banner holder, the trumpeter, the chief of an *otog,* and the wives of the *Darkhads* with special credentials, were all given similar honorific titles and privileges.[11]Judging by this, such titles as the *yambatan, güüsh, khonjin, shireet örlög, khötöltön* and the *khia* all indicated officials of sorts in those times.

2.4 *The Military*

The strict military administrative structure had been dismantled, which later assumed the form of an administrative, military set-up, and still later merely became a purely administrative structure. However, the army during this period was primarily concentrated under the authority of the Khan and the princes of the *Tümed.* By this time, the *Tümed* no longer had the obligation of supplying ten thousand soldiers to the Khan. The States or each of the single *Tümed* had their own separate armies. For example, Altan Khan had an army of three *Tümen* or the equivalent of thirty thousand elite soldiers. But when the Great Khan became more powerful and stronger, the chiefs or the Khans of the *tümen,* under the decree of the Khan, had the responsibility of leading their own army in war or to take part in hunting, which was still popular then. There were instances of rejection of the Khan's decree, especially when the Khan had become weaker and his rule had become weak. For example, when Altan Khan did not follow the orders of *Tümen* Zasagt Khan and failed to partake in the invasion against Liaodong, the relations between them soured.

There is almost no documentary evidence about the fate of the *khishigten,* who were considered the backbone of the Great Mongol Empire.

11 Kh. Perlee, Sh. Bira, Two rare documentary sources related to the history of culture of the Mongols and Cenrtal Asian nations, Ulaanbaatar, 1974, p. 111.

However, there were a group of people who were called the *khishigten* among the Tsakhar *Tümen*. It appears that the Tsakhar *Tümen*, who were under the direct domain of the Khan, apparently continued to carry out some of the responsibilities of the *khishigten*. However, the *khishigten* of this period were not like the *khishigten* during the time of the Great Mongol Empire, as the *khishigten* carried out the duties of guards and sentries. Judging by historical sources, the Khan had under him the so-called "thirty-three *örlögtön*," "sixty-one *khiirten*," the suites and bodyguards to the Khan,[12] which was a new kind of set-up. Apart from them, there were the so-called princes, aides and comrades that served in the *ger* of the Khan. The army of the Mongols during this period did not have a single organisational arrangement that would stand up as one powerful force when needed by the Khan, but the tactics, the weapons they used and their military skills had not become inferior. This is evidenced from, for instance, the incident of the capture of the Tümü fortess of the Ming Dynasty (1449), the battle of Batmönkh Khan against the Uriankhais at Dalan Tergüün, as well as the repeated submission of the Ming Dynasty to Altan Khan.

2.5 *State and Religion*

Although Buddhism was the State ideology of the Yuan Empire, it had not quite fully penetrated among the indigenous Mongols, who inhabited the lands beyond the mountain pass, that is, present-day Mongolia, the Inner Mongolia Region Autonomous of the People's Republic of China and the southern parts of Siberia in Russia. At this very juncture, the Yuan Empire disintegrated and consequently the links between Mongolia and Tibet, which was the centre of dissemination of Buddhism, were temporarily disrupted. Therefore, shamanism continued to remain the prevailing belief of the entire Mongol race.

It became increasingly clear that shamanism had failed to become the ideological instrument for putting an end to the wars and crises that had continued for more than two centuries among the Mongol noble princes and aristocrats. This state of affairs was deeply understood by Tümen Zasagt Khan and Altan Khan, and they were of the unanimous opinion that Buddhism was the most sophisticated and powerful ideology that could help unite the entire Mongol race and put them under a single rule.

In 1576, in the Year of the Red Mouse, Tümen Zasagt Khan invited Ilduni Sanggiduktshi Garma Lama of the Red Hat Sect of Tibetan Buddhism from Tibet to visit, became his disciple and organised the dissemination of Buddhism among the Chakhar and Khalkha people. This was not an

12 *History of the MPR*, in Three Volumes, Book One, Ulaanbaatar, 1966, p. 444.

unplanned act, as this move not only considered the traditional links between the State and religion pre- and post the Great khan era, but also the fact that the Red Hat sect or the *karma-pas,* were becoming extremely powerful in Tibet, both politically and ideologically.

In the next year, 1577, Altan Khan of the *Tümed* and Crown Prince Khutagtai Setsen (1542–1588) invited the head of the karma-pa sect Sodnomjamts or *Sonam Gyatsho* (1542–1588) to visit Mongolia. After this a monastery was built at the port of Tsavchaal near Hoh Nuur, and both Altan Khan and Prince Khutugtai Setsen, taking the lead, converted the Mongols of south Mongolia to Buddhism. Altan Khan conferred on Sonam Gyatsho lama the title of *Dalai Lama* and the Third Dalai Lama Sonam Gyatsho permitted Altan Khan to use all the honorary ranks and titles of the Khubilai Khan. Having analysed these developments that occurred within a period of just one to two years, scholar N. Ishjamts wrote "...Sonam Gyatsho was proclaimed the Dalai Lama following which Altan Khan developed the relationship of a teacher and disciple with the Dalai Lama, and the fact that the Tümed and the Ordos Mongols were converted into Buddhism was far from an expression of disagreement with Altan Khan and even perhaps, rivalry between the two. Mongol khans and nobles, in order to forge an alliance between the state and the Tibetan religion, brought the most influential representatives of either the Red or the Yellow Hat sects, and pursued a policy of fully backing and taking advantage of the most advantageous amongst the two sets, and had to all likelihood distributed their own respective responsibilities in this manner. This is because, Altan Khan and Prince Khutugtai Sesten did not show displeasure when Tümen Zasagt Khan adopted the Yellow Hat sect of Tibetan Buddhism, while Tümen Zasagt Khan did not oppose Altan Khan and Prince Khutugtai Setsen's conversion to the Yellow Hat sect. What is more, Tümen Zasagt Khan and Abtai Khan sent invitations to the Dalai Lama to visit Mongolia, and immediately converted the Chakhar and the Khalkha Mongols into Buddhism...".[13]

Also during this period Mergen Tevne of the Oirads also adopted the Yellow Hat sect of Buddhism and in 1580–1590 sent his son to Lhasa, the capital of Tibet, to study Buddhism. Having mastered Buddhism he became popular under the name of Neij Toyin, and was instrumental in spreading Buddhism in Western Mongolia. In this manner, Buddhism was firmly established in the mind and spirit of the entire Mongol race

13 N. Ishjamts, "State and religion policy of Tümen Zasagt Khan", *"East-West" Journal*, No. 1, p. 27.

and became a central State ideological instrument of the Mongols and their khanates.

3 The Law

3.1 *Legal Sources*

The period under review is extremely rich in terms of law and legality. In particular, during the rule of *Tümen* Zasagt Khan, high-ranking Mongol nobles brought together the West and *Dzüün Gar Tümed* in order to ensure unity and to bring to order the domestic situation of the Mongol nations, and there are even historical references that the great State law, *The Great Yassa,* was amended and renewed. Regrettably, the above-mentioned amended *Great Yassa* has not come down to us. Nevertheless, the new amended *Yassa* became the backbone, the central fulcrum, of the Mongol State and in keeping with this amended *Yassa* some of the Khans and nobles of the *Tümeds* passed sub-laws of the *Yassa,* which were enforced in their own domain and jurisdiction.

The evolution and development of law in the 14th–17th centuries can be seen in the *Altan Khaany Tsaazyn Bichig* (meaning the "Code of Law of Altan Khan"), *Khutugtai Setsen Khuntaijyn Sashni Tsaaz* ("Religious Code of Prince Khutugtai Setsen') and *The Mongol-Oirad Law.* The fact that many codes of laws were instituted during this period is connected to the following factors: 1) the Mongol khans and nobles during this period had inherited a very rich tradition of law; and 2) there was growing demand in the society to pass and enforce laws; in other words, the Mongols, who were scattered and fragmented, realiSed the importance of a law-governed State that would unite the scattered Mongols, and this was also, perhaps, what the Mongol people in general desired.

3.2 *The "Code of Law of Altan Khan"*

Altan Khan of the *Tümed* (1507–1582), basing himself on *The Great Yassa* by the *Tümen* Zasagt Khan, instituted a special code of law to be enforced among his own *Tümed,* and named it the "Small Yassa." We have inherited this code of law not in the Mongolian language but in Tibetan translation, and that too in the *kyug-yig* ("fast letters"; or *chuyig*) style. This code of law was studied and revived through comparative means by S. Bira together with some other scholars and researchers.

When we compare this code of law with the codes of laws that were adopted at a later period, we find a number of distinctive features. First, the code of law of Altan Khan, in terms of its substance and style, more or less adapted the customary laws of the Mongols of the steppes, for it was far from being fully refined. Second, the difference in the social class and strata had not been distinguished clearly. Third, the central clauses and provisions do not show any sign of having any religious influence; and fourth, it is intricately linked with codes of laws adopted at a later period of the Mongol Empire.

Altan Khan's Code of Law, in all likelihood, had 13 Chapters, as the Code ends with the note "Thus ends the thirteen Code of Law approved by the Supreme Master *Gegeen* (meaning Altan Khan)."[14] The Code of Law in reality does not have clauses and provisions. However, scholar S. Bira, who has closely studied it, has classified the Code into several categories according to their subject matter and in this respect, the following explanation can be furnished.

In the Preamble of the Code of Law, Altan Khan decreed that each and every Mongol should unite and consolidate their unity under the blessings of Buddhism, and strictly abide by the laws, customs and traditions. He defined the relationship between the State and religion in the following manner: "A written law is like an indestructible *vajra* (thunderbolt) that will not weaken like a *cloth amulet*; the might and power of the law of the Khagan is as strong as a yoke made of gold,"[15] which is copied from the book *Tsagaan Tüükh* or *The White History – the Book on Ten Noble Deeds*, and this reflects the continuity of the code of laws of the Mongols. Altan Khan's Code of Law, however, was not about the principle of duality, but emphasises the law of the Khan or the State, and in this respect this Code of Law is substantially different from the codes of laws that were in place in the sixteenth century, such as *Tsagaan Tüükh* or *The White History,* and the *Khutugtai Setsen Khuntaijyn Sashni Tsaaz* ("Religious Code of Prince Khutugtai Setsen").

The Preamble of the Code of Law of Altan Khan says, "Thou art the leaders of the 40 banners and 5 *aimags* of the Mongols, examine carefully in thy minds and thoughts, and ascertain (*your allegiance to the Code of Law. Tr.*). Be wary that thou shalt, with any flicker of doubt, accept severe punishment under the principle of duality as decreed by the *Erlig Nomun Khan* (The King of the Underworld). Thus, in thy minds and thoughts examine carefully and ascertain (allegiance)."[16] Judging by this it can be concluded that each and every Mongol was obliged to abide by and respect the Code of Law and anyone who dared to contravene it awaited se-

14 Sh. Bira, *Study into the History, Culture and Historiography of Mongolia*, Vol. 3, Ulaanbaatar, 2001, p. 124.

15 *Ibid.*, p. 125.

16 *Ibid.*, p. 125.

vere punishment that could only be handed down by the *Relic Noun Khan* – the King of the Underworld, meaning that the "iron fist of the State" would spare no-one who dared to go against the law.

Let us now look briefly at the fundamental clauses and provisions of this Code of Law.

1 **A case of homicide.** The Code of Law has a general provision under "murder," "homicide," which spells out the principles of meting out punishment by classifying homicides cases according to their types and severity. For instance, included in the homicide cases are premeditated murder, someone losing their life by interfering in a brawl between two people although the victim had not been asked to interfere, an honest person losing their life by trying to intervene between two adversaries, an act of filicide, a criminal act when the adopted parent kills their adopted child, the case of a person who dies in a fire caused by the fault of another person, the case of a person killed due to arson, the case of homicide committed by a mentally unstable person, and other cases of killing and murder, both human or animal-related. A criminal convicted of homicide was either thrashed, or punished by confiscation of the convict's private property, livestock etc., which in Mongolian was termed *Yüs, Tav Torgokh* (literally meaning "nine, five penalties"), and there was a punishment called "substitution" and from among all kinds of punishment, the most common was the *Yüs Torgokh,* the severity of which was graded according to the severity of the crime. And if a person, who interfered in the brawl with fair intentions was killed, then the guilty person was meted out the severest of punishments under *Yüs Torgokh*

Of particular interest is the fact that Altan Khan's Code of Law does not make any mention of sentencing a person convicted of homicide to capital punishment.

Researchers and scholars have different interpretations of the punishment "substitution." For instance, D. Dashtseden writes: "'Substitution' meant that "a close relative of the murderer could be put to death."[17] However, in our opinion, "substitution" meant that if the murderer was a noble or from a family of the upper elite, then one of his subjects would be handed over to the victim's family as a slave, a servant, or perhaps the wife or one of the children of the subject would be given away to serve as a servant in the victim's family. Once someone was given as a slave-servant, the new master decided how he would treat his new subject. If a person who had given rise to the case of "substitution" and had not actually murdered someone else, then that person would be sold as a slave and

17 E. Avirmed, D. Dashtseden, G. Sovd, *Mongol Law,* Ulaanbaatar, 1997, p. 48.

that would mean he would lead a very miserable life. There is also a punishment, which says "substitute together with camels," which did not, perhaps, mean that the guilty person was penalised by giving camels to the family of the victim, but rather actual camels were used as a "substitution" for the punishment.

2 **A case involving physical injury.** If someone had intentionally or accidentally caused serious physical injury, such as, damaging someone's eye leading to blindness, breaking someone's teeth, hitting someone with a long, sharp stone or wood, whipping and even kicking someone hard causing physical injury, pulling their hair and beard and causing facial injury, these were considered grave crimes, which also included causing someone's death if the injury and death caused were not premeditated or intentional. Anyone guilty of the abovementioned crimes was whipped, penalised with the so-called *Yüs, Tav Torgokh* and even the punishment of "substitution" and for some very serious cases, many of the means of punishment were given in combination. Judging from the above, the ancient principle of retribution – "A life for a life, an eye for an eye, a tooth for a tooth" – was no longer practiced, which meant that the legal system during the time of Altan Khan had become much more refined, and perhaps much more "humane."

3 **Theft and robbery.** Provisions related to theft and robbery occupy a significant place in the Code of Law of Altan Khan. This section in the Code of Law specifies in great detail everything related to livestock breeding, which was the mainstay and the source of livelihood of the Mongols, and so the kinds and forms of punishment related to, say, stealing an animal, were spelled out in a highly detailed manner. A person who was found to have committed the smallest of crimes, related to the stealing of an animal, for example, had to repay at least one small animal (a sheep or a goat, which is collectively called the *bog – бог мал* in Mongolian) or one large animal (a horse, a cow or a camel, called the *bod – бод мал* in Mongolian), while someone who had committed a much more serious crime was punished according to the above forms of punishment, such as the *Yüs, Tav Torgokh* and even "substitution." For example, the Code of Law of Altan Khan stated: "Take one sheep in fine for stealing a wooden chest, animal wool and hair, animal hair scraper and scarifier, writing brush, pen, and animal collar,"[18] and punish a person "guilty of stealing material property, a horse, a cow by subjecting him to the *Yüs, Tav Torgokh* and the 'substitution' punishment." From the above, we can learn that a person

18 S. Badarch, *History of the State and Laws of Mongolia (Legends and Illustrations)*, Ulaanbaatar, 1989, p. 129.

guilty of theft and robbery awaited the severest of all punishments. The Mongols held hunting birds in high esteem and prized them, which is evidenced by the punishment meted out to those who dared to "steal kite, eagle, bearded vulture, and condor." They were punished with dual *Yüs Torgokh*. It appears that anyone who was caught stealing anything made of metal was punished and had to pay a high penalty.
The Code of Law points out "A life for a life, and a non-living thing for a non-living thing," which was one kind of punishment given to a person guilty or convicted of a felony.

The Code further specified that "A person who is below the age of ten is not a thief, but those who are above the age of ten and is guilty of thievery is a thief," which can be explained by the fact that the Code considered a child under the age of ten to have committed a misdemeanor and so the child was not convicted. But if a thief was murdered, the person guilty of murder would not receive capital punishment. However, if the perpetrator either tried to justify himself or the crime or if the act of murder was carried out with someone else, then the guilty party would receive a much more severe punishment.

4 **Marriage and family relationship.** The related section in the Code of Law deals with the issues of protection of women, giving girls an opportunity to express their opinion if they were about to be given as a wife in marriage, non-tolerance of promiscuity and domestic violence, welcoming of daughters-in-law, marriage and family relations. For example, the Code spells out a punishment of *Yüs Torgokh* (nine penalties) if a pregnant woman is hurt and has a miscarriage, if a man and a woman are guilty of immoral behavior, then they would be given a sentence of *Doloo Yüs Torgokh*, i.e. nine penalties seven times etc. And it is very interesting that there were provisions in the Code that upheld and protected the rights of young women, such as "Punish the parents with *Yüs Yüs Torgokh* or 9 times nine penalties if the parents are guilty of having married off their daughter in an indecent manner," "If such a married off girl returns home, she is not punishable," "A person who has defiled a virgin of young age and if the parents of a girl have forced their daughter to marriage", in both cases, the offenders were put to death.[19]

5 **Types of crimes in the relationship between master and servant.** The section dealing with this relationship mentions "capital punishment," which is not to be found under any other provision in the Code of Law. For example, the Code says "Execute (by strangulation) a Chinese

19 Sh. Bira, *Study into the History, Culture and Historiography of Mongolia*, Vol. 3, Ulaanbaatar, 1997, p. 132.

servant who is responsible for managing foods and supplies," and "Show sympathy while executing capital punishment if a servant ... is guilty of thievery,"[20] which is proof that social origin and class difference had found reflection, to a certain measure, in the Code of Law of Altan Khan. However, further on there is a clause which says that "if a servant of foreign origin, who is honest and decent to his master, shall be treated as a Mongol servant," meant that a servant or a slave, who served his/her master honestly, was given less punishment and even treated as an equal of a commoner Mongol.

6 **Cases related to the dead and epidemics**. The Code of Law, besides prohibitionary provisions related to the prevention of infectious and other serious communicable diseases, also contains many provisions that have religious and customary shades and undertones. Take, for example, the following: "Flog and impose *Yüs Yüs Torgokh* or 9 times nine penalties if a person with infectious disease visits another household and spreads the disease that leads to death, and impose a *Gurvan Yüs Torgokh* or 3 times nine penalties if there is no death. If a person affected with infectious disease does not pass on the disease to another, the infected person shall have to give one camel as a fine, and if someone contracts the disease from the infected person and loses eyesight, then the infected person shall be flogged several times, and also punished with *Yüs Yüs Torgokh* or 9 times nine penalties."[21] Also if a person who has just buried a dead person visits a household, who has disturbed the remaining bones of the deceased, who takes the items used for the burial, who takes possession of the horse and the sacrificial horse of the dead, and if a person has intentionally taken such horses and put them in a different place, this guilty person shall be fined with livestock and even *Yüs Yüs Torgokh* or 9 times nine penalties. There are also some provisions related to religious belief and rites, such as burning incense during a burial ceremony for cleansing and purifying purposes.

7 **Safeguarding livestock animals from various threats and risks**. Altan Khan's Code of Law codified encouragement and incentives for people who did a good deed by protecting livestock from various natural disasters. For example, a person who saves sheep and goats from wandering away in a heavy snow blizzard or sand-storm, or anyone who prevented an attack on livestock by wolves, who rescues animals from flood, landslide and fire was rewarded with sheep, cows and horses, while a person who used animals for entertainment purposes and got them killed by

20 *Ibid.*, pp. 132–133.
21 *Ibid.*, p. 133.

drowning was punished under *Gurvan Yüs Torgokh* or 3 times nine penalties.

8 **Protecting and saving wild animals.** People who hunted wild ass, wild horses, antelope, male and female roe deer, moose, royal stag, doe, wild boar, mountain goats, ibex, muck deer, wolverine, badgers and hare were mostly fined in kind, which meant that hunting of these animals had not been fully prohibited, for they were hunted during special seasons and times. According to the Code of Law, the hunting of small fish, kite, crow, and magpie was permitted throughout the year and there was no ban on their hunting.

9 **Assisting one another.** In this section, a human being was considered invaluable and incentives and rewards were codified for a person who saved the life of another person. Take, for example, the following:

- Give in reward a steed to a person who has helped a lost child;
- If it is a girl, reward the person with a servant;
- If a Mongol is saved from fire and water, give two steeds in reward;
- If an internal Chinese (*Chinese slaves were divided into three categories - internal, middle and inferior. Tr.*) is saved, reward the person with a horse, and if a middle Chinese is saved, then reward the person with a horse as well;
- If an inferior Chinese is saved, reward the person who saved the Chinese with a cow.

Although these provisions were discriminatory in terms of class in society, they impart the notion that the life of even a servant or a slave was invaluable, and in this sense, these provisions are humane in nature.

10 **Related to envoys and official dealings.** Special attention is given in Altan Khan's Code of Law to envoys and emissaries, whose role in the conduct of administrative and civilian matters was important. Judging by the Code of Law, the envoys were classified as State, common and sentinel. An official State envoy would be accompanied by two ministers and two attendants. Depending on their role and responsibility, the envoys were also classified into two categories - emergency and conditional. Judging by the fact that a person who was guilty of "beating an envoy" was given the punishment of *Tav Torgokh* or 5 times nine penalties, and a person guilty of "hurting an envoy with an arrow or with a dagger" was given the punishment of one *Yüs Torgokh* or one time nine penalties, plus a penalty of one camel, it is clear that envoys enjoyed special immunity and special privileges. However, should the envoys violate established rules and regulations, they were punished instead. For example, if an envoy set up his camp beyond a herd of horses, or a camp of nomads, the envoy was fined with one horse. The Code of Law declared that being given the job of an

envoy was an important state assignment, "anyone who dared to act as an imposter would be put to death like a thief."

11 **Regarding fugitives and deserters.** The Code of Law of Altan Khan specifically deals with the issue of fugitives and deserters; this may be because there were numerous instances of people becoming fugitives who had committed the crime of entering into conflict with their masters. It is perhaps in order to buttress the principle of master-subject that those who dared to shelter or give refuge to slaves or subjects belonging to other masters were given harsh punishment, and no distinction was made with respect to the origin or status of a person who had helped a subject flee from his master, who would be pursued and punished.[22] In this manner, the Code of Law of Altan Khan is one of the most unique and rare monuments of ancient laws and legislation that legalised and codified central aspects and elements of the social relations of the Mongols in the 16th century.

3.3 *"Khutugtai Setsen Khuntaijyn Sashni Tsaaz" (Religious Code of Prince Khutugtai Setsen)*

Khutugtai Setsen Khuntaiji (1540–1586) was a lawyer, and an outstanding and shrewd statesman. This is why he bore a special title, "The Truly Sanctified and Wise *Taiji*," and he is remembered in historical manuscripts and sources as a "Sage who scrutinises the past and predicts the future."

Khutugtai Setsen Khuntaiji deeply researched the sutra, *The White History or the Book on Ten Noble Deeds* (in Mongolian *Арван Буянт Номын Цагаан Түүх*), written during the reign of Khubilai Khan, compared and analysed it with other books and at the instruction of Altan Khan and the Dalai Lama wrote a book of law on religion and belief. Although the original copy of this law did not come down to our times, we can gain an idea of this book of law on religion by the Mongolian version as quoted by Sagan Setsen in his book *Erdeniin Tobchi* or the "Bejeweled Summary," or from the Tibetan version as quoted in the biography of the Third Dalai Lama Sodnomjamts, which was composed in 1646 by the Fifth Dalai Agvaanjamts (Ngawang Lobsang Gyatso, 1617–1682). The contents of these two important historical monuments were the subject of comparative study by the Mongolian scholar Sh. Bira, who has revealed that their contents concur.[23]

22 *Ibid.*, p. 135.
23 *Ibid.*, p. 125.

The Religious Code compiled by Khutugtai Setsen Khuntaiji composed the relationship between the State and religion to please the mind and sight of both the clerical and lay nobles and the aristocrats, and laid the legal foundations confirming that the Yellow Faith of Buddhism would be the central ideology of the Mongol State. The Tibetan version of the Religious Code begins with a kind of Preamble as follows: "Glory to the convergence of the Place of Worship, and the Lord of Gifts, the pathway to Supreme Faith (Religion) has been opened and the ocean of blood has been turned into an ocean of milk and therefore, the Chinese, the Tibetan and all the Mongols in the vanguard, must live and exist under the Ten Glorious and Noble Virtues."[24] This is an expression of a central idea that boils down to providing the legal guarantees for laying the firm foundations of spreading the Yellow Faith of Buddhism among all the Mongols, both lay and clerical, commoners and noblility, who had become disciples of the Dalai Lama.

The following code of conduct was established in the Mongolian language version of the Religious Code:

- Those who use camels and horses as *death-escorts* when a deceased is buried shall be put to death by execution;
- Practice fasting and only eat vegetarian dishes, and do not slaughter animals for food every year and every month;
- Grant *Tsorji* (a lamaistic title) equal rights to those of a Crown Prince, a *Rabjamba* (lamaist doctor of theology) and a *Gabji* (lamaist clerical degree) equal rights to a *Taiji* (title of a Mongol nobleman), a friar equal rights with the son-in-law of a nobleman, and a lama of a rank of *Taiji*, a nun, *Ubashi and Ubasanz (a lay man and a lay woman who has taken certain religious vows)* with that of a *Taiiji* (a nobleman) of lower rank, if a common person dares to lay hands on them or insults them, then punish that person similarly to someone who manhandles a Crown Prince;
- If a Buddhist lama breaches religious principles and if he gets married, the lama must be thrown out of the monastery. If a lay man or a lay woman, who has taken a certain religious oath, slaughters an animal, he/she must be stripped of his/her religious oath and made lay again, and if a noble lady and a lay woman who have taken religious vows consume alcohol, their entire property must be confiscated.

These ideas are contained in the Tibetan version of the Religious Code and what is interesting is that some of these prohibitory provisions are outlined in fine detail. For example, sections dealing with the disposi-

24 *Ibid.*, p. 98.

tions and responsibilities (sanctions) related to the banning of the disgraceful ancient funeral practice among the Mongols called the *Khoillog* (*хойллого* in Mongolian. *According to this practice, when a nobleman died, he would be buried along with the clothes and other items he had been using, including his horse, sheep, concubine and servant, who were all buried alive. Such a practice continued until the fifteenth and sixteenth centuries, but was banned towards the end of the 16*th *century. Tr.*) and also the banning of the practice of attacking, raiding and instigating a war, as compared to the Mongolian version of the Religious Code, are exhaustive and detailed. To conclude, some of the outrageous practices in shamanism, which had become sticking points in promoting the spread of Buddhism in the land of the Mongols, were banned; and the power and authority of high-ranking Buddhist monks were supported by law and put on a par with those of the nobles and princes, and behaviourial norms for the Buddhist monks were also introduced.

3.4 *The Golden Horde Manuscript on Birch Bark*

In 1970, a Mongolian-Russian research expedition, led by a prominent Mongolian scholar, Kh. Perlee, and a Soviet geologist, E. V. Shavkunov, found an extremely rare and important manuscript written on birch bark in the ruins of an ancient town called *Kharbukh,* situated on the territory of the present-day Dashinchilen *soum* in the Bulgan *aimag*. The manuscript included copies of a collection of 18 codes of laws that were discussed and adopted during 18 assemblies of the Mongol nobles of the four Khalkha banners, the six banners and seven banners covering the period from the second half of the 16th century to the 40s of the 17th century. In 1973, Kh. Perle reprinted them in a book called *The Newly Discovered Monumental Works of Codes of Laws*. From among these codes of laws, the most interesting one is *The Great Yassa of the Seven Khalkha Banners,* which can be classified as a summarised version of all the other 17 codes of laws.

High-ranking nobles and *taijis* from the Khalkha four banners, six banners and seven banners, who were State officials, were primarily involved in the adoption of the laws. Some of the more prominent and important nobles, who were actively involved in the process were Khündelen Tsüükher Tümenkhin of the Tüsheet Khan *aimag* and Setsen *Taiji* of the Zasagt Khan *aimag*. As Tüsheet Khan *aimag* was situated in the heart of the land of the Khalkhas and also because this *aimag* was actively engaged in the political affairs of the Khalkha Mongols, Tüsheet Khan's subjects were predominantly active in the assemblies of all the Khalkha banners.

One specific concept that is repeated over and over again in the code of laws is the idea of putting an end to feuding and disunity by respecting unity and harmony. In the aforementioned code of laws, this idea is expressed in this manner: If anyone is guilty of a wrong deed, whoever that person may be, shall be punished and dealt with as spelled out in the code of law.

Scholar Kh. Perlee culled the following crimes that were included in the 18 codes of law from *The Golden Horde Manuscript on Birch Bark*:

1 Crimes about the rights to possession and utilization of land and water;
2 Crimes related to open and covert stealing of livestock animals, raiding and plundering, as well as crimes related to the stealing of household items, work instruments and weapons;
3 Crimes such as homicide, bloodshed, thrashing, bashing, using knives and sharp-edged weapons, cursing, and quarrelling;
4 The case of multiple fugitives;
5 Crimes committed against an envoy, an emissary;
6 Crimes related to an eye-witness;
7 Crimes related to nobles and high-ranking aristocrats;
8 Crimes related to wars and enemies;
9 About lamas and crimes related to them;
10 Crimes related to the administration and the community;
11 Crimes related to marrying off an underage girl, daughter-in-law and disruption of a matrimonial bond;
12 Crimes related to the right to belief and religion;
13 Crimes related to inheritance, possession and taking over ownership of property;
14 Crimes related to the relationship between the nobles and their subjects; and,
15 Crimes related to complaint lodging, convicting a criminal, passing or repealing sentence etc.[25]

If we analyse the classifications made above, we find that in 1603 a special code of law on *Otogs* was adopted, designed primarily to stabilise the administrative divisions and to confirm the principles of relationship between a master and his subject. Under this law, the councils of all the *Otogs* were disbanded and as much as the *Otogs* constituted the primary administrative units, the law ensured that the *Otogs* should be stable in order to strengthen the principle of master and subject. Anyone who violated this law posed a risk to the stability of the *Otogs* and was severely

25 Kh. Perlee, Sh. Bira, *Two rare documentary sources related to the history of culture of the Mongols and Central Asian nations*, Ulaanbaatar, 1974, p. 8.

punished. From the above we can see that the *Otog* and the land (territory) were mutually and inseparably interdependent.

Those subjects who had run away from their masters and owners were described in the codes of laws as fugitives, and their movements were strictly banned. Such provisions were critical in bolstering the principle of master and subject.

The codes of laws of the six banners attempted to regulate relations concerning ownership and utilization of territorial land and water: "If anyone attempts to take by force water that has already been under the ownership of another person, the guilty shall be fined with one horse … a horse to be fined if a person who has completed watering his animals refuses to give other person to water his animals…"[26] There also are provisions related to the protection of the nature and environment, which have been formulated as "if a person has contaminated water then he must be fined with a fawn and a cow, and reward a person who has witnessed the act with a cow."[27]

Also it was prohibited to kill any animal by making a horse trample and crush the animal under its feet, and a violator was given a harsh sentence. The code of law of the six banners stated: "Reward the corresponding number of horses to a person who has inherited the house (ger)", which meant that anyone who did not inherit the property without any consent or without a will was fined the corresponding number of horses according to the number of members in that household. This code of law also contained a provision to fine a person a cow should the person sell or misuse the inherited asset. In this way, the codes of laws contained clear-cut, albeit concise, provisions related to inheritance rights.

According to the "Manuscript on Birch Bark" there were mechanisms to regulate relations connected with the type of economy the Mongols were engaged in. Also, it is clear that among the livestock animals, horses were held in high respect, followed by camels; cattle and sheep are mentioned indiscriminately. Anyone who stole livestock produce (dairy produce, meat, hides, wool etc.) was punished and in compensation had to pay back as many as one to nine heads of livestock animals to the owner. Thieves who stole household items made of metal awaited severe punishment and they were considered as serious offenders. If someone stole a metal brazier, the guilty person was fined 27 heads of livestock animals, and a thief who stole a steel knife was fined one horse. All the codes of laws in the "Manuscript on Birch Bark" touched upon the official duty of

26 *Ibid.*, p. 109.
27 *Ibid.*, p. 109.

an envoy and a member of a horse-relay service; for instance, anyone who dared to oppose and physically hurt an envoy was doomed to capital punishment.

These codes of laws contain numerous clauses and provisions legitimatising and consolidating the privileges of the princes and nobles. For example, if small ranking Khans quarrelled amongst themselves within a *ger* they were fined one hundred head of horses and ten camels; if a servant physically assaulted a noble and his wife, the servant was severely punished, which was evidence of the policy of protecting and consolidating the ranks and image of the small ranking Khans, who had come into being with the direct involvement of the Dalai Lama in the affairs of the Khalkha Mongols.

Changes occurring in social life were accompanied by some very strange forms of crimes, which were regulated in the Khalkha codes of laws. For example, a code of law on the novice lamas of the *Four Banners* mentions crimes related to temples, monasteries and lamas, such as missing a number of relay horses, cooking utensils belonging to the clergy and monastery, non-submission of duties to the monasteries, as well as absconding from monastic duties etc., and even defines the kinds of punishment for each of these crimes. There were incidents of destroying property and statues of temples and monasteries, and those involved in this kind of "crime" were dealt with harshly.

The code of law of the *Six Banners* as well as the code of law passed in 1620, the Year of the Monkey, could be regarded as a reflection of the worsening living conditions and standards of the common people and the looming threat of mass hunger.

One common thing in all the aforementioned codes of laws are the repeated clauses and provisions of marriage-related offences committed against women and girls. The code of law of the *Six Banners* says "Stop a wedding without any witnesses. May the witnesses be found." This code of law says that when a girl who has reached the age of twenty is given for marriage, the concerned person must notify his master and the master of his own son-in-law, and we can find a similar provision also in *The* Great *Yassa* adopted in 1620, the Year of the Monkey. During this period, traditional wedding rules were disregarded and consequently related crimes began to rise. This is why the codes of laws passed in the Year of the Iron Pig (1611) decreed that anyone who abducted a nobleman's betrothed lady and gave her in marriage to another person should receive a fine of a livestock animal and tea, and the betrothed woman should be returned. The code of law of 1613 or the Year of the Water Cow says that if a minor Khan takes the betrothed woman of a commoner subject, the latter should be compensated with either one camel or armour. If the son of a noble, although he is going to have a wedding, gives his to-be-wife to a stranger, he is to be punished by fifty heads of livestock and a sizable amount of tea (*Tea was imported and a rarity, but a daily beverage, and ten bundles of tea was equivalent to a camel, eight bundles of tea to one cow, and one bundle of tea was equivalent to two horses. Tr.*) If there is no wedding, then the confiscated animals must be returned.[28]

One of the codes of law in the "Manuscript on Birch Bark" mixes up the different kinds of punishment for different crimes and offences, but nonetheless it goes into detail about the nature of the committed crime, the kinds of punishment, the severity of the punishment etc. In terms of the nature of the punishment given, fining a guilty person livestock animals was apparently the common form of imposition of a penalty. And so, the "Manuscript on Birch Bark" was an extremely important legal instrument that regularised the social relations of the Khalkha people during the reign of the Mongol Khanates, when the Mongols were no longer a united nation under a single Khan.

3.5 *The Mongol-Oirad Laws*

In 1635, Erdenebaatar, Crown Prince of the Oirads, who succeeded his father Prince Kharkhol and ably continued his father's policy and actions, founded the Choros Khanate. During his reign, the situation of the Oirads stablisied and subsequently a policy facilitating the unity of all the Mongols was pursued actively. At the initiative and direct involvement of Crown Prince Erdenebaatar a grand assembly of the Khalkhas and Oirads was held at a place called Ulaan Buraa of Travagtai in early August 1640. Some 28 State and religious figures of the Khalkha Mongols and the Oirads, such as Ochirbat Tüsheet Khan Gombodorj, Eredene Zasagt Subadai, influential nobles of the Setsen Khan *aimag*, Crown Prince Erdenebaatar, Khöndlön Ubaashi of the Oirads, and Güsh Khan of the *Oirad Banners* or better known as *Tör Baikh*, monk Tengerei, as well as representatives of nobles and princes of Mongols in Hoh Nuur and Volga River came for this grand assembly.

At this assembly, they considered and unanimously adopted the famous code of laws called the *Mongol-Oirad Laws*. At that time, the Oirad script had not yet been invented and so the code must have been written in the Uighur Mongol script. However, to date, the original of the *Mongol-Oirad Laws* has not been found and so for our research purposes we used the sole copy of the law preserved in the Republic of Kalmykia in

28 *Ibid.*, p. 115.

Russia in the *tod* (clear) script (*Clear Script is an alphabet created in 1648 by the Oirad Buddhist monk Zaya Pandita for the Oirad language. Tr.*). In terms of its structure, the *Mongol-Oirad Laws* began with a Preamble and had 120 paragraphs in the original form when it was first passed, as the Laws were amended several times between 1640 and 1761. As far as we know, 15 paragraphs were added to the original Laws by two separate decrees passed by Galdan Boshogt Khan of the *Züün Gar* Oirad. Research carried out in Inner Mongolia, China, established that Khan Donrovrash (Dondogdash) of the Torghuts (1741–1761) added 53 paragraphs of amendments to the *Mongol-Oirad Laws,* which means that the Law almost had some 190 paragraphs.

The *Mongol-Oirad Laws* as well as the "*The Great Laws of the Forty and Four*", as mentioned in historical sources, were extremely important documents in legal terms. They were adopted to raise the awareness of the people about the threats of external aggression in that extremely difficult historical period, promoting the unity and harmony of all the Mongols, elevating the influence and reputation of the Yellow Faith of Buddhism and beefing up its authority, strengthening the principle of master-subject, and based on the above, providing legal regulation for the multi-faceted social relations of the times.

The Preamble of the *Mongol-Oirad Laws* begins: "We bow in reverence to Vajradhra, an embodiment embodying void and ultimate emptiness (*Śūnyatā in Sanskrit*) emanating from the tenet that all things are empty of intrinsic existence and nature (*Śūnyatā in Sanskrit*) (*meaning God Shakyamuni or Siddhartha Gautama, Tsonkhapa – an influential Tibetan Buddhist monk, philosopher and tantric yogi, Panchen Erdene Lama, Dalai Lama. Authors*),"[29] which in essence is a call to the Mongols to wholeheartedly pay veneration to Lord Buddha's teachings, and to bow in reverence to the founder of the religion and the great successive saints of Buddhism.

Paragraph one states: "Anyone who dares destroy this state and breakaway with a chunk of the state by pillaging and killing, then Mongols and the Oirads will come together to deal with the dissident, confiscate all his properties and assets and shall divide them into two to take possession over them. If a handful of people in the remote areas breakaway from the *aimag,* the dissident shall be made to pay in compensation one hundred armours and camels, and one thousand horses, and all the property and

29 K.F. Golstunskii, *Mongol-Oirad Laws of 1640, supplementary decrees of Galdan Boshogt Khan, and laws adopted for the Kalmyks living on the Volga during the reign of the Kalmyk Khan Donrovrash (Dondogdash).* Kalmyk texts in Russian translation and notes. St. Petersburg, 1880, Vol. 1.

animals taken by them shall be taken back."[30] This paragraph basically reflects the intent of the Mongols and the Oirads to join forces and so unite the internal forces to protect the country from all alien aggression; should a third party invade them, they would come together to withstand the invasion. Also, if any element violates the established legal regulations, and brings about social disturbance by way of attacking either the State or any one of its *aimags* under its jurisdiction, then such action, on a broader scale, would have serious implications for the State, and warns that even a minor disagreement among the nobles of the *aimags* and *banners*, although they may appear to be a local matter, could lead to crisis and discord at the level of the entire State.

With the objective of putting an end to local disputes and disagreements among the local nobles over their territory and subjects, the *Mongol-Oirad Laws* clearly stated that should there be fugitives who have left their master nobles and taken sides with another, the matter would be resolved through talks and negotiations.

According to one provision of the law: any fugitives identified as Barags, Baats, or Khoids, between 1617 and 1628, during the assembly, become subjects of the noble of the region where they are located, whether in Mongol or Oirod. For fugitives from other tribes, they must be handed over and accepted without any hindrance. Violators of this provision will be severely punished.

It was also decided that a fugitive who initially belonged to the Khalkha Tsogt Taiji would remain in their new domicile. This was perhaps because, on the one hand, there was no official successor to claim back the subjects that once came under the jurisdiction of Tsogt Taiji, and on the other hand, the cost of repatriating a fugitive back to the Khalkha was too costly an undertaking. On the whole, the aforementioned paragraphs were designed to bolster the principle of master and subject.

The *Mongol-Oirad Laws* also contained provisions and paragraphs emphasising the importance of vigilance and alertness; prohibiting robbery and cowardly attack of one member of the confederation against the other member; stressing the importance of immediately notifying each other should there be any danger from alien enemies and should one have such an intelligence, and of immediately coming to each other's support should there be such a threat; prohibiting one *aimag* from giving shelter to a fugitive from another *aimag*; stressing the importance of a community of ten households to form a small army unit who would gather at their master's place if they are summoned to do so; subjecting to public

30 *Ibid.*

humiliation a defector by making the man put on a woman's gown and making him walk through the public; confiscating the entire property of a person, and putting him to death, who although he knew that the enemy was at their doorstep, had failed to warn about the danger; and ensuring that a person who has witnessed how an enemy had drawn away their livestock to go after the raider to bring back the lost livestock animals. Anyone who dared to contravene these legal provisions was given harsh punishments: "Destroy from one generation to another a person who although has seen the enemy coming but had not warned of the danger; Confiscate half of the livestock animals owned by a person who, although had seen the bandits, but had not informed the others about the robbery." In this manner, the *Mongol-Oirad Laws* made the protection of the country's independence and sovereignty an obligation of each individual, all the classes and groups of the society, thus putting high civil responsibility on each and every Mongol.

There are many paragraphs in the *Mongol-Oirad Laws* that elevated Buddhism as the State ideology and consolidated the status of the Buddhist temples, monasteries and lamas. For instance, if high-ranking Buddhist lamas were given power and rights similar to those of the high-ranking nobles and aristocrats in the "*Khutugtai Setsen Khuntaijyn Sashni Tsaaz*" or the Religious Code of Prince Khutugtai Setsen, the *Mongol-Oirad Laws* put in place additional special rights for the high-ranking Buddhist lamas and provided better protection of their rights by proclaiming that "if the цорж are insulted and attacked, the guilty shall be punished by *Yüs Yüs Torgokh* or 9 times nine penalties, and if a lama who is the teacher of a noble is insulted and attacked, then the person who has committed the offence shall be punished by *Tav Yüs Torgokh* or 5 times nine penalties." The laws further stated that pilgrims should be provided with meat and foodstuffs by the people and anyone who had encroached on the property and knowledge of the lamas should be punished harshly. During this period, efforts were made to drive out shamanism from the life of the Mongols, as anyone who invited a shaman to carry out a shamanistic ritual, would be punished in a severe manner. In order to keep Buddhism taintless, the lamas were obliged to strictly follow their monastic vows and their violators were punished severely.

The *Mongol-Oirad Laws* took care of livestock breeding, basic means of livelihood of the Mongols, as well as hunting of game and service in the horse-relay stations, which was their supplementary means of livelihood. For example, the *Mongol-Oirad Laws* had provisions that emphasised the need for jointly organising actions related to livestock breeding, increasing livestock population and production, organising game hunting and for this purpose, using different kinds of both lethal and non-lethal kinds of traps, protecting the hunting grounds of the Khans and nobles, and the need for improving horse-relay services. Apart from the above, there were provisions that focused on the need to protect livestock animals, specifically, male animals, such as male camels, bulls and stallions, and that also put in place safeguard measures against such animals, as well as protecting the people from rabid dogs and wolves etc.

The *Mongol-Oirad Laws* also touched on the legal aspects of administrative rule, civilian and family affairs. For instance, the Laws contain some unique solutions for solving conflicts arising among family members and they emphasise the importance of respecting parents in-law, parents and the older siblings in a family. Take, for example, such provisions as "A person guilty of manhandling his/her teacher and parents would be subject to one *Yüs Torgokh* or nine penalties to even three *Yüs Torgokh* or 3 times nine penalties," and "If a son beats his wife to teach her a lesson, then the in-laws of the girl would not be punished, however, if the son physically abuses his wife for no reason, then the parents of the boy would be given a *Yüs Torgokh* or nine penalties."

The *Mongol-Oirad Laws* put special emphasis on combatting robbery. According to Professor E. Avirmed, the Laws contain some 20 paragraphs related to robbery and the following robberies would be considered as a serious offence:

- Stealing of weapons, uniforms, in particular, bows and arrows, swords and shields, helmets and armours;
- Stealing of camels, horses, cattle, sheep and gestating livestock animals;
- Different kinds of carpets and rugs, and clothes;
- Household items, furnace and stove, and kitchen utensils;
- Tools and implements used for production purposes;
- Personal items of others;
- Draft animals, such as horses, camels as well as implements used for transportation when using draft animals as well as food items;
- If a single unmarried and homeless person steals, he/she would be detained and given to the household from where he/she has stolen to work as their servant;
- A person who has intentionally erased material evidence of a thief and who has given shelter to the thief shall be punished;
- Crimes committed by a gang of bandits;
- A person who has witnessed a crime of robbery or knows the perpetrator is obliged to come forward to give evidence; and there are other provisions in the *Mongol-Oirad Laws* that outline the processes

and procedures of revealing a case of robbery and the manner in which such crimes should be resolved.

A closer look at the section in the *Mongol-Oirad Laws* on the types and kinds of punishment and justice meted out to perpetrators of crimes reveals that the measures of punishment had become much more refined and specific. There were many kinds of punishments, for example, after the suspect was arrested, all the livestock animals that the culprit had stolen was returned in full to the rightful owner and depending on the severity of the crime, the guilty person was given sentence, which were numerous and of different types. It transpires that a person who had stolen a certain number of livestock animals was made to recompense the victim, and if someone had stolen horses, camels, sheep and goats, then the suspect received harsher punishment, from flogging to recompensing with many more numbers of livestock than the person had actually stolen. Sometimes, the thief's family was also punished, as that family's property was confiscated and distributed among the victims and for more serious crimes, the suspect's fingers and ears were cut off, and he could even be condemned to death by execution. However, during this period, the number and kinds of punishments became fewer as alternative forms of punishment were given. More than condemning a guilty person to death, the convict's personal household properties were confiscated; he/she was made a servant in the house of the victim, which was beneficial to the country as well as the nobles and princes.

Let us take a few examples related to thievery as defined in the *Mongol-Oirad Laws*. "Dismember one finger of a person who is found guilty of stealing one of the following: the traditional Mongol style of knife, arrow, file (tool), tether, hobble, leather strap, bridle, hammer, halter, high quality hat, bedding, slacks, pair of scissors, iron stirrups, wooden saddle, overcoat, mantle, felt saddle-cloth, crupper, gown, belt, cotton sash, encasement for armour and helmet, pole axe, dairy produce, a whole sheep mutton, a household *del* gown, saw, intricately carved wooden bowl, pincers, high quality rings, bait, saddle cloth etc. If the convicted person desires that his punishment is revoked, he would instead have to give in compensation two large cattle, such as a horse, a cow, or a camel and two sheep."

Later, a number of changes and amendments were made to the *Mongol-Oirad Laws*. In this respect, special mention can be made of the will and decrees of Galdan Boshogt Khan. It is believed that there are at least two amended versions of the *Mongol-Oirad Laws*; however, the date when the first version of the amendment was adopted is uncertain. This version of the Laws included prohibitionary provisions outlawing people from roaming around the land aimlessly without coming under the jurisdiction of any one administrative unit, and also consolidated the principles of serfdom, and renewed administrative divisions. It can be assumed that these amendments including decrees were inserted in the Laws immediately after Galdan Boshogt became the Khan. The first decree passed by Galdan Boshogt Khan included rules and regulations for reforming the administrative actions and work methods for combating thievery, resolving civilian cases, and addressing the issue of loans and dues.

Galdan Boshogt Khan passed his second decree in 1678, according to which the Khan urged an end to bribery and corruption, especially inducing or influencing judges, resolving the dispute between the Oirads and the Khotons (*Turkic ethnic group of people. Tr.*), regulating family relationships between them, and ways to settle their litigations. The amendments made to the *Mongol-Oirad Laws* by Prince Donrovrash (Dondogdash) of the Torghuts cover a wide range of issues, such as, strengthening the State and government, regulating religious ideology, standing up to alien enemies, issues related to envoys and relay service, rules and procedures for settling cases of thievery, dues and loans, combating fugitives and deserters, witnesses in criminal and civil cases, the issue of ethics and morality, game hunting, as well as livestock animals. And so the *Mongol-Oirad Laws* are an extremely valuable legal source that reflect and represent the complete stage of development of laws and legislation among the Mongols in this period.

5 The Administrative Structure and the Laws of Mongolia under Manchurian Rule (17th Century–20th Century)

1 Historical Summary

Disputes and power struggles among the Mongol nobles and princes weakened the once powerful Mongols, while the Manchus, descendants of a sedentary farming people known as the Jürchen, a Tungusic people who lived around the north-eastern region of China, were becoming stronger towards the close of the 16th century. In 1575, Nurhaci proclaimed himself the Khan of the Manchus and started forcibly bringing into his fold the neighbouring tribes and ethnic groups of people. And in 1616 he founded the so-called Great Golden State (Great Jin Empire). The Manchus rid themselves of the Ming Empire, and their might and strength grew literally day by day as they became an aggressive power ready to swallow their neighbours.

Given the circumstances, Ligden Khan of the Mongols started looking for allies to counter the ever-strengthening Manchus and thus in 1619 he entered into an alliance with the Ming Dynasty. However, the latter was pursuing an insidious policy to set the Mongols against the Manchus for its own gain. Although Ligden Khan had the lofty ambition of uniting all the Mongols against the Manchus, he failed to garner the support of the leaders of the Khorchin, Dörvöd (Dörbet), Jalair and Gorlos tribes, who instead surrendered to the Manchus. Ligden Khan undertook a failed punitive expedition against the Manchus and fled westward to die in 1634. His son Eiji Khan fought the Manchu soldiers who had pursued his father, but his army could not withstand the powerful army of the Manchus and surrendered to them in 1635. Tsogt Taiji, a noble from northern Khalkha, was the only Khalkha to join Ligden Khan against the Manchus.

In 1636, the Mongol nobility of Inner Mongolia held their assembly where they proclaimed Abakhai (Hong Taiji) of the Manchus as the Khan of the Mongols. Soon after, other tribes of Inner Mongolia acceded to the Manchus and this is how Inner Mongolia came under alien occupation.

Some important Mongol Khalkha nobles, when they were faced head-on with foreign aggression, joined forces and sought ways and means to fight against the Manchus. They were also supported by the Oirad nobility. To illustrate, in 1640. the Khalkha and Oirad nobility gathered for an assembly at the initiative of Baatar Hong Taijing of the Oirads, where they adopted the *Mongol-Oirad Laws*.

Important Khalkha nobility, with the objective of ensuring the spiritual unity of the people, proclaimed Zanabazar, the son of Tüsheet Khan Gombodorj, as the head of the Yellow Hat Sect of the Khalkha Mongol. He became famous in history as the First Bogd Jebzundamba Khutugtu or Öndör Gegeen. Simultaneously, efforts were made to win over some nobles of Inner Mongolia and even to establish links with Russia. However, two very important Khalkha statesmen – Tüsheet Khan Gombodrj and Setsen Khan Sholoi, who formed the backbone of the above policy initiatives – passed away in the 1650s only to be succeeded by an unreliable young nobleman. This had a pernicious impact on the political situation of the Khalkha and Oirad Mongols, which sparked off a crisis in their camp. As was mentioned earlier, the Manchus were conducting a policy of pitting the Khalkha and the Oirads against each other to prevent them from uniting. The dispute between Tüsheet Khan Chakhundorj and Galdan Boshogt of the Oirads exacerbated and flared into a war in 1688 between the Khalkha Mongols and Züün Gar (Dzungar). Galdan Boshogt emerged victorious in the war and Tüsheet Khan Chakhundorj and important Khalkha nobility led by Öndör Gegeen became dependent dignitaries of the Manchu Qing Dynasty.

In May 1691, an assembly was held at Dolon Nuur (*of Seven Lakes, which today is a town and the county seat of Duolun County, Xilin Gol League in the Inner Mongolia Autonomous region, China. Tr.*) to integrate the Khalkha Mongols into the Manchu (Qing) dynasty, there Enkh Amgalan (Kangxi Emperor) of the Qing dynasty passed an edict wherein he decreed that the Khalkha Mongol should be administered in accordance with the Collected Statutes of the Qing dynasty (Da Qing Hui Dian) and their precedents that were then introduced in 49 banners of Inner Mongolia. In this manner, Mongolia was overtaken by the Manchus primarily for two reasons: first, the two Mongols of Outer and Inner Mongolia had utterly disregarded their vital national interests; and second, they were at conflict with each other, and consequently, they became easy prey for alien forces.

From among the Mongols, the Züün Gar (Dzungar) Khanate remained the last stronghold of the independence of the Mongols as such. After Galdan Boshogt, his successors Tseveendash (1679–1727), who was the Khanate of the Züün Gar and his immediate successor Galdantseren at times stood firmly against the Manchus, and when circumstances demanded, they made friendship with them. However, after the death of Galdantseren, the struggle for the throne took a nasty turn and the Mongol khans never came to terms with each other. Finally, in the seventh month of 1755, the Züün Gar (Dzungar) Khanate was completely overtaken by the Qing dynasty. And so the last bastion of Mongolia's independence and sovereignty collapsed and all the Mongol tribes came under the direct rule of the Manchus.

The Mongols did not sit, arms folded, under the oppression and exploitation of the Manchus. They continued to fight for their freedom and independence. Among such struggles, the most important and major armed resistances were masterminded and led by Amarsanaa of the Oirads and Chingünjav of the Khotgoids and continued from 1755 to 1758. But the Mongol resistance was suppressed in a most brutal manner by means of arms by the Manchu lords.

Between the 20's of the 17th century and the second half of the 18th century, the Manchus brought under their central administrative control strategically important Mongol territories and lands, which put an end to the possibility for the Mongols to not only engage amongst themselves, but also with other peoples and tribes; and in general, the Manchus pursued a policy of turning Mongolia into a benefactor ally. However, starting from the mid-nineteenth century, the nature of this policy changed and by the twentieth century the Manchus proclaimed the so-called "new government policy" under which the Qing dynasty set out on a mission to sinicise the Mongols.

2 Administrative System and its Organisational Set-up

2.1 *The Manchu (Qing) Emperor*

When Mongolia was under the Manchu occupation, the supreme lord of the Mongols was the Manchu (Qing) Emperor. In 1636, the Manchus occupied southern Mongolia and Ambakhai Khan or Daiqing Gurun was proclaimed the Emperor of the Mongols. Before him, Nurhaci Taizu (1616–1626), the Exalted from the Heaven, ruled the later Jin Dynasty for ten years, followed by Setsen the Clever Taizun's (1627–1635) eight-year rule, and 19 years after the foundation of their dynasty, the Manchu brought the Mongols under their submission.

Below is a list of Manchu Khans who ruled over Mongolia:

1. The Grand Progenitor Nurhaci Taizu (1636–1643), who ruled for seven years;
2. The peacemaker Xidu Khan (1644–1661), who ruled for 16 years;
3. Enkh-Amgalan Xinzu Khan (Kangxi Emperor), who ruled for 61 years (1662–1722);
4. Harmonious Justice Xidun khan (Yongzheng Emperor), who ruled for 12 years from 1723 to 1735;

5 The Supporter of Heaven Govzun Khan (Qianlong Emperor), who ruled for 59 years from 1736–1795;
6 Saishaalt Yüroolt Rezun Khan (Jiaqing Emperor), who ruled for 24 years from 1796 to 1820;
7 The Shining State Xaon Zun Khan (Daoguang Emperor), who ruled for twenty-nine years from 1821 to 1850;
8 The Plentiful Wen Zun Khan (Xiafeng Emperor, 1851–1861), who was in power for ten years;
9 The Total Renovator Muzun Khan (Tongzhi Emperor), who ruled for 12 years from 1862–1874;
10 The Glorious Succession Dei Zun Khan (Guangxu Emperor), who was in power from 1875 to 1908, ruling for 33 years; and,
11 Proclamation of Unity Xuan Tong Emperor (1909–1911), who was the last Manchu Emperor who ruled for two years.[1] They were all the supreme lords of the Mongols.

The *Emperors of the Manchu Qing dynasty* were the masters over the lands of the Mongols, and they distributed territorial banners to the governor nobles, and extended to them successive rights of possession of these lands. The Manchu Emperors also considered the Mongol nobility as their benefactor allies and accordingly, the Mongol nobilities were decorated with titles and privileges, granted hereditary rights, the right to dismiss officials, to establish provinces and banners, demarcating their territories, passing codes of laws etc. Thus they held supreme power over the Mongols, who would grant permissions and favours only by signing with a red brush.

2.2 *Administrative Changes in Inner Mongolia*

At an assembly of the Inner Mongolian nobility, held in 1636, the Manchu Emperor passed a decision on the institution of an administrative centre and local bodies for enforcement in Inner Mongolia. A so-called Central Office of Mongolian and Tibetan Affairs, known as *Mongol Yaman* or *Zongli Yamen* was established. Not very long after its establishment, it was expanded and renamed to *Regulations of Lifan Yuan* or *The Board for the Administration of Outlying Regions* (The Board) with one Prime minister, two Vice Ministers overseeing the matters of the Eastern and Western wings, and the Ministers were all of Manchu origin, and in addition, a new post, that of a Mongol Minister of the Wings was instituted. This institution, on the one hand, was responsible for conducting a policy overseeing the domestic administrative affairs of Inner Mongolia, and on the other hand,

1 J. Ölzii, *Brief History of the Manchu Race*, Ulaanbaatar, 1995, p. 32.

enforcing a policy viz the Khalkha Mongols, Tibetans and Hoh Nuur. By 1661, the Board's status had been elevated and brought on a par with that of the six central ministries. In other words, the Board assumed the right to pass edicts on matters related to Mongolia on behalf of the central government of the Manchu Qing dynasty.

In 1675, after the revolt of the Chakhar Mongols against the Manchus was quelled, they were divided into 8 banners, East and West wings and put under the control of the Mongol Amban (*Manchu: "Minister"* or civilian governor, *Tr.*) residing in Peking. The Qing dynasty installed Manchu commanders at Hoh Hot in 1693 and in Suiyuan in 1737, and appointed an *Amban* at Khölönbuir (*During the Qing dynasty, 1644–1912, Khölönbuir was part of Heilongjiang province. Tr.*) in 1773, the overall command was given to the imperial commanders in Heilong (Black Dragon) River and Shenqin (Mukden).

The Manchus tore apart the 24 *aimags* of Inner Mongolia and replaced them first with 24 banners, which were later reorganised into the following 6 *chuulgans* or leagues.

1 The Jirim league, which included 6 Khorchin, Jalaid, Dörvöd and 2 Gorlos banners, a total of 10 banners;
2 The Josotu league, which included 3 Khorchin and 2 Tümed banners;
3 The Juu Uda league had a total of 11 banners, including the Aokhan, Naiman, Ar Khorchin, Khishigten (Kesigten), Züün Khalkha, and 2 banners each of Baarin, Jaruud and Onginuud;
4 The Shilingol (Xilin) league had 10 banners, such as 2 each of Üjemchin, Khuuchid, Sönöd, Abga and Abganar banners;
5 The Ulaan Chab league included 6 banners, including 1 banner each of Dörvöm Khüükhed, Myy Myangan and Baruun Khalkha, and 3 Urad banners;
6 The Ikh Juu league, which included the 7 Ordos leagues.[2]

Each *chuulgan* had a chief, and a number of deputies, and so *chuulgan* offices were set up. The *chuulgan* convened once every three years to discuss and consider the grievances and cases of the banner subjects.

The *aimags* of Inner Mongolia, who had submitted to the Manchus without any kind of resistance, were made "Outer affiliated" banners; their rulers were given hereditary rights. However, those Mongol *aimags* that resisted the Manchus were turned into "Domestic affiliated" banners, which were governed not through hereditary right but through either military or civilian governors called the *Amban*.

2 *Brief History of the Mongol People*, Hoh Hot, 1988, p. 101.

2.3 *Administrative Structure of Outer Mongolia*

This consisted of the central military and administrative body, territorial units and the *aimags, banners* and the *shabi* (means "disciple" in Mongolian) of the khutugtus.

DIAGRAM 7 Administrative structure of the Manchu Qin Empires in Khalkha Mongolia (1691–1754)

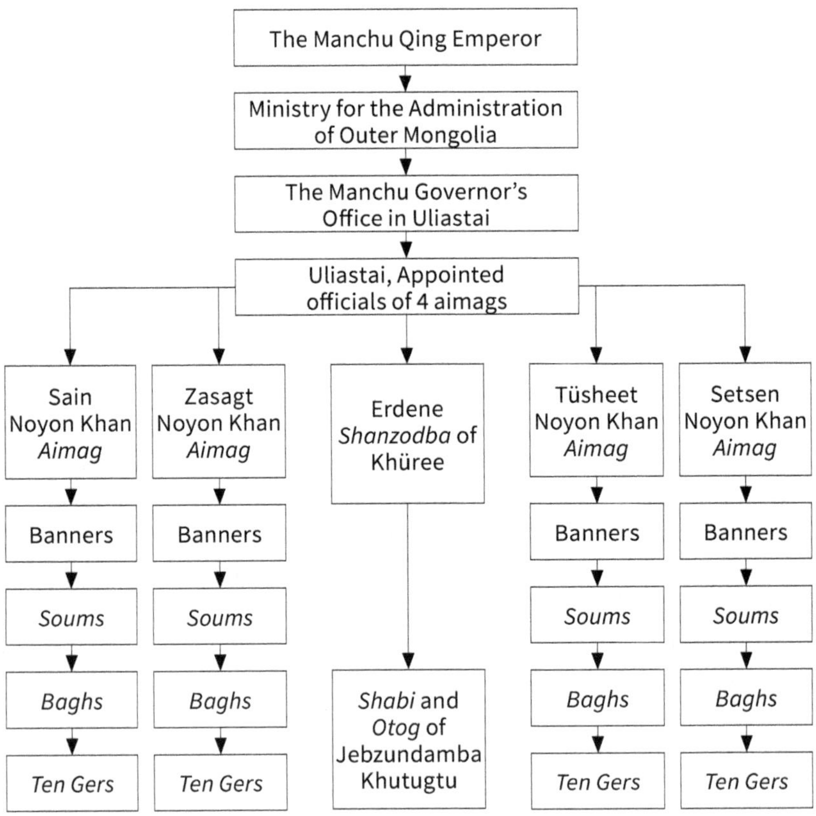

The *Board (Ministry) for the Administration of Outlying Regions* was the central State body of the Manchu Qing dynasty that administered Mongolia. It was headquartered in Peking and consisted of the *Board for National Minority Affairs, Court of Territorial Affairs, Board for the Administration of Outlying Regions, Office for Relations with Principalities, Office of Barbarian Control, Office of Mongolian and Tibetan Affairs,* and *Court of Colonial Affairs.* The Ministry administered Outer Mongolia through the military governor in Uliastai, and the civil governors in Ikh Khüree and Khovd (Khobdo). In certain cases, they would directly engage with and manage the *aimag*

chuulgan. The Board was responsible for conferring on the governors and *taiji* imperial titles and privileges, the right to their inheritance, overseeing the contribution of tributes and corvee, organising official ceremonies, enforcing laws and making changes and amendments to them, and reporting to the emperor etc.

2.4 *The Office of the Uliastai Military Governor*

This was the highest office of the Manchu Qing Dynasty with special authority that was set up in Outer Mongolia. As it was headquartered in the town of Uliastai the governor was also called the "Uliastai Governor" or the "Uliastain *Amban* Governor." A letter sent by the Uliastai Military Governor to the Setsen Khan *aimag chuulgan* mentions that the "Uliastai Governor... shall consider important matters related to the Outlying Regions, administer the military preparedness of the four *aimags,* supervise the sentries of relay stations, arrest and investigate fugitives and escapees."[3]

In the beginning, a few Mongols were appointed as the Governors of Uliastai, but later on they were replaced entirely by Manchus. The advisory officials under the Uliastai Governor included both the Manchus as well as Mongols.

The Office of the Uliastai Governor had four departments, including the Internal Affairs Department (Dorgi), Military Affairs Department (Chokhai), Financial and Administrative Department (Buigan), and the Mongol *Jurgan* Department to administer and supervise the banners. Mostly Manchu and Chinese people worked in the Office of the Uliastai Governor besides a handful of Mongols, who were primarily low-ranking officials and clerks.

The Office of the Uliastai Governor directly administered the entire so-called outlying regions of Outer Mongolia until the establishment of the Ikh Khüree and Khovd ministries, after which the affairs of Zasagt Khan and Sain Noyon *aimags,* as well as the Uriankhais of Khövsgöl Nuur Lake and Tagna (Tannu) came under his direct jurisdiction. Nevertheless, the higher office that administered the affairs of Outer Mongolia continued to remain and function in general.

2.5 *The Ministry of Ikh Khüree*

In the beginning there were no Manchu ministers (*ambans*) in Ikh Khüree; however, under the pretext of providing services to the Bogd Khan Manchu aides and clerks were appointed, whose primary duty was to keep an

3 Central National Archives of Mongolia, Fonds-2, Series-16, p. 183.

overall supervision. Later in 1758 a Mongol minister and then in 1761 a Manchu minister was appointed and subsequently an office of the minister (ministry) was set up. Ikh Khüree's Mongol minister in the beginning had extra authority and rights, but later the Manchu minister was given extra authority. He would generally manage all official matters to take the upper hand in the line of authority. An edict of the Manchu Qing Emperor defined the Manchu minister as "an official, appointed under the Emperor's decree to Khüree who would manage all matters." By the late nineteenth and early twentieth century, the Ikh Khüree minister's office had more than 170 staff and had become a bulky bureaucracy with its annual budget topping 10 thousand *taels* of silver.[4] Mongol officials and clerks who served in the office would work for a period of 4 months alternately from the two eastern *aimags*.

Tüsheet Khan, the minister of Ikh Khüree, besides managing the affairs of the Setsen Khan *aimag* and the *Shabi* of Bogd Jebzundamba Khutugtu, also managed the commanders in Ikh Khüree and the Khiagt *jurgan*, and he was also responsible for matters dealing with Russia.

2.6 *The Office of the Manchu Minister in Khovd (Khobdo)*

The Manchu Qing Empire, with the objective of administering the government affairs of the Mongols in the outlying region of Khovd, opened an office of the Manchu minister in Khovd In 1762, which according to an edict of the Manchu Emperor was defined as "The Minister to manage affairs as appointed by a decree to Khovd." In common language, the minister was better known as the "*Khovd Amban*" or the "Khovd Minister." This minister had such departments as the Military *jurgan*, Finance *jurgan*, Mongol affairs *jurgan* and the Secretariat.

This minister had the overall responsibility of administering government matters of the two Dörvöd *aimag*, 7 banners of Altai Uriankhai, 2 Torguud banners, and one banner each of Zakhchin, Miangad and the Ööld. The treasuries of the 4 Khalkha and 2 Dörvöd *aimags* functioned under the Khovd minister, and they would be responsible for collecting dues and corvees from the relevant departments and the population.

2.7 *The Office of the Commissioners in Ikh Khüree and Khiagt (Kyaktha)*

The Manchu Emperor, for the purpose of administering matters of the traders and merchants in the key trade and commercial centres in Khalkha Mongolia, set up its own administrative offices in Ikh Khüree in 1719 and in Khiagt in 1727.

---

4 *History of the MPR*, Three Volumes, Book One, Ulaanbaatar, 1968, p. 182.

These administrative offices were called the "Khüree *jurgan* commander's office" and the "Khiagt *jurgan* commander's office," but given the duties they were performing, they were better known as the "Khüree commissioner's office" and "Khiagt commissioner's office." They were not only responsible for administering and managing the affairs of the Chinese people, but were also administering justice in disputes between the Manchus, Chinese and Mongols. The commissioner's offices employed a number of officials, including the commander of a *jurgan*, bannerman, minister, clerk, military officer etc.

2.8 *Aimags*

From history we know that the term *aimag* originated very early on. During the period after Mongolia was occupied by the Manchus the term *aimag* became the name of a large administrative division. The 7 Khalkha banners that existed from the mid-sixteenth to late seventeenth centuries were divided into East and West wings, Tüsheet Khan, Setsen Khan and Zasagt Khan *aimags*, which came under the jurisdiction of three important noble princes.

Abatai Sain Noyon Khan of the Khalkhas (1554–1588), on the instructions of Tümen Zasagt Khan, visited Hoh Hot in 1577 where he met with the Third Dalai Lama Sodnomjamts (Sonam Gyatso in Tibetan) and was converted into Yellow Sect Buddhism, and the two agreed to spread the Yellow Sect in the land of the Khalkhas. In response, the Dalai Lama gave him the title of *Ochirai Batu Tüsheet Khan* and this is how he was better known in history as the Khalkha Tüsheet Khan. Not very long after, another prince of the Khalkha East wing, Sholoi (1577–1662), the grandson of Amin-Dorai, the fifth son of prince Gersenj, proclaimed himself the Khan and became popular as Setsen Khan. Also, Laikhor, an influential prince of the West wing, proclaimed himself the Khan and he became known in history as the Zasagt Khan. In this manner, three Khans were almost simultaneously proclaimed in Khalkha and started administering the Khalkha Mongols.

At an assembly, which was held in 1691 at Dolon Nuur (Seven Lakes), Outer Mongolia was made a subject under the Manchus and three *aimags* were formed that were put under the administration of the aforementioned three Khalkha Khans, which were called the Tüsheet Khan *aimag*, Setsen Khan *aimag* and the Zasagt Khan *aimag*. In 1692, in accordance with the military policy of the Manchu Qing Empire, the Tüsheet Khan *aimag* was made into the Northern post of the Khalkhas, the Setsen Khan *aimag* into the Eastern post and the Zasagt Khan *aimag* the Western post of the Khalkhas.

Recognising the merit of Chin Wang Dashdondov in his war against the Oirads, in 1725 Sain Noyon gave him 19 banners of the Tüsheet Khan *aimag*, which was turned into another new *aimag*. The new *aimag* was named the Sain Noyon *aimag* and was made into the Central post of the Khalkha, and this is how there came to exist four Khalkha *aimags*.

Administratively, an *aimag* consisted of banners and *shabi* of a recognised khutugtu carrying a seal. In this respect, Tüsheet Khan *aimag* had 20 banners, Setsen Khan *aimag* had 23 banners and 1 khutugtu *shabi*, Zasagt Khan *aimag* had 19 banners and 3 *shabi*, while Sain Noyon *aimag* had 24 banners and 7 khutugtu *shabi*.[5]The four Khalkha *aimags*, in terms of their human and livestock populations, were relatively similar.

After the Manchus occupied the Oirads, the Dörvöds were further divided into East and West wings, two new *aimags* were created and put under the jurisdiction of the Khalkhas. The East wing was named the Dalai Khan *Aimag*, and the West wing as Ünen Zorigt Khan *Aimag*. And so Outer Mongolia had six *aimags*. Apart from this, the Altai, Khövsgöl Lake and Tagna (Tannu) Uriankhais, Ööld, Miangat, Zakhchin and Torguuds did not come under the jurisdiction of any *aimag* and became independent administrative posts.

In 1728, the Manchus turned each Khalkha *aimag* into *chuulgans* (leagues, assemblies) and determined the place where they would meet. In the beginning, the *aimag* Khan was appointed by an order by the *aimag's chuulgan* chief, but later this practice was changed, and any one governing prince of a given *aimag* was appointed to the post. This drastically lowered the power and authority of the *aimag* Khan, who became no different from the other governing princes who came under the jurisdiction of the *chuulgan* chief.

The places where the *chuulgans* were to meet were given names after lakes and rivers in the area, for example, the *chuulgan* of Tüsheet Khan *aimag* was called the "Khan Uul *chuulgan*," the *chuulgan* of Setsen Khan *aimag* was called the "Kherlen Bars *chuulgan*," the Zasagt Khan *aimag chuulgan* "Binderiya Lake *chuulgan*," and the Sain Noyon Khan *aimag chuulgan* was called the "Tsetsergel *chuulgan*." But the 2 Dörvöd *aimags* were divided into Eastern and Western wings, and so they were called the Eastern and Western wing *chuulgan* of the *aimag*.

An *aimag chuulgan* was a consultative decision-make body, which considered all matters related to the given *aimag* under the direct control of the Manchu Governor and the *amban*. The convening of a *chuulgan* was

5 Ts. Sodnomdagva, *Government and Administrative Structure of Outer Mongolia Under Manchu Rule, (1692–1911)*, Ulaanbaatar, 1961, pp. 47–48.

termed as "the coming together of the *chuulgan* or the convocation." According to the law, a *chuulgan* was supposed to convene once every three years. An *aimag chuulgan* was chaired by the chief of the *chuulgan,* and the commander. Apart from them, the *chuulgan* was attended by all the ruler princes of all the banners. Other officials and clerks, who had come as a part of the ruler prince's entourage, could neither take part in the deliberations, not partake in the decision-making process, as their role was restricted primarily to giving advice.

A report on the registration of soldiers was submitted for consideration to an *aimag chuulgan,* based on which the number of relay services, sentry households, and soldiers that each banner had to provide was decided upon and the distribution was done equally and in a fair manner. The *chuulgan* also decided on the demarcation of the territory of the banners, and taking decisions about settling disputes etc. If there were matters on which the *chuulgan* chief or the commanders were in no position to take decisions, they were discussed and a decision was taken on the basis of consensus. A *chuulgan* did not pass any special resolutions, as the rule was to only register and record the issues on the agenda and the manner in which they were addressed. At times all the four Khalkha *aimags* would convene for the *chuulgan,* or two *aimags* would meet for the *chuulgan* to distribute evenly the dues that were to be paid by the *aimags,* resolve territorial disputes, identify the next reincarnation of Bogd Jebzundamba etc., that is, matters of common interest and concern to all the *aimags.*

Failure to attend the *chuulgan* was met with serious disciplinary action. The Mongol Code says that "Should the governor, *wang, beil, beis, güng, taiji* and their son-in-law not attend the *chuulgan* when it's announced … their ^ month wages would be deducted. Those taiji and son-in-law who do not have a salary, shall be obliged to submit 10 horses in punishment, and for each day of absence, additional one horse has to be given as penalty." Even other officials who accompanied the Governor to the *chuulgan* were fined as well.

The chief of the *chuulgan,* apart from performing general administrative duties in the given *aimag,* was also responsible for carrying out judicial functions.

Each *aimag* also had special officials overseeing military matters and they were called the "assistant *aimag* commander" and "Hebei," who directly reported to the Uliastai commander and enjoyed similar rights with the *chuulgan* chiefs. Every *aimag* commander had his own seal and banner. The *aimag chuulgan* chief, in special cases, also had the right to directly engage with the Board (Ministry).

During the period of Manchu occupation, a non-traditional form of office called the *jasaa* was established in a number of places in Outer Mongolia, where the governors and officials of the four Khalkha *aimags* would serve alternately for a period of 3 to 6 months, hence the term *jasaa,* which in Manchu meant "a shift." For example, there existed the so-called "*Aimag Da* and commander's *jasaa,*" "Permanent and Temporary *jasaa* at Khüree," "The Uliastai four aimag *jasaa,*" and "Khalkha *jasaa* of Khovd."

The "*Aimag Da* and commander's *jasaa*" was also called the external *jasaa* of the *chuulgan* chief and the external *jasaa* of the commander. These *jasaa* were obliged to carry out the orders of the chief of the *aimag chuulgan* and the commander as they were central executive bodies. Some of the *aimags* did not have a central settlement and the concerned officials would follow the *chuulgan* chief and the commander to carry out their official duties and functions.

The so-called permanent Khüree *jasaa* was set up for the purpose of administering various matters related to people from other *aimags* who had moved and settled in Khüree, and it was staffed with representatives of Tüsheet Khan and Setsen Khan *aimags* and their prime duty lay in speedily disseminating the decisions of the Manchu minister and implementing them in their respective *aimags.* This permanent *jasaa,* as compared to the *Da,* and commander *jasaa* had restricted rights and responsibilities, and had fewer staff members. At a later period, when the number of migrants moving to Khüree from Zasagt Khan and Sain Noyon Khan *aimags* increased significantly, similar *jasaa* were also established there. Such a *jasaa* was also permanent and temporary, but the *jasaa* established in these two *aimags* had fewer duties and responsibilities as compared to the aforemenioned four *jasaa.*

The *jasaa* of the Uliastai four *aimags* had the duty of enforcing the orders of the Uliastai *amban* and commander in the four *aimags* and it was an important and responsible organ of the *aimag chuulgan.* Since the commanders of the four *aimags,* after receiving their respective seals, alternately staffed the *jasaa* for a period of three months each, and so they were also called the "commanders of the Uliastai *jasaa.*" The *jasaa* commander, on behalf of their respective *aimags* administered the *jasaa* of the four *aimags* and were responsible for managing the census of the military-age males and the sentries for the relay stations. They were also given the responsibility of tending the select breeds of livestock of the Manchus, and livestock belonging to the *amban* in Uliastai.

The Khalkha *jasaa* of Khovd was a unique *jasaa* that had the responsibility of carrying out various functions of the Manchu rulers on behalf of the four *aimags.* The governor and the official of this *jasaa* were appointed alternately from Tüsheet Khan, Zasagt Khan and Sain Noyon *aimags*, but Setsen Khan *aimag*, which was distantly located, was relieved of these duties. The *jasaa* was responsible for managing the crops, ensuring that the relay stations were adequately staffed, taking care of the officially-registered livestock animals, and acting as messenger, bringing notices to relevant *aimags* and banners. Having created such a managerial and organisational network in Outer Mongolia, the Manchus made it possible for them to politically suppress the Mongols who bore the brunt of all their spending.

2.9 *Banners*

In order to establish their suppressive rule in Mongolia, the Manchus borrowed the traditional administrative models of the Mongols with the military and administrative set-up at its centre. They divided Khalkha Mongolia into seven "Khalkha *banners*," which were given over for administration and management to the seven sons of Gersenj, the sons of Batmönkh Dayan Khan. Later in 1665, one more banner was added bringing the total Khalkha *banners* to eight and this is how Khalkha Mongol was divided into four *aimags* and eight *banners* during the rule of the Manchu Qing dynasty.

In 1691, a great convention was held at Dolon Nuur (Seven Lakes) where the Khalkha Mongol *banners* were divided into 34 smaller *banners*, which were divided further for administration by the Tüsheet Khan, Setsen Khan and Zasagt Khan Khalkha *aimags*. In 1725, when the Sain Noyon *aimag* was being established, the entire Khalkha Mongol was divided into 12 *banners*. The division of the *banners* into smaller and many units was a part of the vicious policy pursued by the Manchu Qing Empire to prevent the Mongols from politically rallying and uniting. This process in principle was completed by the second half of the 18th century and the Khalkha Mongols and the Dörvöds had a total of 102 *banners*. If we add to this the 23 *banners* of the Khövsgöl Lake and Tannu Uriankhais, as well as the Khovd frontier region, there were 125 *banners* in all.[6] However, the Dariganga, an Eastern Mongol sub-group, carried on with their responsibility of herding select livestock animals, primarily horses, of the Manchu Emperor, and they were under the jurisdiction of the special *amban* in Zhangjiakou (Kalgan). It did not have any *banner*, but had a unique administrative set-up called "The Five Hands of Dariganga."

6 Ts. Sodnomdagva, *Government and Administrative Structure of Outer Mongolia under the Manchu Rule, (1692–1911)*, Ulaanbaatar, 1961, p. 74.

DIAGRAM 8 Structural set-up of *banners*

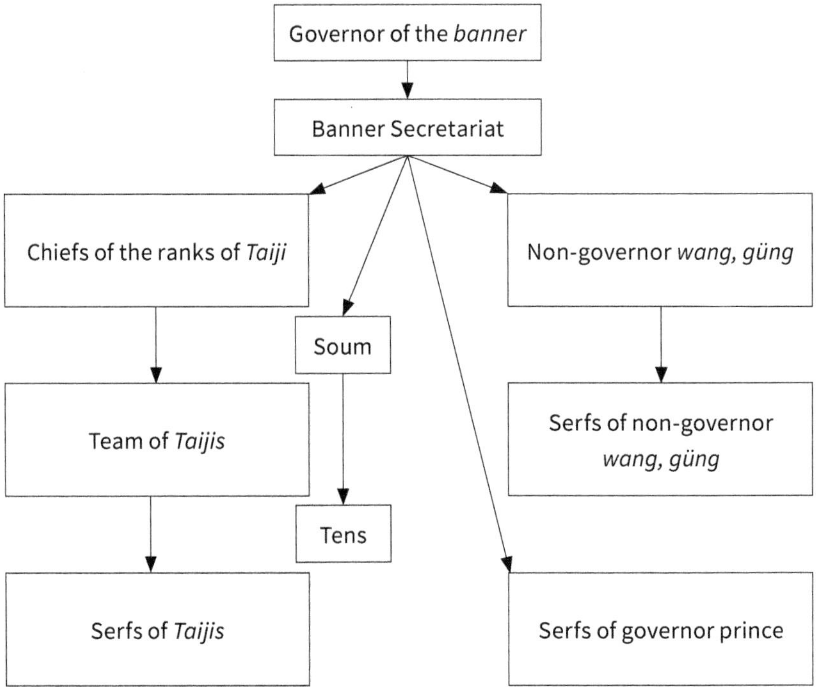

The size and status of the population and livestock herds of the *banners* were relatively non-identical. As of 1858, Prince Dashdorj's *banner*, which was the smallest *banner* of Tüsheet Khan *aimag*, had 36 households with more than 160 people, more than 5,000 heads of livestock, while the largest of the *banners* in the *aimag*, that of Prince Baldandorj had more than 5,400 households or over 25,000 people and 15.7 thousand livestock animals. According to a census carried out in 1858, one *banner* of Tüsheet Khan *aimag* on average had more than 1,250 households, that is, more than 6,130 people and more than 12,350 livestock animals.[7]

The *banners*, which were administrative-military units, were ruled by hereditary *Governor Princes*, appointed by the Manchu Emperor, and with the support of the secretariat they would administer the respective banner and also manage judicial matters. The Governor Princes, as a rule, normally had the title of *Wang* or Prince, *Beil* or Prince of the Third Rank, *Beis* or Prince of the Fourth Rank and *Güng* or Prince of the Sixth Rank (in Manchu times). There were cases when some *banners* did not have ranked

7 Central National Archives of Mongolia, Fonds-13, Series-1.

Governor Princes, who were called the "Governor of the first rank *Taiji*." The sons of the Governor Princes would succeed their father. If the Governor Prince did not have a successor son, the ranks and the tiltes were handed over either to close family related *Taiji* or the son of a *Taiji* would be adopted to succeed him. The *banner* governor was directly accountable to the chief of the *aimag chuulgan* and the commander.

The Governor Prince had an office composed of low-ranking officials and clerks, who would assist him in all the daily business of the *banner*. Such an office was called "The Office of the *Banner*." The office had one assistant called the *tuslagch*, a managing commander called *zakhiragch zangi*, a so-called *meeren* commander (a banner official below the rank of the assistant *tuslagch*) and an officer in the relay service called the *zalan zangi* in Manchurian, one permanent *tuslagch*, 4 to 8 intern clerks and 2 courier messengers called the *takhar*. Depending on the size of the *banner*, the banner offices would have one or two less or more officials working.

The *Banner Tuslagch* was the second highest rank after the Governor Prince, who was the chief of the *banner* office, which is why mainly close relatives of the Board's Governor Prince were appointed to this post. The *Tuslagch* oversaw all the officials and clerks of the *jasaa* and he would act as a proxy when the *banner* governor was either appointed to another post or during his leave of absence. Some of the bigger *banners* had at least two assistant *tuslagchs*.

The Commander or *Zakhiragch* was responsible for the administrative matters of the *banner*. A commander was called *Zakhiragch Zangi*. As mentioned earlier, a *Zangi* in Manchurian meant the leader, the head, an executive.

The *Meeren* was responsible for the military affairs of the *banner*. The *Zalan* was also responsible for military affairs, but he was more or less an assistant to the *Meeren*. In the Manchu language *meeren* actually meant "the shoulder", and so this signified that the *Zalan* would be accountable to the *Meeren*

The basic unit within a *banner* was called the *soum*. In 1691 when the Manchus introduced the notion of *banner* and *soum* in Outer Mongolia, the *soum* became the primary administrative unit in that *banner*. The *soum*, in terms of its organisational set-up, was basically a combination of military and administrative units taken together. According to Manchu laws, a *soum* was formed if there were at least 150 young men of military age. Men between the ages of 18 and 60, with the exception of lamas and shabi serfs, must be considered soldiers. If there were less than 150 young men of military age a *soums* would be created, but it would be called a semi-*soum* and it had a special term called the *Khondog*, which in Manchu meant half a *soum*. The *soums* did not have their own names, but they would rather be called after the commander *Zangi*. A *soum* had the following three types of officials: a *Zangi*, an official called in Manchu *Boshog Khünd* and a messenger called the *Khöögch*. The *Zangi* was the head of the *soum*. The number of *soums* under the jurisdiction of the *banners* was never the same. There was another official called the Zizalan Zangi, who was responsible for administering six *soums* at one time, especially in those *banners* that had numerous *soums*.

The *soum* was further sub-divided into a unit of tens, and this unit called "The Tens" was headed by a chief, who was appointed from among the ten men-folk in that given *soum*.

The *Taiji*, according to their rank, were in charge of the serfs, and they were not organised into *soums* or *gers*, but were formed into a special *otog* or a group. After 1705, a foreman was appointed and these foremen were directly accountable to the Office of the *Banner*.[8]

DIAGRAM 9 Banner Office and Its Secretariat

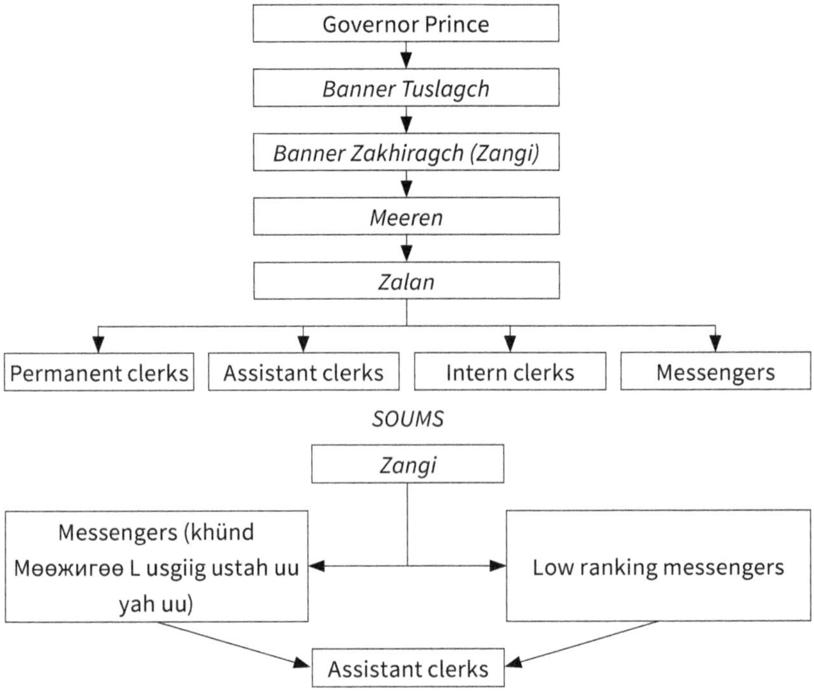

8 *History of the MPR*, Three Volumes, Book One, Ulaanbaatar, 1968, pp. 177–178.

2.10 *The* Shabi *(Ecclesiastical Estate) of Jebzundamba Khutugtu*

In 1639, when an assembly of the Khalkha princes was held at a place called *Shiree Tsagaan Nuur* (Shiree White Lake), many nobles and princes contributed their subjects to Öndör Gegeen or the First Bogd Jebzundamba Khutugtu, and these subjects led to the formation of the Bogd Khan's ecclesiastical estate called the *shabi*. After submission to the Manchu Qing dynasty, the size of the population of the *shabi* multiplied. For example, in 1710, the Bogd Khan's *shabi* had 3,786 households with a population of 17,000, which in 1825 increased to 16,653 households and 83,687 people. Later Bogd Khan's *shabi* increased to almost one hundred thousand; however, on average, it hovered around 90 thousand.[9] Some noble princes also started contributing their subjects to the *shabi*. Therefore the Manchu Emperor started regulating matters related to *shabi*, and in 1837 passed an edict introducing new rules for the creation of *shabi*. Although the people in the *shabi* were ostensibly related to the Bogd in terms of their faith and belief, in reality they were nothing other than common serfs in terms of the duties and functions they performed.

In order to distinguish the *shabi* of the Bogd Jebzundamba Khutugtu from that of other khutugtus and reincarnates, it was called the *Bogd Shabi* or the *Ikh* (meaning Great) *Shabi*. A so-called Erdene Shanzodba Ministry was established in 1723 specifically to administer matters related to the *shabi* – the personal estates of the Bogd Khan, which in 1822 already had the status of an *aimag chuulgan*. The Ministry's responsibility lay in administering the households within the *Shabi*, managing the so-called "Nine White" tributes paid by Bogd Jebzundamba to the Manchu Emperor, and also arranging for the offerings to be given to the Bogd Khan by the four Khalkha *aimags* and organising religious prayers and sermons; it was also involved in criminal and civilian-related judicial matters within the *shabi*.

The Shanzodba Ministry had direct jurisdiction over all the *otogs* within the *shabi* of Jebzundamba Khutugtu, the 30 *aimags*, 10 religious schools of Ikh Khüree, the Western Khüree, Amarbayasgalant and Erdenzuu monasteries, as well as the Bogd Khan's treasury.

The Shanzodba Ministry was primarily responsible for managing the administrative affairs of the *shabi* and the ministry was headed by Erdene Shanzodba. In addition to the Shanzodba, there was also a religious authority called the *Khambo Nomun Khan*, whose rank was the same as that of the Shanzodba. His deputy's position was instituted in 1767, and he was

9 *Международные отношения в эпохе империализма (International Relations During the Era of Imperialism)*, 1780–1910, Moscow, 1938, p. 182.

called the Da Lama, and there were two deputies. The Khambo Nomun Khan also had his personal assistant called the Vice Khambo. The Ministry had more than 50 officials called the *zaisan,* about a dozen clerks, and other staff. The Ministry was also known as the "The Ministry of the Great *Shabi."* The *zaisans* of the ministry worked in rotational shift of one to three months each according to a pre-drawn list.

The Bogd Khan's treasury served as the financial and economic department responsible for managing all expenses, supplies and procurements related to religious functions, events and prayer ceremonies of the Bogd Khan, the Ministry of the Great *Shabi* and its affiliates. The Treasury had two external and internal departments. The revenues of the former department primarily came from the taxes and duties paid by the *otog,* while the latter's revenues were composed of offerings made to the Bogd Khan primarily by the devotees. By the end of the nineteenth century, the *shabi nar* (personal estate of the Bogd Khan) had paid in taxes an average of 700,000–800,000 *lang* or *tael* (*a measuring unit for silver, and one lang of silver is equivalent to 37.2 grams. Tr.*). The "Great *Shabi*" was divided into *otog* and there were 17 great *otog* besides the so-called *Black Darkhad.* There were also some 30 special *bagh* or groups, which were not part of the *otog,* but were directly accountable to the Shanzodba Ministry.[10] The Great *Otog* also was divided into *baghs* and in each *otog* there worked officials called the *Shüülenge* (*an official in the fourteenth-twentieth centuries who oversaw the livestock assets, taxes and tributes of the high-ranking lamas. Tr.*), a *demch* (*a warden of forty households*) and a messenger.

2.11 *The* Shabis *of the* Khutugtus *with Stamps*

In Khalkha Mongolia, besides Bogd Jebzundamba, there was another layer of nobles of the Yellow Hat sect, who were consecrated as reincarnated *khutugtus.* There were two types of *khutugtus,* depending on the number of *shabi* under them and whether they held officials stamps or not. According to Manchu law, if the number of subjects in a *shabi* of a *khutugtu* reached 700, a separate administration was set up, and its leader was given official stamps. Accordingly, such official stamps were given to Yegüzer *Khutugtu* of Setsen Khan *aimag* in 1864, to Jalkhanz *Khutugtu* of the same aimag in 1824, Nomunkhan *Khutugtu* in 1853, Zaya Pandit *Khutugtu* of Sain Noyon *aimag* in 1737, Chin Süjigt Nomunkhan *Khutugtu* in 1751, Naro Panchen *Khutugtu* in 1772, Erdene Mergen Noyon *Khutugtu* in 1826, Erdenepandita *Khutugtu* in 1737, Naran *Khutugtu* in 1897, and

10 Sh. Natsagdorj, *The Right of the Mongols to Inheritance,* Ulaanbaatar, 1971, p. 227.

Khambo Nomunkhan *Khutugtu* in 1807, respectively. They were apportioned part of the territory of their banners together with the common subjects therein and the respective offices of the Shanzodba were established. As a matter fact, in Khalkha Mongolia there were 13 *Khutugtu* with official stamps, and almost 50 *Khutugtu* and reincarnates not holding an official stamp. After the death of a *Khutugtu* or a reincarnate, a boy child of any one household would be recognised and proclaimed as the next reincarnation of the deceased. This was done through a set process, according to which three to four boys would be identified as the possible reincarnation, their names would be written on a piece of paper, which would be put inside a specially-made golden urn and one of the papers would be picked with a chopstick made of gold and silver. This act was performed by a special representative appointed from among Manchu, Mongol and Tibetan lay and secular nobles. The recognised reincarnation would be called a *khuvilgaan* when the child comes of age, and would be called a *khutugtu* from age one to eight.

Khutugtus with stamps were the owners of the most influential and important Khalkha temples and monasteries, which were also named after their owners, such as Zaya's Khüree, Chin Süjigt Nomunkhan's Khüree, Yegüzer's monastery, Jalkhanz's Khüree, Lamyn Gegeen's monastery etc.

The *Khutugtu's* with stamps and their *shabi* or disciples were not included in the list of men folk of the *soum*. They had their own special registries, seals, geographical maps, autonomous administrations, and they enjoyed similar rights to those of the *banners* and were directly accountable to the *aimag chuulgan*.

The next in the rank after the *Khutugtu* was an official called the *shanzav*, who oversaw the administrative affairs of the *shabi* disciples, who were called "the *shanzav* of the *shabi*-disciples of this and that *khutugtu*." The *shanzavs* also had their own office. The *shanzavs* from the given *khutugtu* had the authority to nominate influential lamas to the *aimag chuulgan*. The *shanzavs* were appointed to the post for an indefinite period by an edict of the Manchu Emperor. The *shanzavs* also had the authority to consult with the relevant departments administrative and judicial matters within the *shabi* and submit the case to a higher instance for final decision.

There were a number of lower-ranking officials called the *zaisan* under the *shanzavs*. They would serve in the office of the *shanzavs* in turns for a definite period of time.

The *shabi*-disciples of the *khutugtus* holding stamps were duty-bound to take part in the official business of the *aimags* and *banners*, and render services to the relevant *khutugtus*, but they were relieved of performing duties under the Manchus, and so were different as compared to the common subjects of the *soums*.

2.12 *Courts and Administration of Justice*

The court was one of the constituent components of the military and administrative regime of the Manchu rulers in Mongolia. The Banner Prince was the primary instance of justice administration. It was mandatory to apprise the Banner Prince about any case or dispute, and the concerned Banner Prince was duty bound to complete the investigation and court procedures.

If the Banner *Wang, Güng,* royal son-in-law, assistant or the *Taiji* had not been able to disclose a crime and mete our justice, he would be immediately dismissed. As mentioned in the "Code of Law of Outer Mongolia," if the aforementioned failed to expose and catch a criminal who had been given the death penalty, they would be deprived of their three-year wages; if a person convicted to death by dismemberment was not caught then their wages would not be given for two years, one year's salary would be deducted if a person who was to stand court martial or be exiled was not seized, and a half year's wage would not be given in the event a person who had been convicted to beating and thrashing had not been apprehended. The above appear to be important provisions in terms of accountability if someone was careless or unprofessional. The aforementioned officials were given the possibility to resort to excesses to force a suspect to admit guilt and subject the guilty person to severe punishment and even torture.

The second level where the judgment passed by the relevant Banner Prince was monitored was the office of the chief of the *aimag chuulgan*, whose decision was final and could not be appealed. However, if a Banner Prince handed down a death penalty, the Uliastai commander, Khüree and Khovd *ambans* must be immediately notified through the chief of the *chuulgan*, who would submit the judgment for examination to the Outer Mongol *jurgan* department and finally submit it to the Emperor who passed the final judgment. The Law of the Qing Empire stated that "The banner prince shall take a decision on death penalty, this decision must be notified to *jurgan* and the latter together with the three justice ministries shall pass the sentence. If the death sentence is to be carried out in fall after the convict spends time behind bars, then the final decision shall be taken in consultation with nine Manchu ministers." Judging by the above, we can assume that the administration of justice during the period of the Manchu rule was five-tiered as follows: 1. Banner Prince; 2. Chief of the *aimag chuulgan*; 3. Uliastai commander, and the Khüree and

Khovd *ambans*; 4. The Mongol *Jurgan* of Outer Mongolia, and 5. Manchu Emperor. Apart from them, the *soum* and relay station commanders, to a certain extent, were also involved in court proceedings and applied torture as punishment.

The Erdene *Shanzodba* Ministry, like the *aimag chuulgan,* had the right and authority to conduct court proceedings and administer justice. In other words, this Ministry examined and passed sentences for any criminal and civilian dispute and case among the subjects of the *shabi*. Sentences were passed in accordance with the *Khalkha Jirum* (a monument of the eighteenth century Mongolian feudal law, that is, the Code of the Laws of the Khalkha) and the *Khalkha Jirum* of the Ministry of *Shabi* of East Khüree, and for minor offences committed by the members of the *shabi* an official document called "Ulaan Khatsart or the Red Cheek" was followed. But all disputes among the common folk of the *shabi* and *aimag* banners were settled together with the relevant *aimag* and banner in keeping with the Mongol Code.

The *shabi otogs,* like the banners, did not have *ger*-type (*gers were the traditional felt tents of the Mongol nomads. Tr.*) detention centres, which were termed the "black *gers,*" and so they did not adjudicate grave crimes and these criminals were handed over to the *Shabi* Ministry. The Erdene Shanzodba Ministry had a centralised prison as compared to the *aimag chuulgan.*

During the Manchu rule in Outer Mongolia, testimony by the suspect was regarded as the key evidence in criminal proceedings and the suspects were tortured to confessing. There were nine types of torture that were used and they were called the "Nine Torture." These nine types of torture were executed using special implements that were particularly damaging to the life and health of the tortured, which in fact was the most obnoxious method of forcing someone to confess against his/her own will. They included the following:

1. **The *Shaakhai* or the slippering method**: This is a form of torture in which thick hard layers of leathers, made like the sole of a shoe, which are stitched together with leather straps, was used for punishing a criminal, whose two hands would be strapped at his back, his head resting on his two knees, and hitting his two cheeks 40 times with this leather sole.
2. **The *Tuivan* or the caning punishment**: The executor of this form of torture, half kneeling before the standing victim, would use a bamboo stick or a short wooden plank to strike his thigh once to fifty times.

3 **The *Chavchirag* or Spanking using a plank:** Here the executioner would be standing and would hit the back of the thigh 60–100 times with a long heavy wooden plank.
4 **The *Khülekh* or the Strappado:** is a form of torture in which the victim's hands are tied in the form of a cross, and the tied hands are pulled as far as possible.
5 **The *Saraalj* or the Seesaw method:** The hands of the suspect under investigation would be tied around a wooden pillar, he would be made to kneel down either on a mat of gravel and stones or a wooden bar, whose upper part is carved sharp like a knife-edge, and a long round wood would be thrust in between the hollow of his knees on which two men would stand and move as if sitting on a seesaw.
6 **The *Düüjin* or the method of suspension:** The victim is suspended by a rope attached to both his thumbs, and the support under his feet would be removed and the fingers stretch slowly.
7 **The *Khöshüüreg* or the cross-bar method:** The victim would be made to put his wrists and shins in two large holes made into two thick wooden planks, which are then tied together, and the criminal is made to stand up bending and would remain in this position for up to 24 hours.
8 **The *Töönüür* or the moxibustion:** A burning special incense stick, called the "Red Head" was used for scalding the thick parts of the thigh and the back three times each.
9 **The *Khavchuur* or the forceps:** This form of torture was called the "*Savslaga*" when applied to women. Three wood with knife-sharp edge are used, one of them is placed in between two legs and the other two outside and the three are roped tightly and the rope is gradually tightened. While the women victim's four fingers are tightened with two knife-sharp edged woods, which are gradually made tighter. This method of torture, in most cases, made the victims physically disabled because when this method of torture is used for the first time, it is intended to slice off the skin, the second time, it is meant to cut the flesh and break the sinews, the third attempt is designed at crushing the bones. This is why, the Manchu law had banned the application of this method of torture not more than twice.

Besides these nine types of torture, three other forms of torture were applied, such as, whipping the criminal with heavy wooden or bamboo whip (*which was mostly used when riding a horse. Tr.*), hammering bamboo nail or pointed bamboo and placing a fresh liver either on the spine or the chest. In the first case, the victim was made to lay down on the ground face down and the executor standing would whip the victim. In the case of the second method of torture, pointed bamboo nail would be thrust into the victims nail and finger until it pierces through, which was called the method of nailing. And in the third case, fresh animal liver would be placed either on the spine or the chest, and after it dries up, the dried liver was pulled, which would also peel off the skin of the victim.

In this manner, 12 different methods of torture were used during the rule of the Manchu Qing Empire in Outer Mongolia.

Psychological methods were also applied to pressure the victim mentally, and especially for male criminals, another severe method of torture was used, which in Mongolian was called *Shakhaa* or pressure, which was also known as the "Torture of Oath Taking." According to the *Khalkha Jirum* (Code of the laws of the Khalkha), this kind of torture had also existed in the past. For example, a victim undergoing such a psychological torture had to, in essence, take the following oath: "I am under pressure to confess my truth having lied to thee Bodhisattva, the only son of all the gods of the three times, and the Great *Yaksha* (*a class of demigods. Tr.*), the shape Thee have taken to pacify all the beings in the time of ordeal, have I thy servant thus subject to conflict between the eight great heavens, the eight great water-spirits, the eight great planets, the twenty-eight stars, the four great khans and the one that drink of the blood and eat of the flesh. Should I be telling the untruth, may you do away with me within seven days, consume of my flesh, skin me, drink of my blood, crush my bones and wrench out my heart. Should I be right, may the same fate await that person who has accused me. May thee protect this and next life of mine."[11]

When a person, who has been detained without any evidence or a witness is sentenced to the psychological torture of *shakhaa* the accused must take the above vow and should the accused desire not to take the oath, then he had to perform the following rites in a place called *Nokhoi Khötöl*. He had to hang 2 bows, 2 arrows, 2 swords, heads of 2 camels, 2 horse heads, 2 shoes, 2 *bog* or small cattle heads, 2 pelvic bones, 1 hobble, a total of 18 items on a rope, which is one short culbit long and two hobbles long. The victim who has been condemned to *shakhaa* had to utter the above oath and then crawl under the ropes with these items, and finally drink dog blood from a human skull. At a later period, one more item, a trouser of a widowed woman was also hung on the rope. Judging by the above, such a shameless method used in a criminal procedure during the rule of the Manchu Qing Empire evidences that the rights of the people

11 G. Sovd, *Historical Evolution of the Law of Criminal Procedure*, Ulaanbaatar, 1977, pp. 161–162.

in the occupied lands were flagrantly violated and they acted arbitrarily as they wanted.

2.13 *Social Structure, and the Rights and Privileges of the Noble Aristocrats*

In the 18th to 19th centuries, Mongolia's society was made up of two large groups, the noble aristocrats and the common folk. The first group of noble aristocrats included princes and *taiji* with various ranks and titles, and this group also included the higher-ranking lamas of the Buddhist temples and monasteries. According to the law of the Manchu Qing Empire, the Mongol nobles were given many such ranks and titles as *Chin Wang* (Prince of the First Rank), *Jün Wang* (Prince of the Second Rank), *Beil* (Prince of the Third Rank), *Beis* (Prince of the Fourth Rank), and *Tüshee Gün* or Prince of the Fifth Rank. Nobles who had excelled in their service would be twice given the title of *Ching Wang*. A noble prince (*Zasag Noyon*) in one sense was the key local representative of the Manchu Emperor. The *zasag noyons* had to greet the Manchu Emperor during the New Year, personally visit the *jasaa* for the New Year celebrations, pay a courtesy call on Qian Ching-Men once in three to fourth years, and take part in the imperial hunt. The Manchu Emperor, besides putting tough demands on the Mongol noble princes, also awarded them lavishly to ensure loyalty and obeisance on their part. According to the Manchu law, a Khan and a *Chin Wang*, who had taken part in the imperial new year celebrations, would be given in award 430 taels of silver, a *jün wang* 300 taels, a *beil* 200 taels, a *beis* – 150 taels, and 100 taels of sliver were given to a *tüshee gün*. While other officials, such as the banner chiefs, who did not have any rank or title, were given 70 taels of silver, *taijis* of first and second rank, and their assistants were given 60 tales of silver each, while *taijis* of third and fourth ranks were given in incentive 53 taels of silver. In addition, the noble princes, depending on their ranking, would annually receive salary in money and also silk. For instance, a *Chin Wang* annually received 2500 taels of silver and 40 rolls of silk; a *Jüng Wang* was given 1,500 taels of silver and 20 rolls of silk; a *Beil* – 300 taels of silver and 9 rolls of silk; a government assistant *güng* 200 received 200 taels of silver and 7 rolls of silk, respectively.[12] These nobles and princes were also awarded special ranks that came with finials, use of two-eyed peacock feathers, and fur coats with encircled dragon patterns.

The *Taijis* were in essence the direct descendants of the Mongol Khans. During the rule of the Manchu Qing dynasty, the number of *Taijis* was

12 *History of the MPR*, in Three Volumes, Vol. 2, Ulaanbaatar, 1968, p. 176.

increased and they were divided into four different ranks. The sons of the Khalkha Khans and *Ching Wang* were regarded as the *taijis* with the highest first rank, while the sons of the *Jün Wang* and *Beils* were given the second rank, and the sons of the *Beis* and *Chin Wang* were *Taijis* of the fourth rank. The *Taijis,* as compared to the princes did not get any kind of remuneration as the *Taiji* administering the banner only was entitled to wages.

There were two kinds of *Taijis,* one who had close family relations, and the other, who were subjects. The former types of *Taijis* were, in most cases, descendants of Chinggis Khan and his sons, or the sons and grandsons of Khans and *Wangs,* while the subject *Taijis* were the descendants of Chinggis Khan's son Bilgüüdei. In the early period under the Manchu rule, the *Taijis* did not pay tributes and duties, but starting from the early 19th century, they were taxed, and there were impoverished *Taijis* called the "Khokhi" (*which in Mongolian literally means 'a misfortune.' Tr.*)

Khutugtu's carrying officials stamps were rightly part of a major social grouping of the noble aristocrats.

The second largest social group in Mongolia during the rule of the Manchu Qing Empire were the common folk who served as serfs, subjects or *shabi*-disciples. When the Manchus first invaded and occupied Inner Mongolia and established *banners* and *soums,* the Mongol *wangs, beil, beis* and *güngs* were distributed serfs who were called the "attendant men." Later in 1652, the *taijis* of the four ranks were also given serfs, for example, according to the Manchu law, a Mongol *chin wang* was given 15 serfs, a *beil* was given 40, a *beis* 35, and a *güng* 30 retainers. Similarly, the *Tiajis* of different ranks were also distributed serf retainers; for example, a *taiji* of first rank 15 serfs, second ranked *Taiji* 12, 8 serfs to a *Taiji* of third rank, and the fourth ranking *Taiji* 4 serfs. Besides these princes and *taijis* of different ranks and with various titles, the son-in-law of the State and other sons-in-law were also given retainers, but many more than them. Just one or two retainers were also allotted to the *banner* commanders, *meeren* and other *banner* and *soum* officials to assist them in their daily work. According to an 1814 statistic, Governor Dugartsembel of Setsen Khan *aimag* had 375 serfs, and *beis* Miyürdorj had 325 serfs. The serfs of the princes were exempt from all kinds of taxes, and only had to pay their dues to their own masters, and assist in the daily household chores.

The *albat ard* or the common serfs (slaves) were responsible for carrying out government-level duties. They made up from the bulk of the common people. Men aged 18 to 60 of the common folk were organised into military set-ups. These *albat ard* would take part in the ceremony when the Mongol noble princes would pay their annual dues in gifts to the Manchu Emperor, take part also in the hunts, tend livestock animals, look after the herds of horses, grow food for the soldiers, serve in the army, the sentry and the relay stations, and also collect dues and tributes for the treasury of the Manchu administrations in Mongolia; that is, they were responsible for carrying out many kinds of different government duties also with their own assets and physically. Alongside this, they were obliged to pay taxes to their own nobles and princes. The Manchu rulers had set the size and the limits of the taxes that were levied on the common folk, the *albat ard*, of the Mongol nobles and princes. The size of the tax, for example, included one sheep for anyone who had more than 5 cows, 2 sheep from every 40 sheep owned, and this kind of due was to be paid every year. Owners of two cows had to pay in tax 6 cauldrons of millet, and 3 cauldrons of millet had to be paid by those who had 3 heads of cattle. Alongside this, every 10 households had to come up amongst them with 2 bullock cars when the noble Prince travelled to pay his tribute to the Manchu Emperor, to attend assemblies, when the Prince moved in search of pastures, and even when the Prince welcomed his daughter-in-law or when he married off his daughter, and in addition to the above, households with more than 3 cows had to give a sizable volume of milk, one bottle of distilled milk spirit if a household owned 5 and more cows, and a household that had more than 100 heads of sheep, had to surrender one roll of felt.

One group of commoners were serf-disciples working for the Bogd Jebzundamba and the other high-ranking reincarnate lamas; in the previous sections, we have given a detailed description of the *shabi*-disciples. During the rule of the Manchu Qing Empire, besides the serfs, *albat ard* and the disciples, there was also a group of people called the "free *ard*," which included young men of non-military age, and older and elderly people who were over and above the military-age. As they also came under the jurisdiction of the noble princes, they were also obliged to pay duties. And in some banners there were foreign soldiers who were taken captive, who were call the "household slaves," besides the savants sent as bridal-companions of Manchu princesses, but their number was few and so they did not have an important share in the social structure as a whole. As a matter of fact, based on the Western theory of generational social strata, there were instances of integration of these social classes and groups of Mongolia in the given period, but this phenomenon was not that common.

2.14 *Duties and Taxes During the Rule of the Manchu Empire*

Duties and taxes constituted the central economic duty during the rule of the Manchus, which were levied on their subjects, the common people. In the early period after the Manchus took over Khalkha Mongolia, all the Mongols were not subject to pay duties and taxes as they were primarily mobilised to serve in the army as sentries and guards. However, after the subjugation of the Oirads, the last stronghold of Mongol independence, levying of taxes and duties was uniformly applied across the board.

Key offices that were responsible for overseeing duties and taxes of this period included the offices of the subjects that had taken an oath of allegiance to the Manchu Empire (the Peking Office or *jasaa,* which was more of a ceremonial nature, where the subjects served on a rotational basis), services that were responsible for managing the economy and business of the dynasty (taking care of herds of horses, growing crops and food), services of a military nature (soldiers, guards and law enforcers), the administrative offices, and the relay services that helped links and coordination among all the above.

All these offices and services were designed to bolster the army, the system of serfdom and the regime of the Manchus as a whole. The so-called "Nine White" tributes included one fully grown gilded camel with its neck fully covered with sable skins and with an intricately designed silver nose-peg, and 8 young white horses with yellow halters and decorated with *khadak* (*Khada* – offering a silk scarf) in five colours. Bogd Jebzundamba together with other Khalkha Mongol Khans and princes from six *jasaa* would travel to Peking once a year to present the "Nine White" gifts to the Manchu Emperor, which was called the *jasaa* of the Mongol nobles.

The *jasaa* office of the Khalkha nobles was established when Enkh-Amgalan Khan (Kangxi Emperor) subjugated Khalkha Mongolia, and the number of *jasaa* multiplied, starting in the second half of the 18th century. Accordingly, special rules were introduced to regulate the size of the tributes to the Manchu Emperor, which were done on a rotational basis. Apart from such kinds of tributes, there also existed duties that demanded physical labour, such as taking care of and herding the horses and other livestock animals of the Manchu Emperor. The livestock were primarily raised for the use of the Manchu oppressive soldiers, who were manning the borders of the Manchu Empire. The entire banner was responsible for compensation should there be a non-productive loss of livestock animals. The bulk of the livestock herd of the Manchu Empire was concentrated in Dariganga, a flat fertile land in the east of Outer Mongolia. There were a total of 198 large herds of select livestock animals that were raised in 4 *aimags* and the livestock population growth depended on how the animals were selected. The common Mongols bore the brunt of providing the costs of maintaining the Manchu oppressive army in Outer Mongolia, their remuneration and food, and also transporting the food and weapons. In 1762, crop farming was revived in Khovd and 400 people from Khalkha Mongolia, including soldiers of the Green Banner were mobilised and were made to toil in large tracts of crop fields, almost 57.6 meters in size.[13] The life of the soldiers working on the crop field was miserable. It was the duty of Zasagt Khan, Sain Noyon and Tüsheet Khan *aimags* to ensure the mobility of the soldiers. For this purpose more than 1000 heads of horses and almost 10,000 goats were mobilised during the period from 1811 to 1813.

One of the government duties that the Mongols carried out during the rule of the Manchu Qing Empire was the maintenance and manning of the sentry services, which had two functions: national and local services. There were more than 1,200 soldiers serving in the so-called *ger* watch-posts and their annual budget was approximately equivalent to almost 110 thousand taels of silver.[14] The *soum* watch-posts, which were set up later, were manned by 1,000 soldiers in rotation for a period stretching up to three years. By the middle of the 19th century, the annual budget of a *soum* sentry-post had been estimated at more than 40 thousand taels of silver.[15]

Relay services or *Örtöö*, as they were called in Mongolian, were set up at main highways between Outer Mongolia and the Manchu Qing Empire, and their maintenance, such as provision of horses, food and housing, as well as managing the related logistics, were all made the sole responsibility of the common people living in and around the *Örtöö*, which was a huge burden on the locals. Let us take just one example. There were 120 relay stations from Kalgan (Zhangjiakou) to Uliastai, which were annually supplied for food and logistics purposes with 47,000 camels. 250,000 horses and 53,000 sheep, that is, almost half a million heads of livestock animals.[16] Dozens of local sub-*soum Örtöös* were also set up, which further branched off into other smaller *Örtöös* and once again the common people were responsible for their maintenance. Besides these "official" duties and services, the Mongols were also obliged, under the so-called

13 *Ibid.*, p. 198.
14 *Ibid.*, pp. 124–125.
15 *Ibid.*, p. 201.
16 N. Ishjamts, *The Armed Struggle of the Mongol People for Independence in 1755–1758*, Ulaanbaatar, 1962, p. 49.

"unwritten Manchu laws" to pay "non-official tributes." For example, the commoners had to contribute to the so-called tributes for "currying favour" given to the visiting Manchu *ambans*, military commanders and government officials; the tributes paid by the Bogd Jebzundamba and other high-ranking incarnate lamas; and contributing to the provisions for use during the journey to Peking by the *aimag* khans and princes, and *banner* nobles when it was their turn to visit Peking to pay their obeisance to the Manchu Emperor. This kind of contribution by the commoners included physical contribution of material provisions and also silver. Volume Two of *The History of the MPR*, defining the duties and taxes to the Manchu Empire, states conclusively: "As the Manchu taxation policy became more severe, the life of the Mongols increasingly came under greater threat, which paved the way for the Chinese merchants and money-lenders to reinforce their presence and pressure that ultimately led to each and every single Mongol indebted to the Chinese. As the taxation policy of the Manchus became more severe, the exploitation by the Chinese merchants and usurpers became equally severe leading to the multiplication of the burden of debts by the Mongol officials as well as the common people."[17]

2.15 *State and Religion*

The Manchus resorted to Buddhist ideology as the key tool to tighten their control over the Mongols. The Manchus, on the one hand, encouraged and supported the religious head of the Mongol, Bogd Jebzundamba, in order to make Buddhism part and parcel of the spiritual life of the Mongols and use it for their own benefit; and on the other hand, conducted a policy to contain the reputation of the Bogd Jebzundamba to mitigate his influence as a political force unifying the Mongols. In order to restrict the Bogd Khan's influence, the Manchu rulers supported the idea of identifying the important reincarnates and *khutugtus* by the Mongols themselves. And one very interesting aspect of this policy lay in the understanding that the reincarnation of the Bogd Khan would not be identified from Mongolia but rather from Tibet. This ulterior motive with political objectives was in essence put in place and practiced with the identification of the Third Bogd Lama.

The Manchu rulers also conducted a policy of buttressing the Buddhist temples and monasteries economically, thanks to which, the *jasaa* of the temples and monasteries became more powerful, and the number of both local *khutugtus* and reincarnates with and without official stamps multiplied together with the number of their *shabi*-disciples, as well as the size

17 *The History of the MPR*, Three Volumes, Book Two, Ulaanbaatar, 1968, p. 213.

of their lands and livestock animals. Most of the temples and monasteries in *Khüree* were receiving large amounts of allowances from the treasury of the Manchu Qing Empire.

The Manchu Emperor, from time to time, bestowed titles and ranks on the Bogd Jebzundamba and even honoured him with the so-called "Green Leaf" award. In order to maintain obedience and loyalty, important Mongol *khutugtus* were regularly invited to the Manchu court in Peking, where they were welcomed and showered with different awards and honours.

The ideological and organisational set-up of the *Gelug* or the Yellow Sect of Tibetan Buddhism became stronger during the rule of the Manchus, to unconditionally dominate the spiritual life of the Mongols. The number of lamas began to proliferate. Since the lama, as compared to the common people, enjoyed many more privileges, there was an increasingly large number of people who wanted to become lamas. Roughly one third of the adult male population had taken celibacy vows and consequently, they increasingly retreated from productive labour and subsequently, the burden of taxes and dues became much heavier on the common people. This is why, at a later period, a new rule was introduced according to which one could become a lama only after getting due permission from the banner government. In this manner, the Manchu occupiers took advantage of religion for their own interests and used it as an instrument to achieve their gains at all costs. The Manchu rulers, in fact, were bent on spreading Buddhism not because they had respect for the religion, but because they were intent on using it for their own political ends, and their policies and actions were tailored accordingly. As a consequence of this, the teachings of Buddhism and its holy precepts were subject to a breach that led to its decay and decline.

Starting in the early 19th century, the lamas themselves came forward with criticism related to the decline and decay of the Yellow Sect of Buddhism. These reformists, guided by their social and political convictions, set out on a mission to, first and foremost, prevent Buddhism from becoming a weapon in the hands of the Manchus to achieve their state colonisation policy of assimilation, and to keep religion away from state matters and to develop it in its initial form of purity. However, a handful of high-ranking lamas, who colluded with the Manchu aggressors, opposed the reformists, blamed them for the decline and did not want to break with the past.

3 The Law

3.1 *Legal Sources*

When we study the State, administration and law of Outer Mongolia during the period under the Manchu rule, the key codes of this period obviously become the legal sources. The primary legal sources of this period can be divided into the following three categories: General codes of laws that were enforced at the level of the Manchu Qing Empire (this includes all the laws that were enforced by the edict of the Manchu Emperor); codes of laws developed and adopted by the Mongols themselves (The *Khalkha Jirum*); and, finally, Manchu laws that were enforced in order to rule and administer Outer Mongolia, as a whole, (the Mongol Code, the Law of the Ministry for the Administration of Outlying Regions, etc.). The laws of Mongolia during this period, on the one hand, attempted to preserve, as much as possible, the state and legal traditions of the Mongols, but on the other hand, the Mongols had to yield to Manchu and Chinese legal principles and schools of thought. Although the interests of the Empire were the top priority concerns, since the legal documents of this period regularised the social relations of Mongolia, the legal traditions and the legal sources of the Mongols had also to be taken into consideration.

From among the above-mentioned codes, let us take a closer look at the *Khalkha Jirum* and the Law of the Ministry for the Administration of Outlying Regions.

3.2 Khalkha Jirum *(The Code of the Laws of the Khalkha)*

This is one of the most important monuments of eighteenth-century Mongolian feudal law. A Mongolian Professor, S. Jalan-Aajav, who specifically researched this code of the laws of the Khalkha Mongols, defines it as the "apex" of all the code of laws. [18] Another Mongolian scholar, Jamsrangiin Tseveen, marked a watershed in the study of the *Khalkha Jirum*.[19] Russian scholars, B. Ya. Vladimirtsov, S. D. Dylykov and A. V. Ryazanovskii, and Mongolian scholars, Sh. Natsagdorj and Dr. B. Sodsüren, having studied the *Khalkha Jirum*, touched upon many extremely important issues.[20]

---

18 S. Jalan-Aajav, *Khalkha Jirum bol Mongolin khhuli tsaazin dursgalt bichig mun*, Ulaanbaatar, 1958, p. 3.

19 Жамцарано Ц.Ж., Турунов А.Н. Халха Джирум – описание памятника // Сб. тр. Гос. Иркут. ун-та.– Иркутск, 1923. – Вып. 6. – 18 с.

20 Б.Я. Владимирцов. Общественный строй монголов. Монгольский кочевой феодализм. // Л.: Изд-во АН СССР. 1934. XII+224 с.; Жамцарано Ц. Ж., Дылыков С. Д. Халха Джирум. Памятник монгольского феодального права XVIII в. 1924; Рязановский В.А Монгольское право, Харбине. 1931; Sh. Natsagdorj, History of Khalkh, Ulaanbaatar, 1963.

From among the aforementioned studies, the most fundamental ones are the books by S. Jalan-Aajav called *The Khalkha Jirum is an Ancient Monument of the Mongolian Laws* and *Khalkha Jirum.*[21]

The Manchus were wary of enforcing their own laws in Mongolia, and Enkh Amgalan (Kangxi Emperor) of the Qing Dynasty passed a decree ordering that "The Mongols, who had been just subjugated, should be given an opportunity to follow their own law."[22] Such cautiousness was not without reason, for the Manchus were not oblivious of the fact that the Mongols were capable of regulating their own social issues, and that the Mongols had their own legal traditions as well. The Khalkha nobles tried their best not to lose this opportunity of retaining their right to continue with the traditional law.

Khalkha nobles, princes, and important state and religious authorities met more than 20 times in various places and finally agreed on the *Khalkha Jirum.* It was the Code of the Laws of the Khalkhas, an important monument of eighteenth-century Mongolian feudal law, which incorporated some of the important provisions of the old Mongol codes.[23] However, another Mongolian scholar B. Bayarsaikhan maintained that there never was a code of laws called the *Khalkha Jirum*, even if the various laws that were enforced in 15 other Khalkha banners were compiled, as this was a name given by the official who had compiled the codes of laws.[24]

Enforcement of the *Khalkha Jirum* gradually slackened after the Manchus adopted and enforced the so-called Law of the Ministry for the Administration of Outlying Regions in 1789, and only the Great *Shabi* and its subjects followed and applied the *Khalkha Jirum.* This is evidenced by an official register, better known as the "Red Cheek" maintained by the Great *Shabi* Ministry to record resolved cases, and also from the Ministry's book on rules and procedures.

Today we have inherited two, in principle identical versions of the *Khalkha Jirum*, one called the *Khalkha Jirum* of West Khüree and the other called the "Rules of the *Khalkha Jirum* of the *Shabi* Ministry of Ikh Khüree." Scholar S. Jalan-Aajav was the first to attempt to transliterate the *Khalkha Jirum* from the traditional Mongol script into Cyrillic. He classified and compiled the code into 14 chapters and 301 sections, and commented on

21 S. Jalan-Aajav, *Khalkha Jirum bol Mongolin khhuli tsaazin dursgalt bichig mun*, Ulaanbaatar, 1958; S. Jalan-Aajav, *Khalkha Jirum*, Ulaanbaatar, 1995

22 S. Jalan-Aajav, *Khalkha Jirum*, Ulaanbaatar, 1995, p. 5.

23 D. Gongor, *The Khalkha Summary*, Vol. 1, Ulaanbaatar, 1978, p. 23.

24 B. Bayarsaikhan, "Terms and terminology in the Mongol Code", National University, Law College, "Law" journal on Theory, Practicals and Information, Issues No. 2–3, 2007 (16–17), p. 156.

some of the terms therein. Based on this, let us now take a brief look at the contents of the *Khalkha Jirum*.

The *Khalkha Jirum* was an anthology of different legal norms and standards that codified a gamut of different aspects of social life in Mongolia when it was transformed into a frontier region by the Manchu Empire.

The *Khalkha Jirum* specifically focused on the legal aspects of the administrative liabilities, especially in the case of relay stations, and other forms of crimes and criminal activities. While regulating this relationship, the *Khalkha Jirum* clearly classified the messenger passing through the relay stations according to their ranks and titles, and also fixed the number of horses and provisions, the food and meat they were entitled to, and also spelled out the penalties, their size and severity, according to the gravity of the flaws and errors committed, say if the messengers were delayed or if their mission was disrupted. To begin with, whenever the *Khutugtu Gegeen* (meaning the First Bogd Jebzumdamba Zanabazar) travelled and passed through the relay stations, he and his entourage were entitled to an unlimited number of horses and food provisions, as agreed upon in the early times at the Assembly of the Seven *Banners*. The stipulated punishment for the breach of this provision included the confiscation of all assets from the guilty and "contributing them to the treasury".[25] Next after the Bogd came the *aimag* Khan, his queen, *wang, beil* and other noble officials with lower ranks, who were all entitled to a fixed number of horses for transport and food provisions. It was prohibited for the officers manning the relay stations to provide a lesser number of horses than was supposed to be provided, give horses for transport that were stolen, replace sturdy animals with weak ones, causing bodily harm to envoys and messages with sharp implements or treat them to alcoholic drinks. It was also not permitted for the envoys or messengers to divert from their fixed route to visit their families, mobilise young horses for transport purposes, use animals and horses that belonged to the reincarnated lamas, use extra numbers of transport horses or consume alcoholic drinks, and the violators were either fined with dozens of livestock animals or had to face other, more severe punishments.

Crimes related to theft occupied a major place in the *Khalkha Jirum*. There were different kinds of punishments for anyone who was found guilty of stealing livestock, grain, government assets, and valuable items. For example, the property of the guilty was confiscated, he would be subject to thrashing, whipping, fined with several scores of livestock animals, and even condemned to wearing a cangue, and other forms of

25 S. Jalan-Aajav, *Khalkha Jirum*, Ulaanbaatar, 1995, p. 12.

severe punishment when the guilty had but to confess. There were other forms of punishment, for example, a guilty person was forced to lie prostrate in prayer several thousand times or make circumambulation. In other words, secular and religious forms of punishment were meted out to the guilty. For the first time ever, we come across a new form of punishment in the *Khalkha Jirum*. For example, first time offenders were made to pay 20 heads of large livestock, of which 10 could be a four-year-old horse, or ten horses in the third year or the same number of cows, and for second and third time repeaters, the severity of the punishment was increased.

Provisions in the *Khalkha Jirum* regularising marriage and family relations were formulated in such a manner as to outlaw promiscuous behaviour, safeguarding and strengthening the family.

Noble princes and their son-in-laws were not permitted to have a second wife. The nobles were not allowed to receive betrothal gifts from each other. A noble prince was allowed to receive betrothal gifts from a common man from among three banners. The princes were not allowed to marry other prince's wives; a prince could not marry a woman of one of his subjects; a common man could not marry a noble woman; a common man could not marry the woman of another commoner; attempted rape and sexul assault were prohibited; a woman could not go to bed with another man other than her husband; a woman who was already engaged to someone else could not be given in marriage to a prince, and a commoner could not ask the daughter of a Khan in marriage. Anyone who violated these prohibitionary provisions was punished severely, from paying in compensation several heads of livestock to having their property confiscated or being subjected to harsher punishments: either they were given as a servant to another servant, and in extreme cases, the guilty awaited the death sentence. Promiscuous behaviour was considered a taboo and a person guilty of rape or sexual assault was subject to *Yüs Torgokh* (nine penalties), and if a wife was found guilty of going to bed with another man, she would be subject to *gurvan yüs* or three kinds of penalties.[26]

The following clauses will reveal that family descent and origin played a powerful role in marriages and family relations.

- If a commoner asked the daughter of a Khan for her hand in marriage, he was supposed to give a white camel with a nose-peg made of silver, a white horse, a silver cup filled to the brim with alcoholic drink and a solid pearl without a hole for stringing, after which the consent would be given.

26 *Ibid.*, p. 26.

- If a prince asked for the hand in marriage of the daughter of a royal son-in-law, he would only have to send to the father of the girl a silver cup, a pearl and alcoholic drink.
- If a commoner married the daughter of another commoner, it would be sufficient to exchange alcoholic drink and the offal of an animal, which would mean consent for marriage was given.

The matter of fugitives was dealt with separately in the *Khalkha Jirum,* which was designed to bolster the master-subject relationship. There were different forms of punishment for those who saw a fleeing fugitive but did not report this, if the fugitive returned to his old master, and if a fugitive had committed some kind of crime. The punishment ranged from submission of a few heads of livestock animals to severe beating and whipping. The majority of fugitives during this period were those who had either committed some kind of felony or who simply wanted to escape their abusive and exploitative masters.

In the *Khalkha Jirum,* Buddhist temples, monasteries and lamas were given the status of special legal subjects, and they were given more privileges than any other class in the society then. Anyone who was guilty of encroaching on the wealth and property of a monastery was given extremely harsh punishments. Take, for example, this statement: "If anyone dare to lay hands of the property of a monastery, may his filthy body be banished, and if a common is guilty of this crime, may his filthy body be perished and confiscate all his property."[27] What is more, the lamas were entitled to choose and own the best lands with plenty of water and rich pasture after the noble princes had done so. The *Khalkha Jirum* not only gave special privileges to the lamas, but also codified the importance of strictly following the rules and precepts of Buddhism. A separate law was passed concerning the lamas and those of a rank of a *taiji.*

Different cases of crimes against men and their health were considered at length in the *Khalkha Jirum.* For instance, a prince could not murder his own subject, nor the subject of another prince; kill someone in revenge or just for fun; blind someone, break another's teeth; nobles could not draw sharp pointed weapons against each other; the princes were not permitted to squabble amongst themselves and to quarrel with a *taiji,* verbally insult each other, exchange fists; a *taiji* could not whip, draw a sharp weapon against and swear against a commoner; a prince could not insult a lama with the rank of a *taiji,* attack a commencing monk or even any comer with a sharp-pointed object. A government minister

27 S. Jalan-Aajav, The *Khalkha Jirum is an Ancient Monument of the Mongolian Laws,* Ulaanbaatar, 1958, p. 60.

and officer was not allowed to physically assault an accused person in a way that could fracture the person's bones, injure the flesh and skin; a high-ranking official and a *taiji* could not use a sharp-edged instrument against a commoner, assault him physically; no-one was permitted to verbally attack his guru or parents; a person with a communicable disease was prohibited to transfer the disease by concealing the truth, which could lead to the death of the other person; leaving a travel companion to die without giving him help and support; if a person died of a dog bite or the bite of a dog with rabies; if a person knew that his dog had rabies and nevertheless allowed the dog to attack the livestock of a neighbour or a stranger; if a mad person kills someone innocent, and if a prince drives away a stranger without giving him shelter who dies due to cold, then all those who were considered guilty were given different kinds of punishment from paying fines to performing social duties etc. However, the severity of the punishment largely depended, in all likelihood, on the person's family origin and social status.

The *Khalkha Jirum* had many clauses and provisions related to nature and the protection of the environment. For instance, there are such clauses as, "It is forbidden to fell green trees in places where a *khüree* (meaning a community) has been set up," "It is not permitted to cut down green trees beyond the white and the black land (meaning a piece of land where nothing has grown)," "Do not kill a healthy horse, young goose, snake, frog, duck, baby antelope, dog, skylark," and the violators were punished with the confiscation of their implements, and in addition they had to submit several heads of livestock animals in compensation.

The *Khalkha Jirum* codified the civil and administrative legal norms and standards, primarily focusing on the ownership and usage of pasture lands, public and private property, their inheritance rights, conducting of commercial and trading activities, taking credit and settling loans, that is, all types of property relationship. In particular, there are clauses that are clearly related to the unique mode of life of the primarily nomadic Mongols, such as "If a flock of sheep are driven away by a pack of wolves or by a storm (rain, snow, sand) then the people pursuing after the lost sheep, if they find them they can use one sheep for food from a hundred sheep," "If two folks going out to collect dung (for fire and cooking) fight over the dung that they have found, then the person who found it first has the right to collect the dung." The *Khalkha Jirum* also had special provisions related to horse races and in this respect the *Khalkha Jirum* can very well be classified as a truly Mongol Law.

Changes and amendments were made in the *Khalkha Jirum* prohibiting the consumption of liquor, which applied specifically to the Buddhist lamas and officials carrying out official duties. And those who had given them alcohol or those who had concealed the fact about alcohol consumption were also subject to punishment with one to two horses.

3.3 *Special Features and the Historical Significance of the* Khalkha Jirum

As compared to earlier applied codes of laws, the *Khalkha Jirum* made more specific the mechanisms of regularising different aspects of social life, and equally, the types of punishment for each different kind of offence.

1. 18 years after coming under the occupation of the Manchus, the fact that the Khalkha Mongols themselves developed this code of laws is convincing proof that the Mongols had constantly stood up for the preservation and continuation of the State and legal traditions, even at a time when they had lost their independence.
2. If we compare the methodology of the development of the *Khalkha Jirum* and its contents with the then existing international practices, we can conclude that the Mongols, in terms of the level of their legal mental development, were in no way inferior as compared to other nations and peoples.

One of the important legal sources of the Mongols in the 18th century is the *"Mongol Tsaazyn Bichig"* (*Mongγol čaγaǰin-u bičig or the Mongol Code of Law, which consisted of a set of statutes enacted for the Mongols under the Manchu Qing dynasty. Tr.*). Although this was a Manchu government legal document, it adapted a substantial number of the legal provisions of the Mongols. Consisting of 12 books and 209 articles, the original copy of the *Mongol Tsaazyn Bichig* is preserved at the National History Archives of Mongolia. Doctor B. Bayarsaikhan has ascertained that the *Mongol Tsaazyn Bichig* is an independent code of laws that originated during the reign of Enkh-Amgalan Khan (Kangxi Emperor) of the Manchu Qing dynasty. He made the following observations:

1. The *Mongol Tsaazyn Bichig* formed the basis of the laws for the administration of small vassal states such as Mongolia and Tibet;
2. Some of the terms and phrases were either modified or combined, and formulated, although in less detail;
3. The *Mongol Tsaazyn Bichig* created the foundations for the advancement of the legal knowledge and thinking, and contributed to the formation of state-related ethics of the Mongols;
4. The Mongol Code reflected in every possible way that the Manchu administration was an absolute monarchy;

5 Punishments stipulated in the Mongol Code were a kind of state coercive measure of the Manchu Emperor, which gave the relevant authorities the ability to impose certain kinds of restrictions on passing sentences according to the provisions contained in the law; thus if a suspect was found guilty of a crime, his/her rights and freedom were restricted as provided for in the law;
6 The *Mongol Tsaazyn Bichig* made some attempt to classify and regularize some of the social and even legal relations in the society. This made it easier to classify them,[28] B. Bayarsaikhan wrote, "In the final analysis the natural development of the *Mongol Tsaazyn Bichig* was the Regulations of the Lifanyuan (of 1815)."

3.4 *The Mongol Code*

This was changed and amended a number of times during the reign of Emperor of the Era of Health and Glory, Enkh Amgalan Khan (Kangxi Emperor), and was printed in 1785. Later in 1789, it was reprinted during the reign of the Heaven-Blessed Khan Yongzheng Emperor, and in 1811, by an ordinance of the Saishaalt Yüroolt Khan (Jiaqing Emperor) it was reviewed for the final time and the Code was approved in its entirety in 1817. In this sense, the Mongol Code was a complete collection of codes of laws of the Manchu Empire for the administration of Mongolia as a whole. The Mongol Code was first drafted in the Manchurian language and was later translated into Mongolian. Owing to the fact that it underwent years of redaction, some of the articles of the Code contradicted each other, and the Ministry for the Administration of Outlying Regions even had to admit to this error.

The Mongol Code consisted of 63 books in total. If we look at its structure, key contents and direction, we find that Books 1 to 8 deal with the administrative structure of Outer Mongolia, the inheritance rules of the Mongol nobles and princes, their titles and privileges. Books 13 to 15 cover the wages and benefits to the Mongol *wang, beil, beis, güng, taiji*. Matters related to soldiers were under the common heading "Male compensation." Topics such as government grain, farming, market, tax etc. are covered in Books 10 to 12, containing provisions regularising economic and related relations. And Books 16 to 23 cover norms and standards related to state and government matters. For example, paying of tributes, paying courtesy calls, marriage, award giving, procedures for entourage during travels, welcoming ceremony etc. are dealt with in detail. Books

28 B. Bayarsaikhan, *Legal Research into the Mongol Tsaazyn Bichig*, Ulaanbaatar, 2010, pp. 157–162.

26 to 26 and 28 are about the stamps and seals, establishing family relations through marriage, amnesty and reward, that is, etiquette rules and procedures. Books 31 to 33 set out the rules and punishments related to relay services, and from these Books, we can know that ensuring safety and order on the highways was given particular attention.

The last more than 20 Books of the Mongol Code define the procedures and policy viz criminal activities and related forms of punishment. About this we can learn a lot more from such Books, such as "Human life," "Snatch theft," "Covert theft," "Execute within the prescribed limits," "Grave digging," "Have sexual intercourse," "Conducting ta rial," "Penalising," "Arresting and escaping," "Taking ransom," "To go against capital punishment, "Petty crime" etc.

The last Book 63 of the Mongol Code is entitled the "Russia Code" and covered a wide range of issues. For instance, the Russia Code covers such matters as conducting trade in the areas neighbouring with the Russian frontier, rewarding and punishing the commanders and soldiers of the sentry posts, auditing the Khiagt border sentries once every 10 years, punishing Russians who have illegally crossed the border, inspecting official licenses authorising Russians to trade at Khiagt. The chapter on the protection of frontier borders and regulating border area crossings stipulates: "if there is a Russian border post on the territory of Khiagt District, and if there is a Chinese border post on the top of the Orkhoit Mountain, then divide this territory into two equal and turn them into southern and northern market places."

In this way, the 63rd Book entitled the Russia Code was introduced as a sign that the sphere of influence of the Manchu Qing Empire was extending also into Tsarist Russia, which increasingly came under pressure from the Manchu Empire.

The Mongol Code also defined the types and forms of penal punishment. According to this Code, capital punishment included dismemberment, slicing, slow slicing, decapitation and hanging the victim's body on gibbets for public display. There were other forms of punishment, such as putting the convicted person to penal labour, banishment to places with tough environmental and weather conditions, giving the person as a slave, tattooing the criminal's face etc. Apart from the above, the traditional penal punishment used by the Mongols, the so-called *Yüs Torgokh*, (*a form of penalty which was increased according to the severity of the crime, which included whipping, thrashing, clubbing etc. nine times. Tr.*) and the penalty was multiplied nine, seven, five and three times, and the penalty in most cases involved livestock animals.

Summarising the above brief observations, it can be argued that the Mongol Code, although in some aspects drafted with due consideration of the legal Mongol traditions, was in fact a code permeated through and through with the chauvinistic command policy of the Manchu Qing Empire. Dr. B. Sodovsüren, a Mongolian scholar who has thoroughly studied the Mongol Code, drew the following conclusion: "The Mongol Code is a historical legal document manifesting the many years of policy carried out in Outer Mongolia by the Manchu state."[29]

29 B. Sodovsüren, *Pre-Revolutionary Mongol State and Codes of Law,* Ulaanbaatar, 1988, p. 23.

6 The State and Laws of "Exalted by All" Mongolia (1911–1920)

1 Historical Summary

The Manchu Qing Dynasty, towards the end of the 19th and the beginning of the 20th centuries, started carrying out a so-called "New Administration Policy." Under this policy, it was planned to resettle huge numbers of Chinese in Outer Mongolia, sinocise the Mongols, work the grasslands for cultivation, exploit the natural resources together with major powers, and turn Outer Mongolia into an integral part of the Manchu-Chinese administration. The so-called "New Administration Policy" went against the vital interests of the Mongols, which prompted them to rise in armed liberation struggle. The scale and scope of the liberation struggle can be very well illustrated by the revolt of more than two thousand soldiers of common people in Uliastai in the early part of the twentieth century, the movement of the people of *Beis* Sansraidorj of Setsen Khan *aimag*, and the revolt by the lamas and commoners in Ikh Khüree in 1905–1907 and 1910, respectively. These uprisings, which took place one after the other, in different corners of the country, grew in size, bringing together the insurgents. By 1911, the Year of the White Pig, they had grown into a national liberation revolution.

In July 1911, *Chin Wang* Khanddorj of Tüsheet Khan *aimag* and Da Lama Tserenchimed, a prominent lama of the Great *Shabi*, during their oblation ceremony, the Bogd Gegeen, agreed in principle to call a secret congress of the important Khalkha nobles and lamas to discuss the revival of the country's independence with the support of Tsarist Russia. It was then decided to send a delegation including *Chin Wang* Khanddorj, Da Lama Tserenchimed and Khaisan, an Inner Mongolian noble, to Russia to seek assistance. Although their expectations were not fully met, Tsarist Russia promised small help and support, which facilitated the mounting of a revolution opposing the Manchu rule in China. Under such circumstances, a so-called Provisional Office of General Administration of Khalkha Ikh Khüree Affairs, which was in principle the headquarters for the organisation of the national liberation movement, was set up November 1911. The office, which had a status similar to the Provisional Government of Khalkha, mobilised soldiers from Tüsheet and Setsen Khan *aimags* and Sando, the Manchu Amban of Outer Mongolia, was driven out of the country.

Bodg Jebzundamba *Khutugtu* was declared the Khan of the newly established State on 29 December 1911 and the reinstatement of Mongolia's independence was proclaimed. Mongol soldiers under the command of Magsarjav and Damdinsüren liberated Uliastai In December 1911, after which they liberated Khovd in August 1912 and simultaneously during this time movements were spreading fast in Khölönbuir in the East of Outer Mongolia and in Shilin Gol in Inner Mongolia to unite with the Mongols in Outer Mongolia. In this way, the more than 200 years of Manchu rule in Mongolia was put to its death bed. All social classes and strata of Mongolia were drawn into the national liberation movement. Important and influential Khalkha nobles and aristocrats took over the political leadership of the liberation movement, and bore the burden of the struggle. From among them, *Chin Wang* Khanddorj and Da Lama Tserenchimed, with their education and knowledge, valour and courage, and political ingenuity and wisdom became the practical revolutionary leaders, while Bogd Khan Jebzundamba, who was the head of religion, provided spiritual leadership.

Although the fledgling country persevered in its efforts to seek the recognition of its independence from foreign countries, Tsarist Russia and China, in October 1913, reached a secret deal to retain Outer Mongolia as an autonomous region of China. The Mongolian government delegation opposed, in every way possible, the pressure and blackmail of Russia and China at the Russia, Mongolia and China 8-month-long marathon trilateral talks, which were held in the town of Khiagt in 1915, yet the other two negotiating partners were nevertheless able to impose their will on Mongolia. Thomas E. Ewing drew a constructive conclusion of the above situation, emphasising that geographical location and the vulnerable military and political status of Outer Mongolia hindered its foreign policy activities.[1]

Although Autonomous Mongolia acknowledged Chinese suzerainty, in essence, it had become a State dependent on Russia. The Mongols call the given period the establishment of the "Exalted by All Mongolia," which can also be referred to as the "Mongol Khaganate." The Government of this Khaganate carried out the necessary socio-economic and political reforms in the country in the years spanning 1911–1919.

1 Thomas E. Ewing, *Between the Hammer and the Anvil? Chinese and Russian Policies in Outer Mongolia 1911–1921,* 1980. p. 259.

2 State Structure

2.1 *The Government System and the Bogd Khan*

The newly established independent State was a State of absolute monarchy based on serfdom, where a dual religious and secular State system existed. The country opted for this form of government, which, on the one hand, was an effort to continue with the ancient traditional concept of Statehood (the dual policy), and on the other hand, a crucial part in the choice was influenced by the fact that the Bogd Gegeen was revered as a “Living Buddha.”

The Eighth Bogd Jebzundamba Khutugtu was the absolute monarch of the newly established Mongolia. He was born in 1870 to a Tibetan nobleman’s family, who served as an accountant at the Dalai Lama’s court. He was crowned the Eighth Bogd Jebzundamba Khutugtu of Ikh Khüree, Mongolia in 1875. He actively supported the great cause initiated by *Chin Wang* Khanddorj and Da Lama Tserenchimed, and provided leadership to the 1911 national liberation revolution. When he ascended the throne, he was proclaimed “The everlasting Bogd Khan, the hierarch and ruler of the Mongol religion and state.”

The Provisional Office of General Administration of Khalkha Ikh Khüree Affairs had the following set-up: 1. Bogd Gegeen provided leadership to the 1911 national liberation revolution; 2. Bogd Jebzundamba, as the hierarch of Mongolian Buddhism, was the spiritual leader of the mass devotees; 3. He was considered a member of the *Altan Urga* (Descent from Chinggis Khan) as he was the reincarnation of Öndör Gegeen Zanabazar; 4. In terms of the number of *shabi*-disciples, serfs and wealth, he was the richest person in Khalkha Mongolia; 5. There were no Mongol nobles and aristocrats who were on a par with him to claim his crown, for he was surrounded by supporters coming from all the social segments of Mongolia. Based on all this, he was made the first hierarch and ruler of Mongolia.

What is more, taking stock of the evolving situation then, national liberation revolutionary leaders, such as banner commander Chagdarjav, realised that there could be a power struggle amongst the major Khalkha nobles and aristocrats if anyone other than Bogd Gegeen was proclaimed the ruler of Mongolia, which could enfeeble the united national force leading to dissension and chaos. Tüsheet Khan Dashnyam was against crowning Bogd Gegeen as the theocratic ruler of Mongolia “Compared to Jebzundamba, who is of Tibetan origin, I am the most senior amongst the descents of Lord Chinggis Khan,” but he failed to canvas support. And so it can be said that the crowning of Bogd Gegeen as the theocratic ruler of Mongolia was not accidental for the move had taken into consideration many external and internal factors.

Bogd Jebzundamba was the ultimate theocrat and secular ruler, and his ordinances formed the legal basis of the state and government activities of the country. "The Mongol Code of Ordinances" proclaimed: "Enforce in the entire lands under jurisdiction all matters that have been regulated by the edict of Bogd Jebzundamba. Should a judicious amendment be required owing to circumstances, promptly report about it and seek a decree to carry out the amendments. Ministries, without submission of notice, shall not revoke. Violators of the edict shall be brought to the book."[2]

The resolution of vital national interest issues, appointment and dismissal of top government posts, conferring of titles, ranks and privileges for outstanding services to the state, ratification of treaties and agreements with foreign countries, and appointment of envoys to foreign nations were all decided through the ordinance of the Bogd Khan, who after reviewing appeals and supplications, the Bogd Khan would sign them off by writing "Be it according to the edict."

After Bogd Jebzumdamba Khutugtu became the ruler of Mongolia, he had 55,479 *shabi*-disciples, which increased in number to reach 89,362 and his annual revenue amounted to 900,000 taels of silver.[3] All this displayed the level of his State authority and economic capacity.

2.2 *Highest Executive Body and Government Ministries*

The Provisional Office of General Administration of Khalkha Ikh Khüree Affairs, after taking care of laying the basic foundations of the fledgling nation, such as promulgating the country's independence and enthroning the Bogd Gegeen as the supreme religious and state leader, worked to transfer the provisional government into a fully fledged standing administration. Soon after Bogd Khan was proclaimed the country's supreme head, the Government was formed with four ministries, Interior, Foreign, War, Finance and Law, and their ministers and deputies were immediately appointed. The Interior Ministry was the apex ministry and its chief minister, in some sense, fulfilled the duties of the head of the Government.

Da Lama Tserenchimed was appointed the Interior Minister, and according to the law, his Ministry "was responsible for administering and

2 *The Mongol Code of Ordinances*, Ulaanbaatar, 1995, p. 136.

3 *History of the Mongolian People's Republic*, in Three Volumes, Book Two, (1604–1719), Ulaanbaatar, 1968, p. 575.

managing all key issues related to the country's internal affairs."[4] The Ministry had a number of departments, including the Department of Officials, which was primarily overseeing inheritance rights of the numerous *wang, güng,* and *taiji,* monitoring and maintaining written records, maintaining registration of nobility, religion and lamas; the Protocol Department, which was responsible for state protocol matters; and the Central Department, which oversaw matters related to historiography, drafting laws and legislation, maintaining population census, and matters related to local relay stations.

In the second month of the Second Year of the *Exalted by All* (1912), when the ranking of the ministries was conducted by an edict of the Bogd Khan, the Foreign Ministry was elevated to the rank of second most important government office. Its first minister was *Chin Wang* Khanddorj. The Foreign Ministry's Southern Department oversaw matters related to China, the Northern Department dealt with issues of relations with Russia, and the Central Department was responsible for undertaking cross-cutting ministerial issues dealing with foreign affairs, which were discussed and agreed upon through consensus.

At the initial stage of its establishment, the War Ministry was given in charge to *Jün wang* Gombosüren, and in terms of ranking, the Ministry was the third most important government office and as laid out in the law "Its primary jurisdiction lay in managing all matters related to the military."[5] One of its departments was responsible for drafting military-related bills and enforcing them; another department oversaw matters related to maintaining registration of military personnel and their mobilisation, managing interior forces, police and their weapons, and their training; and the third department was charged with the task of determining the ranks and titles of officers and soldiers, their award and incentives.

The first Finance Minister was *Jün wang* Chagdarjav and the Ministry's mandate, as outlined in the law, was "to manage all financial affairs"[6] of the country. The Ministry's Internal Financial Department was entrusted with the task of managing income and expenditure; the External Financial Department was responsible for managing revenues generated from

4 *The Mongol Code of Ordinances,* Ulaanbaatar, 1995, p. 13 (As transcribed into the Cyrillic script from the traditional Mongol script by O. Batsaikhan, Z. Lonjid and Ch. Khajidsüren).

5 *Ibid.,* p. 13.

6 *Ibid.,* p. 14.

properties leased to foreigners; and the Customs Department was managing all matters related to customs.

The fifth in ranking government agency was the Law Ministry and its First Minister was *Jün wang* Namsrai, whose Ministry, as stipulated by law, "was responsible for ensuring law and order, and all matters related to the judiciary."[7] The Ministry was responsible for conducting inquiry and investigation, conducting court proceedings, and passing sentences.

The central State organs of the Khaganate Mongolia were not restricted to these five ministries, as another new ministry with the general mandate of administering and managing all matters related to customs and duties was established in 1912, bringing the total to six ministries. Bishrelt *Beil* Dorjtseren, who was serving as the Vice Finance Minister, was charged with the task of leading the new Ministry. It opened its branches in Khiagt, Uliastai and Khovd and began collecting taxes from both Mongols and foreigners, which was instrumental in augmenting the state treasury.

Bogd Khan, with the objective of streamlining and strengthening the executive government, set up a new Ministry called the "General Management Ministry" in 1912, which in fact was the institution of the post of the Prime Minister and Sain Noyon Khan Namnansüren was appointed to this new post. However, high-ranking lamas, who were interested in installing their own representative, apart from the Bogd Khan but a little higher in position than the Prime Minister, established a new ministry, the so-called Ministry for Facilitating Religion and State. Da Lama Dashzeveg was appointed as its new Minister, giving him the mandate to supervise and monitor the Prime Minister.

The Mongol Code of Ordinances also determined the organisation structure of the ministries. For instance, the Interior Ministry had one Minister, two Vice Ministers, one managing director, two deputy managing directors, two protocol officers, six writer officers, and twelve professional clerks. Following the examples of other monarchies, the state ministers took oath of office before the Bogd Khan. For example, when the Foreign Minister *Chin Wang* Khanddorj, together with his two deputies, took the oath of office, they pledged to "... shall not seek the simple way when carrying out services for the benefit of the religion and state, we shall not shun challenges, and pledge to abide by this oath, and cherish the state like the apple of eye and mirror of heart."[8]

---

7 *Ibid.*, p. 16.
8 Central National Archives of Mongolia, Fonds-2, Series-2, p. 1.

DIAGRAM 10 State structure of the Exalted by All Mongolia

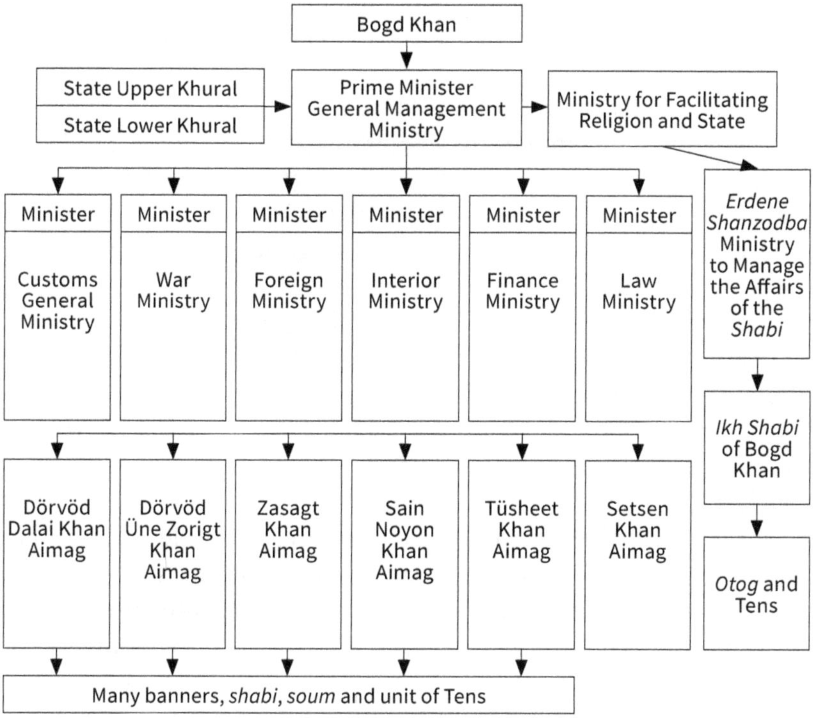

An undeniable proof that an absolute monarchy was established, which promoted the "dual principle" (that is, the parity of power and dignity of religion and State in political affairs) was evident from the substance and the form of the government. For example, the War Ministry had as its deity Red Namsrai, the God of Wealth; the War Ministry's deity was Red Jamsran, God of War; and the Foreign Ministry's deity was Red Ayüsh (Amitābha), the God of Longevity.[9] All the commencement and the conclusion times for all important state or government events were determined by means of numerological astrology, and such events were preceded by chanting prayers, burning incense and making offerings by Buddhist lamas. The Bogd Khan, apart from passing edicts on matters related to the State and government, held religious sermons for the believers and devotees, preaching them Buddha's teachings and religion as a whole.

9 J. Urangua, *Reforms of Outer Mongolia in the Early 20th Century*, Ulaanbaatar, 1997, p. 41.

The aforementioned ministries, in their capacity as the central state administrative bodies, accomplished impressive gains in their respective areas for the promotion of political, social and economic reforms.

2.3 *The State Upper and Lower* Khurals

A significantly important new development in the political life of Mongolian society was the establishment of the State Upper and Lower *Khurals* in February 1914, with the objective of "critically and collectively discussing all tough political issues and synthesising the collective policy."[10] The Upper *Khural* included the heads of ministries, their deputies, *zasag* and *non-zasag wang, güng, beil and beis,* as well as government officials called the *tüshmel,* authorities of the *Ikh Shabi,* and also leaders of Dariganga, Khölönbuir and Chakhar.The Lower *Khural* included the vice *tüshmel,* draughtsmen *tüshmel,* the Ministry of Erdene *Shanzodba* of *Ikh Khüree,* commanders of the four aimags, and the officials of the *jasaa.* The Upper *Khural* had 50–60 members and the Lower *Khural* had 70–80 members. In 1914, the Bogd Khan ratified eight-point internal rules of the *Khurals,* which contained procedural provisions, outlining the mandate of both the houses of the *Khural.* According to the rules, members of the Upper *Khural* met every Sunday at 11 in the morning and the members of the Lower *Khural* met every Friday at the General Management Ministry. Article Two of the Rules clearly outlined the relevant mandate of the two *Khurals* as follows: "The ministers and nobles of the Upper *Khural* shall hold consultations on important political matters, outline policies, and submit report on relevant issues, and take final decisions on those matters that are relevant. The Lower *Khural* shall be given for its consideration and the process shall be monitored. After the Lower *Khural* considers all the matters, relevant decisions shall be taken. The officials of the Lower *Khural* shall table motions of political significance and discuss then and submit a report. If no common consensus is reached on the considered issues, then each issue must explained and the relevant report shall be submitted."[11] Judging by the above, although some of the critically important issues were considered and decisions taken, it can be said that the Upper *Khural* was an organ with consultative rights, in particular, on matters related to foreign relations, which were submitted to the Bogd Khan for his consideration and final decision. The Lower *Khural* did not

10 The Document Called the Shin Toli (New Mirror), 1914, No. 12.

11 *The 1911 Struggle of the Mongolian people for National Freedom and Independence,* Compilation of documents, (1900–1914), Compiled for publication by A. Ochir and G. Pürev, p. 160.

take any final decision on matters considered, for it was responsible for proposing suggestions and recommendations to the Upper *Khural*.

Progressively minded people had been making evidence-based concrete proposals from the rostrum of the *Khurals* on matters related to socio-economic reforms in the country. For instance, Dalai Choinkhor *wang* Tserensodnom proposed to conduct an integrated taxation policy and a policy of supplement the state treasury by adopting an economising policy, while *Meeren* Dorj tabled a motion on establishing a motorised relay service.

At the start, both the Upper and Lower *Khurals*, in keeping with the rules, were beginning to regularly meet 47–48 times a year, but later on they failed to meet regularly and started breaching their internal rules more frequently. On 25 October 1919, the Lower *Khural* was dissolved by *Shanzodba* Badamdorj when the *Khural* members refused to deliberate an ultimatum by a Chinese military officer to terminate the autonomous right of Mongolia.

The fact that the Upper and Lower *Khurals* were active was facilitated by three factors, namely, 1) they were a direct continuation of *Ikh Khurildai*, *Chuulgan of the Nobles*, and the *Banner Chuulgans* – traditional methods of managing the State by the Mongols since early times; 2) the Mongols were earnestly interested in institutionalising parliamentarianism in the country in keeping with international practice; and 3) the idea of a bourgeois republic was beginning to take shape in the country.

However, neither *Khural* was elected, for they were formed primarily on the principle of ancestry, lineage and the rank and position held. A 1914 document on the formation of the State Upper and Lower *Khurals* hints at a gradual transition to electoral democracy, which articulated that "Although there have been assertions that the head and the representative of our *Khural* have not been elected even once, but since the relevant ministers and officials are familiar with the state of officers in their respective areas, it is appropriate, first and foremost to establish a bicameral Upper and Lower *Khurals*."[12] Articles published in Mongolia's first print newspapers "*Shin Toli*" (New Mirror) and "*Newspaper of Niislel Khüree*" convey a similar thought. The Eighth Bogd Jebzundamba himself was contemplating transition to a constitutional form of government.

2.3 *Some Changes in Rural Administrative Bodies*

The forms and structure of local administrative divisions, which existed during the times of the Manchu rule, had been retained in almost their

12 *Ibid.*, p. 159.

original form, but notwithstanding, local administrative units started functioning under the direct leadership of the Mongol Bogd Khan and its government, rather than under the control of a foreign authority or the *ambans*. However, minor changes had been effected in the local administrations: for example, the Khan Uul *chuulgan* was changed to Bogd Khan Khairkhan mountain *chuulgan*, the *chuulgan* Binderya Lake was changed to Khan Taishin *chuulgan* and the Kherlen Bars town *chuulgan* was transformed to Khan Khentii mountain *chuulgan*. At the same time, the Tsetserleg town *chuulgan* was not altered, and the Bat-Yüroolt Tögs Khölög Dalai Khan *aimag* of the Züüngar of the Dörvöd and the Ünen Zorigt Khan *aimag's* right wing were to determine the place they would convene for their assembly on an individual basis. The *chuulgan* of six *aimags* would convene once every three years, and would consider *aimag*-level important matters, such as the alteration of offices and promotion of *chuulgan* head. The *chuulgan* head would be elected from among the *Zasag* khans, *wang, beil, beis* and *non-zasag* khans and their appointment would come into force with an edict of the Bogd Khan. The office of the *chuulgan* head had the relevant numbers of officers working, and the *chuulgan* head's authority lay in endorsing the officials of the *banners*, supervising and monitoring the government functions in the *aimag*, coordinating the work of the relay stations, and attending to all matters that do not come within the competency of the *banner* governments. Military matters were managed by the *aimag* commanders, and similarly like the *chuulgan* head, the commander was appointed through an edict of the Bogd Khan. According to the "Code of Laws," the commander of the Tüsheet Khan *aimag* was given a plain white banner (standard); a plain yellow standard was given to the commander of the Setsen Khan *aimag*; a plain red banner was given to the commander of the Zasagt Khan *aimag*; a plain blue banner was given to the commander of the Sain Noyon Khan *aimag*; the commander of the Dörvöd Dalai Khan *aimag* was given a bordered white standard, while the commander of the Dörvöd Ünen Zorigt Khan *aimag* was given a bordered yellow banner. They were also given marked arrows and 12 shafts of arrows each.[13]

General administrative ministries were set up at Uliastai, Khovd and Khiagt. The highest decision-taking authority – the local minister – was selected by the Interior Ministry, whose office was equivalent to that of a Vice Minister of the central government. The General Administrative

13 *The Mongol Code of Ordinances*, Ulaanbaatar, 1995 (As transcribed into the Cyrillic script from the traditional Mongol script by O. Batsaikhan, Z. Lonjid and Ch. Khajidsüren), p. 27

Ministry had 13–14 officials, such as a chief administrator, writer-official, clerk, doctor, interpreter and a messenger.

The "Code of Laws" defined the administrative structure of the Kingdom of Mongolia, which consisted of the 30 *otog* of Bogd Jebzundamba, 21 banners of Tüsheet Khan *aimag,* 25 banners and 2 *otog shabi* (of Erdene Ilguulsan Khutugtu and Yegüzer *Khutugtu)* of Setsen Khan *aimag,* 20 banners and 2 *otog shabi* (Jalkhanz *Khutugtu* and Ilguulsan *Khutugtu* and Nomun Khan *Khutugtu),* Sain Noyon Khan *aimag's* 25 banners and 8 *otog shabi* (of Zaya Bandida *Khutugtu,* Erdene Bandida *Khutugtu,* Chin Süjigt Nomun Khan Eredene Khamba Noyon *Khutugtu,* Erdene Mergen Noyon *Khutugtu,* Naro Banchen *Khutugtu,* Naran *Khutugtu,* Khamba *Khutugtu* Nomun Khan and Shiva Shreet *Khutugtu),* the Züüngar Dörvöd Bat-Yüroolt Tögs Khölög Dalai Khan *aimag*'s 12 banners and 15 banners of Ünen Zorigt Khan *aimag's* right wing. And so the Exalted by All Mongolia had 6 *aimags,* 118 banners, and 56 *otog shabi* of Bogd Jebzumdamba and the *Khutugtu's* with seals.[14]

2.4 *The Military*

After throwing off the Manchu yoke and driving them out of the country, soldiers who were mobilised from central and local areas, such as the Tüsheet Khan and Setsen Khan *aimags,* became the foundation of the armed forces of the newly established Mongolia. The commander of the Tüsheet Khan *aimag, Chin Wang* Khanddorj, Khalkha's Magsarjav and Barag's Damdinsüren were instrumental and played a decisive part in driving away the Manchu aggressors from the land of the Mongols.

Soon after the establishment of the War Ministry, the Government immediately set about in earnest to set up a permanent army. The First Regiment composed of soldiers from the Tüsheet Khan *aimag* was stationed at Khujirbulan, and the Second and Third Regiments were deployed at the corner of Songino Khairkhan Mountain, while all the soldiers from the Setsen Khan *aimag* were divided into three regiments and were stationed also at Khujirbulan.

Men from these regiments were picked to serve as the Bogd Khan's bodyguards. And so, beginning from 1920, the first military units and regiments of the national army were created.

Not very long after this, relevant laws and legislations were passed and enforced. In December 1912, the draft of a 23-article "Provisional Rules and Procedures of the Mongol Soldiers" was submitted for consideration by the Bogd Khan, who endorsed it. This was a very important document,

14 *Ibid.*, pp. 6–11.

which outlined the basic principles underlying the structure and set-up, war methods, and the legal premises of the country's military. Issues taken up in the provisional rules and regulations were further specified in Chapters 37, 38 and 39 of the "Code of Laws."

Every 50 out of 150 military-age men from the six *aimags* were enlisted into the army, while the remaining 100 were active reserves. The army was divided into the central and local military and the latter was commanded by the *aimag* commander. The office of the *aimag* commander and the central military as well as all military-related affairs were managed by the War Ministry. The basic military unit consisted of the tens with ten servicemen, a military unit of 50 men and a regiment with 200 servicemen.

Each of the tens, units and regiments had their own commanders, and besides this, each regiment had a ranking officer. The commander of the tens was appointed by the unit commander, while the unit commanders were appointed by the office of the commander of the armed forces, and their appointment were subject to consideration and approval by the War Ministry. Each regiment had a standard with the insignia of the Soyombo symbol, and the *aimag* commanders had their own banners showing their individual specific features.

Russia provided financial and personnel assistance in the formation of the army of the Bogd Khan Mongolia. In April 1912, Tsarist Russia extended a 10-year soft loan of 100,000 roubles for this purpose. Russia also provided military instructors. One such first military instructor was a Cossack military officer, Vasilyev from Trans-Baikalia.

In February 1913, Mongolia concluded an exclusive agreement with the Russian Government according to which Mongolia would receive additional support in the establishment of a modern armed forces. Russia, for example, rendered help in setting up a contingent of 1,900 men-strong brigades consisting of 2 cavalry regiments with Russian cannons, machine guns and rifles. It also committed additional weapons and for this purpose agreed to provide 2 million roubles in loan. On top of this, 49 officers and non-commissioned officers were assigned to Mongolia to train Mongol soldiers and bolster military schools.

By early 1912, the military school in Khujir Bulan was inaugurated. It played an important part in educating Mongolian soldiers, training them in handling weapons, which was an important milestone in building the foundations of a modern military in the country. A number of Russian officers including instructor Sushminovich were awarded the Order of *Erdene Ochir.*

Some patriotic and progressive-minded statesmen like Manlai Baatar J. Damdinsüren tabled many significantly important proposals designed at augmenting the defence forces and establishing a modern army for the country.

2.5 *The Court and Court Proceedings*

The monarchy did not stop at reforming the country's judiciary, but went further to make some sweeping changes in the courts and court proceedings. The Law Ministry, which was established in 1911, acted as the highest judiciary body authority of the country. The “Code of Laws” specified that the judges, court officials and clerks “shall administer justice with regard to all disputes and wily acts concerning human lives, theft, defraud, committing adultery, engaging in brawl, and after finding all the factual truth, shall take written statements and confessions, which shall be submitted to the verification department and thereafter prosecuted. The verification department inspect and pass judgment on all the petitions and statements submitted by all the relevant offices, and absolve all the suspects who can be pardoned, determine the kind of penalty, hold court proceedings and process all the related written court documents.”

One of the key judicial system reforms was taken up in Chapter 47, entitled “Petty Crimes and Punishment by Law” in the “Code of Laws.” According to the law, Tüsheet Khan, Setsen Khan and the *Ikh Shabi* reported to the Foreign Ministry all homicide and theft cases related to foreign nationals, and the Foreign Ministry together with the Law Ministry investigated the cases and passed judgement, while other kinds of crime related to theft were to be handled by the relevant local officials, who had the authority to condemn the suspect to cangue and other forms of punishment of less severity. Punishment more severe than banishment was first decided by the local *zasag* and *chuulgan* leaders, who would present the case to the Ministry of Erdene *Shanzodba,* which in turn indicted the guilty party and handed them over to the Law Ministry for its review. If the *chuulgan* chief and the Erdene *Shanzodba* were not able to formally charge a suspect of manslaughter and other similar severe crimes, the suspect was delivered to the Law Ministry, where they would be tried and indicted accordingly. Given the proximity of both Tüsheet Khan and Setsen Khan to Uliastai, criminal cases were handed to the jurisdiction of the minister overseeing judicial matters in Uliastai for its review and conviction. Also cases from the *aimags* of Bat Yüroolt Dalai Khan and Ünen Zorigt Khans of the Dörvöd had to be handed by the relevant official in Khovd to the concerned minister in Uliastai. The fact that the dominion of cases was determined taking into consideration the proximity of geographical location and in coordination with the mandate and direction of authority of the relevant ministry was central to the judicial reform that had been effected.

The death penalty was carried out by an edict of the Bogd Khan. The "Code of Laws" states that "When the death penalty is awarded, the due processes, such as reviewing, recording and sentencing by the *zasag* officials and submission of sentence to the *chuulgan* chief, shall be completed, thereafter the case shall be submitted for review to the Law Ministry, which shall make the final decision and seek petition for the carrying out of the sentence."

Execution in the capital Niislel *Khüree* was carried out in a place called Shar Khad (Yellow Cliff) in the eastern district of the town.

A multi-tier judicial system, starting with the *banner* leader, *chuulgan* chief, Khovd, some relevant ministers and government offices in Uliastai and Khiagt, and the Law Ministry was established during the period of the Bogd monarchy. In this manner, a commoner who was indicted was given the opportunity to fight his case at different levels of the judiciary, which marked the progressive aspect of the judicial reform that was carried out then.

2.6 *The State and Ceremonial Systems*

Soon after the establishment of a khanate Mongolia, the Government immediately set about putting in place the State and ceremonial systems and began using a state symbol clearly exhibiting the national traditions and techniques. The supreme symbol of the newly established State was determined as the Soyombo (*derived from Sanskrit svayambhu, meaning self-created. Tr.*). The Soyombo symbol was placed with esteem in the state flag and state stamps as an epitome of independence and sovereignty of the country. The Soyombo symbol (originating from the Soyombo script, invented by the First Bogd Öndör Gegeen Zanabazar in 1686) has ten elements in columnar arrangement of abstract and geometric symbols and patterns. They are fire, sun, and moon (symbolising universe, organic world), two triangles, two horizontal rectangles, the *Taijitu* or as we commonly know them, yin and yang, and two vertical rectangles.

Mongolia during this period used a state seal, on which were inscribed the words, "This is the seal of Bogd Khan – The Dual Policy Ruler and the Giver of Sun," which was made of jade. The seal was stamped on all kinds of ordinances and edicts, clemency writs, certificates of honour, letters of accreditation, which were as a rule written on yellow silk. The Bogd Khan, in his capacity as the country's theocratic ruler, used a different seal with the inscriptions: "This is the Golden Seal of Jebzundamba Lama, defender of the faith, giver of happiness, salvation and hope to sentient beings, the personification of Vajradhara," which was used on documents related to religious affairs.

From early times, the Mongols had been using the Nine White Banner, the Black Banner and a black and white banner (*The Nine White Banner called the "Yösön Khölt Tsagaan Tug" in Mongolian, was composed of nine flag poles decorated with white horse tail hairs hanging from a round surface with a flame or fork-like shape on the top. Tr.*) But in 1911, keeping abreast of international practices, Bogd Khan's Mongolia introduced a national flag made of cotton, 210 x 210 cm in size. The flag was yellow and bordered with red fabric on three sides, one near the flagpole; it had three tongues made of red cloth, one at the top, middle and bottom, and inscribed on the top and bottom tongue were tantric words *Um Aa Hom*, and the middle one had tantric lines in the Soyombo script, which meant prosperity. The Bogd Khanate also had a war standard, which carried symbols extolling the grandeur of the Mongol State. After ascending the throne in August 1911, Bogd Khan Jebzundamba also created the so-called "Seven Jewels" (*Seven jewels or the seven emblems of royalty, included the wheel, the white elephant, the deep blue horse, the sacred jewel, the jewel woman, the merchant-artisan, and the military commander, which are the seven possessions of a universal monarch. Tr.*). This traditional state emblem of the ancient Mongols was later used in ancient India and Tibet as well.

After 1911, Mongol nobles and officials, as well as ranking lamas started donning State ceremonial dress. During this period, Mongolian military uniform was also introduced, about which we can find a detailed definition in the "Code of Laws." One of the newest introductions in ceremonial dress during the period of "Exalted by All" was the ceremonial robe for the Bogd Khan. The robe incorporates the best of Oriental design, more specifically, Indo-Tibetan aristocratic wear infused with the Mongolian traditional method and motives of clothing, designed to display the glory of the theocratic ruler. High-ranking officials, according to their rank, also had their own specific robes, headgear, topcoat, sash, and even seat cushion and recliner chairs. Their garments differed according to the number of buttons, and peacock feathers on their hats and overcoats. At this time, the dress worn and headgear including ceremonial hats used by the Mongols were very much similar to the Manchus, different according to the rank and position held, and in particular the difference was displayed according to the design of the buttons, as the buttons of higher ranks were studded with pearls.

During the period of the Khanate Mongolia, the order in which the nobles and princes were to sit in the court, the kind of horse-drawn carriage, the shade of the horse, even the *ger* and the fence around it were all codified. For example, ministers would sit in the front row, in the second row the four Khalkha khans would sit, then the two Dörvöd khans, and even their back-rests were all different.

The annual award of the Bogd Khan was called the "Exalted by All" and the Bogd Khan's Government started using the Mongol lunar calendar and that is why the annual Mongolian New Year called *Tsagaan Sar* (White Month) was observed as a celebration of the country's independence. The pompous *Tsagaan Sar* celebrations included the Great Celebration in the Bogd Khan court, while the *aimags* and banners celebrated their own official *Tsagaan Sar* procedures, and the commoners had their own simpler form of celebration.

One of the main celebrations of the newly established Mongol Khanate was a *Naadam,* a sports festival held for the benefit of the Jebzundamba *Khututgu,* which was called the *Naadam to Offer the Bat-Orshil.* This festival first originated during the ceremony of enthroning the First Bogd Jebzundamba, when the seven Khalkha banners got together for this grand celebration, which was better known as the *Danshig Naadam of the Seven Banners.* This festival was further codified in the "Code of Laws" during the reign of the theocratic rule of Bogd Khan, according to which the grand festival was held in the capital of Niislel Khüree, and the mass celebration was organised at a place called Khüi Mandal near the Khiagt relay station in the north of the country. The Khan's guard of honour would line up temples and monasteries where the Bogd Khan's Lunar New Year celebration was planned to be held on special occasions.

Since the dual principle – the parity of power and dignity of religion and State in political affairs – had become a *de facto* policy principle, State celebrations with elements of religious etiquette became a common feature. For example, in the last month of spring a huge procession was held to revere and pay homage to God Maitreya (*According to Buddhist tradition, Maitreya or Maidar in Mongolian, is a bodhisattva who is prophesied to appear on Earth, achieve complete enlightenment, and teach the pure dharma. Tr.*) for the benefit of the coming future, and this procession was called *Maidar Ergekh.* The Bogd Khan, identifying an auspicious day on the last month of the spring every year, visited the palace at the Gungaachoiling Monastery, and again identifying an auspicious day in the last month of fall, would return to the main palace. A religious mask *Tsam* dance was held, archery contests were held, and prayers were offered to the mountains, some ancient rituals that are conducted in keeping with strict established codes and procedures.

One of the latest State symbols that was instituted in 1913 was the *First, Second and Third Class Order of Erdene Ochir.* Foreigners were awarded the Order of First Class, while the Second and Third Class Order of Erdene Ochir were given to Mongol nobles and officials.

These State and ceremonial systems were evidence, symbols of the existence of the independence, sovereignty of the State of Mongolia.

3 The Law

3.1 *The Beginning of Legal Reform*

Mongolia, after regaining its independence, set out to carry out some national-in-form reforms in the political and legal sectors. A Mongolian scholar B. Sodovsüren, who studied the State system and law of this period, writes that the work to replace the Manchu laws and legal system was carried out in two stages. In the first stage, which covered the period from 1911 to 1915, efforts were made to replace the Manchu administration and its system, put in order the government apparatus, conduct a new economic and financial policy, establish a culture and education department, streamline the judicial system, and put in order laws and legislation. In the second stage, 1915–1918, work was done on the draft bills: they were submitted for consideration to the State Upper and Lower *Khurals,* their approval by the Bogd Khan was secured, and finally they were printed for distribution and for compliance.[15]

The key sources of the Mongol Khanate in the early twentieth century were the edicts and ordinances of the Bogd Khan, laws considered by the Upper and Lower *Khurals,* and approved by the Bogd Khan, as well as legal acts of rules of a procedural nature. At one time, there were authors who wrote and claimed that the Mongol Khanate under the Bogd Khan was never involved in efforts to reform the laws, and that the old codes and laws adopted by the Manchus were being applied, but these assertions are being rebuffed by many hard facts and evidence from original sources. In late 1911, Bogd Khan gave consent to provisionally apply some of the clauses and provisions of the "Code of Laws of Outer Mongolia" up until their adoption *à la* Mongol law, having thoroughly reviewed the bill submitted by the Law Ministry. Therefore, up until the adoption of news laws and legislation of new Mongolia, the Government and the Ministry enforced legislative acts on the basis of edicts passed by the Bogd Khan to whom draft bills had been submitted for his consideration and approval.

15 B. Sodovsüren, *State System and Law of Pre-Revolutionary Mongolia, (1911–1920)*, Ulaanbaatar, 1989, p. 41.

For instance, on 12 February 1915, such forms of punishment as rodding, clubbing and even the death sentence, which were given to elderly people, under-age minors and sick people, were replaced by paying of ransom and the size of ransom was fixed. Laws that were in force during the period of the Manchu rule were abrogated on 21 April 1915. Banishment for stealing livestock animals and other's property, punishment of putting a suspect in shackles for one month and flogging 100 times with a wooden whip of the mastermind of stealing 1–21 livestock animals, flogging his accomplice 100 times, thrashing a person 90 times, who had taken a share from the stolen animals, and banishing the mastermind of a crime of stealing 3–5 heads of animals were all revoked and the criminals were made to wear a cangue for half a year. Similarly, the perpetrator of the crime of stealing 6–9 animals was made to wear a cangue for nine months, and those who had stolen 20 or more animals were tortured and amputated, the sentences were revoked with one year imprisonment or wearing a cangue for two years. Those criminals who had masterminded the crime and their accomplices who had stolen 30 or more number of livestock animals, were in the past sentenced to death through amputation, and this form of punishment was replaced by either two years in jail or two years with cangue. All other kinds of death sentences were revoked, while some of them were replaced with a lighter form of punishment, which proves that the legislative policy of the Khanate Mongolia was significantly different from that of the policy that was carried out during the rule of the Manchu Qing dynasty.[16]

The Bogd Khan Government set up a 16-member legislative commission on 5 May 1915 composed of educated state officials and important religious personalities. On 14 July of the same year, instructions were sent to all the ministries, the four *aimags* and the five *shabi* to name the old laws and make recommendations on relevant changes and amendments, and submit their proposals and suggestion to the bills in the making to facilitate the work of the commission.

The Bogd Khan Government of Mongolia was conducting a policy of aligning its State and legal system with international good practices. A Mongolian scholar Jamsrangiin Tsedev drafted the concept of a Constitution by a decision of Mongolia's Prime Minister Sain Noyon Khan Namnansüren. The decision ordered to "Draft a summary of the clauses and provisions that come under the competence of the Government by studying different laws and regulations of big and small countries around the world, the prerogatives and principles of foreign policy, as well as the

16 *Ibid.*, p. 42.

inter-relationship between the highest state and local authorities."[17] A Russian journal *"Dal'nii Vostok"* (Far East) in its September 1913 edition reported that Mongolia's Constitution had been drafted by an edict of the Bogd Khan. According to *"Dal'nii Vostok,"* the draft Constitution, apart from proclaiming the immunity of Bogd Jebzumdamba *Khutugtu*, contained a provision which specified that should the Bogd Khan declare a state of emergency, Tsarist Russia must be informed of this act without delay. The journal also wrote on the legal aspects of the relationship between the Bogd Khan and the Parliament.

The fact that the concept of a Parliament was in the making bears witness to the fact that the authorities of the newly established Khanate Mongolia were determined and committed to intensifying the process of legal reform in the country.

The Law Ministry, from the very days after the founding of the "Exalted by All" Mongolia, introduced a register called "A Summary of General Affairs," which registered submissions by different ministries as well as special edicts that were passed. The record contained 63 documents of a legal nature that were adopted or passed by the Bogd Khan over the period starting in 1911 to April 1917.[18] One of them was the so-called legislative act with 12 paragraphs known as "Mandatory Laws and Rules," which was a compilation of laws and rules which were drafted and enforced by the five government ministries in the years between 1913 and 1919. Let us take a look at these 12 paragraphs:

1 Paragraph One. The rules on notifying Erdene *Shandozba* beforehand if criminal proceedings are contemplated against the lamas belonging to a monastery, its school or those who are serving there, such as the *miangatan* (commander of 1000 men), *gelen* (monk), *Getsel* (commencing monk below the ranks of *gelen*), clergymen or khans, who belong to a monastery in Niislel Khüree or schools, and are involved in religious prayers and functions at *aimags*.

2 Paragraph Two. Rules prohibiting the employment of officials serving at the relevant ministry of the *shabi*, and in the treasury section in several posts at the same time, and the rules of reviewing them on a case-by-case basis, and the due process of notification of such a decision, if it has been taken.

17 The Document Called the Shin Toli (New Mirror), 1914, No. 12, p. 36.

18 *The Mongol Code of Ordinances*, Ulaanbaatar, 1995, p. 13 (As transcribed into the Cyrillic script from the traditional Mongol script by O. Batsaikhan, Z. Lonjid and Ch. Khajidsüren), p. 56.

3 Paragraph Three. Rules on sentencing violators of laws, and on replacing the sentence with a ransom, and determining the ransom as per the rules.

4 Paragraph Four. A rule commuting the sentence of one year of shackles for a criminal sentenced to death or banishment for cattle theft.

5 Paragraph Five. Rules on settling debts owed to a foreigner and a local individual by a person who has defaulted and making the relevant *otog* or the suspect's close relatives repay the loan and on closing the case.

6 Paragraph Six. Rules on forbidding a government office or ministry to arbitrarily alter or repeal all rules and regulations that have been adopted by previous orders and instructions, and on informing beforehand, should there be any changes necessitated by circumstances.

7 Paragraph Seven. Rules on locally handing down punishment for offences related to alcohol consumption, betting and gambling.

8 Paragraph Eight. Rules on stopping and outlawing the buying of sheep, livestock animals, milk, butter, hay and fuel for burning, coming from the rural areas, before they can reach the market by any well-to-do-trader and merchant.

9 Paragraph Nine. Rules on collecting fines in penalty by the relevant authorities from people who have been fined for stealing livestock animals commensurate with their market price.

10 Paragraph Ten. The Codes of Ordinances for enforcement in resolving cases related to thievery and fraud.

11 Paragraph Eleven. Rules on equating the rank of Erdene *Shanzodba* of Niislel Khüree with that of a *chuulgan* chief, and that of senior and junior chiefs of an *otog* with that of a *zasag taiji* and a *zangi* (Commander of a *soum)* and on imposing a fine of compensation by giving livestock animals.

12 Paragraph Twelve. Thirty-two point rules on punishing any lama who ia involved in indecent activities in areas belonging to lay inhabitants.[19]

If we summarise the subject matter of the above 12 paragraphs, we can see that criminal law-regulated relations concerning the state system, religion and the lamas, have been addressed in them. The duties and functions of the monarchy government have been taken up in detail, and the authority and duties of the ministers in Uliastai, Khovd and Khiagt, the

19 *Mandatory Laws and Rules, (1913–1918)*, (Compiled by J. Urangua and B. Bayarsaikhan), Ulaanbaatar, 2004, p. 12.

heads of the *aimag chuulgans* and their structural and organisation set-up have been codified.

Relations related to the lamas and the clergy that have been regulated and codified in the "Mandatory Laws and Rules" have a number of interesting features. First, it incorporated the special features of the older laws and codes; second, it embraced to a certain extent the idea of the principle of the dual policy; and third, rites and rituals of Buddhism were shielded and preserved on the level of legal concept.[20]

The rules regulated such criminal law relations as consumption of liquor, engaging in gambling, carrying out trading before the merchandise reacedh the market, burglary and cheating, and stealing of livestock animals etc. Lamas as well as lay people, who breached the rules, were as a rule penalised by offering livestock animals in fine, submitting nine herds of animals, stroking, and passing sentence to the lamas by threatening them that they would be forced to give up their celibacy. Study into the original source of the "Mandatory Laws and Rules" (1913–1918) has been conducted by Dr. J. Urangua and Dr. B. Bayarsaikhan.

It would be appropriate to note here that a book called *Elements of International Law,* authored by an American lawyer and diplomat, Henry Wheaton, was translated into Mongolian in the early 1990s under the title *Common Laws of Multitude of States.* So far, it is unclear who translated the book and when it was translated. Academician J. Amarsanaa has noted that "This book played no small part in facilitating Mongolia to grow and develop, similarly like many other countries around the world, into a similarly sovereign and independent country in the early 20th century, securing their recognition by world countries, and promoting Mongolia as equal partners in relationship with them, which is evident from the envoys dispatched to Tsarist Russia and Japan, mutual exchange of communications, as well as such historically important events as the tripartite Treaty of Khiagt, signed between Russia, Mongolia and China in 1915. Proceeding from this premise, this book can be viewed as one of the first historical legal sources of common international law of Mongolia."[21]

The subject matter of the translated book *Common Laws of Multitude of States* includes, 1) the means and methods of forming the competent state authorities, their structure, prerogative rights and functions; 2) norms and standards for the defence of the country, and the policy during time of war; 3) principles, methods and forms of foreign policy; 4)

---

20 *Ibid.,* p. 21.

21 Henry Wheaton, *Elements of International Law,* (compiled by J. Amarsanaa, B. Bayarsaikhan and Tachibana Makoto), Ulaanbaatar, p. 71.

the order, procedures, traditions applied in international relations; and 5) wide-ranging topics on foreign trade status and transportation

Thanks to the due functions carried out by the legislative commission, a book of 65 laws called the "Code of Ordinances of Mongolia" was drafted. After relevant changes and amendments were added following consideration by both the Upper and Lower *Khurals,* it was approved by the theocratic ruler of the country. Besides relying on the legal traditions of Mongolia in the drafting of the bill, laws and legislation of foreign countries, such as the one mentioned earlier, were comparatively analysed and used. The bill was drafted between 1915 and 1918 and its chapters were adopted one after the other in a sporadic manner, to be finally compiled into one solid law during these three and more years. Movable-type printing technology was used for printing some parts of the law, while some other remaining parts were handwritten, the copies of which we have inherited. The printer's copies of the 58 books are kept at the National Archives and the National Central Library, and Mongolian historians Z. Lonjid and O. Batsaikhan transliterated the law in the classical Mongolian script into the Cyrillic script, which was published in 1995. Thereafter, the law has been printed several times by the National Law Centre, the Law College of the National University of Mongolia and the Ministry of Law and Home Affairs.

Doctor O. Batsaikhan found and brought from Japan the missing 8 books of the "Code of Ordinances of Mongolia", which were translated from Japanese into Mongolian by translator Almas and put to the print. Some of the books that were not found earlier were found and completed, which was not only a monumental work but also a work worthy of appreciation.

3.2 *The "Code of Ordinances of Mongolia"*

As characterised by Dr. G. Sovd, the "Code of Ordinances, depending on both the evolving domestic and external factors in the given period, with its structure, basic objectives and substance matter, similarly like the laws of other countries in the period of feudal system, was an integrated law that regularised various aspects of social relations."[22]

If we classify the various aspects of social and legal relations contained in the many laws of the Code of Ordinances, we get the following: Six books of the law deal with the State structure of Mongolia; nine books cover the issue of State administration; three books codify rites and rituals of Buddhism; six books are related to civilian affairs, including cus-

22 E. Avirmed, D. Dashtseden and G. Sovd, *Mongol Law*, Ulaanbaatar, 1997.

toms duty and taxes, land farming, and family relations; three books regularise military relationships; there are thirteen books on criminal law and court proceedings, and one book covers the topic of foreign relations.

Although the Code of Ordinance, in terms of content and principle, relied quite substantially on the "Code of Laws of Outer Mongolia" and attempted to incorporate as much as possible the unique and special features of the Mongol society and political relations, its language and its formulation came very close to international legal terms, and in this sense, it truly became a Mongol law. The Code of Laws, first of all, defined the territorial and administrative divisions of Mongolia, the organisational and structural set-up of the government and its ministries, their basic duties and functions, as well as the principle of inheritance and succession. Since this topic has been taken up in the previous section, we would like to refer to a couple of examples of how the Code of Laws regulated relations concerning government officials. The Code determined the size of the staff of the government ministries and the ranks and positions of the concerned officers. For example, government officials were ranked as chief, deputy, officers of third, fourth, fifth and six ranks etc., and accordingly, they were entitled to wear on their hats button knots (*similar to knife lanyard knot. Tr.*), which differed in size and colour to distinguish the rank, grade and position.

Rules were introduced, according to which all officials of ministries, below the rank of the deputy officer, had to undergo a performance review once every three years, for promotion and/or demotion. The chief officers, that is, the ministers, had the responsibility of monitoring and reviewing the performance of their subordinates, and at times, this was done involving also their deputies. According to the established procedure, first a list with the names of the officials was drawn up, who had to appear for a written test of writing a one-page composition on a topic concerning a topical national issue. According to the Code of Laws, a number of competency criteria were considered before taking a decision on promotion or demotion. For example, they were tested for their competency, discipline, business initiative and age. It also defined 8 types of behaviour unfit for a government officer, including, being greedy, brutish, inert, neglectful, having frail health, being obsequious and ill-educated. Government officers were examined according to these criteria, and it was decided whether they could be promoted, demoted, or neither of them.

During the period of the Manchu rule, a key selection criteria included the level of loyalty to the Emperor, but during the period of Bogd Khan Mongolia, as determined in the Code of Law, professionalism, skills and principled behaviour of an officer were given due respect. The Mongol

Khanate under Bogd Khan regarded the appointment and placement of professional, skilled, educated and upright officers as the earnest and strong foundation of the principle of statehood.

Books 1 to 10 of the "Code of Laws" reflect the national traditions and unique aspects of State administration and in this sense, the Code can be rightly qualified as the fundamental code covering the entire spectrum of State relations. As a matter of fact, Book 51 of the Code, in its entirety, seemingly is a redaction of the provisions of the old Manchu law while taking into due consideration the traditions and special features of Mongolian Statehood. But six books of the Code, entitled "Welcoming Guests," "Code for Storehouses," "Reporting the Timely News", "The Law on Offering Sacrifice," "The Code of Protocol", were newly drafted. Laws pertaining to State ceremonies and protocols, the ceremony of welcoming and bidding farewell to guests(s), diplomatic envoys, paying visits, attending a ceremony at a ministry for official duties, holding meetings, paying courtesy calls on the high-ups, presenting a gift to the Bogd *Khutugtu,* as well as other ceremonial issues, such as dress code, and special protocol during Lunar New Year celebrations were all codified strictly according to Mongolian traditions and customs. The books on the "Code for Storehouses" and "Reporting the Timely News" contain financial rules and procedures, the date when the calendar has to be developed, as well as, celestial astrology, yin and yang principles.

The authors of the "Code of Laws" followed the principle of either summarising or defining in detail some of the provisions, depending on their social and economic importance, contained in the laws adopted during the Manchu period. For example, the Manchu law on state cereals had defined the importance of government-owned cereal in three paragraphs, while the "Code of Laws" extended it to 11 paragraphs. The Manchu "Law on Lamas and Their Affairs" had 54 books and 108 provisions, which were reduced to 3 books with 30 provisions in the "Code of Laws."

The privileges of the Eighth Bogd Khan Jebzundamba, the theocratic ruler of independent and sovereign Mongolia, was codified in Book 33 and several others books of the "Code of Laws." For example, Book 33 of the Code contains specific clauses and provisions related to the safety of the Bogd Khan's food, the security of his palace, as well as protocols on seeking audience of the Bogd Khan, making their strict compliance mandatory.

Although some of the penal provisions in the old Manchu laws were adopted in the "Code of Laws" to a certain extent, in most cases, the penalties were moderated. For instance, under the Manchu law, methods of execution included amputation, slow slicing and quartering were listed, whereas the Code of Laws" specified execution by shooting. There were the following types of punishment: removal of someone from an official post, deduction of wages, imposing nine fold penalty, whipping, wearing the cangue, imprisoning, and execution by a firing squad. Given the fact that commodity-money relations were developing, the law also permitted the remitting in payment of a certain amount of money instead of a number of heads of livestock animals.

Books 49 to 55 of the "Code of Laws" basically include provisions of a regulatory nature, but it must be noted that other books also contain ample provisions of this nature.

Book 65, which was recovered from Japan, codified the regulatory mechanisms of different kinds of criminal offences emanating from the new relationship that had evolved together with the process of revival of the country. For example, this book covers offences which had never been considered before, such criminal acts as deliberately setting fire to electrical mains, forging seals and stamps, accidently burning treaties and agreements, weapons, destroying roads and bridges, desecrating graves and their headboards, and specifies the types of penalties for such felonies. The book also contains provisions related to providing medical service and treatments to employers, servants and paid labourers, which could be explained by the development of a commodity-money relationship in the society, a brand new element of social relations. Other forms of punishment included fining with livestock animals, whipping, banishing to a remote location, stripping a noble of his rank and privileges, imprisonment, and indemnifying by paying physical assets.

The drafting of the "Code of Laws" was completed between 1915 and 1918, and because of circumstances, it was not implemented fully in the social life of the country. But the "Code of Ordinances of Mongolia" was not only the central legal document that regulated social relations in the short period after Mongolia regained its independence through the national liberation revolution of 1911, it was also a significantly important document that laid the foundations of the law of Mongolia in the twentieth century.

7 The State and Laws in the Period of Struggle for the Establishment of a Constitutional Structure in Mongolia (1921–1924)

1 Historical Summary

The late 1910s and the early 1920s were periods when Mongolian society was riddled with crises, and when profound changes were taking place in the country's domestic and external environment. The Socialist revolution triumphed in Russia in 1917, which in one way or the other impacted neighbouring Mongolia as well. At this time of trouble, Mongolia's southern neighbour China started hatching plans and schemes to ensure it did not lose any of its old sphere of influence in the country, and waited for an opportune moment to occupy Mongolia. Bogd Khan and his close associates, after carefully assessing the evolving situation and the existing circumstances, set out to seek the patronage and protection of major powers to preserve, at the very least, the country's autonomy, and if at all possible, its independence and sovereignty. Top leaders of the country began to look for partners and support in this case. For example, Prime Minister *Shanzav* Badamdorj believed this objective could be obtained with the help of China, while Jalkhanz Khutugtu Damdinbazar and other *khutugtus* and reincarnates wanted to lean on the United States, and still other nobles and princes wanted to ask for help from Japan. As a matter of fact, practical efforts were being made towards this end.

However, finally towards the end of 1919, Mongolia was taken over by the Chinese aggressors and the country lost its independence, leading to the establishment of an aggressive and tyrannical regime of Chinese military. The abolition of Mongolian autonomy in 1919 reawakened the Mongolian national independence movement. A striking demonstration of this was the formation of a number of anti-Chinese underground resistance groups in the capital Niislel Khüree. They included the so-called "Consular" group headed by a journalist and lama D. Bodoo in late 1918; the "Khüree" group under the leadership of S. Danzan, an officer at the Finance Ministry in the summer of 1919; and the so-called Group of "Aristocrat Nobles," which included many influential clergy and lay nobles and princes, such as Da Lama Puntsagdorj, and Jalkhanz Khutugtu Damdinbazar. The underlying goal of all the three groups were almost the same, to revive the independence of Mongolia for the benefit of the religion.

The first two groups "Consular" and "Khüree" merged on 25 June 1920 to found a revolutionary organisation called the "Mongolian People's Party", which was officially established on 1 March 1921, and was the forerunner and the foundational base of the country's political party – the Mongolian People's Party.

The compatriots for the great cause founded the People's Provisional Government of Mongolia on 13 March 1921 and set about preparing for the national democratic revolution.

Mongolian revolutionaries established contact with the Comintern (Third International) and the Russian Soviet Federative Socialist Republic. They united all the progressive and democratically minded people and mounted a determined struggle for the country's independence and sovereignty, which led to the triumphant National People's Revolution of 1921, and restored the Bogd Khan to the throne of the constitutional monarchy.

The People's Government and the constitutional monarchy together carried out substantial political, social and economic transformations in the country in the years from 1921 to 1924, which created the necessary preconditions for a constitutional, People's Republic.

2 Re-establishing Independence and Laying the Foundation for a New State System

Mongolian revolutionaries, from the very beginning, conducted a policy of "upholding religion" and gave priority attention to developing a well-grounded concept defining the type, form and characteristics of a planned future State system. An agitation note, which was hung on the doors of Xu Shuzheng (*In 1919 Xu assumed command of the Northwest Frontier Defense Army, which invaded newly independent Outer Mongolia in October. On November 17, he forced Outer Mongolia to withdraw its declaration of autonomy, thus temporarily bringing Mongolia back under Chinese control. Tr.*), was a warning petition. "... following in the footsteps of the ancestry, we shall put an end, once and forever, the hereditary practice of the banner *zasag*, remove the present incoherent government and build a government on the examples of many foreign nations around the world."[1] The note was a clear hint that Mongolia wanted to establish a government of a bourgeois democratic republic. The formulation that the country would "build a government on the examples of many foreign nations around the

1 Documents Pertaining to the History of the MPRP (Mongolian People's Revolutionary Party), (1920–1949), U

world," was a clear indication of the plan to build a Republic, not only along the pattern of the Russian Soviet Federative Socialist Republic, but also akin to Western capitalist republics.

Two of the revolutionary groups held a joint meeting on 25 June 1920, where they founded a revolutionary organisation called the "Mongolian People's Party" and adopted a so-called "Oath of Allegiance of the Party People" (Намын хүмүүсийн дагаж явах тангарагийн бичиг – in Mongolian), which outlined the priority objectives of the national democratic revolution as "to liquidate the foreign enemy which is hostile to our religion and race; to restore lost rights; to improve sincerely the internal government; to give total attention to the interests of the poor and lowly masses; to preserve forever our internal rights; and to live neither oppressing nor being oppressed,"[2] thus clearly proclaiming that the country's would have a people's government but class-based in nature. The very formulation that "the good of the poor and common people would be sincerely considered" meant that state matters would be approached from a class perspective.

As the Mongolian revolutionaries began to acquire a better grasp of the notion of State and as their ideology took firmer shape, they began to develop a much more precise concept of statehood. A letter sent to the Mongolia-Tibet Department of the Secretariat of the 10th Far East Comintern in November 1920 by the Mongolian Revolutionaries, who were in Irkutsk, said "...we, representatives of the People's Party, having received enormous assistance of Russia on behalf of the People's Party, and with the help of select authorities and military force, we have regained our autonomy, we have restored the constitutional monarchy of our Khutugtu and through all this, we shall snap the rule by the hereditary nobles ... and as soon as an opportune moment comes when we see signs of improvement, we shall once again wage a revolution in one to two years, and undo the authorities in minority "[3] clearly defining the framework of a future State.

In this letter, the Mongolian revolutionaries defined their fundamental policy direction. Firstly, they used the term "Regain Autonomy" not merely as the revival of autonomy, but also as common terminology understandable for the masses, and resorted to a tactical policy of involving different social classes, groupings and strata in the cause of the Revolution. Secondly, taking into consideration the balance of forces within the country, and the clout and influence of the Bogd Khan, they set the

2 *Ibid.*, p. 7.
3 *Ibid.*, p. 11.

objective of establishing a constitutional monarchy in form only. Thirdly, after the Revolution, after taking multi-faceted socio-political and economic measures and strengthening the external and internal situation, it is formulated that the main direction is to abolish serfdom and declare a People's Republic.

A newspaper *Mongolyn Ünen* (Mongolian Truth), which was first launched on 10 November 1920, played an important part in developing the concept of the new State and government. Such articles, which were carried by the *Mongolyn Ünen,* as "The Benefits of Mongolia's Resurrection," "What type of government is good for Mongolia?" "Basic guidelines for the establishment of a new people's government in Mongolia," and "The benefits of a people's new central and local governments of Mongolia" in essence outlined the basic principles of a new future government and its structures. The article called "Basic guidelines for the establishment of a new people's government in Mongolia" criticised the capitalist democratic State as a government of minority exploiters, and outlined the contours of a law-governed government as follows: "...the newly emerging, sovereign government of Mongolia shall be a special government where a handful of people, who have been elected by the masses, shall serve and manage the government through consultation and consensus and there shall be relevant laws under which the elected few shall be accountable for their performances."[4] This can be interpreted as follows: 1. The new government would be rule by the people; 2. it would be a government that would give freedom to the people and build a new life; and, 3. it would be elected and formed by the people, and be accountable to the people. The article "The benefits of a people's new central and local governments of Mongolia" outlined the basic rules and procedures for the establishment of central and local administrations of the new government, which have been defined as the people's khural (assembly).

The first Policy Guidelines of the MPR, which were adopted in March 1921, indicated that "first and foremost, it would be appropriate to transfer government powers into the hands of the people, and establish a country (power) that promotes election to the people's khural."[5] This was a succinct definition of the concept of State by the revolutionaries. One point that needs special mentioning here is that the majority of the Mongolian

4 "*Mongolyn Ünen*" (Mongolian Truth), Compilation of newspaper articles and news, Ulaanbaatar, 1971, p. 39.

5 Resolutions and Decisions of the Congresses, Conferences of the MPRP and the Plenary Meetings of the Central Committee, Part One, Ulaanbaatar, 1956, p. 16.

revolutionaries basically approached the issue of a new State from the perspective of a national democratic idea, but as their engagement with the Comintern and the Russian Bolsheviks became stronger, they slowly but gradually shifted gears towards a strict class mentality with regard to the question of the type of State and government. This period of evolution of the concept of a new State and government coincided with the revival of Mongolia's autonomy by Baron Ungern (*Nikolai Robert Maximilian Freiherr von Ungern-Sternberg, often referred to as Roman von Ungern-Sternberg or Baron Ungern, was an anti-Communist general in the Russian Civil War and then an independent warlord who intervened in Mongolia against China. Tr.*).

2.1 *The "Restored" Khüree Government*

Baron Ungern, who entered into Mongolia by its eastern frontier in October 1920, drove out the Chinese occupation forces after a five-month long battle, and advanced on Niislel Khüree and liberated it in December 1921. And so, not very long after the abolishment of Mongolia's autonomy, Baron Ungern proclaimed the restoration of Outer Mongolia's autonomy from the State Yellow Palace on the 15th day of the Lunar New Year of 1921 (22 February 1921) and restored the Bogd Jebzundamba Khutugtu to the throne. The Government with its five Ministries was restored and their chief ministers, their deputies and the commanders were reinstated, and some people who contributed to the routing of the Chinese Kuomintang forces were decorated with awards.

After the formation of the Government, Jalkhanz Khutugtu Damdinbazar was made the Prime Minister and Chief Interior Minister; Luvsantseren, who organised the recruitment of Mongol soldiers and who had invited Baron Ungern was given the portfolio of Finance Minister; *Wang* Dorjtseren was made the War Minister; Khatanbaatar Magsarjav was appointed the Commander in Chief of the army; *Shanzodba* Dambajav was given the portfolio of Foreign Minister; *Beis* Chimedtseren was made the Law Minister, and simultaneously, their deputies were also appointed. Bogd Khan conferred on Baron Ungern the rank of Khan, the titles of *Chin Wang*, Restorer of the State, Supreme Commander and his General Rehuni was given the title of *Chin Wang*, Distinct Military Commander, the Buriad Jigmedjav Jambalo the title of *Chin Wang* and Truly Diligent. The chief ministers, their deputies, and officials were proportionately appointed from the *aimags* and the *shabi*. The Bogd Khan issued an edict of 23 February 1921, which read "The Restorer of the State – the Supreme Commander, the Khan ranked *Chin Wang*, General Baron Ungern is a celebrated personality with exceptional meritorious services who annihilated the Chinese Kuomintang army, making selfless sacrifice for the restoration of the sovereign rights of our state. He, therefore, deserves all respect from the state and even now, is leading the army in all directions killing the remnants of the Chinese Kuomintang troops. Therefore, should Baron Ungern befall the need to mobilise soldiers, horses, food and provisions in any and all parts of the country, relevant local *zasag*, officials and people promptly and immediately comes to his assistance. This order and edict must be respected and complied with without fail."[6] As a result of such a mobilisation by the Bogd Khan government, new military units were formed under Baron Ungern's command, which were commanded by Luvsantseveen *Tergüün*, Sundui *Güng*, Baljinnyam *Güng*, Bayar *Güng*, and Dari Ekh Lama of Kharaa.

Although the Bogd Khan and Baron Ungern, in public, pretended to be on friendly terms, they were at serious loggerheads in terms of vital interests and farsightedness. The reinstated Bogd Khan Government, having regained the country's autonomy, intended to make it a sovereign State and further unite all the Mongols, while Baron Ungern had other plans, to set up a so-called confederative State uniting not only the Mongols but also other felt dwellers such as the Kazaks. On this basis he intended to revive the Russian Empire and for this purpose, he apparently contemplated exploiting the Bogd Khan Government as a bridgehead for accomplishing his plans. The Bogd Khan Government, first and foremost, made every effort to diplomatically explain the existing situation to both Mongolia's northern and southern neighbours. On 25 February 1921, for instance, in a letter addressed to the People's Commissariat for Foreign Affairs of the Russian Soviet Federative Socialist Republic, the Bogd Khan mentioned about the restoration of autonomy and the reinstatement of the Bogd Khan to the throne of Mongolia, and pointed out that "From early times the land of great Russia has been providing extensive help and has been protecting Mongolia and in recognition of the assistance in granting autonomy to Mongolia, our Government commits that the free people of Mongolia wants continued strong friendship with the Russian people," and further continued that "ministers together with their armies, who had violated the law and breached the truth, have been driven out of Mongolia's capital Khüree together with the Russian forces. We are in the know about the Russians, who disagree with you the Esteemed Commissariat. The Russian soldiers, who disagree with the Russian government, are attempting to flee westward and our Government is confident that there is no obstacle coming in the way of friendship between Russia and

6 *Revolutionary Measures Taken in 1921–1924*, Ulaanbaatar, 1954, p. 76.

Mongolia."[7] He offered to conclude a bilateral trade agreement, exchange envoys and ambassadors, and forge good-neighbourly relations.

On 2 March of the same year, in a letter sent to the President of the Republic of China, Bogd Khan expounded his reason for briefly exploiting Baron Ungern and noted that it was not the Republic of China, but rather Chinese warlords headed by Xu Shuzheng who had abolished Mongolia's autonomy. "The Mongols had no choice but to join ranks with the army of Baron Ungern since the war minister Gao Silin, who is engaged in brigandry, was planning to breach the sovereignty of the Republic of China. Now that the war minister Gao Silin has escaped from the frontiers of Mongolia with his troops, we since it is inappropriate to maintain the foreign Russian troops, we have also sought their departure, which has been notified to military commander Baron Ungern... who has agreed and has given commitment to leave the country and move northward." The letter expounded Mongolia's collaboration with Baron Ungern, and also described how Xu Shuzheng and his war minister Gao Silin abolished Mongolia's autonomy. The letter further recounted how Chen Yi, the new Chinese command of the Northwest Frontier Defense Army and official representative of the Republic of China was locked up, and how the Government of Mongolia and the Bogd Khan were blackmailed and even how Xu Shuzheng and Gao Silin seized power by force and forged a letter claiming that the Bogd Khan had voluntarily relinquished his authority. "The Bogd Khan did not seal the letter and so request that this matter be resolved. The Peking Government did not approve of the actions of Xu Shuzheng and his military minister Gao Silin. The Government of Mongolia is in the know that Xu Shuzheng had been called back to Peking, but when he escaped a large amount of cash award was promised to anyone who captured Xu Shuzheng, and Chen Yi was rehabilitated."[8] The letter from the Mongolian Government obviously sought to condemn the intrigues of the Chinese military officer and tactically, it was an attempt not to brush aside the authority of the masters of the Republic of China. However, in reality, the Bogd Khan Government contemplated not only to secure total independence of Outer Mongolia, but also unite the entire Mongol race. The Interior Ministry of the Bogd Khan Government sent a letter to six *chuulgan* or banners of Inner Mongolia on 16 April 1921, through which the Bogd Khan Government called on them to unite and set up a religion-based Confederation. "As mentioned before, Mongolia has two foes – China ... and the renegade Russian soldiers from the north,

7 Central National Archives of Mongolia, Fonds-4, Series-621, pamphlet 6.
8 Central National Archives of Mongolia, Fonds-4, Series-621, pamphlet. 6.

and by force we shall not allow these mercenary criminal aliens plotting to occupy our (Mongolia) land and sabotage the foundations of our religion... Our Government pleas to your Esteemed Lord, with due consideration of your origin and aristocratic fame, unite with us of the same race to establish a super Confederative state, we shall be able to deliver from oceans of suffering the Mongol people, who have been worshipping the devotedly following the religion of Buddha from ancient times, this would be helpful in bringing them happiness."[9]

In order to accomplish his schemes, Baron Ungern resorted to blackmail, threats, cajoling, deception and simulation. He tortured and executed any of his commanders and soldiers whom he suspected of any slight fault and of having any kind of relation with the Kuomintang army and even seized all their property. He did not want to see Khatanbaatar Magsarjav anywhere in the neighbourhood of Ikh Khüree and so he had Magsarjav sent to the western frontiers and even spied on him. Baron Ungern even feigned being pro-Mongolian by donning a Mongolian del (gown) with shoulder straps of a general, and converted to Buddhism, and would join crowds of believers by chanting mantras and prostrating himself before the statues of the Buddha. High-ranking clergy and lamas, who wanted to curry favour with him, spread rumours that Baron Ungern was a "holy reincarnate." Baron Ungern even hatched plans to take advantage of the Russian White Guard and Japanese military rulers in the Far East to achieve his crafty designs.

From the perspective of class-based interests, both the Bogd Khan and Baron Ungern had something in common with respect to the Russian Soviet Republic and Mongolian revolutionaries. However, their attitude in this respect was dissimilar, for the Bogd Gegeen, making national interests his priority, was conducting a slightly softer and flexible policy, whereas Baron Ungern pursued a reactionary policy determined to destroy them by all means. It is worth pondering on a comment written on this matter by Prof. L. Jamsran. "... Mongol patriots led by Bogd Khan, with respect to achieving the final goal of breaking the shackles of Chinese oppression, uniting the many different Mongol tribes and establishing a united Mongolia, they sought assistance from foreign powers, but they were also politically smart enough to decide as to from whom, from among the two warring parties in Russia, they should seek assistance."[10]

9 Central National Archives of Mongolia, Fonds-4, Series-621, pamphlet. 12.

10 L. Jamsran, *The Revival of the State Independence of Mongolia*, Ulaanbaatar, 1997, pp. 129–130.

2.2 *The Establishment of a Provisional Government of Mongolia, Its Government Structure, Set-up and* Modus Operandi

Mongolian revolutionaries did not recognise the so-called "Reinstated" Khüree Government, and lost no time in drawing up a plan for an armed struggle against the Chinese Kuomintang and the Russian White Guards for the liberation of the country. This plan was discussed at a consultation of representatives of the MPP, held on 9 February 1921, who preliminarily appointed Damdiny Sükhbaatar as the Army Commander, assigning him the task to manage the organisation of the People's Party's Army.

In late 1920 and early 1921, the Army of the People's Party was formed, which within a brief spell of time, was able to grow in numbers and strength. The Mongolian People's Party held its First Congress on 1–3 March 1921, where it officially confirmed the establishment of its political party and defined the objectives of liberating the country. The Army Headquarters of the People's Party was also established at the Congress. Members of the Army Headquarters held the third extended meeting of the Central Committee of MPP on 6 and 7 March, 1921, where they decided to first liberate Khiagt and rename the People's Party Army into "People's Army." The People's Army was restructured according to the Mongolian military traditions and the commanders of the first four regiments were appointed. They were B. Puntsag, Ts. Khasbaatar, Yü. Tserendorj and Ch. Bazarsad.

A meeting of the MPP, the People's Army, and representatives of the border area *aimags*, banners and the *shabi* was held on 13 March 1921, where the People's Provisional Government was formed. According to the resolution of the meeting, "The Provisional Government is hereby instructed to… call the Congress of the people's representatives of Mongolia, establish a permanent government, and adopt the fundamental laws and rules of the country." A seven-member Provisional People's Government was formed, Dambyn Chagdarjav was appointed the head of the Government, Damdiny Sükhbaatar was appointed as its member officer, and the government members included Dogsomiin Bodoo (in absentia), Namsrai Bilegsaikhan, Lavaryn Sumiya and Khorloogin Choibalsan, and the eight Government-member was to be appointed from the Uriankhai frontier region. The Government in Niislel Khüree was informed about the formation of a People's Provisional Government and a Manifesto was issued addressed to the entire people of Mongolia. The Manifesto outlined the mandatory duties of the people in preparing for a revolution and urged that "… the orders issued and the materials demanded by the People's Government must be provided without any let or hindrance and without any delay" and defined the legislative objectives of the People's

Government to "... form the country's government in a fair manner, respect and rally the authority of the people, and ensure the enforcement and strict compliance of laws and legislation."[11]

And so the People's Provisional Government was a powerful implement in organising the struggle of the people, leading the national democratic revolution to its victory, and political structure and the first and primary source of the people's democratic government with the goal of forming a permanent government. The fact that the People's Provisional Government was formed by a people's congress attended by different social classes, groups and strata of the Mongolian population was a significant development in itself. The Mongolian revolutionaries officially informed the Bogd Khan Government of the establishment of the People's Provisional Government. And so, the country then had two governments, thanks to the efforts of the people who wanted to establish an independent and sovereign Mongolia. Things did not move as simply on the political front as Russia, on which both the groupings in the country staked hope and on which they relied, internally had hostile political forces, the Reds (communists) and the Whites fighting against each other.

The People's Provisional Government with honour carried out its responsibility of organising the liberation of Khiagt and the Provisional Government moved from Deed Shivee to Khiagt on 19 March 1921. The Second Conference of the People's Provisional Government, which was held on 24 March 1921, established the Interior Ministry with four departments, including the general, judiciary, foreign affairs and mutual conveyance departments; the War Ministry with two departments, war and conscription departments; and the Finance and Economic Ministry with the food, provisions and trade departments, their presidium members and managing officers were appointed.

11 *Revolutionary Measures Taken in 1921–1924*, Ulaanbaatar, 1954, pp. 8–10.

DIAGRAM 11 Structure of the People's Provisional Government

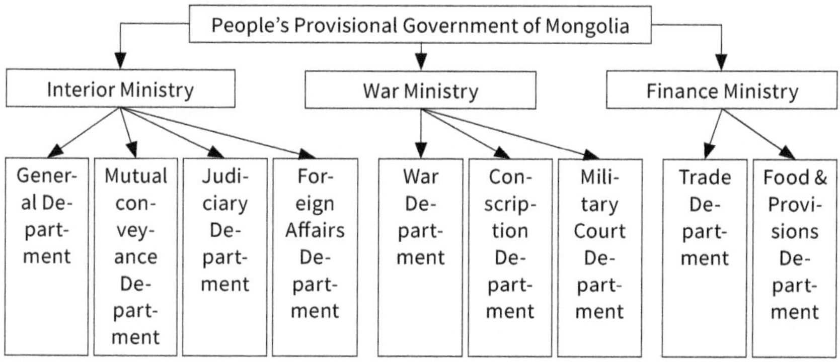

The conference decided to appoint a representative in the Government from Western Mongolia but three people – Khasbaatar, Dambadorj and Ölziikhand – were to be entrusted to this office. They had gone to the western frontiers and had established a People's Provisional Government of Western Mongolia in July 1921. This was an expression, on the one hand, of the flexible policy conducted by the representatives of the Provisional Government in attracting and mobilising patriotic and progressive forces, and on the other hand, local ruling clerical and secular nobles were, in one way or the other, supporting the cause of the revolution.

An All Mongolia Military Council called the "*Mongolyn boshgiig khalakh doh tsergiin khural*" or the "All Mongolia Revolutionary Military Assembly" was formed by a resolution of the People's Provisional Government, passed on 10 April 1921, and Damdiny Sükhbaatar, Khorloogiin Choibalsan and Erdene (P.I. Litvintsev), an officer at the War Ministry, were appointed the members of the Council. The resolution of procedural nature stated that "... although the military affairs ministry can be continued in its old format led by Sükhbaatar, and in the event of a military emergency, all arising matters should be considered and decided upon by a meeting of the All Military Council in the attendance of commander Sükhbaatar and Choibalsan. The chief of the Headquarters shall report directly to the military commander and the All Military HQ is the centre for devising war policy, procurement and supply of military equipment, and manage military units and sections, and emerging general official matters. Matters discussed and agreed upon at the All Military Council meeting shall be complied by the All Military Commander, who shall ensure their implementation."[12] This was the first norms and standards legal act that had sought to introduce democratic principles in the *modus operandy* of the state administrative organs, and reinforce and legalise the rights and duties of the concerned authorities. The People's Provisional Government put a lot of effort into augmenting the People's Army, ensuring their combat and political preparedness, and prepared in earnest for the struggle to free the country of the Russian White Guards.

Rules and regulations on the internal organisational set-up of the People's Provisional Government were adopted on 23 April 1921, followed by regulations on the pay for government office workers, and people's army military commanders and soldiers, which were adopted on 23 May. On 20 May, the Government introduced a seven-hour working day and one day off in one week. In the middle of April, when Chagdarjav was assigned as the plenipotentiary representative in Darkhad, Bodoo was appointed the Premier of the People's Provisional Government.

Some of the significant actions of the People's Provisional Government to introduce legislation was its adoption of the "Rules of the Government Representatives," which was approved on 28 May 1921. According to the Rules, Government Representatives, on the one hand, were responsible for monitoring, on behalf of the people, activities of the old local administrations, and on the other hand, implementing in a limited manner the command and order duties of the Provisional Government. The Rules said that "the age, property and means of living, and names of the people under the particular administrative jurisdiction must be examined and anything which is false must be eliminated. The (Government Representatives) are duty bound to economise on all spending related to taxation, cash and seal, and the local governments." In addition to this, the Government Representatives were given additional rights and duties to make democratic changes in rural areas that were acceptable to the people, in particular, encourage the education of girls and boys, ensure equal rights to people, without distinction of any kind, such as national and ethnic origin, and to stand firmly and decisively against any kind of national or social oppression. Alongside this, the Government Representatives warned against neglecting their duties and abusing their rights.

The People's Provisional Government carried out social and economic changes in the liberated areas and also effected some actions of a legal nature to augment the transformations. The People's Provisional Government held a meeting on 19 March 1921, where it considered the issue of

12 *Compilation of documents and materials related to the life of D. Sükhbaatar*, Ulaanbaatar, 1964.

"Measures on protecting goods and merchandise from the fire that broke out in the town of Naima," and decided to forge trade relations with the Far Eastern Republic (sometimes called the Chita Republic). This was, for the People's Provisional Government, a maiden legal act of an international nature.

In May and June 1921, the People's Provisional Government passed a decision on taxing foreign traders and farmers, and levying customs duty and rent for the exploitation of natural resources, and nationalised the land. A decision on land ownership, which was not only of economic, but also of political significance, stipulated that "The entire land within the borders of our Mongolia is the property of the Mongolian people, and it has been agreed through consultation that hereafter all common local and foreign individual shall be banned from forcefully occupying the land of Mongolia as their own."[13] At this juncture when the first epicentre of the national democratic revolution was in the making, the foundations of a revolutionary democracy judiciary were laid. To illustrate, a Judiciary Department was added to the organisational structure of the Interior Ministry, while the War Ministry was advised to set up a Military Court Department. These measures, which were undertaken by the People's Provisional Government to set up the judiciary system, were in essence designed at structurally replacing the old judiciary with people's courts and judicial institutions.

The Khüree Government of Bogd Khan did not sit, arms folded, with regard to the above measures taken by the People's Provisional Government. Both the governments launched massive public propaganda to justify their respective actions and policies. For example, soon after the People's Provisional Government issued a Manifesto, the Interior Ministry of the Khüree Government in a notice circulated on 28 March 1921, extolled Baron Ungern as a "Liberator" of Mongolia and pointed out that the Government he had helped restore was in compliance with the Tripartite Khiagt Treaty and emphasising that the Bogd Khan Khüree Government was the sole legitimate government to conclude a treaty with the Russian Soviet Federation. The notice even attempted to portray the People's Provisional Government and the Mongolian People's Party as as good as enemies of the Mongolian people. Also, a letter to the so-called "Khüree Comrades," sent by Luvsantseveen to a Mongolian delegation to the Russian Soviet Federation, in a way hints at this idea as well.

The People's Provisional Government took the leadership role to plan the liberation of Niislel Khüree and ensure the victory of the national peo-

13 Central National Archives of Mongolia, Fonds-1, Series-1, p. 2.

ple's revolution. The People's Provisional Government on 10 April 1921 officially sought military assistance from the the Russian Soviet Federation in the fight against the common enemy, the White Guards.

The Central Committee of the MPP and the People's Provisional Government held an extended meeting on 28 June 1921, where they decided to liberate Niislel Khüree, and the People's Provisional Government designed a Niislel Khüree liberation plan under the command of D. Sükhbaatar and A. Neiman.

As the Mongolian and Soviet soldiers approached Niislel Khüree, they were met by representatives of the Khüree authorities, who tried to convince them that there was no longer need for military movement as peace prevailed, and even tried to win them to their side, but their offer was rejected by the People's Provisional Government. And so the first contingent of Mongolian and Soviet soldiers entered Niislel Khüree on 6 July 1921, dismantled the so-called "Baron-restored Government" on 10 July 1921 and took over the government affairs and seal.

Bodoo, the Chairman of the People's Provisional Government, addressing the Mongol nobles and princes said, "Our people's representatives, as desired by the Bogd Khan and the many lamas and nobles, received assistance from Russia, destroyed the foreign aggressors, and have taken over the land and the country. The People's Provisional Government, which has been already established by the people through their selfless contribution to advance the people's freedom, has decided to change the country's government, coming here ... we pay our courtesies as you all, lamas and nobles, have not opposed the revolution, and with due consideration of the country's situation we have proclaimed the Bogd Khan as a Khan with constitutional authority, and as a People's Government will be jointly formed, it would be adequate if the old government ministries out of reason hand over and transfer your seals."[14]

The People's Provisional Government was renamed the Government of Mongolia, and B. Bodoo was appointed its Prime Minister, while Da Lama Puntsagdorj was appointed the Chief Minister of Interior Affairs, Damdiny Sükhbaatar as Defence (Chief) Minister and Commander-in-Chief of the army, S. Danzan was made the Chief Minister of Finance, D. Bodoo was concurrently appointed as Foreign (Chief) Minister and Kh. Magsarjav was made the Chief Minister of Law. This was a transitional government championing national unity.

Bogd Jebzumdamba *Khutugtu* was proclaimed the Khan of a constitutional monarchy and enthroned at the State Yellow Palace. A constitution-

14 *Historical Development of the MPRP*, Ulaanbaatar, 1995, p. 26.

al monarchy was proclaimed for a number of reasons, including: 1. The Bogd Khan continued to enjoy enormous authority and influence among his devotees; 2. The revolutionaries conducted a tactical policy of taking advantage of the authority and influence of the Bogd Khan and assuaging any probable opposition by the lama; 3. Some revolutionary leaders believed that a constitutional monarchy was the unique way of the country's development; and, 4. It grew out of the policy of championing national unity.

The People's Government issued a Resolution on 16 July 1921, which resolved that "It is appropriate that the Government has been termed as government until the many *aimags* and banners would be notified for the convocation of a state *khural*, which shall consider and take a final decision on the matter ... and in the official document, the word provisional can be omitted should there be a need, and so it has been so decided that the government would be called the People's Government."[15] And so, the People's Government remained the key executive administrative of the country until the preparations for the convening of the State *Ikh Khural* were completed and until the proclamation of the Republic. In this sense, M. Sandagdorj has defined this government as a "Transitional Government."[16]

2.3 *The Structure and Authority of the Constitutional Monarchy and the Government*

The government established with the victory of the 1921 People's Revolution (national democratic revolution), in form, was a constitutional monarchy. According to a Resolution adopted by the People's Government on 23 July 1921: "There is no reason for the Khan to violate the decision of the government and as the Khan would be submitted all the laws and legislation, that would be adopted either by the provisional or the Ikh Khural, and so it resolves that the ministries and the frontier ministers should they have any issue to be raised with the Khan should only go through the Government."[17] Thus the main power was concentrated in the hands of the People's Government.

In order to augment and strengthen the people's power, it was vitally important to regulate the relations between the People's Government and the Bogd Khan, and validate their rights and authority by law. To-

15 *Revolutionary Measures Taken in 1921–1924*, Ulaanbaatar, 1954, p. 22.
16 M. Sanjdorj, *History of the People's Government*, Ulaanbaatar, 1974, p. 43.
17 *The MPRP in the Struggle for the Triumph of the People's Revolution*, Ulaanbaatar, 1971, p. 26.

wards this end, a framework document called the "Oath Taking Treaty" was passed by a Resolution of the People's Government on 1 November 1921, which outlined the prerogative rights of both the Bogd Khan and the People's Government. Article One indicated that "Jebzundamba *Khutugtu,* the Bogd Khan of Mongolia shall become the Bogd ruler of the Yellow Sect of Buddhism, whereby he will not have any doing with the political affairs and so hereby declare that the Bogd Khan shall manage without any limitation all matters related to religion."[18] Further on, Article Four read "The laws and legislation that the People's Government would draft and made public, the Bogd Khan, Ye shall be notified as per the rules, and the Bogd Khan does not have the authority to either reject and breach them.," thus demarcating the liabilities and the rights of the People's Government and the Bogd Khan. The fact that all and any decision of the People's Government would be reconfirmed by the Bogd Khan's edict further reinforced the legal basis of the documents concerned. Article Nine said that "These rules have been adopted to ensure the solidity of the people's state ... and with the objective of ensuring internal harmony and unity, externally aggrandising the country, and making the people happy, the Bogd Khan and the People's Government hereby commit and approve these rules and enforce them in the most justifiable manner."[19] This paragraph was a clear manifestation that the People's Government was a transitional form of coalition government that promoted national unity as its priority objective. Hence, the "Oath Taking Treaty" cannot be viewed simply as a civil treaty but rather as legislation of the type of a Constitution that limits the right of involvement of the Bogd Khan in state political matters and consolidates the full authority of the People's Government. Although the People's Government, in the event of rejection of a decision by the Bogd Khan, unilaterally validated and implemented the decision, it positively responded to and considered a big share of motions and requests tabled by the Bogd Khan. This proves that the letter and spirit of the "Oath Taking Treaty" were being complied with and followed as appropriate. The Treaty automatically became invalid after the death of the Bogd Khan in 1924.

A gathering was held in August 1921 attended by common people, nobles, princes, and lamas from many different banners and representatives of the MPRP who articulated their support for the People's Government and agreed to set up a Provisional State *Khural* with consultative powers

18 *Laws of the Mongolian People's Republic and Compilation of Some Related Legal Acts, (1921–1940)*, Book One, Ulaanbaatar, 1972, p. 39.

19 *Ibid.*

in the interim period until the convocation of the State *Ikh Khural*. On 20 November of the same year the People's Government adopted the rules and procedures of the Provisional State *Khural* proclaiming that it was not a legislature but an organ with consultative power. According to the rules and procedures, a Provisional State *Khural* was instituted with 56 members composed of common people, the military, nobles and princes, which held its first meeting on 28 October 1921. The meeting's agenda included the discipline and behaviour of the lamas, issues related to economising stationery costs of ministries and departments, and streamlining military rules and procedures, and accordingly the People's Government was instructed to take the necessary relevant measures. The Provisional State *Khural* examined and discussed matters raised by the People's Government and also issues the *Khural* itself had initiated. During its existence, the Provisional State *Khural* held 60 sessions and carried out its historical duty in a meaningful manner. The Provisional State *Khural* was in a way a democratic, national unity institution that expressed the views, opinions and desires of different social classes and segments. The Provisional State *Khural,* having fulfilled its historical mission of setting the stage for the convocation of the State *Ikh Khural,* was dismissed at the end of 1923.

The establishment of the People's Government together with its first five core ministries signalled the creation of firm foundations of the state's central administrative system, the seeds of which were sown during the early years of the People's Provisional Government. The "Interim Rules of the Khural of the People's Government of Mongolia," which were adopted on 3 March 1922, legitimatised the legislative and executive rights and authority of the People's Government. Article One of the Rules stated that "The *Khural* of the Chief Ministers is the People's Provisional Government, therefore, the Government *Khural* should retain the right to draft, announce and enforce the country's laws and legislation, and settles lawsuits in the interim period until the convocation of the State *Ikh Khural,* when it freely and earnestly, in the spirit of the Mongol people, discusses and decides on the state of affairs of the country, and establishes the highest ruling authorities of the country." According to this provision, the People's Government was not only a legislature and the executive, it was also the country's judiciary. Professor M. Sanjdorj notes that the "Interim Rules of the *Khural* of the People's Government consolidated the norms and standards of authority adopted in such state legal documents as the 'Rules and procedures of the Provisional State *Khural*' and the 'Oath Taking Treaty,' which were adopted earlier." These rules became the starting source for such legal documents as the "Rules of the State *Khural,*" and

"Instructions for Calling the State *Khurals* to Session," which were adopted in 1923. In this respect, the Interim Rules of the *Khural* of the People's Government was an exceptionally important documents related to the evolution of Mongolia's revolutionary democratic power, an important legal act that had enormous impact on the growth of the state and power of the country, and it was a document of Constitutional nature."[20] The interim rules had been followed in some 160 sessions held since March 1922.

2.4 *The Structure, Composition, Rights and Duties of the Government Ministries*

New ministries and departments of the People's Government, based on traditions of statehood, and in particular the experience accumulated during the rule of the Bogd Khan and the early period of the People's Provisional Government, began their work.

The People's Government ministries and departments recruited literate people who were committed to the cause of the revolution and who had some organisational skill, and government officials, who were serving in the former administration, were selectively recruited as well.

Work began on reforming the structures, staff strength, rights and responsibilities of the State ministries and departments relying on the already existing structures that were created by the People's Provisional Government. The Law Ministry's structural set-up was fortified and two new departments, the General and Sentencing Departments, were added to the Ministry on 15 November 1921 by a decision of the People's Government. A Training Department was set up under the Interior Ministry in April 1922, which became the foundation for the People's Education Ministry that was established later in 1924. The People's Government passed a Resolution on 18 July 1921, according to which the Finance Ministry was given additional responsibility to oversee the Electrical Committee of Niislel Khüree, the Manual Milling Service, and the State grain stocks; the War Ministry, artillery maintenance and repair, and the calf leather processing plants; while the Interior Ministry was made responsible for managing the boats plying the Kherlen and the east and west Tuul Rivers. The People's Government took a number of decisions in the second half of 1922, according to which the War Ministry was given jurisdiction over the Commandant's Committee, the General Committee of Posts and Telegram was assigned to the Foreign Ministry, the Interior Ministry was given the responsibility of managing all the relay services and guards in the

20 M. Sanjdorj. *History of the People's Government*, Ulaanbaatar, 1974, p. 57.

country, and the Central Committee of the MPRP was given jurisdiction over the Printing Committee and managing all matters related to printing and publication. These Government resolutions also determined the location of the offices of all the ministries and departments.

A lot of effort had gone into completing the orders and procedures of the government officials, which reflected the kind of State the new People's Government was to have. Starting on 19 July 1921, the People's Government was given a schedule defining the days of the week it would hold it sessions, and not very long after, new rules were introduced, which spelled out disciplinary and other actions that would be taken against anyone who was late for the Government meetings. For example, for every 10 minutes late a fine of 5 *tsen* (*measure of weight equivalent to one tenth of a tael. One tael was equivalent to 50 grams or almost 13/4 ounce. Tr.*) was imposed, and any motion for inclusions in the agenda of the government session, according to the new set of rules, had to be submitted beforehand. Starting on 1 November, it was decided that the ministries and their departments would start work at 9 a.m. in the morning and end at 4 p.m. in the afternoon. Alongside this, the old practice of shifts in the ministries and government offices, as well as the approval by the Bogd Khan personally of appointing assistants of *banners* were scrapped. Other disciplinary actions were introduced between 1922 and 1923 designed at improving the efficiency of government offices, according to which fines were imposed on government officials for intentionally concealing official documents, time limits were introduced for attending to official cases, a two family membere were not permitted to work in one office, and the death sentence was also introduced for bribery and corruption.

The People's Government, starting in 1922, replaced the seals and stamps of the ministries with new ones, signalling and symbolising the revival of a new statehood. In 1921, a special supervisory commission was set up to monitor established posts within ministries and departments, which was an action to review the competency and efficiency of the government officials, and the institution of the commission was considered at a Government meeting held in April 1922. Following this meeting, it was decided that the Government would have a staff strength of 35, the Interior Ministry of 40, the War Ministry of 116, the Foreign Ministry 35, the Finance Ministry 79 and the Law Ministry would have 58 posts. Again in late 1922, the People's Government once again reviewed the posts within its ministries and departments, removed the posts of the Vice Ministers and Deputy Chairmen of departments, and the relevant responsible officials were made members of the People's Government.

New rules on the salary and supplies of ministry and department officials were introduced in August 1921. According to the rules, the monthly salary of the chief executives of the ministries was fixed at 80 *lang (One lang is equivalent to almost 1.33 ounce)*, responsible officers were given 80 *lang*, 40 *lang* to clerks, and the messengers received a monthly salary of 30 *lang*, depending on the workload and work responsibility. As the role of the People's Government grew, so the number of government agencies and departments increased. For example, the General Committee of Posts and Telegrams was established in July 1921, later in November the Institute of Letters, a research institute, was set up, and in December of the same year the Mongolia Cooperative Agency, responsible for managing national and cooperative commercial transactions, was instituted. In June 1922, the State Control and Monitoring Department was established. These ministries and departments became the backbone of the newly established People's Government ensuring its smooth and efficient functioning.

2.5 *The Final Establishment of the Mongolian People's Revolutionary Army*

The People's Government was confronted with the task of reinforcing the gains of the revolution, and for this purpose formed permanent armed forces. The People's Government and the Party Central Committee decided to reorganise the military volunteers into a permanent army, and accordingly introduced mandatory military service and determined the number of years a man had to serve in the army. Within this process, new military units were added, the military arsenal was improved, army units were specialized, combat and political training of servicemen was made regular, and measures were taken to improve discipline in the military. In this respect, the War Minister D. Sükhbaatar announced the first ever enlistment plan in July 1921, which was the introduction of compulsory military service for all men of military age. According to the plan, more than 7,000 men were to be mobilized. But the failure of the Government decision to reach local, especially remote parts of the country, the weakness of the old existing administrative units as well as the poor condition of roads and communication, meant that by the year 1922 only about 2,000 men were enlisted into the army. Alongside this, the old military structures were reorganised and work began on setting up new military brigades, units, squadrons and platoons. By 1924, the Mongolian army had 2 border units and 2 divisions, and one cavalry brigade, one machine-gun and artillery unit and an officer's school in Niislel Khüree."[21]

A permanent military principle took hold in the Mongolian army of the People's Government with limited authority, and the army was divided into central and frontier troops. The central army included the All Military Council, the Training Bureau, Office of Internal Security, Foreign Intelligence Section, two units of cavalry division, artillery unit, machine-gun unit, communication platoon, and an officer's and communication school, and one electrical motor committee, Judging by this, the Mongolian People's Revolutionary Army (MPRA), besides the cavalry units, there also appeared new military units and action was taken to arm them with new weapons and hardware.

An Interior Protection Agency (IPA) was set up under the All Military Council on 16 June 1922. The IPA was expanded and strengthened and in 1924 it became an autonomous agency directly under the Government. The MPRA carried out police and customs duties until 1924. Customs units and committees were set up at the border points and trade centres between 1922 and 1924 with the purpose of setting up the customs office, and towards this end, the customs control and monitoring were beefed up, which helped increase revenues earned from the customs. The People's Government took a decision on 17 July 1921 to institute the State police agency called the "Police Force," whose duty was to strengthen law enforcement and public order, and to ensure public peace and quiet. One of the important components of the MPRA was the frontier troop. In a situation when China posed aggression, Commander D. Sükhbaatar personally gave top priority to strengthening security in the country's Eastern frontier. By 1924, 4 units and 2 divisions were dislocated at Bayantümen, Tamsagbulag, Dariganga and Khovd with a total 2,260 military personnel and servicemen.

One of the important measures taken by the People's Government between 1921 and 1924 was the introduction of a military and people's education and training system. To begin with, a temporary school called the "People's Army Officers' School" was built in October 1921, which was expanded into a permanent school with a one-year training course in 1922 and it had cavalry, political and artillery classes. After several graduations, staring in the 1923–24 school year, it was renamed as "All Army General School" and it started training sergeants and non-commissioned officers. Revolutionary army officers and military personnel were also being trained in the Russian Soviet Federation. The MPRA gave

21 *The History of Mongol Soldiers*, Book One, Ulaanbaatar, p. 136.

priority attention to training military command personnel and also educating and training rank and file soldiers. This task was managed by the "Department for Training Soldiers," which was set up in 1921, and whose responsibilities lay in enlightening and educating the soldiers, and introducing and propagating the Government's policies. The Way Military, and Commander D. Sükhbaatar personally were responsible for improving knowledge-based discipline among the ranks of the army, and they also issued a number of orders and guidelines related to the principle of command and subordination, and military discipline.

Codified acts, such as the Rules of the All Military Council, rules of the military commanders, rules on personnel discipline were adopted in 1922 and 1923 designed at bolstering the legal foundations of internal affairs and the organisational set-up of the MPRA. They were instrumental in adding impetus to the consolidation and development of the permanent army. The military's rear supply infrastructure was enhanced, and new military factories and hospitals were established to support the soldiers and army.

Mongolian-Russian military and political ties played a very important role in the evolution and strengthening of the Mongolian People's Revolutionary Army. These ties were being implemented through the military collaboration between the two countries, expert assistance from the Russian Soviet Federation to the soldiers of the Mongolian Revolutionary Army and through military hardware assistance.

2.6 *The Courts and Justice*

The establishment of the Law Ministry on 10 July 1921 sped up the process of replacing the old justice system that exited during the period of serfdom in the country. "The Law Ministry shall be wholly responsible for managing all criminal and civil cases within the country concerning human lives, theft, defraud, committing of adultery and engaging in promiscuous activities, and also setting up courts in different parts of the country, an adopt related rules and regulations."

During the period under review, the Law Ministry was an agency with a primarily dual responsibility, that is, it acted as a central organ of the state administration and as the supreme court of the country. The Law Ministry was entirely responsible for the courts and court proceedings across the length and breadth of the country, while in the local areas, such cases continued to be handled by the *Banner Zasag* and its secretariat. But the overall monitoring and regulation were provided by the People's Government.

Organisationally, the Law Ministry had three key departments. 1. An Internal Department, which was responsible for investigating criminal cases and resolving civil disputes. 2. An External Department, which was responsible for investigating criminal cases of foreign nationals, and also settling disputes among foreign subjects. 3. A General Department, whose jurisdiction lay in administering justice and overseeing jails and issues related to the notary.

The People's Government passed a decision on 16 July 1921, according to which the Law Ministry was given the responsibility of managing all civil cases and passing related justice. A special military court called the "Commandant's Committee" was set up at the War Ministry, which was assigned the task to judge and pass sentence related to political cases, and all court-related matters within the army. The People's Government overhauled the state court system with its distinctly class-based nature, introducing the principle of equal before law and courts, attaching paramount importance to the humane and educational nature of sentences. For instance, according to a decision passed on 14 July 1921, class-based courts were abolished, and irrespective of origin, similar sentences were passed for similar types of crimes.

Use of torture was completely outlawed in the process of investigation in December 1922 and in the court proceedings in February 1923, which was a move to showcase the humane and compassionate nature of the People's Government. In order to invalidate old laws and codes, and draft new laws and legislation, a so-called Department of Systematising Laws and Legislation was set up under the People's Government in 1922. And in 1923, grievance-addressing departments were set up anew at the *aimags,* banner ministries and their secretariats.

2.7 *The Reorganisation of Local Administrations*

The People's Government carefully handled the reorganisation of local administrations, and conducted an extremely flexible tactic in this respect, although the matter had been in the making for quite some time before. A commission to develop the related policy for local administration restructuring had already been set up by the People's Commission towards the end of 1921, which came up with a final product called "Key Document for the Establishment of a Rule-of-Law based Mongolian Government." Under this document, *khurals* of all levels of the local administrations were dismissed, the principle of hereditary inheritance was abolished, administration officials of all levels were selected and appointed, discrimination based on origin was done away with, and all the inhabitants of the given locality were defined as the *ard* or the common people.

Accordingly, the work of overhauling the legal foundations of the local governments was in principle completed by the end of 1922, and subsequently, the People's Government passed a number of important related documents, such as the "Rules on the Rights and Authority of the Many Mongol *Zasag* and *Zasag Wangs* and *Güngs*" (1922), "Rules on the Local Administrations of Mongolia" (1923), "Rules of the Administration of the *Ikh Shabi*" (1923), the "Rules of the Khovd Territorial Administrations" (1924), and the "Rules of the Dariganga Territorial Administrations."

The "Rules on the Local Administrations of Mongolia" states: "Given that Mongolia has already established a People's Constitutional Government, it is hereby decided that starting with a *bagh* with more than ten households (*ger*), *soums, banner, aimags* and the central government individually shall elect representatives of the people to form a *khural,* which shall be formed in a consecutive manner, which shall have the mandate to review and consider all related issues, and take decisions on the basis of a majority of votes and on this basis, uphold the right of the people." This provision in the rules gives priority importance to the vital interests of the *ard* (people) and proclaims that the wishes and desires of the *ard* shall be the basic duty and function of the organ of the people's representatives. According to the Rules, the head of the primary administrative unit, who was called the head of ten households, has direct jurisdiction over the inhabitants of the given administrative unit, irrespective of whether they were *wangs, güngs, khutugtus* or incarnates, *taijis* or nobles, and also introduces the right to elect and be elected irrespective of social class or group.

And according to the "Rules on the Rights and Authority of the Many Mongol *Zasag* and *Zasag Wangs* and *Güngs*" the seals used by the *zasag* princes, *taijis, khutugtus* and reincarnate lamas to control their serfs were seized and serfdom was abolished, which encouraged social and political activity among the common masses and which, in its turn, helped consolidate the People's Government.

The work to abolish and reorganise local administrations on democratic principles continued from late 1924 to the fall of 1924. As per the "Rules on the Local Administrations of Mongolia" the *khurals* of ten households (ger) were convened first, and the *khurals* of *baghs, soums* were held consecutively, the chairmen of the *khurals* of representatives of *baghs, soums* and *banners* were elected, which were involved in considering issues discussed and agreed upon by lower level *khurals,* and defined future goals and objectives. The *khurals* of *banners* and *shabi* were also held on a similar pattern, which elected their representatives to the *aimag khurals.* Following the *khoshuu khurals* (assembly), the assemblies of the four Khalkha *aimags* and the *Ikh Shabi* were held separately in early December 1924. These assemblies, which were attended by 30–50 elected representatives, guided by the rules of the local administrations discussed in a democratic manner a number of the broad-ranging political, economic and organisational issues of their respective *aimags*. The *aimag khurals* through secret ballot elected their respective *khural* chairpersons; their deputies and office bearers responsible for resolutions and issues, grievances and financial matters were elected, who in turn, elected representatives to the First State Congress (*Ikh Khural*), and they also set up their local relevant ministries. More than 90 per cent of the nobles and principles of the local administrations were replaced by elected people's representatives as a result of elections conducted. However, in some places, there were revolutionary excesses under the pretext of abolishing the old and the obsolete.

There were 9,456 ten *gers*, 1,833 *baghs*, 540 *soums*, 83 *otog*, 106 *banners* in the four Khalkha *aimags*, the *Ikh Shabi* and in the Uriankhai and Tariachin *banners* in Khövsgöl and Khovd in 1924, where a total of 11,960 local *khurals* were set up and roughly 20 per cent of their total population were directly involved in the local *khurals*.[22]

The successive establishment of *khurals* of representatives of ten *gers*, *baghs*, *soums*, *banners*, *aimags* and *shabi*, a system to ensure the broadest involvement by the people's masses in directly running state and government affairs, was instrumental in laying firm foundations for the evolution and growth of an integrated system of organs of people's representatives.

22 M. Sanjdorj, *History of the People's Government*, Ulaanbaatar, 1974, pp. 116–117.

DIAGRAM 12 State structure of Mongolia (1923)

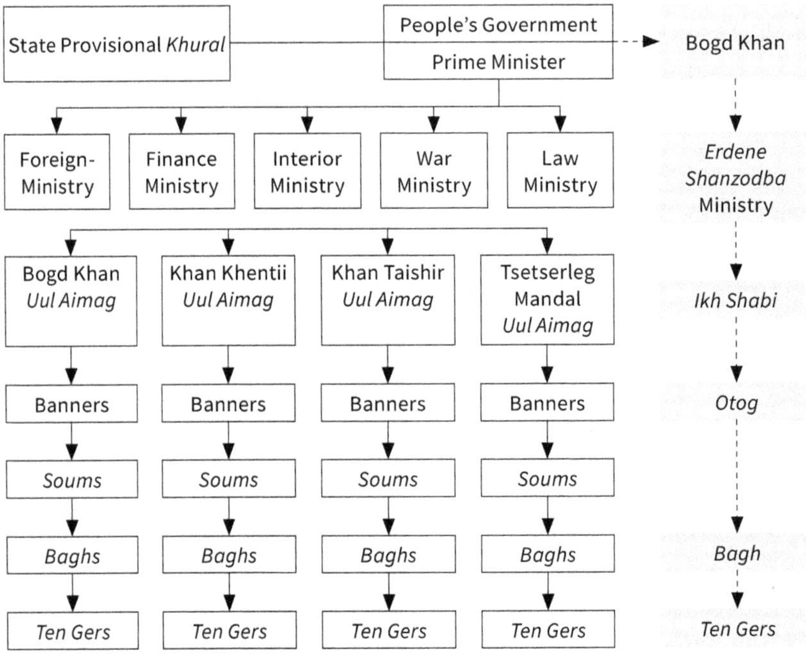

3 The Foundation for the Constitutional Institution is Established

3.1 *Constitution Drafting Process and Progress*

The process of drafting the First Constitution of Mongolia was directly connected with the "Oath Taking Treaty," because on 10 October 1921, the Central Committee of the MPRP and the People's Government, at their joint meeting, set up a special commission to review and adopt the fundamental laws, the rules of the People's (constitutional) Government, and they decided that these documents would be enforced for good. The Commission was directly responsible for drafting the "Oath Taking Treaty" with the Bogd Khan and the first draft of the "Constitution of the People's Limited Government." Hence, there is every reason to believe that the work on drafting the country's Constitution had already begun in the fall of 1921. But the Commission, which was tasked with the assignment to draft the Constitution, was actually formed on 19 May 1922 by the People's Government in its resolution, and the Chief Executive Minister of the Law Magsarjav was appointed to head the Commission. The 39th Session of the Government of Mongolia, which was held on 1 November 1921, issued a Resolution concerning the work of the Commission, which pointed out that "It is recommended to summarise the Constitution of such constitutional republics as England and include it in the draft Constitution of Mongolia tailored in such was to conform with the policies being conducted by the present government."

In keeping with the Government recommendations and guidelines on drafting the Constitution adapting the model of bourgeoisie parliamentarianism, the Commission set about its task. As instructed from the top, the Institute of Letters (*later the Mongolian Academy of Sciences) Tr.*) translated into Mongolian the Constitutions of England, Sweden, Belgium and the Netherlands for use by the constitution-drafting commission. The Government was not happy with the slackness of the Commission and it was dismissed by a Resolution adopted on 29 December 1921, and the work was transferred to its own "Department of Systematising Laws and Legislation." The delay in the drafting of the Constitution was in no way related to the dysfunction of the Commission but was because some of the authorities under the pretext of "reviewing and considering the constitutions of advanced European countries," were trying to designify the relevance and importance of the Soviet Union and its Constitution, and disagreed about accepting the draft of the Constitution. In other words, there was disagreement among some of the competent authorities in terms of the draft and the concept of the Constitution, and also because of pressure on the part of the Comintern and the Soviet Union as well.

A Resolution (Resolution One) passed by the People's Government on 5 November 1921 was important in helping outline the fundamental principles for the drafting of the Constitution and to expedite the drafting process as such. Soon after the adoption of this Resolution, legal experts from the Soviet Union were invited to Mongolia and one such expert was P. Vsevyatskii. Prime Minister D. Tserendorj was assigned as the Constitution-Drafting Commission Chairperson by the People's Government through its Resolution that it had adopted on 24 October 1921. The Commission members included Elbegdorj Renchino, Tseveen Jamsrano and Gombobadamjav.

The following legal documents were referred to in the drafting of the Constitution:

1 Constitution of the Soviet Union, which was referred to as the central document, and
2 The experience of the People's Government accumulated in the last 3 years as well as legal acts of a constitutional nature, which were adopted during this period.

Political, social and economic measures undertaken by the People's Government in the period from 1921 to 1924 became the foundational stones for the establishment of a Constitutional Republic.

3.2 *The First State Congress* (Ikh Khural)

Besides the above-mentioned objective reasons, some factors of an internal and external subjective nature contributed to the delay in addressing pending challenges. The development of a constitutional monarchy was interrupted by the Eighth Bogd Khan Jebzundamba on 20 May 1924, which basically paralysed the influence of the opposition force that had made up the coalition-type-government. Likewise, on 31 May 1924, Lev Mikhailovich Karakhan, a Soviet Armenian diplomat and Wellington Koo, the Foreign Minister of the Republic of China signed an "Agreement of the General Principles for the Settlement of the Questions Between the Republic of China and the Union of Soviet Socialist Republics" in which the USSR recognised Mongolia as part of the Republic of China and confirmed that the USSR shall respect Chinese sovereignty over Mongolia. The Treaty shocked the national democratic-minded Mongolian leaders and led them to come to a common understanding that it would make sense to proclaim to the world, without delay, the existence of an independent Mongolia as a Republic. The Central Committee of the MPRP, which met for its Presidium meeting on 3 June 1924, passed a decision to establish a Republic, which was considered and approved by the Party Central Committee's plenary meeting held on 7 June 1924. The Party Central Committee plenary meeting decided that "A Government of People's Republic would be set up, but a Premier, the so-called Da Juntan, would not be elected, and since the highest state and government authority shall be retained with the State *Ikh Khural* and the Government elected by the Khural."[23]

The First State Congress (*Ikh Khural*) was held in Niislel Khüree on 8 November 1924 of the Solar (Georgian) Calendar, attended by 77 delegates representing various *aimags, banners* and the *shabi.*

The Congress first reviewed the performance report of the People's Government, followed by the reports of the ministries, *aimags, shabi* and special *banners.* The Congress endorsed the outcome of the year performance of the People's Government and issued a related Resolution: "Our People's Government, despite the serious backwardness of our country's domestic situation and the far too many national issues pending imme-

23 *Laws of the Mongolian People's Republic and Compilation of Some Related Legal Acts, (1921–1940),* Book One, Ulaanbaatar, 1972, p. 92.

diate solution, it relied on truly national traditions and did not waver to forge ahead to establish a sovereign Republic of the people, that fully concurs with the country's ideology, and the formation of such a state is correct."

The Congress, following the report by the Economy Ministry, came up with an important recommendation on promoting the national financial and economic policy, livestock economy and industry. Much time was devoted to a discussion of economic development both from the point of view of improving the traditional livestock herding and also the creation of new industry and the exploitation of national resources like minerals and forests.

The Congress passed a special resolution on inclusivity. It emphasised the need to draw the poor and middle sections of the population into "genuinely *ard* associations." The Resolution stipulated that the association would be accessible to self-employed people and poor servant lamas, including artisans and smiths from the towns and rural areas. However, the Resolution exposed ideas that could push it to become a resolution with a class-inclination.

The Congress deemed it important and appropriate to concentrate in the hands of the Government the country's banking and credit policy, which would be conducive to improving the commercial activities of all the cooperatives, which would gradually squeeze out foreign private capital from the country. The Congress instructed the Government to oversee the work of cultural establishments by increasing the number of schools at *banners*, laying the foundations for technical vocational education, enlisting research institutions in carrying out research into important economic issues and starting schools for adults. The most important decision taken by the Congress was the issue of approving the First Constitution of the Mongolian People's Republic.

3.3 *The Adoption of the First Constitution and the Proclamation of the Mongolian People's Republic*

B. Tserendorj, Prime Minister and Chairperson of the Constitution drafting Commission made a brief presentation on the draft Constitution at the Congress session on 24 November and motioned the discussion of the draft Constitution article by article. More than 60 Congress delegates commented (some of the delegates spoke more than once) on the draft Constitution, and at the conclusion of the discussion, relevant changes and amendments were included in the draft. The changes and amendments suggested by the Congress delegates, among others, included the provisions that the State *Baga* (Small) *Khural* would be fully accountable to the State *Ikh* (Great) *Khural,* and should the decision of the *Ikh Khural* contradict the Government policy and existing laws, the *Ikh Khural* would annul the decision, and further, the amendments stipulated that the Government, in its activities, would be directly accountable to the *Baga Khural.* There were many different suggestions regarding the name of the country's capital city and finally the Congress delegates agreed to rename the capital city Ulaanbaatar (*literally meaning Red Hero. Tr.*). Finally, after prolonged debate and scrutiny, the First State Congress (*Ikh Khural*) unanimously approved the Constitution at 16.17 p.m. on 25 November 1924. A mass meeting of working people of the capital city was held at the central square on 26 November, where the new Constitution was promulgated and the Mongolian People's Republic was officially proclaimed. Celebrated Mongolian writer Dashdorjiin Natsagdorj, as a witness and a participant of the Congress, later wrote that "This was a wonderfully unprecedented event which touched the hearts of many."[24]

The Constitution proclaimed Mongolia as a sovereign People's Republic. Article One of the Constitution read: "Henceforth Mongolia shall be named the Mongolian People's Republic, the highest state powers shall be given to the true common people – the *ard,* and all national matters shall be considered and decided by the State *Ikh Khural* and they shall be executed by the Government elected by the *Ikh Khural.* Therefore, revere and abide." This meant that the government powers would be in the hands of the people through the *Ikh Khural* and the Congress also stipulated that *Ikh Khural* should be the political foundations of the people's government. Article Two of the Constitution outlined the aims of the Republic to wipe out the so-called feudal-theocratic regime and its ideology, tailor the political administrative functions to serve the needs of the people, which would help bolster the foundations of a new republican order.

The First Constitution, besides defining the factors imperative for strengthening the political foundations of the People's State, also emphasied the importance of its economic foundations. It declared that all land, minerals, forests and water within the bounds of the territory of the Mongolian People's Republic were the property of the people, and ruled out the possibility of their private ownership.[25]

The Constitution proclaimed and legalised the democratic freedom and rights of the citizens. It proclaimed that the citizens of the MPR had

24 D. Natsagdorj, Brief History of Mongolia, Shini Toli Journal. 1936, No. 3–4, p. 577.

25 *Laws of the Mongolian People's Republic and Compilation of Some Related Legal Acts, (1921–1940),* Book One, Ulaanbaatar, 1972, p. 119.

equal rights irrespective of their origin, belief and gender. It provided for freedom of speech, press, demonstration and meetings, formation of and joining associations, access to free education by all, non-exploitation of other's labour, and the right to elect and be elected by all citizens who have reached the age of 18. Church and State were declared separate and religion was made a matter for the individual conscience.

The Constitution applied the principle of division of state power, by declaring that the "State *Ikh Khural* shall be the supreme power in the Mongolian People's Republic. During the breaks in between sessions of the *Ikh Khural* this authority shall be vested with the *Baga Khural*, and during the period between the sessions of the *Baga Khural* it would be appropriate to allocate this right to the Presidium of the *Baga Khural* and the Government." According to the Constitution, the State *Ikh Khural* became the supreme power of the country and the supreme body of the representatives of the people. The Constitution also stipulated that the representatives to the *Ikh Khural* would be elected by the *khurals* from representatives of people of different levels, that is, the *gers* of ten, *bagh, soum, banners,* and the *aimags.* The State *Ikh Khural* and during its recess, the State *Baga Khural* were given the authority to represent the country in dealings and engagement with foreign countries, ratifying and abrogating treaties and agreements, accrediting and withdrawing ambassadors in foreign countries, modifying the state borders, declaring war and friendship, declaring emergency for the defence of the country, conducting military mobilization.

Some researchers have defined the term "real *ard,*" which can be met with quite frequently in the Constitution, as meaning subjects or nationals of the country. Although such an explanation can be justified, if we interpret this explanation in the context of the other chapters and provisions in the Constitution, as well as some resolutions of the First State Congress (*Ikh Khural*), we can conclude that the country was gradually shifting towards a strict class-oriented stance. For instance, a special decision gives the poor and middle-class of the population to join "genuinely *ard* cooperatives" while those who lived by exploiting others, such as traders, usurers, former princes, Buddhist incarnations, lamas who lived permanently in monasteries, the insane and people who had been condemned of a crime such as theft by a court of law were deprived of the right to elect and be elected. This provision of the Constitution clearly violated human rights and set limits to Democracy, therefore, it does not comply with the national democratic principles that the People's Government had declared. Butler noted that there were close affinities between the Mongolian Constitution and that of the RSFSR, and to some extent, the USSR.[26]

The First Constitution of the Mongolian People's Republic, on the whole, for the first time in the history of the country's statehood, abolished the monarchy, legitimised the national democratic transformations, critical legal principles and the brand new political system, and proclaimed to the world the sovereignty and independence of the country, in this sense, it is a truly historically significant document. The First State Congress (*Ikh Khural*), guided by the Constitution, elected the 30-member State *Baga Khural*, whose composition included 23 members who were *ard* (commoners), 6 who were *Taijis* and only one member was a lama. The State *Baga Khural* held its first session on 28 November 1923 and elected its Presidium with five members, who were all commoners-*ard*. P. Genden was elected the Chairperson of the State *Baga Khural*, which formed the Government and B. Tserendorj was approved as the country's Prime Minister.

When we look at the decisions of the First State Congress (*Ikh Khural*) from today's perspective, we find that although there were some historical restrictions, the historical significance of the Congress can be summarized as follows:

1. The transition from a theocratic, absolute monarchy to a people's constitutional monarchy, and then to a republican government was indeed an extremely significant progressive phenomenon.
2. Mongolia, for the first time ever in its entire history, had its own Constitution. The principles of national Democracy lie in the core of the Constitution's basic concept.
3. This Constitution, again for the first time, comprehensively and broadly legitimatised human rights and freedoms. In particular women were granted equal rights with men, which was unprecedented in the whole of Asia. Mongolia thus preceded the United States, where Democracy is promoted in its classical form, in granting women equal rights with men.
4. For the first time in Mongolia parliamentarianism was introduced with the formation of the State *Ikh* and *Baga Khurals*.[27]

26 W.E. Butler, *The Mongolian Legal System: Contemporary Legislation and Documentation*, The Hague, 1982, p. 174.

27 Although this right was promulgated in the United States in 1919, black women were not granted equal rights with those of black males.

8 The State and Laws during the Period of the First Constitution (1924–1940)

1 Historical Summary

During the years of the First Constitution, the pro-national democracy and pro-orthodox communist forces were still entangled in a nasty controversy over Mongolia's social set-up and the country's future development. Mongolia had become a centre of social experiments.

Starting in the mid-1920s, the Comintern, having assessed the national democratic course of the MPRP, conducted a policy of intimidating pro-national democracy Mongolian leaders such as Ts. Dambadorj, N. Jadambaa, B. Tserendorj, A. Amar and J. Tseveen. They were branded as "rightists" and the Eighth MPRP Congress, held in 1928, removed most of them from the ranks of the party leadership. They were replaced by the so-called "leftist" pro-Comintern young people who were poorly educated, incompetent, and ultra-revolutionary minded. This gave the Comintern the possibility to carry out their experiment of building Socialism in Mongolia. The Comintern, at the Eight MPRP Congress, held in 1930, defined Socialism as a practical objective in Mongolia's development, and set out to carry out their plans under the slogan of building a socialist society in the country.

Beginning from this period onward, the political policy of the ruling party and government became class-based and the Comintern, with utter disregard for the unique characteristics of Mongolia and the ongoing social, economic and cultural reforms that were being carried out, imposed the Soviet model of Socialism on the country and were determined to accomplish their goal at all costs. This adventurist move by the leftists was totally alien to the then realities of the social system of Mongolia and it was totally Utopian in nature. Consequently, by early 1930, Mongolia's society plunged into a deep crisis that sparked off uprisings and social disturbances.

Due to the appreciation by the social progressive forces of Mongolia and the realisation by the Comintern that events were not going according to plan, the Central Committee and the Central Control Commission of the MPRP jointly held their Third Emergency Plenary Meeting in late August 1932, and the Seventeenth Special State Conference, which was held soon after, passed decisions to rectify the leftist deviation and errors. These decisions have gone down in history as the "New Turn Policy."

Politically, the New Turn Policy sought to ensure a proper coordination of the party and state activities in the social management system. Economically, it aimed to pull the country out of economic crisis by way of encouraging the initiative of the masses, and promoting the development of the industrial sector. In social terms, the New Turn Policy set the task of uniformly improving the living standard of the private entrepreneurs and all social segments, and ideologically, it sought to find the correct centre line of the pluralistic views, such as National Democracy, Socialism and religion. The New Turn Policy was not a brand new policy; it was in fact the revived continuation of the national democratic policy, which was being pursued before 1928. During these years, private livestock owners became increasingly interested in increasing their animal population, goods exchange became livelier in the domestic market, and private trade developed. In 1932, the country had 16.2 million heads of livestock, which had increased to almost 26 million by 1940. Foundations were laid for national industry. Industrial plants and Central Power Stations were built in the capital city and a wool washing factory was built in the town of Khatgal with Soviet assistance, heralding the development of the country's industrial sector. National culture and education also made headway. In 1935, only 5.6 per cent of Mongolia's population was literate, which jumped to 20.8 per cent by 1940. National professionals, who received education in the Soviet Union, Germany and France, spread culture in both urban and rural areas. The numerous measures that were taken during the years of the New Turn Policy, from the standpoint of socialist, Stalinist theory, meant retreat; however, from the standpoint of national democratic ideas, they meant real progress and introduced a new trend. Regrettably, national democratic reforms and the natural changes in the country were slowly and gradually cut short by excessive communist ideology and course. The most damaging outcome of the activities carried out by supporters of communist policy was the persecution of thousands of innocent Mongolians with the direct interference of foreign forces.

Party, government and military leaders, to begin with, became the political victims. 86 per cent of the MPRP Central Committee members, almost one half of all the State *Baga Khural* members, and 86.4 per cent of top military officers, with ranks similar to those of generals of the People's Revolutionary Army, were arrested and the majority of them were executed. Among such victims were leading Mongolian politicians and statesmen P. Genden, A. Amar, D. Dogsom, S. Dovchin and many others. During this mass persecution, 17,004 lamas were arrested, of whom 13,679 were executed, while the remaining lamas were sentenced to different terms behind bars. To be precise, 10.9 per cent of the adult male population was persecuted. Lamas and commoners, who were increasingly subject to mass arrests, impregnated the entire society with a feeling of distrust, suspicion and fear.

This marked the beginning of the establishment of a totalitarian regime in the country. Public fear and suspicion were fanned further by the unprovoked war of Japan against Mongolia in 1939, which became a heavy burden on the common people. During this period the policy of the government and the party was directed primarily at safeguarding and strengthening the hard-fought national independence of the country, and addressing critical social and economic issues and natural challenges. For instance, the policy was aimed at leading the country towards social progress by regulating the relations between different social groups, which were formed of common people and former nobles and *taijis*, as well as between the poor and rich segments of the private entrepreneurs by way of conducting a tough and decisive course designed at establishing a regime of people's dictatorship for the benefit of the poor and middle-class people. It was believed that as long as the end objective of the policy was noble, it did not matter how that goal was achieved, and the Mongolians blindly followed the Stalinist theory that as the process of building a new society deepened, the class struggle would become more intense, which explains the appearance of the earlier briefly mentioned impudent social phenomena.

2 State Structure

2.1 *Administrative and Territorial Divisions*

A number of changes were made in the country's administrative and territorial divisions during this period. Before 1924, administrative divisions in the country were of a military administrative nature, but in the given period, economic and administrative types of divisions were made.

Local state administrations were set up replacing the old system of ruling the *banners* through succession. There also appeared new *banners*. In 1918 there were 102 *banners* in the four Khalkha *aimags*, that had increased to 116 by the year 1924. In early 1923, watch posts were dismantled and their lands were given to *banners* ruled by the aristocrats, and the guards working there, at their own initiative, remained as subjects in the *banners* that they earlier served.[1]

1 M. Sanjdorj, *History of the People's State*, Ulaanbaatar, 1974, p. 195.

Starting in 1924, the number *banners* was reduced when actions were taken to merge those with smaller populations and territory.

The *Ikh Shabi* was dismissed and replaced with the formation of a new *aimag* called the Delger Ikh Uul *aimag,* while the *Shabi Otog* were reorganised into *banners.* The *shabi* of the *khutugtus* with seals were likewise either reorganised into autonomous *banners* or merged with the neighbouring *banners.* However, the Delger Ikh Uul *aimag* was dismantled for it did not have its own land and territory. Further, the *baghs* were pulled down in 1927 and small *banners* with four and fewer *soums* were merged with the neighbouring *banners.* And in 1929, the soums were enlarged with 300 households, while the units of tens were reorganised into the unit of twenty (*gers* or households).

Doctor M. Sanjdorj, in his book *History of the People's State,* studied in detail in chronological order the changes in the administrative and territorial divisions during the period of the First Constitution. He has observed that as a result of the aforementioned administrative and territorial divisions carried out in the Mongolian People's Republic in 1925–30, the former *banners* had been practically destroyed with significant changes in their internal organisational set-up, population, territorial borders, and the size of the *aimags* and *banners* were large.[2]

A Mongolian leader D. Dogsom, commenting on the changes effected in the administrative and territorial divisions, noted that this measure was undertaken to "put an end to the breaking up and cutting off the *banners* by the feudal lords in the interests of the needs and requirements of the people." The action was important given the poor status of the country's treasury and the shortage of professional cadres, since it was designed to make savings in the economy, trimming the number of administrative staff and improving the efficiency and services of the administrative organs.

Not very long after, some of the larger *aimags* and *banners* complained that these measures were not helpful in carrying through the country's economic and cultural policies, and harmful to state administrative actions, and started suggesting a review of the administrative and administrative divisions.

Accordingly, the Government started conducting a policy of reorganising the bigger *aimags* into smaller ones, doing away with the *banners* and strengthening the status of the *soums.* The dismissal of the *banners* was justified by arguments that they were not compatible with the revolutionary democratic social and political system, as the *banners* were formed

2 *Ibid.*, p. 197.

to bolster the feudal system and the *banners* were merely serving as an intermediary between the *aimags* and *soums*. However, in actual fact, the *banners* were important units in terms of their geographical location, the environment for practicing livestock industry, and demographic policy.

A legislation called "Law on Re-Classification and Division of the Country's Territory" was adopted on 6 February 1931 and the law was put into action, according to which the *banners* were dismissed, and 5 *aimags* and 513 *soums* were either divided or merged into 13 *aimags* and 113 *soums*. Some changes were carried out in the following years: the Altai *aimag* was dissolved in 1934 but it was reorganised in 1940; some *soums* in Selenge and Khövsgöl *aimags* were separated and merged in 1938 to form the Bulgan *aimag*, while a new *aimag* called Bayan-Ölgii was established, the inhabitants of which were predominantly Kazakhs and Uriankhais.

2.2 *The Evolution and Growth of the State Ruling Bodies*

The ruling representative organs, like the territorial and administrative divisions, were also changed. According to a new approved schedule, the newly set up system of People's *Khural* was organised into a four-tier institution:

1. *Bagh* and *Khorin,*
2. *Soum* and *Khoroo,*
3. *Aimag and Town,* and
4. State *Ikh Khural.*

State and law scholars, such as M. Sanjdorj, S. Jalan-Aajav, E. Avirmed, D. Sangidanzan, I. Dashnyam and B. Pürev have carried out specific research into competent representative political organs of the country and have written thematic articles and textbooks.[3] Let us now summarise, based on the works by these scholars, the objectives and course of the state ruling representative bodies today.

The objective of the People's *Khural* lay in outlining and defining concrete social, political, economic and cultural development policies and goals, monitoring and reviewing their implementation, electing the ex-

---

3 M. Sanjdorj, *History of the People's State*. Ulaanbaatar, 1974; S. Jalan-Aajiv, The main direction of the legislative activities of the People's Revolutionary State. Ulaanbaatar, 1968; E. Avirmed, *State rights of the People's Republic of Mongolia*. Ulaanbaatar, 1969; D. Sangidanzan, *The main roles of the people's state in the democratic stage of the revolution: 1921–1940*. Ulaanbaatar., 1974; I. Dashnyam, *State authorities of the People's Republic of Mongolia*, Ulaanbaatar, 1978; B. Thursday, *The implementation of Lenin's doctrine of the power organization of the representatives of the socialist state in the People's Republic of Mongolia*, Ulaanbaatar, 1981.

ecutive organs of the State, and providing them with an overall management.

The basis for of activities of the People's *Khural* was the *khuraldaan* or the session. Although the *Khurals* were not permanent, they would meet regularly, and at times, the sessions would continue for a long time. According to the regulations of the State *Ikh Khural,* it would be inaugurated in Ulaanbaatar every year on 1 November and it was established that the agenda should be considered within one month and if necessary, the sessions could be extended for one more month. In this way, the sessions of the *banner* (before 1931), *aimag khurals* and that of the State *Ikh Khural* were held within a month, and in an eventuality, they were extended from 15 up to 30 days (for example, the Seventh State *Khural* Congress was in session for 39 days). The agenda of the State *Ikh Khural* was planned and presented by the Presidium of the State *Baga Khural* and the Government, while relevant *aimag* ministries, *banners,* secretariats, *soums* and *bagh* administrations were responsible for drafting the agenda for the local People's *Khurals.* Alongside this, representatives of *khurals* of all levels enjoyed the right to initiate motions and submit them for consideration.

The State *Ikh Khural* occupied a special place in the system of organs of representatives. The State *Ikh Khural* was the highest authority of the country, which had the sole right to amend and adopt changes to the Constitution and address central development issues of the country.[4]

The State *Ikh Khural,* in keeping with the rules on electing representatives of the *Ikh Khural* of the MPR, which were adopted by the Second Conference held in 1925, held its sessions composed of representatives of the *aimags,* towns and the military through the People's *Khurals* of representatives (multi-stage process). These rules of the *Ikh Khural* were based on the principles of the First Constitution, which had revoked electoral rights of certain sections of the population, and in this sense, they can be characterised as replete with class-based ideology. To clarify, people who were deprived of their right to elect and be elected included the so-called people coming from the feudal class, that is, aristocrat *taijis,* lamas and the clergy, and private entrepreneurs who were employers.

The State *Ikh Khural* held a total of 8 sessions in the years from 1924 and 1940, but not a session was skipped in the years between 1924 and 1930. But the Eighth State Congress (*Khural*), which was held in 1934, decided

4 M. Sanjdorj, *History of the People's Government*, Ulaanbaatar, 1974, p. 173.

that the *Ikh Khural* sessions would be held once every three years and the relevant changes were made to the Constitution.[5]

The State *Ikh Khural* considered and passed decisions on all key domestic and foreign policy issues, and also reviewed and discussed the progress reports of the State *Baga Khural* and its Presidium, the Government, all government ministries, special departments, *aimags* and city municipalities. The Fourth State Congress (*Khural*), for example, which was held in 1927, considered and discussed the progress reports of all 16 government institutions, such as the ministries and special departments, and passed a special Resolution. The Law on the annual state budget was also approved by State *Ikh Khural*.

Article 9 of the Rules of the State *Ikh Khural* specifies that the State *Ikh Khural* and the Government members can be asked any question related to their respective functions, and it was mandatory to answer each and every question without exception. Furthermore, Article 10 of the Rules states that should the State *Ikh Khural* deem it necessary, it can set up a special commission to review the question, process and consider it, after which a relevant decision will be taken.

The State *Ikh Khural* transferred to the State *Baga* Khural all the matters immediately after completing its work. The *Baga Khural* of the Mongolian People's Republic, which was elected by the State *Ikh Khural* played an important role in the country's socio-political life. The Second State Congress (*Khural*), which was convened in 1925, amended the Constitution, according to which instead of the 30 elected members of the State *Baga Khural*, more than 30 members were to be elected. The State *Baga Khural* was the highest state power in between the sessions of the State *Ikh Khural* and it was one type of organ of representatives that considered and took decisions on vital national development issues. The working style and principle of the State *Baga Khural* were almost identical with those of the State *Ikh Khural*. The term of office of the State *Baga Khural* was one year until 1934, which was changed to 3 years starting in 1934. This, as mentioned earlier, was related to the term of office of the State *Ikh Khural*. The Constitution specified that the regular session of the State *Baga Khural* would be held twice a year and it would report only to the State *Ikh Khural* and had the prerogative right to elect the Presidium of the *Baga Khural* and members of the Government, and to review and discuss the performance reports of State and government organs of all levels. In the years from 1925 to 1939, there were 7 State *Baga Khurals* of the MPR

5 S. Jalan-Aajav, *Basic Line of Legislative Activities of the People's Revolutionary State, (1921–1949)*, Ulaanbaatar, 1967, p. 138.

and it met for a total of 22 sessions, which discussed the reports of the *Baga Khural* Presidium, the Government, its ministries and departments, and also the reports of the *Baga Khural* members, thus addressing and taking decisions on important domestic and external policy matters of the country.[6]

The Presidium of the State *Baga Khural* had a unique place in the highest state power of the country during the period under consideration. The Presidium of the *Baga Khural* was elected from among the *Baga Khural* members, who were fully accountable to the Presidium. The rules of the State *Baga Khural* Presidium were first approved in 1925 and again later in 1935. According to these rules, the Chairman of the *Baga Khural* Presidium was concurrently the Chairman of the State *Baga Khural,* who served as the Head of State in between the sessions of both the *Ikh* and *Baga Khurals* and according to the rules of the State *Baga Khural* Presidium the Chairman enjoyed total immunity. This definition gives us to believe that the State *Baga Khural* Presidium could very well be qualified as the institute of the Head of State.

During the First Session of the *Baga Khural,* which was elected by the *Ikh Khural,* the Presidium of the *Baga Khural* was elected exclusively from among the *Baga Khural* members as the Chairman, Vice Chairperson and Executive Secretary. Later, the Presidium of the *Baga Khural* was enlarged. The 1933 Rules clearly and specifically listed the powers of the *Baga Khural* Chairperson or Chairperson of the Presidium. They included, among others, calling of the meeting of the *Baga Khural* Presidium, presiding over the meetings, accepting letters of credence of foreign envoys and ambassadors, as well letters of their withdrawal, presentation of high state awards on behalf of the Presidium, and signing the resolutions of the Presidium together with the Deputy Chairperson and Executive Secretary. All issues of national concern were decided upon only by the highest representative body.

If a Government resolution contradicted the relevant law, the Presidium of the State *Baga Khural* reserved the right to order the Government to refrain from or invalidate the resolution. As stipulated in Article 15 of the 1933 Rules, laws and rules approved by the Government came into force only after their approval by the *Baga Khural* Presidium. The Presidium exercised the powers to call the *Baga Khural* to session, draft the *Baga Khural* agenda, monitor the implementation of the *Ikh* and *Baga Khural* resolutions, ratify and annul treaties and agreements concluded with foreign countries, and give high state awards at the personal initiative of

6 M. Sanjdorj, *History of the People's Government*, Ulaanbaatar, 1974, p. 174.

meritorious persons or at the request of the Government. The Presidium, in between the sessions of the *Baga Khural,* also had the prerogative right to appoint and dismiss ministers and chairperson of the central state administrative organs. The resolution was the legal act of the *Baga Khural* Presidium.

The State representative authority, the *Baga Khural* and the legal status of its members constitute important components of the Constitution. The "Special Rules of the *Baga Khural* Members," which were adopted in 1925, and the Second Rules on the *Baga Khural* Members, passed in 1933, outlined their powers.

Competencies as defined by the 1925 Rules:

1. To inspect and review the work of industrial plants;
2. Take part in the local People's *Khural* in a consultative capacity;
3. If a member has been given the authority, he/she has the right to take part in the working of the local People's *Khural* on behalf of the State *Baga Khural.*

DIAGRAM 13 People's State structure (1924)

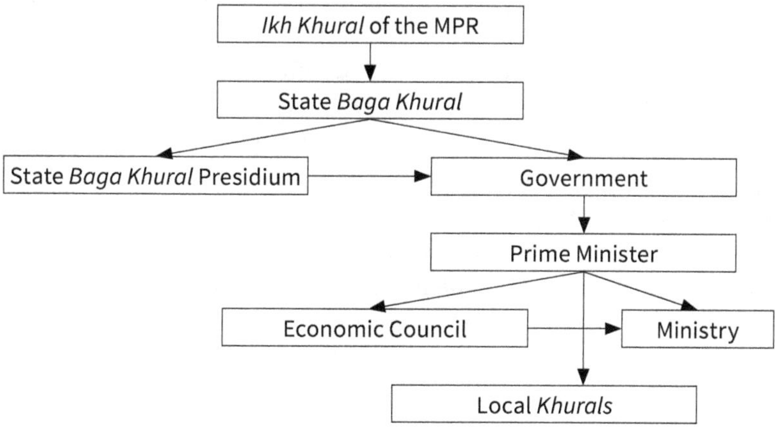

The 1933 Rules not only clearly specified the rights and responsibilities of the *Baga Khural* members, it also outlined their prerogatives. *Baga Khural* members were to be delivered importations of resolutions of the State *Baga Khural* Presidium and the Government, they were entitled to free transportation from the government car pool while going to official assignments, and were also entitled to a fixed monthly salary.

One of the important guarantees entitled to the *Baga Khural* members for exercising their authority was their immunity. The aforementioned rules spelled out that *Baga Khural* members, without the permission of either the Presidium of the *Baga Khural* or its Chairman, could not be investigated or summoned to the court and sentenced. The *Baga Khural* members were given ID cards and they had the right to put on badges as special state officials of the Mongolian People's Republic.

2.3 *The Supreme Central State Administrative Organ*

The People's Government was renamed as the Council of Ministers of the MPR on 2 July 1932 by a decision taken at the Twelfth State Congress (*Khural*). This was not merely a change in name. It was a striking expression of the changes and progress in the organisational structure and activities of the People's Government, but also a hallmark of its democratic nature, and the reinforcement of the principle of collective leadership in considering and passing decisions on all important national problems.[7]

The organisational set-up and activities of the Government were regulated by the "Rules of the Government," adopted by the Second State Conference held in 1925 and the "Rules of the Council of People's Ministers of the MPR," approved in 1933. Article 1 of the 1933 Rules defined that the Council of Ministers shall be the highest state administrative organ of the country. Previously, all the central state administrative organs were included in the structure of the Government, but under the new rules, the State *Baga Khural* instituted the Council of Ministers, which included as its members the Prime Minister, Deputy Premiers, ministers, and the chairman of the internal security department.

The primary duties of the Council of Ministers were to manage the national economy, ensure the implementation of the state budget, manage domestic and foreign trade, culture, education, health and foreign affairs, take national defence measures, ensure public order and safeguard the rights of the people. Given the prerogative right of the Council of Ministers to give directions and instructions, it was given the exclusive right to independently decide all matters and in this respect, it was accountable to both the State *Ikh* and *Baga Khurals*. This meant that the Council of Minister, reporting to the state representative authority, was an organ enforcing laws and decisions, and it was the highest executive authority when dealing with other state administrative organs.

The Council of Ministers was also directly responsible for guiding and regulating the work of the ministries, special departments, and other executive organs of state administration. The Council of Ministers, within

---

7 M. Sanjdorj, *History of the People's Government*, Ulaanbaatar, 1974, pp. 180–181.

its own competencies, had been issuing resolutions compatible with the law.

As the economic and humanitarian functions of the State grew and ever-new economic sectors appeared, there arose the need to set up new independent ministries or special departments in order to regulate their operation.

A number of ministries and departments were formed anew in 1925–26. Within its framework, the Finance Ministry was bifurcated with the formation of a new Economics Ministry, which was given the management responsibility for industry, trade and agriculture. A new Data Section was set up at the Interior Ministry, which was an important move that laid the foundation for the future Statistics Service in the country. In 1925, a so-called *Mongol Teekh Nevtrüülekh Khoroo* or the Committee of Mongolia on Transportation and Transition was established, which was the first state administrative body to manage transport and transportation. The Council of Ministers also laid the foundations for a Weather Department and the Construction Administration.

An administrative body that was responsible for inter-sectoral management was the Economic Council, which drafted national economic policy, and was wholly responsible for regulating, managing and monitoring financial matters.

In order to improve the protection and utilisation of state property, and to ramp up the monitoring of discipline and liability of the human resources, the Government augmented its control and monitoring section into a Control and Monitoring Ministry. Later, although this Ministry was dismissed and reorganised a number of times, the Government had to reorganise the Ministry taking into account social demand, although its name and organisational set-up changed.

The Second State Congress (*Khural*) held in 1925 outlined the basic duties of the Control and Monitoring Ministry as follows:

1. Monitor state organisations whether they are performing their core duties in a responsible and fair manner or not;
2. Combat bribery and corruption, and string pulling;
3. Combat embezzlement and squandering of state property.

The Economics Ministry was reorganised by the Fourteenth State Conference held in 1929 into the Trade and Industry Ministry, and the Livestock Breeding and Agriculture Ministry. And the Sixth State Congress held in 1931 established a new Health Ministry, while the Eighteenth State Conference of 1931 renamed the Interior Ministry into Home Security Authority, but the Twentieth State Conference, which was held in 1932, once again established the Interior Ministry. And in 1936, the Trade and

Industry, Transportation and Transition Ministry was reorganised into the Ministry of Trade and Transportation, the Industry Ministry and the Constitution Ministry.

While carrying out organisational changes in the State central administrative system, the Government, given the deficit in government income, had been making efforts to trim expenditures, and to retain the cost of maintaining human resources given that the country then had a manpower shortage. For instance, the Seventeenth State Conference, which was held in 1932, took a number of important measures in order to cut by 50 per cent State apparatus spending.

1 The Council of Minorities was dismissed and its powers and functions were transferred to the Presidium of the State *Baga Khural*.
2 The Hunger Commission and its offices were dissolved.
3 The Women's Commission and its secretariat were dismissed and their powers and functions were transferred to a public organisation.
4 The Economic Council was replaced with the "State Registration Authority for Planning and Adjustment."
5 The Latin Script and the Cultural Offensive Committees were dismissed and their duties and functions were put under the jurisdiction of the Education Ministry.
6 The law section of the Government was dismantled and its duties and functions were put under the Justice Ministry.
7 The Physical Culture Council was dissolved and its duties and functions were transferred to a public organisation.
8 The State Defence Council was pulled down and its competencies were transferred to the Council of Ministers.[8]

Judging by the above, the structure of the State central administrative organs was not fully developed and had not yet become strong and stable, and consequently, and they were reorganised and restructured many times over.

2.4 *Local* Khural *and Administration*

During the period under review, the legal foundations of the local *khurals* and administrations include the "Rules of the Newly Established Local Administrations of the MPR" approved in 1925 by the Second State Conference, and the "Rules of the *Aimag Khurals* and *Aimag* Ministries (Executive Administrations)," the "Rules of the *Soums Khurals* and Administra-

8 S. Jalan-Aajav, *Basic Line of Legislative Activities of the People's Revolutionary State, (1921–1949)*, Ulaanbaatar, 1967, pp. 176–177.

tions," and the "Rules of the *Baghs* of the MPR," which were all adopted in 1933 by the Presidium of the State *Baga Khural*.

The Aimag *Khural* of Representatives was formed by representatives elected from the *Soum Khural* of People's Representatives. The *Aimag* People's *Khural* had been electing the *Aimag* Ministry's (Executive Administration) with 5 full and 2 deputy members. The 1925 Rules defined that the Deputy Chairman and Head of Department of an *Aimag* Ministry would be members of the *Aimag* Ministry, but the 1933 Rules do not make any mention of the composition directly. The *Aimag* Ministry was elected by the *Aimag* People's Representative *Khural* and it was headed by a Chairman who was officially endorsed by the Government. The 1933 Rules determined the organisational set-up of an *Aimag* Ministry as having the following departments:

1 Animal Husbandry Department;
2 Finance Department;
3 Military Department;
4 People's Education Department, and,
5 A Literacy Class.

The basic functions of the *Aimag* People's *Khural* were:

a Manage and run the *aimag* on the basis of the laws in force in the country;
b Execute laws, resolutions and orders of higher authorities;
c Plan and implement relevant measures designed at promoting the development of such national economic branches as animal husbandry, hay mowing and crop farming, trade, transport and communication, and industry;
d Take measures to improve the cultural education of the working masses, and to make them literate;
e Approve local budgets and monitor budget implementation.

Powers of the *Aimag* Ministry (Executive Administration):

1 Monitor the implementation, within the breadth and length of the *aimag's* territory, laws and resolutions adopted by higher authorities, and help in the organisation of their implementation;
2 Announce the meetings of the *Aimag* People's Representative *Khural* and draft its agenda;
3 Conduct election campaigns in accordance with the relevant laws and instructions;
4 Manage and guide the *Soum* administrations;
5 Manage population and livestock census;
6 Organise the relay service;
7 Enforce the Tax Law;

8 Guide and manage the trade, services and economic entities under its jurisdiction;
9 Render assistance and support in developing the people's livestock economy, and manage the establishment of industrial cooperatives;
10 Organise the work of mowing hay and crop farming;
11 Manage schools and hospitals;
12 Take measures related to national defence.

One point that needs to be especially emphasised is that according to the 1925 Rules, the *Aimag* Ministry had the right to legal procedures but according to the 1933 Rules, this right was removed as the administrative and legal procedure functions were announced at the level of the aimags.

The People's Representative's *Khural* of *soums* were being established with the representatives who were elected by the *Bagh* People's *Khurals.* According to the 1925 approved Rules, the *soum* administrations were being established with a chairman, an assistant and a secretary, appointed by the *soum khurals,* but according to the 1933 Rules, the *soum* administrations were to have 3 members and 2 deputies, based on which a collective leadership organisation, the *Soum* Administration Members' *Khural* (meeting), was set up.

The *soum* administrations were elected by the *soum* administration meetings, which were headed by a chairman endorsed by the *Aimag* Ministry or the Executive Administration. The *Soum Khurals* and *Soum* Administrations were guided by the principle of accountability before the electors, on the one hand, and on the other, the *Aimag Khurals* and the *Aimag* executive administrations, and within this framework, they managed their territorial economic, social and cultural entities, ensured public order and discipline, enforcement of laws, safeguarding the rights of their citizens, and carrying out local economic, social and cultural activities and measures.[9]

2.5 Bagh Khural *and* Bagh *Chairman*

The Rules of *Baghs* stipulated the formation of a *bagh* with as many as 30 to 100 households. The highest authority of a *Bagh* was *the Bagh Khural.*

The power and authority of the *Bagh Khural* and its chairman included the following:

1 Execute the orders and instructions of the *soum* administration, the *aimag* executive administration and the central Government;
2 Address local issues and problems within the domain of the *Bagh*;

9 S. Jalan-Aajav, *Basic Line of Legislative Activities of the People's Revolutionary State, (1921–1949),* Ulaanbaatar, 1967, pp. 176–177.

3 Mobiilse people in the eventuality of fire and flood etc.;
4 Manage the horse-relay services as per the *soum*-assigned schedule;
5 Conduct and maintain a record of *Bagh* population and livestock animals;
6 Take measures to protect the human population and livestock animals from contagious diseases;
7 Plan and execute measures to annihilate wolves and other predators that pose a threat to animal husbandry;
8 Teach literacy to the people, assist parents in enrolling young-age children in schools, and carry out hygiene, sanitation educative work;
9 Collect taxes as stipulated by laws;
10 Ensure the strengthening of revolutionary principles, peace and safety within the *Bagh*.

The related rules clearly defined that the *Bagh* chairperson was the head of the primary administrative organ to engage directly with the people. It stipulates that the *Bagh* Chairman is the government representative in the given *Bagh,* and so the entire people in the *Bagh* are duty-bound to comply with and implement the decisions of the *Bagh* Chairman, which have been taken on instructions from higher government authorities and the *Bagh Khural.*

2.6 *The Judiciary*

The State *Ikh Khural* (1925) instructed the Government to immediately set about setting up democratic judicial institutions by separating judicial responsibilities from the local administrative organs. This decision was pursuant to the ideas of the party programme, which was adopted by the Fourth MPRP Congress, held in 1925. The programme then set the objectives that “judicial institutions must be set up elected by the true *ard* (common people) … torture and excesses practiced during the occupation governments must be destroyed, legal processes laws and legislation must be streamlined and improved for the benefit and in the interests of the masses.” This provision, in principle was important in as much as torture was abolished and the independence of the court was promoted, but decisions were taken to set up the judiciary on the principles of a class approach, which had far-reaching implications in the years ahead.

Soon after the Second State Congress, pursuant to the implementation of its decision, the Government passed Resolution 42, according to which provisional courts were established in the country. Its objective was to hold trials and pass decisions regarding crimes of treason, sabotage, embezzlement, corruption and counterfeiting. The so-called “Provisional

Court" was initially established under the name "Legal Proceeding Authority on Political Cases," which had a chairperson and several members on board, and it was first chaired by Khorloogiin Choibalsan.

Its rules (adopted in 1926) had six basic provisions, which outlined crimes against the State, such as, treason, attempts to mobilise foreign armed forces against the nation, espionage to gather and disclose state and military secrets to be used against the revolution or for personal gain, share information with the enemy, tax avoidance and compulsory military service shunning by way of fanning disloyalty among the people.

In January 1927, the authority of this Special Court was accredited concurrently to the Chairman of the Department of Legal Proceedings of the Supreme Court, and consequently, the Provisional Court was dismantled.

"Rules of Setting up Prosecuting Departments," which were adopted by the Presidium of the *Baga Khural* of the MPR on 16 April 1926, became the legal framework for developing the judiciary in the country into an independent state institution. According to the 1926 Rules, the initial structure of the courts included the following:

1 *Banner* People's Courts;
2 *Aimag* and Town Courts;
3 Special Courts;
4 Supreme Court of the country.

The *Banner* People's Courts remained the primary judicial units of the country's judiciary system until 1931. These courts with one judge and two people's elected representatives tried lighter cases other than those that were tried by the *aimag* and town courts. In those times, the judge was called the Court *Tüshmel* (Officer), who was elected for a term of one year by the *Banner* People's Representative *Khural*.

According to the Constitution, the Court *Tüshmel* enjoyed electoral rights and according to the rules, the Court *Tüshmel* could be a male or a female, who served not less than two years in any one government, party and youth organisation, who was literate, as a citizen of the country had the right to elect and be elected, and had not been convicted before. This provision was applicable to all court officials of all levels.

The people's courts, which were set up during this period, in autonomous towns like Altanbulag, Javkhalant and Ulaanbaatar, and also such autonomous *banners* (which did not come under the jurisdiction of an *aimag*) as Dariganga did not report to the *Aimag* People's Courts but the prosecuting department of the Supreme Court, and in this sense, these courts were primary level courts. One of the differences of these courts as opposed to the *Banner* courts was that they had the authority to hold legal proceedings and pass judgment at a primary level similarly to any court that was under the direct jurisdiction of the *banner* and *aimag* courts.

The *aimag* courts, within the framework of their authority, besides resolving cases as per primary court rules, reviewed the cases that had been appealed against the ruling of the *banner* courts and took legally viable decisions. As mentioned earlier, besides the Special Court, the country also had military tribunals.

The prosecuting department of the Supreme Court had a general oversight of the prosecuting departments of the people's courts and military tribunals, and the courts at the higher instance reserved the right to make the final judgment in full compliance with the law. In other words, the department while conducting legal proceedings according to the procedural laws also led the country's judicial system, monitored legal proceedings and was responsible for ensuring an integrated judicial policy. In the beginning, the prosecuting department of the Supreme Court had one chairperson and 4 members, and the organisational set-up included the "All Member Meeting" and two-sub-departments.

Although this initial set-up of the court was built on strict class-based principles, legal procedural principles, the authority of individual judges and their mode of working were specifically defined, which can be characterised as certain legal progress.

Following the establishment and operationalisation of the independent judicial system, changes were effected in the country's territorial and administrative divisions, and owing to the tenets of the evolving developments the *banner* courts were dismantled in 1931–1933 and replaced with class-based courts and additional *aimag* courts were also set up. For example, *aimag* courts were set up in all the *aimags*.36 people's courts were established under the aimag (provincial) courts. Soon after, the *soum* and *khoroo* leaders were given additional charge as court chairperson, and accordingly, people's courts were set up at *soums,* and later at the *khoroos,* and the People's Courts were abolished in 1933 and 1934 in keeping with the resolutions of the Presidium of the State *Baga Khural*. These courts were abolished in order to bring the courts closer to the people and also to save on funding, according to many researchers and studies.[10]

Starting in the 1930s, under the pretext of waging an all-out war against the intrigues of the so-called class enemies, laws were grossly and flagrantly violated, which basically put an end to the idea of fair trial and monitoring by the prosecutors.

---

10 *Courts of the MPR – On Guard of Protecting Socialist Gains*, Ulaanbaatar, 1977, pp. 27, 47, 60.

This was a time when the country's powers were fully concentrated in the hands of Kh. Choibalsan alone, and with instructions and involvement of Stalin's yes-men hundreds and thousands of innocent people were persecuted on trumped-up charges between 1937 and 1939. The so-called *Extraordinary and Plenipotentiary Commission* was exploited, which forcibly took over the authority of the court procedure bodies. The Commission held 54 sessions, 28,451 people were tried of whom more than 20,000 men and women or 73 per cent were executed by shooting.

Kh. Choibalsan and his stooges accused and convicted innocent people, branding them as anti-revolutionaries and Japanese spies or members of Japanese spy networks and in so doing, the flawed and spurious theory and concepts of Andrey Ya. Vyshinskiy, the State Prosecutor under the Soviet leader Stalin, were being followed by the Mongolians. According to which, the mere admission of guilt under duress was considered sufficient to convict a suspect, and in order to pressure someone to admit guilt, the victims were subject to torture, they were given neither food nor drink, they were beaten badly, blackmailed, and fabricated evidence was produced against them. Soviet advisers and instructors, who were working with the Home Ministry, played a key role in spreading such unlawful practices, who instructed their Mongolian subordinates to make false accusations and admit to trumped-up charges and even personally attended the sessions of the Extraordinary and Plenipotentiary Commission. Kh. Choibalsan, while conducting an arbitrary policy of persecuting people en masse, the Home Ministry was put outside of the control of the Prosecutor's Office, thus put in place an "ideal" environment to widely apply illegal actions.

2.7 *The Procurator's Office*

This was established in 1939 primarily to control and monitor the compliance of laws by legal bodies, in particular the Home Ministry and its departments. In the beginning, the Procurator's Office was set up within the system of the Law Ministry and a post of Vice Minister to head and manage the office was created. Procurator's Offices were set up in *aimags* and the towns between 1930 and 1931. The Procurators of the *aimags* and towns were appointed by the State Procurator. The "Rules of the Procurator's Office of the MPR," adopted in 1930, became the legal basis for the organisational set-up and *modus operandi* of the Procurators' Offices, which outlined the power and authority of the Procurators' Offices as follows:

1. Monitor the compliance of law by the public, all cooperative organisations and the people in the name of the State, and transfer a suspect to the court after thorough investigation;

2 Monitor and supervise the working and functions of the Home Ministry and its agencies and departments;
3 Manage the investigation departments, including execute preventative actions;
4 Monitor legal proceedings by way of reviewing the court judgment;
5 Take part in a court proceeding with the purpose of protecting the right of the *ard*;
6 Monitor and supervise enforcement of judgments and the working of places of confinement;
7 Undertake general control and monitoring within the country to combat and prevent crime. The Rules assigned to the procurators' offices additional power and authority to protest court decisions and judgments.[11]

The Rules were revised in 1934, redefining the authority and power of the Procurator's Offices, which included redefinition of the *aimag* Procurator's Offices. According to the 1930 Rules, the Procurator had the right to monitor the activities of the Home Ministry, but the 1934 Rules provided that the investigation functions of the Home Ministry would be supervised.

By the mid-1930s, the Home Ministry was basically out of the control of the Procurator's supervision, which gave the Ministry a free hand for serious dereliction of duty. Kh. Choibalsan submitted to the Secretaries and the Presidium of the MPRP Central Committee a petition on 1 June 1934, which was neither an application, a complaint, nor a proposal of information. "There is not a single instance of a staff member of the Home Ministry who had made false or framed-up accusations. However, the courts and the procurator's office, instead of assisting in our duties, continue to put spokes in the wheels. Allow me to present the following seven cases – Gelsen's case, the sausage plant case, the case of Adiyasüren and Davaajargal from the Seventh military detachment, the case of "Red" Pürev, and the case of Gombo, representative assigned at temples and monasteries. We are closing our eyes to offenders and criminals. Instead of telling us about the fallacies in our duty, false stories are being invented to weaken our agency and I cannot but call those who are doing runners as people with ill-intentions." When the Presidium of the Party Central Committee discussed the matter, the State Procurator Ch. Choidogsüren made a statement. "Such a situation has arisen because our Procurator's Office is not being involved in the process of investigation

11 S. Jalan-Aajav, *Basic Line of Legislative Activities of the People's Revolutionary State, (1921–1949)*, Ulaanbaatar, 1967, pp. 176–177.

by the Home Ministry when Kh. Choibalsan was informed that we had received complaints from victims that officers of the Home Ministry had pulled their hair, burnt them with cigarette butts, and were beaten, he replied saying such allegations should be believed in. When we urged him to elicit testimony from offenders and witnesses according to the law, but, he together with Nasantogtokh (the Deputy Home Minister) asked 'What unlawful action have we taken?' and rejected our offer." Further, the State Procurator Ch. Choidogsüren explained why the case records were legally incorrect. Choibalsan spoke on two occasions, damning the Procurator and ordered that he be reported as the convicted person who had dared to file a complaint. What is more, a Resolution, which was adopted at this meeting, suggested that "... an end must be put immediately and forever to such rumours calling to question the Home Ministry alleging its unlawful actions, for this could tarnish the good name and reputation of the Home Ministry, which would only play into the hands of the anti-revolutionary elements." In this manner, the supervisory role of the Procurator's Officer to monitor the process of investigation being conducted by the Home Ministry was made inefficient and eventually put an end to this responsibility. State Procurator Ch. Choidogsüren was arrested on 11 September 1937 and he was handed the death sentence by shooting by Resolution 1, passed by the Special Commission of the Home Ministry on 25 October 1937.

3 The System of Law

3.1 *The Evolution and Formation of the System of Law*

A new system of law developed in the country during this period, which was accomplished simultaneously with the abolition of serfdom and restructuring of the feudal system of law. Furthermore, this period witnessed the regulation of many different kinds of social relations that had not been touched, and they were replaced with many new norms and standards. The foundations of the law system of this period took its source primarily from the legislative measures that were taken during the people's constitutional monarchy, which was established as a result of the 1921 national democratic revolution.

Professor I. Dashnyam has defined the legal system that was established between 1921 and 1940 as a new legal system. He believes that the quantitative and qualitative changes that occurred in the laws and legislations make up the key criteria for classifying the development stages of Mongolia's new law system, arguing that marked progress and changes took place in the content and standard of laws and legislation thanks to the regulation of the developing social relationships, as well as in the external from of the laws and legislation.

Proceeding from this premise, Professor I. Dashnyam divided the evolution process of the new system of law into the four following categories:

1 Stage One: when a struggle was waged to establish a new republican system in the country, which resulted in the creation of the foundations for the development of a new system of law;
2 Stage Two: The formation of an elementary legal system according to the Constitution;
3 Stage Three: The impact of the "Leftist Deviation" social crisis on the law;
4 State Four: The law system during the period of corruption and distortion of legality.[12]

The first stage of the new law system continued for 4 years and although it covered a relatively brief span of time, the system occupied an independent place in the overall development of law and had a novel effect on the social life as well. It was no easy task to define the central course and principles of a new law system at a juncture when the old system was being abolished and efforts being made to establish a new one, and lay the foundational sources expressing its substance and basic direction. Equally challenging was the matter of finding theoretical and methodological solutions to attempts to evolve and develop the primary elements and components of a totally new legal system. These challenges and objectives were addressed in the first few years of the process of the establishment of the law system, and based on this, this period has been classified as a stand-alone stage. Consequently, the system acted as a legal tool for regulating outstanding legal and social relations, and addressing the priority objectives of the State and Government. Hence, there is no reason to believe that the new system of law evolved and developed devoid of any concrete policy and objective.

A new legal system, covering almost all, without exception, elements of life evolved in the country emanating from the objective of laying the legal foundations of a new society, state system and regime, and improving and strengthening them further. Although the laws in this period could not have reached a higher level of perfection in terms of their content, form and system, they nevertheless contained some progressive and new

12 I. Dashnyam, *The Abolition of the Medieval Law System and the Formation of the First Modern Law System in Mongolia, (1921–1940)*, Ulaanbaatar, 1994 (Doctor's Dissertation), pp. 78–79.

elements, which were instrumental in the further growth and development of the legal system.

When we analyse the legal acts in the early stage of the evolution of the new system of law, we can identify the following 5 special features:

- The aforementioned legal acts were not legislatures that were officially formed, rather they were acts that were produced by the highest state administrative body accredited with legislative powers or which had been produced in agreement with the legislative monarchy.
- Legislative acts had not taken the form of "law," which passed through such types of legal acts as "resolutions" and "rules."
- These legal acts were in a state of transition in conjunction with the historical circumstances of the country when it was in a state of struggle for deciding on the country's path of development and the establishment of a Republic.
- The relations that had been regulated and the system that had been therefore created had not become fully refined and perfect in terms of their structure and substance.
- They, however, created the necessary groundwork for the drafting of the Constitution, and the formation of a new legislative system.

The second stage of the new system of law begins with the adoption of the First Constitution, which continued until the end of the 1920s. Key gains of this period were the evolution of new judicial branches, and the formation of a whole system composed of these new branches.[13]

The norms and standards of the country's social and political system, economic foundations, foreign policy directions, basic rights and duties of people, the structure and organisational set-up of the State, the principles and processes of their *modus operandi*, which had been defined in the First Constitution of Mongolia, became the foundational stones and the starting point for the evolution and growth of the new law system and its types and branches. As a result, brand new, closely mutually inter-related civil, criminal and judicial branches of law developed in the country covering issues related to the State, government administration, finances, labour, family, cooperatives and ecology.

The Comintern, from the very beginning up to the end of the 1920s made attempts to impose the "socialist model" in Mongolia, which assumed a much more official policy and which was in reality implement-

13 I. Dashnyam, *The Abolition of Middle Age Legal System and the Formation of the First Modern Law System in Mongolia, (1921–1940)*, Ulaanbaatar, 1994 (Doctor's Dissertation), p. 108.

ed starting from the 1930s. This policy directly and indirectly influenced the process of formation of a new legal system during the middle period of the implementation of the First Constitution, as well as the substance and form of the legal system, which were manifested through different means, and their impact was to have a long-term fall-out. One such impact was that of the "Leftist" policy and actions on the legal standards and the substance of the laws and legislations, which would become the determining legal environment for their enforcement.

The majority of the acts passed during this period incorporated, in one way or the other, the so-called "Leftist" policy. In this respect, suffice it to mention laws, rules, resolutions and instructions related to confiscation of property of the so-called feudal lords; the introduction of the system of contractual herding of livestock animals belonging to the *jasaa;* the imposition of tax on the assets and animals of temples, monasteries and the *jasaa;* the establishment of communes and cooperatives; stripping some citizens of their electoral rights; purging of civil servants; banning of religious rites and ceremonies of Buddhist temples and monasteries; forcing of lamas to give up their monkhood; and also regulations related to trade, caravans, transportation, animal husbandry, agriculture, tax, finances and credit etc.

Legal acts that projected or which were intentionally forced to project the "Leftist" line pushed the legislative system into crisis, and the process of the implementation of law and their legality were distorted and misinterpreted.

The second type of impact was connected with the process of reforming the legislation. Recognising the fault in and the fall-out from the distortions created by the "Leftist" policy and actions, they were opposed, and faulty laws and legislation were invalidated in order to overcome social crisis, and many new and different legislative acts were adopted to rectify the errors thereof. Almost 300 laws, rules and instructions were drafted in two years from 1932 to 1934, which constituted the bulk of the legislative reform that had been set in motion.

Although judicial branches developed and legislations were revised and renewed, their future course towards consolidation and perfection came up against monumental challenges and obstacles from the mid-1930s, which were directly connected with the political persecutions that had begun to gain momentum from 1937 onwards.

Not only was there a decline in the number of legislative acts that were being passed between 1935 and 1940, the share of resolutions of the State *Ikh* and *Baga Khurals,* laws and rules in these legislative acts had also shrunk significantly, and on the contrary, there was an increase in the number of resolutions and orders coming from the highest and central organs of state administration. During this period, the country did not have a single specialised law concerning any specific judicial branch. The State *Ikh Khural* stopped meeting for its sessions, the number of *Baga Khural* sessions also decreased together with its composition, several important government and state posts were concentrated in the hands of a single individual. The Home Ministry, which was the central state administrative agency, was deprived of its state control, and what is more, the Ministry no longer was monitored either by the court of the Procurator's Office, and a special Commission with exclusive judicial powers was instituted. All the above created favourable pre-conditions for mistakes and deviations in the process and implementation of the legislation.[14]

Let us now briefly look into the key judicial branches of this period.

3.2 *Tax*

Tax legislation was directly linked with the goals and objectives of the State and the policy of the ruling party with regard to tax and taxation. The MPRP Action Plan, adopted in 1925, defining the tax policy had instructed that "charging of tribute should be regularised simultaneously with the scaling up of dues relevant to the size of the assets, and the burden of official liabilities of poor and impoverished people should be reduced." This policy guideline became the basis of the country's tax policy until 1940.

The issue of tax had been reflected, to a certain measure, in the resolutions and decisions of both the State *Ikh* and *Baga Khurals.* Professor I. Dashnyam, after studying the tax laws and legislation during this period and the practice of their enforcement, defined the following taxes that were levied during this period.

1. Animal husbandry tax;
2. Private industry and traders' profit and turnover tax;
3. Workers and office worker's profit tax;
4. Customs duty;
5. Tax imposed on enterprises of temples and monasteries;
6. Special military tax;
7. Rural tax.[15]

14 I. Dashnyam, *The Abolition of the Medieval Legal System and the Formation of the First Modern Law System in Mongolia, (1921–1940)*, Ulaanbaatar, 1994 (Doctoral Dissertation), pp. 119–124.

15 I. Dashnyam, *The Abolition of the Medieval Legal System and the Formation of the First Modern Law System in Mongolia, (1921–1940)*, Ulaanbaatar, 1994 (Doctoral Dissertation), pp. 221–222.

In the same year, the Third State Congress (*Khural*) approved the rules for graded tax levied on the livestock of the Government and the *jasaa,* which was, in fact, the maiden integrated rules on livestock animal tax. According to the rules, farms that owned up to 6 *bod* (in Mongolian) *or* large animals or *bod,* such as horses, cows and camels were exempted from tax (a horse and a cow were calculated as two *bods,* seven sheep and 14 goats were defined as one *bod,* one camel was equivalent to two *bods,* a donkey and a mule were one *bod,* which adds up to six *bods*). Similarly, businesses owing 6–10 *bods* initially had to pay in tax 3 *bods* and those with 11–20 *bods* were liable to pay in tax 2 *bods* were also exempted from paying tax, while farms that had 5–100 *bods* had to pay a 3 per cent graded tax, and those with 101–150 *bods* were liable to pay a graded tax of 6 per cent. Under the same rules, young animals that were born in the same year were not to be taxed, while farms that had select breeds of animals were levied preferential tax.

According to the tax rules, in 1927, a total of 5.5 million *tögrög* was generated in tax, which increased to 15.7 million *tögrög* in 1928. This was equivalent to 1.20 *tögrög* for each one *bod.*[16]

Livestock animals were valued under these rules and accordingly new policies and procedures were introduced regarding the size of tax on livestock animals corresponding to percentage of animals that were privately owned. Accordingly, some animal husbandry farms where 20 per cent of the livestock were privately owned were given tax waivers, a certain percentage of preferential tax was levied on farms where 21–50 per cent of all the livestock were private-owned, and if 51–100 per cent of all the animals were private, the farms were given some tax waivers without increasing the size of the levy. Similarly, the percentage of tax was set at 5 for whose farms where privately owned animals constituted 101–150 per cent of all the livestock, 10 per cent tax on animals if the share of privately owned animals was 151–200 per cent, and those where more than 501 per cent of all animals were private, the tax was 355 per cent. Also tax size was defined for revenues earned from hay mowing and crop harvesting. Furthermore, one per cent tax for every 90 *tögrög* earned per annum was introduced for farms whose assets were more than 50 per cent.

In the same year, the Presidium of the State *Baga Khural* and the Council of Ministers introduced a Law on Animal Husbandry and Agriculture Tax. Accordingly, with due consideration of the local rates, the annual taxable rate on revenue was set at 7–10 *tögrög* for one cow, 15–20 *tögrög*

16 B. Gonchigsüren, *Official Tax Policy Implemented by the MPRP*, Ulaanbaatar, 1973, p. 27.

for a camel, 5–8 *tögrög* for a horse, a sheep 1.5 to 2 *tögrög* and 1–1.15 *tögrög* for every goat. While foals, calves and camel calves up to 2 years old and lambs and kids less than one year old were not subject to taxation, a farmer who had mowed hay and prepared fodder, built animal sheds and barns, and whose one son was serving in the army was liable to tax waiver, and other tax waivers were included covering such aspects as the productivity of animals, the closeness and the distance of a farm from the market etc.

Another law "Law on Animal Husbandry Tax," which was approved in 1933, also determined the size of tax according to the number of livestock animals, whether they were father or mother animals or not. There were many progressive elements in the aforementioned laws, however, they were permeated with class-ideas, and contained discriminatory provisions viz the well-off segments of the rural society.

Animal husbandry tax collected from the feudal and people's farming businesses amounted to 10.5 per cent of the total budget income in 1924, which had grown to 36.6 per cent in 1928, but decreased to 14.2 per cent in 1940.[17]

Customs duty occupied an important place in the legal tax system. Internal customs levied on trade, which was practiced since 1926, was abolished, and a new system of imposing customs duty was imposed whenever there was an export and import at the country's border. However, until the end of 1930, the country's tax policy was aimed at taxing live animals, raw materials and goods intended for export by foreign traders, who, during this period, besides customs duty, were liable to pay excise duty, turnover tax, and rent for using animal pastures and land. The size of customs duty was 10–50 per cent of the monetary worth of the export goods and raw materials, and 6–30 per cent of import goods. In this manner, the purpose, form and size of customs duty were clearly defined in the customs rules and regulations adopted in 1921, 1923, 1926, 1930 and then in 1939.

Researchers have noted that income tax from private entrepreneurs, traders, workers and office workers contributed to the consolidation of the budget, finance and tax laws. Some of the legal acts that were adopted and enforced include, "Rules on Levying Tax on Buildings in the Town," (1929, 1931), "Rules on Taxing Trade Centres and Licence Dealers" (1931), "Resolution on Income Tax from Office Workers" (1930), "Profit Tax Regulations" (1930), "Regulations on Profit" (1932), Vehicle Tax Regulations"

---

17 B. Dolgormaa, *МНР – Государственный бюджет и планомерное сторительсво, (MPR – State Budget and Planned Development)*, Moscow, 1967, p. 10.

(1932), "Regulations on Collecting Road Tax" (1933), Rules on Collecting Tax from Traders and Industrialists" (1938).

During this period, in addition the basic tax imposed on the livestock animals and assets of temples, monasteries and the *jasaa*, supplementary taxes were collected, which was a part of the policy to undermine and destroy them. As an example, according to a law on tax levied on *jasaa* livestock animals and assets, adopted in 1935, the practice of imposing tax only on livestock animals was changed and additionally other income, building structures of the *jasaa* were subject to duty. But building structures of physical temples and monasteries, and religious implements were not taxed. A special tax that was introduced during this period was the so-called special military tax, which was enforced for almost a decade from 1930 to 1940.

In 1930, the Government issued directives according to which a special military tax was levied on men who were not entitled to serve in all the units of the Red Army, according to which the nobility, such as the *wang, güng, taiji* and noble officials, who did not go for military service, people whose electoral rights had been scrapped but who were of military age, as well as lamas of all ranks and title were liable to pay special military tax.

3.3 *Civil and Family Law*

The central civil and family legislation, the so-called Civil Code, was enforced during this period. The Civil Code was drafted in parts in the years from 1926 to 1929 and the Government considered and approved them piecemeal. As the Civil Code was adopted in separate parts, each of them had their own names too. This goes to show that it was not easy for the Government to regulate property- and non-property-based social relations, which were extensive in nature, but the Government had no choice but to adopt them piecemeal without any delay as soon as they were drafted one by one.

The "Civil Code" of the MPR included the following laws:

1. Law on Protecting and Taking Care of Orphans and Poor People. 4 Chapters and 28 Articles (1926).
2. Law on Inheritance of All Kinds of Wealth and Property. 2 Chapters and 21 Articles, (1926).
3. Chapter 3 of the Civil Code on the Rights and Duties of Families. 28 Articles, (1929).
4. Article 4 of the Civil Code on Unions, Cooperatives Set up by All Officially Authorised Individuals and Cooperative Organisations Established by Common People. 111 Articles, (1929).

5 Chapter 5 of the Civil Code on All Kinds of Household Effects and Other Assets. 36 Articles, (1927).
6 Chapter 6 of the Civil Code on the Time Limit for Making an Appeal Regarding Disputes between Citizens on All Kinds of Loans and Liabilities. 9 Articles, (1927).
7 Chapter 7 of the Civil Code on Giving in Collateral All Kinds of Property and Items. 18 Articleы, (1929)
8 Chapter 8 of the Civil Code on Authorised Personnel to enter into and conclude all Kinds of Treaties and Agreements. 28 Articles, (1929).
9 Chapter 9 of the Civil Code on All Kinds of Treaties and Agreements with 14 articles. (1929).
10 Chapter 10 of the Civil Code with 22 Articles on Instruments of Credit and Liabilities regarding All Treaties and Agreements Duly Concluded was approved by the Sixteenth Meeting of the Government, held on 17 May 1929 and ratified by Resolution 46 of the State *Baga Khural* Presidium.

The first Civil Code affirmed and consolidated the legal basis of the legal competency, capacity of citizens, and that of a legal entity as well. Article 80 of the Law, for example, stated that "All persons with due authority, irrespective of their sex, origin, religion and ideology, with due compliance of laws and legislation have the right to take into private possession, us, transfer to others any item and asset, and to conclude work contracts." The Law also specified the imperativeness of adopting legally-approved rules and procedures qualifying someone as a legal entity. Chapters 8 to 10 of the Civil Code also defined the legal content of civil treaties and agreements, the principles of their conclusion, the rights and responsibilities of the contracting individuals, the guarantees for honouring the treaties and agreements, and determining the time frame of their validity, and when they would be rendered invalid. According to the Law, dialogue, treaty and agreement would be held between two and more individuals and/or organisations. The Law also made it mandatory to outline the mutual rights and responsibilities of those coming into contract, outlining the guarantees for their implementation, and defining the date when the deals come into effect and when they expire etc.

Alongside this, the Law defined that illegitimate treaties and deals are those that have breached legal provisions, used banned language and terms, and that include provisions and clauses that may pose a threat to the interests and traditions of the people and the country. They included attempts to avoid tax, deliberately reducing the amount of tax, clauses that pose serious threat to human rights, deliberately inflating the value of essential goods and the credit cost, shunning from honouring payment liabilities, and for this purpose, engaging in sham disposal and transfer of personal property and wealth, concluding contracts with people without legal capacity, and concluding contracts by use of pressure, deceit and blackmail

Some of the special measures to ensure the honouring of the commitments taken were also strengthened, which included the introduction of pre-payment, fine, security and collateral.

Property jurisdiction constituted an integral of the first Civil Code. The Law defined three kinds of property: state-owned (which included the land and its wealth, forests, water, fauna etc.), private property (included assets and household items owned privately), and collective property (this included property owned jointly by a number of individuals and the property of the cooperative). The Law also substantiated what is moveable and immoveable property. During this period, legal mechanisms for regulating lawful property relations of citizens were weak in some aspects. For instance, the Civil Code did not carry any provision or clause regulating the issue of copyright of authors and investors, and the matter of protecting the honour and reputation of citizens and institutions had been somehow overlooked.[18]

This Civil Code with 10 Chapters and 217 Articles, which was adopted in 1929 was in force until 1952.

Issues central to family and family relations were included and consolidated in Civil Codes and legislation, about which mention has been made earlier. Three chapters of the "Civil Code of the MPR on the Rights and Duties of Families" are regarded also as the first law on family and family relations in the country.

Article 58 of the Civil Code consolidates matrimonial principles, which stipulates that any citizen who has reached the age of 18, irrespective of origin, background, religion and belief, and if the male is a lama or not, can knot matrimonial ties on the mutual consent of the male and female entering into wedlock. The legalisation of matrimonial principles put an end to the centuries-old inequality that prevailed in matrimonial relationships, and introduced a progressive and humane element into this human relationship, which was a significantly important development. The Law also defined not only prohibitive practices but also non-prohibitive practices in marriages, for example, a married man or woman could not marry another person and stated that a man and a woman can have

18 I. Dashnyam, *The Abolition of the Medieval Legal System and the Formation of the First Modern Law System in Mongolia, (1921–1940)*, Ulaanbaatar, 1994 (Doctoral Dissertation), p. 252.

only one life partner; furthermore, persons coming from same family relations could not marry each other, which was an important provision designed at safeguarding the genetic fund of the Mongolian population. The above laws, which regulated family legal norms and standards, included provisions on the rights and duties of family members, their property relations, the basis and procedures for filing and seeking divorce, the duty of a family to assist and support other members and close relatives of the family, the procedures for child adoption, registration of family name etc.

Based on the above, we can deduce that the legal foundations of a family had been already built.

3.4 *Labour Law*

In the period when the Constitution was in force, Labour Laws were passed a number of times. The first labour law was the "Regulations on Assessing One's Labour," which was adopted at a Government meeting held on 14 February 1925. Article 1 of the regulations stated that these regulations must be complied with by all departments and sections of a ministry, government offices in town and settlements, private cooperatives, wholesale and retail trading and industrial enterprises, which equally applied to the rural agricultural firms. This meant that the regulations were relevant to not only government institutions and enterprises, but also to other organisations and businesses of different forms of ownership. This meant that labour relations in both the government and private sectors were regulated by this law.

The "Regulations on Assessing One's Labour" had 27 paragraphs, which covered the most important labour law institutes, such as labour contract, duration of work days and weeks etc. The work day was fixed at 8 hours and the regulations indicated that all workers shall have a day off on Sunday and the duration of the working day on Saturdays shall be less by 2 hours from the normal working days. Article 10 of the regulations said, "Following shall be the days when it would not be mandatory for people to work: 1. New Year – First of January; 2. Foundation Day of the People's Party; 3. One day holiday on the Day of the Establishment of the People's Government and the People's State; 4. 5 day public holiday for the Military *Naadam* Festival; 5. World Revolution Day, including, a. One Day in observation of the Paris Commune of 18 March, b. 1 May, and c. 7 October (Day of People's Revolution of Russia)."

If we compare the first Labour Code of Mongolia or the "Regulations on Assessing One's Labour" (meaning an Employee) with the modern regulatory mechanisms, such labour related issues as labour discipline, labour safety, resolution of labour disputes, abrogation of labour contract, the justification and rules for ending a labour contract, pensions and benefits for the disabled, social insurance, the term of service etc. had not been included in it. But scholar L. Baasan, who specializes in the study of the evolution of labour codes and regulations, argues that the first Labour Code (Regulations) introduced new norms, standards and regulatory mechanisms that did not exist in the country before, and concludes that they set the tone and became the foundational stones for the upcoming laws regulating labour relations in Mongolia.[19]

The Labour Codes were changed and amended three times during this period in 1930, 1933 and 1934. The sphere of the legal coverage of these laws was almost the same, for they were all, without exception, designed to regulate labour relations of people working at government-run industrial and business enterprises, as well as in the private sector. The 1930 Code had 11 chapters with 96 articles, the 1993 Code had 9 chapters with 44 provisions, and the 1939 Labour Law had 10 chapters and 70 paragraphs. All these laws introduced new rules and procedures designed at regulating contractual agreements between the worker and the administration (that is, the employer), which meant that these legislations amounted to legal guarantees of the citizens to free labour. The 1930 Code, for example, defined a labour contract as an employee contract, while a collective contract was defined as a "social contract."

Concerning labour discipline, these laws, in effect, regulated such matters as the duties and responsibilities of a worker and the administration, working time regime, material and monetary liabilities etc., they did not define any kind of disciplinary action. According to Article 77 of the 1933 Code, and Article 64 of the 1934 Law, labour disputes were reviewed and tried by the courts. The issue of labour safety had been defined in separate paragraphs in the 1930 Law as "protecting the life of the assessor of one's labour (an employee) while on work" and the 1933 and 1934 Labour Code contained separate provisions which obliquely meant labour safety.

These laws outlined the kind of actions Trade Unions could and should take to uphold the labour rights of manual workers and office workers. One of the key directions of activities of the Trade Unions, during this period, was the responsibility to organise specific activities designed at improving labour discipline, which was essentially incompatible with the key objectives of the Trade Unions, and consequently, they could simply turn into passive followers of what the administration said and decided. These laws also, in one way or the other, attempted to introduce elements

19 L. Baasan, Labour Law, (General Clauses), Ulaanbaatar, 1996, p. 163.

of worker's social insurance. The 1930 Law touches on the mechanisms to regulate such issues as rendering support and assistance to an employee who had lost the capacity to work due to ill health or physical disability, and similar rights issues of office and manual workers were touched on in the 1933 and 1934 Labour Codes.

According to the 1930 Labour Code, a system was introduced under which social insurance and benefits were given to families, whose member(s) had A. temporarily lost the capacity to work; B. who were pregnant; C. who had given birth; D. who had become physically handicapped, and E. who had passed way. And all the Labour Codes that were adopted since 1933 contained provisions according to which the employers had to pay social insurance premiums; for instance, according to the 1934 Law, an employer had to pay 2 per cent of the salary in premium for an employer who was temporarily unfit to work, and 1 per cent premium for an employee who had become physically handicapped.

3.5 *Ecology Law*

The First State Congress (*Ikh Khural*) paid attention to the protection and rational utilisation of the country's forest, fauna and fish resources, and passed a resolution which "banned unauthorised cutting of trees within the territory of the country, and especially within the bounds of the capital Niislel Khüree, and in the Yüroo and Onon river lake areas, developing rules and instructions for the public on how to protect and use forest resources, and setting up forest management units at appropriate locations and in the number that ws suitable.

Many laws and legislations were passed designed at protecting ecologically important sites. For example, the Government at its meeting held on 25 December 1925, adopted Resolution 25, according to which it approved the "Fishing Regulations" and the "Cedar Nut Harvesting Regulations," and "Provisional Hunting Rules and Regulations" were adopted in keeping with Government Resolution 41 of 29 October 1926. While the Presidium of the State *Baga Khural* passed Resolution 11 on 27 March 1931, according to which the "Forestry Law" was adopted, the "Law on Hunting and Finish within the Territory of the MPR" was passed under its Resolution 15 of 27 March 1931, and through its Resolution 20, which was passed on 3 March 1933, the State *Baga Khural* adopted the revised version of the "Forestry Law." Government rules and regulations on the utilisation of land and pasture lands (under a 1926 Resolution), provisional regulations on use of pasture lands within the territory of Mongolia (1928) and the regulations on use of grazing lands and water (1935) were enacted.

The Government, through its Resolution 19 of 1929, put a 5-year ban on the hunting of sables in Khentii, Onon and Kherlen Rivers, and a 2-year ban on hunting stags.

Ecological law expert, Mongolian scholar O. Amarkhüu, has pointed out that in keeping with the aforementioned laws and resolutions, many new and important standards were introduced designed at promoting the rational utilisation and protection of the land, fauna and forest resources of the country.[20] Let us, as an example, review the two forest laws that were enacted in 1931 and 1993, respectively.

The 1931 Forestry Law defined that the entire forest resources on the territory of the country and the integrated forest fund were state property, and divided the forests into national and local and accordingly, separate forest exploitation regulations were put in place. The Law, for the first time, established exclusion and protection forest zones in order to improve the protection of forests. Exclusion zones included, i. Parts (forest territory) of forest under special protection; ii. Forests to protect water; and, iii. Forests to preserve natural beauty and those that are helpful in protecting the health of the people, which cannot be exploited. It was also prohibited to cut down trees for poles as well as young trees, and for every cut tree, it was mandatory to plant a new sapling. The 1933 Law classified the forests into state and local, and accordingly both state and local forests were placed under the control of relevant forestry units, and rules were introduced according to which trees could be felled only between 1 October and 1 April through special permission, and the areas from where trees had been cut had to be cleaned up and handed over to the relevant forestry unit.

The 1936 regulations on utilisation and protection of water and spring water were the key legal acts that were adopted then in the sphere of usage and protection of water. The regulations made it mandatory to enact special rules for the utilization and protection of water, ensure cleanliness and repair water springs and wells in both the urban and rural areas, and violators of the rules were handed fines and other penalties. The Ministry of Health had been given the responsibility for the utilisation and protection of mineral water used for medical treatment, while the Animal Husbandry and Agriculture Minister was made responsible for maintaining national-level water registration, and the *aimag* and city executive administrations were responsible for the local level water re-

---

20 O. Amarkhüu, *Some State and Legal Theoretical Issues Related to the Protection of the Surrounding Environment*, Ulaanbaatar, 1979, p. 61.

sources, which were important actions to protect water resources at the national and local levels.

A number of laws and legislation were adopted with regard to the protection and utilisation of land. In this connection, let us look at the "Provisional rules on utilising grazing lands within the territory of Mongolia." Procedures were introduced, according to which local administrations allotted plots of lands to the people relevant to the number of their livestock animals. There were also procedures for the utilisation of water and pastures within the allotted plot of land. Furthermore, they outlined guidelines discouraging the use of water and pasture lands by trespassers, destroying water sources and grazing fields belonging to poorer households with few heads of livestock animals, and who did not have the resources to move far and wide by letting animals, belonging to others, into their pasture fields for grazing and watering, and during a natural calamity, with the permission of the local authorities, the farmers could water and feed their animals in reserve areas.

Besides regulatory rules applicable to animal grazing lands, new rules were introduced for the utilisation of land for agricultural purposes (193) and for mowing hay and cultivating grain and vegetables (1933). Mongolian citizens and organisations, according to these rules, were entitled to free use of land for growing crops, vegetables and making hay, and for an indefinite period of time, while the rules made it mandatory for foreigners to pay rent for these purposes. Rules and procedures were further clarified with regard to resolution of land-related disputes, according to which the government had the right to expropriate land. It was prohibited to lease the allotted land through a third party, and separate chapters were also introduced concerning the protection of crop and vegetable fields.

Many important legal acts were enacted during this period designed at protection of the country's fauna resources, and among them the Law on Hunting and Forestry Within the Territory of the MPR holds a central place in terms of its significance. Concrete time frames were introduced for hunting, prohibitions were applied to hunting of some kinds of wild rare animals, use of hunting methods which endangered wild animals, and monitoring and punishment mechanisms were put in place especially for those who breached the law. A total ban was imposed on the hunting of sables, Khavtgai or wild camels, wild ass, Przhewalski horses, saiga, roe deer, martens, sables, swans, she elks, does and their young ones. Cocking a gun, laying trip-bows, digging holes, destroying bird's nests, using explosives and poison for fishing were also outlawed.

3.6 *Co-operative Law*

The foundations of the Co-operative Law were laid during this period as well. Agricultural, industrial, trade and services co-operatives were set up in the country. In order to review the evolution of laws related to co-operatives, it is important to study the legal basis of the different co-operatives individually.

When the country had elementary communes based on mutual assistance among the people (from late 1920s to early 1930s) and during the period when people's co-operatives were established (from the early 1930s to the middle of the 1950s), important legal acts were adopted, which strengthened the activities and organisational set-up of these co-operatives that helped regulate the evolving social relations.

A legal act, which augmented the operational and organisational foundations of co-operatives, was the Rules on Improving People's Enterprises, adopted in October 1929. Its primary objective lay in facilitating joint and collective effort as communes and co-operatives alone could not single-handedly manage the tasks, and also helping people understand the importance of joint effort and mutual assistance, and finally its objective lay in improving the lot of the people, as a whole.

Simple forms of communes were in a way co-operatives where people came together with their individual labour voluntarily without socialising their livestock animals and property. Soon after, the Government made a serious "Leftist" blunder by bringing the majority of people into co-operative farms, and realising its mistake, the Government started conducting a policy of mending the mistakes by further developing co-operatives in the form of elementary forms of collective farms. This is evident from a Regulation on People's Production Associations approved by the Council of Ministers of the MRP, according to which such associations were planned to be set up for the purpose of mowing hay for animal fodder, grazing livestock animals, engaging in joint caravans, building animal sheds and barns, hunting, fishing and growing crops. Working norms and standards, distribution of income, forming labour teams etc. were regulated by a new set of rules for compliance by people's production associations, which were adopted by the Council of Ministers in 1939. Soon after in 1942, model rules of people's agricultural production associations were introduced, which contained specific provisions about capital assets and production implements of the associations. Scholars are of the opinion that labour distribution, remuneration mechanism, and sharing of incomes and profits of these production associations of the people were quasi-socialist in nature.[21]

One of the most important sectors of co-operatives was the trade co-operative. The first joint stock consumer co-operative was established in December 1921, which signaled the beginning of a co-operative economy of the country. A key objective of this co-ooperative was to promote barter trade by procuring animal-origin raw materials from the people and in exchange supplying them with consumer goods at the government rate.

Resolutions of both the State *Ikh* and *Baga Khurals* were instrumental in laying the legal operational and organisational foundations of consumer co-operatives.

Another form of co-operative law is the industrial co-operative law. This form of co-operative helped in the development of cottage industries and the the construction sector, and their legal backings were provided by resolutions of the State *Ikh* and *Baga Khurals,* and the rules of *artels* or crafts co-operatives. They included the "Rules of Construction Co-operatives," "Rules of Cottage Industry Associations and Unions," "Rules for Co-operatives of Lamas," as well as Government resolutions, such as the Resolution on "The Establishment of Cottage Industry," "Regarding Cottage Industry Co-operatives," "Work Given to Craftsmen by Cottage Industry Unions," etc.

Artels (in Russian) or crafts co-operatives were the basic form of industrial co-operatives in the country then. According to their rules, the *artels* would have members, and an individual who had reached the age of 16 could join the *artel* after paying the relevant admission fee. The meeting of the members was the highest authority of an *artel,* and in between its meetings, the General *Artel,* elected from among the *artel* members, would manage its operations.

3.7 *Criminal Law*

The criminal law of this period was called the "Court Law Document" and it was changed and amended three times in 1926, 1929 and 1934, respectively. Criminal justice scholars G. Sovd, B, Sodovsüren, J. Avkhia and R. Günsen have specifically noted that the 1926 "Court Law Document" was the first independent criminal law. Special chapters of the law were approved by the Third State Congress (*Khural*) held on 11 January 1926, and its General Clauses were adopted and enforced on 15 January 1926 at the First Meeting of the Government.

21 T. Sengedorj, O. Amarkhüü, D. Lündeejantsan, *Agricultural Cooperative Law of the MPR*, Ulaanbaatar, 1987, p. 7.

The Law's general clauses consisted of 7 Chapters and more than 40 Provisions. Chapter One dealt with the limitations and restrictions regarding regulation and enforcement of the Court Law Document; Chapter Two specifies the means and methods of improving on sentences passed and rehabilitation, and protecting the people against committing serious crimes; Chapter Three focused on discussion of a sentence; Chapter Four was about punishing those who have attempted to commit a crime; Chapter Five dealt with mitigation of and relieving from punishment; Chapter Six dealt with aggravating punishment, and Chapter Seven dealt with remission and releasing of the prisoner before the end of the sentence period, and granting of clemency.

The Chapters of the Court Law Document had 24 Parts and 187 Clauses, which are in fact Chapters 7 to 31 of the Court Law Document. They cover a whole set of crimes such as, political dissent, sabotaging the country's ties and friendship with foreign nations, opposing the state administrations, contempt of court, violation of laws and legislation on people's health, protection of wealth and property of the people. They also define crimes related to roads and communication, non-fulfillment of the civic duty to protect border marks and posts, carrying out splinter propaganda, and engaging in counterfeiting and making of fake security papers, interfering with weighing scales. They cover crimes committed by government officials, corruption and bribery, embezzlement of government property, destroying of people's assets and wealth, causing physical harm to a person's life and health, physical assault, refraining from rendering help to old people and children in harm's way, insulting others, involvement in illegal sexual behaviour, destroying other's property by stealing, robbing and snatching, misuse of religion for political ends, and violation of the law on the separation of the State and religion etc.[22]

The minimum age for a person who can be convicted for any crime was set at 11 years. Under this criminal law, a person guilty of a crime would alone be judged and convicted. Article 37 states "Sentence shall be handed to the perpetrator alone, and shall not be extended to others." One of the specific features of the Court Law Document is that the crime against the State was included in several chapters, which goes to show the class-based nature of the legislation.

The Government, without making changes to the structure and composition of the 1926 Court Law Document but only clarifying its norms and standards, adopted a new court law at its Thirtieth meeting and the Four-

22 B. Sodovsüren, *Evolution of Criminal Laws and Legislations of the MPR*, Ulaanbaatar, 1973, pp. 43–44.

teenth State Congress held in 1929. The main changes in the new legislation, as compared to the 1926 Court Law Document, were that Chapters 5 and 6 of the General Clauses on deferral and remission of punishment were merged into one new chapter on ways and means of educating the offenders.

The new law set the minimum age for criminal justice at 14 years, and persons who had not reached the age of 18 or lactating mothers, who were convicted of guilty of a crime, were not awarded the death sentence. In the 1929 legislation, a time limit was set for fully or partially curtailing rights of a convict, which was changed to curtailment of right with a time limit. For example, the right to elect and be elected; b. the right to manage an election; c. the right to manage the people's representative of a people's court and the right to transfer to another court were curtailed for 1 to 1.5 years.

As noted by B. Sodovsüren, there arose the need to amend the Court Law Documents several times in view of the new changes in the country's economic situation. For example, the Government bureau responsible for machine-operated transportation issued a Resolution on 7 April 1932 on registration of the country's machine-operated transport operators, the training of concerned human resources and the liabilities of such operators, which introduced a set of new standards. For example, a driver who was guilty of drunk driving was liable for criminal punishment; drivers were liable to criminal justice for breaking traffic rules and thus causing damage to the vehicle and additionally were responsible for compensating for the damage caused to the vehicle company, and the Law Ministry instructed the submission of the amendments for consideration to the Government.

Relying on the experience of the implementation of the 1926 and 1929 court laws and legislation, the new 1934 Court Law was approved at the Thirteenth Meeting of the Council of Ministers in 1943 and the Seventeenth session of the Presidium of the State *Baga Khural*. L. Dendev, commenting on the rationale behind the 1929 Law amendment made in 1935, noted that "In 1934 the law was renewed and the necessary amendments were made in view of the many factual errors in the law. For example, different kinds of crimes were mixed up with relevant causes in different chapters of the law, crimes related to anti-revolutionary activities were covered in several chapters, and punishments for abuse of power, and in particular, sex-related crimes were lenient and slack." [23]

---

23 L. Dendev, Early and modern Mongolian legal history, (translated from Mongolian script by B. Bayarsaikhan), Ulaanbaatar, 2002, p. 91.

The new “Court Law Document” included 6 chapters and 41 articles. A breakdown of the chapters: Chapter One. Objectives and purpose of the law; Chapter Two. Limits and restrictions on enforcement of the law; Chapter Three. General provisions of the court policies; Chapter Four. Penalties; Chapter Five. Procedures on carrying out punishment; and, Chapter Six. On suspended and conditional sentences.

The special chapters of the law, structurally, included a total of 8 parts. Part One. Crime against the revolution; Part Two. *Lese majeste* challenging administrative rules and other related crimes; Part Three. Official crime; Part Four. Economic crime; Part Five. Crime related to violation of the law, rules and procedures on the separation of the state and church; Part Six. Crimes against human life, health, liberty and reputation; Part Seven. Property crime; and, Part Eight. Violation of law and rules on guaranteeing people’s health, public peace and public order and discipline.[24]

Soon after the adoption of this Law, during the dark years of personality cult and mass political persecutions in the country, the Law was changed and amended several times, which created the legal basis for the violation of human rights and persecution by trumped-up charges. For example, military crimes and some crimes related to the breach of administrative rules and regulations were classified as crimes against the revolution and those found guilty were severely punished.

3.8 *Law on Criminal Procedure*

Legal acts defining new rules and principles of procedures, in keeping with the letter and spirit of the First Constitution, were adopted and enforced in the country. The Presidium of the State *Baga Khural* at its First Session, held on 15 June 1926, approved the model guidelines for court sessions trying suspects guilty of involvement in political activities. According to G. Sovd,[25] these guidelines became the corner stone of the first criminal procedure legislation of the country, which outlined the rules for criminal proceedings, the rights and liabilities of the participants in the proceedings, the level and limits of issues on the agenda of the court. The guidelines divided into four stages the process of criminal proceedings. Stage one covered the issue of preparation for the court hearing, stage two related to investigation and debate, and the final stage concerned the court judgment.

---

24 B. Sodovsüren, *Evolution of Criminal Laws and Legislations of the MPR*, Ulaanbaatar, 1973, p. 51.

25 *Courts of the MPR – On Guard of Protecting Socialist Gains*, Ulaanbaatar, 1977, p.165.

An integrated law with 9 chapters and 3 articles, establishing the legal procedural norms and standards was adopted in 1926 by a Government Resolution 26.6 on court proceedings in Mongolia. Chapter One of the law called "Court proceedings" defined the types and structures of the courts and regulated their inter-relationship.

The Chapter called "Guidelines for primary inquiry" defined the rights and authority of the primary investigation agencies, the basis for instituting proceedings, types and classification of evidence materials, forms of preliminary inquiry, rights and responsibilities of the investigator or examining magistrate and the defendant.

Chapter Three "Guidelines of civil processes," defines the norms and rules for regulating civil processes; Chapter Four outlines the procedures for summoning the parties concerned to the court and the investigation agency, and Chapter Five, called "Preparations preceding all court proceedings", defined the basic preparations that must be completed before the court is called to session. Chapter Six called "Court session" dealt with such basic matters as procedures and principles of a court session, agenda of the trial, the rights and responsibilities of the parties, procedures for assigning of punishment and court ruling. While Chapters Seven and Eight concern the procedures for appealing against the ruling of the primary court, the appellate court term, and defined the rights and responsibilities of the court of second level to review the case and take judgment. The final chapter outlined the rules and procedures for implementing the court ruling.

A special thing about this Law was that both criminal and civilian proceedings were regulated by this Law, and its importance lies in the fact that this was the first law that clearly defined the democratic principles of conducting investigation, inquiry and court sessions.

During the years when the First Constitution was in force, substantial changes and amendments were added to the criminal procedural legal sources. In 1935, the Thirtieth session of the State *Baga Khural*, passed Resolution No. 30, and according to paragraph 5 of the Resolution, the law on criminal procedure was amended into a new legislation called the "Law of the MPR on investigating and passing sentences on all criminal cases." Some of the procedures that were included in the previous law were overhauled and made more specific, and new court proceeding rules were introduced. Chapter One of the new law named the competent authorities to conduct inquiry, dedicated departments under these authorities, monitoring of investigation and inquiry by the procurator's office, inquiry schedule, time and protocol, the rights of the defendant, rules and procedures for interrogating under-age individuals, and the justifications for refusal from filing a criminal case.

The law defined the following six competent authorities, which had the power to conduct an inquiry: 1. Procurator's Office; 2. International Security Department; 3. Military Procurator's Office, 4. Secretariat of the *soums* and *khoroos*, 5. the police, and 6. the courts. *Soum* and *khoroo* administrative offices, the police had to complete their investigation and inquiry within a fortnight, while other agencies had to complete their investigation within two months, while the Procurator's Office was given the authority to extend the inquiry period. The concluding Chapter 14 regulated the issue of restoration of the case owing to new evidence and circumstances surrounding the case.

A Resolution of the Twenty-Second State Conference (1939) discontinued the practice of investigation and court proceedings by the administrative offices of *soums* and *khoroos*, and this jurisdiction was transferred to the relevant courts.

During the period when the First Constitution was in force, although the criminal procedure legal mechanisms became more refined and definite, and although the basic principles of legal proceedings, such as rule-of-law, democracy, humaneness, non-violability of human rights and the principles of equality had been consolidated, regrettably, they only remained empty slogans, especially at a time when a single-party dominated and a totalitarian regime got a tight grip on the country. To illustrate, during the mass persecutions that began in 1937, the so-called non-court, powerful Special Commissions were instituted, which in utter disregard for laws and legislation, flagrantly violated the established judiciary processes and arbitrarily decided the fate of tens of thousands of innocent people.

3.9 *Criminal Penal Law*

The Law of the Mongolian People's Republic on Correctional Activities Conducted by the State for All Convicts, which was adopted in 1931, was the first comprehensive penal act, which was a constituent of the legislation on the enforcement of court decisions. The Law had 15 chapters with 126 articles. The purpose of the Law was defined as "to set up detention or correctional centres within the bounds of the territory of the country to detain criminals, execute forced labour in lieu of serving a jail term, and correctional methods as applied to a convicted criminal."

Convicted criminals at correctional centres were made to work and at the same time, they were given educational classes, and it was forbidden to torture or harass them, whip them, shackle their legs and hands in iron chains, confine them in a dark room, and to give them less food than normal, and correctional officers were not permitted to make prisoners work for them privately, and these standards were important in organising the labour of the prisoners.

The Law clearly defines that not less than 25 per cent of the earnings from such labour would be paid to the prisoner, and 25 per cent will go to the state coffers.

Convicted criminals were not only made to serve their sentence, but they were also educated and trained, so that they would be able to adjust to a new life in the society after they were released when they had completed their term of sentence, which was one of the important regulatory provisions in the law. When a convict was released after he/she had completed his/her prison term, the correctional centre would have already opened a bank account in their name, their registered personal items and documents would be returned to them, and it was the legal duty of the relevant *aimags* to assist the released prisoner in finding a suitable job, which according to the law, was overseen by the general manager of the department of correctional centres and special commandants at the Law Ministry.

There were quite a few class-based discriminatory provisions in the Law. For example, provision of cash and material assistance to both the detainee and the released was class-based, and similarly, helping the released in employment was class-inclined.

One important aspect of this law was the use of firearms against convicted criminals. In an emergency situation, prison officers were permitted to resort to the use of firearms if they were attacked by the prisoners, if a convict had repeated a serious crime while behind bars, and if a prisoner had attempted an escape. Guidelines for the use of firearms were issued, according to which, a. the prison officer had to first seek permission to use weapon from the relevant higher authority, and if this was not possible, the prison officer had the right to first use weapons and then report the incident to the higher authority, b. make a written recording of the use of firearms and submit it to the procurator without delay, and c. before use of weapons, warning must be given three times before the weapons are used.

Control and Supervisory Commissions were set up at each penitentiary under the law, which also defined their duties and responsibilities. The Commissions were responsible for receiving applications and grievances of the prisoners, conducting activities at their own initiative, monitoring incorrect sentencing, violation of prison conditions, depositing the earnings made by prisoners by working at the gaol in a wrong bank account, careless handling of the prisoner's suggestions and requests, brutal behaviour towards the prisoners, giving orders to rectify mistakes made, and even relieving prisons before the term of their sentence, and all decisions taken were done collectively by the officials of the correctional centres.

Scholars A. Lhagva and S. Jantsan have established that the importance of the Law lay in the fact that it was the first law that regulated the criminal penal system of the country, on the one hand, and on the other, many provisions in the Law on the matter have been continued not only as a tradition, but are being even applied in practice.[26]

26 A. Lhagva, S. Jantsan, *Criminal Penal Law of Mongolia*, Ulaanbaatar, 1969, p. 24.

9 The State and Laws during the Period of the Second Constitution (1940–1960)

1 Historical Summary

Mongolian society, after going through the hell of mass political persecutions and having withstood the challenges posed by the Khalkha Gol Battle, welcomed the year of 1940. Given the gravity of the situation, Kh. Choibalsan realised full well the importance of preparing in a proper manner the Tenth MPRP Congress and the Eighth State Congress so that they could come up with decisions that would bolster the courage and excite the expectations of the people, and in order to accomplish his objective he went to Moscow in November 1939. His Moscow trip lived up to his expectations as the Soviet side assisted in the drafting of the Party and State congress documents, and committed to lay a railway line from the Soviet border of Naushki up to Ulaanbaatar, and to build a meat processing plant, an auto-mechanical plant and a cement plant in Mongolia. This commitment did not come without strings attached, however. In return, the Soviet side ordered that Mongolia supply 40 thousand tons of wool and cashmere by 1940.

The MPRP held its Congress at the end of March and early April 1940, adopted the Party Action Programme, which set the party's goal to complete the preparation for the country's transition to a Socialist society. The Eighth State Congress was held the same year in June, which adopted the new Constitution of the Mongolian People's Republic. Just as the party and the country were gearing up to implement these decisions, the Great Patriotic War began in the Soviet Union. The State and government spearheaded a nation-wide campaign to manage the country's economy and culture in conditions of war, and to render assistance to the Soviet people. The Yalta Conference of the leaders of the Soviet Union, United States and Great Britain, held in February 1945, agreed to maintain the *status quo* of Mongolia at proposed by the Soviet Union, which was a watershed event in the country's history as this marked the international recognition of Mongolia's independence and sovereignty. Towards the end of the Second World War, the MPR mobilising all its potential and resources, took part in the routing of Japanese militarism.

The first national referendum of the independent and sovereign Mongolian People's Republic was held on 20 October 1945.

After World War II, the country turned its attention towards its peaceful development. The Twelfth Congress of the MPRP, held in 1954, promoted the concept of "full-scale development of socialism," and the entire spectrum of political, social and economic policies and activities of the party and the State were devoted to this huge goal.

The MPRP during this period had succeeded in consolidating itself, through the Constitution, as the leading political force, and accordingly took actions to establish a universal, direct, equal electoral system with secret ballot casting. On the other hand, the cult of personality around Kh. Choibalsan continued to grip the country until the beginning of 1950, and all-important party and state documents were named after him, such as, the "The Constitution of Marshal Choibalsan," "The Five-Year Development Plan of Marshal Choibalsan" and so on and so forth, while the authoritarian regime and the rule of commandism took firmer hold in the country.

The legislature, the executive and the judiciary of the country were ruled and led successively by Kh. Choibalsan, G. Bumtsend, J. Sambuu, Yü. Tsedenbal and D. Damba according to the natural law as well as the law of political competition and rivalry, and in principle, a state-party political system was created in the country.

After the death of I. V. Stalin and Kh. Choibalsan, some changes occurred in the social and political life of Mongolia, which gave hopes for the revival of democratic sentiments, but they were doomed not to be realised.

Economically¸ the private sector was squeezed out by the state co-operative sector, which gradually became stronger day-by-day. Private rural businesses were joined into co-operatives in late 1959, which both had a positive and a negative fall-out. Virgin lands were developed, and crop farming became an independent agricultural branch, which was undoubtedly a very important accomplishment for the country. Light food and mining industries were newly built and some of the existing industrial plants were modernised.

In terms of the country's *cultural and spiritual life*, a brand new people's education system was put in place, one of the primary objectives of which was to combat illiteracy among the population. Regrettably, national culture and traditions were suppressed and criticism by the intelligentsia and their ideas were branded as a delusion and motivated by nationalism, which were branded as going against Marxism-Leninism and even Stalinism.

In its *foreign relations,* the Mongolian People's Republic received recognition by countries of the global Socialist system and some Asian and African countries that had gained their freedom and independence, and this was a period when Mongolia gradually broke its isolation and seclusion from international relations.

These were years when the entire Mongolian people toiled earnestly and very hard for the implementation of the First and Second Five-Year and Three-Year's national economic and cultural development of the country.

The Constitution of 1940 was put up for nation-wide discussion. The draft of the new Second Constitution of the country was based on such legal acts as the Rules of the Council of Ministers, the Rules of the Local Administrations, Rules and Regulations of the Courts and the Procurator's Office, as well as the Labour Code. In the course of the discussion, some changes were made to the draft of the fundamental law and soon after, the Eighth Congress of the State was convened, which adopted the Second Constitution of the Mongolian People's Republic of 30 June 1940. The new Constitution was made up of 12 chapters and 95 articles.

- Chapter One. Social System
- Chapter Two. State System
- Chapter Three. State *Ikh Khural*
- Chapter Four. State *Baga Khural* and its Presidium
- Chapter Five. Council of Ministers
- Chapter Six. Rural Administrative Organs and Their Governance
- Chapter Seven. The Courts and the Procurator's Office, and their organs
- Chapter Eight. Revenue and Spending of the MPR
- Chapter Nine. Electoral System of the MPR
- Chapter Ten. Basic Rights and Responsibilities of the People
- Chapter Eleven. State Emblem, Flag and the Capital City
- Chapter Twelve. Rules and Procedures for Amending the Constitution

The Second 1940 Constitution of the country has been regarded as a law that consolidated the gains of the struggle of the Mongolian people to make a gradual transition from democratic revolution to socialist revolution, having accomplished the goals and objectives of the primary stage of the people's revolution. In this sense, the 1940 Constitution was made in the model of a socialist legislation, which was deeply permeated with class-based ideology. The Constitution legalised and reinforced the form of state structure of the MPR, its goal, objectives and functions.

In Chapter One, the objective of the State was defined as "ensuring the development of the country along the non-capitalist road of development since the country would be building a socialist system."[1] Article Four also defined and legalised the objectives of the State of the MPR. "The reformation of the economy, culture, education and the overall status of the MPR shall be guaranteed through the implementation of the relevant plans and programmes by way of government support and assistance for the development of the people's economy, assisting the voluntary rural co-operatives of the working people by establishing hay-mowing machinery and horse units, and the government's goals shall be met through the further development of animal husbandry, industry, communication and transport." This can very well be qualified as the establishment of the basic foundations for the development of a centrally planned economy.

An analysis of the content of the Constitution leads us to the following conclusions regarding the form of state structure of the country during this period.

1 In terms of the form of government, Mongolia was a Parliamentary Republic.
2 In terms of state structure, Mongolia was a country with an integrated centralized government.
3 In terms of political system, it was not a democratic but a totalitarian regime.

Although the 1940 Second Constitution, in its form and style, was *a la* socialist, this was more declarative in nature; in form, and as implemented in practice, it was democratic in nature. For instances, Articles 2 and 3 state that "The basis of the state of the MPR is the Great People's Khural, and the power and authority of the Government shall be vested in the hands of the urban and rural working people through the Great People's *Khural*." Judging by this, although the principle of representative democracy had been proclaimed in the Constitution, this principle was based on class-policy, and in this sense, the Constitution had rejected democratic values in essence.

Although the Constitution promulgated the democratic development of the State and government, actions were taken to bring the *khurals* closer to the people by reducing the number of people's representatives in the relevant people's *khurals* of all levels. In 1934, one representative was elected to the State *Ikh Khural* from every 5,000 people, but according to the new Constitution, this number was reduced to 1 elected representative from every 1,500 people. The terms of reference of all People's *Khurals* of all

1 *Constitution of Mongolia*, (Compiled and commentary by J. Amarsanaa and O. Batsaikhan), Ulaanbaatar, 2004, p. 141.

levels were legalised individually, their power was expanded and their duties and responsibilities were defined.

The state structure of the country, as established by the First Constitution, was consolidated in Articles 2 and 7 of the new 1940 Constitution with some changes and amendments. As indicated in the Constitution, the highest local administrative power was the working people's *Khurals* of the *aimags*, towns, *baghs, soums and khoroos*, and in the *aimags* and the capital city of Ulaanbaatar, their *Baga Khurals* executed the role of the relevant administrative power in between the sessions of the working people's *Khurals* of the *aimags* and Ulaanbaatar. The presidiums of the *Baga Khurals*, elected by the relevant *Baga Khurals* were responsible for managing the day-to-day activities of the highest administrative organs. As the *Khurals* of *soums, baghs, khoroos* and *khorids* did not have their *Baga Khurals*, executive administrations were set up to run the government in the local areas.

The Constitution had separate chapters on the judiciary, the courts and the Procurator's Office, and the development of their concepts were guided by the 1926 rules on the court proceeding establishments and the 1934 rules of procedures of the Courts and the Procurator's Office respectively. Articles 5 and 7 and Article 6 of the Constitution have provisions that protect the two kinds of ownership, that is, public and co-operative property, as well as the eight of working people to private ownership. This is why the period spanning 1940 to 1960 is also defined as a period when three kinds of ownership prevailed in the country. However, the right to private ownership was restricted to a few types of properties, which was the beginning of centralized planned economy of the country with state property dominating the economy.

Human rights issues were taken up quite broadly in the 1940 Constitution, which was no doubt a progressive move. The rights were not only legalized but their guarantee mechanisms were also defined in detail. The extensive human rights issues, such as the right of citizens to rest, education, and equality, manual labourers' right to seek government material support, the right to belief, the right to form unions and associations, submit complaints to state organisations and government officials, the right to free movement, the right to choose the place of domicile, the right to free speech, press, the right to meetings and oral speech, the right to demonstrations in the streets, the right to inviolability of a person's life, the right to privacy at homes and posts and communication, and the right to migration were all covered.

An important aspect of the new 1940 Constitution was that economic and legal terms and terminology were almost identical or similar to international practice, which was not the case in the First Constitution. However, most of these rights in the new Constitution were of a declarative nature.

The 1940 Constitution promulgated almost all the basic rights and freedoms of the citizens, but at the same, time, it legalised their duties and responsibilities, including the duty to strictly comply with all the state laws, maintain state and labour disciplines, wholeheartedly devote one-self to social causes, protect the country, work for the benefit of the country and society, and serve in the army. From among these mandatory rights, the right to labour and service in the army was considered a noble duty of the citizens of Mongolia.

The MPRP was defined in Article 82 of the Constitution as the "central leading force of the country and all social organisations," which in principle legalised the country's political system with the party in the centre as the sole vanguard of the country.

The chapter on the electoral system indicates that all citizens of the MPR, who have reached the age of 18, irrespective of their age, gender, religion and belief, skills and competencies, property, whether they are nomads or lead a settled way of life, have the right to elect and be elected. However, electoral rights were restricted for money lenders, previous *khutugtus* and reincarnates, other feudal lords and *Taijis* who had serfs and subjects, influential male and female shamans, soldiers of the Russian White Guards, people who had been involved in anti-revolutionary activities, people with mental disabilities, and people whose electoral rights have been curtailed by courts. In this manner, some segments of the population were deprived of their political rights and freedom.

The state symbol, emblem, and the national flag of the MPR were renewed and changed. Although revolutionary ideas inspired their design, the traditions and long-established way of life of the Mongols were fully included in them, making the state symbolics much more meaningful, which was appreciated by the masses. However, during the period of the Second Constitution, the state symbols were altered and modified a number of times.

The national flag, as defined in the Constitution, was rectangular in shape. According to the Constitution, the ratio of the length to the height (width) of the flag was 1:2, made of red fabric, the state emblem was to be in the centre of the flag flanked on two sides with the words "Mongolian People's Republic." In 1945, the name of the national flag was changed to "Red Flag." It is a vertical triband with two red stripes (2/3 of the flag size) at each side and a blue stripe (1/3 thee size of flag) in the middle, with a five-pointed star in yellow on the top part of the red stripe close to the flag pole and underneath the star would be the Soyombo emblem in yellow but without the lotus flower. The letters "Mongolian People's Republic" inscribed under the Soyombo emblem was in the classical Mongol script, which was replaced in 1955 with the Cyrillic script. Similarly, beginning from 1 January 1946, all publications and official dealings were conducted using the new Cyrillic script in conjunction with the joint resolution of the Council of Ministers and the Central Committee of the MPRP, passed in 1945, as well as the resolutions adopted by the Tenth Congress of the MPRP and the Eighth State Congress.

The new National Anthem of the MPR was approved in 1945 with lyrics by Ts. Damdinsüren, and music by B. Damdinsüren and L. Mördorj.

As a Constitution is the foundational basis of all laws and legislations, they were changed and amended reflecting the opinions of professional institutions and the general public. The changes and amendments that were made to the latest Constitution were done with not less than two thirds of the vote of approval by the State *Ikh Khural* members.

The new Constitution, during a span of 20 years from 30 June 1940 to 6 July 1960, had been changed and amended basing on the resolutions of the 1949 and 1957 State *Ikh Khurals*. Besides this, in breach of the Constitution, it was also amended through various acts, such as ordinances, and resolutions of the Presidium of the State *Ikh Khural* and also of the Presidium of the State *Baga Khural*, the Council of Ministers of the MPR as well as the Central Committee of the Mongolian People's Revolutionary Party.

2 The State System

2.1 *The Evolution of the State Power Institutions of Mongolia*

Article 13 of the 1940 Constitution of the Mongolian People's Republic provided that the State *Ikh Khural* shall be the highest organ of state power of the Mongolian People's Republic. The State *Ikh Khural* shall be called into session once every three years by the State *Bag Khural* and the emergency session of the State *Ikh Khural* shall be convened at the discretion of the State *Baga Khural* or at the demand of the local administrative organs representing not less than one third of the population. The powers of the State *Ikh Khural* included the approval and amendment of the Constitution, defining and approving the basic principles and measures related to the country's domestic and foreign policies, and electing members of the State *Baga Khural*.

According to Article 17 of the Constitution, the State *Baga Khural* acted as the highest organ of State power in between the sessions of the State *Ikh Khural* and according to Article 22, during the break of the session of the State *Baga Khural*, the state power was managed by the Presidium of the State *Baga Khural*.[2]

The State *Baga Khural* was elected for a period of 3 years composed of one member elected from every 10,000 population and it was mandatory for the *Baga Khural* to meet for its sessions once every year. As defined in the Constitution, the State *Baga Khural* exercised the following power and authority:

- Call the session of the State *Ikh Khural;*
- Form the Council of Ministers, endorse and change the newly established ministries and state budget organs;
- Approve the laws adopted by the Presidium of the State *Baga Khural* during its break;
- Monitor the country's state revenues and spending.

The Presidium of the State *Baga Khural* was composed of a chairperson, elected from among the *Baga Khural* members, deputy chairperson, a secretary and four members, a total of 7 Presidium members. The Presidium members exercised the following rights and authority: call the session of the *Baga Khural*, elect its members, adopt new legislations until their ratification by the *Baga Khural*, provide commentaries to the laws and legislation in force, grant amnesty and pardon, award state orders and medals, appoint and relieve diplomatic representatives etc.

The State *Baga Khural* Presidium reported to the State *Baga Khural* and the *Baga Khural* in turn reported directly to the State *Ikh Khural*.

The Ninth State Congress was convened in 1949 and considered the issue of democratising the election system of the MPR and it decided that the election to the State *Ikh Khural* would be conducted on the basis of direct, equal and secret balloting, and the deputies to the *Ikh Khural* would be elected through constituencies. In view of the changes in the election system, amendments were made to the country's Constitution, the State *Baga Khural* was dissolved, and the Congress declared that the State *Ikh Khural* was the highest organ of state power and the highest legislature of the country. The Congress decision pointed out that the State *Ikh Khural* would carry out its functions through sessions, standing commissions and through its own Presidium.

B. Bayarsaikhan wrote a book called *Constitutional Traditions of Mongolia*[3] in which he made some interesting observations. "The Constitu-

2 *Constitution of Mongolia*, (Compiled and commentary by J. Amarsanaa and O. Batsaikhan), Ulaanbaatar, 2004, pp. 360–362.

3 B. Bayarsaikhan, *Constitutional Traditions of Mongolia*, Ulaanbaatar, 2017, p. 73.

tion was adopted in the MPR in 1949. Even today, we continue to accept that the changes and amendments to the 1940 Constitution made up the 1949 Constitution, which in turn contributed to the legal development and traditions of the Constitution of Mongolia as a whole. Historical sources, archive materials and compilations of documents, reports presented by politicians to sessions of competent organs, as well as research materials have not made any mention about the adoption of the Constitution of Mongolia in 1949, and so this matter has been taken up in this book. While studying historical documents related to the Constitutions of 1924, 1940, 1960 and 1992, I have discovered material evidences that the Constitution was adopted in 1949. The changes and amendments made to the Constitution since 1949 prove that a Constitution was actually adopted in 1940."

The first election to the State *Ikh Khural* was conducted on 10 June 1951 on the basis of the new election system. According to the law on making changes and amendments to the Constitution, which was approved by the State *Ikh Khural* on 3 April 1957, Article 14 of the Constitution was amended as "There shall be one deputy for every 3,500 people, who shall be elected by the people of the MPR to the State *Ikh Khural* from electoral constituency."

On 6 July 1957, the Presidium of the State *Ikh Khural* passed a Resolution according to which Article 15 of the Constitution was amended as "The State *Ikh Khural* shall be elected for a term of 4 years," and accordingly, Article 2 and 10 were also amended as "The State *Ikh Khural* shall elect the mandate commission to review the term of office of the deputies of the MPR, and also elect the Foreign Affairs and the Budget commissions."

These progressive decisions were designed at improving the representation of the people at the State *Ikh Khural* and strengthening parliamentarianism in the country.

2.2 *State Administrative Organs*

The period between 1940 and 1960 witnessed significant progress in the evolution and growth of the state administrative organs of Mongolia. The Second Constitution provided that the "Council of Ministers of the MPR is the highest executive and administrative power of the MPR."[4] The Council of Ministers was formed by the State *Baga Khural* and the Council was composed of the Council Premier, Vice Premiers, heads of planning, statistics and control departments, and Ministers of the MPR. As per the First Constitution, the Council of Ministers together with the Presidium

4 *Constitution of Mongolia*, (Compiled and commentary by J. Amarsanaa and O. Batsaikhan), Ulaanbaatar, 2004, p. 363.

of the State *Baga Khural* used to be the highest state authority of the country during the recess of the State *Baga Khural,* and took part in legislative and policy planning activities, but according to the 1940 Constitution, the Council of Ministers not only became the highest state administrative organ of the country but also reported to the State *Baga Khural* directly.

During this period, the central State administrative system was composed of ministries and special departments. The 1940 Constitution of the MPR determined that the country would have 11 ministries, that is, the ministry of defence, foreign affairs, animal husbandry and agriculture, industry and construction, trade, finance, home affairs, education, health and law, and five special departments directly accountable to the Council of Ministers. They included the department of planning and statistics, control, general department of communications, arts, science and the State Publishing House.

The central State administrative system of the country underwent numerous alterations in the years between 1940 and 1960. A new Ministry of Food and Fodder Industry (Food Ministry) was established in 1941 by the Presidium of the State *Baga Khural.*

One of the major changes in the central State administrative structure was the approval of the Rules of Collegium at the government ministries in 1941. Accordingly, the Council of Ministers passed a Resolution and 7–9 member Collegiums were set up at each of the 11 ministries. These Collegiums were ministry-level consultative centres, which were managed by the Minister. The Collegium regularly met 3–4 times every month to consider the functional operations of the relevant ministry, local agencies of the ministry and industrial plants under the ministry. The Rules of Collegium also determined the *modus operandi* of the Collegiums, and their decision-making process.

A so-called Department of Local Administration Affairs was set up under the Council of Ministers in 1945, which was later reorganised into the Organisational and Instructions Department in 1956.

The Department of Planning and Statistics, and the Department of Control were reorganised and merged into the State Planning Commission in 1945, but in 1947, the control and monitoring functions were separated, on the basis of which, the State Inspection Agency was set up, which was again reorganised and named the State Control Agency in 1952. In 1960, the Statistics Department was separated from the Planning Commission and was made an independent agency, and two more new ministries, the Ministry of Communications (1955) and the Ministry of Culture (1956) were established.

In keeping with the changes and amendments made to the Constitution in April and July 1957, the number of ministries increased, while the names of some of them were changed, and as a result, there were 12 ministries: the Ministry of Agriculture, Industry, Foreign Affairs, Transport and Communication, Military and Social Security, Trade, Finance, Control, Education, Culture, Health and Law. The Government also had a total of 7 agencies, including the Planning Commission, State Bank, Institute of Science and Higher Education, Physical Culture and Sports Committee, Construction Committee, Geological Research Agency, and the Press and Literature Control Agency. Soon after, the Geological Research Agency was dismantled and replaced with the establishment of the Ministry of Geology and Mining Industry, and the Trade Ministry was bifurcated into the Ministry of Foreign Trade and the Ministry of Procurement.

The Culture Ministry was dismantled in 1959 and in its stead the Committee on Art Affairs was instituted, and soon after several new agencies were established, such as the State Standards and Metrology Agency, Information and Radio Agency, and the Publishing Committee. As a result, the number of ministries and agencies increased quite substantially and the government structure became quite cumbersome, and the Bureau of the Council of Ministers was made up of ministers and chairperson of "some" ministers and agencies.

2.3 *Local* Khural *and Administration*

According to the 1940 Constitution, the MPR was divided into 14 *aimags* and the capital city of Ulaanbaatar. The *aimags* were further divided into *soums*, the *soums* into *baghs*, while Ulaanbaatar was divided into sub-units of *khoroo*, *khoroos* into *khorid*, thus a new administrative and territorial division was introduced.

The *Khurals* of the Working Peoples were the highest organ of power in the local (rural) areas of the country. The *khurals* of the *aimags*, city, *soum* and *khoroos* were elected by representatives from the lower administrative levels, however, the *bagh* and *khorid khurals* were made up of everyone in the *bagh* and *khorid* who held elective rights. In Ulaanbaatar, one representative from every 200 people of the population was elected to the relevant *khural*, which was 1 representative for every 50 people in a *soum* and 1 representative from every 400 people of an *aimag*.

The *Khurals* of the *aimags* and Ulaanbaatar held their session once every three years, while that of the *soums*, *khoroos*, *baghs* and *khorid* convened once every year. These *khurals* reviewed and considered the annual reports of their relative administrative organs and elected representatives to the *khurals* of their respective higher organs.

In 1946, administrative rules were issued designed at mobilising inhabitants of *aimags,* the town and *soums* into administrative work, and animal husbandry, cultural and educational, health protection, finance and tax, co-operative trade, local economy and town development sections were set up. The rules were changed in 1954 and the sections were reorganised into Standing Commissions of the *Khurals* of Working People's Deputies of the *aimags,* town, *soums* and *khoroos* with new rules.

The *aimag* and Ulaanbaatar city *Baga Khurals* and their Presidiums, elected by the *Ikh Khural* and the local state administrative organs, acted as the *soum, khoroo, bagh* and *khorid* local administrations in between the session of the *Ikh Khural.* The 1940 Constitution, in this respect, noted that the "In between the recess of the *aimag* and Ulaanbaatar city *khurals,* the highest organ of power of the *aimags* and Ulaanbaatar shall be the *Baga Khurals* with members elected for a term of three years from every 1,000 people, who have been elected by the *Aimags* and Ulaanbaatar City Working People's *Khurals.*"

In order to carry out their daily duties, the *Baga Khurals of the aimags* and Ulaanbaatar City elected their respective Presidiums consisting of 7–13 members from among their own local assembly members and the Presidium had one chairperson, one deputy and members.

The *soum, khoroo, bagh* and *khorid's* executive administrative organs of the Working People's *Khurals* served as the local administrations composed of 3–13 members elected for a period of one year by the relevant *khurals* and their composition included one chairperson, a deputy, a secretary and members of the administration.

The administration heads provided overall management of the administration's functions and duties, and they had the authority to call for sessions of the administrative *khurals* and also preside over them. The Constitution also stipulated that the Presidium of the *aimag* and town *Baga Khural* Presidiums would have the following 5 sections, namely, animal husbandry and agriculture, finance, health, people's education and military.[5]

2.4 *The Judiciary*

Changes were also made in the judiciary system in view of the changes in the social and political life of the country. The 1940 Constitution stated that court proceedings shall be carried out by the State Supreme Court,

5 *Constitution of Mongolia,* (Compiled and commentary by J. Amarsanaa and O. Batsaikhan), Ulaanbaatar, 2004, pp. 365–366.

Ulaanbaatar City Court, the *Aimag* Judicial Unit, and the People's Court in the local rural areas.

The Constitution also legalised the democratic principles of the judiciary and court proceedings as follows:

1 Court proceedings shall be conducted only by the courts;
2 If not otherwise specified, the court shall involve a representative of the people in the court proceedings;
3 Court proceedings shall be conducted in the Mongolian language, and if a defendant does not know the language, he/she shall have the right to seek the help of an interpreter;
4 The trial shall be open;
5 The accused person had the right to have an attorney;
6 The court shall not be indirectly influenced and shall be strictly guided by the law.

Beginning from this period onward, the State *Baga Khural* elected the Supreme and Special Courts for a term of four years, and the *aimag* and local people's courts were elected for a three-year-term by the relevant *Aimag Baga Khurals.*

In order to guarantee the independence of the judiciary, the country set about to implement the decisions of the Eighteenth State Conference and the provisions outlined in the 1940 Constitution, that is, it was imperative to 1. Relieve the *soum* administration head of his/her functions to conduct trials, and 2. Establish local section courts. The Council of Ministers reviewed this matter at its meeting in 1943 and decided to postpone the implementation of the above actions in view of the preparatory complexities. The State *Baga Khural* Presidium passed a Resolution in 1943, according to which chairpersons of *aimags* and *khoroos,* who were concurrently responsible for conducting court trials, were relieved of this additional responsibility, and the cases under consideration were transferred to the higher level courts and their branches.[6] The Resolution further instructed to "Set up public courts in the *soums* to try small insignificant cases that do not call for criminal responsibility and small property related cases." However, the implementation of this provision of the Resolution was delayed until 1945 and it was partially accomplished.

A Resolution adopted by the State *Baga Khural* in 1943 clearly defined the power and authority of the State Supreme Court, and measures were taken to overhaul its organisational set-up. The Supreme Court as the highest judiciary in the country had the duty of monitoring court pro-

6 *The Constitution of the MPR and Compilation of Related Legal Acts*, Book One, Ulaanbaatar, 1972, p. 494.

ceedings and carry through the integrated policy of the judiciary. According to the rules of the Law Ministry, which were passed in 1941, the Law Ministry was responsible for inspecting and guiding the work of all the judicial organs in the country, and this responsibility was changed by the aforementioned Resolution. This became a major step forward in guaranteeing the independence of the courts.

The basic duties and responsibilities of the Supreme Court were:

1 Review all the adjudicated cases to verify their legality and issue a *certiorari*;
2 Issuing a *certiorari* in the event of an appeal against the judgement of the *aimag*, town and military courts.

The law also provided for the review of special cases by the Chairperson of the Supreme Court or by its members together with 2 representatives of the people. In keeping with the changes in the rules, Collegiums were formed under the Supreme Court, which were given the authority to review all criminal, civilian and military cases that had been considered by primary, appellate and review level courts. The Plenum of the Supreme Court granted the Collegiums the power to review all adjudicated cases against which writs had been issued by the competent officials. The judicial reform, which began in 1940, had been carried through in principle by 1947, thanks to which not only an integrated but also an integrated system of judicial organs was established in the country.

Starting from this period onward, the judicial system of the MPR was made up of district courts, *aimag* and city courts, special courts and the Supreme Court. These changes were consolidated by the 1949 Law on Organisational Structure of Courts.

People's District Courts were planned to be set up at the relevant *soums* and *khoroos*, in keeping with the changes made in the Constitution, as well as the Law on Organisational Structure of Courts and so the Presidium of the State *Baga Khural* approved the Rules on Election of the People's District Courts in 1953. According to these rules, the People's District Courts were to be formed for a term of three years through an election conducted by the inhabitants of the relevant *soums* and *khoroos* through secret votes on the principles of equality and the participation of all the people in the given areas. The Rules also introduced new provisions that the judges and the people's representatives would be elected from among citizens of the Mongolian People's Republic, who had reached the age of 23 and who had not been convicted before.

As regards the special courts, there was only the military tribunal, but the Presidium of the State *Ikh Khural* passed a Resolution in 1955, according to which a special Railway Court was formed at the Ulaanbaatar

Railways with a chairperson, one member and 50 people's elected representatives.

On 22 September 1958, the Presidium of the State *Ikh Khural* of the MPR passed a decree, through which the Law on the Organisational Set-up of Courts of the MPR was renewed, which also reflected the changes that had taken place in the judicial system since 1949.

The Law on the Organisational Set-up of Courts of the MPR had the following distinguishing differences as compared with the 1949 Law.

1 Procedural provisions concerning the nomination of judges were eliminated and the judges were made liable to report back to their electors;
2 The duties and functions of the primary and appellate courts were delineated;
3 A Railway Court was added to the system of special courts.

"Rules of Public Courts" was approved in 1960 under which public courts with 5–9 members were instituted, which were responsible for reviewing trivial offenses and the suspects were handed disciplinary responsibilities. And so by 1960 the court system of the Mongolian People's Republic had developed to maturity and had become relatively independent.

2.5 *Public Procurator*

This institution was a part of the court system, and Article 57 of the Constitution provided that a "Public Procurator (enforcer of law) had the responsibility of monitoring and controlling the strict observation of laws and legislation by the country's government ministries, central and local government agencies and departments, their affiliates, as well as government officials and the general public as a whole." This was the legalisation of the general control set-up of the Public Procurator's Office. Public procurators of the MPR were appointed by the State *Baga Khural* for a term of 5 years, and at the level of town, *aimags, soums* and *baghs* the town and *aimag* procurators, who have been appointed by the procurator for a period of four years, were responsible to carry out their duties.

Article 57 of the Constitution further indicates that procurators in the local rural areas shall be accountable to the State Procurator, but shall conduct their activities independently. With the adoption of the 1940 Constitution, the Procurator's Office, which initially together with the courts were under the jurisdiction of the Law Ministry, were given relative independence, and the State Procurator no longer served as the Vice Minister of the Law Ministry, as he/she was appointed by the State *Baga Khural*.

The Rules of the Procurator's Office of the MPR were adopted in 1941, and simultaneously the duties and responsibilities of the State Procurator, his/her deputy and assistant, *aimag* and city procurators, and investigating officers were defined and enforced.

Organisational restructuring of the State Procurator's Office was carried out in 1944, an assistant procurator responsible for applications and petitions was added and the All Military Procurator was concurrently assigned to serve as the Deputy State Procurator.

The Rules of the Procurator of the MPR was renewed in 1945, according to which, the State Procurator had to report to the State *Baga Khural*, and the *aimag* and town procurators were given the authority to set up district procurator's offices, which also concurrently were responsible to serve as assistant procurators. The State Procurator had three deputies, responsible for general control, special cases and military cases, and departments of investigation and courts, operational matters, and new human resources were set up which were headed by assistant procurators.

The State Procurator also had his/her own two investigating officers, senior and full-time.

2.6 *The New Election System*

According to the part dealing with election rules of 1940, all citizens of the MPR, who had reached the age of 18, exercised the right to election irrespective of their age, gender, religion and belief, skills and education level, property, whether they were nomads or settled. However, electoral rights were restricted for money lenders, previous *khutugtus* and reincarnates, other feudal lords and people who had serfs and subjects, influential male and female shamans, soldiers of the Russian White Guards, people who had been involved in anti-revolutionary activities, people with mental disabilities, and people whose electoral rights had been curtailed by courts. In view of this, there were some 8,000 people who had no electoral rights. However, this kind of restriction, which applied to some citizens, did not continue for long.

The Presidium of the State *Baga Khural* through its Resolution, which was passed in 1944, with the objective of expanding the democratic rights of the people, restored the electoral rights of the people, with due consideration of the fact that the majority of those who had been deprived of their electoral rights were regarded as wasted force who no longer posed any threat to the gains and development of the people's revolution as they accounted for only 0.08 per cent of the entire population of the country, and further, the majority of them, in the last decade, were involved in socially-beneficial labour and had in principle joined the ranks of the working masses, but this change did not apply to those citizens who were mentally ill or whose electoral rights had been curtailed by the court, which was, undoubtedly, a major change in the country's election system.[7]

Legal acts of a procedural nature, which were called instructional guidelines for reviewing the performance reports of the *soums, khoroos, baghs* and *khorids* as well as conducting election campaigns, were adopted in 1941.

DIAGRAM 14 New election system of the Mongolian People's Republic (1949–1960)

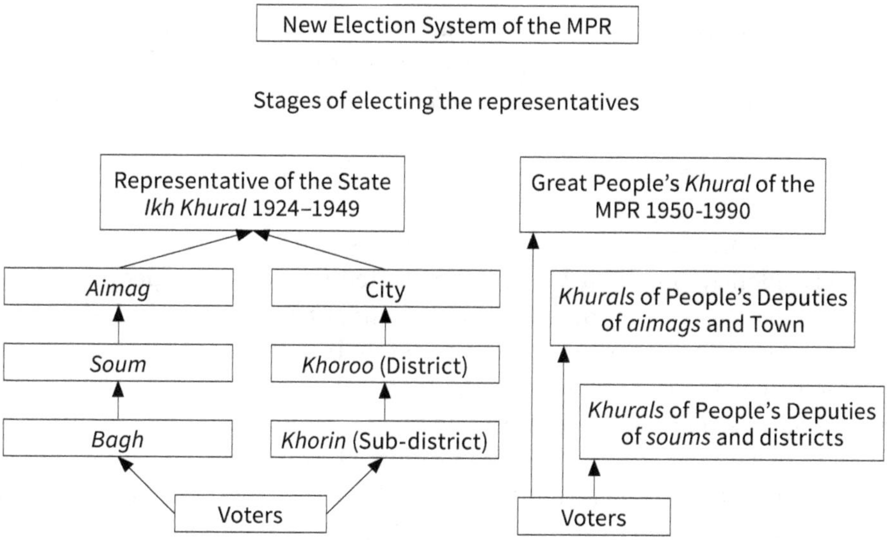

The Ninth State Congress was convened in 1949 and had many issues on its agenda; the most prominent among the agenda issues was the question of democratising the election system of the MPR. The Congress discussed the report of Yü. Tsedenbal and from among the multi-stage and open election system, the Congress chose to institute a new election system of conducting *Ikh Khural* elections directly and equitably, and through secret balloting. The Congress also deemed it appropriate to elect the Deputies of the State *Ikh Khural* through constituencies. Election equality means that all voters have equal right to vote, meaning that no-one had special rights to vote over other voters. Election constituencies were formed with equal numbers of population, and the voters had to cast their ballot on one and the same day in favour of a deputy nominated from one constit-

7 *The Constitution of the MPR and Compilation of Related Legal Acts*, Book One, Ulaanbaatar, 1972, p. 493.

uency or one district. Also the voters had to be registered once and were entitled to cast their vote only once as per the registration.

The citizens of Mongolia were given the right to direct election to all levels of *khurals*. In other words, direct election is a system of choosing political officeholders in which the voters directly cast ballots for the persons that they desire to see elected without the mediation of any organisation or representative. Voters were also given the right to cast their ballots in secret, which meant that the citizens of the MPR were guaranteed the right to cast their vote without any outside influence.[8]

The renewed election system of the State *Ikh Khural* was endorsed in 1950, and constituencies were set up from where 2 deputies would be elected from every 2,500 people. Soon after this, the new election rules of the worker's deputies' *khurals* of *soums, khoroos, baghs* and *khorood* were adopted.

While electing the *aimag* and the town *khurals,* the relevant constituencies were set up with due consideration of the size of population and in such a manner that 30 deputies would be elected from up to 30 thousand residents, one deputy was to be elected for every 600 people, if the population was more than 30,000 in the *aimags,* and in the capital city of Ulaanbaatar, the constituencies were set up in a manner that one deputy would be elected from every 375 resident of the city. However, in the case of *soums* and *khoroos,* there would be 30 constituencies if the population was up to 3,000; one deputy would be elected from every 10 people, if the population of that constituency was more than 3,000; and in the *baghs* and *khoroos,* there were 7 constituencies if their population was up to 400, and one deputy would be elected from every 50 people if the population was more than 400 people.

At this time, a majoritarian system was applied in both the State *Ikh Khural* and the local elections. Public organisations, such as the party, co-operatives, the Trade Unions, youth organisations, people's communes, the Cultural society etc. had the right to nominate candidates to deputy.

New rules for the election of People's District Courts were adopted in 1953, according to which elections were conducted at *soums* and *khoroos,* the judges and people's representatives were elected from among citizens with electoral rights, who were 23 years of age and more, and who had not been sentenced before, and they were elected for a term of three years by the entire inhabitants of the given *soum* and *khoroo.* One judge from one constituency was elected, while 30 to 70 people's representatives were

8 E. Avirmed, *State Power of the MPR,* Ulaanbaatar, 1969, pp. 198–199.

elected in accordance with the number fixed by the executive administration of the *aimag* working people's deputies.

New rules related to election of *aimag,* town, *soum, khoroo, bagh* and *khorin* worker's deputies were approved in 1954, which included some trivial changes of a procedural nature, as compared to the previously adopted rules.

The Presidium of the State *Ikh Khural* issued an edict in 1956 regarding rules and procedures for holding by-elections of the local *khural* deputies. The edict outlined the processes for holding by-elections. It said that if a local *khural* deputy has been transferred, if a deputy has submitted an application asking for relieving him/her of his/her duties as an elected officer, who has died or who has been sentenced on criminal charges, then only by-elections would be held, and the timeframe had been also defined similar to that applied in by-election provisions in the general rules of elections.

In keeping with the 1957 changes and amendments to the Constitution, 1 deputy from every 3,500 people could be elected to the State *Ikh Khural,* which also legalised the percentage of deputies eligible to run in local assembly elections.

3 System of Law

The legal system of Mongolia in the given period was totally overhauled and renewed in conjunction with the adoption of the new Constitution. Specialised laws were adopted, which contributed to developing branch of laws in the real meaning of the word. They included, among others, the Criminal Code passed in January 1942, the Criminal Proceedings Law of 1949, the Civilian and Civilian Proceedings Law approved in 1952 and the Labour Code, which was passed in 1941.

3.1 *Criminal Law*

In the period under review, criminal legislation also changed and developed in view of the changes and reforms in the social life of the country, as well as the nation's political goals and objectives.

Measures were taken to renew the Code of Courts of the MPR and in this connection, the Twenty-Fifth State Congress, which was held in 1942, approved the code as the Criminal Code of the Mongolian People's Republic, which was the first specialised law in the criminal law branch. Its general part included 6 chapters with 54 articles, and the special part consisted of 10 chapters and 165 provisions.

The *general part* of the Code outlined the objectives of the legislation, the scale and scope of its application, general evolution of the political policy, sentences handed to criminals, rules on the application of punishments for correctional purposes by the courts, matters related to suspended sentence and release on bail.

The *special part* included chapters on anti-revolutionary crimes, crimes against administrative regulations, abuse of power, criminal offences of violating the law and rules of separating the state and the church, economic crime, crimes against human life, health, liberty and reputation, property crime, crimes of violating the law and regulations on safeguarding public peace, order and discipline.

The 1942 Criminal Code reflected the changes and amendments made to criminal legislation in the country after 1934. It was changed and amended 15 times during its period of validity.

The changes made to the Criminal Code, in keeping with Resolution 56 of the Presidium of the State *Baga Khural* in 1943, covered such topics as deduction of certain percentage of earnings from penal correctional labour, awarding of severe to the severest punishment to a recidivist, the rules for applying additional punishments, and they also set the time limit for confinement in jail as maximum 25 years, and the maximum period for correctional labour as one year.

While making changes to the Criminal Code, the State *Baga Khural* Presidium passed a Resolution in 1945 defining what is a military crime and stated that it would be considered a crime if a person voluntarily leaves his workplace, office or an industrial site, during the time of war. Also the amendments made in 1947 defined as a crime against the state any encroachment on public and co-operative property.

During the period when the Second Constitution was in force, the most important changes in the criminal legislation were the changes made in keeping with Resolution 66 of the Presidium of the State *Baga Khural*, which was passed in November 1947. According to these changes, minors aged between 14 and 16 would be considered as subjects having committed a crime for certain types of offences. A new provision was also added, according to which imprisonment for a term of not less than 3 years would be imposed on anyone who engaged in propaganda against the People's Revolutionary Government of the MPR, who spread rumours, disseminated and stored anti-government books and articles, and called for committing crimes against the state.

The size of the penalty given to persons guilty of violating the tax law was increased, and so was the penalty for such offences and crimes as crimes against businesses, sexual abuse, crimes against propert. However, in the name of tightening criminal sentences, in particular related to combating property-related crime, errors and excesses were made whereby hundreds of innocent people were wrongly sentenced. A new Chapter 11 was added to the Code in the course of the changes and amendments made therein, called "Concerning crime related to the vestiges of moral behaviours of blood relatives and the feudal system."

One of the special features of the criminal legislations during the period from 1940 to 1960 was the fact that besides the Criminal Code the country also established the legal norms and standards crimes, and independent codified acts were complied. They included, among others, Resolution 5 on safeguarding state, public and co-operative property, passed by the Presidium of the State *Baga Khural* on 4 February 1947; Resolution 93 on commuting the death sentence, which was passed on 5 August 1953 by the Presidium of the State *Ikh Khural*; the 1954 Law on Safeguarding Peace; Decree 120 on prescribing criminal responsibility for divulging state secrets; Order 126 of the Presidium of the Great People's *Khural* of 1957 on railway security measures; the 1956 Law on tightening measures for protecting people's property; and the 1956 Law on preventing embezzlement of public property,

The criminal laws and legislations that were passed from 1940 to 1960 had a powerful impact on eliminating backwardness in the mentality and lifestyle of the people, and they are regarded as powerful factors that helped prevent anti-socialist onslaughts, and raise the rights mentality of the working people.

The *law of criminal (penal) procedure* was overhauled and renewed with the adoption of the Constitution in 1940. This Constitution legalised the basic norms and standards of the criminal procedure law, and in particular, Chapters 7 and 10 of the Law, basic principles of criminal procedure law were defined and backed by law, which were the fountain source of the penal procedure law. In this manner, criminal procedure legal standards of the MPR were renewed and developed in accordance with the letter and spirit of the new Constitution, and also with due consideration of the changes in the country's social and political life. In this respect, the "Law of the MPR on Criminal (Penal) Procedure" which was approved by the Order 4 of the Presidium of the State *Baga Khural* Presidium on 30 July 1949 holds a significantly important place. This Law was made up of 5 parts, 26 chapters and 440 articles.

Part One deals with the case jurisdiction, composition of the court, objection by the parties, types of and classification of evidence materials, about protocol, duration of a procedure, and the cost of the court. Part Two deals with competent organs for carrying out preliminary inquiry, methods and forms of investigation, rights and responsibilities of the participating subjects during an investigation, work methods for ending the investigation. Part Three deals with procedures for making preparations for trying a criminal case by the primary court, and the manner and basic principles of a court hearing, the rules and procedures for the size of the issue on the agenda, and the final judgment of the judge. Part Four deals with procedures for appealing against the sentence passed by the primary court, the timeframe of the appeal, procedures for reviewing the legally-binding judgment, and the procedure for issuing justification for reviewing the case in view of a new emerging situation. Part Five deals with the rules and procedures for carrying through the final validated judgment of the judge, the agency responsible for its execution, its rights and obligations.

This Law, as well as the changes and amendments made therein during the period from 1940 to 1960, were important in further clarifying and augmenting the relevant provisions of the Constitution, for they defined the fundamental principles of adjudication, the democratic principles of a criminal procedure, the inviolable rights of people's private life and the right to housing, the right of the defendant to seek the help of an attorney and the principle of rule-of-law.

In this manner, the Law of the MPR on Criminal Procedure became much more democratic than the previous legislations, which made it possible for a productive collaboration between the courts, the Procurator's Office and the investigation agencies.

3.2 *Labour Code*

The 1940 Constitution defined the duty of the people to labour as a noble responsibility, which also guaranteed economic support to earners. Accordingly, measures were taken to reform labour-related codes and regulations and the State *Baga Khural*, which convened in February 1941, adopted the Labour Code of the MPR with 19 Chapters and 156 Articles.

This Labour Code was in force at a time when the country had a mixed-economic system and so the Labour Code was applicable to the workers in state-owned industrial enterprises and government establishments as well as common citizens and those engaged in private production. At this time, the role of labour contracts became more significant and in view of this the role of the Trade Unions in regulating labour relations was legalised and consolidated; however, the operational orientation and direction of the work of the Trade Unions were hijacked and although it was a public organisation, its activities became hugely politicised.

In the previous labour codes, labour contracts had different names, such as "labour and production contract", "wage earning contract" etc., and in the new Labour Code the term "labour contract" was used for the first time. Concrete time schedules were included in the contract as the Code made it possible for the contracting parties to agree on the term and schedule of the contract. Furthermore, a probationary period was introduced before hiring a worker/labourer, and the right to abrogate the contract was left with the administration and the job seeker, and a new system of monitoring the abrogation of the labour contract on account of reduction of the work force by the Trade Unions was introduced, and they had to give their consent if the contract was cancelled according to law.

Different daily work hours were prescribed, for example, people engaged in intellectual work, young people under the age of 18, and people working in health hazardous conditions had 6-hour-working day, while ordinary workers had 8-working-hours in one day. The Code also clearly specified the duration of the rest hours, and the maximum of extra hours of work a person can do.

The size of labour wages was established either through the labour contract or complementary to the hours of works to be done in one day. Labour discipline issues were regulated in an interesting manner in the Labour Code. According to this labour law, the following disciplinary actions were defined, which included warning, reprimand, dismissal, transfer to another work with reduced monthly pay for up to 3 months, or demotion. If a worker was guilty of repeated labour-related offences, the person concerned was transferred to the so-called "friendly court" and if the offences were repeated then the person had to face different kinds of punishment, such as, receiving criminal charges, forced correctional labour and deduction up to 10 per cent of the monthly wages. Such measures were taken in view of the fact that labour and work were legally consolidated as a matter of honour.

The issue of labour safety was considered in two chapters on the labour of under-age people and labour safety. Further, the issue of labour safety, especially for under-age people and women, was regulated in a detailed manner.

The issue of social insurance was regulated under the chapter called "Regarding protection from social dangers," according to which social insurance premiums were deducted with due account of the relevant economic sector, rather than as provision of benefits and pensions as follows:

1 Coal mines: 9 per cent;
2 State and local budget government offices: 3 per cent;
3 Offices and factories with commercial accounting: 8 per cent;

4 10 per cent of the salary and wages of people engaged in physical labour was deducted as premiums for the pension and benefits fund. Also it was codified that employees shall pay the social insurance premiums.

The 1941 Labour Code laid the foundation for the establishment of the pension and benefit system in the country.

The Labour Code pointed out that the Central Council of the Trade Unions and its local organs shall monitor the implementation of the Code.

This Labour Code, from among all the labour codes that were adopted in the course of the history of socialism, was the most comprehensive and democratic law.

3.3 *Ecology Law*

The country, during this period, passed many laws and legislations and also amended quite a few of them designed at protecting and rationally utilising the country's natural resources. The Forest Law of the MPR, which was adopted under Resolution 67 passed by the Presidium of the State *Baga Khural* on 14 December 1940, consolidated the previously adopted norms and standards in this regard and defined new norms and standards for the rational utilisation and protection of the forest resources as a new policy objective of the country. In order to improve control over the nursing, protection and utilisation of forests, special inspection units were set up and determined that lumbering should be done only between 1 November and 1 May and only with the permission of the Forest Department.

This Law for the first time demarcated the territory of the green belt of Ulaanbaatar at 50 square kilometres.[9]

The Presidium of the State *Ikh Khural* passed a Resolution 31 on 13 March 1957, according to which the Forest Law of the MPR was amended adding a new provision "On the Protection of Forests of the MPR." The Law provided for the establishment of prohibited areas to protect forests and to prevent rivers from drying up, and the creation of green zones in towns and settlements to ensure a healthy environment. To ensure this, the Law put a ban on the cutting of young trees, plants, shrubs, and also mowing hay, and digging mud and soil inside the forests and within a perimeter of less than 100 meters from the forest fringe in protected areas, other than for cleaning and taking care of the forest environment.

9 O. Amarkhüü, *Mongol Customs and Laws Regarding Environment Protection*, Ulaanbaatar, 1999, p. 86.

An amended law called "Law of the MPR on Land Holding" was passed on 6 February 1942 by the Presidium of the State *Baga Khural* through its resolution, which was in force for 30 years until 1972.

A key conceptual idea about this Law was the rational utilisation and protection of land under holding and in this sense, the amended law, as compared with the previous laws and legislation (1928, 1933, 1955) was an important move forward as it consolidated all related past legislations and rules into one single legislative act.

The Law prohibited the sale or acquisition, and also renting of land, and specified that all land holders must be properly registered and provided with proper land hold certificates. In accordance with this Law, the Council of Ministers in 1956 passed a Resolution on "Carrying out organisational changes in the lands of the agricultural co-operatives and state farms", and in keeping with the Resolution, the relevant land organisation was carried out at more than 200 co-operatives and state farms, demarcating the land hold they were entitled to. Later in 1959, the borders of the *soums* were properly demarcated.[10]

One of the key legislative acts that regulated social relations dealing with hunting of wild animals, engaging in proper hunting practices and also regarding hunting trophies was the "Law on Hunting and Fishing on the Territory of the MPR," which was approved by a Resolution of the Presidium of the State *Baga Khural* through its Resolution 19, passed on 3 March 1944.

The law banned the hunting of some of the rare animals and birds, such as, beaver, sable, otter, marten, muskrat, Przewalski Horse, reindeer, saiga, doe, female elk, swan and nightingale, while the government promised to encourage and financially support those who fed and protected deer, doe, elk, wild ass, Przewalski Horse and reindeer. The Council of Ministers was given the authority to ban the hunting of some types of wild animals in the rural areas. The Law also specified administrative and criminal liability for hunting animals and birds that posed dangers to fauna resources, their habitat and geographical distribution (such as, use of explosive materials, fire, using booby traps, chasing down deer etc.), and collecting eggs of fowls, destroying their brooding nests, was banned.

10 O. Amarkhüü, *Mongol Customs and Laws regarding Environment Protection, (Issues of Traditions and Reform)* Ulaanbaatar, 1999, p. 86.

10 The State and Laws during the Period of the Third Constitution (1960–1990)

1 Historical Summary

The 1960s were years of great activity in the history of world socialism, when the ruling parties of the Soviet Union and other European socialist countries held their congresses, which proclaimed their ideological goal of building the material and technical bases of Communism (USSR) and transitioning to developed Socialism (European socialist countries). This enthusiasm and fervour did not by-pass the Mongolian People's Republic (MPR), which in its 1960 Constitution and the Fourth Programme of the Mongolian People's Revolutionary Party (MPRP) put forward the objective of completing the construction of Socialism in the foreseeable future in order to "build perfect socialism and then build communism" in the country.

Let us now summarise some of the more significant evolutionary changes that occurred in the entire gamut of social life of the MPR in the period extending from 1960s to the 1990s.

A bureaucratic commandism system was formed in the political sphere. The social and cognitive foundations of this system were the absolute weight given to centralisation, a cautious attitude towards democratic methods and distrust in the masses. Yü. Tsedenbal and his close associates who were at the highest helm of party and state leadership for more than 40 years, shielding themselves under the name of MPRP, contributed further to the deepening and consolidation of the command system.

The Party played the role of the State, and the State heavily influenced by the Party ultimately ended in the weakening of the distribution of functions between the Party and the State. Consequently, public organisations lost their independencye and an absolute domination of one party took over the country.

In the *economic and social spheres*, there were predominantly two kinds of social ownership – state and co-operative. The economic drive behind the country's goals to complete the construction of Socialism was based on the plan to lay the material and technological foundations of Socialism first, that is, transform the country into an industrial-agrarian State. In pursuit of this objective, Mongolia stuck with the policy of relying on the technical and economic assistance of and cooperation with the Soviet Union and other socialist countries. In this respect, centralised planning was coordinated with the socialist countries, led by the Soviet Union, speeding up the process of economic integration with them. During a span of more than 30 years from 1960, new industrial centres, such as Darkhan, Erdenet and Choibalsan were built to promote the development of the extractive and processing industrial capacities, and in particular, developing the fuel, energy and mining sectors, thanks to which key economic indicators improved and progressive changes occurred in sectoral structures. In 1960 industry accounted for 14.6 per cent of the revenues generated, which grew to 39.5 per cent in 1993. However, the share of agricultural produce had plummeted to 19.1 per cent, which can be explained by the growing share of the industrial and other sectors in the overall social production set-up.[1] However, in terms of key economic and social development indicators (national income, growth in labour productivity) the country was lagging far behind as compared to global developed nations. This was simply because the Soviet Union, which had made the MPR economically dependent on it, was itself far behind in terms of development as compared to other countries around the world.

In the *social policy sphere*, although the Party and State provided such social services as free education and medical assistance, central social protection issues were of low priority as the Party and the State focused more on a policy called "economic-man." The social structure was restricted to three classes, namely, the working class, the co-operative people and the working intelligentsia, while at the same time not paying heed to other elements of social structure.

In the *spiritual sphere*, pluralism was discouraged, social thinking was ideologised and Marxism-Leninism was propagated and promoted as the only true ideology. Although there were such limitations, the education, cultural and science spheres accomplished a good deal of progress. By the end of the 1980s, every one person, working in the national economic and cultural sphere, had acquired higher and/or special secondary education.

In terms of *foreign policy*, the international prestige of the MPR grew, and the country established diplomatic relations with over 100 countries, and maintained economic and cultural relations with dozens of countries. Mongolia became a member of the United Nations in 1961, and the country made enormous efforts to prevent and eliminate nuclear war, and establish lasting peace throughout the world. However, owing to the increasing ideologisation of international relations, the system of foreign relations of the socialist countries became ultra-conservative with almost no future.

1 *Twentieth Century Mongolia*, Ulaanbaatar, 1995, p. 182.

1.1 *The 1960 Constitution of the MPR*

Twenty years after the adoption and promulgation of the Second Constitution of the Mongolian People's Republic in 1940, the First Convocation of the Fourth Great People's *Khural* election the Third Constitution of the MPR was adopted on 6 July 1960, with a Preamble, 10 Chapters and 94 Articles. Chapter One was on the nature of the State and its general organisational principles; Chapter Two spelled out the basic economic principles of the State; Chapter Three was about the highest state power; Chapter Four was about the highest and central state administrative organs; Chapter Five covered the local governing and administrative organs; Chapter Six concerned the courts and the Procurator's Office; Chapter Seven focused on basic rights of the citizens and their guarantees; Chapter Eight was about the duties and responsibilities of the citizens; Chapter Nine defined the state symbol, flag and the capital city; and Chapter Ten defined the principles of amending and nullifying the Constitution. This Constitution defined the class nature of the State as class-based that the "Mongolian People's Republic is a country of workers, co-operated *art* (livestock herders and farmers) and the working intelligentsia, and its foundation is the union of the working class and the co-operated *ard*."[2] According to this fundamental law, the state foundations of the MPR were the *Khurals* of People's Deputies of all levels.

The Great People's *Khural* of the MPR, as defined in the Constitution, had the sole right to create legislation and it was the highest state power, and noting that in between the sessions of the Great People's *Khural* its Presidium would be the highest state authority, while the highest executive is the Council of Ministers, and in the rural areas, the highest authority of power were the *Khurals* of People's Deputies of the given levels. The Constitution defined that the Supreme Court of the MPRP was the highest judiciary in the country, which would have *aimag* and town courts, special courts and the people's district courts. The Constitution established that the State Procurator shall have the power of controlling the enforcement of law in the country. Accordingly, the organisational set-up, the basis of their functions, and the term of office and power of these branches of power were approved. In a nutshell, this Constitution defined the state system of the MPR.

In accordance with Article 18.2 of the Constitution, which specified that "The *modus operandi* principles of the Great People's *Khural* and its affiliates shall be defined through the regulations of the Great People's

2 *Constitution of Mongolia*, (Compiled and commentary by J. Amarsanaa and O. Batsaikhan), Ulaanbaatar, 2004, p. 249.

Khural and other laws that have been passed in compliance with the Constitution of the MPR" (This paragraph was included in the Constitution with amendments made on 21 November 1980) new laws and acts were passed, through which the organisational structure of state organs and their functions were further legalised, with the adoption of such laws, such as the Law of the Council of Ministers of the MPR, the Law on the *Khurals* of People's Deputies of *aimags* and towns, and the Law on the local *Khurals* of People's Deputies of *soums, khoroos* and districts.

The Constitution defined that socialist property, made up of commonly owned industrial means, was the bedrock of the economy of the MPR.[3] This was a provision that directly rejected private ownership but exaggerated the absolute and leading role of state ownership.

Chapter 7 focused on the basic rights of the citizens and the guarantees related to the rights the citizens are entitled to, their responsibilities and how they can be guaranteed. For instance, it noted that citizens of Mongolia, irrespective of their gender, race and origin, religion and belief, as well as their social status all have equal rights. The right of citizens to rest, citizens who have become disabled or those who have lost their bread earners have the right to seek and receive economic assistance from the Government. It also specified other socio-economic and cultural rights, such as the right to education, equal participation in state, economic, cultural, social and political activities, and also freely taking part in the government, social and economic management of the country through their representative organs. Further, unless otherwise medically confirmed that a person is mentally unstable, all Mongolian citizens were given the right to elect and be elected, submit both written and oral complaints and petitions against all state organs and government officials for their illegal activities, red-tape and bureaucracy to the governing bodies and administrations. The citizens were given such political rights, as the right to speech, press, hold meetings, rallies and demonstrations, hold ceremonial acts, and form public unions and associations. The Constitution in this chapter legalised such personal rights as the freedom of belief and non-belief, carry out anti-religion propaganda, and privacy, housing, letters and communication were inviolable, and no-one could be arrested without a court decree and procurator's permission, and in addition the guarantees for ensuring these rights and freedom were specified collectively or individually in the Constitution.[4]

3 *Constitution of Mongolia*, (Compiled and commentary by J. Amarsanaa and O. Batsaikhan), Ulaanbaatar, 2004, p. 249.

4 *Ibid.*, pp. 261, 262.

Defining the right of citizens to education, Article 80 of the Constitution promulgated that the "citizens of the MPR shall be guaranteed the right to free education, the number of general education schools, special professional secondary schools and institutes of higher learning shall be increased, vocational proficiency of the citizens shall be facilitated and students of vocational secondary schools and colleges shall be entitled to government stipends." In this manner, although the rights and their guarantees had been legalised and consolidated, the issue of human rights and freedom, in a broader sense, had not been included in the Constitution, such as filing a petition with the court if the life of an individual (citizen) is under threat, or if a citizens believes that his/her rights and freedoms have been violated, not to testify against oneself and family members, parents and children, defend oneself in a law of court and seek legal advice and assistance.

Article 89 defined the duties and responsibilities of the citizens of the country. For example, a person (citizen) was obliged to devote his/her ability, knowledge and skills for the cause of Socialism, strictly abide by the Constitution, uphold law and serve in the People's Army of the MPR, which were considered noble obligations of each and every citizen.

The Constitution proclaimed that "The leading and guiding force of the state and society of the MPR is the Mongolian People's Revolution Party, which in all its activities is guided by the all-triumphant Marxist-Leninist theory,"[5] which is a striking illustration of the fact of the strong proliferation of the theoretical formula and practical aspects of the ever-growing leadership role of the Communist Party in all socialist countries.

A number of principally new qualitatively changes and amendments were made to the 1960 Constitution by the Law on Making Changes and Amendments to the Constitution of the MPR, which was adopted on 21 November 1980. During the previous socialist system, it was argued that these changes were made in order to augment the "socialist democratic development gains" of the country.

Let us now look at some of the amendments including the changing of the procedure for conducting of business by the Great People's *Khural* of the MPRP and its organs in Article 18 by part 2 regulations and other laws of the Great People's *Khural* that were adopted in conformity with the Constitution of the MPR; Article 20 on state control by the Great People's *Khural* was paired with public control to set up the People's Control Committee and specified that the rules of the committee's organisational

5 *Constitution of Mongolia*. Documents. (Compiled and commentary by J. Amarsanaa and O. Batsaikhan), Ulaanbaatar, 2004, p. 361.

set-up and functions shall be defined by the law; the procedures specified in Article 37 on the power, organisational structure and *modus operandi* shall be defined by the Law of the Council of Ministers of the MPR, which were adopted in conformity with the Constitution of the MPR and this amendment was in two sections; it was also decided that the election constituencies would be set up with one deputy each from 4,000 people; further on, the term of the Great People's *Khural* was changed from 4 to 5 years and specified that it shall be composed of 370 deputies elected from constituencies with similar number of population.

The 1960 Constitution of the Mongolian People's Republic was a socialist-type fundamental law and scholars are unanimous in their view that this Constitution consolidated the gains of the country in its development towards socialism by-passing capitalism.

2 State Structure

2.1 *Highest State Governing Body*

The Constitution promulgated that the highest state governing body of Mongolia is the Great People's *Khural* and its Presidium. The Great People's *Khural* was at the head of all state organs, meaning that it ruled the entire system of *Khurals* of People's Deputies of all levels and had the authority to directly set up all other highest state and central bodies that were responsible for managing and running the country on behalf of the State, control and monitor them, and adopt the Constitution and other laws.

The Great People's *Khural* (GPKh) of the MPR (it was called the State *Ikh Khural* before the enforcement of the 1960 Constitution. Authors) was elected and formed 11 times in the period from 1951 to 1990. In between the sessions of the GPKh, the Presidium of the GPKh of the MPR, elected by the GPKh itself, was the highest standing organ of state authority. The GPKh Presidium included the Chairperson, deputy chairpersons, a secretary and presidium members. The GPKh Presidium reported to the Great People's *Khural* and had the authority to take decisions on some of the important issues under the jurisdiction of the GPKh during its recess. For example, a law that had been approved by a decree of the GPKh Presidium was submitted for consideration to the session of the GPKh, which would ratify the law that unfortunately made this important process a mere formality. Besides the Mandate Commission, the GPKh had more than a dozen Standing Commissions on planning, budget, law drafting, national issues, agricultural industry, culture, education, health and youth.

2.2 *State Administrative Organs*

The structure of the state administrative organs of the MPR consisted of three parts, namely, the Highest, Central and Local Organs of State Administration. As specified in Article 37 of the Constitution and Article 1 of the Law of the Council of Ministers of the MPR, the Council of Ministers was the highest state executive organ. The Council of Ministers was accountable and reported only to the Great People's *Khural* and its Presidium and carried out the functions of the State executive administration by way of providing collective leadership to the central and local State administrative organs on the basis of enforcing the laws and decrees passed by the GPKh and its Presidium.

As indicated in the Constitution, the Council of Ministers was formed for a period of 5 years from the first convocation of each regular election of the Great People's *Khural* of the MPR. As soon as the term of office of the Council of Minister expired, it transferred its power at the First Session of the Great People's *Khural* and submitted its performance report for consideration and the newly formed Council of Ministers submitted its plan of action to the GPKh session for consideration and endorsement.

Article 42 of the Constitution and Article 4 of the Law of the Council of Ministers defined the composition of the Council of Ministers, which would have the Chairman of the Council, one first deputy chairperson, several deputy chairpersons, and Ministers of the MPR and heads of State Committees. According to the above laws, it was decided that the authorities of other central organs of state administration would be included in the Council of Minister as proposed by the Council Chairman to the Great People's *Khural*. Common issues related to the power and authority, and the term of office of the Council of Ministers were regulated by the Law of the Council of Ministers, and its power and authority over relevant state administration branches were regularised through sectoral laws and decrees.

The basic *modus operandi* of the Council of Ministers was its (cabinet) meeting. In other words, the Council of Ministers and its Presidium discussed issues under its jurisdiction domain through meetings and decided on by a majority of votes. The Council of Ministers met for its meeting not less than once every quarter, the Presidium meeting was convened when required, and the meeting of the Council passed resolutions and directives (of the Chairperson).

The work apparatus (office of administration) provided effective, efficient and economical administrative and business services to the Council of Ministers in executing its office. The office of administration of the Council of Ministers included the Secretariat, Organisational and Supervisory office, and other organisational structures, which executed their daily duties and functions in keeping with the rules approved by the Council of Ministers. Besides the aforementioned apparatus or office of administration, the Council of Ministers also had a Standing Commission overseeing vital matters of state management, it also had the authority to set up temporary commissions or working groups to draft requisite issues, review and discuss any divergent views on them, and execute other necessary tasks. To illustrate, the Council of Ministers had a so-called Commission on COMECON or Council for Mutual Economic Assistance *(an economic organisation from 1949 to 1991 under the leadership of the Soviet Union that comprised the countries of the Eastern Bloc along with a number of socialist states elsewhere in the world, including Mongolia. Tr.)*. These commissions operated under rules and regulations approved by the Council of Ministers.

2.3 *Central Organs of State Administration*

Ministries predominantly constituted the central organs of state administration. Ministries were formed by the Great People's *Khural,* which were headed by the minsters, members of the Council of Ministers, and who managed definite state economic, social, cultural, administration and political structures and in this sense, the ministries were the state central administrative organs. The legal status of the ministries was defined by the Constitution, the Law of the Council of Ministers and the relevant rules and procedures adopted by the Council.

As indicated in the Law of the Council of Ministers, the ministries of the MPR managed the sector they were responsible for and were wholly accountable for the sector's status and progress, and addressing the issues confronting them and that may arise before their relevant sectors. The ministries were also assigned the dual responsibility of managing inter-sectoral management. As per Article 21 of the Law, the ministries were headed by ministers, who were accountable and reported to the Council of Ministers of the MPR for managing all the tasks assigned them.

The Minister's composition included the First Vice Minister and other Vice Ministers, who were responsible for efficient management of the businesses of the different sectors under the jurisdiction of the ministry and were accountable to the Minister for their performance and outcomes.

The administration of the ministry was responsible for managing the functions of the ministry and the structure of the ministry administration was determined by the Council of Ministers of the MPR, which included departments, sections, autonomous bureaux, units etc.

The state central administrative organs also included state committees and special agencies/departments, which were formed by the Great People's *Khural* had the authority to coordinate state central administrative and local organs. For instance, the State Planning Commission drafted the consolidated long-term and annual national economic and cultural development plans, assign by distribution the state approved plans, monitored and assessed their implementation and it was the key organ in the centralised planned economic structure coordinating inter-sectoral plans and their implementation.

Besides the ministries and state committees, the Council of Ministers also had under it special agencies/departments (for example, General Department of Road Transport, State Arbitration Department etc.), which were also part of the state central administrative structure, and were established by the Council of Ministers. The special agencies and departments were responsible for independently managing administrative functions that were not under the jurisdiction of the ministries and the state committees.

2.4 *State Local Organs*

During the period under review, changes were made in the structure and organisational set up of the local organs of state in conjunction with the development of all the economic sectors, in particular, in agriculture and industry. By the end of the 1950s, the *soums*, in terms of agricultural production, primarily constituted one entire agricultural co-operative or an agricultural state farm and in view of this the *baghs* were dismantled in August 1959, as a result of which the *soums* and *khoroos* became the primary local state organs.

Taking into consideration the growth and increase in the population of the capital city of Ulaanbaatar, its *khoroos* (districts) were replaced with the so-called *raions* (a Russian word meaning a district) and subsequently the Executive Administration of the *Khurals* of People's Deputies of *Raion* became the primary state organ of the capital city, which was divided into four *raions* or districts of Sükhbaatar, Oktyabr (a Russian word meaning October), Nairamdal (Friendship) and Ajilchin (Workers).

Towns in the country, according to their jurisdiction, were classified into State and local towns. The local *Khurals* of People's Deputies of *aimags,* towns, *soums, khoroos, raion* were the local organs of power. The *Khurals* of People's Deputies of Ulaanbaatar, Darkhan and Erdenet towns, and of the *aimags* were the higher local administrative organs of the relevant *soums, khoroos,* and *raions*. That is, the *soum, khoroo, raion* and rural town's *Khurals* of People's Deputies were the primary level state administrative organs. These two-tier *Khurals* of People's Deputies led the state organs functioning in their respective territories, and were guided by common principles of exercising rural authority and organisational activities.

The sessions of the *aimag* and town *Khurals* of People's Deputies were convened by the executive administration not less than twice a year, while the sessions of the *soum, khoroo, raion* and rural town's *Khurals* of People's Deputies were convened not less than 3 times a year. The Presidium of the Great People's *Khural* of the MPR passed a Resolution on 8 June 1978 and accordingly a Law of the *soum, khoroo, raion* and rural town's *Khurals* of People's Deputies was adopted and enforced on 1 January 1979, which laid the legal foundations of the representative organ of governance in the country's rural areas.

This law defined the basic principles of the organisational set up and functions of the *soum, khoroo, raion* and rural town *Khurals* of People's Deputies and also regularised the prerogative rights and responsibilities, as well as the organisational structure of the local *khurals.* As indicated in Article 2 of the Law, the local *Khurals* would be elected for a period of 3 years by citizens of the MPR who had reached the age of 18 and who lived on the territory under the jurisdiction of the given *Khural* and the elections would be held on the basis of equality and direct secret voting.

The Executive Administrations of the *Khurals* of People's Deputies, their departments and divisions were under the direct jurisdiction of the local state administrative organs and also the government ministries. The Executive Administrations were the executive and command organs of the *Khurals* of People's Deputies. The Executive Administrations of the *soum,* khoroo and rural town *Khurals* of People's Deputies and their compositional structures were elected at the First Session of the respective *Khurals* of People's Deputies, that is, the chairperson, deputy chairperson, a secretary and without the members, and the *aimag,* town and *raion* Executive Administrations were elected and installed with members, the chairperson, deputy chairpersons and an executive secretary. The Executive Administration of the *aimags* and towns enjoyed the right to amend and/or invalidate resolutions and directives of the lower level *Khurals.*

DIAGRAM 15 State structure of the Mongolian People's Republic (1960–1990)

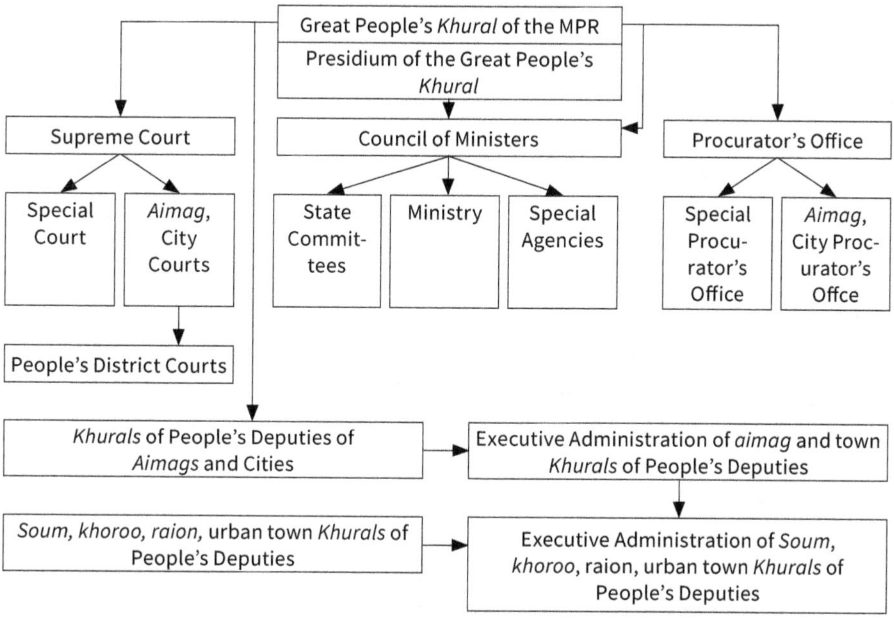

2.5 *The Courts*

According to the Third Constitution of the MPR, court proceedings in Mongolia were to be carried out by the Supreme Court of the MPR, *aimag* and town courts, special courts, as well as the people's district courts. As a result of the establishment of a party-centric political system, the ruling party had, time and again, passed resolutions and had given instructions regarding the organisational set-up of law-enforcement agencies, including the courts. For instance, in accordance with a Resolution 303 of the Central Committee of the MPRP, which was passed in 1961, recommended that urgent measures must be taken without delay designed at strengthening the democracy of courts, and streamlining the organisational management and control functions of the courts. Accordingly, the highest state authority made the necessary changes in the structure and composition of the judiciary. Later, on 3 October 1961, the Presidium of the Great People's *Khural* of the MPR passed an order number 262, under which the Presidium of the Supreme Court of the MPR was formed, which was assigned the entire responsibility of court management. Furthermore, the *aimag* and town courts were given additional supervisory right, that is, they were given the authority to review and pass judgment on valid decisions of a district court based on the remonstration presented by the competent court and procurator's officials.

During this period, primary courts were also reorganised. In accordance with Order No. 315 passed by the Presidium of the Great People's *Khural* of the MPR on 28 December 1961 on reorganising the local judiciary, the people's district courts in all places and *aimags*, other than Ulaanbaatar alone, were dismissed and replaced with the so-called *aimag* mobile courts. Also with due consideration of the increasing number of rural towns and settlements, rural town courts were established. To illustrate, in 1962 the District Court of the mining town of Nalaikh near Ulaanbaatar was reorganised as a Town Court, while new town courts were established in the town of Züükharaa in Selenge *aimag* and in Tosontsengel of Zavkhan *aimag* in 1963. Also in view of the new division of Ulaanbaatar and the creation of *raion*-districts, the Presidium of the Great People's *Khural* of the MPR passed Resolution 117 on 11 August 1965, Ulaanbaatar's District Courts were dismissed and *raion* people's courts were established in all the four *raions*-districts of the capital city. In this manner, the primary courts of the country were divided into the *aimag* mobile court, rural town courts and in Ulaanbaatar – *raion*-district courts. Alongside this, special military tribunals were reorganised as per the requirements of the country's armed forces. For instance, besides reorganising the military tribunals into courts of the People's Army, two new tribunals under the border and home forces were established under Order 92, passed on 8 May 1972 by the Presidium of the Great People's *Khural* of the MPR, which also issued an Order No. 13 on 26 January of the same year, according to which a Military Collegium (Board) was established under the Supreme Court of the MPR, which was an attempt to improve control over the performance and functions of the aforementioned tribunals. A Mongolian Railway Court was also formed under Order No. 25 passed by the Presidium of the Great People's *Khural* of the MPR on 3 February 1975, and in this manner the country then had the above-mentioned three kinds of courts within the special judiciary system.[6]

A Law on the Courts of the MPR, incorporating and reflecting these reforms and changes in the organisational set-up of the courts of the country, was ratified on 25 December 1978 by a Resolution the Presidium of the Great People's *Khural* of the MPR. Structurally, this Law had 6 Chapters and 65 Articles. As defined in the Law, the Supreme Court of the MPR, the *aimag* and city special courts, as well as the district, *raion* and rural town people's courts had the authority to conduct court proceedings. The tasks of the courts, as defined in the Law, were to pursue the objective of not

6 *Courts of the MPR – On Guard of Protecting Socialist Gains*, Ulaanbaatar, 1977, p. 9.

only punishing criminals, but also taking corrective measures to reform a criminal, prevent crimes and breaches of law, and eliminate factors giving rise to crimes and criminal activities while passing penal sentences.

Some of the basic principles of the courts were codified, such as, the equality of the citizens before law, the judges to adhere to the principle of collectivism while holding a hearing, the judges must be impartial and be guided by law only without coming under anyone's influence, and ensure that the defendants exercise their right to an attorney, and follow the language of the court as applied in the law at all levels of courts. Although these principles defined the substance of the court proceedings, the law, however, did not specify those provisions that would prevent the courts from exercising their impartiality, or be guided by or influenced by someone else, in other words, the law was devoid of the political and legal guarantees that ensured the independence of the judges.

2.6 *The Procurator*

The Procurator's Office of the MPR, as defined in the Constitution, was responsible for guaranteeing the Procurator's control in the judicial matters of the country. New and amended laws of the MPR, done in accordance with the Constitution, which regulated key social relations were designed at improving the monitoring of the implementation of the country's laws and legislation by the Procurator, and strengthening the rule of the law.

The ruling party, on several occasions, passed resolutions and decisions concerning the organisational set-up and the functions of the Procurator's Office. To illustrate, we can name Resolution 169 passed by the Political Bureau of the MPRP Central Committee in 1963 on the functions and performances of the courts and the Procurator's Office; Resolution 96 of 1972 on some measures to strengthen the courts and the Procurator's Office, and accordingly concrete policy guidelines and instructions were given, which provide evidence that the courts and the Procurator's Office were being used by the party to carry through its policies. The Procurator's Office set up a research institute, which was given the task to investigate the motives behind and the circumstances of crimes and developing preventative measures in this regard. A class for training investigators was opened in 1979 at the Law School of the National University of Mongolia and also the number of scholarships to Law Colleges and universities in the Soviet Union was increased, which were important measures to strengthen the Procurator's Office in the country.

The Great People's *Khural* of the MPR in 1976 passed a law on the Procurator's control functions, thus defining the basic principles of the organisational set-up and activities of the Procurators. The Law with 6 Chapters and 65 Articles included principally new legal norms and standards that had never been identified in all the previous laws and legislation, and in this sense, the new law on Procurators can be rightly called a highly efficient legal act.

The Law made it legally binding for the Procurator's Office to combat crimes and other offences, study and analyse the motives and circumstances that led to those crimes taking place, plan actions and measures to prevent crimes and offences, improve the legal knowledge and understanding of the working people.

The Law also specified important norms and standards, principles and guidelines for the local Procurator's Offices, which were directly under the jurisdiction of the Procurator's Office of the MPR, ensuring that they take full responsibility for a strict compliance of laws. The Law specified the terms of reference for the recruitment of Procurators and investigators. For example, it clearly states that people who can be recruited should be able to strictly abide by the law, reliably stand up for the interests of the society and the working people, who are citizens of the MPR with higher and medium-level law education, who are upright and honest, and well-behaved, in other words, the best of the best could only be taken to work as a Procurator and an investigator. The Law prohibited the recruiting of anyone who had been convicted before. In this way, the Law, besides specifying the requirements of the Procurators, also indicated that the organisational set-up of the local Procurator's Offices would be approved by the Great People's *Khural* of the MPR, also the Procurators and investigators would be accredited once every 3 years, and the Law defined the hierarchy, the ranks and titles of the Procurators and investigators working in the system of the Procurator's Office of the MPR.

3 The System of Law

The process of law reform began in a stage-by-stage manner starting in 1961 in accordance with the new Constitution. A key feature of the legal system of this period was the adoption of laws with "purely socialist content" within the framework of carrying through the party's overall goal of building Socialism in the country. The party had concluded that socialist production relations had triumphed in the country and accordingly, the party was guided by the ideology that the economic and social structures of the country had entered the higher stage of Socialism, and so the country required a new higher level of socialist legal system. Indeed, during this period the country's laws, in terms of their quality and substance, improved substantially, and in particular, independent and specialised codes were adopted, the footprints of which were an important watershed in the legal system of the country.

Let us now look at some of the important laws and legislation that were adopted during this period.

3.1 *Civil and Civil Procedure Law*

The new Civil Code, which appertains to the period when the Third Constitution was in force, was approved by a Resolution passed by the Presidium of the Great People's *Khural* on 9 February 1963, and which came into force effective as of 1 April 1963. The Civil Code of the MPR, as the Act was called, had a General Section with 6 Chapters and 158 Provisions, and a Special Section with 7 Chapters and 407 Articles.

The Law became the foundational base for the consolidation of a centralised, planned economy and created the legal grounds for a preferential development of state property by restricting the right to equal development of different forms of ownership. Nonetheless, it helped improve different aspects and elements of property-related and also non-property relations as well as the civil legal relations, and provided enhanced legal guarantees for the protection of the rights and interests of the citizens of the MPR.

The country's Law on Civil Procedure was approved by a Resolution of the Great People's *Khural* of the MPR on 29 June 1967, which came into force on 1 October of the same year. This Law was designed to regulate each and every civil procedure in the courts, that is, the procedures for considering civil cases by the courts were defined by this Law. For example, according to Article 3 of the Law, every interested party had the right to give evidence to the court to protect their legitimate rights and interests if they were considered to be in breach of law, or if they were contentious, and what is more, immutable principles that had to be followed during every stage of civil procedure were also spelled out clearly. For example, during a trial every citizen was equal before the law and the court, the legal proceedings had to be conducted by elected courts, the language used during a trial was clearly specified, the law provided for open and continuous trial, and noted the obligatory nature of the judge's sentence etc.

Compared to the laws in force today, there were no provisions that permitted the judges to take unilateral decisions in a civil procedure, and the law provided that all types of civil cases would be tried by a judge together with two representatives of the people. This kind of collective decision taking in all civil proceedings was compromising, on the one hand, to the significance of the court proceedings, and on the other hand, undermined the principle that all disputes should be considered and settled only by professional lawyers/judges.

3.2 *Penal Law and Law of Criminal (Penal) Procedure*

In keeping with the process of reforming the laws and legislations of the country under the Third Constitution of the MPR, the Criminal Law of the MPR was adopted on 31 January 1961, which came into force as of 1 April of the same year. Threats that no longer posed a danger to the society, or the actions or non-actions that no longer were occurring in the country were written off as a crime. For example, the special Fifth and Eleventh Chapters of the 1942 Criminal Law had not been included in the 1961 Law, which concerned violation of the laws and rules of separating the church from the State, and criminal activities related to moral remnants of relationship by marriage and the feudal system. Instead new chapters on crimes against socialist property, crimes against the socialist economy, and crimes against court proceedings were added to the 1961 Law, thus systematising them in the General Clauses of the Law with 5 Chapters and 44 Articles, and the Special Clauses with 11 Chapters and 117 Provisions.

The highest sentence passed under the General Clauses of the Criminal Law was confined to 10 years imprisonment. But under the Special Clauses, only for certain serious crimes, the highest penalty was 15 years in jail, thus reducing the 25-year jail sentence for serious crimes as defined in the 1942 Criminal Law.

Some new and important penal law norms and standards were introduced, such as the procedures for acquitting and/or vindicating a person from criminal charges, transferring their case to a public court etc.

26 years after the adoption and enforcement of the 1961 Criminal Law, a revised and edited version of the Criminal Law of the MPR was adopted on 5 December 1986 and was enforced on 1 July 1987. The revised and amended law had 7 Chapters and 59 Articles in its General Clauses, and the Special Clauses had 13 Chapters and 301 Provisions, which defined some 30 kinds of actions and inactions as a crime and the relevant sentences were also specified. Two new chapters were added the Special Clauses of the Law, including Chapter 7 on crimes against the natural environment and the procedures for protecting natural riches, and Chapter 12 on crime against traffic safety, while Chapter 3 was changed into Chapter 2 concerning crimes that endanger human life, health, freedom and reputation, and Chapter 3 on crimes against socialist property.

In addition to the criminal jurisdiction being improved in this manner in the given period, the procedural law on the application of the criminal code or the Law on Criminal (Penal) Procedure was approved at a session of the Presidium of the Great People's *Khural,* held on 24 December 1963, which came into force across the entire territory of the country effective on 1 June 1964.

The Law of the MPR on Criminal (Penal) Procedure had 7 Parts with 35 Chapters and 403 Articles, which clearly outlined and defined the entire gamut of general issues related to criminal (penal) procedure, such as the jurisdiction of a crime, instances when criminal procedures cannot be conducted, the rights and responsibilities of those involved in the trial, the material evidences, preventative measures, protocol and other documents, period of limitation, cost etc.

3.3 *Family Law*

Twenty-two years after the adoption of the Law of the MPR on Marriage and Family Status, which was adopted in 1951, the new Family Law of the MPR was adopted under a Resolution of the Great People's *Khural* of the MPR, which was passed on 19 April 1973. The new Law with its Preamble, 13 Chapters and 113 Articles came into force as of 1 October of the same year. It must be noted that the Presidium of the Great People's *Khural* of the Mongolian People's Republic adopted procedures for the enforcement and compliance of the law.

The Law was replete with ideology prevalent in the Mongolian social fabric during that period. The Law proclaimed the importance of strengthening the socialist family, further improving family relations, and guaranteeing the right of women in family matters. The Law also outlined provisions designed at regulating relations concerning marriage and divorce, personal and property relations between the bridal couple and their parents, children and other members of the family, procedures for giving a child for adoption, adoption of a child, relations concerning care for and support to citizens, and the registration of civil families.

As pointed out in Chapter 4 of the Law, couples who were entering into wedlock were obliged to register their marriage, and if couples failed to do so, they would not have the relevant rights and responsibilities as spelled out in the Law. The new Law also specifically defined as invalid marriages, which were registered with the Civil Family Registrar of the MPR and those who were married before 1951, and if the marrying couples were able to prove that they were married before the new Law came into force, then they had the right to register their marriage as per the date of their nuptial.

The 1963 Family Law played an important role in providing legal protection to family relations viz their property and non-property, and strengthening equality within a family.

3.4 *Labour Code*

Labour relations during this period were regulated by the Labour Code of the MPR, which was approved on 3 July 1973 at the First Convocation of the Eighth Elections of the Great People's *Khural* of the MPR. Compared to the other previous laws, the new Law, in terms of its structure, was voluminous, with a Preamble, 15 Chapters and 223 Articles. However, it was inferior to the previous laws in terms of labour regulations. For example, the new Law was designed in such a way as to regulate social relations only if the country's citizens were employed on contract with state-owned industrial enterprises, government offices and other government institutions. The previous laws regulated all relations of labour related to contractual workers in all branches of the national economy.

Whatever the case, the 1963 Labour Code defined all institutes of labour relations other than joint labour disputes, contracts and agreements, while joint contracte were dealt with in a separate chapter. But the definition of a labour contract, additional guarantees for legalising labour contracts and their dissolution, as well as the legal rights of the workers were compromised in the new Labour Code. There were, however, some new elements of labour norms and standards in the Law, including deeming as invalid a labour contract that is contrary to law, workers were not made to carry out work that was not included in the contract or that was hazardous to life and health, a potential worker could not be required to submit documents that were not listed in the Law. It was also prohibited to invite a worker by a public organisation to assist in any kind of elections or mobilise a worker into compulsory military service. A worker who was temporarily relieved of his/her duties because of an industrial accident and who had convalesced and was fit to continue to work must be restored in his/her previous job. It was also mandatory to seek the permission of the Trade Unions when a labour contract was abrogated at the initiative of the administration; it was prohibited to dismiss a worker on grounds of health, when he/she was on his/her legal annual leave, on outside-office assignment, and for all other compelling reasons; and the Law specified that the day when a worker tenders resignation or quits his/her job should be considered his/her last day on duty. The 1973 Law for the first time ever regulated the issue concerning the enhancement of the education and proficiency level of a worker, which can rightly be regarded as a progressive part of the new Labour Code.[7]

The procedures for the application of certain provisions of the 1973 Labour Code were regulated by the Council of Ministers of the MPR through

7 O. Jambaldorj, L. Baasan, *Labour Code of the MPR*, Ulaanbaatar, 1986, p. 182.

consultation and consensus with the central state administrative organ overseeing labour, wages and salary, as well as the Trade Unions.

3.5 *Ecology Law*

The Government encountered the task of renewing and improving laws and legislation related to land holdings, comprehensive protection of the natural environment, efficient utilisation of natural resources, and their rehabilitation. Proceeding from this premise, the Fifth Convocation of the Seventh Election of the Great People's *Khural,* which was held in November 1971, adopted the revised version of the Law on Land Holding of the MPR. This Law sought to introduce the mechanism that would ensure a comprehensive and rational use of lands and their protection, taking measures that would help improve land fertility, taking into equal consideration the interests of the State, the society and the citizens in their land relationship, and most importantly, augmenting the rule of law in the land relationship.[8]

With the objective of renewing laws and legislation related to protecting and rationally utilising wild animals, and also catching game, the Hunting Laws of the MPR were renewed twice, first in 1962 and again in 1972. During the 10 years that the 1962 Hunting Law was in force, relevant changes occurred also in the resources and distribution of wild animals, making it imperative to better protect this natural wealth, and to organise hunting and catching of game on a scientific basis. With due consideration of this requirement, the Presidium of the Great People's *Khural* issued an order on 6 January 1972, according to which the Hunting Law was approved in a new form, which was an important act on the part of the State and the government to streamline nature protection legislation. The 1972 Law had a greater advantage as compared to the previous laws as it contributed to instituting a better system of protecting the resources of economically valuable wild animals, birds and fowls, and fish, transferring and acclimatising them in new geographical locations, and monitoring their reproduction under strict plans.

The Presidium of the Great People's *Khural* issued an order on 1 July 1974, according to which laws and legislation relating to the protection and rational utilisation, and rehabilitation of forests and their resources were renewed to primarily improve the system of protecting, increasing and utilising forests and their resources. Laws and legislation on the protection and use of water, an important constituent of the nature environ-

8 O. Amarkhüü, *Foundations of Land Holding Law of the MPR*, Ulaanbaatar, 1973, pp. 82–83.

ment law of Mongolia was also given priority. This is evidenced by the adoption of the Law on Water Use of the MPR, which was passed under a decree issued by the Presidium of the Great People's *Khural* of the MPR on 27 March 1965.

This water law was in force until 1974, when it was renewed by the Presidium of the Great People's *Khural* on 1 July 1974 with the objective of protecting and rationally using surface and underground water and its resources on the territory of the country. The Law put in place some very new standards related to the rational utilisation of both surface and underground water by the population, for livestock breeding, farming and other national economic branches, and protecting water from being polluted and ensuring there was no shrinkage in water resources.[9]

The issue of determining and protecting protected areas occupied an important place in the numerous measures carried out by the State and government to protect the natural environment. In this respect, it is important to mention the Resolution "On some measures to improving the protection and use of the Bogd Uul Mountain," which was passed by the Council of Ministers on 20 July 1974; the resolutions of the Council of Ministers, issued on 21 March 1975 "On measures to protect the nature in the Great Gobi Preserve"; the Order of the Presidium of the Great People's *Khural* on "Establishing the Great Gobi Preserve," which was issued on 14 April 1975.[10] Given the increase in the discovery and exploitation of mineral resources in the country, and also given the immediate social need to study and analyse the country's mineral resources, the Council of Ministers for the purpose of improving the research base of studying, exploiting and protecting the mineral resources passed a Resolution on 12 May 1972 specifying measures on carrying out research in the mining and energy sectors. The Resolution provided the necessary guidelines for the establishment of a mining and energy production research and designing institute, and the terms of reference of this institute.

One of the most important features of this period with regard to the evolution of ecology law was that the sectoral legislation and legal standards covered all the nature environment protection-related projects and the laws became comprehensive and all-embracing.

---

9 O. Amarkhüü, *State and Legal Theoretical Issues of Protecting the Surrounding Environment*, Ulaanbaatar, 1979, pp. 96–97.

10 O. Amarkhüü, *Foundations of Land Holding Law of the MPR*, Ulaanbaatar, 1973, p. 99.

3.6 *Corrective Labour Law*

The country first adopted a law on reforming criminals and convicts in 1931, and in continuation, corrective labour laws of the Mongolian People's Republic were subsequently passed in 1966 and 1981, which were important contributions to the further development of the penal sentencing in Mongolia. The 1966 Law was designated as "confidential" and so it was used only by the Ministry of Social (Public) Security of the MPR and its affiliate the governing body of corrective labour organisation, its units and penal colonies, and they were intended for other state organs, but this classification was made null and void by the 1981 law.

The 1996 Law had 8 Chapters and 55 Articles, and the 1981 Law had 5 Sections, 22 Chapters and 117 Provisions. Key penal system relations were legalised and regulated and they all had their own specific features, such as, basic method of reforming a convict, the involvement of the public in their re-education, types of corrective labour institutions, the difference in their daily regime, volunteer organisation of prisoners, professional and vocational training for them, incentives and disciplinary actions against them, services for the inmates, medical services, compulsory medical treatment, material responsibility of a criminal etc. The 1966 Law had defined its purpose and objective as "to ensure that the sentence passed by the court is meted out in accordance with the law, the convicts are re-educated to respect and abide by the law, educate them to adjust to the socialist way of life and labour, and to prevent them from committing another crime and pose a threat to the society." A new point "educate and re-educate the convicts in the ideology of respecting socialist law and order" was added to the above objective in the 1981 Law. Similarly, brand new clauses were added, for example, to Article 2 of the 1981, which stipulated that "the procedures and conditions for undergoing sentence at a disciplinary unit of the Armed Force of the MPR shall be determined by the laws and legislation of the MPR." The new addition in Article 10 was about the "control and monitoring by the Procurator's Office on serving a sentence" and about "administrative control of convicts on probation."

The Presidium of the Great People's *Khural* passed an Order No. 5 on 11 January 1988 on "Making changes and amendments to the Corrective Labour Law of the Mongolian People's Republic" to the 1981 Law, according to which, new articles – 25.1, 76.1 and 102.1 were added to it, while more than 30 articles were amended stylistically.

11 The State and Laws during the Short Transition Period of the Constitution (1990–1992)

1 Historical Summary

At the crossroads of the end of the 1980s and the early 1990s, Mongolian society came headlong up against the imperative historical need to carry out reform and reconstruction in the country. The world socialist system, born of the 1917 October Revolution, entered into deep crisis and found itself at a dead end. The Mongolian People's Republic was part and parcel of the global socialist system and the crisis and impasse did not pass it by. Socialist development in Mongolia came to a dead end owing to a number of external and domestic factors, including the following:

1. The socialist ideology that was born in Europe, and in particular the theoretical basis of Marxism and Leninism, did not quite suit the conditions in the Orient, including in Mongolia.
2. The revolutionary changes that were carried out in the country did not take their source directly from Capitalism, from which the embryo of Socialism was born. Mongolia cut short this embryo and attempted to directly replace the feudal social system with Socialism, which was characterised as the "Non-Capitalist Path of Development."
3. The world socialist system, Mongolia included, which was directly dependent on the Soviet economy, could not continue along the path of building Socialism when its very foundation – the Union of the Soviet Socialist Republics, the bedrock and support of the socialist system – began to shake in the powerful wave of reconstruction. A common reason why Socialism came to a dead end is because the socialist theory and teachings themselves were riddled with crises, and they failed to become a practical reality in the society of the Socialist States. The Democratic revolution that took place in Mongolia at the juncture of the 1980s and 1990s was not a matter of cognizance by a political force or a smart person; it was a matter of understanding by the entire Mongolian society, the effect of the cognizance by the world socialist system, and the outcome of the efforts of the people of Mongolia who were waiting for such an impact.

Let us summarise the overall situation in Mongolia on the eve of the reconstruction (*perestroika*):

- The system of commandism was in full strength in the country, where a one-party rule was established;

- Different forms of property/ownership, in particular, private property were not recognised, a free-market mechanism was in principle denied and a stiff policy of centralised planning was pursued;
- One single ideology held sway over social spiritual life, and pluralism was strongly discouraged;
- The country primarily conducted a single-polar foreign policy and its foreign policy relations were basically confined to the Soviet Union and other socialist countries.

These were the internal factors that necessitated that the country carry out reform and restructuring. The process of reconstruction in Mongolia was not only a political process but it also became the basic method of restructuring the society in a progressive manner.

2 Reform and Restructing of the State System

2.1 *The State Governing System*

Mongolia's single State governing system prior to 1990 suited the development level, and the specific socio-economic, geographical and population features of the country; however, the rights as enshrined in the laws were not fully exercised, and the activities towards this end did not match expectations.

The command-bureaucratic regime in the country restricted the democratic nature of the State organs of power and its representational nature, policies were imposed from the top (the Party) without considering the opinions and requirements of the masses from below, which became a cumbersome ideological mechanism that only acted by giving orders and command. At times, the regime was influenced by the executive administrative organ, created non-constitutionally prescribed new officials posts, overstepped the line drawing the separation of state power by concentrating all the highest state authority in the political party. Instead of enacting laws that reflected the wishes and desires of the people, the regime adopted legislative acts that protected the rights and interests of the apparatus, which were approved only after seeking permissions from the highest party authority. The people did not have the right to choose their representatives, whose names were already decided at the top and who ran for elections without any rivalry, thus creating a so-called post of a "deputy" with all the immunities possible. Such deviations and excesses in the functioning of the highest state authority were the direct reflections of the distortions and perversions in the country's social and political systems, which pushed the country into a dead alley and crisis.

The country came up against the imperative task to set aright these distortions and perversions and set about reforming and overhauling the state highest governing authority, which marked the beginning of the reform and reconstruction process in Mongolia. Proceeding from this premise, the Ninth Convocation of the 11th Election of the Great People's *Khural* of the MPR (held in May 1990) enacted the Law on Amendments to the Constitution of the MPR. Accordingly, work began to reform the state governing system, delineate the functions of the party and the State, the State was made the nucleus of the political structure, the State's functions were strengthened in all aspects and the power of the State was expanded, the role and responsibility of law were augmented, and measures were taken to establishing an integrated parliamentary system and promoting the development of democracy in the country.[1] As part of this restructuring effort, besides the Great People's *Khural* of the MPR, a permanent Parliament – the *Baga Khural* (Small *Khural)* of the MPR – as well as the institute of the Presidency were created ensuring that their power and authority are distributed in a balanced and a complementary manner. With these structural reforms, the Great People's *Khural* became the supreme organ of power of Mongolia, fully expressing the rights of the Mongolian people.[2]

The Great People's *Khural* of the MPR was elected for a term of 5 years by the people and was composed of elected deputies. The Great People's *Khural*, within its prerogative right and authority, considered and took decisions on the following matters only:

1 Adopt the Constitution of the MPR, and make changes and amendments to it;
2 Elect and relieve the President and the Vice President of the MPR;
3 Elect the *Baga Khural* of the MPR and make changes to its composition;
4 Establish a Control Commission of the Constitution of the MPR, and make changes to its composition;
5 Appoint and dismiss, as proposed by the President of the MPR, the Prime Minister of the MPR, the Procurator General of the MPR, and elect and dismiss the Chairman of the Supreme Court of the MPR;
6 Define the basic guidelines of social and economic development of the MPR.

---

1 J. Boldbaatar, *The Role of the Mongols in the Regional and Global History*, Ulaanbaatar, 2007, p. 63.

2 *Constitution of Mongolia*, (Compiled and Commented by J. Amarsanaa and O. Batsaikhan), Ulaanbaatar, 2004, pp. 333–339.

The Great People's *Khural*, besides the above, also had the prerogative right to consider and take decisions, enact laws and legislation, at its own initiative, on all matters related to the domestic and foreign policies of the country.[3]

The basic organisational and operational activity of the Great People's *Khural* is its Session. The Session of the Great People's *Khural* was held twice between 1990 and 1992. At the first Session, the State *Baga Khural* was formed, the President of the MPR was elected, the country's Prime Minister and the Procurator General were appointed, and the Chairman of the Supreme Court was elected. The First Session of the Great People's *Khural* also formed the Standing Commissions of the Great People's *Khural*; however, this Session did not consider the establishment of the *Constitution Control Commission.*

The Second Session of the Great People's *Khural*, which opened in 1991 and continued in 1992, discussed and adopted the new Constitution of Mongolia and the Supplementary Law of the Constitution, which was a historical event in the country's statehood, and during this brief period, the Great People's *Khural* of the MPR occupied a special place in the structure of the highest state organ of the MPR.

The State Baga *Khural* in its nature and *modus operandi* was the permanent highest state authority, which exercised the prerogative right to pass bills, control them and organise their enforcement. In this sense, the State Baga *Khural* was primarily responsible for creating parliamentarianism in the country, in the real sense of the word, and it held its regular sessions once every half a year, and the session continued for 75 days.

The State *Baga* Khural as a principle form of Parliament, had the authority to nominate Parliament members as the political parties have the relevant number of mandates based on the number of votes received in the election.

The nominees could be a serving deputy of the Great People's *Khural*, or could be a non-deputy also. The Great People's *Khural* considered each and every nominee and those who received the majority of votes became members of the State Baga *Khural*. Ballots were cast in secret as per the rules.

The State *Baga Khural* had a chairperson, one deputy chairperson, one secretary and 50 members, three fourths of whom had to be elected from among the members of the Great People's *Khural*. The Chairperson of the

3 *Constitution of Mongolia*, (Compiled and Commented by J. Amarsanaa and O. Batsaikhan), Ulaanbaatar, 2004, p. 333.

State *Baga Khural* was concurrently the Vice President of the MPR. And so during this brief spell of time, the country had one Vice President.

The State *Baga Khural* exercised the following prerogative rights:

1 Enact legislation and make changes and amendments to them;
2 Call the session of the Great People's *Khural*;
3 Appoint and dismiss the Prime Minister and the Procurator General, elect and dismiss the Chairperson of the Supreme Court by submitting their nomination for endorsement during the recess of the Great People's *Khural*;
4 Establish the Permanent Committees of the State *Baga Khural*, and change its composition;
5 Approve and change the composition of the Government as proposed by the Prime Minister;
6 Elect and change the composition of the Supreme Court as proposed by the Chairperson of the Supreme Court;
7 Appoint and dismiss deputies of the Procurator General as nominated by the latter;
8 Control and monitor the Constitution of the MPR at the submission of the Constitution Control Council, and also at its own initiative, control and monitor the enforcement of the laws of the MPR, as well as the decisions of the Great People's *Khural* and the State *Baga Khural*;
9 Make changes to the administrative and geographical divisions as recommended by the Government;
10 Determine the legal basis of the organisational set-up and activities of the Local *Khurals* of People's Deputies;
11 Approve the National Social and Economic Development Plan, the integrated state budget, and their performance reports;
12 Determine the basic guidelines of the country's financial and credit policies;
13 Invalidate the decisions of the Government, *aimag* and rural town *Khurals* of People's Deputies if they are incompatible with the law;
14 Consider the reports of the Government, the Supreme Court and the Procurator General, and that of the Presidium of the *aimag* and rural town *Khurals* of People's Deputies, ministries, special committees and agencies;
15 Grant amnesty;
16 Ratify and cancel international treaties of the MPR;
17 Hold national referendum of draft bills and vital issues related to the social and political life of the country;
18 Hold national referendums;

19 Institute honorary titles, orders and medals of the MPR, highest military titles and other ranks and titles.[4]

The State *Baga Khural* also had the right to consider and take decisions on all domestic and foreign policy matters other than that coming within the jurisdiction of the Great People's *Khural.*

As the State *Baga Khural* was elected by the Great People's *Khural,* the former was directly accountable to the latter. The Second Session of the Great People's Khural (1911–1992) considered and discussed the performance report of the State *Baga Khural.*

The primary organisational and operational form of the State *Baga Khural* was its Session. Also Standing Committees were set up to ensure the uninterrupted functioning of the State *Baga Khural,* submit for consideration draft bills and resolutions to the State *Baga Khural,* and to ensure that the State *Baga Khural* carried out its control and monitoring functions. The State *Baga Khural* then had five Standing Committees on State Structure, Economy, Social Policy, Law, Women, and Children and Youth. The State Structure Standing Committee had a sub-committee of local *khurals* and administrations, while the Standing Committee on Economy had three sub-committees on finance, monetary and credit policy.

The country's President was one of those state institutes with an important mission of implementing the highest state order. The Law on Amendments to the Constitution had defined that the President is the Head of the People's State, the Guarantee of the Independence of the MPR and the unity of the Mongolian people."[5]

The President was elected by the Great People's *Khural* through secret ballot, a citizen of the MPR, who has the reached the age of 40, a person who is knowledgeable about the life, customs and traditions of the Mongolian people, one who has resided permanently in the MPR in the last at least 5 years. The Law provided that two or more candidates could be nominated to the post of the President, who shall be considered elected if the presidential candidate receives the majority of votes of the deputies of the Great People's *Khural.*

The President took office after taking an oath at the Great People's *Khural.* The term of office of the President was 5 years and according to the Law, the President could stand for re-election for another second term only.

4 *Constitution of Mongolia,* (Compiled and Commented by J. Amarsanaa and O. Batsaikhan), Ulaanbaatar, 2004, pp. 335–336.

5 *Constitution of Mongolia,* (Compiled and Commented by J. Amarsanaa and O. Batsaikhan), Ulaanbaatar, 2004, p. 336.

Punsalmaagiin Ochirbat was elected the first ever President in the history of Mongolia. He won the majority of votes of the deputies at the First Session of the Great People's *Khural* held in 1990.

The President had the prerogative right to pass edicts, grant clemency, announce the elections of the Deputies of People's *Khurals* of all levels, and sign the laws of the MPR, veto laws and other decisions passed by the Great People's *Khural* and the State *Baga Khural*. The President was the Commander-in-Chief of the Armed Forces and had the duty to guarantee the defence and security of the country. The President had the right to enter into talks and conclude treaties on behalf of the MPR, if deemed necessary secure the resignation of the Prime Minister and table a motion on the dismissal of the Government. The President had the power to award honorary titles, orders and medals of the MPR, grant high military ranks and other titles and ranks, grant and withdraw citizenship, appoint and recall the heads of the plenipotentiary representatives accredited to foreign countries and international organisations, and accept the letter of credence of envoys accredited to the MPR from foreign countries.

The President also had special rights to call military mobilisation, declare an emergency, take special measures to enforce public order, and have the last say in regulating and directing the mutual activities of the highest legislature and the executive authority.

The Law on Amendments to the Constitution, besides specifying the prerogative rights of the President, also defined the justifications and procedures for reporting to the Great People's *Khural* and for the President's resignation. Significant changes had been made in democratising the organisational set-up and *modus operandi* of the People's Khural, which were the key forms of self-governance by the people in the highest state power system, expanding their power and authority, and ensuring that they were able to carry out their term of office to the fullest. Presidiums were instituted at the local *khurals* in order to ensure their uninterrupted and permanent functioning, the budgetary rights of the local *khurals* were expanded, and the necessary conditions were created for their independence of activities.

The Law on Amendments to the Constitution also renewed the structure of the offices of the Presidium of the Great People's *Khural* and its executive administrations, their terms of reference. The Chairman of the Presidium was no longer given the responsibility of simultaneously serving as the secretary of the party organisation. This was an important decision on delineating the functions of the political party and the state organ.

A new post of Chairman of the Presidium of the *Soum* and *Khoroo* People's *Khurals* was created, who was concurrently assigned to carry out the functions of the chairman of the executive administration. The practice of assigning heads of agricultural co-operatives and state farms dual responsibility of serving as the chairperson of the Executive Administration of the *Soum* and *Khoroo* People's *Khurals* was altered. This decision was taken to augment the functions and performances of the state organs as state and economic activities, especially in the rural areas, were becoming one and the same, which was a cause of concern as the reputation of the State was at stake.

2.2 *The Formation of a Multi-party System*

The People's State, which was established as a result of the 1921 national democratic revolution, became a guarantee of the country's independence and sovereignty, and an embodiment of the unity of the people, and led the country on to the path of global modern civilisation. However, owing to various domestic and external factors and influence, objective and subjective reasons, the People's State in the course of its evolution and growth, underwent distortion and deviation, which rendered it incapable of carrying through its goals and objectives along democratic lines, and it lost its own social and democratic orientation, and consequently, the power and authority of the People's State shrunk, and its activities became merely symbolic.

The Mongolian People's Revolutionary Party, which alone carried out the role of the country's political leadership over the course of the entire 70 years since the establishment of the People's State (1921–1990), drew conclusions from the situation arising from the wishes and demands of the people, spearheaded an initiative to carry out reform and reconstruction in the country, on the basis of promoting democracy and openness in all areas of social life, which facilitated the liberalisation of the political sentiment of the society and created positive preconditions for the development of the country on the principles of pluralism. New political organisations, such as the Democratic Union of Mongolia, also played an important part in this respect. As a result, the MPRP unilaterally rejected the Constitutional provision of being the sole organiser and leader of the Mongolian society. This move laid favourable grounds for the formation of a multi-party system in the country. With due consideration of these practical circumstances, the Ninth Convocation of the Eleventh Election of the Great People's *Khural* of the MPR, which was held in 1990, adopted the Law of Mongolia on Political Parties, thus consolidating the legal foundations for a multi-party system.

And so, by May 1990 there were already six political parties that had been officially registered by the judicial division (Collegium) for civil cases of the Supreme Court of the MPR.

1 The Mongolian People's Revolutionary Party (MPRP). It was registered on 16 May 1990 under Resolution One of the judicial division for civil cases of the Supreme Court of the MPR. The MPRP was first formed out of two revolutionary underground groups in Niislel *Khüree* when the two groups merged on 25 June 1920 and was officially declared a political party at its First Congress, which was held on 1 March 1921.
2 Mongolian National Progressive Party (MNPP). It held its first constituent congress on 11 March 1990 and was officially registered by the judicial division for civil cases of the Supreme Court of the MPR under its Resolution Two on 22 May 1990.
3 Free Labour Party of Mongolia (FLPM). This party held its constituent congress of 12 March 1990 and was officially registered under Resolution Three of the judicial division for civil cases of the Supreme Court of the MPR on 23 May 1990.
4 Mongolian Democratic Party (MDP). It held its first congress on 18 February 1990 and was registered under Resolution Four of the judicial division for civil cases of the Supreme Court of the MPR on 24 May 1990.
5 Mongolian Social Democratic Party (MSDP). This party was formed on 2 March 1990 and was registered on 25 May 1990 under Resolution Five of the judicial division for civil cases of the Supreme Court of the MPR.
6 Green Party of Mongolia (GPM). It held its first constituent congress on 9 March 1990, and was officially registered by the judicial division for civil cases of the Supreme Court of the MPR under Resolution Six issued on 26 May 1990.

2.3 *Changes in the Election System*

Changes of principle nature were made in the system of electing the State organs of power, during this brief period in the country's history. 99.67 to 99.99 per cent of the total eligible voter population of the country turned up for the elections to the Great People's *Khural* and the local *Khurals* of People's Deputies that were conducted since 1951, which was one of the definite proofs of the truly democratic nature of the election system of the country expressing the interests of the people.

However, this was democracy only in form with respect to the then existing social and political life of the country. The entire process of nominating a candidate to a deputy to the conducting of the elections, during the years when a command and bureaucratic system prevailed, as the elections were regulated and instructed from the top, the social status of the deputies was determined beforehand, and the names of the top government and state bureaucrats and ministers, who "had to be elected" were already allocated to respective constituencies. Consequently, the voters were unable to elect the person they wanted to be elected, since they had to cast their vote for the person who was "destined" to be elected as determined at the top. The voters, therefore, had no choice but to cast votes for the only candidate. What is more, the election process had become quite cumbersome as every single voter was persuaded to go to the polls. And so the elections became formalistic and the heart and soul of a democracy election was distorted, that is, competition among many contenders and the right to choose one of them of your choice. This state of affairs necessitated the reform of the election system and the democratisation of the election regulations as such. The Law of the MPR on the Election of Deputies to the Great People's *Khural,* which was adopted at the Eighth Session of the Eleventh Elections of the Great People's *Khural* held in 1990, was based on the universal democratic principles with due consideration of the multi-party system that was taking roots in the country, the traditions of statehood, the specific features of the administrative and territorial divisions, as well as the best practices of the election system of other countries around the world.

The new election system that was put in place with this Law, besides maintaining the basic election principles, such as secret balloting and direct voting by all eligible voters on the principles of equality, also introduced new regulations on preparing for and holding free and democratic elections. With the extension of the number of candidates that could be nominated, entire communities, workers of industrial enterprises, work collectives of organisations and their affiliates, primary party and public organisations, and also military personnel had the right to individually or collectively nominate candidates for election to the Great People's *Khural,* and what is more, a citizen of the MPR was given the right to nominate himself/herself. This helped do away with the old election system when the candidates were "nominated" from the top and who, as many then suspected, were being awarded for currying favour with their superiors. However, it must be noted that the voters were challenged and quite seriously during the 1990 free and democratic elections as there were too many candidates to choose from each election district.

Since constituencies were set up in each and every administrative and territorial unit for the elections to the Great People's *Khural* there were almost 430 candidates running for election from the *soums, khoroos,* rural town and Ulaanbaatar and its districts. The many numbers of deputies were even put down as "deputies from a gully" by some political forces.

The 1990 election was held through party vote, that is, voters voting for a list of candidates proposed by a party. Based on the outcome of the votes, the number of seats to which a political party was entitled was distributed from every 50 members of the State *Baga Khural.* This was the first time that the country had used the proportional system of election.

In this election the Mongolian People's Revolutionary Party won 60 per cent of the votes, that is, it received a mandate for 31 seats in the State *Baga Khural* to become a majority, followed by the Mongolian Democratic Party with 13 mandates, and three mandates each won by the Mongolian Social Democratic Party and the Mongolian National Progressive Party.

During this brief period in the history of the transition of the MPR, the parliamentary parties formed a coalition government.

3 The Beginning of Judicial Reform

The State *Baga Khural* – the highest permanent legislature of the country, which was formed in keeping with the Law on Changes and Amendments to the Constitution – marked the beginning of legal reform in Mongolia. The most important central objective set before this new legislative body was to begin the drafting and considering the new Constitution of Mongolia, and submit the draft for consideration to the Great People's *Khural.* In the course of carrying through this historical mission, many laws covering many different aspects of state structure, socio-economic issues of the country, were either amended or adopted anew.

To begin with, laws of the State *Baga Khural,* the President and the Government were enacted, which helped strengthen the legal foundations of activities and organisational set-up of the highest state institutes of the country. Within the objective of making a transition from centralised planned economy to a free market economy, state economic management was conducted not by giving centralised orders and command, but by ensuring that State projects and economic goals were accomplished through free competition, through consensus and negotiations. This brief period witnessed the abolition of the singular domination of State ownership, all forms of public and private property were recognised, and law backed the right to ownership.

The State *Baga Khural* effected changes and amendments to the Civil Code of the MPR in 1990. The chapter on ownership rights, which had consolidated the domination of socialist ownership with two forms –

state and collective property – was fundamentally changed in terms of its doctrine, and replaced with two forms of ownership, private and public. Public property included state, religious institution and public (mass) property and the law also acknowledged the possibility of mixed- ownership.

The next step included property owned privately by the citizens. The country was faced with the challenge of providing equal opportunity to its citizens, and in this respect, the next challenge was to privatise public and agricultural co-operative property. In order to tackle this historical challenge, a Law on Privatisation was passed to promote the so-called big and small privatisation schemes. In the process of implementing the Law, although some portion of public property wss given to private ownership by the citizens, the valuation of the assets was reduced and the monitoring of the process was slack, which led to many mistakes and irregularities. What is more, the Law without clearly specifying the methods and mechanisms of privatisation, left the privatisation of co-operative wealth, that is, the assets of agricultural co-operatives, in the hands of the co-operative members themselves to decide. As a result of this, privatisation in the agricultural sector proceeded haphazardly, causing the loss and even embezzlement of enormous amounts of wealth.

In keeping with the afore-mentioned changes in property relationship, a new challenge came to the fore, that is, the country had to find a way to manage business and to overhaul the system organisationally. In order to address this challenge, the Law on Economic Entities was passed, according to which an economic entity in the country existed in the form of either a company, a co-operative or a private enterprise.

This brief period also saw the enactment of the Law on Tax (1990). The purpose of this legislation was to codify social responsibility of equal and fair involvement of industrial enterprises and organisations of all forms of ownership, including the population in forming the budget of the MPR, the centralised reserve for economic and social development of the country, and regulating relations arising out of the effort to carry through the specified responsibility. The Law specified that there would be two kinds of tax – direct and indirect tax. Direct tax included corporate tax, income tax and wealth tax, and indirect tax included sales tax, tax levied on utilisation of land and natural resources.

In view of the changes that took place in ownership and economic entity relationships, some important changes and amendments were made to the Criminal Code. According to the "Law on Making Changes and Amendments to the Criminal Code of the MPR," enacted on 28 December 1990, provisions in Chapter Three of the Special Clause (crime against socialist property) of the Criminal Code, and provisions in Chapter Five (crime against private property of citizens) were consolidated, and Chapter Three of the Special Clause (property crime) was changed and amended in keeping with the transition to a multi-ownership economy and in accordance with the objective of guaranteeing equality to all the different forms of property. The title "Crime against socialist economy" in Chapter Six was renamed "Economic crime."

The country started following the new Labour Code as of 1 July 1991. The purpose of this law was to regularise labour relations of people working in the economic sector, based on different forms of ownership, and codify the right to free labour replacing the mandatory legal provision according to which people of working age had to work, and in special circumstances, they were either forced to work.

The 1991 Labour Law had 10 Chapters with 96 Articles; previous labour laws had fewer numbers of chapters and clauses. With this Law, the precedent was set to regulate social insurance or pensions and benefits by the social insurance law, rather than the Labour Code.

Before the enforcement of the package of social insurance law on 1 January 1995, the key legal act in this regard was the Law on Pensions, which was passed in 1990. This was the first legislation that was enacted by the State *Baga Khural* at its fall session in 1990. According to this Law, there were two types of pensions – *employment* (old age, disability, loss of bread winner), and *social welfare*. Under the Law, the so-called state and local special pensions, which were given to competent authorities, were discontinued. Of special interest are the clauses included in Chapter Two on Old-Age Pension, according to which males who have reached the age of 55 and who have worked for a total of 32 and more years, females who have reached the age of 55 and who have worked for 27 and more years, and mothers who are 50 years of age or who have worked for not less than 20 years, and who have four and more children of their own or have adopted children 3 years of age, and have taken care of and raised them to the age of 6, irrespective of their age were entitled to retire and register for pension. This Law, although it put in order the national pension system to comply with the rights and interests of the citizens, undersestimated the sources for the formation of the pension fund and as a consequence hundreds and thousands of liable pensioners were negatively affected. The depreciation of the national currency as well as inflation added to the woes of the pensioners.

12 The State and Laws of Present-Day Mongolia (1992–Present)

1 Historical Summary

Following the adoption and implementation of Mongolia's new Constitution, the elections for the State Great Khural have occurred 9 times, while elections for the President and local Khurals have taken place 8 times each. The 1992 State Great *Khural* election marked the end of the turbulent years of challenges coupled with social reforms, and the beginning of a new stage in the country's development.

This is to say that Mongolia accomplished the transition from one social system to another new system, and the life of the country and the people revived under totally new principles and concepts. Their foundations were laid by the new, Democratic Constitution of Mongolia and in the period since, the gains and the progress made were reinforced in the political, social, economic and cultural spheres of the country, and like a living organism the country became capable of surviving on its own.

The post-reform political life of Mongolia was characterised by the existence and continuation of the State and government, based on the principles of division of state powers – the legislative, executive and the judiciary. Today, Mongolia is able to guarantee on its own the country's political stability, free from any outside pressure or influence, and with its legal and organisational capacity it is capable of addressing contradictions and challenges within its own internal harmony and unity. And competition, rivalry and consensus grown out of pluralism have become a reality. The MPRP attained a parliamentary majority in 1992 and 2000, while the Democratic Union Coalition of the MNDP and the MSDP were elected the majority in the Parliament in 1996; and in 2004, the MPRP and the Motherland-Democratic Coalition became the parliamentary majority and formed a coalition government. After this, the MPRP and other political parties also formed the Government of National Unity. Although the MPRP won the majority of votes in the 2008 parliamentary elections, it chose to form a coalition government together with the Democratic Party (DP). None of the major parties received the majority of votes in the 2012 elections, and the DP, which had won the highest number of votes, formed a coalition government with the newly formed Mongolian People's Revolution Party during the first two years of its term of office, and in the remaining two years of its term of office, the DP formed a coalition government with the Mongolian People's Party (*which was formerly MPRP and had changed its name to its original one at its Twenty Fourth Congress in 2021. Tr.*). But in the 2016 and 2020 parliamentary elections, the government was formed unilaterally by the Mongolian People's Party (MPP), which secured a landslide victory in both the elections.

Multi-form ownership was legally recognised in Mongolia starting in the 1990s, and the country transitioned to free market relations with no turning back, and privatisation was carried out consistently. In the past period, many important measures were taken designed at laying the legal foundations of free market relations, conducting a single budget, a financial, monetary and credit policy, and freeing both the exchange rate and prices, which yielded and continues to yield tangible results for the good of the country and the people as a whole.

Today, Mongolia is carrying out state administrative and economic structural reforms, creating rational economic structures with a socio-ecological and export orientation. The country is now self-sufficient in energy and fuel, and key food items. It is promoting the rapid development of export-oriented production capacities and services sectors. The country has started developing large mineral deposits. Today, it has an economy with a relatively independent structure, and is coping with its strategic tasks of occupying its rightful place in regional development.

2 The Substance and Significance of the New Constitution

The country's most immediate task in the context of recognising the new choice of development of the country, developing the necessary legal foundations and ensuring the invariable march towards further development, was to adopt the country's foundational law, the Constitution, and to enforce it.

The State *Baga Khural* set up a Commission to Draft the new Constitution of the country and appointed the President of the MPR, P. Ochirbat, to spearhead the Commission. The Commission, after reviewing and studying the proposals and suggestions put forth by scholars and professionals, independent versions of the Constitution, as well as the examples of Democratic constitutions of different countries, made a draft of the Constitution, which was submitted for consideration to the State *Baga Khural*.

The State *Baga Khural* decided to present the draft Constitution for nation-wide discussion. More than 7,000 institutions and organisations, and work collectives discussed the draft of the new fundamental law involving more than 900,000 people and cumulatively more than 200,000 proposals and suggestions were made. The State *Baga Khural* itself twice reviewed the draft Constitution, after which it was submitted for consideration to the People's Great *Khural*.

The draft of the new Constitution was discussed for 76 days by the Second Session of the Twelfth Election of the People's Great *Khural* of the MPR, which was opened on 11 November 1991, and it was adopted at 11.35 hours on 13 January 1992. The new Constitution of Mongolia came into force effective as of 12 February 1992. It had 6 chapters and 70 articles besides the Preamble. It had a schedule on the transition and enactment of the Constitution of Mongolia from the Constitution of the Mongolian People's Republic.

2.1 *The Objective of the New Constitution*

The new Constitution promulgated as its noble goal to strengthen the country's independence and sovereignty, cherish human rights and freedoms, justice and national unity, inherit the traditions of national Statehood, history and culture, respect the accomplishments of human civilisation, and aspire toward the supreme objective of developing a humane, civil, democratic society in the country. The country's name was declared Mongolia by removing the word people.

Chapter One of the new Constitution legitimatised the independence of the country and proclaimed that Mongolia is an independent and sovereign Republic. It stated that the supreme principles of the activities of the State shall be to ensure democracy, justice, freedom, equality, national unity and respect of law. Structurally, according to the Constitution, Mongolia is a unitary State and the territory of the country shall be divided into administrative units only. It promulgated that State power shall be vested in the people of Mongolia. The people shall exercise State power through their direct participation in State affairs, as well as, through the representative bodies of State power elected by them. The chapter stated that the territorial integrity and frontiers of Mongolia shall be inviolable and the frontiers of the country shall be safeguarded by law. The chapter provided that the country shall have an economy based on different forms of property, which takes into account universal trends of world economic development and national specifics, it recognises the equality and inviolability of private and all other forms of property, protection of intellectual property, and defined that the State shall respect religion and religion shall honour the State. Mongolia is committed to adherence to universally recognised norms and principles of international law. The Constitution outlines the national defence and national security policies, and also defines the State symbols of the independence and sovereignty of Mongolia. Article 12 of the Constitution proclaims that:

1 The symbols of the independence and sovereignty of Mongolia are the State Emblem, Banner, Flag, Seal and the Anthem;

2 The State Emblem, Banner, Flag and the Anthem shall express the historical tradition, aspiration, unity, justice and the spirit of the people of Mongolia, and in the succeeding article describes in detail the State emblem, banner, flag and the seal.

One very important aspect of the new Constitution is the fact that it outlined and codified the mechanisms for guaranteeing human rights and freedoms within the internationally-recognised norms and principles such as those in the Universal Declaration of Human Rights (1948) and the International Covenant on Economic, Social and Cultural Rights (1966).

The Constitution, in accordance with the principle of separation of powers, divided the state power into legislative, executive and the judiciary. The issue of the administrative and territorial units of Mongolia and their management were all legally defined and included in the Constitution. It states that "The territory of Mongolia shall be administratively divided into *Aimags* and the capital city; *Aimags* shall be subdivided into *Soums*; *Soums* into *Baghs*; and the capital city shall be sub-divided into districts and districts into *Khoroos*."

The formulation that the governance of the administrative and territorial units of Mongolia shall be organised on the basis of a combination of the principles of both self-government and central government was a very important democratic gain of the Constitution.

Another important feature of the new fundamental law was the introduction of the constitutional control mechanism. A so-called Constitutional *Tsets* (Court) was instituted, which would be the competent organ with powers to exercise supreme supervision over the enforcement of the Constitution, to decide on any breaches of its provision and adjudicate any constitutional disputes, and it was defined as the guarantor for strict observance of the Constitution.

With the promulgation of the new Constitution, the Mongolian people in principle did away with the old system, thus determining the direction, basis and principles for the further growth and progress of the Mongolian State and social structures on the principles of Democracy. The Constitution also laid the foundations of the political and legal principles and norms to be adhered to.

The new Constitution of Mongolia, as defined by contemporary liberals, became an exceptionally striking phenomenon in the State and legal mindset of the Mongolians by consolidating the rights and freedoms of the citizens of the country as the new fundamental law. Compared to previous Constitutions, which were either declarations or programmes, it truly became the basic law or a treaty of social consensus of the people of

Mongolia, and the fountain source of a truly social, democratic, political system."[1] The new democratic Constitution achieved the following:

- The independence of the country;
- Freedom for the people;
- Equality for the population;
- Market economy in the country;
- Democratic regime in the State and state affairs;
- Self-governance in the local areas;
- Brought judiciary control and stability to the Constitution; and,
- Fully restored the international prestige of Mongolia.[2]

The key goal of the Constitution was to consolidate and strengthen Mongolia's independence, sovereignty, security and territorial integrity, develop the nation, and create favourable conditions for the rights, freedoms and happy life of the citizens.

There arose the need to amend Article 22.2 as there was an instance when a Caretaker Government had to function for 6 months, because after the elections the State Great *Khural* was unable to, for an extended period, form a new Government and there was no accountability mechanism in such a circumstance. Further on, according to Article 26.2, Sessions of the State Great *Khural* and sittings of its Standing Committees were to be considered valid with the presence of a majority of its members; however, parties and coalitions with even 50 seats in the State Great *Khural* had difficulty ensuring the necessary quorum, which led to the disruption of the Sessions of the State Great *Khural*.

In view of such practical challenges changes and amendments were made twice in Article 6.7 of the Constitution in 1999 and 2000, which helped overcome the above-mentioned challenges.

The constitutional changes and amendments that were made in 1999 and 2000, as mentioned earlier, helped address some of the challenges that were encountered by the Mongol State and brought about certain progress in the strengthening of parliamentarianism, but these changes and amendments came under strong public criticism and they were dubbed "The seven crippling amendments," which is related to the following provisions:

1 Regular sessions of the State Great *Khural*, as stipulated in Article 27.2, which were to continue for not less than 75 working days, were

---

1 D. Lündeejantsan, *Common Principle and Models of World Constitutions*, Report, 2019.

2 B. Chimid, *Some Pressing Issues of Legal Development of the Constitution of Mongolia*, Report, June 2011.

reduced to 50 working days. This amendment, in some sense, contributed to impairing the permanent nature of Mongolia's Parliament, the State Great *Khural*.

2 Under Article 29.1, no ceiling was set on the number of members of the State Great *Khural* who could concurrently become a member of the Government (Cabinet Minister). As a result, almost all cabinet members were members of the Parliament, which led to the breaching of the balance between the legislative and the executive powers, and the disruption of the control mechanism.

3 Article 27.6 was amended according to which the quorum of the parliamentary session was determined at 50+1 and issues considered at the session were considered valid with a majority of votes, and this formulation drew criticism that laws were being passed with a minimum of votes by only 26.3 per cent of the State Great *Khural* members present.

4 The previous formulation in Article 27.7 was amended as "Decisions on appointment of the Prime Minister and members of the Government, as well as other issues, unless otherwise provided by law, shall be decided by open vote." This amendment was criticised because a mechanism had been introduced through which a political party could put pressure on its members in the Parliament.

These changes and amendments made indistinct the delineation and differences between the legislative, executive and judicial powers, and the system of accountability, as specifically defined by the Constitution, was being eroded. This kind of criticism prevailed and continued from one parliamentary term to another between 2000 and 2016.

2.2 *Changes and Amendments to the Constitution of Mongolia*

The State Great *Khural*, which was formed as a result of the Seventh election to the Parliament, submitted proposals for making changes and amending the Constitution, which were considered and discussed 36 times over the course of five months thereafter at the Regular Sessions and meetings of the Standing Committee, on which the members of Parliament spent a total of 106 hours. Members of the State Great *Khural* conducted discussions around the draft changes and amendments in 21 *aimags* and nine districts of Ulaanbaatar, in the course of which 306 proposals were received from the people around the country.

Besides this, a number of discussions were organised involving State and non-governmental organisations, political parties, scholars and researchers, who tabled more than 600 suggestions. These suggestions were carefully studied one by one and the changes and amendments to the Constitution were approved by the State Great *Khural* on 14 November 2019.

The following changes and amendments were made to the Constitution:

1 The seven changes that were made to the Constitution in 2000 were all revised. Changes were made only to 6 of the 7 amendments, including the one concerning the election of deputy speakers from each parliamentary party and coalition;

2 The provision that natural resources in Mongolia shall belong exclusively to the people and shall be under state protection was defined more precisely, specifying that the exploitation and use of subsoil resources shall cater to the common interests of the citizens, and such resources shall be distributed equally and fairly to the people;

3 The changes ensured the continuity and stability in state development policy and planning irrespective of which political party comes to power. Although the State Great *Khural* had the right to change the revenue and expenditure structure in the state budget during its discussion and approval, the amendment specified that the State Great *Khural* did not have the right to increase the budget spending and the size of the deficit as submitted by the Government;

4 Limitations were set on the rights of the President, members of the State Great *Khural* and the Government to initiate and draft bills, and a ban was put on holding any national referendum that attempts to reverse the independence and territorial integrity of the country;

5 The changes and amendments to the Constitution called for the guaranteeing of the stability of the State Great *Khural* election law, called on political parties to present and implement national level policies, specified that a political party could be established jointly by people who constitute not less than one per cent of all the eligible voters of the country, and called for transparency in all financial and related transaction matters;

6 The number of working days of parliamentary regular sessions was increased to not less than 75 working days. The amendments stipulated the formation of a Provisional Control Committee involving the representation of the minority in the State Great *Khural* to consider concrete issues concerning public interests. It was decided that regular sessions and the meeting of the Standing Committee shall be considered valid if the majority of the members are present and that issues on the table shall be decided upon by a majority of votes of all the members of the State Great *Khural*. However, the amendment

specified that a law of Mongolia shall be adopted by a majority of votes or by not less than 38 members of the Parliament;

7 A ceiling of 4 was set on the maximum number of State Great *Khural* members serving simultaneously as a cabinet member, and the Prime Minister was given the authority to appoint, dismiss and seek the resignation of the cabinet members by himself/herself;

8 The age limit for a Presidential candidate was increased to 50 years, and the candidate would serve only one six-year term;

9 With the objective of guaranteeing independence and impartiality of the judges, and increasing their responsibility, the procedure for the formation of the General Council of Courts, the Judicial Disciplinary Committee, was established and these changes made it possible to introduce the principle of judges working according to a round robin policy system;

10 It was decided that the legal basis of self-governance and the organisational set-up of towns with national and local status within an administrative and territorial unit, as well as that of the villages shall be established through legislation. The State Great *Khural* was given the right to take decisions on the matter of transferring some functions of administrative and territorial units and their management to towns and villages, if motioned by the Government.

Almost 28.5 per cent of the Constitution was amended, that is, 19 paragraphs and 36 provisions of 90 articles were either changed or amended. The Constitutional changes and amendments were enforced throughout the country effective as of 12 noon of 25 May 2020.

3 The Substance and Signifcance of the New Constitution

The country's most immediate task in the context of recognising the new choice of development of the country, developing the necessary legal foundations and ensuring the invariable march towards further development was to adopt the country's foundational law, the Constitution, and to enforce it.

The State *Baga Khural* set up a Commission to draft the new Constitution of the country and appointed the President of the MPR, P. Ochirbat, to spearhead the Commission. The Commission, after reviewing and studying the proposals and suggestions put forth by scholars and professionals, independent versions of the Constitution, as well as the examples of democratic constitutions of different countries, made a draft of the Constitution, which was submitted for consideration to the State *Baga Khural*.

The State *Baga Khural* decided to present the draft Constitution for nation-wide discussion. More than 7,000 institutions and organisations, and work collectives discussed the draft of the new fundamental law involving more than 900,000 people, and cumulatively more than 200,000 proposals and suggestions were made. The State *Baga Khural* itself twice reviewed the draft Constitution, after which it was submitted for consideration to the State Great *Khural*.

The draft of the new Constitution was discussed for 76 days by the Second Session of the Twelfth Election of the Great People's *Khural* of the MPR, which was opened on 11 November 1991, and it was adopted at 11.35 hours on 13 January 1992. The new Constitution of Mongolia came into force effective as of 12 February 1992. It had 6 chapters and 70 articles besides the Preamble. It had a schedule on the transition and enactment of the Constitution of Mongolia from the Constitution of the Mongolian People's Republic.

3.1 *The Objective of the New Constitution*

The new Constitution promulgated as its noble goal to strengthen the country's independence and sovereignty, cherish human rights and freedoms, justice and national unity, inherit the traditions of national Statehood, history and culture, respect the accomplishments of human civilisation, and aspire toward the supreme objective of developing a humane, civil, democratic society in the country. The country's name was declared Mongolia by removing the word people.

Chapter One of the new Constitution legitimatised the independence of the country and proclaimed that Mongolia is an independent and sovereign Republic. It stated that the supreme principles of the activities of the State shall be to ensure democracy, justice, freedom, equality, national unity and respect of law. Structurally, according to the Constitution, Mongolia is a unitary State and the territory of the country shall be divided into administrative units only. It promulgated that state power shall be vested in the people of Mongolia. The people shall exercise state power through their direct participation in state affairs, as well as, through the representative bodies of state power elected by them. This chapter stated that the territorial integrity and frontiers of Mongolia shall be inviolable and the frontiers of the country shall be safeguarded by law. The chapter defined that the country shall have an economy based on different forms of property which takes into account universal trends of world economic development and national specifics, it recognises the equality and inviolability of private and all other forms of property, protection of intellectual property and defines that the State shall respect religion and religion shall honour the State. Mongolia committed its adherence to universally recognised norms and principles of international law. The Constitution outlines the national defence and national security policies, and also defines the state symbols of the independence and sovereignty of Mongolia. Article 12 of the Constitution proclaims that:

3 The symbols of the independence and sovereignty of Mongolia are the State Emblem, Banner, Flag, Seal and the Anthem;

4 The State Emblem, Banner, Flag and the Anthem shall express the historical tradition, aspiration, unity, justice and the spirit of the people of Mongolia, and in the succeeding article describes in detail the state emblem, banner, flag and the seal.

One very important aspect of the new Constitution is the fact that it basically outlined and codified the mechanisms for guaranteeing human rights and freedoms within the internationally-recognised norms and principles as in the Universal Declaration of Human Rights (1948) and the International Covenant on Economic, Social and Cultural Rights (1966).

The Constitution, in accordance with the principle of separation of powers, divided the state power into legislative, executive and the judiciary. The issue of administrative and territorial units of Mongolia and their management were legally defined and included in the Constitution. It states that "The territory of Mongolia shall be administratively divided into *Aimags* and the capital city; *Aimags* shall be subdivided into *Soums*; *Soums* into *Baghs*; and the capital city shall be sub-divided into districts and districts into *Khoroos*."

The formulation that the governance of administrative and territorial units of Mongolia shall be organised on the basis of combination of the principles of both self-government and central government was a very important democratic gain of the Constitution.

Another important feature of the new fundamental law was the introduction of the constitutional control mechanism. A so-called Constitutional *Tsets* (Court) was instituted, which would be the competent organ with powers to exercise supreme supervision over the enforcement of the Constitution, to make a conclusion on the breach of its provisions, and to decide constitutional disputes, and it was defined as the guarantor for strict observance of the Constitution.

With the promulgation of the new Constitution, the Mongolian people in principle did away with the old system, thus determining the direction, basis and principles for the further growth and progress of the Mongolian state and social structures on the principles of democracy. It also laid the foundations of political and legal principles and norms to be adhered to.

The new Constitution of Mongolia, as defined by contemporary liberals, became an exceptionally striking phenomenon in the state and legal mindset of the Mongolians by consolidating the rights and freedoms of the citizens of the country as the new fundamental law, and as compared to previous Constitutions, which were either declarations or programmes, truly became the basic law or a treaty of social consensus of the people of Mongolia, and the fountain source of a truly social democratic political system."[3] The new democratic Constitution achieved the following:

- The independence of the country;
- Freedom for the people;
- Equality for the population;
- Market economy in the country;
- Democratic regime in the state and state affairs;
- Self-governance in the local areas;
- Brought judiciary control and stability to the Constitution; and,
- Fully restored the international prestige of Mongolia.[4]

The key goal of the Constitution was to consolidate and strengthen Mongolia's independence, sovereignty, security and territorial integrity, develop the nation, and create favourable conditions for the rights, freedoms and happy life of the citizens.

There arose the need to amend Article 22.2 as there was an instance when a Caretaker Government had to function for 6 months, because after the elections the State Great *Khural* was unable to, for an extended period, form a new Government and there was no accountability mechanism in such a circumstance. Further on, according to Article 26.2 Sessions of the State Great *Khural* and sittings of its Standing Committees was to be considered valid with the presence of a majority of its members, however, parties and coalitions with even 50 seats in the State Great *Khural* had difficulty ensuring the necessary quorum, which led to the disruption of the Sessions of the State Great *Khural*.

In view of such practical challenges, changes and amendments were made twice in Article 6.7 of the Constitution in 1999 and 2000, which helped overcome the aforementioned challenges.

The constitutional changes and amendments that were made in 1999 and 2000, as mentioned earlier, helped address some of the challenges that were encountered by the Mongol State and brought about certain

3 D. Lündeejantsan, *Common Principle and Models of World Constitutions*, Report, 2019.

4 B. Chimid, *Some Pressing Issues of Legal Development of the Constitution of Mongolia*, Report, June 2011.

progress in the strengthening of parliamentarianism, but these changes and amendments came under strong public criticism and they were dubbed "The seven crippling amendments," which is related to the following provisions:

5 Regular sessions of the State Great *Khural,* as stipulated in Article 27.2, which were to continue for not less than 75 working days was reduced to 50 working days. This amendment, in some sense, contributed to impairing the permanent nature of Mongolia's parliament – the State Great *Khural.*

6 Under Article 29.1, no ceiling was set on the number of members of the State Great *Khural* who could concurrently become a member of the Government (Cabinet minister). As a result, almost the entire cabinet members were members of the Parliament, which led to the breaching of the balance between the legislative and the executive powers and the disruption of the control mechanism.

7 Article 27.6 was amended according to which the quorum of the parliamentary session was determined at 50+1 and issues considered at the session were considered valid with a majority of votes, and this formulation drew criticism that laws were being passed with a minimum of votes by only 26.3 per cent of the State Great *Khural* members present.

8 The previous formulation in Article 27.7 was amended as "Decisions on appointment of the Prime Minister and members of the Government, as well as other issues, unless otherwise provided by law, shall be decided by open vote." This amendment was criticised that a mechanism had been introduced through which a political party could put pressure on its members in the Parliament.

These changes and amendments made indistinct the delineation and different between the legislative, executive and judicial powers, and the system of accountability, as specifically defined by the Constitution, was being eroded. This kind of criticism prevailed and continued from one parliamentary term to another between 2000 and 2016.

3.2 *Changes and Amendments to the Constitution of Mongolia*

The State Great *Khural,* which was formed as a result of the Seventh election to the Parliament, submitted proposals for making changes and amending the Constitution, which were considered and discussed 36 times over a course of five months thereafter at the Regular Sessions and meetings of the Standing Committee, on which the members of Parliament spent a total of 106 hours. Members of the State Great *Khural* conducted discussions around the draft changes and amendments in 21 *aimags* and nine districts of Ulaanbaatar, in the course of which 306 proposals were received from the people around the country.

Besides this, a number of discussions were organised involving State and non-governmental organisations, political parties, scholars and researchers, who tabled more than 600 suggestions. These suggestions were carefully studied one by one and the changes and amendments to the Constitution were approved by the State Great *Khural* on 14 November 2019.

The following changes and amendments were made to the Constitution:

11 The seven changes that were made to the Constitution in 2000 were all revised. Changes were made only to 6 of the 7 amendments, including the one concerning the election of deputy speakers from each parliamentary party and coalition;

12 The provision that natural resources in Mongolia shall belong exclusively to the people and shall be under State protection was defined more precisely, specifying that the exploitation and use of subsoil resources shall cater to the common interests of the citizens, and such resources shall be distributed equally and fairly to the people;

13 The changes ensured the continuity and stability in state development policy and planning irrespective of which political party comes to power. Although the State Great *Khural* had the right to change the revenue and expenditure structure in the State budget during its discussion and approval, the amendment specified that the State Great *Khural* did not have the right to increase the budget spending and the size of deficit as submitted by the Government;

14 Limitations were set to the right of the President, members of the State Great *Khural* and the Government to initiate and draft bills, and a ban was put on holding any national referendum that attempts to reverse the independence and territorial integrity of the country;

15 The changes and amendments to the Constitution called for the guaranteeing of the stability of the State Great *Khural* election law, called on political parties to present and implement national level policies, specified that a political party could be established jointly by people who constitute not less than one per cent of all the eligible voters of the country, and called for transparency in all financial and related transaction matters;

16 The number of working days of parliamentary regular sessions was increased to not less than 75 working days. The amendments stipulated the formation of a Provisional Control Committee involving the representation of the minority in the State Great *Khural* to con-

sider concrete issues concerning public interests. It was decided that a regular sessions and the meeting of the Standing Committee shall be considered valid if the majority of the members are present and that issues on the table shall be decided upon by a majority of votes of the entire members of the State Great *Khural*. However, the amendment specified that a law of Mongolia shall be adopted by a majority of votes or by not less than 38 members of the Parliament;

17 A ceiling of 4 was set on the maximum number of State Great *Khural* members serving simultaneously as a Cabinet member, and the Prime Minister was given the authority to appoint, dismiss and seek the resignation of the Cabinet members by himself/herself;

18 The age limit for a Presidential candidate was increased to 50 years, and the would serve only one six-year term;

19 With the objective of guaranteeing independence and impartiality of the judges, and increasing their responsibility, the procedure for the formation of the General Council of Courts, the Judicial Disciplinary Committee was established and these changes made it possible to introduce the principle of judges working in a round-robin policy work;

20 It was decided that the legal basis of self-governance and organisational set-up of towns with national and local status within an administrative and territorial unit, as well as that of the villages shall be established through legislation. The State Great *Khural* was given the right to take decisions on the matter of transferring some functions of administrative and territorial units and their management to towns and villages, if motioned by the Government.

Almost 28.5 per cent of the Constitution was amended, that is, 19 paragraphs and 36 provisions of 90 articles were either changed or amended. The constitutional changes and amendments were enforced throughout the country effective as of 12 noon of 25 May 2020.

4 The State System

In keeping with the new Constitution's relevant laws, the legislative, the executive and the judiciary powers of the country were adopted and accordingly, their new structures were put in place. Local governments were newly organised with the legalisation of the legal status of the capital, rural and urban settlements, towns and villages. Separation of state powers was effected in the country, which made it impossible for the establishment of an autocracy and the control of state powers by a group of people, for which relevant state laws were put in place. The constitutional provisions that a person cannot be elected as President more than once, and the restriction that the President cannot hold another office, paid or unpaid, outside of the terms of office specified in the Constitution in fact closed the doors for an individual to hold government offices at the same time, thus potentially restricting the possibility that one individual concentrate enormous powers individually.

Social life would definitely necessitate one of the legislative, executive and judicial powers to take a leadership role arising from the vital rights and interests of the people. In the present conditions, when the country is committed to being a law-governed State, the Parliament is that institution that can guarantee the balance of power and stability of the State. Today, under the principle of separation of powers, there is a clear distinction of functions between the three organs of the State and also checks and balances between the three organs. The law has regulated any overlaps in functions, personnel and powers between the three, and also the complementary nature of the three branches of power. Mongolia opted for the softer version of "separation of powers" according to which the Government or the executive is slightly more or directly dependent on the legislative. Depending on the strict or the liberal version, according to State and legal theory, there are two forms of democratic government system: Presidential and Parliamentary, and in this sense, it can be said that in Mongolia the State system is a Parliamentary Republic with a Constitutional Head of State.[5]

Let us now look at the current State structure of Mongolia according to its State power and authority.

4.1 *The Legislative*

Article 20 of the Constitution states that "The State Great *Khural* of Mongolia shall be the highest organ of State power, and the legislative power shall be vested exclusively in the State Great *Khural*." To be precise, the State Great *Khural* is the quintessence of the highest authority of the country, an institution that sets the foundations of the state's domestic and foreign policies, and is the highest supervisory organ. The adoption and amendment of the Constitution and other laws and legislations of Mongolia lie within the framework of its prerogative rights. This put in proper arrangement the irregularities that existed when legislative powers were under the jurisdiction of different organs at the same time. Looking at the

5 D. Lündeejantsan, Ch. Enkhbaatar, *The Law of the Constitution of Mongolia*, Ulaanbaatar, 1996, p. 98.

concepts behind the Constitution and the Law of the State Great *Khural* we can name the following basic functions of the State Great *Khural*.

a It is the principal subject to exercise legislative power. To be precise, it can initiate and draft laws, (a member of the State Great *Khural* has the right to initiate a law), review draft bills submitted by competent organisations and officials, take the final call whether to approve the bill or not, supervise the enforcement of adopted laws and other decisions.

b While exercising its legislative power, the State Great *Khural* shall define the legal foundations of the organisational set-up and operational activities of the executive and the judiciary powers.

c Strictly abide by the State laws and respect the rights and interests of the people.

The functions of the State Great *Khural* are based on the principles of protecting Mongolia's independence and sovereignty, build and strengthen a rule of the law State, ensure the wishes and desires, interests and unity of the people of Mongolia, guarantee democracy, justice, human rights and freedoms.

The Law of the State Great *Khural* of Mongolia and the Law on the Procedure of the Parliamentary Sessions of the State Great *Khural* of Mongolia are the central legal instruments of the Mongolian parliament's organisational set-up and operational activities. The initial Law of the Legal Status of Members of the State Great *Khural* was enacted, which was merged with the new revised version of the Law of the State Great *Khural*, and was adopted in 2006. The goal of the Law of the State Great *Khural* is to create the guarantee framework of the powers of the State Great *Khural*, its organisational set-up, the composition, the powers and immunity of the members of the State Great *Khural*, and regulate other relations conneted with the functions and activities of the Mongolian Parliament.

The Law of the State Great *Khural* of Mongolia was adopted in 1992 and since then, during these many years, it was amended only once. The new revised edited version of the Law of the State Great *Khural* of Mongolia was adopted on 6 February 1997, and the issues of the procedure of the parliamentary sessions and the legal status of the Parliament members were regulated through separate laws.

The State Great *Khural* exercised exclusive prerogative rights as defined in Article 25 of the Constitution and also other rights. With the objective of streamlining the legislative functions of the State Great *Khural* (SGKh), a Law on Procedures for the drafting of bills, and other decisions of the SGKh and submitting them for consideration was enacted in 2001. This law was revised in 2015 and named the "Law on Laws and Legislations."

The SGKh is reviewing and taking decisions on draft bills submitted by subjects empowered to draft bills, such as the President, members of the State Great *Khural* and the Government, and all matters related to the national economy and the state structure.

As defined in the Constitution, the State Great *Khural* was vested with the following, among others, exclusive prerogatives to enact laws, and make amendments or changes to them; consider the President as elected, and enact the law recognising his/her powers; determine the financial and credit, official taxation and monetary policies of the State, and the main directives for national economic and social development; approve the Government Programme of Action, the state budget, and their performance reports; determine the structure, composition and the powers of the National Security Council of Mongolia; determine the legal basis of the system, organisational structure and activities of the local self-governing and administrative organs; institute titles of honour, orders, medals and highest military ranks of the State, determine the table of ranks for some special sector officials of the public service; and make decisions on amnesty.

One of the exclusive prerogatives of the State Great *Khural* is to determine the basis of the domestic and foreign policies of the State. In this respect, the SGKh has adopted 51 policy-related documents, such as the National Security Concept of Mongolia, National Development Concept of Mongolia, the Foreign Policy Concept of Mongolia, Military Doctrine of Mongolia, Population Policy etc.

The SGKh is mandated to monitor the implementation of the adopted laws and decisions, and review the performance reports and information of the organisation formed by and accountable to the SGKh. These organisations include the Government, the Central Bank, Financial Regulatory Committee, State Audit, National Statistics Committee, Anti-Corruption Agency, and the Civil Service Council etc.

The State Great *Khural* also exercised the following prerogative rights within the framework of the state structure. Determine and announce the date of elections for the Presidency and to the State Great *Khural* or its members; appoint, replace or remove the Prime Minister, members of the Government (Cabinet Ministers) and the composition of other organs directly responsible and accountable for their work to the State Great *Khural* as prescribed by law, establish the state borders, approve or change the administrative and territorial division of Mongolia as submitted by the Government (Cabinet); ratify or annul international instruments to which Mongolia is a Party, and establish and sever diplomatic relations with foreign states; hold national referendums; and declare a state of war, state of emergency, and a state of war in the entire or some parts of the country in special circumstances.

The basic organisational form of the State Great *Khural* is its sessions. As prescribed in Article 27 of the Constitution, the GPKh holds its regular sessions once every half year for not less than seventy-five working days. Also, the State Great *Khural* carries out its term of office through its Standing Committees, Sub-Committees, party parliamentary groups, and through other organisational forms.

The Standing Committees are responsible for drafting the agenda of the parliamentary sessions, carrying out preliminary discussions of the agenda items, drawing conclusions and within their competency, they have a common duty and function of monitoring the State Great *Khural*. Today, the State Great *Khural* has the following Standing Committees:

1 Security and Foreign Policy Standing Committee;
2 Natural Environment, Food and Agriculture Standing Committee;
3 Social Policy Standing Committee;
4 Education, Culture, Science and Sports Standing Committee;
5 State Structure Standing Committee;
6 Budget Standing Committee;
7 Law Standing Committee;
8 Economy Standing Committee;
9 Ethics and Disciplinary Standing Committee;
10 Innovation and e-Policy Standing Committee;
11 Industrialisation Standing Committee.

The State Great *Khural* sets up party (coalition) groups in the Parliament and the party (coalition) must have at least 8 seats in the SGKh. The party (coalition) group includes only those State Great *Khural* members who were nominated by their party (coalition) and who have been elected to the Parliament. Political parties that have run in the parliamentary elections by forming a coalition can form one parliamentary group provided the coalition has won a minimum of eight seats in the SGKh. Parliamentary members, representing different parties and who have secured not less than 10 seats in the Parliament cannot join to form a parliamentary group. The Law on the State Great *Khural* prescribes that these Parliament members can join any one party or coalition group.

Regarding the composition of the State Great *Khural,* as defined in Articles 21.1, 21.2 and 21.3 of the Constitution, it has one chamber and is composed of 76 members who have been elected on the basis of universal, free and direct suffrage by secret ballot by eligible voter citizens. Today, the State Great *Khural* has a chairperson (Speaker), and deputy chairpersons (Vice-Speakers) representing parties that have groups in the Parliament.

The Speaker of the State Great Khural is responsible for coordinating and regulating the entire work related to the terms of office of the Parliament.

In the period since the enforcement of the new Constitution 8 parliamentary elections were held and during the period between 1992 and 1996 the country had the first standing Parliament, the State Great *Khural.*

Natsagiin Bagabandi, who served as the Speaker of the Great People's *Khural* of Mongolia from 1992 to 1996, addressing the last meeting of the Fall Session in 1996, that is, the concluding Session of the First Election of the Great People's *Khural* said: "The term of office of the present State Great *Khural,* which became the first standing parliament elected in accordance with the new Constitution, is concluding. Today, the people of Mongolia and in the years ahead, history would judge our performance ... Human deeds and actions that appear tall from atop a high mountain can be seen and felt much better than future deeds and actions. I am firmly convinced that the outcome of the sweat that you have dropped and the indefatigable intellect that you have devoted for the motherland and the people will not go to waste for they will be immortalised forever in the pages of the annals of development of the homeland and humankind, and they shall hold a respectful place in the history of the nation."

The Speaker of the Great *Khural* elected in the second Parliament election was Radnaasümbereliin Gonchigdorj, followed by Lhamsürengiin Enebish and later Sanjbegziin Tömör-Ochir as the Third Speakers, in the fourth election, Nambaryn Enkhbayar, Tsendiin Nyamdorj and Danzangiin Lündeejantsan in this order served as the Fourth Parliament Speakers, followed by Damdiniin Demberal as the Fifth Speaker, and then Zandaakhüügiin Enkhbold served as the Parliament Speaker after the Sixth Parliamentary elections, followed by Miyegombyn Enkhbold and later Gombojavyn Zandanshatar became the Great *Khural* Speakers after the Seventh Parliamentary elections, and in the Eighth election Gombojavyn Zandanshatar was re-elected at the Speaker of the State Great *Khural* of Mongolia.

A member of the State Great *Khural* is an envoy of the people elected to the highest organ of state power, who exercises his/her power and authority by respecting and upholding the interests of all the citizens and of the State. Any citizen of Mongolia, who has reached the age of 25, can stand for election to the State Great *Khural* by all eligible voter citizens through universal, free, and direct suffrage by secret ballot.

A member of the State Great *Khural* takes the oath of office before the State Coat of Arms by swearing "I do swear, as a member of the State Great *Khural* and an envoy of the people, to faithfully execute the office of Member of the State Great *Khural* of Mongolia and will to the best of my ability uphold the interests of all citizens and the State, respect the statehood, historical and cultural traditions, uphold and abide by the Constitution of Mongolia, and remain free of corruption and conflict of interests. Should I go back on my oath I shall be accountable before the law." A total of 383 Mongolian citizens have been elected and served as members of the GPKh during the Eight State Great *Khurals* since the adoption of the new Constitution of Mongolia.

4.2 *The President of Mongolia*

The President is the Head of State of Mongolia. As indicated in Article 30.1 of the Constitution, the President or the Head of State is the embodiment of the unity of the Mongolian people. As the Head of State, the President, proceeding from the objective of guaranteeing the independence and sovereignty of Mongolia, within the framework of the prerogatives specified in the Constitution and other laws, shall facilitate the appropriate collaboration between the legislative, executive and judiciary of the country. The President, in the capacity as the embodiment of the unity of Mongolian people respects and upholds national unity and harmony, and when necessary, facilitates the social groups, sections and political forces to reach consensus and understanding.

Presidential elections have been held in accordance with the Constitution and the Law on Presidential Election. An indigenous citizen of Mongolia, who has attained the age of forty five years and has permanently resided in his/her motherland for at least five years, was elected as the President for a term of four years. The age limit and the term of office were revised and changed to 50 years of age and only one term of 6 years respectively with the Constitutional amendments made in 2019. Presidential elections will be organise before the end of the President's term of office, and only parliamentary parties, individually or collectively will nominate one single Presidential candidate each.

At the primary stage of the elections, all citizens eligible to vote shall participate in electing the President and the State Great *Khural* shall consider the candidate who has obtained a majority of all votes cast in the first round of votes as the elected President, and shall promulgate the law recognising his/her powers. Within 30 days after the law is passed recognizing President elect's power, he/she will take oath of office to the State Great *Khural*. Since the adoption of the new Constitution, 7 Presidential elections have been held in the country. In the 1993 election, Punsalmaagiin Ochirbat was elected the President, in 1997 Natsagaiin Bagabandi was elected President, who re-ran for the post in the 2001 election, and

N. Bagabandi was re-elected in 2001 to serve a second term of the Head of State. In the 2005 Presidential election Nambaryn Enkhbayar was elected and in the next election in 2009 Tsakhiagiin Elbegdorj was elected and in 2013 he was re-elected to serve his second four-year-term as the President. Khaltmaagiin Battulga won convincingly in the Presidential election held in 2017 to be elected as the Head of State of Mongolia.

Basing on the Constitutional provision on this aspect of the powers of the President, these prerogative were consolidated by the Law on President and other laws and legislations.

Constitutional law researchers have divided the powers of the Mongolian President into the following four groups:

4.3 *Presidential Powers Related to State Structure and Management of the Country*

Call and announce the First Session of the Great People's *Khural* or table a motion on calling an emergency session of the State Great *Khural* to consider pressing national-level issues; Submit to the State Great *Khural* proposal to appoint as Prime Minister, a person who has been nominated by a party or coalition that have secured a majority of seats in the Parliament, and if neither party nor coalition have obtained a majority, then a person who has been nominated by a party or coalition with the largest number of seats, in consensus with other parties or coalitions; Submit to the Parliament proposal on dissolving the Government, and draft a relevant legislation; Veto, partially or wholly, laws and other decisions adopted by the State Great *Khural*; Appoint judges of all levels and hold the State Seal as defined in the law, and many other prerogative rights.

A point that needs to be particularly emphasised is the formulation of the amendments to the Constitution that were made in 2000 with due consideration of the fact that a Prime Ministerial candidate, who was nominated by the Democratic Union Coalition, who were in power in 1996–2000, was rejected several times by the President. This refers to Article 33.2.2 of the Constitution, which specified that if a party or a coalition with the largest number of seats is unable to reach consensus on the candidate nominated for the Prime Minister, then the political parties and coalitions with seats in the State Great *Khural* must consult and within five days submit to the Parliament the nomination of the Prime Minister whose nomination has been agreed upon by a majority. This clause in Article 39 of the Constitution was revised and amended as "A person nominated by a party or coalition with a majority of seats in the parliament, or a person who has been nominated to the post of Prime Minister by any party or coalition that does not have a majority of seats in the Parliament, or a candidate nominated by a party or coalition that has more seats and who in consultation with other parties and coalition have been able to form a majority, and in other cases, if a parliamentary party or coalition, after consultation become a majority and nominate a candidate, then the President will submit a motion to the State Great *Khural* within five days backing the candidate that has been suggested to the post of Prime Minister."

1 *The prerogative of the President to guarantee national security and rights exercised with relation to the country's defence.* The President of Mongolia heads the country's National Security Council and he/she is the Commander-in-Chief of the Armed Forces of Mongolia. The President also has the prerogative to declare a state of emergency or a state of war on the whole or part of the national territory, and issue ordinances on the deployment of the Armed Forces whenever extraordinary circumstances arise, as prescribed in the relevant clauses of the Constitution.

2 *President's prerogatives vis-à-vis the country's foreign relations.* In foreign relations, the President has the right to represent the State with full authority, make statements hold negotiations, conclude international treaties in concurrence with the State Great *Khural* as defined in the laws, appoint or recall, in consultation with the State Great *Khural*, heads of plenipotentiary missions of Mongolia to foreign countries.

3 *Other prerogatives of the President.* Confer state titles and highest military ranks, and award orders and medals, grant amnesty, and take decisions on granting or cancelling citizenship and many other prerogatives.

The administration of the President is the Office of the President. The President appoints the Chief of Staff and his/her advisers.

A state institution that is headed by the President is the National Security Council (NSC) of Mongolia. The NSC is a consultative organ that is responsible for formulating the state policy on ensuring the national security of the country, and coordinating and regulating the implementation of this policy. The NSC, in terms of its functions, scale and scope of operations, is much broader than the previous Defence Council, and its members include the President of Mongolia, who is also the Head of NSC, the Speaker of the State Great *Khural* and the Prime Minister of the country exclusively. The Vice Speakers of the State Great *Khural*, Chairperson of the Parliamentary Standing Committee and President's advisers serve as NSC advisers, and Members of the Cabinet and heads of some regulatory agencies (Chief of the General Staff of the Armed Forces of Mongolia etc.) serve as Rapporteurs of the National Security Council of Mongolia.

As opposed to the Defence Council, which was headed by the General Secretary of the Central Committee of the former Mongolian People's Revolutionary Party, and later which was spearheaded by the President of the Mongolian People's Republic (1999–1992), the present National Security Council has reinforced the legal foundations of the Council with the Constitution of Mongolia and the Law on the National Security Council of Mongolia.

4.4 *The Government (Cabinet)*

The 1992 Constitution defined the role and place of the Government within the executive power of the country, and it augmented the composition and the basis of its powers and authorities. In this respect, the Constitution specifies that "The Government (Cabinet) of Mongolia shall be the highest executive organ of the State."

The Government, in terms of its composition, consists of the Prime Ministers and the Cabinet members. The Prime Minister, in concurrence with the President, submits his/her proposal on the structure and composition, and its changes to the Government (Cabinet) to the State Great *Khural*. Prior to the 2019 Constitutional amendments, the SGKh, individually considered and appointed the candidates nominated by the Prime Minister as Cabinet members. According to the 2019 amendments, the Prime Minister appoints, relieves or dismisses a Cabinet Member only after tabling his/he motion to the State Great *Khural* and the President, and the Cabinet members appointed by the Prime Minister take an oath before the Parliament. The Government was formed on this principle in 2020.

With regard to the issue of structure and composition of the Government, the Law of Mongolia on the Government, has undergone many revisions. The composition of the Government of Mongolia in the Law of Mongolia, adopted on 31 July 1992, were either revised or amended in 1993, 1994, 1996, 2000, 2004, 2005, 2008, 2012, 2016 and 2020, respectively, and the amendments and revisions were all adopted.

The composition of the Government, which was formed in 2002, included, 1. The Prime Ministers; 2. Deputy Prime Minister; 3. Chief Cabinet Secretary; 4. Minister of Nature, Environment and Tourism; 5. Minister of Foreign Affairs; 6. Finance Minister; 7. Minister of Law and Home Affairs; 8. Labour and Social Protection Minister; 9. Defence Minister; 10. Minister of Constitution and Urban Development; 11. Minister of Education and Science; 12. Minister of Road and Transport Development; 13.

Minister of Culture; 14/ Minister of Mining and Heavy Industry; 15. Minister of Food, Agriculture and Light Industry; 16. Minister of Energy; and, 17 Minister of Health.

The composition of the Government had been undergoing constant changes. The Government in office from 1992 to 1996 had 13 ministries and 6 special agencies, but starting in 1996, its composition included the ministries, and regulatory and implementing agencies.

Structurally, the country today has two types of ministries:

a Six General function ministries, including the Ministry of Foreign Affairs; Finance Ministry; Ministry of Law and Home Affairs; Ministry of Nature, Environment and Tourism; Defence Ministry, and the Ministry of Labour and Social Protection.

b Fourteen direction ministries. They include the Ministry of Education and Science; Ministry of Construction and Urban Development; Ministry of Road and Transport Development; Culture Ministry; Ministry of Mining and Heavy Industry; Ministry of Food, Agriculture and Light Industry; Ministry of Energy, and, Ministry of Health.

Besides these fourteen direction ministries, there are 12 Government regulatory and 24 implementing agencies.

In keeping with the general functions of the Government to implement the state laws, and manage economic, social and cultural organs as specified in the Constitution, the Government also exercises specific powers defined in the Law on the government and other laws and legislations.

The powers of the Government include the following:

1 Organise and ensure nation-wide implementation of the Constitution and other laws;
2 Work out a comprehensive policy on science and technology, guidelines for economic and social development, and make State budget, credit and fiscal plans and to submit these to the State Great *Khural* and to execute decisions taken thereon;
3 Elaborate and implement comprehensive measures on sectional, inter-sectoral, as well as regional development;
4 Undertake measures on the protection of the environment, rational use and restoration of natural resources;
5 Guide the central state administrative bodies and direct the activities of local administrations;
6 Strengthen the country's defence capabilities and ensure national security;
7 Take measures for the protection of human rights and freedoms, to enforce the public order and to prevent crimes;
8 Implement the state foreign policy;

9 Conclude and implement international treaties with the consent of and subsequent ratification by the State Great *Khural* as well as conclude and abrogate intergovernmental treaties.

4.5 *The Judiciary*

The Constitution of Mongolia has promulgated the existence of an independent judiciary, which has challenged the State to exercise judiciary power in the country in the real meaning of the word. Article 49 of the Constitution specifically states that "The President, the Prime Minister, members of the State Great *Khural*, members of the Government or the officials of the State, political parties or other public organisations, citizens or anyone else, shall not interfere with the discharge of judicial duties by the judges," which is the constitutional legal guarantee providing for the establishment of an independent and impartial judiciary. The independence of the judiciary does not in the least mean that the courts and the judiciary are outside of criticism and that they can act as they please. It is the common demand of the people that the courts and the judiciary strictly abide by the law, function and perform impartially within the realm of law alone. In recent years, actions have been taken to streamline the functioning of the judiciary by passing many important and key laws and legislation, which form bedrock legal foundations and conditions for the due implementation of the constitutional principles of guaranteeing social order and discipline, human rights and freedoms, and ensuring that everyone is equal before the law.

In line with the amendments to the Constitution of Mongolia, an independent body financed from the court budget "The Judicial Disciplinary Committee" was established in 2019 tasked with the function to suspend, dismiss, and impose other disciplinary sanctions on judges.

The State Great *Khural* adopted the Law on the Court of Mongolia on 4 February 1993, consisting of 6 Chapters and 63 Articles, which was amended a number of times, first in 1994, then in 1996, 2002, 2003, 2007 and 2010. This Law stated that the courts alone shall exercise judiciary powers. It outlines the structure of the judiciary, the procedures for the establishment of courts and appointment of judges. The Law defines the prerogative powers of the judges, principles defining court decisions, composition of the courts, the oath of the judges, the emblem of the judiciary organs, and the exercise of judicial powers. The procedures for the selection and appointment of courts and judges, judicial professional committees, the powers of the judges and the Chief Justice, the organisational structure and operational principles of the General Council of Courts and the Judicial Disciplinary Committee, the terms of reference and the procedures for the appointment of their members, the responsibilities and liabilities of the judges are defined in the Law. Further, the Law has legalised the duties and functions of the court's secretariat, departments, their staff members, and the guarantees for carrying out judiciary functions.

The basic structural set-up of Mongolia's judiciary includes the Supreme Court of Mongolia, *aimag* and capital city courts, and *soum* and *inter-soum*, and district courts. The Law also recognises the establishment of courts specialising in criminal, civil and administrative justice, but the activities and the decisions of the courts cannot be outside of the oversight of the Supreme Court.

There are the following three-tier courts in Mongolia:

1 Primary,
2 Appeals, and,
3 Supervising.

Administrative courts have been set up in the *aimags* and the capital city, and administrative appeals courts have also been established.

The State Great *Khural* reserves the right to form courts. The Chief Justice of the Supreme Court of Mongolia is appointed by the President of Mongolia for a term of 6 years from among the judges of the Supreme Court and the candidates must be a citizen of Mongolia, at least 35 years of age with higher legal education and not less than 10 years' experience in judicial practice. Other judges of the courts are appointed from among Mongolian nationals, who have reached the age of 25 with higher legal education and with at least 3 years experience of practicing law, and who have not been convicted any time before.

According to the Law on Selection and Recruitment of Judges, a candidate who is vying to be a judge, must pass the selection test and must be in possession of the relevant certificate.

The judges of the Supreme Court are introduced to the State Great *Khural* by the General Council of Courts after which they are appointed by the President, while other judges of courts are also Appointed by the Mongolian President after their nomination are submitted for consideration by the Mongolian Head of State.

The General Council of Courts, functions on the principle of respecting the independence of courts. It does not interfere in the work of the courts and in court proceedings but deals exclusively with the selection of judges from among lawyers, protection of their rights and other matters pertaining to the guaranteeing of conditions guaranteeing the independence of the judiciary. Five of the 10-member General Council of Courts are elected from among the lawyers and the remaining five members are appointed on an open basis by the SGKh, for only one term of four years, and the Chairperson of the Councils selected from among the Council members. The performance report of the General Council of Courts, whose duty is to guarantee the independence of the judiciary, is presented for consideration to the Supreme Court.

Today there are a total of 505 judges in Mongolia's 21 *aimags* and the capital city working in 29 appeals courts and 90 primary courts.

4.6 *The Procurator (Public Prosecutor)*

In conjunction with the strengthening of the judiciary, the functions of the public prosecutors have been significantly updated. As indicated in Article 56 of the Constitution, the Public Prosecutor exercises supervision over inquiry into and investigation of cases and the execution of punishment, and participates in the court proceedings on behalf of the State.

As compared with the previous procurator's system under socialism, the duties and functions of the public prosecutors of today's Mongolia no longer exercise highest control (general control) over enforcement of laws, maintain surveillance (court supervision) on measures to prevent crimes and court proceedings.

The Law on the Public Prosecutor's Office of Mongolia, with 6 Chapters and 43 Articles, was adopted in 1993, which codified the structure of the Public Prosecutor's Offices, their principles of operation, their duties related to monitoring case registration, investigation and sentencing procedures, the obligation of a Public Prosecutor to take part in a court proceeding. The Law defined the terms of reference of a Public Prosecutor, the State General Public Prosecutor, the legal forms of monitoring by public prosecutors, and the overall operational functions of the offices of Public Prosecutors.

This Law was revised and adopted in 2002, and it was again changed and amended in 2003 and 2007, respectively, and in 2017 a new revised version of the Law was adopted.

The Public Prosecutor's Offices of Mongolia, on behalf of the State, ensure the implementation of criminal legislation across the entire territory of Mongolia, and are an independent body participating in the exercise of judicial power.

Today, the organisational structure and mode of operation of the country's Public Prosecutor's Offices are based on the principle of single, centralised management, and it must be immune to outside influence and enforce law equally and impartially.

The system of Public Prosecutor of Mongolia is composed of the Prosecutor General's Office, *Aimag* and Capital City Public Prosecutor's Offices, and the *Soum* and Inter-*Soum* or District Public Prosecutor's Offices. The State Great *Khural* reserves the exclusive right to a Public Prosecutor's Office with due consideration of their requirement, the distribution of the population and the geographical location. A special feature of a public prosecutor's offices control duties is the fact that speclalised public prosecutor's office can be set up and operationalised only on the basis of a motion passed by the Prosecutor General of Mongolia, and the Transportation Public Prosecutor's Office was formed through this procedure.

The Prosecutor General's Office also has an investigation authority, which administratively, financially and human resources matters is an independent agency with the power to investigat6e cases falling under the Criminal Procedure Law.

Citizens of Mongolia, who have higher education, have the necessary professional competency and who have not been convicted, are appointed as Public Prosecutors. The Prosecutor General is appointed for a term of 6 years by the President in consultation with the State Great *Khural*. The President of Mongolia, based on the suggestion of the Prosecutor General, appoints the latter's deputies also in consultation with the State Great *Khural*, who are appointed for six years in office. The law stipulates that the Prosecutor General and his/her deputies must be citizens of Mongolia, who have worked as a professional lawyer for not less than 10 years. *Aimag* and Capital City Public Prosecutors are appointed from among law professionals, citizens of Mongolia, who have worked in the field for at least 5 years.

The Prosecutor General's Office includes the Prosecutor General, his/her deputies, Assistant Public Prosecutors and Surveillance Prosecutors. The composition of *Aimag* and Capital City Public Prosecutors' Offices include the Public Prosecutors, their deputies, and also Assistant and Surveillance Prosecutors. The *Soum* and Inter-*Soum* Prosecutors' Offices also have a similar organisational set-up.

Public Prosecutors have the following grades and categories: chief state legal adviser, deputy state legal adviser, accredited legal adviser, senior legal adviser, and legal adviser.

As defined in the Law on Public Prosecutors, the Public Prosecutors have their own uniforms according to their grades and categories.

And so, the consolidation of the structure and functions of the courts and the Public Prosecutors by the Constitution of Mongolia signifies that these institutions have special functions and legal rights within the other judicial organs of the country. Together with the courts and the Public Prosecutor's Offices, crime registration, investigation, police, prison, the Bar and the notary, in their capacity of legal supervisory organs, have played an important part in guaranteeing human rights and freedoms, strengthen law and order, and preventing crime and offences.

Today, laws that have laid the legal foundations of the structure and mode of operation of the aforementioned law agencies, are in force in the country. The country's first *Law on Police* was adopted in 1993, which came into force effective as of 1 January 1994. With 8 Chapters and 53 Articles, this law outlined the structure of Mongolia's police, the functions and responsibilities of their management and central bodies, the duties and administrative obligations of the police to combat crimes, the duties of the police organisation to ensure exigent circumstance operations and their efficiency. The law defines who is a police officer, what are his/her legal rights, guarantee mechanisms to ensure the police carry out their duty efficiently, the assistance and benefits police force are entitled to. It also specifies the weapons and special implements that the police are entitled to carry, the justification for their use, the kind of assistance police force can extend to citizens, business and economic entities, the role of the internal forces in combating crimes and safeguarding public order and discipline, the kinds of surveillance the police and their organisations can and are subject to. Changes were made to the Law on Police on 26 July 1996, which defined that the police structure consists of the central police agency, agencies and departments under it, *Aimag* and Capital City police agencies (departments), and *Soum* and District police departments (and sub-departments).

Until 1997 the activities of the national bailiff agency were regulated by two legislations, the *Law of Correctional Services* (with 7 Chapters and 47 Clauses, it was in force since 1994), and the *Law on Enforcement of Court Rulings*, but this practice was discontinued in 1979 when the bailiff agency was subject to a single integrated Law, which was, however, revised and amended in 2002. The revised Law defines the structure and organisaitonal set-up of the country's bailiff service, and the legal basis and procedures for bailiff services. Accordingly, the national bailiff agency structure included the General Executive Agency of Court Decision of Mongolia, prisons and correctional institutions, and the *Aimag* and Capital City agencies of court decisions.

The Law of Mongolia about Notary was enacted in 1997. The purpose of this Law was to certify acts and documents related to agreements, contracts, ownership rights, and the concluding of contractual documents, to carry out other functions as specified in the Law and regulate relations arising out of the need to protect the interests of citizens and legal entities by way of preventing any possible conflict or argument that may arise thereof. The 1997 Law, as compared to the previous law, which was passed in 1985, recognises the notary service as having both public and private ownership. The notary organisation of Mongolia consists of the Bar Association of Mongolia, and the *Aimag* and Capital City Chambers of Notaries.

The revised and updated Law of Mongolia about Notary, which was adopted in 2011, defines the basic principles of the activities of the notary services, as to uphold the rule of law; be independent; ensure equal rights; observe justice; keep the client's confidentiality and strictly adhere to the code of ethics. The Law also specifies the obligations and commitments of the notary, notary districts, the language used by the notary, seals and certifying stamps, the rate of documents and services, the oath, rights and responsibilities of a notary, registration of notary, validity and the concrete functions a notary can and shall take etc.

The right to defence in legal cases, one of the important aspects of the judiciary, has been legalised in a *Law of Mongolia about Advocacy* passed in 1994. The Law defines the objectives of the defence counsel organisations, their operational principles and organisational structures, the procedure for seeking permission authorising activity, registration of defence attorneys, procedures for relieving or suspending defence counsellors, the prerogatives and guarantees of their functions, pay for their service, and their responsibilities and liabilities.

The Law of Mongolia about Advocacy was revised in 2002, which defined the working principles of defence counsel organisations and attorneys. Their responsibilities have been defined as guaranteeing human rights and freedoms, respecting law and justice, the free choice to seek the service of a defence attorney. The Law stipulates that the activities of the defence counsel shall be under state patronage, and also prohibits any organisation or government official to interfere in their activities, and it has made it mandatory for defence attorneys to invariably protect the rights and legal interests of their customers.

More changes and amendments were made to the Law of Mongolia about Advocacy in 2007 and the law was fully overhauled and revised in 2019, which defined that defence counsel work shall be managed. A professional lawyer who has passed the competency test and has been registered in the integrated registrar of defence counsels and who has received the official right to manage defence counsel work is permitted to work.

4.7 *Basic Functions of the Mongolian State*

The basic functions and duties of the Mongol State today are to promote the development of a free-market economy, deepen the process and strengthen the rule-of-the-law State, and guarantee human rights and freedoms.

Let us now look at the basic domestic and external functions and activities of the State, spearheaded at discharging the aforementioned basic functions and duties.

4.7.1 The Heart of the Economic Functions of the State

This has been, in the course of each of the milestones in the nation's historical development, the implementation of the policies defined and advanced by the State. Articles 5.1 and 5.2 of the Constitution promulgate that "Mongolia shall have an economy based on different forms of property, which takes into account universal trends of world economic development and national specifics. The State recognises all forms of both public and private property, and shall protect the rights of the owners by law." This constitutional provision defines the meaning and direction of the economic reform of the country and lays the legal foundations for a dynamic and decisive implementation of these ambitious goals.

The State *Baga Khural* passed the Law on Privatisation of the Mongolian People's Republic in May 1991, which set in motion the process of privatisation in the country. The grand privatisation process began when 44 per cent of all the state-owned assets, or 22 billion *tögrög* worth of assets, according to a 1990 valuation, were distributed to every single citizen of Mongolia, who were given investment vouchers. The country's first securities market service began through the first Stock Exchange of Mongolia, which was established in 1992 and 241 state-owned industrial enterprises were fully privatised, and some shares of another 234 state-owned economic and industrial enterprises were given over to private ownership. Citizens began to sell their shares by cash through the second securities market, which opened in the second half of 1995. Assets worth 6 billion *tögrög* belonging to the agricultural co-operatives, including livestock animals were given over in private ownership to the co-op members and individual livestock herders.

27.7 per cent of all livestock animals of the country were privately owned by citizens and herders in 1989 and 98.9 per cent of livestock animals had been transferred to private ownership by 2009. A Law on State and Local Property was adopted in 1996 and within this law and the National Privatisation Programme 1997–2000 almost 600 state-owned small industrial enterprises and business entities were auctioned, and more than 250 large businesses were auctioned through sealed bidding.[6]

6 *Mongolia's Development in the Twentieth Century*, Ulaanbaatar, 2005, p. 36.

However, the privatisation process was turned into a mass campaign activity overlooking some important privatisation due processes, such as the post-privatisation economic efficiency, social responsibility, and failed to define if the privatised industrial and service enterprises should maintain their original business profile or not. This was particularly relevant to agricultural and livestock co-operatives, after privatisation of which there was no-one to take responsibility for the thousands of artisan wells and animal sheds as a result of which all of them were either left unmanaged or whatever could be stolen went into private hands for personal use.

The country adopted the "Housing Privatisation Law" in 1996 under which all the housing estates, initially under government ownership, were privatized. Later in 2002 a Law on Privatisation of Land was adopted according to which citizens of Mongolia, for the first time in history, began to own private land.

The liberalisation of prices and the exchange rate became the central pre-requisite for the transition to a free market economy. In January 1990, the Government passed a resolution specifying some measures on transitioning the economy to free market relations and accordingly there was a change in schedule. The Government replaced the ration card system in the fall of 1993 by introducing a free price mechanism in retail trade. In May of the same year, foreign exchange was liberalised and a Government Resolution was passed in this respect which helped determine real exchange rates based on demand and supply. The Government continued to keep a hold on the prices of electricity, thermal energy, petroleum and oil products.

With the development of the relevant legal, juridical, economic and financial environment, commercial banks were opened in the country one after the other. By the end of 1992, the country had 11 such banks and their number had increased to 13 by 1996. During the past period, some of the banks were shut down and in their place new banks emerged, and the number of banks in 2020 had not changed much since 1996.

The Development Bank of Mongolia was established in 2011 to finance mega-projects. State budget occupies a central place in the financial system of Mongolia, and during the reform years, its revenue and expenditure structures changed substantially.

The State Great *Khural* adopted a package of tax laws in 1992–1993, setting in motion the reform of the country's tax system.

The central goal of the State's economic policy goal is to increase the country's real economy. Although the real production outcome of the industrial sector had grown during the more than 30 years of transition, this growth was ensured primarily ensured by the growth in the mining industry sector. This period also witnessed a repaid increase in the country's economic foreign relations. Having completed the period of transition to free-market economic relations, launching work on developing major mining projects such as Oyu Tolgoi and Tavan Tolgoi and simultaneously expanding their related infra-structure network and construction projects, today the country has reached a new stage of rapid economic growth. A lot of work had been done for infra-structure development during the years of transition.

State policies and laws on energy, construction, urban development, road, transport and communications have been adopted and enacted. The Law on Energy was revised in 2011 and the Government passed an Integrated Energy Network Programme, which is now in the process of implementation. Laws related to roads and transport have been revised a number of times and the country is now working on a "Millennium Road" programme. Similarly, many other laws were revised, amended and adopted anew. The revised Law on Communications was enacted in 2001; the Law on Water Supply of Towns and Settlements, and the Use of Cleaning Installations was revised in 2002; the Laws on the Use of Airspace for flights, and State Aircraft were amended in 2003. New laws on water transport (2009), renewable energy (2007), railway transport (2007), state policy on railway transport (2010) were adopted. The revised edited version of the Law on Construction and the new Law on Urban Development were adopted in 2008. The following laws and programmes were also adopted during this period, including the Laws on Development Policy and Planning (2015), State Policy on Food and Agriculture (2003), State Policy of Livestock Herders (2009), "Mongol Livestock" National Programme (2010), and "Water" National Programme (2010), respectively.

The next stage of the economic development course of the State was to draw up a roadmap for guaranteeing the country's economic security. The National Security Concept of Mongolia (1994, 2010) was an important document outlining the basic line of action of the State in the immediate future designed at strengthening the country's independence and sovereignty and guaranteeing free human development and social progress. These had also found their due reflection in the Comprehensive National Development Policy of Mongolia.

Mongolia today has concrete and precise policies and programmes of development. Mongolia will become a truly developed nation of creative people who would create national wealth through labour rather than remain a "rich consumer country" relying on natural mineral wealth, and this would be possible by launching major development projects, expanding the economy and ensuring that every single Mongolian is employed. The central economic objective of the Mongolian State is to ensure the fair distribution of social income in order to prevent social instability when a handful of people in the society may benefit from the gains of economic growth leading to income discrepancy; strengthen the middle class; reduce poverty; and to reduce the income gap in the rural areas and in the sectors. Since 1990, the State and Government of Mongolia have been carrying out important policy programmes and actions designed at laying the legal foundations of market economic relations; ensuring a mutually-coordinated budget, finance, monetary and credit policy; preventing the risks of unbridled inflation; support industry and services by liberalising price; liberalise the national currency tögrög's foreign exchange rate and stabilize the buying capacity of the national currency; and deepen the process of privatisation. Between 1992 and 1996 alone, The State Great *Khural* passed the package of tax laws, the budget law (1992), and considered and adopted the law on excise duty (1993), thus codifying the formation of the State budget. Foreign investment law was revised in a manner to create a favourable environment for foreign investment in the country. The State and Government had done a lot with respect to the development of the country's infra-structure. The country is today following the laws on communications and energy, railways and road safety; a new securities law has been passed and the second securities market has opened with the privatisation process having attained a new level. The Law on State and Local Property has been enforced. The state policy of rural areas has been also adopted and practically all livestock animals are under private ownership today. The country has thus adopted all major laws directed at regulating market economy relations, while some of these laws have been revised and amended. All this has helped put in place legal regulatory mechanisms of economic relations, and the implementation of policy programmes and projects have laid reliable foundations for making the economy healthier and stronger.

4.7.2 The Humane Policy of the State

It is natural that the implementation of human (social) policies improves as the economic strength and capacity of the country grows. As a result of some major political and economic measures taken towards ensuring the transition of the country towards free-market relations, the pre-conditions were put in place to carry out reforms in the social sector. In recent times, the State Great *Khural,* with the objective of creating social safety networks for the Mongolian population in concurrence with the market conditions, passed a package of laws on social insurance and social welfare, and a law on health insurance. The Mongolian parliament approved a comprehensive State population policy, which covers the entire spectrum of issues related to children and youth, women, elderly citizens and the differently abled people, which is being successfully implemented today. Although salary, pensions and welfare benefits are being increased, the living standard of the vulnerable section of the society continues to plunge, and poverty and unemployment continue to remain a serious challenge. In order to alleviate poverty and facilitate a creative labour attitude among the poorer section of the population, and also reduce unemployment, the State believes that it is important not to lower the earnings of the low-income section of the population. In other words, with due consideration of inflation, old age pension indexation was done to increase the size of pension benefits, and the minimum guaranteed level of living standard of the population has been revised and all these measures are part and parcel of the State's duties and functions designed at creating a humane society in the country. The foundational base of the state policies on education, science and culture have been defined and relevant laws and legislations have been enacted, and truly major steps are being taken by the State and Government to develop these sectors compatible with market relations.

In the beginning of the transition, the majority of industrial enterprises came to a screeching halt with their operations stalling, and their fallout contributed to a rise in unemployment. Some of the jobless people, who registered themselves with the newly established labour exchange, became paid labourers, while another group of unemployed people became incomeless and pennyless to join the ranks of the vulnerable section of the population. This proves that poverty is directly connected with employment. This makes it imperative for the State to give top priority attention to increasing jobs by way of supporting small and medium enterprises, besides focusing only on mega-development projects.

The country adopted a Law on Employment Support in 2001. The Law helped create the legal basis for types and forms and activities to support employment, their coverage scale and scope, and their finances; the legal foundations of employment organisations; and it specified the rights and responsibilities of the National Employment Council and employment organisations, the management of government revenue and spending on employment schemes, their accounts balance etc. New clauses were included in the amendment of this Law in 2008, covering services and measures to support labour tailored to the specifics of the differently able citizens, provision of incentive packages to employers who provided jobs to such disabled people continuously for not less than 24 months.

In 2008, the Parliament passed the Law on Labour Safety and Labour Health. The Law defined the basic principles of the state policy on labour safety and health, specified the control mechanisms, and labour safety and health standards at the workplace. The minimum labour wage was revised a number of times, and according to the Law on the Minimum Labour Wage regulated relations related to setting the minimum basic hourly wage (salary) to be observed in employment and other similar contracts.

Besides the traditional pension insurance system, starting in 1999, the system of named pay accounts was codified, and a new policy was introduced for granting pensions in view of the accumulation of deductions from *tögrög*; however, these measures did not bring about any tangible changes in the system.

With the adoption of a revised version of the Law on Social Welfare in 2005, the types of social welfare pensions and benefits, and the coverage of their services were defined, new procedures were introduced for the replenishment of the social welfare fund, and the structure and functions of the social welfare institutions were defined. In accordance with the amendments in the above aw, social welfare schemes were brought closer to the customers – the people – by introducing the so-called "conditional cash allowance" (*Under Article 25.5 of the Family Law caretakers of elderly citizens is special need, differently abled people, and orphan children are provided cash support or conditional cash allowance on special conditions and through certain criteria. Tr.*) and public-based social welfare services.

Other related laws and legislations were adopted, including the revised Law on Social Protection of Senior Citizens (2005), a package of laws on social protection of differently abled citizens (2006), the Law on Allowance for Mothers and Children, and the Law on Providing Cash Assistance to Children, Mothers and Families (2006), the Law on Increments from the State to Elderly Citizens who are either Heroes of Mongolia, Labour Heroes, and have the Honorary Titles of People's and Merited (2008), and the Law on Incentives for Mothers with Many children (2010).

With the passing of the Law on Incentives for Mothers with Many Children, mothers who have given birth to 4 children are given a Motherhood Medal of Second Order called "Mother's Glory" and those who have given birth to six and more children get the Medal of the First Order. The Law on Human Development Foundation was adopted in 2009 and later in 2016 the Law on Foundation of Future Heritage was passed, the objectives of these foundations are to support human development, families, children and their welfare.

During the years of reform and transitions in the country, the government set out to create the necessary legal foundations education, culture and science and in this respect Master Development Plans and National Programmes have been launched. The pre-education system has been revamped, the process of transitioning to a 12-year secondary education system was rolled out, the Law on Professional (Vocational) Education was adopted (2009), and students of vocational and industrial training centres were given monthly stipends by the Government. The higher education system of the country was reformed and as a result today there are two types of higher educational system functioning – public and private. A State Education Foundation has been established, which has started giving loans and gratis aid to college and university students. Both private and public secondary schools are functioning in the country today, and the Government has also put in place the system of non-formal education where school drop-out children and adults are trained and given support. The Teacher Development Law of Mongolia was adopted in 2018. Although many different reforms and measures have been taken, the education system is yet to be fully transformed and reformed.

A healthy way of life, facilitating health protection habits and practices, reducing morbidity and mortality among the population and extension of average life span constitute the key components of the humane policy of the Mongolian State and Government.

The 1998 Health Law, which was amended in 2002, defined the state policy and basic principles of the State in relation to health and relations concerning the right of citizens to protect their health, and access to public health and medical assistance are being regulated through this Law. The State and Government have yet to address the challenges of improving the significance and the impact of health insurance, and drastically improving the quality of medical assistance and services that are being rendered to the population.

One of the special hallmarks of the reforms in the country today are the fact that the social and political views and thinking of the people are changing for the better, national traditions, customs and religions are reviving, thus augmenting the intellectual and spiritual freedoms of the people. The drive to uphold history, culture, national unity and the country's independence, and the mentality to improve personal livelihood through labour are becoming stronger in the mindset of the Mongolian society.

4.7.3 The State's Duties and Functions to Guarantee Liberty and Freedom

One of the bedrock pillars of the new Constitution of Mongolia is to respect and guarantee human and civil rights and freedoms, improve the people's living standard by way of regulating the economy through social-oriented policies, and securely guarantee the development and growth of a Mongol. The heart and soul of freedom is determined by the possibilities made available for an individual to choose his/her life as he/she wishes, and the opportunities made available for developing one's talent and skills. Freedom can only fully serve the interests of the people by avoiding extreme polarisation – either by putting freedom in a tight box and controlling it, or letting it loose that could lead to chaos and disorder.[7] Proceeding from this very premise, all the laws and legislations being adopted by the Mongolian State, in the final analysis, serve the objective of guaranteeing human rights and freedom through the entire gamut of the system existent in the country. During the years of Democracy and transformation, the Mongolian State and Government have adopted dozens of laws designed at reliably guaranteeing rights starting with the equal right of all people legally residing in Mongolia before the law and the court, and to become a legal subject, to personal rights, freedoms, social and economic rights, political rights and an option to choose a free way of life. In this regard, we can enumerate a number of laws having a direct bearing on and related to the rights and freedoms of the citizens, including the laws on criminal, civil and court proceedings, the laws on the right of citizens to travel overseas and also on seeking asylum, the legal status of foreigners in Mongolia, laws related to copyright, patents, culture, education, health and social welfare.

One of the most important elements of the State's functions to guarantee the rights of the citizens is the question of ensuring human security. To this end, the Government adopted the National Security Concept of Mongolia in 2010.

The National Security Concept defines the basis of ensuring human security for Mongolians by creating healthy and safe living conditions and environment, ensuring food security, guaranteeing secure residence and protecting them from becoming a victim of crime or assault.

Mongolia is implementing a Human Rights Programme. The adoption of the Law on a National Human Rights Commission in 2000 became the legal basis for the functioning of the National Human Rights Com-

7 D. Lündeejantsan, *Security, Development, State and Law*, Book One, Ulaanbaatar, 2002, p. 115.

mission. The Law with 6 Chapters and 26 Articles, spells out the rights and prerogatives of the Commission members, their working principles, structure and composition of the Commission. The Commission regulates complaints and takes decisions if businesses, organisations and officials are guilty of violation of human rights and freedoms. Article 3.1 of the Law describes the National Human Rights Commission of Mongolia as "an independent national body responsible for monitoring the implementation of human rights and freedoms set forth in the Constitution, laws and international treaties of Mongolia and protecting and promoting human rights."

The Commission submits a report on the status of human rights and freedoms in Mongolia to the State Great *Khural* once every first quarter of the year. The Commission's annual reports have been published in the "State Information" journal. Other than in 2006 when the Commission submitted its report to the Session of the State Great *Khural* for its review, it has been submitting its reports for consideration to the Parliamentary Standing Committee on Law, which has come up with recommendations and resolutions instructing the Government and its relevant agencies, other relevant law-enforcing agencies to take actions to repair and end human rights breaches.

4.7.4 The State's Duties and Functions to Augment the Rule of Law, Law and Order

A State law is the bedrock of norms and standards for regulating social relations, rule of law is the central principle of strengthening the Statehood, and law and order are the legal demands, and practical enforcement of law, and they are mutually complementary social tools and implements for strengthening a humane, democratic, civil society in the country. The rule of law, law and order and discipline cannot separately be effective and this is why, the Government and State have defined the key functions and activities in this regard, which are clearly spelled out in Article 11.1 of the Constitution, which reads that "The duty of the State is to secure the country's independence, ensure national security and public order."

By the mid-1990s, the country had adopted the "Concept of Strengthening Public Order" and enacted some of the key laws related to judiciary institutions and their *modus operandi* (criminal, civil, civil procedure laws, administrative accountability law, law on combating alcoholism), which became the preconditions to ensure that every individual is equal before the law and the court, and reinforcing public law and order in the country.

Since 2000, the country has enacted many cross-cutting laws and legislation, and many laws have been changed and amended, while some have been adopted anew, which include the following: A revised and amended version of the Law on Combating Alcoholism (2999); Law on Administrative Forced Labour (2000); Criminal Code (2002) with 31 Chapters and 305 Articles; Criminal Procedure Law (2002 with 49 Chapters and 420 Articles); Law on Enforcement of Court Decisions (2002 consisting of 20 Chapters and 144 Articles); Law on Reviewing Civil Cases in Courts (consisting of 20 Chapters and 195 Articles, adopted in 2002);Civil Code with 12 Chapters and 94 Articles (2002); Law on Arbitration (2003, consisting of 8 Chapters and 43 Articles); Law on State Registration of Legal Entity (2003, it has 9 Chapters and 29 Clauses); Law on Combating Domestic Violence (2000); Law on Combating and Preventing Crime of Stealing Livestock Animals (2004); a revised and amended version of the Law on Tobacco Control (2005); Anti-Corruption Law (2006); a revised and edited version of the Law on Selection of Lawyers (2007); General State Registration Law (2009); Law on Forensic Medical Examination (2009); and the Law on Infringement (2015).

The Law on Mediating Reconciliation, which was enacted in 2012, provided legislation that provided solutions to resolving all disputes without going to the courts.

4.7.5 National Security Concept

The National Security Concept of Mongolia in terms of protecting citizens from transnational crime, has specifically stated that its objective is to "Improve the protection of citizens from terrorism and transnational crime or violence; Prevent citizens in particular, children and women from becoming victims of human trafficking, improve the legal environment and maximize efforts to investigate, disrupt and suppress such criminal activities and punish wrongdoers; Improve national capacity to control and monitor the flow of narcotics and substances affecting human psyche and vigorously combat the illegal sale, possession or consumption of all substances as defined by law; and, Intensify training and information campaign to prevent the public from committing crimes and increase international cooperation in this area."

Irresponsibility, discord and calls for justice reflect that enforcement of law is wanting, control over its enforcement is slack, and the system of accountability and responsibility is unable to live up to the expectations and demands of the people.

Therefore, there arose the imperative need to strengthen law and order, and a lot has to be achieved in this regard though.

4.7.6 Science, Technology and State

This function of the Mongolian State and Government is being considered separately because it is directly linked with the state's duties and functions growing out of the natural course of development of global culture and civilisation. Precisely from this premise, Article 38.2.2 of the Constitution clearly specifies that the Government has the power "to work out a comprehensive policy on science and technology, guidelines for economic and social development, and make State budget, credit and fiscal plans, and submit them to the State Great *Khural* and to carry out the decisions taken thereon." Within the framework of rapidly developing science and technology, the priority tasks of the Mongolian State and Government are to objectively appraise the value of the human factor and intellectual output, carry out in-depth research in the country's natural wealth and basic raw materials, manufacture market-competitive products, and introduce state-of-the art technology into production. With respect to the scientific and technological development of the country, there are a number of legislative acts including the State Policy on Science and Technology, the revised and edited version of the Law on Science and Technology (2006), the Law on Technology Transfer (1998), State Policy of State-of-the Art Technology (2010), Law on Innovation (2012) and others.

In the new millennium, the State and Government are primarily responsible for strengthening the national competitive capacity, and promoting the development of a knowledge-based economy. During the years of transformation, the state's policy was primarily focused on maintaining the human resources and their potential by way of giving salary to people working in the science sector, as a result of which the number of people engaged in this sector has decreased threefold in the last 20 odd years, and this was a period marred with declining investment, nevertheless, the State and government were able to conserve the basic structures of modern science, that had reached to a certain level, and also the national science capacity.

Structural reforms were carried out in the science sector by setting up the so-called "Research-Experiment-Development-Business" structure and accordingly technological incubators were established at research institutions, colleges and universities, based on which the State and Government succeeded in revising the priority directions of science and technology.[8]

8 *Mongolia's Development in the Twentieth Century*, Ulaanbaatar, 2005, p. 29.

4.7.7 Ecology and State

Protection of the surrounding natural environment has today become the most pressing challenge and accordingly, the State is stepping up its programme activities in this direction and with every new challenges coming to the fore, the State and Government of Mongolia are approaching the issue of ecology as a stand-along priority area. These functions of the State have been given due consideration in the Constitution of Mongolia, the Law on Protection of Natural Environment, which was enacted in mid-1990s, and other laws and legislations that have been adopted in line with the above. Take for example, the following long list of policy programmes and laws: The Law on Land (It was passed in 1994 and came into force effective as of 1 April 1995); Law on the Bowels of the Earth (with the relevant changes and amendments made on 5 December 1994); The Law on Protected Areas (passed in 1994 and enforced on 1 April 1994); Forest Law (enforced as of 5 June 1995); Water Law (came into effect as of 5 June 1995); Hunting Law (enacted on 5 June 1995); Law on Natural Plants (came into force as of 5 June 1995); Air Law (also enacted on 5 June 1995); Law on Protection against Hazardous Chemical Agents (came into effect as of 5 June 1995), and also the Law about Payments for Cutting and Using Household Wood for Fire from Forests, Law about Payments for use of Natural Plants, Law on Payments for Use of Mineral Water, and the Law on Use of Game Hunting Resources (these aforementioned laws were all enacted effective as of 1 July 1995), and the Law on Land Lease (adopted in 1997). The Law on Use of Air was passed in 2010. Article 5 of the Environmental Law states that the state shall have the function of preventing harmful effects on the environment and disturbing the environmental balance in order to ensure the right of people to live in a healthy and safe environment.

Further the law codifies the functions of the State as follows:

1. Create favourable environmental conditions for human life, work and rest;
2. Develop an ecologically-oriented economy and ensure environmental balance;
3. Ensure conditions for the rational use of natural resources on a scientific basis;
4. Ensure that the decisions and activities to protect the environment and use natural resources are transparent, and,
5. Ensure the inviolability of natural resources.

In the period after 2000, dozens of environment-related legislations were adopted, including the Law on Animal Kingdom and the Law on Hunting (2000); and the revised amended version of the Law on Land (2002), which was amended about a dozen times. The Law on Giving Land for Ownership to Citizens of Mongolia (2002), Law on Mineral Water (2004); Law on Water (2004); Law on Poisonous and Hazardous Chemical Agents (2006); the amended version of the Law on Forests (2007); also an amended version of the Law on Protection of Plant Kingdom (2007); Law on Evaluation of Influencing Factors on Environment (1998), which was changed and amended in 2006; a revised amended version of the Law on Air (2010) and the Law on Air Pollution Penalty (2010).

Mongolia also acceded to and ratified many multilateral treaties and conventions of environment protection. On a broader scale, one of the key elements of the State's ecological functions is to give top priority attention to environment security and safety.

The National Security Concept has stated that maintaining environmental balance, protecting water resources, mitigating climate change and negative impacts of land degradation, preventing biodiversity depletion, and reducing risks of environment pollution, natural disasters and their risks are important pre-requisites for guaranteeing healthy living environment and environmental security.

In this regard, the Concept has outlined in detail the policy and the measures the State should pursue to prevent water shortage, mitigate climate change and negative impacts of land degradation, protect and preserve bio-diversity and prevent depletion of its resources, reduce the level of environmental pollution, and reduce the risks of natural disasters and contingencies.

4.7.8 Foreign Policy Functions of the State

Guaranteeing the independence and security of the country is the *foundational* cornerstone of the State's functions and duties. About this, the Constitution promulgates that "The duty of the State is to secure the country's independence and guarantee national security." For the Mongols, homeland and the independence of Mongolia are the most sacred non-negotiable heritage left behind by our ancestors. Enrichment and advancement of the traditions of the preservation and augmentation of the country's independence must be at the heart of the activities of the Mongolian State. The National Security of Mongolia implies that there must be guaranteed, tried and tested favourable external and international pre-requisites that assure the vital interests of the Mongols. The national interests of Mongolia imply the existence of the Mongolian people, their culture and civilisation, the independence and sovereignty of Mongolia, the inviolability of the county's state borders, relative independent economy, balanced ecological development, and national unity and harmony.

As defined in the National Security Concept of Mongolia, adopted in 1994, respect for a sense of national patriotism is the core of the national security policy. Guaranteeing national security means the protection and consolidation of Mongolia's vital national rights and interests, and pursuing a multi-pronged policy by the State to create an entire array of guarantees. The defence policy of the Mongolian State and activities in this respect are part and parcel of the measures designed at ensuring national security.

These policy principles were further streamlined and defined in the amended version of the National Security Concept of Mongolia, which was adopted in 2010, which determines the following operational principles for guaranteeing the country's national security:

- Upholding patriotism

Incessant creative urge by every individual citizen of Mongolia to contribute to patriotism and the future welfare of the country and the nation by taking pride in national values, become their patrons, carrier and developer are the foundation of the State policy and activities on ensuring national security.

- State-citizen collaboration

Guaranteeing national security is the primary duty of the State. The State must pay heightened attention to ensure that the citizens have broad knowledge and understanding about issues related to national security, and in this respect create the necessary opportunities for and promote collaboration with the citizens so they can contribute to national security guarantees.

- The integrated nature of the Security Policy

National security guarantees can be reinforced if the State succeeds in ensuring mutual coordination and inter-dependency between "Existential Security," "Economic Security," "Internal Security," and "Information Security."

- Knowledge-based approach

The attitude towards security and activities to guarantee security is based on knowledge, information and analysis.

- Realistic attitude

Realistically interpret potential threat and trials, and ensure efficient mobilization of limited resources and opportunities to overcome them.

- Take into consideration globalisation factors

Globalisation, on the one hand, is increasing vulnerability related to dependency of one nation on another, and on the other hand, it is creating opportunities for tapping into external resources and possibilities to safeguard and augment national interests.

The Constitution of Mongolia proclaims that the country "shall have armed forces for self-defence. The structure and organisation of the armed forces and the rules of military service shall be determined by law." In accordance with this, the Law on Defence of Mongolia, which was adopted in 1994, declares that Mongolia shall protect the homeland from external armed incursions and aggressions relying on its own armed forces and with the involvement of the people, and if necessary, Mongolia can seek assistance from another country in accordance with the UN Charter. In time of peace, Mongolia shall have a small and a competent armed forces and other forces compatible with the defence needs and requirements of the country, as well as the capability of the economy.

One of the bedrock foundations of the State defence policy of Mongolia is the Military Doctrine, which was adopted in 1994. It outlines the defence duties and functions of the State as follows:

- The use of force or the threat of use will not be viewed as a means of settling any dispute and Mongolia will not recognise the outcome of such use of force or aggression;
- Mongolia will not, under any circumstance, resort to the first use of weapons against another state, the country will not pose any military danger or threat, and will not take part in any war or armed conflict in cases other than if the country itself becomes an object of outside aggression;
- Mongolia not be a part of any military alliance unless the independence and sovereignty of the country are directly threatened or there is a potential threat; and,
- In the absence of relevant national legislation, Mongolia will strictly adhere to the policy of not allowing foreign troops to enter the country, be stationed in or pass through its territory.

The Mongolian State gives priority to political and diplomatic means while pursuing its defence functions and duties. Mongolia is actively pursuing a policy of promoting ties and relations with the UN Department of Peace Operations, international military organisations and other influential countries. While pursuing this policy, the Mongolian State stands for the strengthening of trust and confidence in the defence relations.

Mongolian servicemen have been actively involved in international peace operations in hotbeds around the world. The Law on Participation in UN Peacekeeping Activities was revised and amended in 2010, and accordingly, personnel of the Mongolian Armed Forces, border and internal forces, the police, the intelligence department, National Emergency

Management Agency and the General Executive Agency of Court Decision of Mongolia have been involved in international peacekeeping missions, and in this respect the purpose of the amended Law is to regulate relations concerning training and supplies of the Mongolian peacekeepers.

"Peacekeeping efforts" mean the guaranteeing of international and regional peace and security, put an end to armed conflict, and to eliminate its consequences. With this purpose in mind, the UN Security Council, in accordance with the UN Charter, passed a resolution providing for the involvement of the United Nations and other regional arrangements and agencies in the maintenance of international peace and security.

A constituent of the foreign policy functions of the Mongolia State is to *maintain friendly relations with different countries around the world.*

The purpose and objective of this function are designed at strengthening Mongolia's international standing by way of following the development process of humanity, and reliably guaranteeing the country's independence and sovereignty by means of forming with influential countries in the region and in the world a network of relationships based on the interdependence of political, economic and other interests. The Concept of Foreign Policy of Mongolia, adopted in 1994, states that Mongolia shall pursue an open and non-aligned policy. While following a policy of creating realistic interest of the developed countries in Mongolia, it will seek to avoid becoming overly reliant or dependent on any particular country, and Mongolia shall augment the interests of foreign countries in Mongolia through political and legal means.

The revised version of the Concept of Foreign Policy of Mongolia, adopted in 2011 declares the following:

1 Mongolia 's foreign policy shall be based on its national interests, as defined in its Constitution, and the Concept of National Security, and the country's specific external and internal situation constitutes the basis for determining its foreign policy objectives, principles and priorities.
2 Mongolia's foreign policy objectives are to maintain friendly relations with all the countries of the world, strengthen political, economic and other ties and cooperation, augment Mongolia's position in the international community and strengthen the country's independence and sovereignty by way of accelerating progress and development.
3 The priority of Mongolia's foreign policy shall be safeguarding its security and vital national interests by political and diplomatic means.
4 Mongolia shall pursue a peaceful, open, independent and multi-prop foreign policy.

5 The unity of foreign policy shall be guaranteed and its continuity will be preserved. The central state administrative organ responsible for foreign relations shall be responsible for maintaining the unity of foreign policy and for coordinating and supervising foreign relations of the central state administrative organs and local governments and territorial units.

6 In developing its relations with other countries, Mongolia shall be guided by universally recognized principles and norms of international law as defined in the Charter of the United Nations, including mutual respect for each other's sovereignty, territorial integrity and inviolability of borders, right to self-determination, non-interference in internal affairs, non-use of force, settlement of disputes by peaceful means, respect for human rights and freedoms, and equal and mutually beneficial cooperation.

7 Mongolia shall, besides, striving to develop priority ties and cooperation with influential countries in the region and in the world, it will seek to avoid becoming overly reliant or dependent on any particular country.

8 In formulating Mongolia's foreign policy and determining its priority directions and objectives, a flexible approach shall be applied.

9 The foreign policy of Mongolia shall consist of three basic mutually interconnected parts, including political, economic, scientific, technological, cultural and humanitarian foreign policy, policy of protecting the interests of overseas Mongolian citizens, and, public diplomacy and policy of foreign publicity and public diplomacy.

With the onset of the 21st Century, globalisation is growing in scale, science and information technology have developed in leaps and bounds, political and economic integration process is deepening and so is the mutual dependency of States and countries. The bipolar nature of international relations in the last half of the previous century has changed drastically. New major development centres have been established and their influence in international relations is growing fast and are like to grow rapidly.

On the other hand, a stark difference began to appear in the rate and level of development of countries, and growing rate poverty and unemployment strangled the poor countries with a frail economy. Some countries are continuing to become nuclear and there is no end in sight to international tensions. Furthermore, climate change, environmental degradation, international terrorism, human and drug trafficking, and the increase in infectious diseases are posing greater danger and challenges.

While Mongolia, a country that respects democracy, human rights and freedom, is moving and developing to become a nation with free market economy, and its foreign relations and cooperation are expanding, and the number of Mongolians studying and working in foreign countries is increasing.

Mongolia has entered the road of rapid development, strengthening its economic potential by way of tapping into its rich mineral resources, increasing employment and raising the living standards of the population.

The State and Government today are faced with the task of extending its foreign relations and increasing its outcome in order to contribute more towards addressing pressing global problems, and carrying through its national development policy.

The objective of the foreign policy of the Mongolian State is to create a favourable external environment to guarantee national security, progress and development, extend diplomatic and consular ties, raise the level of relations with influential countries, energise Mongolia's activities in international organisations, and to make its own contribution to addressing pressing global problems.

The Mongolian State is invariably pursuing the general policy line of staying away from joining any military alliance when there is no external military threat to the country, disallowing the use of its territory and aerial space against another state, and entering, stationing, or transiting through its territory any foreign military force.

As a member of the international community, Mongolia is making every possible effort to contribute to the common universal cause of addressing both regional and global problems and challenges.

- Support all activities and take an active part in them designed at bolstering democracy and guaranteeing human rights and freedoms;
- Facilitate non-proliferation of nuclear and other weapons of mass destruction, promote disarmament, fight against international terrorism and organized crime, and take an active part in the peace-keeping and development missions of the United Nations and other international organisations;
- Mongolia is committed to back and take part in the efforts of the international community to adapt to climate change, minimize its negative consequences, protect natural environment from degradation and prevent the spread of pandemic.

The following policy directions guide the Mongolian State in its foreign policy efforts:

1 Maintaining friendly relations with the Russian Federation, People's Republic of China is the priority direction of Mongolia's for-

eign policy activity. It will strive to promote a balanced, good neighbourly relations with them. In doing so, traditional relations as well as the specific nature of our economic cooperation with these two countries will be taken into account.

2 The second priority direction of Mongolia's foreign policy activity is to promote partnership ties and expand cooperation with the United States of America, Japan, European Union, India, Republic of Korea, Turkey and other countries in the East and the West within the framework of its "Third Neighbour Policy".

3 The third direction of Mongolia's foreign policy activity is to promote bilateral friendly relations and cooperation with other countries in Asia, tape part in multi-lateral cooperation in the Asia, Pacific region, bolster strategic stability in East Asia, North East Asia and Central Asia, and extend security cooperation.

4 Actively continue cooperation with the United Nations, its specialised agencies and international financial trade and economic organisations, and facilitate the augmentation and extension of the role and responsibility of the United Nations in global governance.

5 Simultaneously with promoting bilateral ties and cooperation with the developing countries, Mongolia is committed to promote its international cooperation within the United Nations, the Group of 77, Non-Aligned and other multilateral platforms, and in this respect Mongolia has acceded to and ratified dozens of multilateral treaties, agreements and conventions.

4.7.9 Civil Service

According to Article 46.2 of the Constitution "State employees must be Mongolian nationals. They shall strictly abide by the Constitution and other laws, and work for the benefit of the people and in the interests of the State." This clause becomes the legal heart and soul of facilitating public office in the real meaning of the word. The Law on Civil Service, which was passed in 1994, was revised and amended in 2017.

This law has classified the civil service of Mongolia, the principles of this service, hierarchy in public office, its duties and responsibilities, the legal status of public officers, as well as the requirements and procedures of service, and the guarantees thereof.

In Mongolia, civil service has four categories:

1 Political public office;
2 Administrative public office;
3 Special public office, and,
4 Service public office.

The following political positions are elected to public political offices in accordance with the conditions, procedures and criteria established by the Constitution of Mongolia and other laws, and to work on assignment as a result of these elections, and to serve during their term of office:

1 President of Mongolia;
2 Speaker of the State Great *Khural;*
3 Prime Minister of Mongolia;
4 Vice Speaker and Members of the State Great *Khural;*
5 Cabinet (Government) Members;
6 Chief of Staff of the Office of the President of Mongolia;
7 Chief Cabinet Secretary;
8 Vice Ministers;
9 Advisers to the President, State Great *Khural* Speaker and the Prime Minister of Mongolia;
10 Governors of all levels and Vice Governors of *Aimags,* Capital City, *soums* and districts;
11 Full-time advisers, personal assistance and media officer serving only during the term of office of a political officer;
12 Officials of the offices of the party and coalition groups in the State Great *Khural;*
13 Other officials as specified in the law.

Chairpersons of the Presidium of the *Aimag,* Capital City, *soum* and district *Khurals* of Citizens' Representatives (local assembly), and administrators of towns and villages can be considered as having the same official status like any other political position of the State.

The following are administrative public officials, who have organisational duties and functions as providing professional recommendations in relation to drafting and developing of state policies, and administrative leadership in the implementation of these policies:

1 Chairperson, members, managers and executives of the Civil Service Council;
2 Offices (Secretariat) of the State Great *Khural,* President, Government and the Constitutional *Tsets* (Court), managerial and executive officials of the court administration, and the office of the Public Prosecutor;
3 Executive managers and officials of the Financial Regulatory Committee, National Statistics Committee, General Election Committee, and National Human Rights Commission;
4 Executive Officer and executives of the Secretariat of the National Security Council;

5 State Secretary of ministry, and other top managers and executives of state ministries;
6 Unless otherwise provided by law, top managers and executives of Government agencies;
7 Secretary of the *Aimag,* Capital City, *soum* and district *Khural* of Citizens' Representatives, and *Aimag,* Capital City, *Soum* and District *Khurals* of Representatives and Governors, and their administrative offices, their officials, managerial and executives.
8 Unless otherwise provided by law, top executives and administrative officers of the local administrations under the Governors of *Aimag and* Capital City, which are government financed;
9 Managing and executive positions of the office of the city or village Administrators;
10 Other positions specified in the law.

Positions of State administration have two classifications: officials of State central administration and officials of local administrative central organs.

Mongolia has full-time public office position, which is further categorised as Chief Officer (*Tergüün Tüshmel*), Officer-in-charge (*Erkhelsen Tüshmel*), Senior Officer (*Akhlakh Tüshmel*), Officer (*Des Tüshmel*) and Assistant Officer (*Tuslakh Tüshmel*).

The position of Chief Officers include the Secretary of State of a Ministry and other similar positions. The position of Officer-in-Charge includes the head of the department, head of division and other similar positions; the position of a Senior Officer includes the head of a department of Ministry, senior expert, expert and other similar positions; the positions of Officers include senior specialists, specialists, senior organisers of the Ministry and other similar positions, and, the positions of auxiliary or Assistant Officers include the Ministry's organiser and other similar positions.

The positions of Chief Officer, Officer-in-charge, Senior Officer, Officer and Assistant Officer also have relevant categories, grades and ranks as First, Second and Third Class.

Categories, ranks and grades of the managers and executive officers of the State Great *Khural,* the President, the Government, the Supreme Court, the Constitutional Court, General Prosecutor's Office, National Human Rights Commission, Civil Service Council, National Security Council, General Election Commission, Financial Regulatory Commission, and the National Statistics Office, are determined by the State Great *Khural* based on the proposal of the Central Civil Service Body.

The Government determines the categories, ranks and grades of public administrative positions of ministries and state organisations based on the proposal of the Central Civil Service Body.

Special government positions, as specified the Constitution and other laws of Mongolia include the following positions with the purpose of guaranteeing national and population security, enforcing public law and order, and the rule of the law principle:

1 Members of the Constitutional Court, judges of all levels of courts, and public prosecutors;
2 Secretary of the National Security Council of Mongolia;
3 President, First Vice President and Vice President of the central Mongol Bank, Chairman and full-time members of the Financial Regulatory Committee, Chairperson and Deputy Chairperson of the National Statistics Committee, Chairman and Secretary of the General Election Commission, Commissar and members of the Nation al Human Rights Commission, members and executives of the national and local auditing authorities and the Independent Authority Against Corruption;
4 Management of the Armed Forces, Border and Internal Forces, Emergency Agency, Intelligence Agency, Police, Agency of Court Decision, and the Forensic;
5 Diplomatic service;
6 Officers and sergeants of the Armed Forces, Border and Internal Forces, Emergency Agency, Intelligence Agency, Registration Authority, Investigation Department, Police and Agency of Court Decision; bailiff officers, customs officers, Forensic office experts and investigators.
7 Other positions specified in the law.

Categories, ranks and grades of special government positions are determined as specified in the relevant laws.

State service officers are contracted to ensure that state services are fair, of good quality and accessible. And their job is to facilitate the normal functioning of the state institutions. State service includes the following positions:

1 Assistant officers with the duty to ensure the normal functioning of a state organ;
2 Chairpersons, directors, managers and other managerial and executive officers and auxiliary staff of state financed education, science, health, cultural, arts, and sports agencies
3 Managers, executives and auxiliary staff of state service offices under ministries and agencies.

The Government based on the recommendations of the central civil service agency determines categories, ranks and grades of state service positions.

State officials, other than the State political officials, during their term of service, are not permitted to take part, in any form and manner, in the activities of a political party, coalition and movement, and if the state official is a member of any political party, he/she must refrain from party membership during this period, and the state official is duty-bound to officially notify in writing about this to the relevant administrative office of the concerned organisation and the party he/she belongs to, within seven days after appointment as a state official.

A State official is entitled to receive salary from the government for his/her service in the position during the entire length of service, and is ensured relevant working conditions and guarantees, and such as state official is called a State/government officer.

Within the framework of the classification and categorisation of state administrative and state special position, a Mongolian citizen who is carrying out full-time managerial and executive functions according to the relevant profession and competency, is called a full-time state/government officer.

The legal status of political State official, carrying out the function of a state political position, is regulated by the laws of the State Great *Khural*, the President and the Government; and the legal status of state special officers of the armed forces, the police, courts and public prosecutors and diplomatic officials is regulated by the relevant legislations; and the legal status of the state service officers, similarly, is regulated by the labour and other relevant laws and legislation.

The Law on Civil Service defines the legal status of the state administrative officers. A state administrative officer, before assuming office, takes an oath committing to dedicate his/her knowledge and skills to the homeland and the people, strictly abide by the laws and ethical standards of Mongolia, and swear to discharge duties strictly in concurrence with the vital national interests. The oath-takers vow "Should I break the oath, I shall be held accountable before the law".

Civil service and the management of civil servants come under the jurisdiction of the central civil service agency, which is the State Service Council. The Council is an independent and autonomous body and reports to the State Great *Khural*. The Council functions on the principles of collective leadership, which has a full-time five member. Three of the five Council members are nominated one each by the Secretariat of the State Great *Khural*, the Office of the President, and the Secretariat of the

Cabinet of Mongolia, and the remaining two Council members are nominated by a representative of the civil servants. The nominated candidate must have served as a full-time civil servant for a minimum of 15 years, should have a higher education specialising in either state management, economy, law or education, should not have been convicted and should be a citizen of Mongolia at least 45 years of age.

Full-time members of the State Great *Khural* Council are appointed for a 6-year term in office. The chairperson of the Council is nominated from among the Council members, he/she is elected through secret ballot, and the candidate who has secured the highest number of votes serves as the Council Chairperson for a term of 3 years.

Mongolia has three types of civil service positions: managerial, executive and assistant.

4.7.10 Local Self-government

Administratively, the territory of Mongolia is divided into *Aimags,* and Capital City, the *aimag* is divided into *soums, soums* into *baghs,* the Capital city is divided into districts and sub-districts or *khoroos* as they are called in Mongolian. *Aimag,* Capital City, *soum* and district have their own special functions as provided by the law, and they are administrative, territorial, economic and social complexes having their own functions and administrations. Darkhan-Uul, Orkhon and Gobi-Sümber *aimags* were newly established in 1994. As pointed out in Article 51 of the Constitution, governance of administrative and territorial units of Mongolia shall be organised on the basis of combination of the principles of both self-government and central government.

As per the changes and amendments to the Constitution of Mongolia, the legal status of towns and villages located on the territories of administrative divisions, as well as the legal foundations of self-governance and organisational set-up of villages shall be defined by law.

The Constitution points out that the transfer of administrative and territorial units, and some of their management functions will be considered and decided by the State Great *Khural* as proposed by the Government.

Prior to 1992, *aimag,* town, *soum, khoroo, raion* and rural town *Khurals* of People's Deputies put together were defined as the local state organs of power, but since the adoption of the new Constitution, this status of the *Khurals* of People's Deputies as a state organ of power was replaced with a different basic form of self-governance system, which was augmented. This consisted of the following three types: 1. *Khurals* of Representatives of Citizens; 2. General Meetings of inhabitants of *Baghs* and *khoroos;* 3. Presidium that would be functional in between their sessions. The main legal basis of local self-government is the Law on Administration, Territorial Units and their Management, passed in 1992.

The changes and amendments to this Law were approved by the State Great *Khural* in 2006. This Law regulates issues related to establishing, changing and dismantling of administrative and territorial units of Mongolia, and their management structure, power and authority, principles of their working and also their organisational set up.

The issue of establishment, revision and dismantling of an *aimag, soum* and district is decided by the State Great *Khural* if the Government submits a motion in this regard, which should have taken into consideration proposals by the inhabitants of the given territory, as well as the distribution of population, the economic capacity, geographical location and the state of roads and communication. While the issue of establishing changing and dismantling a *bagh* and *khoroo* is decided by the *Khurals* of Representatives of Citizens of the given *aimag* or Capital City. In the case of endorsing and changing the borderlines of *Aimags*, the Capital city, *Soums* and districts shall be approved by the State Great *Khural* at the presentation by the Government are decided by the State Great *Khural* as motioned by the Government, which bases its decision on the motion by the *Aimag* and Capital City *Khurals* of Representatives of People. In the event *aimags* and the Capital City have different opinion on borderlines, then the State Great *Khural* can, without any restriction, pass a decision.

Land given on tenure as per the law, subterranean and surface natural wealth, local assets, and accumulation from revenues earned by both public and private industry and services, tax, payments and fees.

The administrative and territorial unit management combines the principles of self-governance and central government, and the management independently can address economic and social issues within its territory and while carrying out its functions, the management must be guided by the rule of law that guarantees democracy, justice, freedom, equality and national unity.

Local self-government has the legal capacity to address independently, within the precincts of law, economic and social issues within the territory in the interest of the citizens. The local self-government has its own representatives, who are elected through open election, and it too has an executive organ to which it is accountable.

The Law (revised version) on Elections to Local *khurals*, which was adopted in 2007, had been regulating the system of conducting local *Khural* elections and its procedures until 2016.

The local-government has the following set up:

1 *Khurals* of Representatives of Citizens of *Aimag* and Capital City,

2 *Khurals* of Representatives of Citizens of *soums* and districts;
3 General Meetings of the Citizens of *Baghs* and *Khoroos,* in between their sessions, their Presidium would be responsible for carrying out their functions.

The term of office of the *Khurals* of Representatives of Citizens of *Aimag* and Capital City is 4 years and this term of office will not concern the *Khurals* set up through an extraordinary election.

Representatives of the *Aimag,* Capital City and *Soum Khurals* shall be permanent residents of the given administrative and territorial unit.

Representatives of the Capital City District *Khurals* can be a permanent resident of that particular district, or could be temporary resident, meaning he/she could be working in a business, an economic entity or an organisation in the district.

The term of office of the serving *Khurals* of Representatives ends with the acknowledgment of the term of office of the newly elected representatives of the *Khural.*

The number of elected representatives of the *Aimags,* Capital City, *soum* and districts is fixed with due consideration of the distribution of the population and the structure of the given administrative unit in the following manner:

1 *Aimag Khurals:*
   a 25 representatives for a population up to 50,000;
   b 31 for a population from 50,000 to 90,000;
   c 35 representatives if the population is more than 90,000.
2 Capital City *Khural:* 45 elected representatives.
3 *Soum Khurals:*
   a 15 representatives for a population of up to 2,000;
   b 211 for a population from 2,000 to 9,000;
   c 25 representatives if the population is more than 9,000.
4 District *Khurals:*
   a 21 representatives for a population up to 2,000;
   b 25 for a population from 20,000 to 80,000;
   c 35 representatives if the population is more than 80,000.

The chairperson of the *Aimag* and Capital City *Khurals* is responsible for providing professional and methodological leadership to the *soum* and District *Khural.* The chairperson and the secretary of the *aimag* and Capital City *Khurals* of representatives are full-time government officials.

A Session is the basic form of the working operation of the *Khurals* of representatives of citizens.

The regular Session of the *Aimag,* Capital City, *Soum* and District *Khurals* is called not less than twice a year, and the General Meetings of the *bagh* and *khoroo* are also held not less than twice a year.

An emergency session of the *Khural* can be called as remanded by not less than two thirds of the elected representatives or by a decision of the relevant *Khural* Presidium. The first session of a newly elected *Khural* is announced and convened by the Presidium of the *Khural,* whose term of office is ending, within 20 days after the casting of votes and other sessions are called by the presidium of the relevant *Khural* not less than 15 days before the commencement of the session of the new *Khural.* The first Session elects the chairperson of the relevant *Khural* together with the *Aimag* and Capital City *Khural* Presidium of 7 to 11 members, 5–7 members of the *Soum* and District *Khural* Presidium, and 3–5 representatives of the *bagh* and *khoroo Khural* Presidium.

The first session of the given *Khural* is chaired by the most senior of the elected representatives, while other sessions are chaired by the chairperson of the *Khural* and in his absence, by any one elected representative, who is a member of the give *Khural* Presidium, but as proposed by the chairperson of the *Khural.* A session of *Aimag,* Capital City and *Soum Khural* representatives is considered valid if the majority of the elected representatives are present for the given session. The sessions of the *Bagh* and *Khoroo Khurals* can be organised in parts.

The Governor of an *Aimag,* Capital City, *Soum,* District, *Bagh* and *Khoroo* is the local government representative whose duty it to provide state management over the concerned territory.

Resident inhabitants coming under the jurisdiction of the given General meeting of the given administrative and territorial unit have the right to nominate candidate to the Governor of the *Bagh* and *Khoroo*; and the candidate to the post of Governor of anA*aimag,* Capital City, *Soum* and District can be nominated by the political party or coalition in the given *Khural,* and/or the representatives of the relevant *Khural* can also nominate their own candidates. If the candidate receives more than 50 per cent of the votes of the citizens and representatives taking part in the *Khural* Session, the name of the candidate who has received the majority of such votes will be proposed to the relevant higher level authority for the approval of the candidacy. For example, the Governor of an *Aimag* and the Capital City is appointed for a period of four years by the Prime Minister of Mongolia. The elected Governor of a *Soum* and District will be appointed by the *Aimag* and Capital City Governor, while the Governor of a *Bagh* and *Khoroo* is appointed by the *Soum* and District Governor and all for a term of four years, and this term of office does not concern those

Governors who have been re-appointed. The *Aimag,* Capital City, *Soum,* District, *Bagh* and *Khoroo* Governors have their own secretariats.

The Governors provide the *state management* in the relevant territories of the *aimag,* capital city, *soum,* district, *bagh* and *khoroo.* The Government is responsible for carrying through the decision of his/her *khural* and also performs as the local executive authority and in this sense, such Governors bear direct responsibility for ensuring the implementation of laws and legislation, decisions of the Government and the relevant higher authorities, and they are directly accountable to the Government and the higher instance Governor, and they too have the right to veto the decisions of the relevant *khurals of aimag,* capital city, *soum,* district, *bagh* and *khoroo.*

The *Khurals* of Representatives of Citizens of the *aimags,* capital city and *soums* have the power and authority to consider all matters relavant to the administrative and territorial unit under their jurisdiction and pass relevant decisions regarding them except those matters that are within the power and authority of the higher-instance *khural* or other authorities. *Khurals* of Representatives of Citizens of the *aimags,* capital city and *soums,* however, reserve the right to consider and take decisions on the following matters:

1 Matters related to the territorial economic and social development, relevant long-term plans, local budget and finances, and their implementation and performances;
2 The power and authority of the Representatives of the *Khural;*
3 Electing and dismissing the Chairman and secretary of the *Khural* sessions and the *Khural* Presidium;
4 Submit motion to the higher-level Governor and the Prime Minister on matters related to the nomination of candidate to the post of Governor, his/her dismissal and resignation;
5 If deemed necessary, the *Khural* can consider the performance report of the relevant Governor, assess and evaluate his/her performance;
6 Accept or reject the vote by the Governor of the *Khural* decision.

The Presidium of the *Khurals* of Representatives of Citizens of the *aimags,* capital city and *soums* has the following powers in between the sessions of the *khurals* other than those that come under its prerogatives:

1 Set the date of the *Khural* Session and announce it, ensure its preparations, and draft proposals and decisions related to its organisational and other activities;
2 Ensure the implementation of the *Khural's* decision and monitor the implementation status;

3 Take decisions on proposals, applications and complaints submitted by citizens, business entities and also governmental and non-governmental organisations;
4 Facilitate the conducting of elections of the President, the State Great *Khural* and the *Khurals* of Representatives;
5 Organise public opinion polls, as decided by the relevant authorities, at the relevant territorial level on matters related to bills, and important issues of the state and the society;
6 If it deems necessary, it can consider and take decisions on important economic and social issues of the territory under its jurisdiction;
7 Nominate candidates to high state awards and submit the proposal thereof.

The Governor is the key implementer of state management in the relevant local jurisdiction, and in this respect, he/she exercises the following power and authority:

1 The Governors of *aimags,* capital city, *soums,* districts, *baghs* and *khoroos,* with the objective of comprehensively ensuring the development of their territory, provides leadership in managing the economic and social development plan, long- and short-term programmes, ensuring the approval and implementation of the budget;
2 Improve accessibility to all kinds of services to the population in their respective administrative and territorial units, facilitate, guide monitor the activities of social, cultural and business enterprises, determine and allocate land for tenure, and manage the exploitation and use of natural and other mineral resources strictly in accordance with the law;
3 Combat natural disasters and human and animal infectious diseases, fight fires, mobilise people, transport and communication means and materials during an emergency, and render assistance to those people who are in need;
4 Monitor how people are exercising their rights and duties as specified in the laws and legislations, and organise measures to prevent breach of law;
5 Facilitate ties with the local business and economic entities on the principles of contract and tax policy.

5 The Legal System

A new legal system is developing and taking form foothold as a result of the stage-by-stage legal reform in the country as a whole. As specified in the appendix to the Constitution, the State Great *Khural* confronted the task of fully overhauling the country's laws and legislation by 1996 so the legal reform is compatible with the letter and spirit of the Constitution of Mongolia. The most important primary task of the State Great *Khural* was to reform the country's legal system. Nine sessions of the State Great *Khural* were held between 1992 and 1996, during which the Parliament adopted 369 laws, and passed 374 resolutions, of which 117 laws were brand new ones.

In this manner, the task of fully reforming the country's legal system as defined by the Constitution, its appendices and the legislative policy of the State Great *Khural* of Mongolia, was successfully accomplished. We can draw this kind of conclusion not only by the number of bills passed but also the fact that the issues of basic social relations were regulated on their basis. And so, the legal reform carried out in the country is the most important direct outcome of the work of the State Great *Khural.*

If we look at the legal branches of the country since the promulgation of the new Constitution, we find that the legal basis of the Constitution of Mongolia, administrative, criminal, civil, criminal procedure and civil court procedures, the powers of the courts, and how law is being practically applied, are based on the principles of the Romano-Germanic or the Continental legal systems, but the business law, which related to the "private" legal branch, the country had relied, in one or the other, on the Anglo-Saxon law system.[9]

The State Great *Khural,* has not only primarily adopted laws defining the legal foundations of the legislative, the executive and judicial powers, but has also defined the foundations of the market economic relations (privatisation, economic and business entity, anti-bankruptcy, tax, customs duty, bank, state budget, securities, accounting and book-keeping, statistics, restriction of unfair business competition, foreign exchange regulation etc.) and has adopted these most important and relevant bills, which have all been enacted. The Mongolian Parliament has also passed laws on the issue of guaranteeing the State's independence and sovereignty, the entire gamut of social relations and relations connected with providing social guarantees to the population (package of laws on education, culture and social insurance, state civil service etc.), legislations defining the legal basis of ensuring human rights and freedoms (legal status of foreign nationals, legislation concerning overseas travels by Mongolian citizens, related to migration, copyrights, patents etc.). In this way, the

9 D. Lündeejantsan, *Security, Development, State and Law,* Book One, Ulaanbaatar, 2002, p. 264.

coverage of legal regulations were extended and this signalled a tendency (legal differentiation) towards the appearance of ever new branches of law, and at the same time, there also has been a tendency towards merger and classification (legal integration) of common social relations that are regulated by law.

From an analysis of the existing laws and legislation in force in Mongolia from the standpoint of the following three criteria, that is, regulatory elements, regulatory methods and foundations of laws and legislation, we can conclude that the following legal foundations constitute the law system of Mongolia:

1 Constitutional law;
2 Administrative law;
3 Civil law;
4 Criminal law;
5 Labour law;
6 Social welfare law;
7 Land law;
8 Ecology law;
9 Family law;
10 Financial and credit law;
11 Economic and business law;
12 Co-operative law;
13 Criminal procedure law;
14 Civil procedure law;
15 Administrative procedure law;
16 Executor process law.

The State Great *Khural,* judging it appropriate to continue the process of reforming the law system of the country in the letter and spirit of the Constitution, passed a Resolution 18 in 1998 according to which the "Judicial Reform Programme of Mongolia," and the "Basic Guidelines for Streamlining Mongolia's Laws and Legislation up to 2000" were adopted became important landmarks in reviewing the accomplishments and progress in the law sector and outlining the future plan of action. Since 2000, within the framework of this Programme, the relevant Governments, in concurrence with these programme documents, had thrice adopted Basic Guidelines for Streamlining the Laws and Legislations of Mongolia, thanks to which, more than 400 laws and legislations are in force in Mongolia today.

In 2007, the Ministry of Law and Home Affairs together with law scholars and researchers monitored and evaluated the judicial reform programme and came up with relevant recommendations. They pointed out that although the judicial reform was successful, which was launched in

1992 to correspond new laws and legislations with the Constitution and its principles, the laws that were passed had a weak inter-relationship with substantial discrepancies and loopholes. They recommended the review of the content of all the laws, their text processing and legal terms, and to plan concrete time-bound and measureable actions and measures to better coordinate, systematise and streamline them.

Accordingly, the Government of Mongolia was instructed to "Carefully follow the principles of ensuring that the development of bills are scientifically-based and of high quality and in this manner deepen the process of law reform, and streamline laws and legislation by way of eliminating ambiguities and duplications in them." This is specified in Provision 4.1.1 of the "Action Programme of the Government of Mongolia in the Years 2008–2012," which was approved by Resolution 35 passed in 2008 by the State Great *Khural*. As a follow up, the Government in collaboration with the German Technical Cooperation Agency's (GTZ) project "Guaranteeing legal environment for sustainable economic development" worked to determine duplication, discrepancies and ambiguities in civil and economic laws, and improving their coordination.

In the period since 1992, the Government came up with and implemented concrete policy programmes on the following: 1. Laying the legal foundations of Mongolia's sovereignty; 2. Promoting human rights and freedoms, and their legal guarantees; 3. Streamlining the legal foundations of the state system of Mongolia; 4. Creating the necessary environment for judicial reform; 5. Regarding legal professionals; 6. Mongolia's participation in international judicial regulations. In this regard, the central issue concerning the legal foundations of guaranteeing the sovereignty of Mongolia is to ensure that Mongolia's state structure is unitary and the territory should be divided only into administrative units, and backed by law the inviolability of the state borders of the country, ensure that the government powers are in the hands of the people, and to create the mechanism which would make sure that the principle of rule by the people is direct or is effected through their representative organs.

During this period, judicial foundations were laid for the possession, ownership, utilisation and protection of the land, its bowels, the forests, water, animal kingdom, plants and other natural resources. The Government in this respect also passed laws that precisely and comprehensively outlined the legal basis for the use of land by foreigners and stateless people, as the land is a special object of ownership, and set down to their enforcements. The Civil Code of the country, which codified the legal regulation of property and ownership relations in the country, was revised and streamlined, and on this basis sectoral laws, which regulated specific forms of property and ownership relations, were passed in phases with due consideration of the demands and needs of the society.

The Constitution, in its Article 5.1 and 5.2, had articulated that the country will "have an economy based on different forms of property, which takes into account universal trends of global economic development and national specifics, and the State recognizes all forms of both public and private property, and the rights to ownership shall be protected by law."

The State Great *Khural*, in the "Judicial Reform Programme of Mongolia", which was adopted in 1998, had set the task of comprehensively reforming specific issues of social relations in the Civil Code, and in the plan of actions of the Government Action Programme, adopted in 2000, and within the framework of reforming Mongolia's laws and legislations, had committed to package the Civil Code, Law on Civil Procedure Law and Criminal Procedure Law, drafted the Civil Code of Mongolia, which was submitted to the State Great *Khural*.

While developing the Civil Code, consideration was given to the need to reform it on the basis of the common gains and the standards of the Romano-Germanic legal system, intensify the pace of judicial reforms to match the demands and requirements of a market economy, and to carry out legal regulation of unprecedented new and emerging social life of the country.

The following principles were adhered to in the development of the draft Civil Code:

- Model and codify the development trends of the country's economic and legal relations with that of the universal rules of global development;
- Improve the environment and pre-requisites for guaranteeing equality and fairness of those involved in civil legal relations;
- Accurately determine the juridical mechanism of promoting free and equitable development of all forms of property;
- Accurately define the principle of freedom contract and state regulation in contractual relationship;
- Eliminate duplication and ambiguities in the acting judicial regulations;
- Eliminate the discrepancies in the common and special regulatory mechanisms of civil law, and precisely define their inter-relationship;
- Precisely define the guarantee mechanisms of civil rights.

Many new elements were incorporated into the Civil Code, including the application of civil legislation as follows:

- If an international treaty to which Mongolia is a party provides otherwise than the Civil Code, the international treaty shall prevail.
- In cases other than the International Treaty stipulating that national legislation should be adopted, civil legal relations shall be regulated by the International Treaty of Mongolia.
- In case laws other than the Constitution and this Law contradict each other, the provisions of the Law, which regulates this matter in more detail, or in case of absence of such, provisions of the lately adopted Law shall apply.
- Validity of an invalidated Law shall not be restored if the Law annulling this Law is invalidated.
- If the Law envisages, the legal acts adopted in compliance with this Law by Government, other competent government agencies or officials and containing civil legal norms and enforced publicly, shall be applied.
- Ignorance about the Law or its misinterpretation shall not serve as a ground for its non-compliance or exempt from responsibilities stipulated by the Law.
- In the absence of norms regulating similar relations, the particular relations shall be regulated in compliance with the civil legal content, principles and commonly accepted norms.
- If parties to the contract agree, the newly adopted legislation with better terms and conditions shall apply.

The Civil Code has also defined anew the objects of civil legal relationship as "In accordance with the grounds and procedure stated in the law, material and nonmaterial wealth, which could be valued in terms of money in civil circulation, shall be objects of civil legal relationship."

Participants in civil legal relationships have been clearly specified with new clauses such as: citizens, juridical/legal persons and organisations without legal status shall be participants in civil legal relationship. *Aimags*, the Capital City, *Soums*, Districts, as state, administrative and territorial units, can enter into civil legal relation like other legal entities. Such concepts as grounds for arising and protecting civil legal relationship, exercising rights and assuming duties in civil legal relationship have also been included in the Law.

The State Great *Khural* revised and adopted the Family Law on 11 June 1999 and invalidated the Family Law which was enacted in 1973.

The revised and amended Family Law defined the basis of the marriage relationship, formal requirements, procedures and divorce, and has regulated family property and non-property relations, adoption procedures, the rights and duties of parents to bring up a child, relations regarding maintenance and right to maintenance, guardianship etc.

According to this Law, the age for marriage has been clearly specified. "Mongolian male and female citizens, aged 18 and over, of a Mongolian citizen can marry a foreign citizen or a stateless person on the basis of mutual consent, unless such marriage contradicts the Law." The Law states that a male in Mongolia shall have one wife, and a female - one husband.

Legal notions concerning the end of a marriage relationship and divorce have been clearly specified and defined. In Mongolia marriages are dissolved through either judicial or ministerial procedures on grounds provided by law. But the Civil Code regulates property relations of a family.

Relations between parents and children have been regulated in Chapter Five of the Law. It has codified the conditions of relations arising between the parents and children and for establishing parentage by either ministerial or judicial procedures. According to the Law, both the parents exercise equal rights and the same duties in the upbringing of the child/children.

The 1973 Family Law had only one regulatory provision concerning the exclusion of parental rights. Whereas the 1999 amended Law, besides the aforementioned regulation, has included the provision upholding the interest of the child to the effect that a child has the right to grow up and taken care of in the home he/she was born. With the objective of implementing the UN Convention of the Rights of Child, a new provision was also included concerning the limitation of parental rights up to 6 months.

One of the most important relations that have been regulated by the Family Law is the relationship of maintenance - to maintain and to be maintained. For example, the maintenance rights and duties have been codified, noting that the amount of maintenance shall be determined considering the age of the child. The maintenance may be paid in cash or through property.

In keeping with the objectives outlined in the UN Convention of the Rights of Child, the issue of child adoption, the Law has clearly specified the general conditions and procedures for adoption of a child of Mongolian citizenship by a foreign subject, for example.

The Government of Mongolia, with the objective of liberalising labour relations in the country and abiding by the standards set by the International Labour Organisation (ILO), the State Great *Khural* considered and adopted the "Labour Code of Mongolia" in 1999, which was enacted effective as of 1 July 1999. The Labour Code has 15 Chapters and 142 Articles.

If we compared this 1993 Labour Code with the older Labour Law of the Mongolian People's Republic, we find that the following principle changes were made:

1 14 new terms and terminologies have been defined in the law in order to help the implementers, enforcers and controllers of the law get a better understanding and awareness about the provisions and clauses in the law. For instance, given the substantial qualitative changes in the labour relations subjects, terms such as employer, employee, their representatives, labour contract and collective contract and agreement have been defined and specified clearly from the standpoint of law.
2 Basic principles in establishing collective contracts and agreements and their scope and limitation, their implementation monitoring by the parties concerned have been clearly defined, specifying the key methods or regulating labour relations in a non-centralised manner.
3 Labour agreements, which are important legal facts leading to labour legal relations, have been given priority in the Law. It has specified the forms, the term, basic conditions of labour contracts, general and special conditions for labour contract termination, and the difference in initiating and validation of labour agreement, and besides all this, labour contracts have been classified, and the special regulatory mechanisms of labour contracts and agreements.

A new chapter on working conditions, labour safety and sanitation standards has been added to the Labour Code with the purpose of outlining measures designed at eliminating factors that could have a negative impact on the health and working capacity of an employee while at work or during the course of the contract. This chapter conclusively defines the concept of working conditions, refrains from such classification as manual, poisonous, underground, which are no longer used internationally, and has classified working conditions as normal and abnormal. The Law stipulates that the State shall determine the sanitation requirements and standards, defining that the employer also has the duty to create the working conditions in compliance with the set standards and that they are responsible for creating favourable working conditions and environment. It has precisely defined the basis requirements of labour safety and sanitation conditions, and has codified the system of managing the implementation and monitoring of the law.

A new chapter has been added to the Law on employment of minors disabled person, dwarfs and elderly citizens with the purpose of providing the necessary guarantees for life and creating the normal psychological pre-requisites for minors, elderly people, as well as physically challenged and dwarfs who are unable to work in normal working conditions and who require added attention and support from the State and the society.

Another new addition in the Law relates to management and organisation of labour with the aim of implementing national-level policy on labour and social issues, introducing decentralisation mechanisms, and strengthening the system of collective management, and also codifiing labour management in the local areas. It has also outlined the judicial basis for the establishment of a system of trilateral social consent. As stated in the Law, an *ex-officio* National Committee of labour and social consent shall be established within the Government, which will be composed of representatives of three parties – the Government, national organisations representing the rights and legal interests of the employees, and the employers themselves.

The National Committee of labour and social consent is a consultative body to influence the development and implementation of state policy concerning labour issues, and develop the system of trilateral social consent; settle collective disputes initiated within the scope of protecting the citizens' labour rights and associated economic, social, and legal interests; monitor the implementation of the national agreement of social consent, and consult on common economic and social policy issues.

The "Law on Minimum Size of Labour Remuneration" was approved by the State Great *Khural* on 16 April 2010, according to which, the National Committee of labour and social consent is responsible for determining the minimum labour remuneration.

In the past collective labour dispute were regulated through the "Law on Regulating Collective Labour Dispute", which was invalidated, and this relationship was taken up in a separate chapter on "Regulation of Collective Labour Disputes" in the amended Law, which defines the forms of reconciliation of collective labour disputes, such as inviting intermediaries, reconciliation committee, labour arbitration court.

Since 2001, the Labour Code was revised and amended five times, 25 provisions were invalidated and relevant changes and amendments were made to 15 provisions and articles.

The Bill on Criminal and Criminal Procedure was submitted to the State Great *Khural* by the Government of Mongolia, which was considered at the fall session of the Parliament and the bill was approved on 11 January 2002.

The practice of the Supreme Court of Mongolia commenting on the size of damage caused by a criminal activity was revised and codified by the Criminal Law. The size of damage has been decided to be estimated in the following manner based on the minimum level of one month labour wage in keeping with the law in force when the crime was committed:

1 Small amount – equivalent to 1 to 5 times the amount of the minimum monthly wage;
2 Substantial amount – equivalent to 51 to 120 times the amount of minimum monthly wage;
3 Large amount – equivalent to 126 to 200 times the amount of minimum monthly wage;
4 Especially large amount – equivalent to 102 and more than the amount of the minimum monthly wage.

If harm is inflicted by resorting to self-defence under circumstances excluding social danger of the crime, this would not constitute a crime. A new formulation in the law reads that "Any action specified in the Special Part of this Code to eliminate the danger to defend the interests of the state or society, own or others' right to life or inviolability of an individual, others rights and freedoms shall not constitute crime provided the damage inflicted to the third person is less severe than the one averted and the danger under the given circumstances could not have been eliminated by other means."

According to the 2019 Criminal Law "Items created by way of crime, arms and means used for committing it, or income gained by way of crime and other things incidental thereto that have been seized and included the state budget is defined as punishment by confiscation of property." This formulation was replaced with the following phrase: "Confiscation of property represents a forced free-of-charge withdrawal of the culprit's share property for the benefit of the state in the instances specified in the Special Part of this Code." Another new formulation reads "Seizure of items created by way of crime, arms and means used for committing it, or income gained by way of crime and other things incidental thereto shall be mandatory in addition to the confiscation of property." This sentence is applied as a supplementary punishment and the wrong-doer will be forced to come up with the allotted property.

Regarding conditional sentence, the Law stipulated that If, considering the nature and degree of social danger of the committed crime, the character of the culprit who has been sentenced to imprisonment for the first time for a less serious crime, and the circumstances of the crime, in cases where he/she compensated for the damage or redressed the harm caused, the court deems that the sentence imposed does not need to be served in person it may impose the sentence conditionally and fix a probation for a period of up to 5 years.

Proceeding from the commitments undertaken by Mongolia under international treaties and the realistic demands of the society, new chapters on crimes against security of mankind and peace has been included in the Special part of the Criminal Code.

Under the Criminal Code in force now, the following are not considered as a criminal offence: intentional infliction of severe bodily injury at strong mental impulse, infliction of severe bodily injury by exceeding self-defence limits, use of threat to kill or inflict heavy physical injury, use of vehicles, machinery and transport means for selfish interest and gains, cause damage to other's property accidentally, commit crime against the property of a foreign state and its organisations and their nationals and international organisations were not considered as crime in view of the changes in the property relations in order to concur them with the present-day development of the society. Similarly, these crimes were not considered as crimes: victimise a person who has criticised the person, mishandle livestock animals, seriously breach administrative control, conceal facts that may be detrimental when registering marriage, steal state orders and medals, illegally obtain petrol, fuel and lubricants, mishandle vehicles and machinery, forge travel tickets etc.

Involving persons under legal age in heavy drinking, drug abuse, prostitution, vagrancy and beggary, forced labour, causing hindrance to a journalist's professional activities, utilisation of illegally gained property and money (money laundering), deliberately report falsely about banditry, set up an organised criminal group and be involved in it, misappropriation or embezzlement by an competent official, abuse of power by an official of a non-governmental organisation have all been classified as crime under the new Law.

The coverage of penalties such as imposition of fine, forced labour and arrest has been extended with a view to change the limits of some sentences, apply extra sentence, and give the judges a choice of sentences. In the penal system, for example, a new punishment has been added, according to which a person who is guilty of having committed a minor and severe crime is put under detention for a period of up to six months and the correctional sentence has been changed into a punishment of forced labour for 100 to 500 hours. In order to create conditions so that punishment by imposing a fine is not affected by inflation, the law has stipulated that the size of the fine at the time when the sentence was passed shall be increased by 5 to 500 times the minimum labour wage.

The Law states that the "Special Supervising Judge" would give the permission for forced detention or for taking a suspect into custody. After considering the vacancy of special judges, their location, and work burden and many other factors, it was finally decided in the Criminal Procedure Law that there was no need for such judges, as the judges of the primary courts can pass their routine but final judgment and accordingly such an amendment was made to the law.

A new Article 10 has been added to the Criminal Procedure Law to the effect that "When a suspect is arrested, he/she shall be informed of the reason and grounds for the arrest, and he/she shall be reminded of his/her right to have an defense counsel, to defend him/herself, to lodge a complaint to court and not to give testimony against him/herself."

With the objective of preventing violation of law and putting an end to red-tape, improving the Procurator's (Public Prosecutor) role in monitoring an inquiry and investigation, preventing a Public Prosecutor from unjustifiably putting on hold or dismissing a case and refraining from initiating criminal proceedings, the Law has stipulated that only a Public Prosecutor shall have the right to grant permission for dismissing, abstaining from and reinstating a case. It was decided that the criminal cases would be handed over to the procurator.

A number of new clauses have been added to the Law, which enable the defence counsel to submit petition to collect objects, documents, information and other evidences required for providing legal assistance, or to present them and to have them inspected and included in the file of the case, participate in judicial examination in the court; to be present at his/her will in resolving by court the issue of arrest or confinement under guard of the suspect or accused being defended and to submit comments to the court; to participate at his/her will in the appellate or supervisory instance court hearing.

It was decided that the Public Prosecutor's Office would have a criminal case archive in order to improve the safety of criminal case files and set up an integrated archive system

A new provision in the Law is the term of investigation of a minor with confinement, which states that the total term of investigation with confinement shall not exceed 18 months.

An investigation department has been newly established under the Procurator's Office, the duty of which is to conduct preliminary investigation and inquest into crimes committed by the police, a person conducting inquiry, an investigator, a Procurator and a judge. The Procurator will not carry out any investigation, as a Procurator shall perform its monitoring duty as stipulated in the Constitution and the Law on Procurator's Office.

The number of persons conducting inquiry has been reduced as the officers conducting inquiry have been given this task. This, according to the Code of Judicial Practice, relates to the fact that the initial inquiry officer is responsible for completing the review of the case to its end, and this function requires a trained professional lawyer. An inquiry officer exercises the rights of an investigator and thus enhances the investigator's duties and responsibilities.

Appendix 1
List of Names of Mongol Khans and Other Mongolian Leaders

A **Summary of Mongol Khans**

1 Chinggis (1162–1227). Yesükei Baatar's son. He founded the first Mongol State and ascended the throne of the Great Mongol Empire in 1226–1227.

2 Ögödei (1187–1241). Chinggis Khan's third son. Chinggis Khan's youngest son Tului ruled the State after the death of Chinggis Khan, and Ögödei ascended the throne (1228–1241) as willed by the Great Khan.

3 Güyüg (1206–1248). Eldest son of Ögödei Khan. He reigned the Empire from 1246–1248.

4 Mönkh (1208–1259). Tului's eldest son. He ruled the country from 1251–1259.

5 Khubilai (1215–1294). Tului's son. He founded the Mongolian Yuan Empire, which he ruled from 126?-1294.

6 Ölziit Tömör (1265–1307). Khubilai's eldest son. Ölziit Tömör reigned from 1294–1307.

7 Khaisankhüleg (1281–1311). The second son of Chinghem, who was the son of Khubilai Khan. He succeeded to the throne from 1308–1311.

8 Ayürbalbad Buyant (1303–1324). Third son of Darambal and was the Khan between 1312 and 1320.

9 Shidbal Gegeen (1303–1324). Buyant Khan's son, he was the Khan of Mongolia from 1321–1324.

10 Yösöntömör (1276–1324). The second son of Gamal and his grandfather was Chinghem. He ascended to the throne and ruled the country from 1324–1328.

11 Ashitgev (1320–1328). Yösöntömör's son, who ascended to the throne in 1328 but abdicated one month after he was proclaimed the Khan.

12 Khüslen (1300–1329). Eldest son of Khaisan Khüleg Khan. He was enthroned in 1329 but died the same year he became the Khan.

13 Tövtömör (1304–1332). Second son of Khaisan Khüleg Khan. He ruled the country from 1329–1332.

14 Rinchinbal (1325–1332). Khüslen Khan's son. He died two months after enthronement in 1332.

15 Togoontömör (1320–1370). Rinchinbal's elder brother. He was the Emperor of the Yuan Empire from 1333 to 1368, the "Red Turban Re-

bellion" took place that ultimately led to the collapse of the Mongol Yuan Empire.

16 Bilegt (Ayüshiridar) (1338–1378). Togoontömör Khan's eldest son. After returning to his native land, he set up his capital at Kharkhorum (Karakorum) and ruled Mongolia as its Khan from 1370 to 1378.

17 Tögstömör (1342–1388). Bilegt Khan's son. He was the Khan from 1378 to 1388, and died at the hands of a traitor.

18 Enkhzorigt (1359–1392). Eldest son of Tögstömör Khan. He was the Khan of Mongolia from 1389 to 1392.

19 Elbeg Nigüüslegch (1361–1399). Enkhzorigt Khan's son, who was the Khan from 1392 to 1399.

20 Güntömör (1377–1402). Son of Elbeg Nigüüslegch, he was the Khan from 1400–1402.

21 Ügch Khashiha (.7–1408). He was on the throne from 1403 to 1408.

22 Ölziitömör (1378–1411). Güntömör's son, and he was the Khan from 1408–1441.

23 Delbeg (1395–1415). Ölziitömör Khan's son and was the Khan from 1411 to 1415.

24 Adai (1400–1438). Younger brother of Kharuusag Düüregch, who was enthroned in 1426 to serve until 1438.

25 Taison (Togtabokh) (1422–1452). Adai Khan's eldest son, who was the Khan from 1439 to 1452.

26 Akbarjinjion (1423–1452). Taison Khan's son, who was enthroned in 1452 but was assassinated the same year when he became the Khan.

27 Esen (1407–1455). He was the Prime Minister under Taison Khan. The son of Togoon Taison of the Oirads. In the middle of the 15th century, he united the Oirads and the Mongols and in violation of the traditional Golden Lineage became the Khan of the Mongols, but he was assassinated in 1455.

28 Mercus (Ükhegt) (1446–1456). Second son of Taison Khan. He was enthroned in 1455 but was killed a year later in 1456.

29 Molon (1437–1462). Mercus Khan's younger brother and was the Khan from 1456 to 1462.

30 Manduul (1426–1467). Third son of Adai Khan, who was enthroned in 1463 and was the Khan until 1467.

31 Batmönkh (1464–1517). Manduul Khan's younger cousin, the son of Bayanmönkh Jinon. In 1470, he was enthroned as Dayan Khan and ruled the country until 1517.

32 Barsbold Jinon (1488–1519). Batmönkh Dayan Khan's third son and he ruled from 1517–1519.

33 Bodi-Alag (1505–1547). Eldest son of Törbold and grandson of Batmönkh. He was on the throne from 1548 to 1557.
34 Daraisun Günden (1520–1557). Bodi-Alag Khan's eldest son. He ruled as Khan from 1548 to 1557.
35 Tümen (1539–1592). Eldest son of Daraisun Khan, better known as Tümen Zasagt Khan, who ruled the country from 1548 to 1557.
36 Buyan (1555–1603). Tümen Zasagt Khan's eldest son. He ruled from 1593 to 1603 and became famous as Buyan Setsen Khan.
37 Ligden Khutugtu (1592–1634). Son of Buyan Setsen Khan. He ruled from 1604 to 1634. He was the last Khan in the Chinggis Khan's lineage.

B Exalted By All Mongolia (1911–1919)

1 The Eighth Bogd Jebzundamba Khutugtu, the theocratic ruler of Mongolia.
2 Prime Ministers:
  a Sain Noyon Khan T. Namnansüren (February 1919 to November 1919)
  b Shanzodba Badamdorj (January to July 1921)
  c Jalkhanz Khutugtu S. Damdinbazar (January to July 1921)
3 People's Provisional Government (May–July, 1921)
Chairman: D. Chagdarjav (March 1921)
D. Bodoo (March to July 1921)

C Mongolia Under Constitutional Monarch (1921–1924)

1 The Constitutional Monarch Eighth Bogd Jebzundamba Khutugtu (July 1921-May 1924)
2 Prime Ministers:
  a D. Bodoo (July 1921-January 1922)
  b Jalkhanz Khutugtu S. Damdinbazar (February 1922 to May 1923)
  c B. Tserendorj (August 1923-November 1924)

D Mongolian People's Republic (1924–1992)

1 *Highest State Power*

a State Baga Khural. (November 1924–February 1949)
Chairmen of the Presidium:
- P. Genden (November 1924–November 1927)

- J. Damdinsüren (November 1927–January 1929)
- Kh. Choibalsan (January 1929–June 1930)
- L. Lagaan (April 1930–July 1932)
- A. Amar (July 1932–March 1936)
- D. Dogsom (March 1936–July 1939)
- G. Bumtsend (July 1940–February 1949)

b State Ikh Khural (February 1949–July 1960)

Chairmen of the Presidium:
- G. Bumtsend (February 1940–September 1953)
- J. Sambuu (July 1954–July 1960)

c Great People's Khural (July 1960–November 1990)
- J. Sambuu (July 1960–May 1972)
- Yü. Tsedenbal (June 1974–August 1984)
- J. Batmönkh (August 1984–March 1990)
- P. Ochirbat (March 1990–November 1990)

2 *The Highest Executive Power*

a Government (November 1924–July 1932)

Prime Ministers:
- P. Genden (July 1932–March 1926)
- A. Amar (March 1936–March 1939)
- K. Choibalsan (March 1939–February 1952)
- Yü. Tsedenbal (May 1952–August 1984)
- J. Batmönkh (July 1974–August 1984)
- L. Sodnom (July 1984–March 1990)
- Sh. Gungaadorj (March 1990–November 1990)

E The Brief Period of Transition to Constitution

Mongolian People's Republic (September 1990–July 1992)

1 President: P. Ochirbat (September 1990–February 1992)

2 Chairman of the State *Baga Khural* and Vice President – R. Gonchigdorj (September 1990–July 1992)

3 Government. Prime Minister – D. Byambasüren (September 1990–July 1992)

F **Mongolia (November 1992)**

1 *Presidents:*

- P. Ochirbat (February 1992–June 1997)
- N. Bagabandi (June 1997–May 2005)
- N. Enkhbayar (May 2005–May 2009)
- Ts. Elbegdorj (May 2009–July 2017)
- Kh. Battulga (July 2017)

2 *Chairmen of State Great Khural:*

- N. Bagabandi (July 1992–July 1996)
- R. Gonchigdorj (July 1996–July 2000)
- L. Enebish (July 2000–September 2001)
- S. Tömör-Ochir (September 2001–July 2004)
- N. Enkhbayar (July 2004–May 2005)
- Ts. Nyamdorj (July 2005–June 2007)
- D. Lündeejantsan (June 2007–September 2008)
- D. Demberel (September 2008–July 2012)
- Z. Enkhbold (July 2012–July 2016)
- M. Enkhbold (July 2016–January 2018)
- G. Zandanshatar (January 2018)

3 *Prime Ministers:*

- P. Jasrai (July 1992–July 1996)
- M. Enkhsaikhan (July 1996–April 1998)
- Ts. Elbegdorj (April 1998–July 1998)
- J. Narantsatsaralt (August 1998–July 1999)
- R. Amarjargal (July 1999–July 2000)
- N. Enkhbayar (July 2000–August 2004)
- Ts. Elbegdorj (September 2004– January 2006)
- M. Enkhbold (September 2004–December 2007)
- S. Bayar (December 2007–October 2009)
- S. Batbold (November 2009–August 2012)
- N. Altankhuyag (August 2012–December 2014)
- Ch. Saikhanbileg (December 2014–Juyl 2016)
- J. Erdenebat (July 2016–October 2017)
- U. Khürelsükh (October 2017–January 2021)
- L. Oyün-Erdene (January 2021)

Appendix 2
Chronology of Events in Each Chapter

Chapter 1

- The disintegration of the tribal system in the first millennium BCE.
- In 209 BCE, Modun Shanyu established a State for the first time.
- In 198 BCE, the Hunnu Empire concluded an agreement with the Han Dynasty of China establishing the border of the two Empires along the "Great Wall of China."
- The Hunnu Empire ceased to exist in the year 93 CE and was replaced by the State of Sumbe.
- The State of Sumbe existed in the 2nd to 7th centuries CE.
- Mugulyui's son Charugui established the State of Nirun in the year 30 CE.
- In the year 414 CE, Tatar became the Khan of the State of Nirun by force, and starting from this period onward, the Mongols became better known to the outside world as Tatars.
- In the years around 438–489, Buddhism witnessed a flourishing growth in the Great Nirun State.
- Jarun Khan (Shelun), who became the Emperor in 402–410, introduced a code of law of a military-administrative nature.
- The Great Nirun State ceased to exist after it was routed by the Turkic people in 555.
- A Turkic Empire existed on the territory of Mongolia during the years from 552 to 745.
- The Uighur Empire existed on the territory of Mongolia from the year 745 to 840.
- In the years 907–1125, the Kidan Empire existed in the south-east of Mongolia and along the territory of North China.
- In the 6th to 11th centuries, a section of the Mongol tribes came under the composition of alien tribes, while some others set up their own small but independent empires or existed in the form of tribal confederations.
- Temüjin was born in 1162.
- In 1189, Temüjin was proclaimed the Khan of the Khamag Mongol tribal confederation.
- Mongols States during this period predominantly had ancient nomadic social relations.

Chapter 2

- The Mongol nobility, who had formed an alliance against Temüjin, gathered on the banks of the Ergune River in 1201 and proclaimed Jamukha as Gür Khan.
- In the fall of 1203, Temüjin made a surprise attack on Tooril Khan of the Khereids in a place close to the Tuul River.
- In 1185–1206, Temüjin took part in 32 battles and subjugated 81 Mongol tribes and clans.
- The *Ikh Khurildai,* which was held in 1206, enthroned Temüjin as the Khan of the Great Mongol Empire and honoured him with the title of Chinggis Khan (Lord of Oceans).
- Major *Khurildais,* which had significantly important historical roles, were held in 1189, 1202, 1204, twice in 1206, 1216 and 1219.
- Chinggis Khan died in 1227.
- Ögödei became the Khan of the Mongol Empire (1229–1241).
- Güyük became the Khan of the Mongol Empire (1246–1248).
- Mönkh became the Great Khan (1251–1259).
- In 1246, Güyük Khan sent a letter to Roman Pope Innocent IV.
- *The Great Yassa* – the code of laws – was adopted in 1206 as a direct outcome of the historical event of the establishment of the first united Mongol Empire.

Chapter 3

- After the death of Mönkh Khan, Arigbökh and Khubilai Khan separately called the *Ikh* (Great) *Khurildai* in the year 1206 and simultaneously proclaimed themselves the Great Khans of the Mongol Empire.
- Khubilai moved his capital to Beijing in 1264.
- In 1271, Khubilai Khan changed the name of the Great Mongol Empire into the Yuan Empire.
- The Law of the Yuan Empire was written in 1271.
- The territory of the Mongols during the Yuan Empire included the present-day Mongolia, the Inner Mongolia Region Autonomous of the People's Republic of China and the southern parts of Siberia in Russia.
- *The Veritable Records of the Great Yuan* is a compilation of laws and decrees passed before 1322.
- The Great Yuan Empire declined from the Red Turban Rebellion led by Song loyalists in 1368.

Chapter 4

- 22 Mongol Khans had held the Imperial Seal of the Mongol Empire from 1370 to 1634, which is also called the "Period of the Smaller Khagans" (also referred to as "The Northern Yuan [dynasty]").
- In 1454, Esen Taishi of the Oirads, in violation of the rules and procedures followed by the members of the *Altan Urga* (*Descent from Chinggis Khan. Tr.*), became the Khan of the Mongols and briefly united the Mongol tribes.
- In 1470, Batmönkh was made the Khan with the title of *Dayan Khan* and ruled for more than 40 years.
- Tümen *Taiji* became the Khan in 1558 and was celebrated as the Tümen Zasagt Khan.
- Ligden Khan ruled the Mongol dynasty from 1603 to 1634.
- Tümen Zasagt Khan and Altan Khan were converted to Buddhism in 1576–1577.
- The Mongol-Oirad Assembly was held in 1640. The *Mongol-Oirad Laws* were adopted.

Chapter 5

- Inner Mongolia was occupied by the Manchus in 1636.
- In 1636, the Qing Dynasty was declared when Hong *Taiji* (Abakhai) was proclaimed the Khan of the Mongols at an assembly of the Inner Mongolian nobles and princes.
- War broke out between Khalkha Mongol and Züün Gar in 1688.
- Outer Mongolia became a vassal State of the Manchu Qing Dynasty.
- Western Mongolia or the Züün Gar came under the submission of the Manchus in 1755.
- In 1755–1758, Amarsanaa of the Oirads and Chingünjav of the Khotgoids waged an armed revolt against the Manchu Dynasty.
- The so-called Mongol *Jurgan* or the Ministry (Board) for the Administration of Outlying Regions was established in 1636.
- The Uliastai commander's office was set up around 1723.
- The Ministry of Erdene Shanzodba was established in 1723.
- The Office of the Manchu Ministry was established at Khüree in 1761.
- The Office of the Manchu Ministry was set up in Khovd in 1762.
- The *Khalkha Jirum* was discussed and approved in the years between 1709 and 1795.
- The wooden print of the *Mongol Code* was released in 1787 and distributed, and the Code was completed in its entirety in 1817.

Chapter 6

- Starting in 1901, the Manchu Qing Empire began implementing the so-called "New Administrative Policy" in Mongolia.
- In August 1911, *Chin Wang* Khanddorj and Da Lama Tserenchimed, a prominent lama of the Great *Shabi*, during their oblation ceremony agreed with the Bogd Gegeen to call a secret congress of the important Khalkha nobles and lamas to discuss the revival of the country's independence from the Manchu Qing Empire.
- In 1911 *Chin Wang* Khanddorj and delegation travelled to Russia to seek support for Mongolia's independence.
- On 29 December 1911, Bogd Jebzumdamba was enthroned as the theocratic ruler of Mongolia, and the country proclaimed the revival of the country's independence.
- The army of Magsarjav and Damdinsüren liberated Uliastai in December 1911, and Khovd in August 1912.
- Tsarist Russia and China reached a secret deal in October 1913 and agreed to make Outer Mongolia an autonomous region of China.
- Mongolia was made an autonomous region of China during the so-called tripartite Mongolia, China, Russia Treaty of 1915.
- A new ministry "General Management Ministry" was established in the middle of 1912 and Sain Noyon Khan Namnansüren was appointed the Prime Minister of Mongolia.
- The State Upper and Lower *Khurals* were formed in February 1914.
- National military units and regiments were formed starting in 1912.
- The typically Mongol law called the "Code of Laws of Mongolia" was drafted, which was submitted for consideration and amendment by the Upper and Lower *Khurals* and approved by the Bogd Khan in the years from 1915 to 1918.

Chapter 7

- The Socialist Revolution in Russia took place, which impacted Mongolia through various means and channels.
- The so-called Khüree and Consul revolutionary groups, including political groups of the nobles were founded at the crossroads of 1918–1919.
- In late November 1919, Chinese warlord Xu Shuzheng threatened the Mongolian authorities, abolished Mongolia's autonomy and established a reactionary Chinese regime.
- The Consul and Khüree underground groups merged on 25 June 1920, established a revolutionary organisation called the "Mongo-

lian People's Party" (MPP) and decided to seek assistance from the Russian Soviet Federation.

- A consultative meeting of the MPP was held at Ar Khiagt on 1 to 3 March 1921, where they formally established the party and elected its leaders.
- The People's Provisional Government was established on 13 March 1921.
- The people's volunteer army liberated Khiagt on 18 March 1921, heralding the first national democratic revolution.
- The people's volunteer army together with Soviet army units liberated Khüree and the national liberation revolution triumphed in July 1921.
- The so-called "Restored Government of Baron" was dismissed on 19 July 1921 and the duties and functions of the ministries were transferred to the People's Government.
- The Eighth Bogd Jebzundamba was enthroned at the State Yellow Palace and was proclaimed a constitutional monarch of Mongolia on 11 July 1921.
- A so-called "Oath Taking Treaty" was adopted by a resolution of the People's Government on 1 November 1921, which defined the principles of relationship and the rights and duties of the Bogd Khan and the People's Government.
- A Provisional State *Khural* was established in November 1921.
- The "Provisional Rules of the People's Government" came into effect on 3 March 1922.
- The "Rules on the Rights and Authority of the Many Mongol *Zasag* and *Zasag Wangs* and *Güngs*," were approved in 1922 and the "Rules on the Local Administrations of Mongolia" and the "*Ikh Shabi* Administration Rules" were approved in 1923.
- Local administrations were subject to democratic reforms and transformation starting from late 1923 to the fall of 1924.
- The First State Congress (*Ikh Khural*) opened on 8 November 1924.
- The First Constitution was adopted on 26 November 1924 and the Mongolian People's Republic was proclaimed.

Chapter 8

- The Law on Re-Classification and Division of the Country's Territory, which was adopted on 6 February 1931, abolished the *banners* and instead established 13 *aimags* and *311 soums.*

- The Seventeenth State Conference, held on 2 July 1932, projected the New Turn Policy.
- The Seventh State Congress (*Khural*), which was convened on 20–27 December 1934, decided that the State *Ikh Khural*, which met for its session once a year, was changed and decided that the State *Ikh Khural* session, which would be convened by the State *Baga Khural*, would be held 3 times in one year.
- The mass campaign of political persecutions began on 10 November 1937 across the length and breadth of the country.

Chapter 9

- The Second Constitution of the Mongolian People's Republic was adopted at the Eighth State Congress, held on 30 June 1940.
- A national referendum on the independence of the MPR was held on 20 October 1945, and the Mongolian people voted 100 percent for their country's independence.
- The Ninth State Congress, which was convened in February 1949, considered the issue of reforming the election system of the MPR.
- The First Election to the Great People's *Khural* of the MPR was conducted on 10 June 1951, which elected 395 deputies to the Great People's *Khural*.
- Elections to the local organs of power were conducted in October 1952.

Chapter 10

- The Third Constitution of the Mongolian People's Republic was adopted at the First Session of the Fourth Election to the Great People's *Khural*, which convened on 6 July 1960.
- The Mongolian People's Republic became a full-fledged member of the United Nations Organisation in 1961.
- The Fifteenth Congress of the MPRP, which was held in the middle of 1961, adopted a party programme which had outlined the party's objective to "complete the construction of socialism in the country."
- The Eighth Plenary meeting of the MPRP Central Committee and the Special Session of the Great People's *Khural*, which were held in August 1984, relieved Yümjaagiin Tsedenbal of his official duties, and Jambyn Batmönkh was concurrently appointed as the Secretary-General of the MPRP Central Committee and the Chairman of the Presidium of the Great People's *Khural* of the MPR.

Chapter 11

- The Mongolian Democratic Union was established in December 1989, which organised political rallies and meetings demanding the democratisation of the Mongolian society.
- In accordance with the Law on Making Changes and Amendments to the Constitution, which was adopted on 23 March 1990, the clauses specifying the leading and guiding role of the MPRP, both in the Preamble and Article 82 of the Constitution, were deleted, and the Supreme Court was designated the responsibility of acknowledging and registering political parties.
- The Law on Amendments to the Constitution of the MPR was passed by the Ninth Session of the Eleventh Election of the Great People's *Khural,* which was convened in May 1990.
- The Ninth Convocation of the Eleventh Election of the Great People's *Khural,* held in May 1990, adopted the Law on Political Parties.
- The first free and democratic elections were held in Mongolia in July 1990.

Chapter 12

- The new Constitution of Mongolia was adopted at the Second Session of the Twelfth election to the Great People's *Khural* of the MPR on 13 January 1992.
- Election to the State Great *Khural* was held on 28 June 1992. The first session of the first elections of the State Great *Khural* opened on 20 July 1992 with 76 members taking their oath and entering into office as Parliament members.
- Punsalmaagiin Ochirbat, who was elected as the First President of Mongolia on 19 June 1993, took his oath of office in the State Great *Khural* and the same day the State Great *Khural* passed a law confirming the office of the President.
- The First Session of the Second State Great *Khural* election opened on 19 July 1996 where the members took their oath of office and the same day a decision was passed confirming the term of office of 76 Parliament members.
- Natsagiin Bagabandi was elected the President of Mongolia in the Presidential election, which was conducted in May 1997, who took his oath of office in the State Great *Khural* on 20 June.
- The third election to the State Great *Khural* was held on 20 July 2000 and the first session of the Parliament was convened on 19 July, where its 76 members took their oath of office.

- Presidential election was held on 20 May 2001 and Natsagiin Bagbandi was re-elected, who took his oath of office on 21 June the same year.
- The fourth State Great *Khural* election was held on 27 June 2004 and the State Great *Khural* members took their office on 27 July to begin their four-year term office.
- Presidential election was held on 22 May 2005, where Nambaryn Enkhbayar was elected as Mongolia's President. The new President took his oath of office on 25 June.
- The fifth election to the State Great *Khural* was conducted on 29 June 2008 and its 76 new members took their oath of office at the first session of the new State Great *Khural* on 29 August 2008.
- The next round of Presidential election was held on 24 May 2009, where Tsakhiagiin Elbegdorj came out as the winner and he assumed his office of Presidency by taking his oath on 18 June 2009.
- The sixth election to the State Great *Khural* was carried out on 28 June 2012 and the first session of the new Parliament was held on 6 July, where 69 new members of Parliament took their oath. This was the first time that the parliamentary election was conducted using the mixed system.
- Tsakhiagiin Elbegdorj was re-elected as Mongolia's President in the presidential election, which was held on 28 June 2013. The new President was sworn in on 10 July of the same year.
- The seventh State Great *Khural* election was held on 29 June 1016. The first session of the new Parliament was convened on 5 July, where the new members of the State Great *Khural* were sworn in.
- The regular Presidential election was held on 26 June 2017, (second vote casting was organised on 7 July) and in this re-run election Khaltmaagiin Battulga was elected the President of Mongolia, who took his oath of office on 10 July of the same year.
- Changes and amendments to the Constitution of Mongolia were approved by the State Great *Khural* on 14 November 2019, and the President of Mongolia approved the changes and amendments on 26 November (coinciding with the day the Republic was proclaimed, and the First Constitution was promulgated), and the amended Constitution came into force effective as of 25 May 2020.
- The eighth Parliamentary election was organised on 24 June 2020, the first session of the new Parliament was convened on 30 June and 75 new members of the Parliament were sworn in.

Bibliography

Note to the reader: This Bibliography follows Mongolian tradition, which lists authors by first name or first name initial. Consequently, the alphabetical order of this list is based on the first letter appearing in each bibliographic citation.

"Mongolyn Ünen" (Mongolian Truth) newspaper, (Collection of Articles and News Published in the newspaper, Ulaanbaatar, 1971.

"State Information" Journal, (1990–1992).

"Дальный Восток" (The Far East), 1913, Issue No. 36.

A. Amar, Brief History of Mongolia, Ulaanbaatar, 1989.

A. Damdinsüren, Brief History of the Mongol Arms and Weapons, Ulaanbaatar, 1990.

A. Dumburai, Punishment, Ulaanbaatar, 1992.

A. Kalinnikov, Национально-революционные движения в Монголии, (National Revolutionary Movements in Mongolia), Moscow, 1926.

A. Lhagva, Historical Road of Development from a Penitentiary Squad to General Executive Agency of Court Decision, (1921–2001), Ulaanbaatar, 2001.

A. M. Khazanov, Кочевники и внешний мир, (Nomads and the Outside World), Almaty, Dake Press, 2000.

A. Namsrai, History of the *Züün Gar* (Dzungar) Khanate, Hohhot, 1996.

A. Ochir, Brief History of the Mongol Oirads, Ulaanbaatar, 1993.

A. Tsanjid, Political Science, Ulaanbaatar, 1997.

A.S. Benfeld, Khalkha Under the Manchus, Moscow, 1980.

About the Code of Law of Altan Khan, Institute of Social Sciences of Inner Mongolia, 1984. Issue No. 2, pp. 57–68.

Alan J. K. Sanders, Historical Dictionary of Mongolia, Scarecrow Printing, 1996.

Altan Tobchi – The Golden Summaru, Ulaanbaatar, 1990.

Ancient and Modern-day Legal Courts of Mongolia, Ulaanbaatar, 1936.

B. Baabar, History of Mongolia, Ulaanbaatar, 2017.

B. Baabar, Mongolia in the 20th Century: Migration (Nüüdel Suudal – Gains and Losses), Ulaanbaatar, 1996.

B. Baabar, Mongols: Migration (Nüüdel Suudal), Vol. 1, Ulaanbaatar, 2009.

B. Batsüren, B. Chinzorig, E. Jigmeddorj, Nomadic States and Empires of Central Asia, (6th-12th centuries), Ulaanbaatar, 2017.

B. Batsüren, Early and Ancient Turks, Ulaanbaatar, 2009.

B. Batsüren, P. Delgerjargal, U. Erdenebat, History of the Great Mongol State – the Mongol Empire, Volume One, Ulaanbaatar, 2019.

B. Batsüren, R. Mönkhtulga, Ancient History of the Hunnu and Mongols, Vol. 4, Ulaanbaatar, 2017.

B. Bayanchuulgan, History Linking Manchuria and Mongolia, Manuscript, National Central Library of Mongolia, Book 11.

B. Bayarsaikhan, Constitutional Traditions of Mongolia, (Legal Research Analysis of the 1949 Constitution of the MPR), Ulaanbaatar, 2017.

B. Bayarsaikhan, Dictionary of Law, (History of the State and Law of Mongolia), Ulaanbaatar, 2003.

B. Bayarsaikhan, Law Dictionary, (History of Mongolia's State and Legislation),

B. Bayarsaikhan, Law Dictionary, (History of the State and Law of Mongolia), Ulaanbaatar, 2008.

B. Bayarsaikhan, Legal Research into the *Mongol Tsaazyn Bichig*, Ulaanbaatar, 2010.

B. Bayarsaikhan, Terms and Terminology in the Mongol Code, National University, Law College, "Law" journal on Theory, Practicals and Information, Issues No. 2–3, 2007 (16–17).

B. Bayarsaikhan, The White History of Ten Virtuous Books of Mongolia, Ulaanbaatar, 2002.

B. Chimid, Administrative Law of the MPR, Ulaanbaatar, 1973.

B. Chimid, Knowledge of the Constitution, Ulaanbaatar, 2008.

B. Chimid, Principles of Respecting and Revering the Constitution, (Four Statements Addressed to the Elite and Every Individual), Ulaanbaatar, 2006.

B. Chimid, Today's Politics Through the Eyes of a Lawyer, Ulaanbaatar, 2006.

B. Dash-Yondon, Identifying the System and Presenting It, Ulaanbaatar, 1996.

B. Dolgormaa, МНР – Государственный бюджет и планомерное сторительсво, (MPR – State Budget and Planned Development), Moscow, 1967.

B. Gonchigsüren, Tax Policy of the MPRP, Ulaanbaatar, 1973.

B. Günbileg, Comparative Law, Ulaanbaatar, 2008.

B. Laagan, The Proclamation of the Mongolian People's Republic is the Embodiment of the State Policy of the MPRP, Ulaanbaatar, 1985.

B. Lhamsüren, External Environment and Independence of Mongolia, Ulaanbaatar, 1995.

B. Punsaldulam, N. Khishigt, Mongolia's Revolutions of 1911 and 1921 (Summary of Foreign Historiography), Ulaanbaatar, 2007.

B. Punsandulam, Historiography of the 1911 National Revolution of Mongolia, (1911–2003), Ulaanbaatar, 2006.

B. Punsandulam, N. Khishigt, Mongolia's Revolutions of 1911, 1912, (Summary of Foreign Historiography), Ulaanbaatar, 2007.

B. Pürev, The Application of Leninist Teachings on the Representative Organs of Socialist State Power in the MPR, Ulaanbaatar, 1981.

B. Sanjmyatav, Historical Truth about the Tripartite Khiagt Treaty, Ulaanbaatar, 1991.

B. Shirendev, Biography of Ardyn Khatanbaatar Magsarjav, Ulaanbaatar, 1976.

B. Shirendev, Brief History of the Mongolian People's Revolution, Ulaanbaatar, 1969.

B. Sodovsüren, Criminal Code of the MPR, Ulaanbaatar, 1969.

B. Sodovsüren, Evolution of Criminal Laws and Legislations of the MPR, Ulaanbaatar, 1973.

B. Sodovsüren, Pre-Revolutionary Mongol State and Codes of Law, (1911–1920), Ulaanbaatar, 1989.

B. Sodovsüren, State and Law in Pre-Revolution Mongolia, Ulaanbaatar, 1988.

B. Tseden-Ish, From the History of the Formation of Mongolia's Borders, Ulaanbaatar, 1997.

B. Ya. Vladimirtsov, Общественный строй монголов. Монгольлский кочевой феодализм, (Social structure of the Mongols. Nomadic feudalism of the Mongols), Central Library of Mongolia, Manuscript, 1947.

B. Ya. Vladimirtsov, Общественный строй монголов. Монгольский кочевой феодализм, (Social structure of the Mongols. Nomadic feudalism of the Mongols), Leningrad, 1934.

Batsaikhan, Mongolia's Independence and the China, Russia, Mongolia Khiagt Treaty of 1915, (1911–1916), Ulaanbaatar, 2002.

Baya, Dei Huni, Northern Yuan Dynasty, Inner Mongolian University Printing Institute, 1991.

Bibliography of Hunnu Study (Compiled by. Ts. Turbat), Ulaanbaatar, 2009.

Bibliography of Research Works into the History of Mongolia in the 17th-20th Centuries, Compiled by E. Jigmeddorj, Ulaanbaatar, 2007.

Biographies of L. Bat-Ochir, D. Dashjamts and D. Sükhbaatar, Ulaanbaatar, 1968.

Brief Guide to Archival Documents Related to the History of Bogd Khan Mongolia, (1911–1912), Ulaanbaatar, 1992.

Brief History of the Mongol People, Hohhot, 1988.

C. P. Atwood, Encyclopedia of Mongolia and the Mongol Empire. Facts on File library of old history, New York, NY: Facts on File, 2004.

Ch. Bawden, Modern History of Mongolia, London, 1968.

Ch. Dalai, History of Mongolia. (1206–1260), Ulaanbaatar, 1992.

Ch. Dalai, History of Mongolia. Khamag Mongol (1101–1206), Book One, Ulaanbaatar, 1996.

Ch. Dalai, History of Mongolia. The Great Mongol State (1206–1260), Book Two, Ulaanbaatar, 1994.

Ch. Dalai, History of the Oirads, Book One, Ulaanbaatar, 2002.

Ch. Dalai, Mongolia During the Period of the Yuan Empire, Ulaanbaatar, 1973.

Ch. Dalai, Ögödei Khan. Imperial Fund, Ulaanbaatar, 2000.

Ch. Davaadash, Coup d'état in Mongolia, Ulaanbaatar, 2008.

Ch. Davaadash, The Red History, Ulaanbaatar, 2004.

Ch. Enkhbaatar, Constitutional Law, Ulaanbaatar, 2001.

Ch. Jügder, Social, Political and Philosophical Mentality during the Period of Feudalism in Mongolia, Ulaanbaatar, 1987.

Ch. Jügder, State Ideology and Science of Warfare of Chinggis Khan, Ulaanbaatar, 1990.

Ch. Jügder, The Evolution of Social, Political and Philosophical Thinking of Mongolia at the Crossroads of the 19th and 20th Centuries, Ulaanbaatar, 1972.

Ch. Önörbayar, How the Concept of Constitution was Introduced in Mongolia, (1921–1924), Ulaanbaatar, 2015.

China, Russia, Mongolia Khiagt Treaty of 1915, (Daily Notes), Ulaanbaatar, 1999, (Compiled by O. Batsaikhan).

Christopher Kaplonski, History and Politics in Mongolia, Memory of Heroes, Routledge, 2014.

Civil Code of the MPR, (Edited by D. Zundui, N. Chinbat), Ulaanbaatar, 1988.

Compilation of Chinese Historical Sources about the Mongol State during the Period of the Ming Dynasty, Volumes 1, 2, 3, Compiled by Bayankhüü and Wan Xun, Inner Mongolian University Printing Institute, 1991.

Compilation of Documents and Materials Related to the Life of D. Sükhbaatar, Ulaanbaatar, 1964.

Compilation of materials and reports of a scientific and research conference jointly held by the Social Science Faculty and the Law College of the Mongolian National University, Ulaanbaatar, 2001.

Compilation of Russia-China Treaties and Agreements, Ulaanbaatar, 2001, (Compiled by M. Batchimeg).

Concise Dictionary of Legal Knowledge, Ulaanbaatar, 1986.

Constitution of Mongolia, (Compiled and Commented by J. Amarsanaa and O. Batsaikhan), Ulaanbaatar, 2004.

Constitution of Mongolia. Documents, (Compiled and Commented by J. Amarsanaa and O. Batsaikhan), Ulaanbaatar, 2004.

Constitution of the MPR and Compilation of Related Legal Acts, Book One, Ulaanbaatar, 1972.

Constitution of the MPR and Compilation of Related Legal Acts, Ulaanbaatar, 1972.

Courts of the MPR – On Guard of Protecting Socialist Gains, Ulaanbaatar, 1977.

D. Ankhbayar, The Mongol Il-Khanates, Ulaanbaatar, 2006.

D. Ayalon, The Great Yassa of Chingiz Khan, A Re-Examination (Part A), Studia Islamica, No. 33, (1971), pp. 97–140.

D. Bold-Erdene, Political Party of Mongolia and the Evolution of the Party System, Ulaanbaatar, 2008.

D. Dash, From the History of the Proclamation of the MPR, Ulaanbaatar, 1984.

D. Dashjamts, The Issue of the Evolution and Development of Progressive Democratic Ideas in Mongolia, (At the Crossroad of the 19th and 20th Centuries), Ulaanbaatar, 1976.

D. Enkhtsetseg, Mahagurgis, Molon and Mandul Khans, Ulaanbaatar, 2007.

D. Enkhtsetseg, The Meaning of the Mongol Khutagt Khan, Ulaanbaatar, 2007.

D. Gangabaatar, Constitutional Law: State Structure, Principles and Concept, Ulaanbaatar, 2016.

D. Gombosüren, History of the Armed Forces of Mongolia, Ulaanbaatar, 1998.

D. Gongor, Khalkha Summary, Vol. 1, Ulaanbaatar, 1978.

D. Gongor, The Khalkha Summary, Vol. 2, Ulaanbaatar, 1978.

D. Gongor, Монголия в перехода от родового строя к феодализму, (Mongolia's transition from clan system to feudalism), (Early 11th-12th centuries), Ulaanbaatar, 1974.

D. Lündeejantsan, Ch. Enkhbaatar, The Law of the Constitution of Mongolia, Ulaanbaatar, 1996.

D. Lündeejantsan, Ecology Law: Laws, Legislation, Violations and Liabilities, Ulaanbaatar, 1996.

D. Lündeejantsan, Issues of Relations between Traditions and Reform of the Statehood of Mongolia, "Zasgiin Gazryn Medee" (Government News) newspaper, February 1993, Issue no. 5, 6.

D. Lündeejantsan, L. Ölziisaikhan, Parliamentarianism, Ulaanbaatar, 2005.
D. Lündeejantsan, Powers and Democracy, Ulaanbaatar, 2015.
D. Lündeejantsan, Security, Development, State and Law, (Compilation of Selected Papers and Articles), Book One, Ulaanbaatar, 2002.
D. Lündeejantsan, Separation of State Powers in Mongolia, Ulaanbaatar, 2001.
D. Lündeejantsan, Separation of State Powers in Mongolia, Ulaanbaatar, 2018.
D. Lündeejantsan, The Process of Making a Law and Legal Technology, Ulaanbaatar, 2016.
D. Maidar, Chinggis Khan and the Great Mongol Empire, Ulaanbaatar, 1990.
D. O. Morgan, The 'Great "yāsā" of Chingiz Khān' and Mongol Law in the Īlkhānate, Geschichte und kultur de Altaischen Volker, Berlin, 1974. Basil Blackwell, 1986. The Great 'Great "yāsā" of Chingiz Khān' and Mongol Law in the Īlkhānate BSOAS, Vol. 1, No. 1, 1986. The 'Great Yassa' of Chingigis Khan Revisited in Russian, Amitai and M. Biran (eds), Mongols, Turks and Others, E, J. Brill, 2005, pp. 291–308.
D. Ölziidolgor, The State Stamp of Mongolia, Ulaanbaatar, 1999.
D. Pokotilov, История восточных монголов в пероиде династия Мин (History of East Mongols during the Period of the Ming Dynasty), (Based on Chinese sources), St. Petersburg, 1893.
D. Sangidanzan, Courts of the MPR, Ulaanbaatar, 1967.
D. Tsogzolsüren, Titles, Ranks and State Ceremonial Dresses of the Mongol Nobles and Aristocrats, (1911–1919), Ulaanbaatar, 2003.
Damba, Rise and Fall of the Northern Yuan Dynasty, 1998.
Dariijav, Study into the History of the Mongols Living in the Southern Part of the Gobi during the Period of the Ming Dynasty, Ulaanbaatar, 2000.
Dayama Shieiru (Japan), Social System of the Mongols during the Period of the Qing Dynasty, Hohhot, 1988.
Dictionary of Politics and Laws of the Constitution of the MPR, Ulaanbaatar, 1988.
Dictionary of Some Historical Terms and Chronology of the Mongolian People's Republic, Ulaanbaatar, 1991.
Documents Related to Mongolia and Manchuria Relations in the First Half of 17th Century, Compiled by Li Bao Wen and Nyamka, Transliterated into the Cyrillic Script and commentary by Ts. Törbat and D. Enkhtsetseg, Ulaanbaatar, 2004.
Documents Related to the History of the 1921 People's Revolution, (1917–1921), Ulaanbaatar, 1957.

Documents Related to the History of the 1990 Democratic Movement, Book One, (Compiled by J. Zaankhüü), Ulaanbaatar, 2004.

Documents Related to the History of the MPRP, Book One, Ulaanbaatar, 1966.

Documents related to the Laws of the Yuan Empire. Department of Manuscripts of the Institute of History.

Dornotiv, Chinggis Khan's science of warfare, Huhhot, 1990.

Dornotiv, Khalkha Jirum, Autonomous Region of Inner Mongolia of the People's Republic of China, 1989.

E. Avirmed, D. Dashtseden, G. Sovd, Mongol Law, Ulaanbaatar, 1997.

E. Avirmed, State Power of the MPR, Ulaanbaatar, 1969.

E.A. Belov, Россия и Монголия (История, проблемы, современность), (Russia and Mongolia, History, Problems and the Contemporary), Ulan-Ude, 1997.

E.I. Kychanov, К вопросу об уровне софиально-экономического развития татаро-монгольских племен в XII в. //Роль кочевых народов и цивилизации Центральной Азии, (On the issue of the level of social and economic development of the Tatar-Mongol tribes in the 13th century. // Role of nomadic peoples and civilisation of Central Asia), Ulaanbaatar, 1974

Erdene Daiching Khosoi Chin Wang M. Khanddorj, (Scholarly conference documents), Ulaanbaatar, 2009.

Fifth Plenary Meeting of the MPRP Central Committee, Ulaanbaatar, 1988.

First Archives of the History of the Republic of China, Book on the Mongol Script Related to the First Half of the 17th Century, (Compiled by Li Bao Wen), Ulaanbaatar, 1997.

Foreign Policy Concept of Mongolia, Ulaanbaatar, 1994.

Futaki Hiroshi, Tracing the Historical and Cultural Heritage of the Mongols, Ulaanbaatar, 2002.

G. Bayarkhüü, A Comparative Study of the Laws and Customary Norms of the United Mongol State and the Period Thereafter, (13th-18th centuries), Ulaanbaatar, 1997.

G. Byambasüren, B. Bayarmaa, Mongol State Ceremony, Protocol and National Pride, Ulaanbaatar, 2004.

G. Chuluunbaatar, Evolution and Growth of Civil Society in Mongolia at the Crossroad of the Twentieth and Twenty Frist Centuries, Ulaanbaatar, 2005.

G. Ganbold, Some Theoretical Issues of the Socialist State and Law, Ulaanbaatar, 1990.

G. Kungurov, I. Sorokovikov, Аратская революция, (The Revolution of the *Ard*), Irkutsk, 1946.
G. Myagmarsambuu, Jamhua Setsen, Ulaanbaatar, 1966.
G. Myagmarsambuu, Khans of Khamag Mongol, Ulaanbaatar, 2000.
G. Sovd, A course on the Criminal Rights in the MPR, Ulaanbaatar, 1973.
G. Sovd, Commentary to the Laws on the Constitutional *Tsets* (Court) of Mongolia, (Research and Application), Ulaanbaatar, 1999.
G. Sovd, Historical Evolution of the Law on Criminal Proceedings of Mongolia, Ulaanbaatar, 1977.
G. Sükhbaatar, Ancient Ancestors of the Mongols, Ulaanbaatar, 1980.
G. Sükhbaatar, Chrestomathy of the History of Mongolia, Book One, Ulaanbaatar, 1992.
G. Sükhbaatar, The Nirun State of Mongolia, (350–556 CE), Ulaanbaatar, 1992.
G. Sükhbaatar, Xianbi, Ulaanbaatar, 1971.
G. Zandanshatar, The Movement for Putting in Order, Ulaanbaatar, 2014.
Galdan, Erdeniin Erkhi (Golden Rosary), Ulaanbaatar, 1960.
George Lane, Genghis Khan and Mongol Rule, 2002.
George Vernadsky, Research into the Great Yassa of Genghis Khan and its Content, Ulaanbaatar, 1992.
Hashhara Mamoru, Changes in Khalkha Mongol Laws in the 18th Century. Toyoshikeenkryu, 49.30.1990 (From the translation by T. Mönkhtsetseg).
Hashhara Mamoru, Codes of Laws on Criminal Cases of the Ikh Shabi in Mongolia Under the Manchu Rule, "Erkh Züi" (Law) Journal, No. 2, 3, 2005.
Henry Wheaton, Elements of International Law, (compiled by J. Amarsanaa, B. Bayarsaikhan and Tachibana Makoto), Ulaanbaatar.
Historical Overview of the Evolution of Laws and Legislations of Mongolia, (1911–2008), Ulaanbaatar, 2008.
History of Jin Dynasty, Hohhot, PRC, 1993.
History of Mongolia (Issues of history, theory and methodology), Ulaanbaatar, 2010.
History of Mongolia Vol. 2 of 5, Ulaanbaatar, 2004.
History of Mongolia, (History and Issues of Theory and Methodology), Ulaanbaatar, 2010.
History of Mongolia, 5 Volumes, Ulaanbaatar, 2004.
History of the Evolution of Laws and Legislations of Mongolia, (1911–2008), Ulaanbaatar, 2008.
History of the Mongol Soldiers, Book One, Ulaanbaatar, 1996.

History of the Mongol State and Law, (Selected Works), 4 volumes, Ulaanbaatar, 2006.
History of the Mongolian People's Republic, 3 Volumes,Ulaanbaatar, 1968.
History of the Mongolian People's Republic, Books One and Two, Ulaanbaatar, 2003.
History of the Mongolian Soldiers, Book Two, Ulaanbaatar, 1996
History of the MPR (Mongolian People's Republic), Ulaanbaatar, 1984.
History of the MPR, Book Three, Ulaanbaatar, 1969.
History of the MPR, Vol. 1 of 3, Ulaanbaatar, 1996.
History of the MPRP, Ulaanbaatar, 2001.
Hon Yun Bing, Zen Zhen Peng, Khubilai and the Yuan Empire, Hohhot, 1987.
I. Dashnyam, Election System of the MPR, Ulaanbaatar, 1975.
I. Dashnyam, History of the Mongol State and Laws, Ulaanbaatar, 1997.
I. Dashnyam, The Abolition of the Medieval Legal System and the Evolution and Formation of the First Modern Law System in Mongolia, (1921–1940), Ulaanbaatar, 1994, (Doctor's Dissertation).
I. Dashnyam, The State and Laws of the Empire of Chinggis Khan, Ulaanbaatar, 1997.
I. N. Kradin, Империя Хунну (Hunnu Empire), Moscow, 2001.
I. Saruul, Davaach Khan, Imperial Library, Ulaanbaatar, 2004.
I. Saruul, Tseveenravdan Khan, Imperial Library, Ulaanbaatar, 2002.
I. Tsoodol, Thousand Years of Wonders of Mongolia, Ulaanbaatar, 1992.
I. Ya. Zlatkin, Очерки новой и новейшей истори Монголии (Essays on Contemporary and the Latest History of Mongolia), Moscow, 1957.
I. Ya. Zlatkin, Очерки новой и новейшей истори Монглоии (Essays on the Contemporary and the Latest History of Mongolia), Moscow, 1952.
In the Struggle for the Victory of the People's Revolution of the MPRP, Ulaanbaatar, 1971.
J. Amarsanaa, Facilitator of Social Relations of Law, Ulaanbaatar, 1988.
J. Amarsanaa, Question of Human Rights in International and National Laws, Ulaanbaatar, 2000.
J. Avkhia, People's Great (Ikh) Khural of the MPR, Ulaanbaatar, 1984.
J. Batmönkh, Force Cannot be Used, Ulaanbaatar, 2001.
J. Bayasakh, Two Chinese Sources that Relate to the History of the Great Mongol State, Ulaanbaatar, 2005,
J. Boldbaatar with Caroline Humphrey, The Process of Creation of National Symbols and Their Adoption in the 1992 Constitution of Mongolia, Inner Asia, Volume.

J. Boldbaatar, "Mongols and the Mongolian Empires," Chapter 4, Part I, "The Formation and Naming of the Mongols," World History, Vol. 2, Ulaanbaatar, 2002.

J. Boldbaatar, Annals of the Years Replete with History, Books One and Two, Ulaanbaatar, 2003.

J. Boldbaatar, Ch. Dashdavaa, The Reform Movement and Its Fate, (1952–1966), Ulaanbaatar, 2006.

J. Boldbaatar, Chin Zütgelten Güng Khaisan, Ulaanbaatar, 2002.

J. Boldbaatar, Chinggis Khan, Book Three, Imperial Library, Ulaanbaatar, 1999.

J. Boldbaatar, Da Lama, (The Life and Work of G. Tserenchimed), Ulaanbaatar, 1997.

J. Boldbaatar, Dulaan Khan's Son (About G. Bumtsend), Ulaanbaatar, 2001.

J. Boldbaatar, Dulaan Khan's Son, Ulaanbaatar, 2001.

J. Boldbaatar, Erdene Daiching Chin Wang Khanddorj, Ulaanbaatar, 1994.

J. Boldbaatar, Head of the Government of Mongolia, Ulaanbaatar, 2003.

J. Boldbaatar, Histiography of Mongolia: Reforms and Trends, (From 1990s to Today), Ulaanbaatar, 2008.

J. Boldbaatar, Histiography of Mongolia: Reforms and Trends, (From 1990s to Today), Ulaanbaatar, 2008.

J. Boldbaatar, Minister Amar, Bulgan Town, 1993.

J. Boldbaatar, Mongolian Historiography, Reform and New Trend, (From the 1990s to the Present Times), Ulaanbaatar, 2008.

J. Boldbaatar, Personal Notes, Translated by Asralt Höh-Öndör, Khailar, Cultural Printing Committee of Inner Mongolia, 1985.

J. Boldbaatar, Prominent Sons of the Miangat People, (About B. Baasanjav, Mongolian Statesman and Public Figure), Ulaanbaatar, 2006.

J. Boldbaatar, S. Demberel, Abtai Sain Khan, The Imperial Library, Ulaanbaatar, 2006.

J. Boldbaatar, The Great Mongol Empire, Institute of History and Archaeology of the Mongolian Academy of Sciences, Ulaanbaatar, 2019.

J. Boldbaatar, The Mongol Empire, Evolution, Maturity and Decline, History Study, Vol. XXXV.

J. Boldbaatar, The Role of Mongols in Global and Regional History, Ulaanbaatar, 2007.

J. Boldbaatar, The Role of the Mongols in the Regional and Global History, Ulaanbaatar, 2007.

J. Boldbaatar, The Shape and Nature of the State and Government as Defined in the First Documents of the MPRP, "Namyn Amidral" (Party Life) journal, 1974, Issue No. 3.

J. Boldbaatar, The World Knows About My Backwardness, (Dashiin Damba), Bulgan, 1994.

J. Bor, Some Questions of Foreign Policy and Diplomatic Traditions of Mongolia, Ulaanbaatar, 1988.

J. Ganbold, T. Mönkhtsetseg, T. Naran and A. Puntsag, The Yuan Empire of the Mongols, Ulaanbaatar, 2006.

J. Gerelbadrakh, The Issue of Ranks and Titles of the Mongol Noble Aristocrats in the 15th-17th Centuries, Ulaanbaatar, 1999.

J. Gombojav, N. Jantsan, History of the Formation of the Constitution, Ulaanbaatar, 2001.

J. J. Saunders, The History of the Mongol Conquests, Ulaanbaatar, 1992.

J. Ölzii, Brief History of the Manchus, Ulaanbaatar, 1995.

J. Tseveen, Mongolian Historical Sources of the 10th Century, Translated from Russian and published by E. Pürevjav and S. Chuluun, Ulaanbaatar, 2008.

J. Urangua, Altan Khan, Ulaanbaatar, 2007.

J. Urangua, Mongolia in the Beginning of the 20th Century (1911–1919), Ulaanbaatar, 2006.

J. Urangua, Reform in Outer Mongolia in the Beginning of the 20th Century, Ulaanbaatar, 1997.

J. Zaankhüü, The Regulating Activities of Chinggis Khan and the Issue of Globalisation, Ulaanbaatar, 1976.

J.Boldbaatar and David Sneath, Ordering Subjects: Mongolian Civil and Military Administration (17th - 20th Centuries), Imperial Statecraft. Political Form and Techniques of Governance in Inner Asia, 6th-20th Centuries, Edited by David Sneath, Western Washington University, 2006.

Jack Weatherford, Genghis Khan and the Making of the Modern World, Ulaanbaatar, 2006.

John of Plano Carpini, Istoria Mongalorum, Guillaume de Rubrouck, *Itinerarium fratris Willielmi de Rubruquis de ordine fratrum Minorum, Galli, Anno gratiae 1253 ad partes Orientales*, Ulaanbaatar, 1988.

Ju Yatin, History of Genghis Khan, Ulaanbaatar, 2002.

K. Osson, History of the Mongols from Chinggis Khan to Tamerlane, Vol. 1, Irkutsk, 1937.

K.F. Golstunskii, Mongol-Oirad Laws of 1640, supplementary decrees of Galdan Boshogt Khan, and laws adopted for the Kalmyks living on the Volga during the reign of the Kalmyk Khan Donrovrash (Dondogdash). Kalmyk tests in Russian translation and notes. St. Petersburg, 1880.

Kh. Choibalsan, Brief History of Ardyn Khatanbaatar Magsarjav, Ulaanbaatar, 1942.

Kh. Choibalsan, D. Losol, G. Demid, Concise History of the Foundation of the Mongolian People's National Revolution, Second Edition, Ulaanbaatar, 1974.
Kh. Gündsambuu, Stratification of the Mongolian Society: Evolutionary Trends, (Twentieth Century), Ulaanbaatar, 2002.
Kh. Nyambuu, State Ceremonies and Protocol of the Bogd Khantae Exalted by All Mongolia, Ulaanbaatar, 1993.
Kh. Nyambuu, The Most Revered System of State of Blue Mongolia, 1992.
Kh. Perlee, Issues of Basic Legal Principles in the Secret History, Mongol Study, Ulaanbaatar, 196, Vol. 3, Book 15.
Kh. Perlee, Sh, Bira, Two Rare Documentary Sources Related to the History of Culture of the Mongols and Central Asian Nations, Ulaanbaatar, 1974.
Kh. Perlee, The Kidans and Their Relationship with the Mongols, Ulaanbaatar, 1960.
Kh. Shagdar, History of Chinggis Khan's Wars, (1179–1206).
Khalkha Jirum (Source Study), Book Two, Ulaanbaatar, 2009.
Kim Jon Re, Historical Personality of the Millennium. Historical Figures, Ulaanbaatar, 1999.
L. Baasan, Labour Law of Mongolia, (General Clauses), Ulaanbaatar, 1996.
L. Bat-Ochir, In Search for Historical Truth, Collection of Selected Papers, Ulaanbaatar, 1999.
L. Bilegt, Раннемонгольские племена (Этногенетической изыскания на основе устной истории) (Ancient Mongol Tribes – Ethnogenetic Research Based on Oral History), Ulaanbaatar, 2007.
L. Byambajargal, The Problems and Improvement of Constitutional Review in Mongolia, Kookmin University, Seoul, 2015.
L. Dendev, Commentary on Some Letters in the Official Documents during the Manchu Period, 1954.
L. Dendev, Concise History of Mongolia, Ulaanbaatar, 1935.
L. Dendev, Historical Sources of Mongolia in the 20th Century. Special Documents During the Period of Autonomous Mongolia, (Compiled by O. Batsaikhan).
L. Ganbaatar, The History and Culture of the Hunnu, Ulaanbaatar, 2008.
L. Jamsran, Esen Khan. Imperial Library, Ulaanbaatar, 2000.
L. Jamsran, The Beginning of the Revival of the Mongols, Ulaanbaatar, 1992.
L. Jamsran, The Revival of the State Independence of Mongolia, Ulaanbaatar, 1997.
L. N. Gumilyev, Hunnu in China, St. Petersburg, 1994.
L. N. Gumilyev, The Hunnu, Moscow, 1964.

L. N. Gumilyev, Поиски вымешленного царства, (The search for a fictitious kingdom), St. Petersburg, 1994.

L. Punsag, Study into the Customs in the Secret History, Ulaanbaatar, 2010.

Laws of the Mongolian People's Republic and Compilation of Some Related Legal Acts, (1921–1940), Book One, Ulaanbaatar, 1972.

Li Pyon Re, A Retrospective Study into the Proclamation of the Revival and Independence of the Mongolian Nation in 1911, Ulaanbaatar, 1997.

Luvsandanzan, Altan Tobchi, Ulaanbaatar, 1990.

M. Enkhsaikhan, Political Party, Ulaanbaatar, 1996.

M. I. Golman, Монголоведение на Западе – центры, кадры, общества, (Mongol Studies in the West – Centres, Personnel and Society) Early 1950s of the 20th Century, Moscow, 1977.

M. Murakami, Land of Blue Wolves, World History 8, Tokyo, 1968 (Translation from Japanese into Mongolian by T. Mönkhtsetseg).

M. Onuki, Study into Mongolian History and Our Contemporary, Osaka, Japan, 1984.

M. Sanjdorj, From the History of the Mongolian Statehood, (12th – 14th Centuries), Ulaanbaatar, 1998.

M. Sanjdorj, From the History of the Mongolian Statehood, (13th-19th centuries), Ulaanbaatar, 1998.

M. Sanjdorj, History of the People's State, Ulaanbaatar, 1974.

Magsarjav, Contemporary History of Mongolia, Ulaanbaatar, 1994.

Mandatory Laws and Rules, (1913–1918), (Compiled by J. Urangua and B. Bayarsaikhan), Ulaanbaatar, 2004.

Marco Polo, The Wonders of the World, Ulaanbaatar, 1987.

Materials of the Third-Ninth Congress of the MPRP, 1924–1934.

Mongol Soldiers of the Twentieth Century, Ulaanbaatar, 2001.

Mongolia during the Period under the Manchu Rule (Research Conference, National University, 15 May 2001), Ulaanbaatar, 2004.

Mongolia in the Twentieth Century, Ulaanbaatar, 1995.

Mongolia's Development in the Twentieth Century, Ulaanbaatar, 2005.

Mongolia's First Standing Parliament, (1990–1992), Ulaanbaatar, 2007.

Mongolia's Independence and Tsarist Russia, (1912–1913), (Compiled by Udo Barkmann, J. Boldbaatar, J. Urangua and N. Khishigt), Ulaanbaatar, 2008.

Mongolia's National Security Concept, Ulaanbaatar, 1994, 2010.

Morris Rassabi, Khubilai Khan. His Life and Times, University of California Press, Berkeley, Los Angeles, London.

Morris Rossabi, Modern Mongolia: From Khans to Commissars to Capitalists, University of California Press, Berkeley, Los Angeles, London, 2005.

N. Altanshaa, Three Mongol Khans – Ögödei, Güyük and Mönkh, Hailar, 1985.

N. Ariungoo, Mongol, Chinese Relations in the 14th-16th Centuries, Ulaanbaatar, 1996.

N. Bagabandi, Meaning of Isolation from Globalisation, and Globalisation to Isolation, Ulaanbaatar, 2004.

N. Bagabandi, The Significance of Reform and Traditions in Progress "The President: Policy and Objectives Prior to the New Millennium", Ulaanbaatar, 1998.

N. Ishjamts, State and Religious Policy of Tümen Zasagt Khan, "East-West" Journal, 1993, No. 1.

N. Ishjamts, The Establishment of a United Mongol State and the Formation of Feudalism, Ulaanbaatar, 1974.

N. Jambaljav, Key Issues of State Policy, Ulaanbaatar, 2019.

N. Jantsan, Criminology, (Second Edited Version), Ulaanbaatar, 2004.

N. Khishigt, the 1921 Revolution and the People's Volunteer Army, Ulaanbaatar, 2001.

N. Lündendorj, Evolution Trend of Statehood and Legal Mindset, (Issues of General and Special Theories), Ulaanbaatar, 2002.

N. Magsarjav, Contemporary History of Mongolia, Ulaanbaatar, 1994.

N. N. Cardin, T. Skrynnikova, Империя Чингис-хана, (Chinggis Khan's Empire), Moscow, 2006.

N. Nyam-Osor, About the Great Yassa Code of laws of Chinggis Khan, Ulaanbaatar, 2000.

N. Nyam-Osor, Chinggis Khan's Great Yassa in the Social and Political Life in the 13th century, Ulaanbaatar, 2006.

N. Nyam-Osor, Historical Research into the Development of the State and Statehood of Mongolia in the 13th-14th Centuries, Ulaanbaatar, 2003.

N. Ts. Munkuyev, Chinese Source on the First Mongol Queen, Ulaanbaatar, 2004.

N. Ya. Bichurin, История Тебета и Хунунора, (History of Tibet and Huhnor), I, St. Petersburg, 1833.

Namsrai, The Manchu Rule over Mongolia, Ulaan Khad town, 1983.

National History Archives of Mongolia.

O. Amarkhüü, Foundations of Land Holding Law of the MPR, Ulaanbaatar, 1973.

O. Amarkhüü, Mongol Customs and Laws Regarding Environment Protection, (Issues of Traditions and Reform), Ulaanbaatar, 2000.

O. Amarkhüü, Mongol Customs and Traditions, Laws and Regulations on Nature and Environment Protection – (Issues of Traditions and Reform), Ulaanbaatar, 2000.

O. Amarkhüü, Mongolian Customs, Laws and Legislation on Nature Protection, (Issues of Traditions and Reform), Ulaanbaatar, 1999.

O. Amarkhüü, State and Legal Theoretical Issues of Protecting the Surrounding Environment, Ulaanbaatar, 1979.

O. Batsaikhan, Challenges Encountered Along the Road of Development of Mongolia, (1921–1933), Ulaanbaatar, 1977.

O. Batsaikhan, Mongols on the Road to Becoming a Sovereign Nation, (1911–1946), Ulaanbaatar, 2005.

O. Batsaikhan, The Last Khan of Mongolia – Eighth Bogd Jebzumdamba, Ulaanbaatar, 2008.

O. Batsaikhan, The Mongol Nation on the Path to Becoming a Sovereign State, (1911–1946), Ulaanbaatar, 2005.

O. Bolormaa, The Migration of the Oirads towards the Volga, (16th-1th centuries), Ulaanbaatar, 2008.

O. Dagvadorj, D. Dovchinsüren, The *Great Yassa* of the Great Mongol Empire and the Blue Book of Other Ordinances by Chinggis Khan, (13th century), Ulaanbaatar, 2006.

O. Jambaldorj, L. Baasan, Labour Code of the MPR, Ulaanbaatar, 1986.

O. Lattimore, Nomads and Commissars, Ulaanbaatar, 1995. (Translated by Ts. Batbatar and E. Puntsag).

O. Mönkhsaikhan, Towards Better Protection of Fundamental Rights in Mongolia: Constitutional Review and Interpretation, Nagoya University, CALE, 2014.

O. Oyünjargal, The Administrative Policy of the Manchu Qing Dynasty ion Mongolia, Ulaanbaatar, 2009.

O. Pürev, Concise Dictionary of Geographical Names Related to the History of the Mongolian People's Revolution, Ulaanbaatar, 1983.

Odon, Esen Khan, Hohhot, 1988.

Otahi Matsuvo, Khubilai Khan, Ulaanbaatar, 1991.

P. Amarjargal, The Powers of the Parliament: Trends of its Formation and Growth, Ulaanbaatar, 2016.

P. Delgerjargal, The Early History of Xianbi, Book Two, Ulaanbaatar, 2017.

P. Delgerjargal, The Origin of the Mongols, Ulaanbaatar, 2005.

P. Delgerjargal, Z. Batsaikhan, Ancient History of Hunnu Mongolia, Book One, Ulaanbaatar, 2017.

P. Ochirbat, Time of the Heavens, Ulaanbaatar, 1996.

P. Puntsagnorov, History of Autonomous Mongolia, Ulaanbaatar, 1955.

Procurator Control of the MPR, Ulaanbaatar, 1974.

R. Bold, Mongolia's Independence and the United States of America, (1910–1976), Ulaanbaatar, 2007.

Rashid al-Din, Compendium of Chronicles, Vol. 1, Book 1, (Translation into Mongolian by Sürenkhorloo), Ulaanbaatar, 1994.

Rashid al-Din, Compendium of Chronicles, Vol. 1, Book 2.

Rashid al-Din, History of the Mongols, Part 2, St. Petersburg, 1868.

Rashid al-Din, History of the Mongols, Part 3, St. Petersburg, 1888.

Rashpuntsag, History of Mongolia, in 4 Books, Book Two.

Reform of the Mongolian Society, Second Revised Edition, Ulaanbaatar, 2008.

Regulations of *Lifan Yuan* or the Law on the Ministry for the Administration of Outer Mongolia, National Printing Committee, Beijing, 2006 (As translated and commented by Borjigon Mönkhbaatar).

Resolutions and Decisions of the Congresses, Conferences of the MPRP and the Plenary Meetings of the Central Committee, Ulaanbaatar, 1956.

Resolutions of the State *Ikh* and *Baga Khurals* of the Mongolian People's Republic, the Constitution and Manifestos, 1956.

Revolutionary Measures Taken in 1921–1924, Ulaanbaatar, 1954.

S. Badarch, O. Dagvadorj, S. Chuluun, History of the Judiciary of Mongolia, Ulaanbaatar, 2007.

S. Badarchi, Ancient Mongolian Legal Traditions of How Women Protected their Children, Ulaanbaatar, 1995.

S. Badarchi, History of the Mongol State and Laws, (Legends and Illustrations), Ulaanbaatar, 1989.

S. Badarchi, O. Davaadorj, S. Chuluun, History of the Judiciary of Mongolia, Ulaanbaatar, 2007.

S. Bira, The Establishment of the First United Mongol State, (Report made at the Scientific General Assembly of Members of the Mongolian Academy of Sciences commemorating the 790 years of the first united Mongol State and the 75th anniversary of the People's Revolution), Ulaanbaatar, 1996.

S. D. Dylykov, Халха джурам – памятник Монголькогог феодального права XVIII в, (Khalkha Juram – Monument of the Mongolian Feudal Law), Moscow, 1965.

S. E. Malov, Памятники древнетюркской письменности Монголии и Киргизии, (Monuments of Ancient Mongolian and Turkic Writings), Moscow-Leningrad, 1959.

S. G. Klyashtornyi, T. I. Sultanov, Государство и народы евразийских степей. Древность и средневековые, (States and peoples of the Eurasian steppes – Antiquity and the Middle Ages), St. Petersburg, Oriental Studies of Petersburg, 2000.

S. G. Luzyanin, Россия-Монголия-Китай в первой половине XX в. Политические взаймноотношения в 1911–1946 г, (Russia, Mongolia and China in the First Half of the 20th Century. Political Mutual Relations in 1911–1946), Moscow, 2000.

S. G. Luzyanin, Россия-Монголия-Китай в первой половине XX века. Политические взаимоотношения в 1911–1946г. (Russia-Mongolia-China in the First Half of the 20th Century, Political Relations in 1911–1946), Moscow, 2003.

S. Ichinnorov, Political Life of Khorloogiin Choibalsan and the Times, Ulaanbaatar, 2005.

S. Ishinnorov, Some Issues on the Social and Economic Status of Mongolia at the Crossroads of the 19th and 20th Centuries, Ulaanbaatar, 1986.

S. Jalan-Aajav, Basic Line of Legislative Activities of the People's Revolutionary State, (1921–1949), Ulaanbaatar, 1967.

S. Jalan-Aajav, Khalkha Jirum, Ulaanbaatar, 1995.

S. L. Tikhvinskii, Татаро-Монгол в Азий и Европе, (Tatar-Mongols in Asia and Europe), Moscow, 1970.

S. Narangerel, Basic Questions of Corrective Labour Law of the MPR, Ulaanbaatar, 1985.

S. Narangerel, Introduction to Mongolia's Law System, Ulaanbaatar, 2003.

S. Narangerel, Law Dictionary, (Second Edition), Ulaanbaatar, 2008.

S. Narangerel, Mongolian and Global Legal Systems, (Comparative Law), Ulaanbaatar, 2005.

S. Ölziibayar, S. Enkhbat, The Jujan State, Ancient History of Mongolia. Vol. 3, Ulaanbaatar, 2017.

S. Ölziibayar, Science of Mongolia, Book 27, Ancient History of Mongolia, Ulaanbaatar, 2009.

S. S. Jalan-Aajav, Basic Line of Legislative Activities of the People's Revolutionary State, (1921–1949), Ulaanbaatar, 1964.

S. Tömör *et al*, State Law of the MPR, Ulaanbaatar, 1987.

S. Tömör, Budget Law of the Local *Khurals* of People's Deputies of the MPR, Ulaanbaatar, 1984.

S. Tsedendamba, State of Affairs of Religion in Mongolia, (XX-XXI centuries), Ulaanbaatar, 2008.

S. Tserenbaltav, Ts. Minjin, Biography of Temüjin-Chinggis Khan, Vols. 1–3, Ulaanbaatar, 2006.

S. Tsolmon, Galdan Boshogt Khan, Ulaanbaatar, 1994.

S. Tsolmon, Galdan Boshogt Khan: Social and Political Activities (1644–1697), Ulaanbaatar, 2007.

S. Tsolmon, The Golden Horde of the Mongols, Ulaanbaatar, 2005.

Sagan Setsen, Erdeniin Tobchi, Ulaanbaatar, 1961.

Saishaal, Chinggis Khan's History, Books One and Two, Huhhot, 1967.

Saruul-Erdene, Mongolist of the Indiana University, Bloomington, India, 2005.

Sh. Bira, Research into the History, Culture and Historiography of Mongolia, Ulaanbaatar, 1997.

Sh. Bira, Research into the History, Culture and Historiography of Mongolia, Vol. 1 and 2, Tokyo, 1994 and Ulaanbaatar, 2001.

Sh. Bira, Research into the History, Culture and Historiography of Mongolia, Vol. 3, Ulaanbaatar, 2001.

Sh. Bira, Some Special Issues of History and Ideology of the Great Mongol State, Ulaanbaatar, 2006.

Sh. Bira, The Establishment of the First United Mongol State, (Report made at the Scientific General Assembly of Members of the Mongolian Academy of Sciences commemorating the 790 years of the first united Mongol State and the 75th anniversary of the People's Revolution), Ulaanbaatar, 1996.

Sh. Natsagdorj, History of Chinggis Khan, Ulaanbaatar, 1991.

Sh. Natsagdorj, Khalkha History, Ulaanbaatar, 1963.

Sh. Natsagdorj, Khubilai the Wise, Ulaanbaatar, 1998.

Sh. Natsagdorj, Land Relations in Pre-Revolution Mongolia, Ulaanbaatar, 1975.

Sh. Natsagdorj, Primary Course of Evolution of Feudalism in Mongolia, Ulaanbaatar, 1978.

Sh. Natsagdorj, Right of the Mongols to Inheritance, Ulaanbaatar, 1971.

Sh. Natsagdorj, Soum, Serfs and Shabi People, Ulaanbaatar, 1972.

Sh. Natsagdorj, The Primary Course of Evolution of Feudalism in Mongolia, Ulaanbaatar, 1978.

Sh. Natsagdorj, The Right of the Mongols to Inheritance, Ulaanbaatar, 1971.

Sh. Sandag, Political Foreign Relations of Mongolia, (1850–1919), Book One, Ulaanbaatar, 1971.

Sharavnyambuu Tsedenjapov, Lord Chinggis Khan, Ulaanbaatar, 1991.

Some Documents Related to the History of Mongolia Discovered From the Personal Archives of V. Kotvich, (Compiled for printing by B. Shirendev), Ulaanbaatar.

Some Issue of Historical Traditions and Reform of Mongolia's State and Law, Compilation of Joint Research Conference of the Faculty of the Social Sciences School and the Law School of the National University of Mongolia, Ulaanbaatar, 2001.

Some Issues of State and Legal Mind-set of Mongolia, Ulaanbaatar, 2002.

State and Legal Foundations of the MPR, (Edited by E. Avirmed, B. Chimid), Ulaanbaatar, 1976.
State and Legal Foundations of the MPR, (Edited by G. Sovd, E. Avirmed), Ulaanbaatar, 1966.
State Upper and Lower Khurals, Book One, (Compilation of Documents), Ulaanbaatar, 2003, (Compiled by J. Gerelbadrakh).
Sü. Batbold, Issue of Augmenting Local Autonomy, Ulaanbaatar, 2010.
Sümbe Khamba Ishbaljir, History of Hoh Nuur, Ulaanbaatar, 1997.
T. Altangerel, Mongol Codes of Laws in the 16th-17th centuries, Ulaanbaatar, 1999.
T. Altangerel, Mongol-Oirad Laws and Their Research, Ulaanbaatar, 1998.
T. D. Skruynnikova, Харизм в власти в эпоху Чингис-хана, (Khwarezm in power during the era of Chinggis Khan), Moscow, 1997.
T. Davaakhüü, Finance Law of the MPR, Ulaanbaatar, 1977.
T. Erdenekhishig, Military and Political Relations between the Hunnu and the Han Dynasty, Ulaanbaatar, 2009.
T. Mönkhjargal, History of Civil Codes of Mongolia, Ulaanbaatar, 2006.
T. Mönkhjargal, The Law of Inheritance, Ulaanbaatar, 2009.
T. Sengedorj, O. Amarkhüü, D. Lündeejantsan, Law of Agricultural Co-Operatives of the MPR, Ulaanbaatar, 1987.
The Cambridge History of China. Alien Regimes and Border States, pp. 907–1368.
The Code of Ordinances of Mongolia, Ulaanbaatar, 1995, 2008, (Transliteration from the classical Mongol script to the Cyrillic script by O. Batsaikhan, Z. Lonjid and Ch. Khajidsüren).
The Constitution of the MPR and Compilation of Related Legal Acts, Book One, Ulaanbaatar, 1972.
The Development of the State Structure and Political Thinking of Mongolia. (3rd century BCE to 20th century CE), Ulaanbaatar, 1955.
The Document Called the Shin Toli (New Mirror), 1914, No. 12.
The Early State, (Edited by H.J.M. Claessen and P. Skalnik), The Hague: Mouton Publishers, 1978.
The Evolution and Growth of the State Structure of the Mongols and Political Mentality, (3rd Century BCE–20th Century CE), Volume One, Ulaanbaatar, 1995.
The Great Mongol Khans, Ulaanbaatar, 2010.
The Great Yassa of Chingiz Khan, A Re-Examination (C1), Studia Islamica, No. 36, (1972).
The Great Yassa of Chingiz Khan, A Re-Examination (C2) Al-Maqrizi's Passage on the Yassa under the Mamluks, Studia Islamica, No. 38, (1973).
The Great Yassa of Lord Chinggis Khan, Ulaanbaatar, 1995.

The Historical Road of the MPRP, Ulaanbaatar, 1995.
The History and Culture of the Hunnu, Collective Work, Ulaanbaatar, 2011.
The History of Yuan Empire, Beijing, 1987.
The History of Yuan, Book 210, Manuscripts Department of the State Library.
The Livelihood and Culture of the Ancient and Medieval Mongols, Ulaanbaatar, 2006.
The Mongol Code Introduced by the Manchu Empire, National Central Library of Mongolia.
The People's Republic Government in Mongolia, (Compilation of documents), Ulaanbaatar, 1970.
The Secret History of the Mongols, Ulaanbaatar, 1976.
The Struggle of the Mongolian People in 1911 for National Liberation and Independence, Collection of Documents, (1900–1914), Compiled for printing by A. Ochir and G. Purvee.
The Treatise of Mongolia, Books One and Two, Ulaanbaatar, 1997.
The White History of Ten Virtuous Books, Hohhot, 1981.
Thomas E. Ewing, Between the Hammer and the Anvil? Chinese and Russian Policies in Outer Mongolia 1911–1921, 1980.
Thomas J. Barfield, The Perilous Frontier: Nomadic Empires and China, 221 BC to AD 1757, Cambridge, Basil Blackwell, 1989.
Torbre, Preston M. The Ching Imperial Household Department, A Study of its Organisation and Principal Functions, 1662–1796, (Harvard East Asian Monograph 71), Cambridge, Mass. U London, 1977.
Treatises of the Wang and Güng of Outer Mongolia and Khoton Aimag as Written under Edict, Books 45–46.
Ts. Balkhaajav, The Issue about State and the Revolutionary Activities of the People's State, Ulaanbaatar, 1966.
Ts. Batbayar, D. Gombosüren, Mongolia and Tibet in the First Half of the 20th Century, (History of the Visit to Mongolia by the 13th Dalai Lama Tüvdenjamts), Ulaanbaatar, 2009.
Ts. Batbayar, Foreign Relations of the Exalted by All Mongolia, Ulaanbaatar, 2008.
Ts. Batbayar, Kodama Mitsui, The Japanese in Khüree, (1911–1912), Ulaanbaatar, 1993.
Ts. Batbayar, Mongolia and the Super Powers in the First Half of the 20th Century, (From Khiagt to Yalta: Stalin, Chang Kai-shek and Mongolia's Independence), Ulaanbaatar, 2005.
Ts. Batbayar, Mongolia, Japanese Relations in the First Half of the 20th Century, Ulaanbaatar, 1998.

Ts. Büdkhand, 70 Years of Historical Journey the Procurator, Ulaanbaatar, 2000.

Ts. Dorjsüren, North Hunnu, Ulaanbaatar, 1961.

Ts. Elbegdorj, The White Footprints of Truth, Ulaanbaatar, 1999.

Ts. Enkhchimeg, The Tsagadai Empire of the Mongols, Ulaanbaatar, 2006.

Ts. Enkhee, Researches by Mongolian Historians on Ligden Khan, (17th-19th Centuries), Ulaanbaatar, 2007.

Ts. Gombosüren, Was the Traditional Mongolian Society Feudalism? Ulaanbaatar, 1995.

Ts. Khandsüren, The Jujan Empire and Some Issues of History, Ulaanbaatar, 2005.

Ts. Khandsüren, The Jujan Empire, Ulaanbaatar, 1994.

Ts. Minjin, The Great Yassa (Historical and legal research), Ulaanbaatar, 2009.

Ts. Sarantuya, Legal and Fundamental Concepts of the Constitutional Process and Pressing Challenges, Ulaanbaatar, 2006.

Ts. Sonomdagva, Changes in the Local Administrative Divisions of the MPR, Ulaanbaatar, 1969.

Ts. Sonomdagva, Government and Administrative Structure of Outer Mongolia under the Manchu Rule, (1692–1911), Ulaanbaatar, 1961.

Ts. Terbish, Evolution and Growth of the Mongolian Parliament, (Commentaries, Document Sources and References, 1911–1969), Ulaanbaatar, 2003.

Twentieth Century Mongolia, Ulaanbaatar, 1995.

U. Khürelsükh, Ts. Sükhbaatar, 20 Years of Democratic Movement and Future Tasks, Ulaanbaatar, 2010.

Ulaan Khatsart (The Red Cheek), Ulaanbaatar, 1961.

Ulaan Khatsart, (Red Cheek), Compiled for Printing and Foreword by Sh. Natsagdorj, Ulaanbaatar, 1978.

V. A. Ryazanovskii, Historical Summary of the Legal Documents and Monuments of the Mongols, The Great Yassa, Ulaanbaatar, 2000.

V. A. Ryazanskii, Великая Яаса Чингисхана, (The Great *Yassa* of Chinggis Khan), Harbin, 1993.

V. S. Taskin, Введение. Значение китайских источников в изучении древней истории монголов: материалы по истории древных кочевых народов групуу дунху. (Introduction. The significance of Chinese sources in the study of ancient history of Mongols; Materials on history of ancient nomadic peoples of the Dunhu group), Introduction. Translation and commentary by V.S. Taskina, Moscow, 1984.

V. S. Taskin, Материалы по истории древных кочевых народов, (History Materials of the Ancient Nomadic Peoples), Moscow, 1978.

V. V. Bartold, Сочинения (Compositions), Moscow, 1968.

V. V. Bartold, Сочинения (Compositions), Vol. 1, "Туркестан в эпоху монгольского нашествия" (Turkestan during the era of the Mongol Invasion), Vostochnoi Literatury Publishers, Moscow, 1963.

V. Ya. Sidikhyanov, Маньжурский правитель Китая, (Manchu Rulers of China), Moscow, 1985.

Y. Ishjamts, the 1755–1758 Armed Struggle of the Mongolian People for Independence, Ulaanbaatar, 1962.

Yu. V. Kuzmin, Монголия и Китай начала XX века в оценках российских военных исследователей, (Mongolia and China in the Early 20th Century as Assessed by Russian Military Researchers), Irkutsk, 2007.

Z. Batsaikhan, The Hunnu, Ulaanbaatar, 2003.

Z. Lonjid, History of the Financial Services of Mongolia, (1911–1924), Ulaanbaatar, 2009.

Zbigniew Brzezinski, The Grand Chessboard, Ulaanbaatar, 2003.

История Монголии XX, History of Mongolia – XX Century, Moscow, 2007.

Материалы по истории русско-монгольских отношений. 1636–1654 (Materials on the History of Russia-Mongolia Relations), Collection of documents by G. I. Slesarchuk, Moscow, 2009.

Международные отношения в эпоху империализма, 1870–1910, (International Relations in the Era of Imperialism), Moscow, 1938.

Уголовный процесс МНР, (Criminal Process of the MPR), (Edited by J. Avkhia), Ulaanbaatar, 1974.

Index

www.ingramcontent.com/pod-product-compliance
Lightning Source LLC
Chambersburg PA
CBHW071236230926
51849CB00001B/116
9789083407524